in print
in paperback
only for 15⁰⁰

China in Antiquity

China in Antiquity

by HENRI MASPERO

translated by FRANK A. KIERMAN JR

DAWSON

Published 1978

© The University of Massachusetts Press 1978

Originally published in French as *La Chine Antique*, Volume
IV of *Histoire du Monde*, by E. De Boccard, Editeur, Paris,
copyright © 1927, and in a new edition, upon which the
English version is based, revised by Henri Maspero and
published as part of the *Annales du Musée Guiment*, *Bibliotheque
d'Etudes*, Tome Soixante et Onzieme, copyright © 1965 by
Presses Universitaires de France.

British Library Cataloguing in Publication Data

Maspero, Henri
China in antiquity.
1. China – Civilization
I. Title   II. Kierman, Frank A
931   DS723
ISBN 0–7129–0818–8

Typeset in Great Britain by
Computacomp (UK) Ltd, Fort William, Scotland
and printed by W & J Mackay Ltd, Chatham

Contents

List of Maps

Author's Preface

Despite what is often said, ancient Chinese history does not extend very far back, nor are the texts concerning antiquity of any great value. We have glimpses of certain epochs separated by periods which are virtually unknown, rather than a consecutive history. Thus we are beginning to know what China was like towards the end of the Yin dynasty (about the twelfth and eleventh centuries B.C.), thanks to recent archaeological discoveries which have made it come alive to some degree; but the centuries that follow, those in which tradition sets the apogee of the Chou dynasty, are a void to us. Only towards the end of the ninth century does the darkness begin to lighten; and from the end of the eighth century, for two and a half centuries from 722 to 480, the history is pretty well known, thanks to a chronicle which covers that period. But then the mists return, though less thick than for ancient times, over the following period down to the end of the third century, for which our documents are few and none too reliable. Efforts by European, Japanese, and Chinese scholars are beginning to unravel this history a little, but critical work upon it is still only beginning.

Consequently, in seeking to produce a history of the Chinese world in antiquity which would accommodate recent critical studies, I have had to discard many a hypothesis long accepted as established fact. To avoid lengthy discussions which would have gone beyond the framework of this study, I have often had to limit myself to stating in a footnote the traditional theory which I reject and, for some of the most important cases, briefly noting my main objections.

There is a great variance in the number and arrangement of

references within this volume. In the chapters which are purely historical there are few notes: since we have but a single source, there is no use in citing it at every point. Yet in the chapters on society, religion, and literature it is essential to indicate, as much as possible for every fact, references to passages in texts which are very diverse and very scattered. It has also been necessary to set forth, at least briefly, my reasons for accepting or rejecting the indigenous literary tradition, for considering certain works authentic or not, and for assigning dates to them.

Personal names constitute a considerable difficulty for the period which this book covers. Each individual has a clan name, *hsing*, which is never used except for religious purposes; a family name, *shih*, which may be that of a locality, or a function, or a degree of kinship; a personal name, *ming*, which is given three months after birth; an appellation, *tzu*, which is chosen at the moment when one takes the cap of manhood; and finally a posthumous title. Kings and princes are called by their posthumous titles, other persons by the personal name, sometimes followed by the appellation in parentheses. For names of locality or of function, I have translated them as such, but with 'of' before place names and 'of the' before function titles (as is done for medieval Italian families). Thus the man whose personal name is Tun and whose family, possessing or having possessed the fief of Chao, has taken that as their particular name, will be called Tun of Chao. One who is called by the personal name Hui and whose family, having exercised the function of *shih*, took its particular name from that, will be called Hui of the Shih. After ancient times ended these names of place, function, and so on became true family names; and, since the fact of their being clan names was forgotten, they are generally translated into the modern style, as Chao Tun or Shih Hui. This practice seems to me anachronistic for the age of antiquity, when the proper significance of these names was still known to all.

HENRI MASPERO

Foreword

The original edition of this book by Henri Maspero (1883–1945) was published in 1925. The title was *La Chine antique*, the word *antique* being used to specify the early history of China up to the foundation in 221 B.C. of the unified empire which was to last till 1911, somewhat as we apply the word to the period of European history before the so-called Middle Ages. The author had been working at the book since 1920, when he had come back to Paris to occupy the chair of sinology at the Collège de France, after having spent twelve years in the Far East as a member of the Ecole française d'Extrême-Orient. Maspero's intention was to publish further volumes on later periods of the history of China. In his subsequent career, a large part of his activity was devoted to the collection and elaboration of material concerning China up to the T'ang dynasty; but at the same time he published many papers complementing *La Chine antique* in the fields of economic history, mythology, astronomy and so forth. A complete bibliography of the writings published in his lifetime may be found in the necrology which I contributed to the *Journal Asiatique* (vol. ccxxxiv, 1943–45, pp. 263–80), while the numerous works published after his death are listed in a note to H. Maspero and E. Balazs, *Histoire et institutions de la Chine ancienne* (Paris, 1967, p. vii), or also in the foreword to the revised edition of *La Chine antique* published by the Imprimerie Nationale in 1955 (later included in the collection of the Musée Guimet, Presses Universitaires de France). [See Maspero bibliography, below, 498–511.]

In this 1955 edition, I incorporated the corrections and additions which Maspero had scribbled, mostly around 1930, in the margins of his copy of the first edition. The present English translation is based on this revised edition, with the welcome addition of an index which I had mistakenly deemed unnecessary to provide in 1955; Maspero himself thought that a general index would conclude the volumes which he intended to publish after *La Chine antique*. But these volumes were never written.

The book here presented to the English-speaking public was thus written half a century ago, with some improvements made since. In the meantime the history of early China has been largely recast by important discoveries in archaeology and epigraphy, as well as by the progress of research, particularly through the work of a new generation of Chinese and Japanese scholars. As mentioned above, Maspero himself contributed to this progress; but his premature death, at the age of 62, prevented him from giving a new form to his book.

The Second World War was drawing to its end when he was arrested by the Gestapo, on 28 September 1944, 'suspected of terrorist activities'; and he was deported to the concentration camp of Buchenwald. The charge came about owing to the activities of his elder son, who was a member of the Resistance and had been implicated in a dangerous affair in Paris; he managed to escape the Gestapo and join the American army, only to be killed at the front six months before his father died at Buchenwald.

Maspero was a brilliant specialist in early Chinese history, perhaps the best of his time: 'l'homme de la Chine antique', as his colleague Paul Pelliot dubbed him when paying homage to him after his death. His work was characterized by a strong emphasis on facts as against theories, a sense of living realities, a Latin clarity and critical acumen (his father, the famed Egyptologist Gaston Maspero, was of Italian origin), an encyclopaedic curiosity, and the novelty and originality of his views. He broke new ground in linguistics, in economic history, in the history of sciences and religions (his essays on Taoism have been recently reprinted in a bulky volume, *Le taoïsme et les religions chinoises* (Gallimard, 1971), of which an English translation is in preparation). History of art is lacking in *La Chine antique* because he had reserved that subject for a separate volume which he had undertaken to write for the publishing firm Hachette.

Such as it is, *La Chine antique* remains a classic of lasting value. It has aged well, though bearing the marks of its date in some respects such as archaeology and the like. Maspero did not ignore the Yin inscriptions, as witnessed by his lengthy reviews of Tung Tso-pin's and Kuo Mo-jo's publications in the *Journal Asiatique* for 1933, or his notes to the chapter on the Yin dynasty in both editions of *La Chine antique*. He did not, indeed could not, exploit them systematically as they were then not yet numerous enough nor deciphered certainly enough. A thorough revision of his book to bring it up to date was unthinkable; it would have meant writing a new book. But as regards the main lines of the history of early China, or such special aspects of it as the record of political and institutional events, there is as yet no better handbook available to students or to the general reader. The valiant translators who undertook to tackle Maspero's text with its severe accuracy, its total lack of rhetoric, its nice shades of meaning or subtle understatements, should be thanked for having successfully accomplished a long and delicate task.

Paris, September, 1975.   P. DEMIÉVILLE.

Introduction

Since 1945 Chinese Studies has been one of the most rapidly developing subjects in the humanities. Where, thirty years ago, it was still possible for an individual scholar to keep abreast of what was being done in every branch of Sinology, the sheer volume of publication now makes it impossible to maintain such an overall view. A single person would be hard pressed to cover all the important new work in a single field of history, of art or of literature. This rapid growth, and the number of scholars engaged in research, has tended to make scholarship obsolescent much more rapidly than was the case even a decade ago, and the average undergraduate reading list will contain very little published more than twenty years ago. Why then, should anyone take the trouble to translate and republish a book first issued half a century ago, in a time when modern historical scholarship on China was in its infancy, both in China and in the West?

Moreover, the whole shape of Chinese Studies has changed out of all recognition. In the early 1960s when our profession was beginning to flex its muscles and feel generally euphoric about the progress being achieved in the understanding of China's past, it was fashionable to look back on the Sinology of the pre-war period and write it off as over-concerned with matters of 'antiquarian' interest and obsessed with the pedantic pursuit of philological detail. The modes of scholarship then fashionable advocated the submersion of Chinese Studies in the general 'disciplines' of history, literature, art criticism, and the various social sciences.[1] These criticisms of our predecessors in the days before specialization were largely levelled at the French school of sinology which in the period before 1945 had dwarfed all other activity in Chinese Studies outside the Far East. Why, once again, should it be timely to translate and republish a work by a member of this school, a man who was at once a superb philologist with the most austere standards, and a broad humanist, the very antithesis of the main trends of our own times — of specialization, of reliance on theory derived from non-Chinese models, of insistence on interpretation at the expense of descriptive scholarship?

Perhaps we should answer this second question first. The self-congratulatory views held by some scholars in the early 1960s now begin to look as quaint and dated as the scholarship of the 1920s and 1930s then appeared to them. The new 'disciplinary' approach to Chinese Studies, the gross under-estimation of solid philological scholarship as the foundation for any serious historical study of China, the belief that the social sciences held a set of methodological keys which would miraculously unlock the mysteries of China's past, have had their heyday and can now themselves be seen in perspective. No one would wish to deny the far-reaching effects of these new approaches on the study of Chinese history, but they are now being appraised in their proper role, as techniques and approaches to be used in historical investigation, just as philological scholarship provides a set of techniques without which the literary evidence of the past cannot be adequately interpreted. In the middle 1970s there has been a revival of serious interest among younger scholars in all the fields which were so fashionable in the inter-war years and have since been neglected — the pre-Ch'in philosophers and other early texts; text criticism; the reconstruction of the ancient stages of the Chinese language; early Chinese religion; the study of China's neighbouring peoples; and above all ancient history.[2] All these were subjects that had been out of fashion, in the West at least, and their revival has led to a new interest in and a reassessment of much pre-war scholarship.

Needless to say, the new scholarship in these fields is very different from that of pre-war days. The sciences of archaeology and of linguistics have both been transformed completely in the last half-century, making possible approaches inconceivable in the 1920s. Even as historians our presuppositions are quite different; we have new insights deriving from linguistics and from literary theory; abundant new evidence has become available to us from archaeology, we have the results of decades of textual scholarship in Japan and China to digest, we have more than ever before to meet the scrutiny of our colleagues working on other civilizations, because at long last Chinese history is slowly becoming accepted as a part of the general record of human history, rather than viewed as a separate inward-looking area whose relationships with the rest of the world are conceived only at a very general and superficial level. Maspero's work is relevant to this new scholarship in a number of ways. He was himself among the pioneers of Chinese linguistics, and the first historian to take account of the newly born study of Chinese archaeology. But his greatest importance lies in the breadth of his vision, his conception of China's antiquity as an organic whole, and his provision of a general framework within which each of our specializations finds its importance and which still remains to be superseded.

Maspero, son of a famous Egyptologist, whose own first published work was a study of the financial system of ancient Egypt,[3] was one of the handful of French scholars who between 1890 and 1940 transformed the study of China in Europe. Formerly a field largely dominated by consular officials and missionaries, whose scholarly work, splendid as some of it was (the translations of such men as Legge and Couvreur, for example), was the part-time occupation of busy men whose professional interests lay elsewhere, Chinese studies were to become a branch of academic learning, conducted within the framework of the great universities, in which the most rigorous standards of contemporary scholarship and learning were applied. The scholarship of these men, Edouard Chavannes, Maspero's own teacher, Paul Pelliot and Maspero himself, was extraordinary in its scope. Chavannes, before his premature death, had written widely not only on Chinese history, but also on the history of Buddhism, on popular religions and religious cults, and on China's relations with the neighbouring peoples. In everything he touched Chavannes had established and maintained an austere standard of accurate translation, of attention to philological detail, and a consciousness of the overall context of his subject matter that made him the first truly modern sinologue. Pelliot and the slightly younger Maspero both spent many years in the Ecole d'Extrême Orient at Hanoi, and had the great advantage of long experience in the Far East, but unlike their predecessors enjoyed this in an academic environment undisturbed by irksome official or professional duties.

Pelliot, the chief — and totally undeserving — target for the attacks on pre-war sinology in the 1960s, was a scholar of even greater range than Chavannes. He too wrote extensively on China's relations with foreign countries, particularly on the history of Central Asia, on Buddhism, Manicheanism, and on many aspects of Chinese cultural and political history. He too became the accepted arbiter of standards in our field — not only through his own scholarly virtuosity but by the enormous body of his long and detailed book reviews, covering every subject under the sun and constantly revealing a profound knowledge of unsuspected subject matter. In retrospect, Pelliot's greatest contribution to our field was perhaps his phenomenal knowledge of bibliography. From his time onwards the Western scholar was expected to have as broad a knowledge of the literature on his subject as a Chinese or Japanese contemporary. Moreover, he was able to keep up with, and introduce to Western readers, the growing secondary literature of contemporary Chinese and Japanese scholarship. Western sinology was no longer to be a provincial school of learning divorced from the mainstream of scholarship in the Far East.

When Maspero became Chavannes' successor at the Collège de France in 1920, he had already produced a great range of scholarly work.[4] In addition to some valuable articles on the early history of Chinese Buddhism, he had written extensively on the early history of Annam, had carried out a series of detailed field investigations among the various minority peoples of French Indo-China, and had written at length about their customs, religions and languages. This experience in Indo-China was to be formative, since not only did he continue to work on Indo-China for much of his life, but it also provided him with close experience of a living society in which he saw reflected many of the features of Ancient China, and which inspired him to the extraordinary feat of vision and imaginative re-creation of the past which underlies *China in Antiquity* and many of his later writings. His studies of the linguistic history of Indo-China also motivated his interest, which was again to last throughout his life, in the history of the Chinese language, and in the reconstruction of the earliest stages of its grammar and phonology, a field in which his work has to some extent been overshadowed by that of Bernhard Karlgren, but in which he made an important contribution to this major breakthrough in knowledge.

The next few years, from 1920 to 1926, were spent in the preparation for *China in Antiquity*. To break the ground, Maspero subjected the early sources to intensive text-criticism, pursued the origins of the earliest legends and myths, and worked out the elusive details of chronology and political history. His lectures at the Collège de France ranged over historical criticism, prehistory, early religion and modern folk religion, early philosophy, the reconstruction of the ancient language, Chinese art, the comparative sociology of ancient China and the modern Thai peoples.

The result of this long preparation was a book which still has a good claim to be the best single-volume account of any period of Chinese history. It was written when Maspero was still only 43, but it shows a complete mastery of the subject within the limits imposed by the evidence available at that time.

There is no point here in describing the book. However, it should be mentioned that it was by no means Maspero's last word on Ancient China. He had originally planned to follow it with another volume taking China's history down to the Sui period, but only some parts of this study dealing with the institutions of the Han period were ever completed.[5] In the 1930s Maspero became more and more involved in the study of Taoism, a field in which his achievement was to be even more original than his work in ancient history. But he constantly returned to early China, writing on the text-criticism of early works,[6] the early history of the language[7] myth, religion,[8] forms of judicial procedure,[9] astronomy,[10] early agriculture and early forms of land tenure.[11] Among his posthumous works was a long and extremely imaginative sketch outline of early Chou society, which incorporated much of this later research.[12]

China in Antiquity, then, has a permanent value, as a summary of the views of one of the greatest sinologists on Ancient China, a synthesis which will always provide insights of great value, and which will always rank as a major work of creative imagination and profound scholarship. Like all historical scholarship, however, it is a document of its own time, and it happens to have been written during a decade in which scholarship on early China was undergoing profound changes. While Maspero was preparing *China in Antiquity*, based as it is on a firm foundation of traditional Chinese scholarship, China was experiencing the first fervour of iconoclastic modern historical research. During the 1920s the younger Chinese intellectuals were rejecting their heritage wholesale. The records of the past — particularly those of the distant past — were questioned, doubted and discarded. The very existence of the early Hsia and Shang dynasties was questioned. This highly sceptical approach to the accepted records blossomed, in particular in Ku Chieh-kang's *Ku-shih pien*, the first volume of which appeared in 1926, just as *China in Antiquity* was going into the press. This period of iconoclasm stimulated a great burst of critical scholarship on the texts of

early works, which has gone on down to the present — and
which renders obsolete some of Maspero's datings of early works
— and throws into question the reliance he places for example
on some parts of the *Book of Documents* (*Shang shu*) and *The Rituals of
Chou* (*Chou-li*) which are now thought to be of much later
provenance than was then believed.

This critical, rationalistic, pragmatic attitude to the written
evidence was essentially scholarship very much in the mode of
the great Ch'ing period textual critics, and Maspero himself was
pursuing similar lines in his work on the elements of fictionalized
romance in the *Tso chuan*[13] and in his work on the *Book of
Documents*.[14] Like him, the Chinese and Japanese scholars in the
1920s were much concerned with the problems of the
relationship of early historical writings with their underlying
strata of myth and legend, as were his European contemporaries
Gustav Haloun and Bernhard Karlgren. But Maspero's work
differed from their own in one very important particular, the
comparative approach based on his personal observations in
Indo-China.

Here Maspero was treading, more cautiously, in the path
along which his contemporary Marcel Granet was also
advancing, sometimes recklessly, and without the foundation of
solid scholarship at Maspero's disposal. This comparison of the
China of the early Chou with modern tribal societies was an
important perception, which coincided with the attempts of the
Chinese iconoclasts to destroy the picture preserved in the
traditional histories of the Hsia and Shang and the Early Chou as
great unified empires similar to those of more recent times.
Maspero, Granet, and some of their Chinese and Japanese
contemporaries saw early China as a far more primitive society,
organized on a much smaller scale, with a strong tribal element.
The world pictured in Granet's writings, or in Waley's magical
version of the *Book of Songs*, has more in common with *The Golden
Bough* than with traditional Chinese ideas. Since the 1930s this
conception of Chinese antiquity has in its turn become the victim
of fashion, and it is now again conventional to think of the Early
Chou as a more powerful and better organized political system
than was the case before the War. This attitude — which possibly
may prove to have swung back too far from the iconoclasm of
the 1920s — can be seen exemplified in the recent work of
Professor H. G. Creel.[15]

China in Antiquity was published too soon to have reflected the
dour and sterile controversies over the periodization of ancient
history which have occupied much of the energies of the Marxist

historians in China, and have evolved into long and unproductive debates on such topics as whether the Early Chou was a slave society, and whether China experienced a unique stage of historical development, the so-called Asiatic mode of production. Maspero was, however, fully aware of these developments, and later, in 1933, published a very lengthy and detailed review of Kuo Mo-jo's two early major works on Ancient China, *Researches in the Oracle bone Script*, and *Researches on the Society of Ancient China* (both published in 1930) which, while praising much of Kuo's detailed research, called in question many of his interpretations and heavily criticized the generally poor level of his analysis of early history and his sketchy knowledge of western theories of society and history.[16]

Nevertheless, it must be remembered that *China in Antiquity* was written just as modern Chinese historical scholarship was coming into being in the new Chinese universities. It was also written just at the birth of another field of research, modern archaeology.

If one were to sum up in one word what has happened in the field since Maspero published his great book, the answer would undoubtedly be archaeology. When Maspero wrote, the only archaeological studies to be published were the early reports of Andersson on the neolithic cultures of north-west China. Since then the beginnings of settlement in China have been pushed far back in time with the discovery of Peking Man, and we are even now only beginning to appreciate the great extent and variety of China's neolithic cultures — among which are probably to be discovered the Hsia. On these early stages of Chinese prehistory the reader would do well to consult the monumental volumes of Cheng Te-k'un,[17] and the more recent works of Chang Kwang-chih[18] and the brilliant but controversial recent studies of Ho Ping-ti.[19]

One of the most important archaeological discoveries, the early results of which are mentioned by Maspero, was the discovery in the last years of the nineteenth century of the first Shang period oracle bone inscriptions. One of Maspero's very first publications was a review of the early study of a few of these inscriptions by Chalfant, and in preparing *China in Antiquity* he was able to use the results produced by Lo Chen-yü and Wang Kuo-wei, Jung Keng, Chang Feng and L. C. Hopkins. Although by the 1920s considerable progress had been made in reading the inscriptions, only a small number of bones and tortoiseshells had then been discovered and published. This situation was soon to be revolutionized by the first systematic scientific excavation carried out in China, the excavation of An-yang, the site of the last Shang capital. From this site a huge number of oracle inscriptions were discovered. Many more have been discovered in Shang sites elsewhere, and since the 1930s the study of bone inscriptions — *chia-ku wen* — has become an important and highly specialized field of research. The fragmentary nature of the oracle questions has made it very difficult to derive a systematic body of historical evidence from them, but we are now approaching the time when it will become possible to write a far more detailed and coherent picture of Shang society and the Shang state. For a very full account of these problems, the reader should consult the study of the An-yang excavations by Li Chi.[20]

Archaeology has also added to the written record in the discovery of great numbers of inscribed bronzes from the entire period covered by *China in Antiquity*. Maspero deserves great credit for being the first western scholar systematically to use bronze inscriptions as historical evidence, not only in *China in Antiquity*, but also in his very important later studies on the early system of feudal tenure, the land system, and the place of the oath in early legal procedure. However, since the 1920s and 1930s the science of epigraphy has seen great advances, and both the number and variety of published inscriptions have increased dramatically.[21] The earlier collections of rubbings available to Maspero when writing his studies were mostly taken from bronzes which had been acquired from dealers, and the original provenance of which was unknown. There is now a large corpus of known bronzes recovered in controlled scientific excavations from sites that can be identified and dated, and we thus now have far better stylistic and technical criteria for dating and for establishing authenticity that can be applied to bronzes in older collections some of which, together with their inscriptions, are clearly fakes.

More recently, Chinese archaeologists have excavated textual materials even more important than inscribed bronzes, in the shape of books and documents written on wooden slips or silk scrolls from graves of the Warring States, Ch'in and Han periods.[22] Some of these provide variant early versions of works which have been transmitted to the present day, while others are copies of otherwise lost books which provide us with totally new historical evidence. Among those relevant to the period covered by *China in Antiquity* these include early versions of the *Book of Ceremonial (I-li)* and of the *Book of Changes (I-ching)*, the latter in an arrangement quite different from that of modern texts and including hitherto unknown commentaries; two copies of Lao-tzu's *Tao-te ching* discovered together with four short and hitherto unknown Taoist texts which have been tentatively identified as the lost *Huang-ti ssu-ching* and as originating from southern China in the early 4th century B.C.; fragments of *Kuan-tzu, Mo-tzu* and the *Yen-tzu ch'un-ch'iu*; copies of two works entitled *Rules of Military Affairs (Ping-fa)* by Sun Pin and Sun Wu, with fragments of other early military treatises, *Liu-t'ao* and *Wei-Liao-tzu*; a number of medical, veterinary, calendrical and astronomical manuals, and texts on divination and related matters as yet unidentified and unpublished.

Most important to the historian are two further sets of recently excavated documents. The first are a group of purely historical texts. A fragment, unfortunately heavily damaged, of a historical narrative similar in style to *Tso-chuan* was discovered in one of the Han period graves at Ma-wang-tui near Ch'ang-sha, Hunan. This same grave also contained a very long section of a silk manuscript of the *Chan-kuo ts'e*, including long sections which are not included in the modern texts. Much of this material relates to Su Ch'in (see below pp. 360–62, Notes pp. 443–44) about whose story Maspero published a lengthy study.[23] Lastly, a fragment of an unidentified chronological record covering the period 306–217 B.C. was discovered in a Ch'in period burial at Shui-hu-ti, Yün-meng, Hu-pei, which largely corroborates the bare account of this period in *Shih-chi* but occasionally differs from the accepted record and adds some further detail.

The same grave at Shui-hu-ti also contained the second set of documents of the greatest importance. These are fragments of the codified law of the state of Ch'in, dating from the period prior to the unification of the empire in 221 B.C. Some of the fragments have explanatory commentary, and further documents recovered from the same grave are model cases exemplifying the workings and application of the law. These fragments provide entirely new and invaluable material on the working of law and of administration during the latter part of the Warring States period.

Archaeology has, however, done far more than merely to add to the sum of written evidence available to the historian of the period. Careful examination of the evidence from scientifically excavated sites now enables us to understand far more about the material basis of life than could ever be learned or inferred from textual evidence alone. The new techniques of radio-carbon dating, although so far employed on only a few early Chinese sites, are beginning to provide us with absolute dates for the earlier stages of Chinese culture.[24] Pollen analysis, again used on only a few sites, has nevertheless enabled us to form hypotheses about the vegetation, crops and natural environment at various times in the past.[25] Current work on the history of climate is now giving us an insight into climatic changes in Chinese history,[26] although we are still far from being able to draw the clear and detailed profiles that can now be constructed for Europe and North America.

Careful correlation of textual and archaeological evidence permits us to reconstruct the pattern of crops grown in various parts of ancient China, identify the domesticated animals, and gain a picture of the customary diet of its people. Chinese historians of agriculture using textual evidence, the results of archaeological investigations and even modern field experiments, have begun to piece together a detailed picture of early crops, techniques of cultivation, knowledge of soils and agricultural implements.

Similarly we are far better informed, thanks to archaeology, about every aspect of the handicrafts and of technology. The most remarkable progress has been made in our knowledge of the history of metallurgy. The once common assumption that bronze technology was imported into China from the Near East or Central Asia has now been abandoned, and it is accepted that Chinese methods of bronze casting and smelting were independently developed. We have some clear understanding of the techniques of advanced piece-mould casting employed by Shang craftsmen and ever more evidence of the complexity and sheer size of the artifacts they were able to produce. There are some pieces of evidence that suggest that bronze smelting may have antedated the Shang. We have a clear idea of the historical stages by which bronze technology spread from the central area of the Shang to the rest of China.[27] Equally striking, though not yet so well integrated, is the evidence gradually accumulating about the introduction and spread of iron technology, from the latter part of the Ch'un-ch'iu period. Here too the techniques employed were strikingly different from those in use in the Near East and in Europe, and led to an early use of cast iron, which made possible the mass-production of tools, utensils and weapons from an early date.[28] Since bronze had rarely been used for everyday tools, but reserved for ceremonial and luxury objects, this led to a rapid and radical change in the types of implements available for agriculture and handicrafts,[29] with a major increase in overall productivity, and later to major changes in warfare.

We are also beginning to perceive something of the patterns of communication and trade in early times, and from the sixth century B.C. onward we can see patterns of regional production and specialization in a wide variety of products and manufactures. This growth of commerce led to the development of a variety of copper coinages by the fourth century B.C., the distribution of which tells us something of the extent of inter-regional trade.[30] By that time, money from a great number of places circulated freely together over very wide areas.

With the growth of production and trade went the growth of cities. Archaeology has once again transformed our knowledge of early Chinese urban settlements. Since the discovery and detailed excavation of An-yang many other early city sites have been investigated, giving us much detail not only of the form and construction of cities and their buildings, but enabling us to form an idea of their size, to understand something of their internal organization and of their social setting. We also begin to see a pattern for historical change from the Shang cities, in which a small walled area contained the royal residence, the homes of the great clans, and the administrative centre, and was sur-rounded by a series of settlements of subjects, with specialists in each handicraft living together, to a far larger city, in which not only the ruler and the aristocracy, but a large mixed population, still mostly living in specialized groups, and the markets were enclosed by a wall. By the end of the period covered by *China in Antiquity* such cities were very large; Loyang covered about 9 sq. km, Lin-tzu the capital of Ch'i about 16 sq. km, and Hsia-tu in the northern state of Yen about 30 sq. km.[31]

In addition to the work in recent decades on the reconstruction of the physical appearance and functions of early Chinese cities, there has been much interest in the ceremonial and symbolic aspects of the early Chinese city, and particularly of capital cities.[32] This has largely been the work of historical geographers and sociologists rather than of archaeologists, and it is important to remember that the current interpretations of the archaeological evidence have been much influenced by modern anthropological and sociological theory.

Sociology has itself contributed to other lines of investigation crucial in the historical writings devoted to the early period of Chinese culture. One problem much in Maspero's own mind, and also of great concern to his contemporary Granet,[33] whose importance in the history of sociological theory has recently been reassessed by the late Maurice Freedman, was that of the kinship structures of ancient society, a subject over which Maspero became engaged in polemics with Kuo Mo-jo in the 1930s. This subject has been reworked by such scholars as Ruey Yih-fu and Chang Kwang-chih in the light of modern anthropological theory in more recent years, and these studies have gone some way to clarifying the kinship system used by the Shang royal house and by the Chou nobility.[34]

Studies of social function, of social stratification and of social mobility have also given us a new understanding of the great changes that affected the fabric of society during the Chou period. Hsü Cho-yun's *Ancient China in Transition* (1965) was a very important work of historical synthesis, which put these social changes into a broad context of economic change and of political development from the semi-feudal kingdoms of the eighth century B.C. to the powerful centralized states, staffed by professional functionaries, of the late Warring States period. The organization of the Early Chou state, and its 'feudal' system, has also been the subject of much research since Maspero's day. He himself wrote important contributions to this subject in the 1930s.[35] Much Chinese scholarship has since been devoted to feudal tenure, enfiefment and subenfiefment, while it is worth remembering that the ideas of western scholars about European feudalism have changed very markedly since the 1920s. The reader would be well advised to consult the later writings on this subject of Derk Bodde[36] and H. G. Creel.[37] Besides their writings on feudalism, these two scholars have also made extremely important studies of the development of political institutions in Ch'un-ch'iu and Warring States times, which suggest a rather earlier date for the emergence of the type of bureaucratic institutions usually associated with the rise of the Ch'in state, and draw attention to the fact that these developments took place in several of the states rather than in Ch'in alone.[38]

The section of *China in Antiquity* that is most dated is undoubtedly the last one on literature and philosophy. It is impossible here even to mention the many new translations and analytical studies written on pre-Ch'in literature and thought since the 1920s. These have, in many cases, completely revolutionized our understanding of the texts themselves, and have taken into account the ever-growing modern Chinese and Japanese secondary literature on the field. We now hold different views from those of Maspero on the date and authenticity of many important sources. Other studies, in particular the writings of Needham, have investigated Chinese ideas about the natural sciences as evidenced in early literature, and provide the reader for the first time with an understanding of this important aspect of Chinese thought. There is, unfortunately, no really adequate and up-to-date general treatment of pre-Ch'in literature and thought available in any western language.

The same is true of the early history of religion and myth, to which Maspero made such an important contribution. This is another field in which archaeology and anthropology combined have opened up new perspectives.[39] Studies of motifs used in Shang and Chou ornament on bronzes and other artifacts, which began in the 1930s, have now to be re-examined in the light of the strange and vivid tomb paintings and shrouds discovered in Han tombs which are now considered as belonging to an ancient and complex system of cosmological beliefs and mythology going far back into antiquity. These recent discoveries show links with the strange world revealed in the archaeological discoveries made in the Ch'ang-sha area in the 1930s, including the 'Ch'u silk manuscript' found in 1934 and recently studied by Noel Barnard and other scholars.[40]

These, like the southern poetry preserved in the *Songs of Ch'u*, show striking regional variations in beliefs and even in language, but also indicate that under these regional differences there was a deep underlying cultural continuity between the various regions of early China. Archaeology has constantly underlined this fact, and is progressively extending the area covered by early Chinese culture. The distribution of sites from the various Neolithic cultures, or sites showing Shang characteristics, is now known to be far more widespread than was believed only twenty years ago. A clear basic continuity is also being established which lasted from the Neolithic into early historic times, a cultural continuity that already exhibits many of the characteristic traits of Chinese civilization.

We thus know a great deal more about many aspects of Ancient China than was possible in 1927, particularly about material civilization. Maspero's great work, if it is to speak to the present generation as more than a 'classic in the field', must be read with this reservation in mind. Why has no replacement been written, to bring together all this new knowledge?

The answer is twofold. The spate of discoveries being published in Chinese archaeological journals is such as to inhibit any but the most impetuous scholar. Cheng Te-k'un's monumental three volumes on *Archaeology in China* completed in 1959–63 are already seriously dated, even though a supplement to the first volume was published in 1966. Chang Kwang-chih's *Archaeology of Ancient China*, first published in 1963, was extensively revised in 1968 and has now appeared in a third edition. Since the resumption of publication by Chinese archaeological journals, *Wen-wu*, *K'ao-ku* and *K'ao-ku hsüeh-pao* after the Cultural Revolution, we have been inundated with new data, and any generalization is liable to be rendered obsolete overnight by some new discovery.

The second reason relates to the changes in the style and nature of our scholarship, which make it unlikely that we shall ever again see another Maspero. It is inconceivable in the modern academic world that any single scholar should even keep completely up-to-date with all the fields of research necessary — archaeology, art history, sociological history, religion and myth, philosophy, literature, epigraphy, textual scholarship, historical linguistics — far less make his own significant contributions in all of them. The explosion of knowledge has made a new synthesis of the same magisterial quality as *China in Antiquity* most unlikely, if not impossible, unless it were written by a team of specialist scholars. Any such work of corporate scholarship is hardly likely to have the integrity and guiding intelligence provided by Maspero in his masterpiece.

It follows, obviously enough, that *China in Antiquity*, unique in its own day, remains the finest single volume history of pre-imperial China. Nowhere else is the chronological narrative of the period set out so clearly and so eloquently. Moreover it covers every aspect of early history, describing social and political institutions, religious beliefs and mythology, the growth of literature and the philosophical schools. Every section bears the marks of a penetrating and original mind, and the whole is unified by an individual vision as no historian has succeeded in doing before or since.

Cambridge, 1978   D. C. TWITCHETT

Notes

1 See the series of articles entitled 'Chinese Studies and the Disciplines' in *Journal of Asian Studies*, 23, 3 (1964).
2 Some idea of this renewed interest among younger scholars may be gained from the new journal *Early China* (Vol. 1, 1975; Vol.2, 1976).
3 *Les finances de l'Egypte sous les Lagides*, Paris, 1905.
4 His appointment was announced late in 1919, his inaugural lecture, 'Edouard Chavannes', subsequently published in *T'oung pao*, 21, pp. 43–56, was given on 24 January 1921. For details of Maspero's career see the detailed obituary and bibliography by Paul Demiéville 'Nécrologie: Henri Maspero (1883–1945)', *Journal Asiatique*, 234 (Suite) (1943–45)

pp. 245–80, and the same author's 'Henri Maspero et l'avenir des études chinoises', *T'oung-pao*, 38 (1947), pp. 16–42.

5   Henri Maspero and Etienne Balazs, *Histoire et institutions de la Chine Ancienne, des origines au XIIe siècle après J.C.*, Paris 1967.

6   'Notes sur la logique de Mö-tseu et de son école', *T'oung-pao*, 25 (1927) pp. 1–64; review of Conrady and Waley on the *Book of Changes*, *Journal Asiatique*, 226 (1935), pp. 160–73.

7   'Préfixes et dérivation en Chinois archaïque', *Mémoires de la Société de Linguistique de Paris*, 23 (1930), pp. 313–27.

8   'Mythologie de la Chine moderne', *Mythologie asiatique illustré* (Paris, 1928), pp. 227–365; 'Le mot Ming', *Journal Asiatique*, 223 (1938), pp. 249–56. 'Légendes mythologiques dans le *Chou King*', *Journal Asiatique*, 202 (1924) pp. 1–100; reviews of works by Kuo Mo-jo and Karlgren, *Journal Asiatique*, 222, fasc. annexe, pp. 2–21.

9   'Le Serment dans la procédure juridique de la Chine antique', *Mélanges Chinois et bouddhiques*, 3 (1935), pp. 257–317.

10   'L'astronomie Chinoise avant les Han', *T'oung-pao*, 26 (1929) pp. 267–356; 'Les instruments astronomiques des Chinois au temps des Han', *Mélanges Chinois et bouddhiques*, 6 (1930), pp. 183–370.

11   'Le régime féodal et la propriété foncière dans la Chine antique', *Revue de l'Institut de Sociologie (Bruxelles)*, 16 (1936), pp. 3–36; 'Les régimes fonciers en Chine', *Recueil de la Société Jean Bodin*, 1 (1937), pp. 265–314; 'Les terres désignant la propriété foncière en Chine', *Recueil de la Société Jean Bodin*, 3 (1938), pp. 287–307.

12   'Contribution à l'Etude de la Société Chinoise à la fin des Chang et au début des Tcheou', *Bulletin de l'Ecole française de'Extrême-Orient*, 46 (1954), pp. 335–402.

13   'La composition et la date du *Tso tchouan*', *Mélanges Chinois et bouddhiques*, 1 (1932), pp. 137–215.

14   'Légendes mythologiques dans le *Chou King*', *Journal Asiatique*, 202 (1924), pp. 1–100.

15   Herrlee G. Creel, *The Origins of Statecraft in China*, Vol. 1: *The Western Chou Empire*, Chicago 1970.

16   *Journal Asiatique*, 222, fasc. annexe, pp. 2–18. Kuo Mo-jo published a rejoinder in *Wen-hsüeh nien-pao*, 2 (1936).

17   Cheng Te-k'un, *Archaeology in China*: Vol. 1, *Prehistoric China*, Cambridge 1959; Vol. 2, *Shang China*, Cambridge 1960; Vol. 3, *Chou China*, Cambridge 1963; supplement to Vol. 1, *New Light on Prehistoric China*, Cambridge 1966.

18   Chang Kwang-chih, *The Archaeology of Ancient China*, New

Haven 1963; 2nd revised and enlarged edition, New Haven 1968; 3rd edition, New Haven 1977. *Early Chinese Civilization: Anthropological Perspectives*, Cambridge, Mass. 1976; Chang Kwang-chih (ed.), *Food in Chinese Culture: Anthropological and Historical Perspectives*, New Haven 1977, esp. pp. 1–52.

19 Ho Ping-ti, 'The Loess and the Origin of Chinese Agriculture', *American Historical Review*, 75, 1 (1969); *Huang-t'u yü Chung-kuo nung-yeh ti ch'i-yüan*, Hong Kong 1969. *The Cradle of the East*, Chicago and Hong Kong 1975.

20 Li Chi, *Anyang*, Seattle and Folkestone 1978.

21 A recent work cataloguing some 4030 bronzes with inscriptions is Chang Kwang-chih, Li Kuang-chou, Li Hui and Chang Ch'ung-ho, *Shang-Chou Ch'ing-t'ung-ch'i yü ming wen-ti tsung-ho yen-chiu*, Taipei 1973.

22 These are described in a number of articles in *Wen-wu, Kao-ku* and *K'ao-ku hsüeh-pao*. The texts of *Tao-te-ching* and of the military treatises described below have also been published separately. For a bibliography and some notes see Jeffrey Riegel, *Early China*, 1 (1975), pp. 10–15; a survey of the documents, M. Loewe, *T'oung Pao*, 63 (1978), pp. 99–136. A note on the medical texts from *Ma-wang-tui* by Donald Harper is in *Early China*, 2 pp. 68–9.

23 'Le roman de Sou Ts'in', *Etudes Asiatiques publiées à l'occasion du 25e anniversaire de l'Ecole française d'Extrême-Orient*, Paris (1925) vol. 2, pp. 127–42.

24 On radiocarbon dates established in China since 1965 see Noel Barnard, *The First Radiocarbon Dates from China*, Monographs on Far-Eastern History (Canberra) 8, (1972). Ho Ping-ti, *The Cradle of the East*, pp. 14–21; Chang Kwang-chih, *Early Chinese Civilization*, pp. 38–46; Noel Barnard and Satō Tamotsu, *Metallurgical Remains of Ancient China*, (Tokyo 1975), p. 17 table.

25 See Ho Ping-ti, *The Cradle of the East*, pp. 26–35 and the Chinese literature cited in the footnotes.

26 Chu K'o-chen, 'A Preliminary Study on the Climatic Fluctuations during the Last 5,000 Years in China', *Scientia Sinica*, 16, 2 (1973).

27 Noel Barnard and Satō Tamotsu, '*Metallurgical Remains of Ancient China*; Ho Ping-ti, *The Cradle of the East*, pp. 177–221.

28 J. Needham, *The Development of Iron and Steel Technology*, London 1968, Yang K'uan, *Chung-kuo ku-tai yeh-t'ieh chi-shu ti fa-ming ho fa-chan*, Shanghai 1956.

29 Sekino Takeshi, 'New researches on the Lei-ssu', *Memoirs of the Research Department of the Tōyō bunko*, 25 (1967).

30 Hsü Cho-yun, *Ancient China in Transition*, pp. 122–26; p. 121 gives a distribution map. See also Cheng Te-k'un, *Chou China*, pp. 258–65.
31 See Cheng Te-k'un, *Shang China*, pp. 39–59; *Chou China*, pp. 36–41. Chang Kwang-chih, *Archaeology of Ancient China*, pp. 280–311; *Early Chinese Civilization*, pp. 22–71.
32 See Chang Kwang-chih, *Early Chinese Civilization*, pp. 47–71; Paul Wheatley, *The Pivot of the Four Quarters*, Edinburgh 1971.
33 Marcel Granet, 'Categories matrimoniales et relations de proximité dans la Chine ancienne', *Annales Sociologiques*, (1939); 'La Polygynie sororale et le sororat dans la Chine féodale', in *Etudes Sociologiques sur la Chine*.
34 Feng Han-yi, *The Chinese Kinship System*, Cambridge, Mass. 1948; Chang Kwang-chih, *Early Chinese Civilization*, pp. 72–114.
35 See note 11 above.
36 Derk Bodde, 'Feudalism in China', in Rushton Colbourn (ed), *Feudalism in History* (Princeton, 1956), pp. 49–92.
37 H. G. Creel, *The Origins of Statecraft in China*, Vol. 1 (1970) pp. 317–87. See also Ch'i Ssu-ho, 'A Comparison between Chinese and European Feudal Institutions', *Yenching Journal of Social Studies*, 4 (1948), pp. 1–13.
38 H. G. Creel, 'The Beginnings of Bureaucracy in China, the Origin of the *Hsien*', *Journal of Asian Studies*, 23 (1964), pp. 155–84; Derk Bodde, *China's First Unifier* (Leiden, 1938); Hsü Cho-yun, *Ancient China in Transition* (1965).
39 See Chang Kwang-chih, *Early Chinese Civilization*, pp. 149–96.
40 Noel Barnard, *The Ch'u Silk Manuscript — translation and commentary*, Monographs on Far Eastern History (Canberra) 5, (1973).

Translator's Preface

The task of translating *La Chine antique* into English was begun many years ago by Esson M. Gale, whose translation of *Essays on Salt and Iron* from the Chinese is a standard one. Dr. Gale died in 1964 and the manuscript went through a number of hands before 1971. In that year it came to me, ostensibly as a manuscript nearly ready for typesetting but needing a little polishing here and there. Unfortunately, the polishing ultimately required complete reworking which has left virtually no sentence unchanged; and for two of the books (I and III) I have simply used my own pre-existing translation.

In retranslating I have hewed as closely as I could to Maspero's original, trying to preserve at least the spirit of its elegant but straightforward style. I was extremely fortunate to have a great number of detailed emendations suggested by Mme. Maspero and by Prof. Paul Demiéville; and although keyed to the old and unacceptable translation, these were of enormous assistance. They have also been so kind as to read my own altered version through and have saved me from many a *bêtise*. In addition, my old friend Prof. Frederick W. Mote of Princeton has gone through the final manuscript with a fine-tooth comb, providing an invaluable objective and critical eye. Needless to say, however, any errors or infelicities or failures of standardization that may remain are in no way the responsibility of anybody but myself.

The translation uses simplified Wade–Giles romanization, since that is the most nearly standard system of transcription in English; and a chart explaining that system is on page 489. The maps from *La Chine antique*, which were extremely congested, have been somewhat simplified without sacrificing essential information; Map 2 includes names of relevant modern provinces to help the reader orient himself. Also provided are an index and a chronological chart for reference. In the interests of economy, almost all Chinese and Japanese characters have been relegated to the Bibliography and the Index.

Book I
The Beginnings

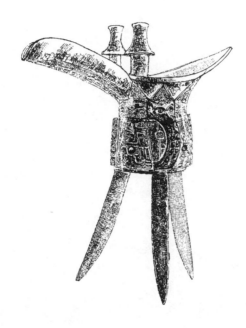

1
The Primitive Chinese World

At about the time when the civilizations of the Near East reached their height, at the other end of the Asian continent, in the broad, low-lying plains which form the shores of the Gulf of Chihli and the Yellow Sea, the agricultural peoples inhabiting the banks of the Yellow River were taking the first tentative steps on the road towards civilized life and, unaware how great the future of their accomplishment would be, were laying the foundations of the Chinese Empire.

Chinese civilization developed with its back turned to the Mediterranean world. At least in its beginnings, it remained outside the influence of that world, knowing nothing of it except what was transmitted through the intermediacy of the Scytho-Siberian peoples, with whom the Chinese had commercial relations from prehistoric times.[1] The civilization of China faced towards the Pacific Ocean from a vast region of high mountains and wide plains which descend from the Tibetan plateau eastward to the sea. Two entirely different worlds, whose soil, climate, flora, and fauna have nothing in common, separated from one another by the lateral barrier of an enormous mountain chain, and each watered by a great river — such is the setting within which China evolved down the centuries.[2] This immense territory is far from being one. On the contrary, it is cut up into quite distinct regions, rather like compartments, between which communication is difficult.

In the north, Shansi forms one of these compartments. Towards the southwest it descends gradually to the Yellow River, the great trough of the lower Fen opening easy access from this side to the rich valleys through which it flows. Towards the south

and east, on the other hand, the T'ai-hang and Wu-t'ai
Mountains raise their peaks like an actual wall between plateau
and plain. The valley of the Ch'in provided the masters of the
plateau with a corridor into the Honan Plain, but it did not by
any means lead the plains people into the heart of the region,
were they to try to ascend it; and farther to the northeast the
passes are few and difficult. Thus we see the rulers of Shansi, the
princes of Chin, constantly in touch and often at war with their
neighbours to the west but having little direct intercourse with
those of the east and seldom descending into the Yellow River
plain except through the valley of the Ch'in, so as to emerge into
what was in antiquity the state of Wey.[3] nox Wei-

At the extreme western end of the Chinese world, the valley of
the Wei constitutes another almost sealed compartment. To the
south the enormous mass of the Ch'in-ling closes it off with a
formidable barrier; to north and west dwell the barbarians, and
beyond them is the desert. The sole link with the rest of China is
the Yellow River, but, after dashing against Hua-shan and being
turned towards the east, the river is of little use for navigation, in
winter because of low water and sandbanks, and in summer
because of too violent a current. Here too geography has greatly
shaped history: the masters of this region, the lords of Ch'in,
mixed rather little with the rest of the Chinese world; but they
struggled ferociously for centuries to seize the opening through
which the Yellow River enters the great eastern plain.

To the south, the basin of the Yangtze is another quite
separate area, clearly marked off on its northern side. It can be
approached easily only along the seacoast, in the plain where in
all ages the Yellow River, the Huai, and the Yangtze have
mingled their waters through secondary channels; but farther
west, where the mountains begin, lines of communication
become few. The Huai Mountains, though not very high, share
the charm of the eastern K'un-lun with their parallel ridges,
abrupt slopes, and passes which are not hard going but stretch
out interminably. The easiest of them, that leading to Nan-yang-
fu, is some forty kilometres long, though it never rises above 450
metres; and the route to Hsin-yang, which the Peking–Hankow
railway follows today, is little shorter and goes through higher
passes. As you go westwards, the passes become ever more
difficult: to go from the Wei Valley to that of the Han the best
routes must cross passes more than 1,000 metres high. Thus the
masters of the Yangtze basin, the kings of Ch'u, secure from
their northern adversaries, could choose their time to raid the
states of the central plain and, having struck their blow, could

retire within their own land; none of their northern enemies dared to pursue through the long passes of the Hua-shan, which were so well suited to ambush. It was only when a powerful kingdom was established on the lower Yangtze, turning the defences of Ch'u, that they became vulnerable.

Finally, to the northeast, the state which was called Ch'i in ancient times, within the present-day provinces of Hopei and Shantung, was also surrounded with imposing natural fortifications. To the north and west it was well protected by the immense and almost impassable swamps through which the branches of the lower Yellow River meandered (its bed being different from that of modern times); to the south it had the massif of T'ai-shan, and this extended eastwards to the sea.

Unlike these clearly defined and naturally protected regions, the great eastern plain is a land of easy communication, where canals crisscross in all directions and where no obstacles impede an army's progress. A region both wealthy and indefensible, fated to be constantly a battlefield and always laid waste, we shall see how, throughout ancient times, it was indeed ravaged by the men of the north, of the south, and of the west, without ever being able to resist any of these invaders. Thus the very configuration of the land imposed inescapable conditions upon the history of ancient China.

The area covered by Chinese civilization at its origin was nothing like so extensive as the vast territory it occupies today, which it took over only very gradually. In ancient times it included only a small area in the north, the middle, and lower parts of the Yellow River basin. Even within this cramped area the Chinese were not by any means the sole occupants. Only the irrigated plain was wholly theirs; all the mountains, even in the very heart of their domain, were in the hands of the barbarians.[4]

The terraced plateaus of Shansi were the land of the Ti.[5] In the south the six tribes of the Red Ti, Ch'ih Ti, dwelt in the land of Shang-tang, on the upper courses of the Ch'in and the two Chang rivers. The westernmost of them, the Kao-lo of Tung-shan, controlled the left bank of the Yellow River at the point where the plain disappears among the mountains pinching in above the modern sub-prefecture of Yüan-ch'ü.[6] To the east were the Lu-shih, who have lent their name to present-day Lu-an-fu; and near them, to the north, were the Liu-hsü, around the modern sub-prefecture of T'un-liu, occupying the southeast corner of Shansi province. Still farther north, the Ch'iang-chiu-ju and the To-ch'en (whose location is not precisely known) lived next to the Chia-shih, the easternmost of the Red Ti, who spread to the banks of the Yellow River in the area where Chi-tse, in Kuang-p'ing-fu, stands today.

North of the Red Ti, the White Ti, Po Ti, divided into three tribes, occupied the entire massif of Wu-t'ai-shan and the lands at its foot in Cheng-ting, Hopei. To the east were the Fei and the Ku, near present-day Hsin-lo, and to the west the Hsien-yü of Chung-shan, near T'ang. The subjugation of these Southern Ti (Red Ti) and Eastern Ti (White Ti) required several centuries. Although the former were brought to heel in about 593 B.C., the last tribe of the White Ti, the Hsien-yü, struggled on in the Wu-t'ai Mountains until almost the end of the Chou dynasty, being conquered only in 296. On the other hand, the entire west and centre of Shansi had been occupied by tribes of the Western Ti whose name is unknown because they had been subdued much earlier.

Since prehistoric times Chinese settlers had held the lower Fen Valley from near where it joins the Yellow River up to P'ing-yang-fu; and they had established small principalities there, such as Keng, Huo, and Chao. At a date which is unknown but certainly very early they had gained a foothold in the rich basin of T'ai-yüan-fu, where from the fifth century B.C. on the lords of Chao held their fief of Chin-yang. Therefore the Ti of the mountains which separate the Yellow River from the Fen, cut off from their eastern kinsmen, offered little resistance. They were brought under control in the beginning of the seventh century, and two forts were erected in their territory: Ch'ü and P'u, roughly where modern Chi-chou and Hsi-chou are.

Only the tribes which dwelt farther north remained independent, and these later founded the small kingdom of Tai, the name of which survives in Tai-chou, a prefecture in northern Shansi. To the north they butted upon the nomads who had lived from the remotest times in the broad steppes of the Mongolian plateau, on the rim of the desert: the Three Hu, San-hu. In the west, on the banks of the Yellow River, these included two tribes of Huns, the Lin or Tai-lin (in the region of Shuo-p'ing in far northern Shansi, where the great autumn assembly of the Huns was held towards the beginning of the Christian era), and the Lou-fan, a little farther south of them around present-day K'o-lan. Then in the east, near the sea, were the Manchus: the Eastern Jung, or Eastern Hu, or Wu-chung. Farther north were the Mo, who had neither cities, nor palaces, nor houses, nor ancestral temples, and who cultivated only millet.[7]

As in the north, the south and west of the Yellow River were infested with barbarians, who in these regions were called Jung.

The mountains which separate the River Lo from its tributary the Yi were the domain of the Jung of Lo, of Yi, of Yang-chü, and so on. From their haunts they dominated the eastern capital of the Chou, Lo-yi, near modern Ho-nan-fu. A little to the southeast the Jung Man, or Mao, inhabited the northwest portion of the Huai Mountains, near Ju-chou, Honan. To the west the plain of the Wei was surrounded by Jung: in the south the Li dwelt on the slopes of the Hua-shan and its spurs right down to the banks of the River itself. Other tribes inhabited western and northern Shensi, in the mountainous massif out of which the rivers Wei, Ching and Lo flow and which separates them from the Yellow River. Here dwelt the Kun-jung, the Jung of Ti-huan near modern Kung-ch'ang-fu, the Mien-chu near modern Ch'in-chou on the Wei. To the northeast were the Wu-shih, around Ching-hsien, and most important the Yi-ch'ü, who for centuries resisted the Chinese and only lost their independence finally in 315 B.C. They had their centre near modern Ch'ing-yang.

These tribes had originally occupied the whole valley. Chinese colonists, coming from the great eastern plain towards the middle of the second millennium B.C., had gradually dispossessed them or more probably had subdued and assimilated the greater part of them. But remnants had been left behind as they vanished, and these still held corners of the plain, small enclaves isolated among the Chinese, such as the Ta-li, the Ch'üan-jung, and the P'eng-hsi of T'ung-chou on the banks of the River Lo.[8]

In the south, the basin of the Yangtze River was the domain of the Man, who had come late under Chinese influence with the conquests of the eleventh century B.C. They had quickly recovered their independence and retained it to the end of the Chou dynasty, becoming civilized by contact rather than by conquest. In the east along the seacoast, the Yi of Huai lived in the marshy plains of northern Kiangsu, on the Shantung border, on the lower Huai, its tributaries, and the lakes which they fed. In the west these Yi were in contact with the Hsü, who had originally occupied the entire area between the Yellow River and the Huai Mountains, on the middle course of the Huai and its tributaries. During historical times, however, attacked alternately by the princes of Lu and of Sung, they had been restricted to the eastern part of their old domain, around Ssu-chou in northern Anhwei, leaving only insignificant remnants in the west. The most important of these, the Hsü-jung, still in the seventh century (they were not conquered until 668 B.C.) held the marshy area out of which the Chi River flowed, between Ts'ao-chou-fu and K'ai-feng-fu, at the point where the boundaries of the three modern provinces of Hopei, Shantung, and Honan converge. Finally, the mountains of the Shantung peninsula were also a barbarian domain; and in historical times the isolated groups of the Lai, the Chieh, and the Ken-mou perpetuated the remembrance of this amidst such sinicized principalities as Chü, Ch'ii, and Chu-lü.

Thus the sphere of Chinese civilization at the dawn of the historical period was clearly delimited. It was divided into two distinct regions, each in one of the Yellow River plains and separated by groups of barbarians. The more important of these, in the lower valley of the river, touched the sea only on a narrow front north and south of the Shantung peninsula, on the Gulf of Chihli and the Yellow Sea. To the west it did not extend beyond the sheer wall of the Shansi plateau and the narrow channel through which the Yellow River squeezes before it reaches Honan. The second, and much less extensive, region was in the small plain where the Wei and Lo rivers flow into the Yellow River, between Hua-shan to the south and the Shensi plateau to the north.

Both regions were surrounded by barbarians; but this term should not be misinterpreted. True enough, in the extreme north the Jung of Wu-chung and of Tai seem to have been Tungus and Huns, as perhaps were also the Lu-hun and other tribes of the central area who continued on into fully historical times. Likewise, in the south, the Man tribes have been considered closely related to the Tibetans of Shu (Szechuan) and the Miao-tzu of Pa and also, no doubt, of southwestern Ch'u. Nevertheless, the majority of the tribes — the Ti; almost all of the Jung, the Hsü, and the Huai; and even the basic population of Ch'u, Wu, and Yüeh — were certainly small Chinese tribal groupings which had remained behind in their mountains, their marshes, or their forests, keeping themselves aloof from the civilizing movement which carried the plains people along.[9] In the same way the Greeks had regarded the Thessalians and Macedonians as barbarians. What distinguished 'the Hsia', Chu Hsia, from their barbarian neighbours were probably no more than social differences, though these became more obvious as writing, political organization, and material progress demonstrated more clearly the superiority of the plains people over those of the mountains. These differences are fairly well summed up in a discourse which the *Tso chuan* attributes to a Jung chieftain of the sixth century B.C.: 'Our drink, our food, our dress differ from those of the Chinese states. We exchange no courtesies with them. Their language and ours are not mutually intelligible.'[10]

In the world 'under heaven', *t'ien hsia*, China was a civilized island amid a sea of barbarians. This situation was naturally reflected in the Chinese conception of the world, its form, and its inhabitants.[11] They viewed it as a chariot, of which the square earth was the body and the round heaven the canopy. Heaven has nine levels, each separated from the next by a door guarded by tigers and panthers, commanded by a gate-keeper of the Lord on High, Shang-ti. The lowest door, the *Ch'ang-ho-men*, is at the boundary between the celestial and terrestrial worlds, and through it the west wind blows on the world below. On the highest level, in the Great Bear, is the Celestial Palace, *Tzu-wei-kung*, the dwelling-place of the Lord on High, from which he governs heaven and earth. This palace is specially guarded by the Celestial Wolf, T'ien-lang (that is, the star Sirius), who slays all who approach. 'A wolf with piercing eyes paces softly back and forth; he tosses men in the air and plays with them as with a ball; obeying the orders of the Lord on High, he casts them into a bottomless pit; and then he may sleep.'

The underside of heaven, despite the nine levels, is not a vault but flat, like a cartwheel. Between it and earth no lateral walls set bounds to the world. There are merely pillars at the eight extremities of the earth;[12] and these support the sky, keeping it apart from the earth and preventing it from falling. On them it rests unmoving while sun, moon, and stars move beneath it. In the beginning these pillars were of equal height, and heaven and earth were parallel to one another; but due to a cataclysm in which the northwest pillar, Mount Pu-chou, was toppled, heaven and earth fell together on that side. Since that time, heaven tilts towards the northwest and the earth towards the southeast, the polestar is no longer in the centre of the heavens, the stars 'flow' each night from east to west, and the rivers on earth flow from west to east. Below the sky flows the Celestial River, *T'ien-ho*, also called the Celestial Han, *T'ien-han*, or Han of the Clouds, *Yün-han* (that is, the Milky Way), which forever separates the Weaving Maiden from her husband, the Herd-boy. By this river the waters of the celestial world go to rejoin those of the terrestrial world in the Great Abyss. Through the firmament there runs a sort of crack, *Lieh-ch'üeh*, through which the lightning flashes; and it is also pierced by doors through which the Celestial Influx can come down to mix with the Earthly Influx: at the North Pole is the Gate of Cold, at the South Pole the Gate of Heat, and so forth.

The sun and the moon are not exclusively celestial beings. The sun, a sort of fireball like a lotus blossom, spends the night on earth. Each morning when he rises his mother, Hsi-ho, bathes him in the Gulf of Sweetness, *Kan-yüan*, also known as the Hsien Pool, *Hsien-ch'ih*. Then he crosses the Valley of Sunrise, *Yang-ku*, where his passage produces the dawn and climbs the heavens by the branches of an immense tree, the *k'ung-sang* or *fu-sang*, a thousand *li* high with leaves like mustard-seeds. Then he commences his daily journey, travelling in his chariot driven by his mother until evening, when he descends again in the west to Mount Yen-tzu. When he has disappeared, the shining flowers of the Jo tree, which are the stars, light 'the earth below'. Sometimes the sun and the moon are attacked in mid-course by monsters, the *ch'i-lin* which eats the sun and the toad with three feet, *tan-chu*, which devours the moon, and that is what produces eclipses.[13] Hsi-ho had ten sons who lived at the foot of the *k'ung-sang* tree and ascended to heaven in turn every ten days of the cycle; but one morning in ancient times all together climbed into the branches of the tree and the earth began to burn up. It was necessary for Yi the Excellent Archer to shoot nine of them with arrows. As for the moon, or rather moons (for there are twelve of them, the daughters of Heng-o), they live on earth in the west and ascend the heavens in turn to light the earth for a month.

Beneath lies 'the earth below', divided into concentric zones. In the middle are the Nine Provinces, *chiu-chou*, of China, with barbarians surrounding them on all sides: the Ti, the Jung, the Man, and the Yi. This is the world inhabited by men. It is washed by the ocean to the south and to the east; but to the north extend vast deserts, the domain of Lady Pa, the Goddess of Drought, from which it is separated by two rivers: on the north the Red Water, *Ch'ih-shui*, which flows eastwards, and on the west the Black Water, *Hei-shui*, which flows southwards. Farther on are the Four Seas, *Ssu-hai*, which are connected with one another and girdle the inhabited world like the River Ocean of the Greeks. Beyond the Four Seas, *hai-wai*, are immense lands peopled with gods and fantastic beings. There dwell the gods of the winds, two of whom are responsible for stopping the sun at the end of his annual journey towards the north, when he rises at the summer solstice and when he sets at the winter solstice. There too can be found the Count of the Water, Shui-po, whose name is T'ien-wu and who has the body of a tiger with eight human heads and ten tails, and the Queen Mother of the West, Hsi-wang-mu, the Goddess of Epidemics, as well as many other gods, goddesses, dwarfs, and monsters. There live the strange beings with which the imagination of the ancient Chinese had peopled the distant deserts, together with those they took over later on from acquaintance with the Greeks and the Hindus, such as holes-through-the-chests (*kuan-hsiung*), long-legs (*ch'ang-ku*), giants (*lung-po*) a hundred feet tall, pygmies (*ch'iao-yao*) five inches high, and so on.

Farther still, since 'the earth being square and the sky round, the four corners of the earth are not covered by the sky', lie the lands where the sun never shines. In the southwest corner is the land of Ku-mang, where heat, cold, day and night are not distinguished and where the sleeping inhabitants wake only once in fifty days. In the northwest corner is the country of the Nine Yin, Chiu-yin, which the sky does not cover and where the sun never shines. In the middle of it stands a god with the body of a serpent and a man's head, the Torch Dragon, Chu-lung, whose body is over a thousand *li* long. He neither eats, nor drinks, nor sleeps; the wind and the rain block his throat; when he opens his eyes, it is day in the land of the Nine Yin; when he closes them, it is night; when he breathes, it is windy; when he inhales, it is winter; when he exhales, it is summer.[14] In the opposite corner, the southeast, yawns the Great Abyss, *Ta-huo*, a bottomless pit into which the waters of the terrestrial world and those of the Celestial River (the Milky Way) hurl themselves without either filling or emptying it. Beyond that is the void: 'Below is a bottomless pit, and there is no earth; above is boundless space, and there is no sky.'

Such was the way the ancient Chinese visualized the world and, like most of the peoples of antiquity, they gave themselves the place of honour in 'the middle country', *Chung-kuo*, of the earth, the sole hearth of civilization amid the barbarian hordes.

What were they like, these Chinese on the banks of the Yellow River, who in prehistoric times had already begun to disengage themselves from the surrounding barbarism? In physical type[15] they do not seem to have differed greatly from their modern descendants in Hopei, in Shantung, and in Honan. They were people of moderate stature, but vigorous; they had that yellow tinge which they have always characterized as white, and straight, glossy black hair; the countenance had a not-very-aquiline nose, high cheekbones, eyes that were prominent and somewhat slanted, a large mouth with strong teeth set somewhat apart, and a scanty beard and moustache.

This is evidenced by the idealized portrait of a distinguished man, such as can be found among writers at about the beginning of the Christian era: 'teeth an inch long, a dragon face, a tiger mouth'; or again, 'eyes like clouds, a nose like that of a dragon, a mouth like that of a square pot, the ears protruding'; or yet more simply, 'a broad forehead, long ears, large eyes, teeth spaced, mouth square'. Thus when, in the fourth century A.D., the Chinese came into contact with Buddhist missionaries coming from India and Iran, they were amazed by the deep-set eyes and prominent noses, like the Chinese of the last century when they saw Europeans.[16]

The depiction of a young woman in the seventh century B.C. is hardly different from that of a young Chinese woman in our day.

> Her fingers are like shoots of white milkweed,
> her skin is like frozen cream,
> her neck is like a white worm,
> her teeth are like melon seeds,
> her brow like [the head of] a cicada,
> her eyebrows like [the antennae of] a silkworm;

or again,

> her black hair is like clouds,
> there are no false locks,
> her brow is white,

and

> how her teeth gleam in her artful smiles!

Tall men were not uncommon. The father of Confucius was very big, and Confucius himself inherited this noble stature. In sum, a walk in the countryside of Honan, or southern Hopei, or western Shantung today would show peasants of the same type as those of the *Shih ching*.

According to the most commonly accepted theory,[17] the Chinese are a branch of the nomadic peoples of northern Asia, Mongols or Manchus, who, having come to the banks of the Yellow River, settled down there and became civilized. But whatever their ethnic origin may have been (and like all historic peoples, their blood must have been very mixed by the beginnings of history), the affinities of their initial culture must be sought in quite the opposite direction. The Chinese language has no relation whatever, not even a distant connection, with the tongues of the northern tribes. Rather, it is very closely related to an important group of dialects spoken by southern tribes: the Thai, who inhabit northern Indochina as well as Yünnan, Kweichow, and Kwangsi. It also shows relations which are less clear, but nevertheless indisputable, with the Tibeto-Burman languages, which are perhaps distant relations or, if not that, have lent or borrowed important elements of the vocabulary — the names of numbers for example — in very ancient times.[18]

From the earliest time that we can trace this Sino-Thai linguistic group, it manifests the most salient characteristics of the modern languages. The words are always monosyllabic, and their phonetism, though rather poor in groupings of consonants, is on the other hand quite rich in diphthongs. Two consonants cannot follow one another immediately except in the initial position, and the second of them must still be a liquid. In the final position only six consonants are tolerated, three oral occlusives and three nasals (gutturals, dentals, and labials). As against this, groupings of vowels into diphthongs and triphthongs are frequent finals. Moreover, one of the essential elements of the phonetic system of these languages is their system of tones. Each word has a tone, the inflection of which was perhaps originally dependent upon the final, while the height was governed by whether the initial was unvoiced or voiced.[19] Each of these monsyllabic words remains absolutely invariable, with no morphology of any kind.[20] The beginnings of a system of derivation, though it was not developed, existed in the asyllabic prefixes which came to be placed before certain initials, and also in a system of tonal changes, perhaps the residue of an ancient suffixation procedure which must have disappeared very long ago both in Chinese and in all the Thai languages. Another procedure of derivation consisted in the reduplication of a word, a reduplication accompanied by widely varying modifications of the original element; but that too was not long continued.

In forming phrases, the construction was all the more rigid since nothing distinguished nouns from verbs and since most words (in Chinese itself, in theory, all words) could be used nominally or verbally with no change in external form. Only their position in the written sentence or (especially in speaking) the use of numerous particles enabled one to make clear the meaning of discourse. In sum, these languages form characteristic groups, which their monosyllabism, the absence of inflexion, and the system of tones set completely apart from all those of northern Asia.[21]

Moreover, language was not the only cultural feature which the ancient Chinese had in common with their southern neighbours. An essentially agricultural and sedentary civilization; a religion tightly linked to agriculture; a political organization basically aristocratic and feudal, rooted in the possession of land; property-holding of a religious character — all these associate them with the southern tribes, Thai, Lolos, Mossos, Miao-tzu, and all dissociate them from the northern tribes. Between the nomadic cattle-herders of the north, the ancestors of the Manchus, the Mongols, and the Huns of historic times, and the irremediably anarchic Mon-Khmer tribes of the Indochinese peninsula (upon whom only a foreign education has sometimes been able to impose social groupings broader than the village), throughout almost all of the territory which makes up China today the diverse tribes which lived there had established, long before history could record them, the same kind of societies: sedentary and agricultural, powerfully attached to the soil by their religion and their institutions. Thus, by a remarkable twist, the progressive conquest and assimilation of the countries to the south by Chinese civilization during recent times seem to be only the re-establishment in a modern form of a prehistoric situation, wherein almost all those who now people the Chinese empire already shared a common civilization.

The Chinese thus appear to be the northernmost branch of these sedentary and agricultural peoples,[22] the western branch of which is composed of the Tibeto-Burman tribes of Tibet, Szechuan, and Yünnan (Tibetans, Lolos, Mossos, Burmans, etc.), the southern branch the Thai of southern China and northern Indochina, and the central branch the Miao-tzu of Hunan and Kweichow.

Life was perhaps harder for these Chinese at the dawn of history than for any of their brethren who lived farther south. It was probably in the great northeastern plain,[23] between the sea and the craggy wall bounding the Shansi plateau, that they began to develop their civilization. From there it spread forth, in that long-vanished epoch, westward into the beautiful Wei Valley, thence up the Fen into the small valleys of Shansi, south towards the Huai and the River Han and the mountains through which one passes into the great valley where the Han flows into the Yangtze. A very harsh climate, torrid in summer and glacial in winter, with gales of chill, sand-laden wind just before the start of spring even more trying than the great cold of winter, with rivers frozen solid or at least full of floating ice throughout the winter but thawing rapidly in the first fine days and changing almost instantly into torrents — all tended to make communication difficult during nearly a third of the year. The great artery, the Yellow River, fast-flowing and cut up by sandbanks, is dangerous to navigate. Its innumerable arms wander capriciously across the low, flat, almost slopeless plains. This is the country which was known as the Nine Rivers because the Yellow River was said to have nine main channels there. It extended over a wide area at the foot of the Shansi plateau, for its course at that time was different from today's and, after a long detour, it flowed into the sea through the modern course of the Pei Ho, near Tientsin.[24]

Each year, moreover, the floods displaced it and sought out new channels. Low-lying areas filled with water, becoming vast swamps which have dried up over time, though some still remain today. In them grew a profusion of aquatic plants — knotgrass, rushes, dolic, valerian — among which wild geese and cranes nested and fish swarmed. All about were larger or smaller areas of land, too damp for farming, covered with tall grass interspersed with clumps of white elm, wild plum, and chestnut. This was not true forest: that existed only on the periphery, on the mountain slopes of Shantung in the east and of Shansi in the west, and with it the domain of the barbarians began. This was thick bush, providing a haunt for great wild beasts — tigers, panthers, wildcats, leopards, bears, wild cattle, even elephants and rhinoceros,[25] wolves, wild boars, foxes — and also small game of every sort — herds of deer and antelope, monkeys, hares, rabbits, and birds of every species, which were hunted in great beats in winter by setting fire to the undergrowth.

Only the borders were put to use, as pasturage for horses and domesticated cattle or as plantations of mulberry trees for silkworm cultivation. The best lands, protected against flooding by dikes and cultivated regularly, produced millet and sorghum in Hopei, rice south of the Yellow River, and wheat almost everywhere. Beans, gourds, indigo, and hemp were also grown.

There were few trees in the fields; in theory there should have been none at all. The fields were divided into squares about one *li* in surface area, called *ching*, divided into nine equal lots which eight families cultivated, each keeping the produce of its lot for its subsistence and giving the produce of the ninth to king or overlord as tax. Nearby, scattered and almost hidden in the plain, stood little clusters of several low huts made of pounded earth: peasant dwellings, each group forming a hamlet, *li*, of two hundred inhabitants, with a mound of the God of the Soil, a school, and a marketplace. This is where the peasants shut themselves up in winter, but they abandoned it entirely in spring, going to live in large sheds in the midst of the *ching*. This continued the tradition of their prehistoric ancestors, who, in the beginning, before permanent fields had been organized, had been obliged to leave the hamlet each spring to go and live far away in the bush, where they cleared the land.[26] All summer they lived almost entirely in the open air, working in the fields, clad in garments of coarse hemp with a sort of straw hat to shield them from the sun, taking turns by night in the watch-huts or on the rounds to drive away the robbers, wild boars, or birds who came to steal the ripening grain before the harvest.

Here and there were the small manors of nobles. There dwelt the lord of the fief, amidst his women, his children, his servants, and his small court of the nobles attached to him (mainly descendants of the junior branches of his family or minor vassals), and finally his priests, scribes, and fighting men. The manor was built according to set ritual principles. Right at the back were the living quarters, and in front of them was a series of three courtyards. The principal one, that in the centre, contained the audience chamber, facing south; and it was flanked on the east by the ancestral temple and on the west by the altar-mound of the God of the Soil. Each court had its high entrance gate. The whole was enclosed by a protective wall and a ditch for protection against unexpected attack. Within the enclosure were granaries, storerooms, and magazines of weapons. Outside it to the north was a large area where the market was held; and on either side of the south gate stood the quarters for counsellors, priests, artisans — all those whose services were a constant necessity to the court.

Sometimes, though not always, a larger outer wall encircled this complex. This was so for the capitals of the Chou dynasty, the western one, Hao, near present-day Sian, which was supposedly founded by King Wen, as well as the eastern one, Lo, near modern Ho-nan-fu, which is traced back to the Duke of Chou; and it was true of other cities as well. Towards the end of the Chou dynasty such double walls seem to have proliferated, though the towns remained quite small. 'If the wall of a city exceeds 3,000 feet in length (about 600 metres), it is a danger to the state.'[27] And Mencius speaks of a city with an interior wall three *li* and an external wall seven *li* around — that is, respectively, about 1,000 and 2,400 metres.[28] The remains of the wall at Shang-ch'iu, the capital of Sung, today trace a square on the ground less than 800 metres around;[29] and similarly the traces of the ancient wall of Yi, the capital of Chin, the state which dominated all others in the sixth and fifth centures B.C., make a square less than a kilometre around.[30] The capital of Eastern Chou, Lo-yi, was 17,200 feet, or less than 4,000 metres, around; and in theory that was the greatest city of the empire.

> The capital is in the shape of a square nine *li* to a side, and each side
> has three gates. Within are nine main avenues and nine transverse
> roads, the former as broad as nine chariot-spans [seventy-two feet, or
> about fifteen metres]. To the left [east] is the ancestral temple, to the
> right [west] the altar of the God of the Soil; in front [facing south] is
> the audience chamber, beyond that [north] the marketplace. ...
> Outside [the palace] stand the nine houses where the nine ministers
> stay when they come to court. ... The gate-towers of the palace are
> fifty feet [high], those at the corners seventy feet, [those of] the
> [external] wall ninety feet.[31]

The Chinese countryside was not thus organized without
trouble, since the land presented enormous difficulties to those
who cleared it. All those fine cultivated fields of millet, rice or
wheat had to be painfully wrested from the bush or from the
waters.

> Ah! they clear away the weeds! Ah! they cut away the brush!
> Their ploughs split the soil.
> Thousands of couples dig up roots,
> some in the low-lying fields, some in the high ground.

Or again:

> Heavy is the toil!
> The thorny brush has been stripped away.
> Why in days of old did they do this task?
> So that we might plant our grain, our millet,
> so that our millet might be abundant,
> so that our millet might be luxuriant.

Or finally:

> That southern mountain,
> it was Yü [the Great] who brought it under cultivation,
> clearing the plains, the damp lands,
> and I, his distant descendant, have laid it out in fields.[32]

Clearing the land had been lengthy and painful. Dikes had to be
built against flooding, canals had to be dug to drain and dry out
the marshes. All these works were so ancient that the memory of
them had been lost in the mists of legend, and they were
attributed to the heroes of high antiquity. At the beginning of
the world they had descended from heaven to earth, following
the orders of the Lord on High, to put it in order so that men
might dwell in it.[33]

Each region had given a particular turn to this legend

according to the particular factors of its local topography, religion, and society. Sometimes, as in the legends of the East, the difficulties were personified by a monster who had to be overcome and killed before any work could be done. In all versions the enormous effort of accomplishment was emphasized by the fact that the first celestial envoy was unable to succeed in his task, and only the second managed to carry through to the end.

In the north of the great plain the struggle between the civilizing heroes and earthly monsters took on an epic air, with the gods playing their part in it. The Yellow Emperor, Huang-ti, descended from heaven to set earth in order, had to strive against the monster Ch'ih-yu, who had a bull's head on a serpent's body. To drive his adversary away, Ch'ih-yu tried to fell the *k'ung-sang* tree, and thus, by preventing the sun from climbing into the sky, to plunge earth into perpetual darkness. Against Ch'ih-yu, who had invented weapons, the Yellow Emperor marshalled armies of fierce beasts — bears, panthers, tigers — and finally sent the Winged Dragon, Ying-lung, against him. Ch'ih-yu then summoned to his aid the gods of the wind and the rain, and the Yellow Emperor had to make his daughter Pa, the Goddess of Drought — who had eyes in the top of her head so that she could not see where she went and who dessicated every spot where she set foot — come down from heaven against them. Ch'ih-yu was overcome and killed; and the Goddess Pa, who could not be sent back up to heaven, was banished to the lands north of the Red Water, which she transformed into deserts; but the world became habitable.

Farther south in the plains there was almost the same legend, though with different names. There the monster Kung-kung, with a serpent's body, a man's head, and red hair, was vanquished by the hero Chuan-hsü and in his rage sought vainly, by butting with his horns, to knock down Mount Pu-chou, the column that supports the northwest corner of the sky, so as to make the heavens collapse. He succeeded only in unsettling it so that even today the earth tilts towards the southeast and the sky towards the northwest.

Between the domains of these two legends, at the foot of T'ai-shan, they tell how the world was set in order by Fu-hsi and his sister Nü-kua. The latter had planted the feet of a sea turtle at the four corners of the earth so as to hold up the sky and she had then melted the five colours from stones so as to complete it. Finally, after having slain the black dragon, she had diked the rivers by heaping the ashes of reeds along their banks.

By contrast, in the western country, with its narrow valleys, tight defiles, and high steep mountains, the hero Yü had made the waters run by piercing the mountains. In the beginning the Yellow River was stopped by a chain of mountains which it could not pass. Kun was the first to be charged with putting the lands in order. On the advice of a tortoise and a hawk, he tried to dike the River. When the water continued to rise, he stole from the Lord on High the 'living earth', which grows and swells up by itself. Furious, the Lord had him put to death. For three years his corpse remained exposed without rotting and, when it was cut open with a sword, his son Yü emerged, after which Kun's body changed into a fish. More fortunate than his father, Yü succeeded in breaching the mountains at Lung-men, the waters flowed, and men 'had a place to dwell'.

The legend of Yü was packed with episodes. One time, he had changed himself into a bear to work at making the waters flow. Since he could not be seen by his wife in this guise, they had agreed that she would approach only after hearing a drum beaten. One day, in rolling some rocks away, he made a noise which his wife took to be the sound of the drum summoning her. She hastened to him but, struck with terror at the sight of this bear, she ran away. He pursued her but, still in a panic, she fell and was turned into a stone. Since she was pregnant with Ch'i, the stone grew little by little until Yü, opening it with a blow from a sword, drew the child forth.[34]

Thus, modifying to local taste an ancient cosmogonic legend common to all the peoples of southeast Asia, the Chinese recounted how, at the beginning of the world, gods and heroes had set the earth in order so that the human race could dwell in it. At the same time other heroes introduced agriculture. T'ien-tsu, the Ancestor of Agriculture, taught men to cultivate fields; Hou-chi, Lord Millet, gave them the most valuable of grains; Shen-nung, the Divine Husbandman, with the head of an ox on a man's body, taught them to make ploughs and to till the soil.

There was not yet perfect order in the world, however, for monsters still abounded. The hero Yi the Excellent Archer delivered men from them.[35] As a child he had lived alone in the forest. When he was five his parents had left him under a tree while they did their work. Returning, they found him surrounded by singing cicadas and, alarmed at this prodigy, dared not take him back. He grew up alone, living by hunting. At twenty he resolved to travel the world, but first he wished to see his family again. He drew his bow, crying out, 'I shall shoot towards the four directions. May my arrow land in front of my door!' He then shot a single arrow which, skimming the earth and clipping the plants, led him to his family's home. Then he set out to wander the world, armed with his bow, and like the Greek Heracles performed superhuman tasks.

One day all ten suns mounted into the heavens together, so that the earth began to burn. Yi struck down nine with arrows and killed them, and their bodies remained at the foot of the *k'ung-sang* tree. He battled against the hurricane and struck the Count of the Wind in the navel with an arrow. He attacked the Count of the River, who seized men and drowned them, and shot out his left eye. In the plain of Ch'ou-hua he slew the monster with a pierced tooth who fed on men, and on the shore of the T'ung-t'ing Lake he killed the great serpent Pa, whose bones make up the Pa Mountains. There are also tales of his adventures as a gallant; while fighting against the Count of the River, he seduced the wife of the Lo River god.

Finally, after an expedition to the west of the Shifting Sands, he became king. But the hero who 'first spilled blood on the earth' could not have a peaceful end. This came after he had killed the monster Feng-hsi, the son of K'uei, which lost him the protection of Heaven: when he offered the victim in sacrifice to the Lord on High, it was rejected. Some time afterwards, betrayed by his wife, he was killed by Feng Meng, who used an arrow made from the wood of the plum tree, the only weapon which could wound him. His body was cut up and boiled in a cauldron by his wife and her lover, who gave it to his own children to eat.

Since ancient times Chinese historians have sought to make historical personages of all these mythological heroes — of Yi the Excellent Archer as well as of Huang-ti who descended from heaven, of Kung-kung with the serpent's body, of Shen-nung with the head of an ox, of Prince Millet, of Yü who changed himself into a bear, of Kun who became a fish, and of Nü-kua who closed up the holes in the sky — and they have tried, by putting these legends together, to derive a history of mankind in its earliest times. In the period when the short discourses which are today collected under the title of *Shu ching* were composed, in about the eighth century B.C. and the following centuries, all of these legends were put together into a sort of connected narrative.[36]

At the beginning came a whole series of sacred personages, *sheng-jen*, creators of rituals and arts, to whom the religious title *ti* was given. First was Fu-hsi, who had discovered the eight trigrams, *pa-kua*, and his sister Nü-kua, who had originated the rites of marriage. After them came Shen-nung, who was the first to make a plough and who taught men husbandry. Towards the end of his reign, enfeebled by age, he became incapable of keeping his great vassals under control. One of these, Ch'ih-yu, was especially unruly and was the first on earth to fabricate weapons and to rebel. Huang-ti defeated and killed him, and then took the place of Shen-nung. Huang-ti in his turn became a sacred emperor: he created the rites, music and the calendar, garments and hairdressing; he constructed the first temples and instituted the division of the land into *ching*. Phoenixes and unicorns came to dance in the courtyard of his palace. After him are placed the hero Chuan-hsü and other emperors whose figures are more blurred.

Two of these, Yao and Shun, precisely because nobody had anything to say about them, became at an early date the saints *par excellence*, those in whom it was convenient to incarnate all the virtues which the philosophy of Chou times attributed to a sacred personage. They were the first ancestors of great families at the Chou court: Yao was ancestor to the lords of Fang, one of whose daughters married King Chao in about the ninth century, and also to the counts of Tu, the last of whom was put to death by King Hsüan in 785. Shun was ancestor to the dukes of Ch'en, the last of whom was dispossessed by King Hui of Ch'u in 478. Of Yao nothing more is known.

Only Shun seems to have possessed a legend, though it is no more than a folk tale. It tells of the orphan persecuted by his stepmother and her son, but triumphing over all hazards and in the end marrying the two daughters of the king. This offered a fine opportunity to fill such reigns with admirable examples of virtue and sanctity. To start with, Shun became a model of filial piety, to which the tale lends itself rather well. Then all the things that a sacred king must do to assist nature in her operations were attributed to him at the prescribed period and in the prescribed order.

> When the Emperor Shun makes a tour of inspection, he goes first to the east, then to the south, then to the west, then to the north. He performs each of these journeys in the month which an association of philosophical ideas links to such and such a direction in space. He remains four years at the capital so as to receive the vassals from the four cardinal directions in proper succession. In the sixth year, which will be the first in a new cycle of five, he will recommence what he had done in the first year.[37]

Nevertheless, despite their sanctity, a cataclysm marred the reign of these two: a terrible flood, which the chronologists were constrained to set in the time of Yao and Shun because the name of Yü was associated with it by legend. By his great works of construction, Yü had succeeded in making the waters flow and he had established a perfect division of the world. After that Shun had relinquished the empire to him. Yü had reigned, and after his death he had for the first time left the throne to his son Ch'i, founding the first dynasty, the Hsia. This was a great topic of discussion among the scholars at the end of the Chou dynasty: whether 'by taking the empire as his own' Yü had not shown himself inferior to Yao and Shun.

The princes of Hsia are named, but we know hardly more about them than their names. However, the fifth and sixth of them, Hsiang and Shao-k'ang, have some substance. The legend of Yi the Excellent Archer was introduced here and a whole romance was elaborated. The hero was transformed into a rebellious noble who had dethroned the king and taken his place, only to end up as victim of his wife's intrigues. In the meantime the wife of the legitimate king, though pregnant, had succeeded in escaping the usurper, and she had borne a son. This boy, raised among the servants, after many adventures as cook in the household of the lord with whom he had taken shelter, had ended by marrying the lord's daughter and reconquering his kingdom. But gradually the princes of Hsia had lost their virtue. The last, Chieh, was an abominable tyrant who, led on by his beautiful wife Mei-hsi, gave himself over to all kinds of debauchery. Their greatest pleasure was to sail about in a barge on a lake of wine amidst an orgy of naked men and women bathing and drinking and eating until they were besotted. One of his great vassals, the Prince of Shang, called T'ang the Victorious, aided by his wise minister YiYin, defeated Chieh, deposed and exiled him, then took the throne and founded a new dynasty, the Shang or Yin.

Again there unrolls a succession of kings who are no more than names, the dynastic Virtue diminishing proportionately as they become more distant from the founder. The last of them, Tsou-hsin, was also a cruel tyrant who delighted in torture. He had the breast of his relative, the sage Pi-kan, cut open to see whether, as was said, the hearts of sages really had seven orifices. He conceived the torture of a metal beam over a blazing fire, along which he made men walk barefoot. He had the bellies of pregnant women opened to see the sex of the infants. One day, seeing some men fording a river in the dead of winter, he had their legs broken to see whether the marrow of the bones had frozen. Once again Heaven withdrew its mandate from the dynasty and sent saints, King Wen of Chou, and then his son King Wu, who killed the tyrant, overthrew the Yin, and established his own dynasty in its place.

Except for the mere fact that the Yin and Chou dynasties did exist successively, all this is pure legend. Part is euhemeristic interpretation of mythological legends; a no less important part is taken from the libretti of the grand ballets which were danced at the ceremonies for the royal ancestors. Every year the kings of Chou, in dances lasting a whole day, mimed the story of King Wu and his victory over the tyrant of Yin. In this they were probably merely imitating the kings of Yin who, before them, must have had similar dances performed to honor the founder of their dynasty, T'ang the Victorious, and others of their ancestors. Their descendants, the dukes of Sung, carried on these dances. The dukes of Ch'i, who claimed to be descendants of the Hsia and were recognized as such by the Chou court, seem also to have initiated ballets of the same sort imitating these and, no doubt, depicting the history of Yü and of Ch'i, and that of Shao-k'ang, the particular ancestor of their line.

Thus there had been created a sort of pattern for the dance of a dynastic founder.[38] Its principal theme was the victory he had won over the last sovereign of the preceding dynasty, with recitations of rhymed verse in his honour and a prose harangue addressed to the troops before the battle. Since Yü had not dethroned his predecessor, the harangue was attributed to his son Ch'i, on the eve of a victory over a rebel, the prince of Hu.

Some legends have obviously been fabricated out of whole cloth after this pattern. It is evident that, of the two legends recounting the founding of the Yin and the Chou, absolutely identical even down to the details, except of course for the names of persons and places, the one is a slavish imitation of the other, though it is impossible to make out for certain which is the prototype. All that Chinese historians tell us regarding the origins of the empire, the first emperors, and the first dynasties is merely a euhemeristic and pseudo-historical interpretation of ancient religious legends, done by uncritical scholars, and it has no historical validity whatever.

2
The Dawn of History: the Yin Dynasty

The Chinese had to spend many centuries in creating the first rudiments of civilization in the great flood plain where the innumerable channels of the Yellow River meander, and in advancing slowly beyond their neighbours, who remained barbarian. When they emerged for the first time,[1] about the eleventh or tenth century B.C., under the last kings of the Yin dynasty,[2] they already enjoyed a fairly advanced culture.[3]

They knew the art of writing: prototypes of the present-day characters were used. If in some religious inscriptions there was a tendency to conserve the old habits of using pictographs rather than the true writing of a later period, this was merely a religious archaism, for that stage had been passed long before, and each word was represented by a special sign which was always the same. The origin of these signs was a series of ideographs: the sun was portrayed by a circle, the moon by a crescent, the earth by a clump set on a horizontal line, sacrifice to the gods by a man kneeling before an altar, a forest by two trees side by side. Man, woman, child, and animals of all kinds were portrayed graphically, some of them stylized, such as cattle and sheep, which were denoted primarily by their horns. Yet already at that time — as today — a number of these ideographs were used only to convey the sound of the word denoting the object they had portrayed, and thus they served to write other words homophonous to the original one. These characters were written on bamboo slips with small pointed rods dipped in a sort of varnish or were engraved on bronze or ivory or, for divination, on tortoise-shell.

The inscriptions tell us nothing about the organization of

society, but it is probable that the division into two classes, an aristocracy of noble families and a plebeian peasantry, existed already at that time as it did in later centuries. For this was one of the characteristics which ancient China had inherited from the primitive culture common to the Far Eastern world, and from which she only slowly managed to free herself. In this highly hierarchized society the king, *wang*, held the first rank: he presided over both religious and lay affairs. He offered all the very numerous sacrifices, not only to divinities of all kinds, but also to his ancestors and their ministers.[4]

In the Great City, *Ta-yi*, or capital, where he lived, his palace was surrounded by temples: the Great Hall, *Ta-shih*, which was the ancestral temple; the Southern Hall, *Nan-shih*, which was probably the hall where the formal audiences were held; the Hall of Blood, *Hsüeh-shih*, which may have been merely another name for the ancestral temple.[5] There was also a mound to the God of the Soil, *she*.[6] From here the king controlled the entire administration.

From the time of the Yin kings, in fact, the Chinese had set up a regular administrative system.[7] At its head stood the prime minister, *ch'ing-shih*. Some of them have become famous: at the end of the dynasty sacrifices were still being offered to Yi Yin, the prime minister of the dynastic founder. Under the prime minister were various high officers of state: the Grand Minister, *ta-ch'en*, who was responsible for the royal pronouncements and orders and also acted as director of etiquette at the great ceremonies, having under him the lesser ministers, *hsiao-ch'en*, who deputized for him at the less important ceremonies; the Chief Scribe, *ta-shih*, who was head of the secretaries, *shih*, who wrote down the royal orders on bamboo slips, keeping a duplicate in the archives (he was also head of the royal archives and guardian of the rituals, which he gave out before each ceremony); the Grand Chamberlain, *tsai*, who was in charge of the royal treasury.[8]

Below these came a whole string of functionaries, *kuan*, officials, *liao*, and department heads, *ssu*, whom we perceive only vaguely, but who show that there existed an organization much like what the Chou would have later on. By chance we know the actual titles of some few of these officials. The palace had its own separate personnel: the household servitors, *ch'en*, who seem to have formed a special class of families attached to the person of the king or his lords, and were employed sometimes as functionaries, sometimes as soldiers, and sometimes as ordinary servants.[9] The Sweeper-Servitor, *sao-ch'en*, seems to have been a sort of lodge-keeper who had to keep the courtyards clean and do watchman's duty at the gates. Within the palace itself there were the pages, *shu*, young boys who waited on the queen and princesses.

In the countryside the administrative organization of agriculture was as rigorous as under the Chou. The inspectors of fields, *chün*, fixed the times of sowing and reaping. The harvest was the chief business upon which the life of the whole community depended, since at all times China has been an essentially agrarian society.[10] They grew chiefly two kinds of millet — one with panicles and one without — as well as wheat and even rice. The state of the crops was also a constant object of concern to the king. The 'archives of the oracle' show him forever consulting the diviners about this: 'Divination of the day *keng-shen*. [The king] asks: Shall I get a harvest of millet? The third month. ...' 'On the day *mou-hsü* [the king] asks: Will my millet produce a harvest?' 'Divination of the day *yi-wei*. Question: Will there be a harvest in the Lung Park? Second month.' He was especially preoccupied by rain, since in north China everything depends on its coming at the right time. Therefore one often finds formulas of this sort: 'Query of the day *yi-mao*. The king asks: Will it rain this month?' The wind, too, was a subject of anxiety; again recourse to the oracle: 'Divination of the day *mou-wu*: it will rain. Divination of the day *keng-wu*: There will be a strong north wind.'

But it was chiefly for hunting that the king was interested in the wind. 'Divination of the day *yi-mao*. Question: Today the king is going to hunt. Will he not be hampered by a strong wind? [Answer:] There will be a strong wind.'

The breeding of cattle, sheep, and pigs was also of great importance. The king went himself to inspect the animals destined for sacrifice. 'The king has personally examined the oxen.' When an animal was pregnant, he was anxious to know in advance the sex of the offspring. 'Divination: Will they be male or female?' The ancestral spirits were asked about finding lost sheep. 'Question: Will the strayed sheep be found?'

The number of animals offered in sacrifice was enormous. There was a special word to designate the hecatomb, *tan* (obsolete in this sense); there was another (which is lost today) to denote the sacrifices of a hundred pigs. There were offerings of ten white pigs or again of ten oxen and ten sheep, or even of thirty or of forty oxen made all at one time to a single ancestor. It is clear that animal husbandry must have held an important place in the Chinese economy of those days.

In theory the power of the king was absolute, but in practice it was constantly limited by the Council of the 'Small and Great', *hsia-shang*. In case of dispute between the king and his councillors the advice of the ancestors was sought by divination. An inscription gives us an example:[11] 'Divination of the day *keng-shen*. ... Question: The king [wishes to?] undertake an expedition against the country of X; [the Council of] the Great and Small does not agree. Shall I not be successful?' If the oracle's answer fell in with the royal wishes, he overruled the council's opposition. In the *P'an-keng*, one of the books of the *Shu ching*, attributed to the Yin era but actually compiled at a much later date, one can read how King P'an-keng, having decided to move his capital, appealed to the oracle in order to break the opposition of his council: 'P'an-keng wished to move his capital to Yin, but the people did not want to go and live there.' He thereupon called before him the malcontents and addressed them as follows: 'Our king [his predecessor Tsu-yi] came and established himself here. Loving my people and not wishing to see them perish in a place where none can protect his life, I have consulted the oracle and have received the following reply: "this [land] is not [good] for you." When the kings of old had any problem, they respectfully obeyed the decrees of Heaven. ... Do not have the audacity to oppose [the response of] the oracle.' And should his ministers not obey him, he threatened to punish them by cutting off their noses or even massacring them and their families.[12] In theory, thus, it was the dead and deified ancestors who governed the empire through these oracles. Their living descendant was merely their proxy and representative, who had to consult them and submit to them in all important matters.

The army consisted of horsemen, of war chariots, and of foot soldiers. As later in Chou times, the latter were probably recruited from among the peasantry, whereas the chariots were driven by the nobles. For arms the soldiers had the bronze sword, the bow — shooting either arrows or pellets — the crossbow, the battle-axe, and the halberd, with a strong, thick, slightly convex blade.[13] This last was the most formidable of the weapons, and from this epoch on the character for it furnished the radical for writing almost all military terms. For weapons of defence, there were shields of hide. Iron was not yet used;[14] it appeared only towards the end of the Chou dynasty, so combat weapons were made of bronze. Stone weapons were no longer used except in certain religious ceremonies: the king's insignia of command was the axe of polished jade.[15] The troops seem to have been organized into units three thousand strong.[16] There is mention, too, of a force of 'three hundred horsemen — left, right and centre', which is to say in platoons of a hundred horse each.

On the return from an expedition, the prisoners were put to death, sometimes all at one time, as can be seen from this inscription: 'The eighth day [the day] *hsin-hai*, 2,656 men were chastised with the halberd [i.e. killed].' Or they were sacrificed separately to various ancestors: 'On the day *chia-yin* lots were drawn to consult the three [ancestors]. In drawing the lots, three sheep … thirty oxen and two prisoners [were offered up?] to Ancestor Keng.' Or again: 'Divination of the day *kuei-wei*: [the king] offers up to Ancestor Keng … thirty oxen … three prisoners.'[17]

There are inscriptions giving some details of an apparently difficult war with a turbulent neighbour, probably a tribe of barbarians from the western mountains, the character for whose name has remained indecipherable.[18] 'The king draws lots on this question: shall he go to help, shall he go to Lai-chou [whose inhabitants] have come three times [to beg aid]? On the seventh day, *yi-ssu*, agreement is given to his going to Lai-chou, starting out from the west.… *Yu-ch'üeh* announces: the land of X has made a raid and carried off five out of the seven of our people working in our fields at ——— for the sacrifices.' This land had an ally, T'u,[19] which was also raiding unfortunate Lai-chou. 'Hsi——— announced: T'u has made an expedition against two villages in our eastern districts; the land of X has made one against the fields of our western districts.' The enemy must have been strong, because, in spite of the oracle's favourable reply agreeing to the expedition, provided it start from the west (on another occasion it was ordered to start from the north), the king is uneasy for his army in the field and he asks again. 'On the day *keng-tzu*, divination through the [ancestor] guest. [The king] puts the question: [I wish] to send three thousand men by chariot against the land of X. Will the expedition be successful or not?' Or again, the expeditions would take place but be unsuccessful. 'The day *mou-wu*, divination through ——— [The king] asks: Three times I have ordered expeditions against X. Will this one be successful?'[20] We do not know how this war was concluded or whether the land was conquered in the end.

Thus, thanks to these inscriptions, the Yin dynasty partially emerges from the mist in which it has been concealed; and if we cannot yet follow its political history, we can at least see the last of these kings in their daily life. They claimed descent from a personage of miraculous birth, Hsieh. His mother, Chien-ti, going with her sister to sacrifice in the countryside, had eaten the egg which a flying swallow had dropped. Thereupon she conceived, and at its birth the child received the clan name Tzu in remembrance of the egg (*tzu*) to which it owed its origin. Later a descendant of Hsieh, T'ang the Victorious, is supposed to have founded the new dynasty by overthrowing the last sovereign of the Hsia dynasty. It is indeed possible that the Shang kings, whose domain lay in the western part of the great plain, took the place of an ancient power whose centre lay farther to the east.

The Yin dynasty had thirty kings. Their descendants in historical times, the dukes of Sung, had carefully preserved the family genealogy, and their traditional list differs hardly at all from what one can draw up from the inscriptions. But its chronology is unknown. Even in Chou times, Chinese historians had no authentic document of that remote period, and the efforts at chronological reconstruction which have been made again and again are of no validity whatever. Some thirty sovereigns can hardly have reigned for over 450 years (an average of fifteen years per reign is greater than any of the historic Chinese dynasties), nor for less than 300 years; and consequently the beginnings of the Yin dynasty can be placed roughly between the fifteenth and thirteenth centuries B.C.[21]

They succeeded in building up a large and lasting empire. It did not include the whole of present-day China, nor even anything like the Chinese world at the time of Confucius. It is hardly possible to make more than an appropriate guess at its true size. According to tradition the ancient kingdom had been broken up after the Chou victory: the southern portion below the Yellow River remained with the descendants of the Yin kings and became the duchy of Sung; the northwest, above the Yellow River, with its capital, made up the principality of Wey; and the northeast, at the foot of T'ai-shan, became that of Lu. This tradition is corroborated by the siting of the ancient capitals of Yin. That dynasty is supposed to have moved its capital no fewer than seven times; but only a few of the locations seem to be definitely known. They are the most ancient, Po (near present-day Kuei-te fu in Honan), which the dukes of Sung reoccupied when they had to abandon their northern domain; and the last two of the seven, Yin (at the village of Hsiao-t'un in Chang-te fu, where the tortoise-shell inscriptions were found), and Ch'ao-ko (near Wei-hui fu), both of these lying north of the Yellow River, in Honan.

The proper domain of the Yin kings thus included both banks of the Yellow River, from where it enters the plain at the foot of

the Shansi plateau to the base of T'ai-shan and the edges of the
Huai basin, perhaps reaching as far as the sea. Besides this territory which directly belonged to them, they must have extended
their suzerainty over all the Chinese territories of the north[22] and
the east. To the northeast they were in contact with Ch'i, the
country stretching from the foot of T'ai-shan north to the Gulf
of Chihli and the River Chi. To the east they made expeditions
against the Yi barbarians of Shantung.[23] To the southeast they
seem to have visited Hsü and Huai (that is, northern Kiangsu and
Anhwei), where the barbarian population must, at least
occasionally, have acknowledged their suzerainty. They went
hunting in Feng, by a lake near modern Kaifeng, or not far from
there at Ch'ii; they went to Hsiang and to Yü, near Ho-nei in
Honan province.[24]

Did the power — at least the nominal power — of the Yin ever
reach westwards into the valley of the Wei? We would have to
think so, if indeed the country of Shao which some twenty
inscriptions tell us the king visited, were the same one that bore
that name later and became famous as the appanage of the chief
minister of the Chou kings Wu and Ch'eng. But this
identification is hardly probable. It was too long a trip for the
king to have made so often. It seems likely therefore, that
another Shao, much closer to the capital, is the one in question.
At the same time, such an extension of their sovereignty, even if
perhaps only momentary, would have been by no means
impossible.[25] The name Chou appears several times on
inscriptions, where one finds the king asking his ancestors
through divination whether he ought to give a certain order —
which unfortunately is not intelligible — to a prince of Chou,
who must be one of the ancestors of the future dynasty.[26]

It was probably about the middle or end of the Yin dynasty[27]
that Chinese farmers started breaking out of the great eastern
plain and creating fresh domains for themselves at the expense
of the barbarians.[28] It was undoubtedly then that they founded
the small domains of the Huai mountains: Ch'en, Shen, Ts'ai,
Hsu, An, Huang and, farther south, Jo, Li, Sui, Erh, etc. The
most important initiative was that which ended with the
conquest of the Wei and Fen valleys — that is, in modern terms,
central Shensi and southwestern Shansi. Already certain clans
neighbouring the barbarians had spread among them. The Chy
clan[29] descended from Lu-chung had crossed the T'ai-hang
Mountains, at the foot of which they had several fiefs — Su, Wen,
etc. — in the plain of northern Honan, around Huai-ch'ing fu;
and they had established some small seigniories, the most

important of which in historical times was that of Tung (near modern Wen-hsi in Shansi). But it was only the fringes of the barbarian lands that were thus breached.

Several large clans, whose fiefs lay near the southwest frontiers of the Chinese world,[30] the Chi, the Ssu, and the Ying, were the principal perpetrators of a complete penetration and a veritable colonization; and among them the Chi clan seems quite early to have played the chief part. In the east it was already an important clan, whose various families dominated the whole country extending from the seacoast to the Yellow River, to the south of T'ai-shan, and to the frontiers of the barbarians. Princes of this clan possessed numerous small fiefs: Ts'ao, Ch'eng, Chi and Kao in the southwestern corner of Shantung; T'eng farther east near T'eng-hsien, and Yang, near Yi-chou, in the southeast of the same province.[31] Farther west they were perhaps established south of the Yellow River, but it is difficult to distinguish between the ancient domains and those that the Chou kings later handed out in this region.

There, moreover, a number of other clans were represented by important noble families: the Tzu clan with the fief of Shang (Sung in Chou times); the Chii clan, descendants of Huang-ti, with the fief of Yen; and so on. Beside and among the lords of the Chi clan, a family of the Ssu clan held Tseng in southern Shantung, and another, Fei, not far from it, near modern Yü-t'ai hsien. Farther west, south of the Yellow River and around Kaifeng (Honan), other members of the Ssu possessed Ch'ii, the name of which has remained attached to a sub-prefecture, and Shen, near Ch'en-liu. A family of the Ying clan held — quite near Tseng, whose overlord was of the Ssu clan — the fief of T'an, in Yi-chou fu (Shantung); but most of the Ying had their lands farther south, in the Huai mountains, where they had enough influence for certain chiefs of the Hsü and the Huai to have taken their name.[32]

Towards the end of the Yin dynasty members of these clans, probably junior members of families, began to migrate westwards to seek their fortunes; and they succeeded in founding principalities in barbarian territory. Members of the Ssu clan settled on the banks of the Yellow River around the temple they had raised to their ancestor Yü at the exit of the Lung-men gorge: at Shen near Ho-yang on the right bank of the river in Shensi (one of the Ssu daughters from here is said to have been the mother of King Wu of Chou); and on the left bank of the river at Tung,[33] Hsia and Ming, in southwestern Shansi. Other members of the Ssu clan even overflowed the Ch'in-ling mountains and founded Pao in the Han Valley. The beautiful Ssu of Pao, the ill-starred queen who ruined King Yu of Chou, was from that area.

Mixed in with them on the banks of the Yellow River between the mouths of the Fen and the Wei were Ying clansmen. There was Keng on the lower Fen; Fei on the right bank near the exit from Lung-men; quite near there Liang or Sha-liang, almost opposite the mouth of the Fen; and still further west, Wang and P'eng-ya on the bank of the Lo River. Outside this central area they founded posts which seem to have been completely separate: to the west Ch'in on the upper Wei; to the east Chao on the middle reaches of the Fen; and still farther east Liang-yü, near Ho-shun in eastern Shansi. But the most extensive lands belonged, it seems, to various families of the Chi clan. All the quadrilateral formed by the Fen and the two branches of the Yellow River belonged to them: Chieh, Hsia-yang, Yü, etc. The Chi clan also had domains throughout the Wei Valley: at Jui near its mouth, at Shao, and at Kuo, near Feng-hsiang fu. The most powerful of all these nobles was the Lord of Chou, whose principality occupied the whole western part of the plain, on the middle courses of the Ching and Wei rivers up to their entrance into the mountains.

The tradition of the Ancestral Temple of the Chou kings indicates that this domain was founded by the twelfth ancestor of King Wu, Duke Liu, who was the first to clear the lands of Pin and who formed a great fief there.[34]

> Dedicated was Duke Liu
> never resting, taking no pleasure
> he allotted the fields, he divided up the land. ...[35]

Life was hard for the Chinese farmers of the Far West, and their descendants several centuries later recalled the time when their ancestors had dwelt in caves dug in the loess.[36] The domain of Pin was particularly exposed, lying as it did on the edge of the mountains where the unsubdued barbarians remained out of reach. After a century or a century and a half the pressure on the Chinese there became so strong that they were forced to withdraw from the area, and the tenth lord, T'an-fu, the old duke, left the marches of the River Ching and migrated south to the banks of the Wei, at Ch'i.

> The ancient Duke T'an-fu
> came in the morning, galloping his horse
> following the banks of the western rivers
> to the foot of [Mount] Ch'i
> there he and the daughter of the Chiang [clan]

together came and searched for a dwelling place.
The plain of Chou was beautiful,
with its violets and sow-thistles sweet as cakes;
there he first consulted [his officers],
there he pierced the tortoise-shell [for divination],
and it answered: Establish yourself here; it answered: Propitious
moment;
build yourself a dwelling on this spot.
He encouraged the people and he established,
and he placed them to the right, and he placed them to the left,
and he divided the fields village by village,
and he dug canals and he measured,
from the west to the east,
everywhere he put everything in order. ...
The oaks and thorn-bushes were cleared,
roads for travelling were opened,
the Kun barbarians fled,
ha! all of them were panting.[37]

To this T'an-fu and his brother Chi-li tradition traces the influence which the lords of the Chou clan exercised in this region. Chi-li was the first to enter into relations with the Yin court; his power aroused the fears of the king, who had him assassinated. His successor, Ch'ang, who later received the posthumous title of King Wen, succeeded in imposing his authority over all the nobles in this western region, and even over the barbarian Jung tribes of Shensi and the peoples of Shu and P'eng in Szechuan. The king of Yin is said to have recognized his authority by granting him the title Count of the West, Hsi-po, and by presenting him with a bow, a battle-axe and a halberd. His hegemony was, however, not won without trouble, and legend has preserved the name of Count Hu of Ch'ung, who slandered the Count of the West to King Tsou of Yin and was thus responsible for his imprisonment.[38]

We can easily understand how tempting the rich eastern plains must have been to the western nobles, when they compared them with their own poor territories always menaced by the barbarians. The storm broke towards the end of the eleventh or beginning of the tenth century B.C. The Count of the West threw his semi-barbarian hordes against eastern China, the capital was seized, the Yin king, Hsin, was slain; and the victors divided up the domains of the conquered. Then, laden with booty, King Wu of Chou returned to his domain on the Wei and re-established himself at his recently built capital of Hao. A new dynasty, Chou, had replaced the Yin.

3
The Chou Empire
(Ninth and Eighth Centuries)

In so far as tradition reveals, the victory of the Chou was decisive, despite the somewhat disconcerting form which the historical interpretation of the great ballets danced at the festivals of the ancestral temple has given it. The kingdom of the Yin was dismembered and the entire northern part detached and given by King Wu to two of his brothers. Their capital and all the territory bordered on the south and east by the Yellow River, with six vassals, became the portion of Feng, Prince of K'ang, and constituted the principality of Wey. Farther to the east, the country on the other side of the River and at the foot of T'ai-shan, with seven other vassals of the Yin, was conferred upon Tan, Duke of Chou.[1] This was the fief of Lu, in the midst of the seigniories of the Chi clan, which had in all periods been preponderant in the region situated between the Yellow River, T'ai-shan, and the sea. The descendants of the Yin retained only the southern part of their former domains, the land which had been, according to their traditions, the cradle of their family and where they had had their first fief and first capital. This was the duchy of Sung. The leading role had decisively passed away from them.

Of the first kings of Chou, immediately after the conquest, we know nothing, not even legends; nothing remains of them except their names and titles, no more: after King Wu, King Ch'eng, then King K'ang. Beyond this we find some stories regarding King Ch'eng, dating from his minority. This is because the regent at that time was the Duke of Chou, the ancestor of the princes of Lu, and the festival rituals which those princes devised in his honour have given birth to a whole cycle of legends;

afterwards there is complete silence.² Tradition seems to regain some solidity only with King Chao and his son, King Mu; unfortunately, towards the end of the dynasty that tradition was defaced by a lot of fabulous literature which took King Mu as its hero.³ Kings Chao and Mu had been great conquerors, who had extended the empire afar among the barbarians of 'the four directions'. Chao perished in the course of one of these expeditions, drowning while he was crossing the River Han.⁴

King Mu, who succeeded him, was not truly his son: the queen had had adulterous connections with the spirit of her ancestor, Chu of Tan, the son of the ancient emperor Yao, and it was due to these relations that King Mu was born.⁵ His reign passed in warlike voyages and expeditions to the four corners of the world,⁶ on a chariot drawn by a team of marvellous horses who covered a thousand *li* a day. His curiosity drove him to the sources of the Yellow River, to which a descendant of the God of the River personally guided him, and where he visited the palace of the Yellow Emperor. He went yet farther and reached the mountain where the sun sets. Near there he visited the goddess of deadly epidemics, who lives in the western part of the world and governs it, the Queen Mother of the West, Hsi-wang-mu. A hundred episodes of these fantastic voyages are told: in one expedition against the land of Yüeh, having no boat to cross the Yangtze, he had tortoises gathered together and they had made a bridge for his army;⁷ another time, during a hunt, he had seen the beautiful Chi of Sheng and had married her, but she died soon afterwards and the king, still sick with love, had given her a splendid funeral.⁸ Yet another time, a sorcerer had kidnapped him to the palace of the Yellow Emperor, at whose court he lived for a long time, and when he came back down to earth, he discovered with surprise that the voyage and the life in heaven had lasted only a twinkling.⁹ Then he died after a long reign of a hundred years.

It is hardly possible to unravel what is due to the romancers' imagination and what belongs to the primitive basis of legend. The sole fact which seems certain is the importance of the century which these two reigns cover and which they alone sum up for tradition. After the approximate half century of readaptation which followed the triumph over Yin and the conquest of the great eastern plain, towards the end of the tenth or the beginning of the ninth century, the kings of Chou broke out of their peace and quiet and almost immediately imposed themselves by force upon their barbarian neighbours, penetrating, probably for the first time, into the Yangtze Valley and subduing the tribes on the banks of the Han River and in the Hupei basin.

At the same time they set themselves to organizing the empire thus created. To King Mu is attributed a reform of justice, and it was he particularly who is said to have introduced the practice of indemnity for punishment. His name has become so thoroughly the symbol of this first empire that his successors, kings Kung, Yii, Hsiao, Yi, and Li,[10] have left behind scarcely more than their names. The last of them was driven from his capital by a faction at his court in 842 and fled to the house of his brother-in-law, the Lord of Kuei, at Che on the banks of the Fen, in southwestern Shansi, succeeding in maintaining authority only over the small territory of that river valley. From this his nickname is derived — King of the Fen, *Fen-wang*.[11] Respect for the royal authority was still such that those who had overthrown him dared neither take his place nor name a successor to him during his lifetime: there could not be more than a single king, 'the Unique Man', in the world. Yet they retained the government for fifteen years (842–828), and it was only at the death of King Li that the Duke of Shao and the Duke of Chou were able to place his eldest son on the throne.[12] He was King Hsüan (827–782).

With this prince the historical period of Chinese history truly begins; he is in fact the first from whom we have some authentic documents. These are verse narratives of several of his expeditions, odes probably designed to be chanted at the ancestral temple to announce victories to the ancestors.[13]

It seems that the empire established by kings Chao and Mu in the preceding century did not last, or at least that it was much weakened. The reign of Hsüan was spent in endeavouring to reconstitute it, on the one hand by maintaining in allegiance the vassals who were always disposed to arrogate complete independence to themselves, and on the other hand through distant expeditions to subdue the barbarians, tribes of whom encircled the Chinese world on all sides.

Most urgent, it seems, was to chastise the Hsien-yün, probably Huns, who lived along the two banks of the Yellow River upstream from Lung-men, in Shensi and Shansi, and who had taken advantage of the troubles at the end of Li's reign to give themselves over to incursions and raids for pillage. In 822 they even had the insolence to plunder the capital, Hao (near Sian), during an absence of the king. The army was sent out in all haste to pursue them; it overtook them at T'ai-yüan, a place the location of which is still unknown, and the barbarians were completely beaten.

In the sixth month, what a tumult!
The war chariots were prepared
with their four vigorous stallions
and the regular equipment was set in them.
The Hsien-yün made a furious incursion
and consequently we had to march in haste;
the king ordained that we leave on the expedition
to deliver the capital. ...
The four stallions were large and stout
and they had broad foreheads!
We vanquished the Hsien-yün
thus accomplishing great exploits. ...
The Hsien-yün had judged badly,
when they occupied Chiao and Huo
and seized Hao and Fang,
going as far as north of the River Ching.
Our standards ornamented with bird designs
fluttered their white folds in the wind;
ten war chariots
went before to commence the march.
The war chariots were well balanced,
as high behind as before, with their four vigorous stallions,
vigorous and well trained.
We vanquished the Hsien-yün, going as far as T'ai-yüan;
in peace and in war [Yin], *chi-fu*
is an example to the ten thousand states!

The most pressing danger thus being averted, the king found himself free to move, and the rich Hupei basin, at the confluence of the Han and the Yangtze, soon attracted him. This was the country of Ching, whose barbarian inhabitants, momentarily subdued by kings Chao and Mu, had long ago shaken off the royal yoke. An expedition was directed against them:

Insolent barbarians of Ching
hostile to the great state!
Fang-shu is very old,
yet his plans are full of vigour;
Fang-shu directed the army,
seized [the chiefs] to torture them and made the enemies prisoners.
The war chariots were numerous,
numerous and finely equipped,
like the rolling of thunder.
Intelligent and loyal is Fang-shu;
in one expedition he vanquished the Hsien-yün;
now the barbarians of Ching come to submit.

After this success, it was still necessary to contend with the

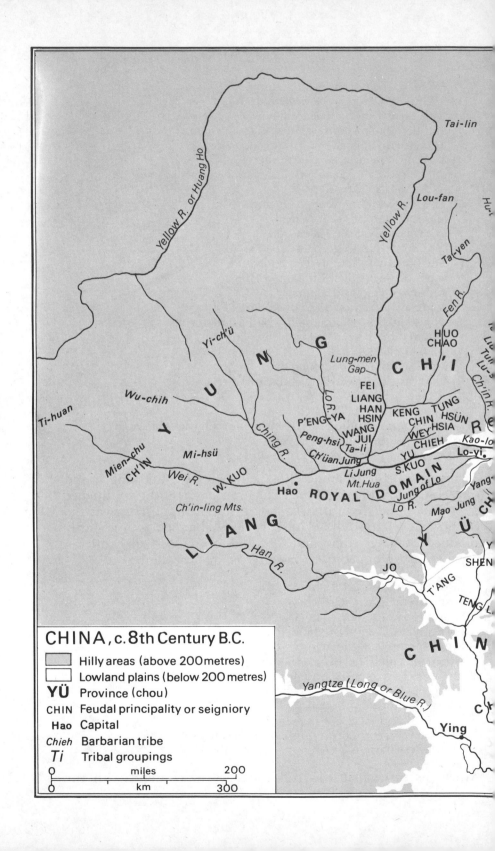

CHINA, c. 8th Century B.C.

Hilly areas (above 200 metres)
Lowland plains (below 200 metres)
YÜ Province (chou)
CHIN Feudal principality or seigniory
Hao Capital
Chieh Barbarian tribe
Ti Tribal groupings

|0 | miles | 200|
|0 | km | 300|

Map labels:

Tai-lin
Lou-fan
Yellow R. or Huang Ho
Yellow R.
Ta-yen
Fen R.
HUO
CHAO
Yi-ch'ü
Lung-men Gap
CH'I
Wu-chih
FEI
LIANG
HAN
HSIN
KENG TUNG
CHIN HSÜN
WEY HSIA
P'ENG-YA
Peng-hsi
WANG
JUI
CHIEH
YU
Ti-huan
Ching R.
Ta-li
Ch'üan Jung
S.KUO
Kao-lo
Lo-yi
Mien-chu
Mi-hsü
W. KUO
Li Jung
CH'IN
Wei R.
Mt. Hua
Jung of Lo
Hao ROYAL DOMAIN
Ch'in-ling Mts.
Lo R.
Mao Jung
Yang-
CH
LIANG
Y
SHEN
Han R.
JO
T'ANG
TENG L
CHIN
Yangtze (Long or Blue R.)
CH
Ying

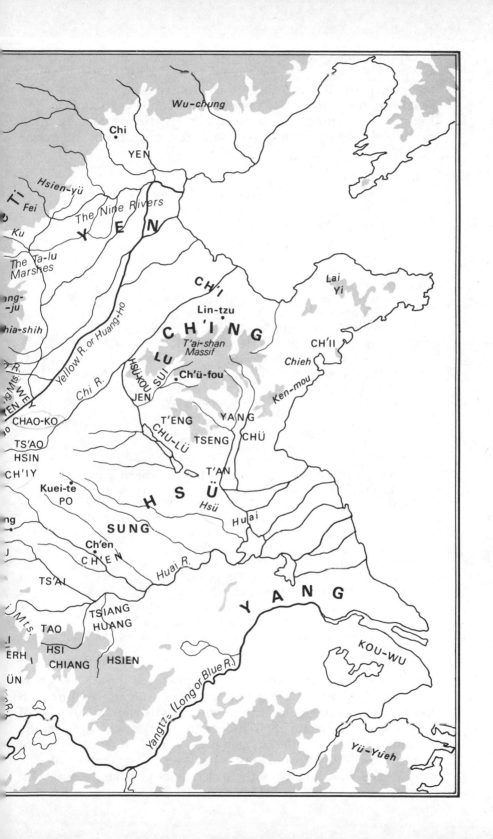

barbarians of Hsü, in the southeast on the banks of the River
Huai, on the borders of present-day Anhwei, Shantung, and
Kiangsu. This time all the royal forces, the six armies, were
mobilized, and the king in person took command of the troops
(821).

> Nobly, clearly,
> the king gave orders to the first minister,
> of whom Nan-chung is the ancestor,
> the Grand Master Huang-fu:
> Arrange my six armies,
> prepare my arms,
> be obedient,
> be prudent,
> go to aid the principalities of the south.
> The king says to Lord Yin:
> I give orders to Hsiu-fu, Count of Ch'eng,
> to right and to left that he set the ranks in order,
> that he harangue my troops,
> that he lead them upon the banks of the River Huai,
> that he inspect this land of Hsü,
> that he not stop, that he not hold back,
> so that the three affairs may succeed one another.
> Nobly and strongly,
> majestic is the Son of Heaven!
> the king advances with calm,
> his troops are neither in masses nor in broken lines.
> The region of Hsü is shaken without interruption,
> it trembles in terror, the region of Hsü
> as before the rolling and the bursts of thunder,
> the region of Hsü trembles for terror!
> The king has displayed his warlike virtue,
> like to a furious thunderclap;
> he makes his guards, the Tigers, advance,
> with air ferocious, like enraged tigers;
> he arrays his troops on the bank of the Huai,
> and thus seizes a throng of prisoners.
> Well guarded was this country on the banks of the Huai,
> when the royal army was there.[14]

We understand the history of this epoch too poorly to know
whether King Hsüan's expeditions show that the empire had
begun to turn decadent, so that the vassals took advantage of
this to try and regain their independence, or whether, on the
contrary, they mark the apogee of its power. But too many of
those expeditions could only impoverish it: none of the
neighbours of China was then rich enough that a successful

expedition could return what it cost in losses of men and of work; and moreover, not all the campaigns were successful. In 789, the western barbarians destroyed an army at Ch'ien-mou.[15]

It was not, however, from without that the blows would come which would put an end to the power of the Chou. King Yu, who succeeded Hsüan in 781, seems to have been one of those insignificant princes who so often follow great sovereigns in oriental monarchies; if we believe the tradition, the intrigues of court and of harem must have filled his reign. One of these was fatal to him. One of the princes whom Hsüan had filled with honours, the Count of Shen, had given his daughter in marriage to King Yu, and he had remained Yu's minister. A palace revolution in which he found himself dismissed to make way for a new favourite, while his daughter was degraded, brought him to form a league with other discontented lords and with the barbarians. They burst into Hao, the capital, and killed the king (771). Then, while they put upon the throne one of his sons, Prince Yi-chiu, who had taken refuge with them, and installed him at the eastern capital, Lo-yi, near modern Ho-nan fu, another lord, the Duke of Kuo (i.e., Western Kuo), chose another son of King Yu's and named him king at Hui (near Sian). Ruined, Hao was no longer habitable.

From this epoch dates the irreversible decadence of the royal power. Naturally, legend came to take the place of historical facts, since those were too few. Since the Hsia dynasty, as the story goes, there had been kept in the palace a fabric filled with dragon spittle, which nobody had ever opened out.

> At the end of King Li's reign, it was opened and examined; the froth flowed through the palace and could not be cleared away. King Li had his women come naked and cry together against it; the froth was transformed into a black lizard and in that form entered the seraglio. Within the harem a little girl of the age when one loses the milk teeth found it. When she reached the age when young girls are given the hairpin, she found herself pregnant without having had a husband. She gave birth and, seized with fear, she abandoned her infant.

The child was taken up by travelling merchants and raised at Pao; later she was offered to King Yu, who became infatuated with her.

> Ssu of Pao seldom laughed. King Yu, wishing to make her laugh, tried a thousand devices, but she did not laugh. King Yu had established a great bonfire to be lit by day and a great drum [to warn of the coming of enemies]. [As if] the enemies were coming he lit the day bonfire and the lords came running; when they arrived, there were no enemies. Ssu of Pao then burst out laughing.

Delighted, the king performed this trick often, so much that the lords no longer bothered about it. When the Count of Shen allied himself with the barbarians and they came to lay siege to the capital, the king lit the bonfire in vain: nobody came, and he was killed.[16]

4

The Court and Administration of Western Chou

The Court

The court of the Chou kings should not be imagined, even in their greatest times, during the ninth and eighth centuries, in the times of Hsüan and Yu, as the locus of refined civilization, philosophy, and hierarchic ritualism which the rituals composed long centuries afterwards are pleased to depict. The ancient texts, quite on the contrary, show it as still semi-savage.

There was a mixture of external pomp and barbaric luxury. Even aside from the great annual ceremonies, the king received the lords with much display.[1] He sat upon a dais, facing south, his arms supported upon stools ornamented with jade, with a black-and-white drapery behind him. At his left hand was the minister charged with helping him in the reception, at his right hand the Grand Scribe. The visitor entered, prostrated himself and, without approaching, remained standing in the middle of the court. When the king had spoken, the minister repeated his words addressing his orders to the visitor, with instructions which the scribe at hand noted on the spot. Then having received the order, the visitor prostrated himself, brow to the ground, and backed out.

At great ceremonies, such as the funeral of a king,[2] all the treasures of the dynasty were displayed. Then were shown off all the barbarian magnificences of the court: the five kinds of precious stones, the red sword, the grand seal, the sceptre with pointed end symbolizing royal severity, the great tortoise-shells for divination, the great drum 8 feet high, and famous weapons — the halberd of Tui, the bow of Ho, and so on.

The principal diversion of the king and his court was hunting, with great beats in which the bush was set afire to make the beasts come out — wild buffalo, tigers, wild boars, wolves[3] — and hunters waiting to take them as they fled or pursue them by chariot. Hunts varied according to the season, but they went on constantly. They were, moreover, a religious affair: they were one of the royal functions, at a time when wild beasts swarmed to the point of being a public nuisance.

Between times, the king and his nobles entertained themselves with archery tournaments, another religious ceremony partly transformed into a pleasure party, in which, following rigid rites and protocol, the king and his favourites shot off their arrows in time to music.[4] All the festivals, all the ceremonies ended in great feasts and drinking bouts, in which the king and his whole court gorged themselves with food and got drunk on millet wine. 'In long draughts into the night we drink, / till all are drunk, there is no retiring,' is said of a royal feast;[5] and at the end of the feast, to express thanks, the guests say, 'We are drunk with your wine.'[6] Likewise after a sacrifice, among the guests, 'None is discontented, all are satisfied, / they are drunk, they are satiated.'[7] And this was a turbulent, bawling drunkenness exceeding all constraints:

When the guests are drunk,
how they shout, how they brawl!
They disorder our plates and bowls, they dance on and on fantastically.
Ah! when they are drunk,
they are unconscious of their transgressions,
caps askew and likely to fall off,
they dance on and on without stopping.
When they are drunk, to go out,
this would be for the best;
[but] to be drunk and not go out,
this is called ruining one's virtue.
To drink is well and good
only when good deportment is kept.
Whenever wine is drunk,
some get drunk, others not.
So an inspector is appointed
with a scribe to assist him:
these drunkards in their shamelessness,
are ashamed for those who are not drunk.[8]

Drunkenness and drunken dancing were the regular upshot of all these feasts: 'they get drunk and then they dance, / thus rejoicing together.'[9]

Certain ritual dances accompanied or followed the official

royal banquets; and since these dances were part of the education of young men, the guests when drunk mixed with the dancers, taking their staggering part. But often the ritual dances of a relatively restrained character were replaced by others of a totally different kind: often sorceresses were called for and made to dance and sing in the palace,[10] under the pretext of driving away evil influences. These were violent dances, often with very rapid steps and patterns, in which the women replaced one another constantly since they were exhausted in a few moments, drinking and singing in the intervals of the dance, until everybody, guests and sorceresses alike, being drunk, the feast ended in an orgy. The orgies of the pool of wine which legend attributes to Chieh, the tyrant of the Hsia dynasty — when he sailed in a barge on a lake filled with wine while three thousand naked youths and young girls bathed in it, drinking and eating the food arranged in piles on the bank — were merely an amplification, within the framework of a popular tale, of the ordinary feasts of the court.

These feasts, violent and ending in drunkenness, were a momentary though certain distraction from the perpetual fears for their lives in which everybody — kings, and their women, and their courtiers — floundered amidst intrigues of all sorts. King Li had, as a personal attendant, a sorceress from the land of Wey who showed him by supernatural means the lords who spoke ill of him, and these were put to death on the spot.[11] And the executions were ferocious: Prince Ai of Ch'i, accused of having vilified King Yi, was seized and boiled in a tripod.[12] This severity did not prevent factions from flourishing, for King Li, driven out of his capital by a court party in 842, had had to flee to Che.

Yet despite these habits, still bearing the mark of a brutal savagery, this was indeed the dawn of Chinese civilization. It was under the last kings of Western Chou that the first flights of literature appeared in verse and in prose, efforts initially timid and tightly tied to liturgy, but freeing themselves little by little to set the scene for a fine flowering of court poetry with popular forms and themes, under kings Hsüan and Yu, and for a prose literature with philosophical leanings, which developed more broadly under the Eastern Chou.

The Central Administration

The growth of the empire had of necessity brought with it a

complete reorganization of the administration. The first kings of
Chou seem to have been content to adopt that of the preceding
dynasty. Their successors probably developed this, but they do
not seem to have changed its principles. A reform of justice is
attributed to King Mu; his successors and King Hsüan seem to
have introduced other reforms, the full significance of which we
can hardly understand. The one thing we know is that the
scribes, in order to simplify official correspondence, which was
already quite busy, adopted in about the eighth century a more
cursive and less complicated script, which is called the *chuan*
script. At the end of the Western Chou, in about the era of kings
Hsüan and Yu, the royal administration seems to have been fully
developed.[13]

To direct this entire apparatus, the king had with him a prime
minister, *ch'ing-shih*,[14] a function and title which went back to the
Yin dynasty, and this officer was, in short, the king's substitute
and replacement in all things. With an energetic king, the prime
minister still wielded considerable power; but when the king was
too weak or too idle to occupy himself with business, it was the
prime minister who managed everything, as the Count of Cheng
did for King P'ing — so this office was a bone of bitter
contention. It tended to become hereditary in certain families. In
the ninth and eighth centuries four dukes of Kuo were vested
with it, and in the seventh century four dukes of Chou succeeded
one another in it. The former were displaced definitively in 655
when their apanage was conquered by the Prince of Chin, the
latter when the last of them fled to Chin in 580. In the sixth and
fifth centuries the post was shared out among the dukes of Shan,
descendants of King Ch'eng, and the dukes of Liu, the first of
whom was the son of King Ch'ing (618–613). Then, at the end of
the fifth century, we see the dukes of Chou reappearing and,
attaining supremacy, they lasted until the end of the dynasty. Yet
it was a new family, that founded by a brother of King K'ao
(440–424), in favour of whom the dukes of Chou had yielded their
ancient titles on the grounds that no legitimate heirs remained.[15]

Below the prime minister the administration was divided into
sections, regular ministerial departments. To start with there
were three ministers responsible for the overall affairs of the
empire: agriculture, war, and public works.[16] These were
ministers of the first rank, who were called collectively the Three
Old Ones, *san lao*, or the Three Chargés d'Affaires, *san yu shih*, or
the Three Great Officers in Charge of Affairs, *san shih tai-fu*, or
perhaps also the Three Officers, *san li*.[17] In the order in which
they were generally listed, probably corresponding to their

precedence, these were the *ssu-t'u*, the *ssu-ma*, and the *ssu-k'ung*.[18]

The Director of the Multitude, *ssu-t'u*, or Master of Agriculture, *nung-fu*, 'protected the people'.[19] He was responsible for directing the common peasants in their daily life. He did this through a complicated local administration which was entirely under his direction. The work in the fields, strictly regulated, was in his hands: his subordinates presided at the allotment of fields, at the sowing, at the harvest, at the threshing; he organized and directed the corvée labour, sometimes in person, allotting the work among the labourers;[20] he followed the peasants even to the market, where all was under his control — police, prices of sale, allotment of places for sellers, and so on. His grip upon the life of the commoners went yet farther: the everyday proceedings of peasant life — marriages, festivals, and assemblies — were regulated by him; and legal proceedings for peasants, at least the less serious, were within his jurisdiction, being judged locally by his subordinates.[21]

The Director of the Horses, *ssu-ma*, or Master (of the troops) of the Royal Domain, *ch'i-fu*,[22] 'suppressed the rebels'. For the peasants of the domain he was master in all things military, as the *ssu-t'u* was in all things civil. He called up and trained levies, assembled them for military instruction and for hunting, and reviewed them. He was their judge in the field, on manoeuvre, or at drill; he directed the great hunts of the four seasons; and he led the armies in time of war. He was the commander of the army,[23] as much of the noble warriors as of the common soldiers. As such, in case of victory, it was he who was received in triumph, at his re-entry into the capital, marching at the head of his troops with flute in left hand and axe in right hand, amidst chants of victory; and it was he who offered up the prisoners to the God of the Soil and to the ancestors. In case of defeat, it was he who went into mourning.[24] His function extended to all things military: weapons and arsenals, chariots, horses, and stud-farms, which he managed in times of peace.

The Director of Works, *ssu-k'ung*, or Lord of the Vast (Works), *hung-fu*, 'established the boundaries'.[25] Unlike the preceding officials, he was concerned not with men, but with land. The peasants themselves were not within his jurisdiction, but the fields, the dikes, the canals, the uncultivated areas, the rivers and the mountains all came under him. He looked after and maintained the great dikes on the rivers, planned the digging of canals, and prevented them from silting up;[26] and elsewhere his subordinates also busied themselves with the small dikes which separated the fields, and surveyed the land for the periodic reallotments. In addition, all artisans, architects, sculptors, metal-casters, armourers, carpenters, embroiderers, and so on came under him.[27]

Below these three ministers of the first rank, three ministers of lower rank had functions hardly less important.[28] Two of them were concerned with the king's personal affairs, the third with criminal justice.

The Chamberlain, *tsai*, or General Chamberlain, *chung-tsai*, or again Grand Chamberlain, *t'ai-tsai*,[29] was responsible for all the king's private affairs. He saw to it that the palace was provided with food, drink, fabrics and clothing, furniture, utensils, and tools of all kinds; he was the overseer for the butchers, cooks, preservers of food, tailors, shoemakers, furriers, dyers, storekeepers, and treasurers; he had the task of managing the palace and commanded the eunuchs and domestics. These functions as controller of the palace and especially as director of the royal treasury placed him of necessity in the first rank. He became indeed prime minister, probably in the first half of the seventh century, and this is the post which the rituals at the end of the dynasty accord him; but this transformation is peculiar to the royal court, and in the principalities he remained controller of the lord's personal domain and minister of finances.[30]

The Grand (Master) of Religious Affairs, *t'ai-tsung*, or Count of Religious Affairs, *tsung-po*, attended to everything dealing with the imperial worship, chiefly ancestor worship. All the court priests, prayer-sayers of all kinds, augurers, diviners, interpreters of dreams, sorcerers and sorceresses, doctors, veterinarians, and so on were under his orders. By the end of the dynasty the whole College of Scribes, which had probably been independent of this dignitary in former times, had also been placed under his control.[31]

The Director of Criminals, *ssu-k'ou*, 'attended carefully to all the public matters that were assigned him' and 'kept the hundred families in check by prescribing punishments [for crimes committed], so as to teach them to revere virtue'. Punishments included what were called the five chastisements, *wu-hsing*; death, castration (or for women confinement within the palace), amputation of the feet, cutting off the nose, and marking with a black tattoo on the face. These could be redeemed, the tattoo-mark for an average 100 ingots of copper, cutting off the nose for twice that (200 ingots), amputation of the feet for more than twice the cost for cutting off the nose (probably 500 ingots), castration for 600 ingots, death for 1,000 ingots. The penal code, *hsing-shu*, set out all crimes and penalties in detail, and each generation made these more precise and consequently more rigid. In Western Chou times the code attributed to King Mu enumerated 3,000 crimes, of which 200 carried the death penalty, 300 castration, 500 amputating the feet, and 1,000 each the two lowest penalties. The code at the end of the dynasty enumerated 2,500 crimes, 500 for each form of punishment.[32] Moreover, various kinds of extenuating circumstances were taken into account for crimes committed by error or accident, as were aggravating circumstances for crimes committed with premeditation, and the penalties were lessened or increased accordingly.[33] The Director of Criminals did not personally sit in judgement upon any cases except those involving the death penalty. Others were judged by his subordinates, the local criminal magistrates. Under him also came the executioners, the prison warders, and so on.

All these ministries had a great number of lower-ranking functionaries: heads of various offices, scribes, workmen, and so on. Even if it did not have such a number of personnel as the later rituals ascribe to it, the administration of the end of the ninth century must have been very complicated. Much was written in that period, to which tradition attributes a simplification of the writing system. These six bureaus also centralized the effective administration of the empire, and it was through them that all business reached the court; but this is not to say that the Prime Minister, the three ministers in charge of affairs, the Chamberlain, the Director of Religious Affairs, and the Director of Criminals formed the king's entire entourage by their seven selves.

The monarch had a sort of council made up of individuals selected sometimes from among the ministers and sometimes from outside them, and they were given titles which set them above any hierarchy, though without assigning them any specific functions. There were the Grand Protector, *t'ai-pao*, the Grand Master, *t'ai-shih*, and probably the Grand Guardian, *t'ai-fu*, who were collectively called the Three Dukes, *san-kung*. Their very names seem to indicate that they date back to the most ancient times, when the kings, imprisoned in their palaces by the taboos attached to their function, needed these advisers to teach them what interdicts to observe, to guide them among the perils of religious observance, and to supervise them in the accomplishment of their sacred duties. In Chou times these were the most exalted positions at court; and tradition ascribes the title of Grand Protector, in the successive eras of kings Wu and Ch'eng, to the Duke of Shao and that of Grand Master to Shang of Lü.

Besides these there existed court positions which, though perhaps of little importance in themselves, took on a greater weight from the fact that they brought the holder near the king's person. The Officer of the Table, *shan-fu*, is noted among the favourites of King Yu, together with the Commander of the Guards, *shih-shih*.[34] There were also treasurers, *ch'üan-fu*; masters of the robes, *chui-yi*; and finally the Grand Scribe, *t'ai-shih*, with his whole army of scribes who wrote down and kept custody of royal orders, religious rituals, and laws. The holders of these offices, often hereditary, were called the Grand Officers, *tai-fu*. This entire world appears later on in the *Chou li* attached to one or another of the six ministries, but it is not certain that they had been so since the beginning.

This organization varied with the times. At the time when the rituals codified it, in about the fourth century, the ministries seem to have become equal and their heads received the collective name of 'the six ministers', *liu-ch'ing*. The ancient and honourable function of prime minister had been absorbed by the Grand Controller, whose importance in his role as treasurer-general had brought him, in about the seventh century, to take over that position. The king thus had six ministers as against the three allowed to the princes, as he had six armies as against their three, or twelve pendants to his ceremonial bonnet as against their nine. But at the same time that the administration was being regularized, its reality was diminishing little by little, with the gradual disappearance of the royal power. And this loss of substance allowed it to present more symmetry than more living, stronger institutions could have supported, though that was well suited to their role, which became increasingly a mystical one. Indeed, as they were deprived of their real powers their function came to consist above all in assuring, by their very existence, the harmony of heaven, earth, and man.

But at the time when the royal institution still existed as something more than a symbol and when the royal domain was still quite extensive, this administration had to fill a double role. On the one hand it managed affairs which concerned the empire as a whole: visits by vassals paying homage, the regular transmission of tribute from the provinces, military expeditions against barbarians or rebels, disputes among feudatories, and so on. On the other hand it administered the king's own domain, the principality which was reserved to him at the centre of the empire and which constituted the Royal Domain. These were two very different tasks, and it was not the least error of ancient Chinese administration that it charged the same men with both the one and the other. Yet this was an inevitable confusion, for if the kings had had a domain reserved to them, they had not thereby renounced their authority over the rest of the world. That remained complete, even over territories bestowed in fief upon distant vassals, and it could not have occurred to them to set certain of their subjects off under a special administration.[35]

The Administration of the Royal Domain

The Royal Domain consisted of the ancient family lands in the Wei Valley, with the former princely capital of Hao (near present-day Sian) where the kings continued to reside during their first centuries, and the territory of the Lo Valley and the middle Yellow River valley, with the new capital of Lo-yi (near modern Ho-nan fu), said to have been founded by the Duke of Chou just after the conquest, to which the kings withdrew in the eighth century. But this domain shrank incessantly under the Eastern Chou. The valley of the Wei, where the kings did not again show their faces after the catastrophe of 771, was definitively lost between 687 and 640. The lands north of the Yellow River were ceded to Chin in 640. And the petty principality which remained dissolved little by little in the course of the centuries, until it came to no more than seventy-two villages when Ch'in brought it to an end by annexing it in the middle of the third century.

The general organization was rather simple. Each capital, with its suburbs, was a separate district which the king was considered to administer himself. A fairly large zone around the capital then formed interior districts, where in theory no apanage would be granted. The balance of the principality constituted exterior districts which were distributed as apanages to princes and functionaries. The administration of the two zones, interior and exterior, was exactly the same, except that the divisions did not have the same names and that for each of them the functionaries were always ranked one degree higher in the former than in the latter.

The territory was divided into regions, *hsiang*, in the interior zone, and circles, *sui*, in the exterior, each with a grand officer, *tai-fu*, at its head. These regions and circles were divided, respectively, into departments, *chou*, and districts, *hsien*, the chiefs of which (*chou-chang* and *hsien-cheng*) were under the orders of the grand officers. Below them, chiefs of cantons, *tang-cheng*, or masters of towns, *pi-shih*, according to the zone, commanded their subordinates: the former masters of localities, *tsu-shih*, the latter chiefs of communes, *tsan-chang*. Finally, each clan area or commune was divided into four villages, *lü*, or hamlets, *li*, of twenty-five families run by village mayors, *lü-hsü*, or controllers of hamlets, *li-tsai*.

These administrators were naturally patricians, the highest ranked bearing the title of grand officer, *tai-fu*, and the humblest mere nobles, *shih*. Chosen by the king probably from among the local nobility, at least for the lower grades, they governed their divisions, made the regular sacrifices, presided over the archery ceremonies, were involved in the reallotment of peasant lands, regulated agriculture, judged civil cases, oversaw plebeian marriages, directed the collection of taxes, managed the land registry and census, especially at the time of the great triennial census review, and so on. At the beginning of each year, the prefects of regions and circles went to learn about the new laws posted by the king at the Sacred Palace, *Ming-t'ang*; and upon their return they posted these in their turn, as they did the regulations which were announced to them each month. Their subordinates went to learn about these laws from the prefects and these they posted in their turn. Furthermore, in order that those who were illiterate should be in step with the laws and regulations, they proclaimed them at the times when sacrifices were made to the God of the Soil, in spring and autumn. At the end of each year, all functionaries gave an account of their administration to their superiors. Moreover, inspectors, *ssu-chien*, went the rounds of the jurisdictions and gave reports to the prefects.

Functionaries of all kinds assisted the administrators: for agriculture, for the exploitation of forests and ponds, for the court of the justice of the peace, and so on. The official go-betweens, *mei-shih*, handled peasant marriages under the administrators' direction; warehousemen, *ts'ang-jen*, managed the granaries, in which the tax revenues in kind were stored; tax gatherers, *lü-shih*, in autumn took in the taxes and fines which were paid in grain and in spring concerned themselves with loans to the distressed; bursars, *lin-jen*, ordered payments in kind, furnishing grain for the sacrifices, for visitors or officers on duty, for troops passing through, and so on; assessors, *chün-jen*, set the rates for taxes according to the value of the lands, based upon the harvest, for a period of three years; collectors, *wei-jen*, gathered the tax from mountains and forests in wood for heating or for construction; directors of the markets, *ssu-shih*, were concerned with the organization of the police and of taxation for the markets, together with treasurers, *ch'üan-fu*, who played the same role with regard to the merchants that the tax gatherers did vis-à-vis the peasants — on the one hand, taking in taxes, and on the other, granting short-term loans.[36]

Yet the greatest task of the district administrators was the regulation of agriculture. It was they who, under the orders of the *ssu-t'u*, decided what crops to plant, gave orders for sowing and harvest, oversaw the labours of all the peasants, and imposed fines upon the lazy. In summer they had all the gates of towns and doors of houses opened and terminated the city and road tolls; in winter they did the reverse, closing everything up and seeing that the peasants shut themselves up, first in the villages and then in their houses. They had the fields demarcated, and the small dikes and canals overhauled; they saw to the census, to the land registry, and to the statistics. Finally, in the case of levies for war or the hunt, they carried out the instructions of the Director of the Horses.

Aside from their civil functions, administrators had judicial responsibilities. Justice[37] was, in fact, carried out by two sorts of judges, according to the gravity of the offences. Crimes and misdemeanours which did not give cause for imprisonment fell to the civil administration and were judged by the local subordinates of the *ssu-t'u*. Those which had to be punished by imprisonment or heavier penalties were under the jurisdiction of the Director of Criminals and his subordinates. Travelling correctional magistrates, the Assisters, *ssu-chiu*, went through the districts to judge the offences of peasants, such as contempt of the aged, insults, disputes, or drunkenness. The ordinary punishment for such faults was flogging; but if they were repeated twice, the delinquents were regarded as incorrigible and were sent off to criminal justice courts to be punished more severely. Unpremeditated crimes were the sphere of the Conciliators, *t'iao-jen*, who were also itinerant. In cases where a compromise could be reached, their task was to have a solution agreed to between the victim or his family and the guilty party; or if the victim had been wounded or killed by a domestic animal — horse, ox, or dog — between the aggrieved party and the owner responsible. Cases of legitimate self-defence were also within their brief. So were vendettas. Vengeance was one of the patrician's duties, whether he took it himself or aided one of his relatives.[38] There also the Conciliator's task was to seek to have a compromise accepted by the victim's relatives, to prevent further murders and to bring vengeance to a halt. When an affair had been concluded, he gave the guilty party a tablet pointed at the upper end, which guaranteed him against further molestation.

Criminal affairs in the jurisdiction of the *ssu-k'ou* also went before different tribunals depending upon their seriousness. Those which did not call for the death penalty were judged directly by magistrates established in the jurisdictions — provosts of region or circle, provosts of department, or, for the apanages, of district. For those offences which did call for the death penalty, the provosts merely carried out preliminary examinations, and it was the *ssu-k'ou* himself who judged them. The provost made a report to the Deputy for Criminal Affairs, *shih-shih*, who examined the dossier and passed it on to the Director of Criminals. The latter adjudicated all criminal proceedings in open court before the Deputy for Criminal Affairs and all the assembled provosts from region, circle, department, and district, each of whom discussed those within his jurisdiction. When the arguments were concluded, the Director of Criminals pronounced sentence, which the Deputy for Criminal Affairs wrote down *in toto* himself from the *ssu-k'ou*'s dictation. He then handed the verdict over to the Subdirector of Criminals, *hsiao-ssu-k'ou*, who deposited it in the archives. Returning to his jurisdiction, on the day set, the provost had the culprit executed, and the corpse remained exposed in the marketplace for three days. The king appeared only if he wished to grant clemency. In that case he attended the open court on the day when the case was to be judged; or frequently he would have himself represented by one of his ministers. The local provosts also had to handle recidivists who had already been* tried by the administrators, so that a heavy punishment would be inflicted upon them. They were exposed for several days in the pillory upon the Beautiful Stone, *mei-shih*, in the Court of External Audiences of the palace, after which they were cast into prison.

No case was purely civil. Plaintiff and defendant always played in fact the roles of accuser and accused, and the one who lost the case was condemned to punishment. Thus to avoid this (or at least to avoid the penalty of a ransom-fine), the two parties often came together to end the litigation without trial, by a settlement ending in an agreement under oath.[39] When no arrangement was possible, one of the parties instituted proceedings by bringing to the audience a bundle of a hundred arrows and a bar of copper.[40] The other had to respond with a similar deposit: if he failed to do so, he was regarded as unsure of his case and lost the trial. Three days later, the *ssu-k'ou* called them both together into his presence, examined their proofs, and gave judgement. If there had been a contract or an agreement between them, the original version was inscribed on a red tablet and kept at the ancestral temple. The Director of Contracts, *ssu-yüeh*, sacrificed a cock, anointed the door of the depository with its blood, opened the door and took out the document. Those whose version did not conform to the original were condemned to the punishment of being branded on the face. If after examination it was impossible to determine where right lay, the king made both parties take an oath and left the gods to punish the perjurer. On the other hand, plaintiffs too poor to get a bar of copper had recourse to the Lung-coloured Stone. They went and stood by it and, at the end of three days, the Deputy for Criminal Affairs came to receive their complaint. There also stood the Kao Drum, after which the outer gate of the palace was named. As soon as the drum had sounded the Grand Steward, *ta-p'u*, received the complaint and informed the king.

Finally the administrators were not only civil chiefs and judges, but also military chiefs, so that in time of war or merely a hunting expedition they came under the control of the Director of the Horses, *ssu-ma*, the Minister of War, and of the Commander-in-Chief.

Military organization was, in fact, closely copied from civil.[41] Each family had to give one man; each group of five families a squad of five men, *wu*, commanded by a non-commissioned officer, *kung ssu-ma*; each village a platoon of twenty-five men, *liang*, under the orders of a platoon commander, *liang ssu-ma*; each commune a company of a hundred men, *tsu*. Five companies formed a battalion of 500 men, *shih*; five battalions, a regiment of 2,500 men, *lü*; and finally five regiments an army of 12,500 men, *chün*. The Royal Domain was divided into six regions, each of which furnished an army, so that the total of the royal forces was 75,000 men and made up six armies. But if these figures mean anything,[42] they represent recruitment figures, not troops actually raised. It was not necessary to call up, out of these 75,000 trained men, more than just the number needed for hunting, for military expeditions, and so on. In theory, only the king possessed the right to have six armies, and he allowed only the most important vassals the right to have three; the less important had the right to only two or one.

The fundamental element in the army was the war chariot ridden by three nobles (the master of the chariot, his charioteer, and his spearman), with a supporting company divided into four platoons, one before, one behind, and two at the sides. Each contingent was led by the chief of the respective territorial jurisdiction: it was the commune chief who led the company, with the village chiefs as officers under his orders. He assembled the men and placed himself at their head. To control them, he had near him the drum which he beat for the signal to advance and the bells with which he gave the order to retreat, and on his chariot was his banner to serve as a rallying point, which he lowered when he sounded the retreat. Similarly, each platoon commander had his guidon to which he rallied his men.

Armies in the field pitched camp each night. They made a barricade out of chariots set up one behind the other with the pole of one resting upon the cab of the next, and with two chariots facing one another and with poles raised and tied together forming the two gates, north and south. Tents were set up for the God of the Soil and the royal ancestor (whose tablets accompanied the army, each on its own chariot), and then for the commanders; and a sacrifice was offered to the local god of the soil.

Combat was not joined at the first contact, nor without ceremony: it was essential that the divination be favourable. In the morning the prince or the commanding general called his officers together. He had a tent set up for consulting the tortoise-shell before the tablets of the ancestors. Then, the tent removed, he gave his orders: if the tortoise-shell gave a favourable response, they prepared for battle; if not, the army waited there until the next day or else retired to seek out a better place. It was then that the adversary sought to entice them into combat by provocation.

There were established procedures for this. A warrior drove his chariot, flag flying, right up to the enemy entrenchment, and returned after having just brushed past it. Or, after having approached the enemy camp, he halted and fired an arrow, while his charioteer dismounted and adjusted the harness of the horses. Or yet again, he halted his chariot at the gate of the camp, entered, cut off an ear and took a prisoner, and then returned.[43] It was hardly possible to restrain an army thus provoked from launching a pursuit of the flouters, so that they would be drawn into combat despite unfavourable auguries.

When the order to fight was given, the officers, back among their troops, arrayed them in ranks and mounted their chariots, each in his own place. When these preparations were complete, they descended from the chariots, accompanied each one by his halberdier, who took his weapon in hand, and went to hear the general's harangue; only the charioteers were left behind. When that was finished they remounted the chariots and then dismounted once again for the prayer. After that, the commanding general's drum gave the signal for combat, which was instantly repeated by the drums of all the commanders from echelon to echelon.[44]

Of field strategy or tactics in combat, there was no trace at all. The armies pushed straight ahead until they met and then they threw themselves at one another until one of them gave, or until night fell to separate the fighters. Thus the simplest stratagems — an advance guard which pretends to be scattered so as to lure the enemy, disorganized in pursuit, upon the main body of the army, as two generals of Chin, Mao of Hu and Chih of Luan, did at the Battle of Ch'eng-p'u (632) — was certain of success amidst the general disorder and lack of coordination.[45] Indeed, the commanders in their chariots scarcely remained with their men: they challenged one another, exchanged courtly messages, engaged in individual combats. In the context of the confused mêlée of chariots and foot soldiers, commanders in chief and army commanders no longer had any control whatever over their subordinates, and their role was limited to beating the drum uninterruptedly, to encourage the men to press forward.[46] At most, before the fighting began, they could give their subordinates certain instructions, though these were of a very general character. It was not until right at the end of the Chou period, in the time of the Warring Kingdoms, when the counts of Ch'in and the princes of Chao had substituted horsemen for war chariots in the makeup of their armies, that the leaders of each element began to be capable of exerting effective command and that preconcerted action became possible, giving birth to a rudimentary strategy.

The weak point of this administration was its financial organization. The absence of a practical medium of exchange required that taxes be levied in kind: grain, pieces of fabric, wood for building or heating, and so on. It was not that money did not exist. Since Yin times cowry shells, *pei*,[47] had been used, and this practice continued under the Chou. But that could not be carried very far and, in everyday life, for important transactions, they used ingots of copper, *wan*,[48] which were probably weighed and cut, or bolts of fabric which were measured; or they had recourse to barter, exchanging merchandise for slaves or horses or chariots or tablets of jade, and so on.

Only towards the end of the fifth century[49] were the first coins, called *pu* or *ch'üan*, cast in the great principalities, in variant forms but quite similar in weight. There were round pieces, pierced with a round hole (the modern 'cash' has a square hole), and ingots in the form of small swords or spades, with or without inscriptions. Each state had its coins. The princes of Ch'i often put the name of their state on the face of their pieces,[50] but they seem to have been alone in this custom.

Ordinarily each city where there was a mint inscribed its name, complete or shortened, on its coins. The most common of these pieces were those of two *chin*, one *chin*, and one-half *chin* (approximately 30 grams, 15 grams and 7.5 grams, though with considerable variations in weight). They remained rather unhandy, but there were some coins still clumsier. The largest pieces in the form of a sword, *tao*, in Ch'i came to 30 *hua* (= *huo*), weighing between 44 and 57 grams. All these pieces seem to have been in rather short supply.[51] Even when their use had spread throughout the entire Chinese world, in about the fourth century B.C., people did not seek to use them to replace taxes in kind, even though these were so unhandy. It was taxation in kind which continued to be the basis for public revenues, both of the king and of the princes.

The most important of such taxes was that on cultivated land, the tithe on the crop,[52] which the tax collectors received in autumn after the harvest. Those who exploited the resources of the mountains and lakes paid a tax equal to 5/20 of their production, in timber or firewood, or in products of the hunt — ivory, rhinoceros horn, feathers, and so on. On houses and enclosures attached to them, taxes varied, depending upon the area. In the capital, houses themselves were not taxed but there was a tax on enclosures of 1/20 of what they produced; in the inner suburbs the tax was doubled; and in the outer suburbs it came to 3/20. Taxes on lands given in apanage to princes or functionaries were paid to the holder of the apanage; but he in turn had to pay 2/10 of that to the Treasury as tax. Moreover, fines levied upon peasants were collected in kind.[53] Hardly any of the taxes were paid in coin, except for the taxes collected in the market; and those probably were replacements for ancient payments in cloth, from which the name *pu*, cloth, comes to be applied to copper coins. These market taxes included fees for setting-up, fees on written agreements, fees on animals killed, fees on linen cloth, fees on silk, and so on. Finally, tribute sent by vassals was a source of revenue, perhaps a rather important one in Western Chou times; but it became precarious under their weakened successors established at Lo-yi, and it moreover diminished steadily, especially after Prince Huan of Ch'i, and then the princes of Chin and of Ch'u, had commenced as hegemons to levy contributions upon the vassals.

Only a very little of what all these taxes produced ever reached the Royal Treasury. The difficulty of communications and the awkwardness of payments in kind had obliged the taxing authorities to agree to the principle that local taxes should be disbursed in the locality, with only the surplus being transmitted to the capital; and many factors contributed to the diminution of this surplus. The tax gatherers loaned grain to the peasants in springtime; the treasurers advanced short-term loans to merchants and peasants; the directors of the markets bought unsold market products on the pretext of regularizing the price; and all these practices forced them to keep the greater part of the taxes in their own hands. One can also guess how much leakage such usages must have engendered, despite controls, not to mention the abuses of all kinds which they invited.

What did get through to the capital, after having climbed the echelons of the administration level by level, was turned over to the Grand Treasurer, *ta-fu*, and his subordinates in the Interior Treasury, *nei-fu*, and External Treasury, *wai-fu*. The Controller exercised a general control. Each operation, each input or output of grain or money, had to be signed for twice, with one slip being retained by the recipient or the donor and the other being sent to his superiors; and the totals from these strings of daily slips were recapitulated into monthly returns. But neither the Controller nor the Treasurer had any direct leverage upon the agents of the fiscal authority, since they fell under the *ssu-t'u*, whereas they themselves came under the Controller-General. Thus the controls must have been quite ineffective.

To simplify accounting, the product of various taxes had been committed to the ordinary expenditures of the king and the court. The tax from the markets went to the king's food and clothing; that from the mountains and lakes went to funeral ceremonies. Taxes in kind were allotted in various ways according to their place of origin: those from the capital district went to the reception of visiting officers; those from the suburbs to the provision of grains and fodder; those from the domain itself to the payment of all kinds of artisans and workers; those from the apanages to sacrifices; and so forth.

The ideal of good government was set forth by an author who seems to have written towards the middle of the third century: 'The prince eats his taxes, the grand officers eat their fiefs, the patricians eat their domains, the common people eat their strength, the artisans and merchants eat the prices fixed by the state, the functionaries eat their functions, the administrators eat their apanages; the government is in order, the people are at peace: wealth is not lacking.'[54] Everyday life was thus assured, after a fashion, but there remained no way to provide against unforeseen expenditures: military expeditions, great public works, famine. The least difficulty was insurmountable; and, at the end of the sixth century, the king was so poor that when, in 510, he wished to restore the wall enclosing his capital, he had to beg subsidies from Prince Ting of Chin. Ting called the sovereign lords together; and, under the presidency of his minister Shu of Wei, he called an assembly of the ministers of principalities together at Ti-ch'üan to set the required contributions from each of the feudatories.

The Provinces

Basically the royal administration, though gigantically enlarged, was scarcely more than that of a rather small principality, the lord of which, 'father and mother' of his subjects, is both religious leader and civil leader, regulates their entire lives, and directs all their actions without too much trouble because he is so close to them. Yet by that very pattern, so punctilious, so careful about details, so lacking in concerted management, it was ill-adapted to a great feudal empire, very extensive and formed out of very diverse elements, with different peoples, languages, and folkways, in which numerous autonomous petty lords having no connections with one another divided the territory among themselves.

In the eighth century, the basin of the Yellow River was divided into at least a hundred little fiefs,[55] not counting the barbarian tribes, who remained more or less independent. The Royal Domain extended over the entire centre of the empire, in the lower valley of the Wei (Shensi) and in that of the Lo (Honan), two valleys of unequal importance, though both fertile and well cultivated. The domain was thus very great, but cut in two by mountains; and the Yellow River, fast-flowing and hardly navigable, was all the more unsatisfactory as a link between the parts since it required making a long detour to get to the mouth of the Lo and then go up to Lo-yi, the eastern capital.

In the west, on the upper course of the River Wei, on the barbarian frontier, the small fiefs of Ch'in, Mi-hsü, and Juan and, below them, the dukedom of Western Kuo were included in the Royal Domain. So probably were the seigniories on the right bank of the Yellow River: the principality of Han, which has bequeathed its name to a sub-prefecture in Shensi, the counties of Jui and Liang. On the other side of the River, on the north bank, and outside the Royal Domain was the principality of Yü. Farther north, at the mouth of the Fen, were Wei and Keng and to the east, up the same valley, the small fief of the Prince of Chin, which the *Shih ching* calls by its ancient name, T'ang. Upstream to the north were Chao and Huo, very close together and next to the Ti barbarians, masters of the Ta-lu basin which would later be called T'ai-yüan, as would the entire eastern part of Shansi as far as the great eastern plain.

At the River's exit from the mountains the plain was divided among several principalities. North of the River was Wey, the former capital of the Yin; the *Shih ching*, following a tradition regarding the conquest, considers the districts of Yung and Pei practically as separate fiefs of Wey. South of the River the descendants of the former Yin kings had retained a portion of their family domains, which formed the duchy of Sung. To the west of Sung, in the first years of the eighth century, the domain of Cheng had been detached from the Royal Domain and had become the apanage of a brother of King Hsüan. To the south Sung bordered upon Ch'en, in the Huai Mountains, the princes of which traced their line back to the Emperor Shun; to the east it extended to the territory of a number of tribes on the seacoast, the Hsü and the Huai; to the north it reached to the county of Ts'ao (the name of which still survives in a district in the southwest corner of Shantung), between the Yellow River and the River Chi; and to the northeast to the principality of Lu, at the foot of T'ai-shan on its southern side, which was, like Wey, a piece detached from the former kingdom of Yin. East of Lu was a series of small fiefs: Chu-lü, Chü, and Ch'ii, bordering the Yi barbarians of Shantung. To the north, on the opposite slope of T'ai-shan, between the Yellow River and the sea, was the important principality of Ch'i and, still farther north, Yen, on the other side of the River in the area where Peking is today and, at least in certain periods, including southern Manchuria. West of Ch'i, between the River, the mountains, and the eastern Shansi plateau, lay small principalities: Hsing, the northernmost of the Chi clan's seigniories, around Shun-te fu in Hopei, and along the River Chi the six petty domains of the descendants of the mythical Emperor Fu-hsi — Jen, Hsü-kou, and so on.

Finally, right down in the south, the edge of the Huai Mountains, which separate the basin of the Huai from that of the Yangtze River and its tributaries, was covered with castles surrounded by small domains, the most important being Ch'en, Ts'ai, and Hsu and such others as Tao, Chiang, Hsi, and Hsien. Some were even established beyond the mountains in barbarian country: Shen, Lü, T'ang, Sui, and so forth. Farther on, the barbarians of the rich Hupei basin, at the confluence of the Han with the Yangtze, were commencing to organize themselves into a Chinese-style state which was to become the powerful kingdom of Ch'u.

Such were the most important of the fiefs which were answerable directly to the king. Their lords comprised the feudal aristocracy, collectively called 'the princes', *chu-hou*. One rank lower were their vassals, *fu-yung*. The princes were so called because the greater part of them did indeed bear the title of prince, *hou*: the Prince of Chin, the Prince of Lu, the Prince of Ch'i, and so on. Yet not all the lords were titled thus: there were other titles, among which a certain hierarchy was established.

Some lords whose ancestors had received the position of local count, *po*, retained that title although the function had fallen away long before (it was in this way that the lords of Ch'in, Cheng, and Ts'ao were called counts) and even though others of the same status (such as Wey and Ch'i) preferred to style themselves princes, *hou*. Moreover, the king's ministers bore the very exalted title of duke, *kung*, and their descendants sometimes retained this, as did the dukes of Chou and of Kuo. The same title was also given to the princes of Sung, descendants of the former kings of Yin, as it was to the descendants of ancient sovereigns: the Duke of Ch'iy, the Duke of Ch'en, and so on. It was also granted, by courtesy, to all dead princes, whatever their rank, that being the title which was joined to their posthumous names to designate them after death. Finally, the chiefs of barbarian tribes who had submitted[56] received the title of sir or sire, *tzu* (the Sire of Ch'u), a polite term corresponding more or less to our 'sir' or 'mister' in everyday conversation, and one which disciples bestowed upon their master: thus Sire K'ung (Confucius), K'ung-tzu, and Sire Mo, Mo-tzu, and so on.

These titles formed a hierarchy of three ranks.[57] That of duke, *kung*, was the highest; then in the second level came those of prince, *hou*, and count, *po*; and in third place those of sire, *tzu*, and baron, *nan*. They can be identified by the number of brevet titles, *ming*, granted: nine for the duke, seven for the prince and the count, three for the sire and the baron. But this hierarchy was purely honorific and did not involve any political superiority of one rank over another.

The kings had tried to impose an organization upon this assemblage of small fiefs. They had divided the empire into nine provinces, *chou*, each having at its head a representative of the royal authority. A document from the end of the Western Chou period, the *Yü kung*,[58] has preserved the names of the nine provinces. In the north was Chi, bounded on west, south, and east by the Yellow River, which occupied approximately the southern half of modern Shansi. Yen, in the northeast, lay on both sides of the former mouth of the Yellow River, in the northern part of Hopei. In the east, Ch'ing was between the Yellow River and T'ai-shan, in northern Shantung. In the southeast, Hsü stretched between T'ai-shan and the Huai River and along the seacoast, on the border of Shantung and Kiangsu. South of Hsü, Yang was at the mouth of the Yangtze, in Kiangsu. On the middle Yangtze and the lower River Han was Ching, in Hupei. In the southwest lay Liang, on the upper Han; in the west Yung, in the Wei Valley, in Shensi; and finally, in the centre, Yü, south of the Yellow River and on the River Lo, in present-day Honan. The Royal Domain was divided between two provinces, Yung and Yü, each with one of the two capitals, which agreed with the tradition, according to which King Wu had divided its administration between two counts: the Duke of Shao in Yung, in the old capital of Hao, and the Duke of Chou in Yü at the new capital which he himself had built, Lo-yi.[59]

To represent him in each province the king named a sort of governor. This was one of the local lords, who received, together with the title of 'count', *po*, or of 'pastor', *mu*,[60] the mission of maintaining order, administering justice, and punishing rebels. The archives of the principality of Ch'i in the seventh century preserved a document, perhaps authentic, but more probably a fabrication of the period composed to justify the ambitions of Prince Huan. In any case this shows well enough what the responsibilities of the pastors were: 'Truly punish the lords of the five ranks and the counts of the nine provinces [when they are at fault], so as to assist and sustain the house of Chou!' And it indicates the approximate boundaries of the province of Ch'ing: 'As far as the sea to the east, as far as the River to the west, as far as Mu-ling to the south, as far as Wu-ti to the north' — that is, from around Tientsin in the north to T'ai-shan in the south.[61] In the time of King Hsüan the Prince of Shen received, together with the title of count, the responsibility of containing the barbarians of the south. This probably refers to his nomination as count or pastor, undoubtedly of Ching.[62] In about the same period the Prince of Ch'i received the task of keeping an eye on the barbarians of the east, the Prince of Han those of the north, and the Prince of Lu the Hsü. This refers perhaps to responsibilities as counts for the provinces of Ch'ing, Yung, and Hsü, though the titles are not mentioned.[63]

The choice of counts from among the local lords was not done to give the royal power really strong bases in the provinces, since it would inevitably mean that the counts would abuse their authority in carrying out their private affairs. Still, as long as the kings were and appeared sufficiently strong — which is to say until about the middle of the eighth century — they maintained dominance over their vassals without too much trouble. On occasion the king dethroned princes for some offence, put them to death, and set up successors to them. Towards the beginning of the ninth century, King Yi had Ai of Ch'i arrested after he was denounced by the Prince of Chi and had him boiled in a tripod, then designated one of the condemned man's younger brothers to succeed him.[64] A century later, in 796, King Hsüan put to death Po-yü, a member of the princely family of Lu who had, eleven years before, assassinated Prince Yi and had taken his place; and the king named the victim's brother to take his place.[65] Yet this was an authority which made itself felt only intermittently, by a kind of sudden convulsion. King Hsüan punished Po-yü only at the end of eleven years; and as for King Yi, when Prince Hu of Ch'i, whom he had himself set upon the throne to replace his brother Ai, was put to death in his turn by another of his brothers, he took no action against the latter.

The most important duties of the lords were homage, tribute, and military service. The rituals, which were compiled later, have endowed the entire organization with a regularity which it seems to have lacked in reality. Visits of homage should have been due theoretically every three, four, five, or six years, depending upon the distance;[66] in actual fact they were far from being that frequent. Thus, according to the tradition of Lu, it was only in 820 that a prince of that country went to offer homage at court for the first time.[67] Here again the royal authority seems to have manifested itself in fits and starts. When the Prince of Han had not yet come to court in the fourth year of King Hsüan (824), the king sent the Lord of Kuei to him, after which the prince, seized with fear, accomplished his duty.[68] But it is observable that even lords quite close to the capital, and ones whose domains were located within the province which was considered peculiarly as Royal Domain, came irregularly.

Tribute, which was relatively light, consisted especially of the characteristic products of each region which were necessary for the various religious ceremonies. We must assume from the *Yü kung*, which notes a single delivery of tribute for each province, that the count gathered together the tributes of the lords in his province and then transmitted them to the capital. Yen sent varnish and silk; Ch'ing sent salt, silk, hemp, lead, pine trees for columns in the ancestral temple and the palaces, and so on; Hsü sent pheasant plumes for the dancers and sounding stones for the musicians; Yang and Ching sent gold, silver, copper, bamboos, ivory, and skins, as well as trees for building and woodworking; Yü sent iron, silver, stones for arrowheads, and skins of bears, wildcats, and so on; Yung sent various kinds of jade, and so forth. Even the barbarians were supposed to send products of their land: those of the upper Yellow River, on the margins of the desert, sent skins and felt, those of Lai in the Shantung peninsula sent the silk of the mountain mulberry, and so on.[69] The very nature of this tribute indicates that it was sent regularly; and the *Yü kung* moreover distinguishes carefully between ordinary tribute and that which was required only when it was specially requested. Refusal of tribute was a sign of rebellion: the fact that the king of Ch'u was no longer sending to Chou the tribute of white grasses which had been required of him was the pretext which Prince Huan of Ch'i invoked for his expedition against that country in the seventh century.

To sum up, the Chou empire in about the eighth century B.C. must have resembled the contemporary empires of the Mediterranean, rather than the symmetrically organized state which the rituals were pleased to describe. The royal authority, based upon effective military power, was obeyed just as long as it could impose itself; almost every king had to give proof of his power anew. Sometimes the vassals in concert succeeded in getting rid of a sovereign who was too energetic or too much enslaved by his favourites, male or female: he was dethroned or assassinated. In wishing to make the immense empire which they had founded obey them, the Chou kings were pursuing a dream which could not be realized. In that period, in a China with difficult communications, with a sparse population, with barbarian tribes entrenched in the interstices between provinces, the constitution of a true state was still an impossibility. It would take centuries for the conditions favourable to the founding of a unified empire to develop.

Book II
Social and Religious Life

1
Society in Ancient China

Chinese society in the Chou period was divided into two distinct classes: below, the common peasantry and, above, the patrician class or nobles, *shih*.[1] In structure the two classes were totally opposite: in the one a kind of gregariousness, a group life in communities within which individuals and families were submerged and did not count; in the other, by contrast, a kind of familial individualism. Within the limits imposed by their duties to their overlords and to their parents the nobles were free individuals. The peasants were restricted within the narrow bounds of an all-pervading organization which left them no initiative. The patrician class had clan names, ancestors, and their own family worship; they could own fiefs and receive official posts. The lower class had none of these things; they could never own land. Even in the ethical rules of conduct the difference reappears: patricians practised rites, *yi-li*; the common man had only customs, *su*. 'Rites do not extend down to the common people.'[2]

The Common People

In ancient China the common people were the peasants, *nung*, belonging to families which in groups of eight worked the fields that were allocated to them periodically by their overlord.

All estates, whether royal domains or those of nobles, were divided into *ching*,[3] i.e., large squares of land, each split up into nine smaller equal lots, of which eight (called 'private fields', *ssu-t'ien*) were distributed, each to a family chief, for the family's support and maintenance on condition that in common they cultivate the ninth lot, the centre or common field, *kung-t'ien*, the product of which went to the overlord.

The size of the *ching* seems to have varied according to the different regions. In the Royal Domain, i.e. in the Lo Valley, it was as a rule one thousand *mou* (roughly 37$^1/_2$ acres), each head of family being allotted a field of 100 *mou* and five more for his house and garden. It was the same on the banks of the Yellow River in the region where it enters the eastern plain between Huai-ch'ing and K'ai-feng. Farther north, around Yeh, family lots were 200 *mou* each. In the estates of Sung the *ching* appear to have been smaller, comprising only 630 *mou*, or seventy *mou* per private or common lot. In Chin, in the Fen Valley (Shansi), the *ching* seems to have been originally still smaller, only something like 400 *mou* (about fifteen acres) for the nine lots; but this system, which had disappeared so quickly that it was completely forgotten by the fourth century, had been replaced by a much simpler system of government by family, each head of a family receiving 500 *mou*, of which he had to cultivate five in lieu of tax.[4]

Though the peasant worked these lands, he did not own them; they belonged to the overlord. The term 'private fields' must not be allowed to mislead us. The peasants of the same *ching* did not each cultivate his own field separately, but worked the nine lots in common. The ideal of peasant happiness is thus described by Mencius, referring to the days of King Wu: 'Around his homestead of five *mou* the space between the walls is planted with mulberry trees on whose leaves the silkworms feed, so that the old people may wear silk clothing. He has five chickens and two sows being raised for the right season, so that the old people have meat to eat. The fields of a hundred *mou* are cultivated so that the family of eight is secure against hunger'.[5] In this way the peasant produced almost all he required: grain, cattle, silk, etc. The surplus was taken to market.

Each town, large or small, had at least one market, which lay to the north of the lord's residence, having been established there by the wife of the first ruler when the fief was created. This remained the chief marketplace, even for the larger towns which had other markets in the eastern and western districts. It was a vast open square. At Lo-yi, the capital of the Eastern Chou, it was 600 feet square, covering an area of nearly 2$^1/_2$ acres.[6] On market days the director of the market, *ssu-shih*, set up his office in the centre of the square and, when all was ready, opened the market by hoisting his flag. The space in the centre had usually to be left clear; around it the peasants and pedlars set up their stalls. Those selling the same kind of goods were assigned to the same quarter, under the supervision of one of their own people, the *ssu-chang*, Head of the Quarter, who had to collect the market tax and see to the policing of his group. There were quarters of grain merchants, sellers of arms and furniture, of earthen vessels, of metalware, dealers in slaves, and so on.[7] The prices for each class of goods were fixed by the Provost of the Merchants (the chiefs of the different quarters were under them), who could also grant or refuse the right to open a stall. The goods on sale were subject to all sorts of regulations: the length and width of rolls of linen and silk were fixed; carts had their exact dimensions laid down; for the fruits and grains the period during which they could be sold was fixed, and it was forbidden to bring them to market out of season; the adulteration of good-quality foodstuffs with bad was punished, if it exceeded 20 per cent. Special inspectors watched for fraud and arrested offenders, while the police kept an eye on the general behaviour and prevented quarrels or fights.[8] All transactions were confirmed by contract. In less important cases a sheet of paper torn in two was enough; in larger business transactions, such as the sale of slaves, a formal deed of sale was drawn up in duplicate by an official guarantor, who levied a tax on it and gave summary judgement in case of dispute.[9]

In the life of the countryside the market played the same important part that it still plays today. It was the centre of exchange, not only of goods, but also of news and ideas. Not only peasants attended it, but also businessmen of every kind, wholesalers and retailers; no commercial transaction could be carried through elsewhere. Market days were divided into three sessions: the morning one for wholesale dealers and the evening for the small retailers; only the afternoon was left to the peasants from the surrounding districts to settle their petty affairs.[10] The morning market especially, when all sorts of strangers met together, must have been a great opportunity for passing on news of all kinds. Here public opinion, if it existed at all at that time, must have been formed. Here the peasant would learn about happenings in the principality and in the empire generally, and would thus come, however slightly, into touch with the rest of the world.

Indeed, it was only by chance encounters at the market that the peasants could have any contact with the exterior world, so much did the establishment enclose them, shut them up in their villages and districts, controlling them and thinking for them. Affairs of state or even of their village were no business of theirs, and even their own personal affairs hardly concerned them. The peasant could scarcely possess even simple family interests, for his family was only a group, a collection of eight persons, parents and children, which in law had no separate identity. Such identity in ancient China depended on a particular worship. In contrast to the patrician class which had family cults, so that each family had an identity of its own, the common people, having no ancestors, had no family cults. The twenty-five families of a hamlet were required to make up, around the hamlet's God of the Soil, *li-she*,[11] a peasant grouping with a cult of its own and therefore its own identity. Within these groupings the greatest possible uniformity had to be maintained in order to obtain the ncessary unity; so no initiative was left to the peasants. His whole public and private life, not for him personally but for the whole community at the same time, was regulated from above by the sovereign and by his delegated officials individually. Each year special agents told the peasant what crops he was to plant, when he was to sow and when to harvest. Others ordered him to leave his winter home and go to work in the fields, or to leave the fields and shut himself up again in his house. Others again looked after his marriage. Others parcelled out the land and distributed any extra portions according to the number of his children. A whole ministry, that of the *ssu-t'u*, was charged with the task of looking after him and of regulating everything for him.

But the one fact that determined the life of the common man, which fixed his character most clearly, was not an administrative fact but a religious and social one. The year was divided into two seasons which were in a way opposed: the season of outdoor activity in spring and summer, that of seclusion in winter. This division, which was of no importance for the noble class as regards religious observances, governed the whole life of the peasantry and was the guiding principle of his existence. Everything changed from one of these periods to the other: place of abode, way of life, occupation, even morals.

In the cold season, when winter approached in the ninth month, the order was given for the peasants to return to the village: 'The cold is coming, in full force. The people have not the strength to stand it. Let everyone return to the houses!'[12] Thereupon each family went and occupied the sun-dried brick hut which was allotted to it in the hamlet, *li*, where twenty-five families, the tenants of three *ching*, grouped themselves into neighbourhoods, *lin*, of five families each.[13] This small group was managed (not hereditarily) by a noble of the lowest rank, a simple *shih*, who had his house and ancestral hall there. To the northeast was the school, to the north the marketplace, and at the southern entrance the altar of the God of the Soil. Each hut had its little orchard of mulberry trees, its pig pen and chicken run, within a small enclosure of 2¹/₂ *mou* (about 400 square metres). Here the peasant family took up its quarters when the work in the fields was over.

> In the tenth moon the cricket enters under our beds;
> we fill up the chinks, and smoke out the rats,
> we close the windows, we plaster over the doors.
> Ah! my wife and my children!
> The change of the year requires this.
> Let us enter and dwell here.[14]

They never left it again till the following spring. Winter was the time when work was done at home,[15] especially women's work: weaving, making garments, and so forth.

In summer the peasants abandoned their village houses entirely:

> In the days of the third month we take our plough in hand.
> In the days of the fourth month we leave [the village]
> together with our wives and our children
> who bring us food to eat in these southern fields.[16]

All of them, men and women, boys and girls, settled down in the open country, on the common fields of the *ching*, as their prehistoric ancestors had done of old, at the initial clearing of the virgin bush. First of all, in the third month of spring and with much ceremony, they 'brought forth the fire' from the main house of the village, extinguishing the old fire and relighting a fresh fire of elm or willow branches, gathered from the forest, in the flat ground levelled off in the middle of the fields.[17] Then they built themselves large huts called *lu*,[18] within which they crowded higgledy-piggledy, in groups of families who cultivated three lots of the same *ching*.[19] Thus they passed the time entirely in the open, working in the fields or enjoying themselves at the seasonal feasts.

For them the difference between summer and winter was not merely that between a season when one was hot and another when one was cold; it was a difference between two periods which had nothing whatever in common, when the whole way of life was ordered in quite a different way. Winter was the period of seclusion, when each family lived in its own home, thrown back on itself, separated from its neighbours and usually

having no contact with them. Summer, on the other hand, was
the time of liberty and open-air life, when the family unit was
lost in the community,[20] when one's own vanished home was
replaced by the communal hut, when the joint cultivation of the
fields took the place of home tasks. Between these phases were
the periods of transition, spring and autumn, when the two
modes of life intermingled.

The common people, possessing neither worship nor rites, knew
nothing of the patrician-style marriage, *hun*; all they had were
unions, *pen*.[21] These, insufficient for a noble who married to
continue a cult, were entirely regular for a plebeian. Since he had
no clan name and therefore no family in the religious sense, the
obligation of exogamy for him took on a form which was special
and quite different from that among patricians.[22]

In the second month of spring, the king having opened the
marriage season by sacrificing to the Divine Intermediary, the
official go-between, *mei-shih*, announced to the peasants that the
time for the union of 'youths and maidens' had arrived. This was
the moment when they were leaving their winter homes for the
summer huts where several families lived together, and it was
also the time of the great spring festivals which preceded the start
of work in the fields. Young men and girls, as soon as they had
reached the age of fifteen, came together to sing in the fields,
sometimes in groups and sometimes in pairs, at places
consecrated by tradition to such meetings. Song followed song,
and it ended with their mating under the open sky. Throughout
the spring and summer the lovers could see one another and
meet without any difficulty.[23] But when winter came and the
families returned to the village, they were parted. The contacts
that had been permitted in summer were now forbidden; and if
they could be re-established, it was in secret. The easy morality of
summer had given place to the strict regimen of winter. In the
following spring most of them began again to sing together.
Some, however, the flighty ones, sought out new partners. This
might continue so for several years, until the young man was
thirty and the girl twenty. In autumn, if the girl was pregnant,
the lovers were married, probably in the eighth month, at a
general ceremony presided over by the go-between. The young
woman then left the house of her parents and went to live with
her husband. From then on she ceased to sing in the spring
festivals.[24] Thus the matrimonial union of the common people,
like all the rest of their lives, followed the rhythm of the year,
divided into two opposed periods.

The Patricians

The distinctive feature of the patrician, *shih*, was that he had ancestors and belonged to a clan, *hsing*.[25] He derived all of his qualifications from the Virtue, *te*, of the earliest ancestor of his clan: this ancestor had been a god, a hero, or an ancient emperor; he had possessed lands, he had held an official post, he had given rise to a cult, he had received a clan name. His descendants were forever after qualified to own land, to hold official positions, to carry on a cult, and to bear a clan name. The clan name was thus the external symbol of nobility.

In historical times the clans of ancient China were not territorial, nor is there anything to show that they ever had been. Some branches of a clan might hold a fief; but the majority did not, and no land was the collective property of a clan.[26] Whatever they may have been to start with (and certain traits seem to show that in their early form they were groups connected on the maternal side),[27] in historical times they were exclusively the collectivity of nobles descending in the male line from a common ancestor to whom they rendered worship. At their marriage daughters left this cult, joined that of their husbands, and took part in his sacrifices. It was a religious grouping whose chief feature was an absolute ban on any sexual relations among its members. Neither lawful marriage nor concubinage was allowed within the clan. The fear of violating this taboo was so extreme that, if anyone had purchased a concubine without knowing her *hsing*, he had to resort to divination in order to make sure that the union was lawful.[28] The number of clans seems to have been very limited, and the traditional figure of 'a hundred clans', *po-hsing*, undoubtedly greatly exceeded the actual number.[29] Ancient texts mention less than thirty and, although this number was probably the minimum, it is not likely that it was greatly exceeded.

The ancestor of a clan was a god or a hero. Thus the Chi clan, that of the Chou royal house, of the princes of Chin, Lu, and Wei, of the counts of Cheng, and so on, all derived their descent from Hou-chi, 'Sovereign Millet'; the Tzu clan, to which the dukes of Sung belonged, from Hsieh; the Ssu clan, from the Great Yü; the Chiang clan, to which belonged the princes of Ch'i, Lü, and Shen, claimed descent from the God of the Eastern Peak, T'ai-shan; the Kuei clan of the dukes of Ch'en claimed descent from the Emperor Shun; the Ch'ii clan of the counts of Tu and the lords of Fang from Emperor Yao; the Feng clan from Fu-hsi. Sometimes an entire group of clans had a single ancestor.

Thus eight clans (Chy, Jen, Ts'ao, Yün, Chi, Szu, P'eng, Mi) claimed descent from the hero Chu-yung and his brother Lu-chung, each having one of the latter's six sons as its particular ancestor.

Such ancestors were not always human beings: the ancestors of the Ssu clan were Kun, a fish, and Yü, a bear; and at the sacrifices in their honour neither the flesh of fish nor bear-fat was offered up.[30] Chung-yen, the ancestor of the overlords of Ch'in and Chao (of the Ying clan) was a bird with a human voice who excelled in driving horses.[31] When the Chien-tzu of Chao dreamed that he visited the court of the Lord on High he beheld the ancestor of the princes of Tai in the form of a mastiff.[32] Sovereign Millet, the ancestor of the Chi clan, and at the same time the god of cereals, who gave millet to mankind, appears actually to have been an anthropomorphic form of millet; and it is the plant itself which seems to have been the original ancestor. These are evidently survivals from very ancient ideas,[33] which by historical times left scarcely perceptible traces. The ideas, however, developed in another direction, and towards the middle of the Chou dynasty, in so far as they euhemerized the ancient legends, trying to turn them into history, the earliest ancestors received genealogies. All the clans were thus linked up with the ancient emperors, above all with Huang-ti, an artificial arrangement which the systematic appearance of the genealogies betrays.

The clan was only of religious importance; otherwise it was the family, *shih*, or branch, *chih*, or house, *tsu*, that formed the chief unit in the patrician world. It was, so to speak, a subdivision of the clan: strictly agnatic like the clan, it was composed of the descendants in the ancestor's male line, as well as their wives. But it was essentially a civil, even an administrative unit. It depended entirely upon the good will of the king or prince who created it by bestowing — upon a relative, a minister, or a favourite — a special name as a mark of honour (usually this was the name of a territory, but sometimes that of an administrative function). In each generation a member of a house could obtain a special name for himself, thus becoming the founder of a new house. Thus in the principality of Chin the houses of Chung-hang and of Chih sprang from the house of Hsün.

Each house had its own head, who was known by the family name alone and had no personal name.[34] The whole family owed him obedience: he could accept or refuse any child born into it; he married off the sons and daughters; and he could even dissolve the marriages of the latter if he wished.[35] He presented the members of his house at the court;[36] and if any of them were given a reward, they were supposed to offer part of it to him.[37] If they committed a crime, he had the right to try them privately without interference by the State.[38] Nor was the tie severed by emigration. Younger sons who had settled in alien territory were bound for the next three generations to report to the head of their house, who had remained behind in their native area, all the main events of their lives — honours, marriage, and so forth.[39] Even after they had established a new house of their own, the heads of these younger branches still owed respect to the head of the senior branch. This they showed by certain outward observances: if their rank was higher than his, they were not to take their symbols of rank along with them when they were visiting for the sacrifices; nor were they supposed to offer up sacrifices to their own immediate ancestors until they had attended the sacrifices of the head of the senior branch.[40]

It was marriage that enabled the clan to perpetuate itself and its worship. For this reason the marriage of patricians was above all a religious act. Its object was to provide a noble with a present helpmate in, and future successors for, the family worship. In their lifetime spouses worshipped the ancestors together; after their death they in turn formed an inseparable couple. A noble was therefore permitted to marry only a single time; this was an inviolable rule, as much for the Son of Heaven as for the ordinary patrician. A widower could not marry again, and cases of second marriages cited by historians were always stigmatized. But of course this rule did not mean monogamy: on the contrary, a young man married not one but several girls at one and the same time. A simple patrician without any rank or title was allowed two, a *tai-fu* three; the king and the princes married nine girls; and according to some traditional practices the king could marry as many as twelve. No matter how many of them there might be, they all had to be of the same clan. One of them was the principal wife, who played her part in the sacrificial rites; the others, who were furnished by the same family to be her attendants, *ying*, were secondary wives, subordinate to the first wife, and destined to replace her if she died, but having no right to her title.

The fundamental rule of patrician marriage[41] was that a noble could never marry a woman from the same clan as his own.[42] This was merely the application of the general rule forbidding sexual relations between men and women of the same clan. It was probably to insure that this exogamic rule was observed, as well as to verify that the omens were favourable, that the

preliminaries were presided over by a go-between, *mei* — not the
official and collective intermediary for a peasant district, but a
relative or a friend chosen for the occasion. His interposition was
essential. A famous poem says: 'To take a wife, what must one
do? Without a go-between one cannot marry.'[43] Without him
there could be no lawful marriage, *hun*; there would be only a
union, *pen*, as among the peasants, and the head of the family
could refuse to acknowledge a girl who had married in that way
and could force her husband to repudiate her.[44] It was the go-
between who superintended all the preliminaries up to the
betrothal. He made the first approaches, asked the young lady's
name, passed it on to the young man's family, and reported to
her family the outcome of the divination. His role ended only
with the betrothal, by which time all had been irrevocably
settled.[45]

When the wedding-day arrived, the bridegroom went in
person to fetch the bride and conduct her to his home. He did
not actually bring her himself, but went through the pretence of
doing so. Holding the reins so as to stop the cart for her to get in,
and, when she had done so, leading it forward for about three
turns of the wheels, he then handed the reins to the carter and
returned to his own cart. As soon as they arrived at the young
man's house, the marriage ceremony took place. It was called
'the agreement by the gourd', *ho-chin*. The young couple
together had a meal of three dishes and they were brought three
cups of wine. The last time the wine was poured into the two
segments of a gourd cut in half, the symbol of their union as an
inseparable couple. Then the secondary wives and the pages of
honour, *tsan*, did their part in the ceremony, the former eating
the remains of the husband's repast and the latter the wife's.
Meanwhile the newly married couple had been conducted to the
nuptial chamber, where they undressed, the husband handing
his garments to one of the secondary wives, and she hers to the
cart-driver who had brought her there, a relative of the
bridegroom. That completed the marriage ceremony, not only
for the principal wife, but also for the attendants.

The next thing was to assimilate the young wife into her new
family, by initiating her into the worship of her husband's
ancestors. On the day after the wedding the husband presented
her to his relatives, living and dead, to whom she went and paid
her respects. This was, however, nothing more than a sort of
courtesy presentation, so that the ancestors should know the
stranger who had come to live with them. It was not till after
three months that the real presentation took place, on the

occasion of a solemn sacrifice, when for the first time she took
her ritual place at her husband's side. Until this final ceremony
she was not really part of the family and could have been sent
back without its really being called repudiation; and to signalize
this the husband's family, during this entire period, kept the
horses of the cart which had brought her there, so that, if
necessary, they could take her back.[46] If she died within the three
months, she was not regarded as a wife and could not be buried
at her husband's side. It was only after the sacrifice to the
ancestors that she became the lawful wife.[47]

All such ceremonies seem to have retained traces of very
ancient rites: in the wedding ceremony, traces of group
marriage, in which all the brothers of a family married all the
sisters of another; in the interval of three months before
presenting the bride to the ancestors, a reminder of former times
— past for the nobles, though not for the peasants — when
young couples who had met freely in spring and summer did not
marry in the autumn unless the girl was pregnant. Among
patricians, too, it was probably the first signs of pregnancy that
in primitive times had made the marriage definitive.[48]

There was no lack of children in families thus constituted, in
which — in addition to the wife and her attendants married
according to the rites — purchased concubines could also be
added, if the husband were rich. The rank of the children varied
according to that of the mother. The eldest son of the principal
wife was always considered the senior, even though there were
brothers actually older than he, but of inferior birth; it was he
who carried on the family line and its worship. But the
ceremonies when they came into the world took little account of
rank.

At the actual birth, quite simple symbolic rites were
considered sufficient: if it was a boy, a bow of mulberry wood
was hung up on the left side of the gate; if a girl, a napkin on the
right side. During the first three days the child was left alone in a
closed chamber which nobody was allowed to approach, not
even to feed it. If it was a boy, it was laid on a bed; if a girl, on the
floor. In its hands were placed symbols of its future occupations:
a jade sceptre, emblem of dignity; or a terracotta spindle, symbol
of women's work.[49] At the end of this time, when the child
showed its vitality by its cries, the head of the family decided
whether to accept or refuse it.[50] If rejected, it was killed or
exposed.[51] If it was accepted, a servant — chosen by divination
after having been purified by fasting during the three days of the

infant's fast — went to get it and carry it to the women's apartments, where the mother or the wet nurse suckled it for the first time. At the same time, if it was a boy, six 'arrows' of coarse grass-stalks were shot off, using the mulberry-wood bow that had been hung up by the gate on the day of birth: towards the sky, the earth, and the four cardinal directions, in order to ward off all calamities. The infant's acceptance, making it a member of the clan, was solemnized by a sacrifice which the father offered and which served to announce the event to the ancestors. But the infant's ordeal was not finished: 'the vital spirit and breath of the child are without strength.' Therefore it had to be kept hidden away for another three months in a separate room, where its mother had to live apart from her husband and the other women until the ceremonial return. Only then was it considered vigorous enough to face the danger of being presented to its father.

A lucky day having been fixed by divination, the child's hair, which had not been cut until then, was dressed — as well as it could be — in the style worn by children, which it would keep till the end of adolescence. A small tuft of hair was kept on top of the head: for a boy, it was braided into two horns on the sides; and for a girl, into a cross in the middle. The mother, carrying the infant in her arms, came to the middle of the main hall; and the woman in charge of the harem said to the father: 'So-and-so, a mother, today ventures to respectfully show you her child.' The father took the child by the right hand and gave it a name, *ming*, which he uttered in a childish voice, so as not to frighten it. Only after it had been given a name could the child be entered in the register of the family of which it was a member.[52]

From the day of its birth the child of a patrician possessed a Virtue, *te*, somehow latent in it, which distinguished it from the commoner and gave it special capacities. But this Virtue could develop fully only after an initiation which brought the child to enter into a new life under a new name. This was the taking of the cap of manhood, *kuan*, for boys and of the hairpin, *chi*, for girls. These ceremonies marked the end of adolescence and the start of adult life. Every patrician, *shih*, had to undergo this ceremony, even the eldest son of the Son of Heaven, for 'in this world nobody is noble, *kuei*, by birth.'[53]

Originally the young of the patrician class seem to have prepared themselves for the initiation ceremony from puberty on by a special kind of life, away from adults: boys away from home, gathered in a house for young men which in historical times became a college; girls, on the other hand, within the home at the ancestral temple. For the latter the discipline was somewhat relaxed: they were allowed to stay shut up in the women's quarters and only made a kind of 'final retreat' at the ancestral temple. But for the boys the regimen remained severe, and they were shut out from their home until they had completed their studies.

The boys received their education in the district school.[54] There they lived, day and night, for nine years, their tenth to their twentieth year, learning the three virtues, the rites and the six sciences: dancing and music, archery, chariot driving, writing and arithmetic. This instruction was divided up into half-yearly courses according to the seasons: outdoor exercises in spring and summer, indoor studies (writing, etc.) in autumn and winter. Eldest sons had the prerogative of attending the royal college in the capital, where the hereditary prince was being educated. The best students from the district schools were also brought there; the course of study there seems to have been the same. The life of these students, confined to the school, retained traces of the time when that institution had been the house in which boys were prepared for initiation and where, being a community of adolescents, they were not supposed to have any contacts with adult society. For this reason the school was situated outside a town or village, to the northwest, and a semi-circular ditch round it clearly marked its separation from the secular world. (Only the ditch round the royal college at the capital formed a complete circle.) Even in historical times, when the old ideas were beginning to weaken, the school remained a sacred spot which was barred to women and where, except for teachers, male adults were allowed to enter only for set ceremonies.

When he had finished his studies the youth returned home and prepared himself to put on the hat of manhood, letting his hair grow. The second month was the ritual period; the day was fixed through divination by the milfoil stalks. The ceremony, having been announced to the ancestors the evening of the previous day, took place with great pomp in the eastern half of the house before a crowd of friends and relations. First of all the hair-style of childhood — two horns on each side of the head — was undone and the adult coiffure, a coil of hair on top of the head tied with a silk ribbon, was made. Thereupon the three main ceremonial hats were solemnly placed on the young man's head, after he had been clad each time with the appropriate garment. The whole ceremony was meant to show that he was being born to a new life. He was given a new coiffure, new hats and robes, and finally a new name, *tzu*, to replace his childhood name, *ming*.

This fact of rebirth was further emphasized by the ritual prayer. As he placed the first ceremonial hat on the youth's head, the priest said: 'In this happy month, on this lucky day, for the first time the hat is placed on your head. Banish all childish thoughts; you must now behave in conformity with the Virtue of a perfect man. May your old age be happy and your fortune ever increase in splendour!' And before giving the new name he said: 'The rites and ceremonies have been carried out. In this auspicious month, on this lucky day, I proclaim your proper name. This name is very favourable; it is the right name for a noble wearing a hair-knot; it is the right name for you who have arrived at manhood. Take it and keep it for evermore.'[55]

For a girl the ceremony, though not so solemn, had the same significance. At the age of ten she was separated from the boys and shut up in the women's quarters, where she was taught a woman's duties: first and foremost obedience, which was her chief duty; then women's tasks, such as pounding hemp, weaving, unwinding silk-cocoons, and so forth; and finally the religious ceremonies in which as a married woman she would have to play her part. When she became engaged, she retired to the ancestral temple for three months, and then received the hairpin and a new name.

With the donning of the hat of manhood a young noble entered the ranks of the grownups. From that time on he had all the duties, but also all the privileges, of his class. He became a warrior; he took part in military expeditions; he could enter the service of his prince; he was fit to be given a post or a fief; he could perform public and private ceremonies; and finally he could take a wife. Nevertheless, although in principle all patricians enjoyed the same rights, in actual fact they were far from being equal. Leaving aside the princes, *chu-hou*, appointed by the Son of Heaven, there was a whole hierarchy ranging from ordinary country nobles, *shih*, to the grand officers, *tai-fu*, who held official posts at court and in the provinces and whose ranks were evidenced by the number of responsibilities, *ming*, that had been conferred on them.

Of a patrician's privileges the most important was his right to own land; but not all of them owned it in the same manner. Some held it as a fief, *kuo*; the king had bestowed it upon them or their ancestors in a solemn investiture, *feng*, 'with earth and grass', handing them a clod of earth from his own God of the Soil to be placed on the mound of the God of the Soil in the fief, the mound established for them at their residence opposite the ancestral temple.[56] Fiefs were of all sizes, from large principalities with rulers more powerful than the king himself down to the small type of fief of a hundred families, such as the one the victorious King of Yüeh wanted to give to his enemy, the King of Wu, after having conquered his kingdom.[57] All fiefs were created in the same fashion, all being property of an essentially religious nature.

Not all the land, however, was held in fief. A certain number of nobles held land, not by feudal tenure, but simply as property. To start with, there were distant relatives of the prince or official to whom an apanage had been granted as emolument for their service. This was called a 'domain', *chia*, or 'village for sustenance', *shih-yi* or *ts'ai-yi*.[58] Such lands were not always conferred hereditarily; for them there was no investiture by earth and grass; on them no altar to a special God of the Soil was erected,[59] so that its acquisition had no religious character. Thus they were not fiefs, no matter how extensive they might be;[60] yet, unlike the allotments of the common peasants, they were fixed once and for all, not changing but comprising a certain definite area, together with the peasants who worked it. Those upon whom they had been conferred had rather the right to enjoy them, a sort of usufruct.

There were, in addition, families granted a kind of 'hereditary emolument', *shih-lu*,[61] which was usually paid in land, like that given to officials. These were families that had an official among their ancestors. Such lands, as the name indicates, were handed down from father to son and were probably parcelled out among their children, for there were some tiny domains. A certain noble of Ch'u, Hsü Hsing, who had come to live in T'eng, himself worked the land that the Prince of T'eng had granted him, which proves that it could not have been very extensive; and he exalted this practice into a philosophical principle.[62] The same thing was done by Chung of Ch'en.[63] There is no reason to suppose that such persons had a right to dispose of the land, which in theory did not belong to them. Nevertheless, it seems likely that in practice ways must have been found at an early date to get around the principle. Thus the laws which from the fourth century on gave the almost universal right to buy and sell land freely were merely recognizing a *fait accompli*.[64] The grand officers, moreover, had set an example by exchanging or selling land which had been bestowed on them and which, having no God of the Soil of its own, had no religious unity.[65]

In this way there gradually arose, from the sixth century on, a class of small landowners whose rights extended over a fixed area of land, but not over any definite locality. They formed an intermediary class between the princes, the grand officers, *tai-fu*, and the vassals, *fu-yung*, all of whom had fiefs, and the propertyless peasants. From the ranks of these poorer nobles seem to have come the writers of the Chou period and also those adventurers who sought their fortunes at princely courts during the period of the Warring Kingdoms. Most of them were very poor. Confucius spent his youth in poverty after the death of her husband deprived his mother of the emoluments from his position and reduced her to her own personal property. And Yen Hui, a disciple of Confucius, 'lived in a narrow alley, eating off a single bamboo plate and drinking out of a gourd; no one else could have stood such hardships'.[66] A writer of the third century B.C. describes a poor noble's dwelling as follows:[67] 'Here is a scholar whose home [house and garden included] measures only a single *mou*; the house itself is only fifty feet square.[68] The outer gate is of pine, with a small arched door at one side; the house-door is of wattle, the window is the neck of a broken jug. He possesses only a single garment which the family uses when one of them goes out. He eats only once in two days.'

On what did all these poor patricians live? Their usual career was to enter the service of their overlord. 'When a son is ready for service, his father enjoins him to be loyal. The son then inscribes his name on a tablet and presents this [as a guarantee of his good faith, together with the body of a sacrificed animal, saying]: "If I am disloyal, may I be killed [like this animal]!" '[69] Thus registered, a young noble became a member of his overlord's household, one of his followers, *t'u*. The lord kept and protected him, and in return the youth waited on him, obeyed him, followed him to war or on missions or, if his lord were disgraced, into exile, sometimes even to death, committing suicide on his patron's tomb. In all the principalities the great lords had whole troops of clients, either younger members of their own family or nobles from their domain, often employed as bodyguards. In 563 in Cheng, after the assassination of Prime Minister Tzu-ssu, and Minister of War Tzu-kuo, the latter's son, Tzu-ch'an, upon hearing the news, closed up his house and put it in a state of defence, summoned his officers, put his men in formation, and set forth with seventeen war chariots — in all some eighteen hundred men.[70] It was from among such followers that a lord chose his squire, *shu*, his charioteer, the halberdier of his chariot, posts much sought after, as they brought the follower into close personal contact with his master.[71] From among the crowd of followers he also chose the officers of his household: priests, diviners, treasurers, masters of the wardrobe, cooks, butchers and so forth, as well as land agents and superintendents of his towns, *tsai*.[72]

Although they were there to carry out all orders, these were not mere bravoes, ready to perform any dirty work at the behest of the master who paid them, but vassals who would go to any lengths in carrying out their duty to their chief. Indeed, a kind of code of honour, called 'ancient rules', *ku-chih-chih*,[73] governed their acts. The first and probably the most important rule was absolute obedience to their patron, no matter what the consequences. 'When the lord has issued his orders, nothing else matters,' was the ancient rule.[74] The prospect of certain death did not deter them. When in 550 B.C. the nobles of Ch'ü-wu, a fief of the Luan clan, were asked what they would do if their exiled and disgraced chief, Ying of Luan, were to return, they replied, 'If we had our lord here, dying for him would not seem to us like dying.'[75]

This same code forbade them to desert their patron if he were in trouble, and this feudal law carried even more weight than filial piety. An example is provided by the conduct of the two sons of T'u of Hu who followed Ch'ung-erh into exile. They let their father be put to death rather than desert their patron by availing themselves of the pardon Prince Huai of Chin (637) promised when he granted the followers of Ch'ung-erh twelve months in which to come in and submit or otherwise see their families slaughtered.[76] The 'ancient rules' governed the relation of these hangers-on to persons other than their patron. They were, for instance, forbidden to fight with a former teacher. Thus Tzu-yü, carrying the fugitive Prince Hsien of Wey in his chariot and seeing they were pursued by his old instructor in archery, cried out: 'If I shoot, I may kill my teacher. If I don't shoot, I shall be killed. Wouldn't it be better to make a mere show of shooting at him?' After having shot two arrows into the armour of the horses, he changed places with his charioteer who, having no such link with his adversary, could shoot to kill.[77]

One of the most serious duties of a young noble was that of family vengeance. He had to pursue without mercy the murderer of his parents or of a brother, and had to give armed help to the avenging party when more distant relatives were concerned. In the case of father or mother this duty took precedence over all others. It even necessitated giving up one's official posts; one had to be ready to kill the murderer anywhere, for the world was not wide enough to hold at one time a son and the assassin of his parents: [78] 'He must sleep on the mourning mat [even when the mourning was over], his head resting on his shield ... ; if he meets the murderer in the marketplace or at court, he should not have to return home to get a weapon to attack him [but should carry one always].'[79]

Vengeance extended even to the dead. When in 506 the generals of the victorious Wu armies, Wu Tzu-hsü and P'i of Po, invaded Ch'u, they dug up and flogged the corpse of King P'ing, dead ten years, who had had their fathers executed.[80] Stories of family vendettas fill the annals of those days.

Service with a prince or other great lord was the usual career of a noble under the Chou dynasty; and it was not easy for them to evade this. Only when they had reached the age of seventy could they ask permission to retire, and even then it was not always granted. Indeed, even when they had been punished for some crime, they did not leave their patron's service: if condemned to castration, they served in the private quarters of the palace; condemned to cutting off the feet, they served as keepers of the palace gates.

Not all of them, however, were suited to military or official duties. Those who did not consider themselves fit for such a career lived from their land, if they could. Others lived by their own knowledge, as priests, diviners,[81] sorcerers, doctors,[82] veterinarians,[83] cooks,[84] and butchers.[85] The luckiest of these also ended up by attaching themselves to the destiny of some prince or other great lord. Others, again, became village schoolteachers, instructing the children of nobles in the art of writing and the rudiments of the rites, music and archery, to prepare them for the district school. A few took up commerce, as Ssu of Tuan-mu (Tzu-kung) did in the state of Wey and as Chuan-sun Shih did in Ch'en before they joined Confucius and became his disciples.[86]

Unlike the peasants, they were not tied to the cultivation of the land nor restricted to the primitive barter system of the nearest market town, and so they were able to do business on a large scale, as did Mu of Tuan-kan who, before studying under Tzu-hsia, had been the biggest broker in the state of Chin.[87] They undertook to sell the salt of Ch'i to all the neighbouring states, they transported grain, silk, cattle, horses, 'awaiting the right moment to move goods, and seeking to make a profit of one tenth.'[88] They would even sail in small boats up the Yellow River as far as Lung-hsi, near modern Ninghsia, to meet the caravans coming from the West. Such a trader was the cattle-dealer of Cheng who, meeting a Chin army, devised a ruse to save his country from a surprise attack.[89] Then there was the merchant, a native of Chin, who in 588 planned to rescue a Chin general, Ying of Chih, who for eight years had been a prisoner in the land of Ch'u, by carrying him off in a bale of merchandise.[90] And there was Li of Fan, who after twenty years as minister to the King of Yüeh left that country and twice made fortunes in business.[91] Some of them helped to manage the domains of lords whose duties kept them at court.[92] Others, however, were reduced to living by their wits, like the parasite in one of Mencius's anecdotes who went around every day watching for funerals, so that he might partake of the burial feast.[93]

No matter what their condition, even if reduced to misery, patricians were still eligible for the highest posts. Fu Yüeh, according to the legend, was working on the land when the king, Wu-ting of the Yin, appointed him minister. If a noble were exiled, it was the custom of the land that took him in to offer him a post suitable to his rank. The distinction between patricians and commoners was never effaced.

The Princes

When a patrician was granted a fief by the king he became a prince, *chu-hou*, if the king remained his immediate suzerain, or a vassal, *fu-yung*, if the king attached him as vassal to some more powerful neighbouring prince. The investiture took place at a solemn ceremony.[94] From the altar of Sovereign Earth, the great God of the Royal Soil, a clump of earth was taken, its colour and the side of the altar from which it was removed corresponding to the compass bearing of the fief from the capital: a green one if it lay to the east, a white one for the west, and so forth. It was sprinkled with yellow earth, wrapped up in white herbs, *mao*, and handed to the new feudatory, who took it back with him to his residence in his principality, where it formed the core of the mound dedicated to the God of the Soil for his fief.

Invested with a fief, whether as prince or vassal, a patrician found that he had acquired fresh rights and duties: duties towards the spirits of his domain — sacrifices to the God of the Soil created for him, to the mountains and rivers, to his own ancestors, who had now become the guardians of his territory; duties towards the people — good government, instruction in the ceremonies, and guidance in the right path; duties towards his suzerain — tribute, military service; and so on.

In the midst of his domain he built himself a dwelling with

three large gates: the Gate of Storehouses, *K'u-men*, leading to the courtyard of the Pavilion of External Audiences, where he dispensed justice; the Gate of Pheasants, *Chih-men*, leading to the second courtyard, where the Pavilion of Internal Audiences was, with the altar of the God of the Soil on the west and the ancestral temple on the east side; and finally, the Gate of the Chariot Lu, *Lu-men*, leading to the private apartments.

Unless his fief was unusually large and affairs of state occupied most of his time, his life would be little different from that of any ordinary noble. Leaving aside his private life (the taking of the cap of manhood, marriage and so on), which was the same for all patricians from the king downwards, his public life had no peculiar character. Although the investiture had enlarged his Virtue, it had not made him a holy person. He was not tied to any special observances, nor hedged in by any taboo applying solely to his rank and position. He remained a simple patrician, even though he had been entrusted with the government of a fief.

Only accession to royalty conferred upon a noble a peculiar aura that princes did not possess. When the large principalities were created at about the end of the eighth and beginning of the seventh centuries, their rulers actually enjoyed as much political power as, and even more than, their suzerain the king. Yet it was on him that their temporal power relied for its religious basis, and their persons remained completely secular at all times.

The King

The king[95] was the universal sovereign: 'Under the wide heavens all is the king's land. Within the seas that bound the earth all are the king's subjects.'[96] Nevertheless, the royal power was always more religious than political. For the king was not merely the first among the princes, the supreme patrician, the one whose Virtue extended farthest and exerted the most influence. Nor was he merely the chief of state, the absolute master of his people, the sovereign overlord of the princes and of all the barbarians. He was, above all, a sacred being whom the Lord on High, Ti, had invested with a special charge, *ming*, the one who had received the Mandate of Heaven, *T'ien-ming*,[97] or, as it is expressed somewhat differently, the one who was the son of Heaven, *T'ien-tzu*.

For the Chinese of antiquity the term 'Son of Heaven' was not, as with moderns, merely a conventional title. The Chou kings truly descended in a direct line from the Lord on High, for the mother of their ancestor Hou-chi had conceived him while walking in the god's footsteps. The dukes of Sung, descendants of the Yin kings, ascribed no less exalted an origin to their ancestor, Hsieh, telling that his mother became pregnant after consuming an egg dropped by a swallow. Some such marvellous origin was the least a person needed to be capable of receiving and exercising the Mandate of Heaven. For the mandate not only entrusted the king with the task of ruling man; it made him the effective assistant of the Lord on High in maintaining the natural order of the world, one who had to assist Heaven by his actions so that all things would be well ordered. This was achieved not so much by his offering sacrifices as by his conducting his daily life in such a way that his influence, his Virtue, contributed to the proper process of the universe, to keeping the stars, the seasons, the alternations of hot and cold, and all else constant in their courses.

A personage sacred as much by birth as by function, the king was subjected to a host of positive and negative obligations. It must be said, however, that by historical times, as his political role more and more outweighed his religious role, the most troublesome duties had gradually disappeared, though without affecting the sacred character of the office.

In prehistoric times the king had been considered so sacred that he could not dwell among his subjects in the crowded city. His residence had been set outside it, in the southwest suburb.[98] It comprised a group of buildings arranged symmetrically in a square around a large central hall which was set aside for the ancestor of the dynasty, so that the king lived always in close proximity to that first member of his family who had received the Mandate of Heaven.

His life there was regulated minutely in accordance with the progression of the year. His place of abode, clothing, and food varied according to the seasons, the cardinal directions, the elements, colours, and flavours. In spring he had to live in the Eastern Pavilion, wear green garments, and eat wheat and mutton; in summer he lived in the Southern Pavilion, wore red, and ate haricot beans and chicken; in autumn the pavilion was the Western one, his clothes were white, and he ate hemp-seed and dog-meat; and in winter he lived in the Northern Pavilion, clothed himself in black and dined on millet and pork. This was because in spring the east and the colour green go together; in summer, south and red; in autumn, west and white; in winter, north and black; and the use of grains and domestic animals was naturally conditioned by the time of year when they were grown or bred. When he went out for the great sacrifices, on a hunting tour, or a military expedition, his chariot and horses were also adapted to the colours for the season. When he made a tour of inspection of the fiefs, the dates and order in which he visited them were fixed on similar lines: he had to go east in the first year, south in the second, and so on, so as to keep his travels following the order of the seasons. His relations with his women were determined by much the same kind of considerations: the night of the full moon was reserved for the queen, whose symbol was the moon. After that the other wives followed in descending hierarchic order to the end of the month, and in ascending order for the first half of the new month.[99]

Otherwise, in communicating with his subjects, he could not address them directly. The old legends show that all the sage-kings of antiquity were assisted by wise ministers who conducted the government on their behalf (Yao handing over the government to Shun; the latter on becoming king leaving all business to Yü, and he again appointing as his minister Po-yi). These legends serve to preserve the memory of the time when the king, fenced round with taboos of all kinds within the sacred world in which his function placed him, could exercise power only through a minister who, coming to receive and transmit orders, was the necessary intermediary between the king and the outside world. Still in historical times, nobody came before the king except bent nearly double, not daring to fix his eyes above the neck or below the belt, and one spoke to him only after having placed a large or a round jade tablet, *kuei* or *pi* — a mark of honour — before the mouth, so that his breath should not defile the king.

By historical times the old prohibitions that kept the king a prisoner in his sacred domain had vanished. The Chou kings lived together with their wives in the centre of their walled capital. That, at least, is where they usually lived, a kind of 'secular residence'. For the ancient palace continued to exist as the only spot where the Virtue of the king, the true reason for his office, could make itself felt. This palace, scarcely more than a survival from the past, was called Palace of the Circular Ditch, *Pi-yung kung*, or also, it seems, Sacred Palace, *Ming-t'ang*,[100] with its terrace for astrological observations, the *Ling-t'ai*. The king no longer lived there, but he went there, as he did to other temples, for certain ceremonies. According to the *Book of Rites*, he went there each month to carry out a pageant of the ancient royal life, in his dwelling, his robes, his food, so that the world should continue in order, the seasons succeed one another regularly, the course of nature be untroubled.[101]

But as the memories of the ancient way of life grew dim, his role lost importance. There was a *Pi-yung kung* in Hao, the capital of the Western Chou, its foundation attributed to King Wen; and its *Ling-t'ai* was still standing near the capital of the Prince of Ch'in in the sixth century. Whether one was built at Lo-yi when King P'ing made his capital there in the middle of the eighth century is uncertain. The chief ceremony of the *Ming-t'ang*, the great audience of all the princes of the empire, was held there on a temporary sacred place, a square altar built especially for the ceremony each time in the suburbs of the capital;[102] and it seems that most of these special rites were transferred to the Ancestral Temple, which gradually became the great centre of religious life.

For their ordinary life, the Chou kings were established, like ordinary overlords, in the middle of their capital. That of the Eastern Chou is said to have formed a small square 17,200 feet in circumference (about 3,500 metres)[103] north of the River Lo, from which it took its name, City of Lo, *Lo-yi*.[104] The encircling wall, a simple earthern rampart surrounded by a ditch, was pierced by twelve gates (three to a side); the principal one, on the south, was for the king's sole use. Near the southeast gate stood the nine famous tripods, *Chiu ting*, which are supposed to have been cast by the mythical emperor Yü the Great; the possession of them symbolized the legitimacy of the royal power. Nine streets crossed the city from north to south, and nine from east to west, except in the centre, about a ninth of the whole area, which was occupied by the palace. To the north lay the chief market, a vast square surrounded by shops. It had been opened by the queen when the city was founded and was larger than the ordinary markets in other parts of the city. To the south rose the ministry buildings, to the west lay the private residences of officials, courtiers, and others who lived by the court.

The palace, which had no religious character, was simply a kind of civil residence of the kings[105] and was but an enlarged version of a noble's home: it had an audience hall to the south, with the ancestral temple on the left and the altar of the God of the Soil on the right; at the back were the living quarters, and the whole was enclosed by a wall with the main gate on the south side. From the time when the kings had been freed from the taboos which relegated them to the Sacred Palace outside their town, they were content to adopt for their own use the style of their vassals' dwellings.[106] Three gates, one behind the other at intervals of a hundred feet, led to the private apartments, through courtyards around which were the various public buildings.[107] The first gate, that of the Kao Drum, *Kao-men*, led to the outer court, at the farther end of which stood the Pavilion of External Audiences. There the king dispensed justice or, to be more exact, had it dispensed by the Director of Criminals. Here, too, he gave solemn audiences, seated facing south. Between the pavilion and the gate the centre of the court formed an open space where officers of state and vassals took up their positions in order of precedence, the former on the left and the latter on the right, the nine ranks of the hierarchy being marked off by as many thorn bushes. At the entrance facing the king stood three acacias, marking the places of the Three Dukes, *san-kung*, the highest court of officials. On either side of the open space stood, on the right the Beautiful Stone, *mei-shih*, where criminals were exposed as if in the pillory, and on the left the Lung-coloured Stone, *fei-shih*, where anyone who complained against an official would stand for three consecutive days.[108]

Farther on, the Ying-men, Gate of the Ying Drum, flanked by two terraced towers, *kuan*, led to a second court. The rear of this was occupied by the Pavilion of Internal Audiences, where the king received his ministers each morning and discussed public business with them. This court opened on the right into an enclosure containing the altar of the Great God of the Soil and that of the God of Grains, *she-chi*. On the left it led to an avenue, to the north of which was the Ancestral Temple, *t'ai-miao*, while across from it, south of the avenue, there rose like a screen the palisade and roof housing the altar of the defunct God of the Soil of the vanquished dynasty, called the warning God of the Soil, *chieh-she*, or God of the Soil of Po, *Po-she*.[109] This was the central gate, near which was the impluvium, *chung-liu*, the residence of the God of the Soil of the palace, as also it was in every house. Thus for fear that the impluvium might be damaged by the wheels, nobody was allowed to pass through this gate in a chariot, under penalty of having his chariot pole broken and his charioteer beheaded on the spot.[110]

Finally, the *Lu-men*, Gate of the Lu Chariot, or *Pi-men*, Gate of the Constellation of the Net, led to the Six Palaces reserved for the king, the *liu-kung*. The first building, *ta-ch'in*, Grand Apartment, or *Lu-ch'in*, Apartment of the Lu Gate, was a reception pavilion. Thirty-five paces long, it consisted of three halls: the *yen-t'ang*, Hall of Feasts, where the king gave state banquets to vassal princes and to ministers; to left and right of it were side chambers in which he was dressed for these ceremonies or where he went to rest after they were finished. Behind this, around the interior courtyard lay the Private Apartments of the king, *Wang-hsiao-ch'in*, his real living quarters, with bedrooms, dressing rooms, storerooms of all kinds, kitchens, and so on. To the rear, farther north, were the women's Six Palaces, *liu-kung,* the arrangement of which seems to have been much the same as that of the king's Six Palaces. In front were the Grand Apartments of the queen, *Hou-ta-ch'in,* where she gave audiences to manage the internal affairs of the palace or issued orders to the servants. This also served as a hall for reception or ceremony; here, for example, newborn infants were presented in their third month. Behind that, around an interior court, lay the Small Apartments, *hsiao-ch'in,* two of which were for the queen herself, while three others were allotted to the three princesses, *fu-jen,* her attendants and concubines of the first rank. Outside the Six Palaces lay the Nine Chambers, *chiu-shih,* divided probably into three pavilions which were inhabited by the two classes of palace maidservants, *shih-fu* and *yü-ch'i,* and also by the slaves, *pei,* women condemned to forced labour within the palace; and by the eunuchs, *ssu-jen,* who were charged with guarding and keeping an eye on all these women. Lastly, other pavilions served as kitchens, storehouses, and so forth. A sort of grand park, as in the modern imperial palaces, seems to have occupied the whole northern portion of the enclosure.

Here the king spent his life among his wives and unmarried children. When they grew up the sons no longer lived in the women's quarters, but each was allotted his own palace: generally, the Eastern Palace for the crown prince, *t'ai-tzu,* the Western, Northern, and other such palaces for his brothers. The king's private life hardly differed from that of all the other great lords: taking the cap of manhood, marriage, funerals — there were no special rituals for him. Where the rites allowed, he enjoyed some advantages: where an ordinary noble married only three wives, and a feudal lord nine, the king had twelve; he regularly worshipped seven ancestors, as against five for princes and three for great officers; and so on. But these were merely surface facts which in no way modified the essence of the rites.

Only after death did a vestige of the ancient distinction reappear: just as the ritual dwelling of the living king, the Sacred Palace, differed from the habitations of ordinary men, so the dwellings of dead Sons of Heaven, their tombs, differed from those of their subjects. Not only was the burial mound much larger, but for the king alone the path of rough stone leading to the innermost burial chamber was a covered alley, *sui.* Princes had the right only to a path open to the sky, though the meaning of this privilege, which the kings guarded jealously, is unknown.[111]

The royal office was hereditary, going from father to son: the eldest son of the chief wife was the lawful successor. But the ritual of succession still retained traces of a more ancient order of succession, when the royal heritage had descended in the female line, so that it was not the son who normally became heir, but the son or brother of the sister. Thus, in order to pass the heritage from father to son it was necessary to use the intermediacy of a minister, who conveyed to the son the royal power which the father had given him for that purpose.[112]

Shortly before his death the king assembled his court with one of the Three Dukes, the Grand Protector, at its head and gave him responsibility for transmitting the royal power to his son and for helping him to rule. Immediately after the king's death, the Grand Protector took general charge: he ordered the officials to make funeral preparations; he had the testamentary charge of the dead king entered in the records by the Grand Scribe; he also ordered that the crown prince be brought to the side of his father to conduct the mourning. Some days later he proceeded to enthrone the crown prince. On that day the Grand Protector, bearing the great tablet of jade twelve inches high which was the royal emblem, and accompanied by the Count of Religious Affairs and the Grand Scribe (as the king was when he gave audience), entered by the steps reserved to the master of the house. Standing with his face to the south, he rendered the royal etiquette, that for reception at an audience, to the crown prince, who entered by the steps designated for guests and conducted himself before the Grand Protector as a subject. The Grand Scribe then read out the order transmitting power to the prince, who refused it twice and then accepted by pouring a libation, after which he received the royal insignia. Thereupon he took the place of honour, facing south, while the Grand Protector retired, took up the jade tablet which was the emblem of ministers, re-entered by the guest steps, and saluted the new king as his subject.[113]

Thus in historical times the royal office retained traces of the time when it had played a role more religious than political. The events during the Chou dynasty that were to deprive its kings of all political power led them back, by a strange turn of the wheel, to an exclusively religious role. But ideas had changed since high antiquity, even though the ritual gestures had remained the same; and the priest-king at the end of the Chou only remotely resembled the sorcerer-king of the times when the royal function commenced.

2
The Ancient Religion: Mythology

The religion of ancient China was essentially aristocratic. It belonged, so to speak, to the patricians, and was their quite special preserve. They alone had the right to worship and, in the widest sense, the right to the *sacra* thanks to the Virtue, *te*, of their ancestors, whereas the common people, having no ancestors, had no such rights. They alone were in personal contact with the gods, or with certain gods at least, and so they alone could address them. This does not mean that the common people were denied the blessings of religion. On the contrary, they were excluded only from worshipping; but once this was done, they benefited as much as the patricians did. Religion was, above all, an affair of the group, and not of the individual: one had to be head of a community, however small, to have a worship to carry on, not for oneself, but for the entirety of the community over which one presided. Thus the king worshipped for the whole empire, each prince for his principality, fief-holders for their fiefs, administrative heads of hamlets for their hamlets, and heads of families for those families. In this way the relations between gods and men were exactly laid down, and everyone knew to which of the innumerable deities he could and must address himself.

The Gods

The ancient Chinese had indeed peopled the world with a throng of gods and goddesses whose favour had to be sought, of spirits who had to be conciliated, and of good or evil influences which had to be attracted or warded off. They were of all kinds. Some were entirely personal, heroes whose histories were known and whose adventures were recounted; but most were less clear in makeup, belonging to numerous categories in which all were alike but indistinct, even to impersonal powers which exist even though one cannot say exactly under which form. The Chinese have never troubled much to discuss the nature of their gods. Philosophers and poets have turned their attention to other more immediate and accessible problems. They had no general name for the gods but bracketed together in one term the two words for ghosts and spirits, *kuei-shen*, or two others, spirits of heaven and earth, *ch'i-shen*.

Popular belief seems to have seen these quite simply as ordinary human beings, more powerful no doubt yet not all-powerful, with an understanding that was limited, though superior to ours. Their essential nature was not so very different, as they could be wounded (Yi wounded the Count of the River and the Count of the Wind with his arrows) or even put to death. In other ways too they were similar to human beings: quick to take offence and often vindictive. Dead gods, like dead men, still existed: the dead God of the Soil of the Yin dynasty received worship in the Chou capital. All such ideas remained rather vague, unformulated and exercising only slight influence over a religious sentiment which concerned itself rather with the worship itself and with those who rendered it than with the objects of that worship. But one thing was common to all these beings and powers: this was their sacred character, personal or impersonal, which was called *ling*.

The deities mentioned in ancient texts are so numerous that it would be tedious to give the names of them all. The forces of the physical world were all deified: there were Hsi-ho, the Mother of the Sun and Heng-o, the Moon Goddess;[1] Feng-po, Count of the Wind, also called Fei-lien, a kind of bird with a deer's head, who produced the wind;[2] the Lord of Rain, Yü-shih, who was called Ping-yi and produced rain by croaking;[3] Lei-shih, the Master of Thunder, also respectfully called My Lord Thunder, Lei-kung, whose other name, reminding one of the reverberation of thunder, is Feng-lung, a dragon with the head of a man who beat his stomach to produce the peals of thunder,[4] or according to other versions held in his left hand a drum which he tapped with a mallet;[5] or the Masters of the Night for the Lord on High.[6] Then there were local divinities: the Count of the River, Ho-po, who was named P'ing-yi, Lord of the Waters; the gods of the Four Seas, with the bodies of birds and the heads of men;[7] the gods of the Four Peaks and of mountains, rivers, forests; and finally gods for each of the Five Primordial Elements.

Anything that had to do with human life, with society, with the various human activities had its gods. Some presided over fate, the Great and Small Directors of Destiny, Ta shao ssu-ming;[8] others over marriage, Kao-mei or Chiao-mei, the Go-between.[9] Others again were the five household gods: the God of Interior Doors, *hu*; My Lord Hearth, Tsao-kung; the God of the Impluvium, *chung-liu*, who acted as god of the soil for the house; the gods of the entrance gate, *men*, and of the well, *ching*, or some say of the street, *hsing*.[10] Others presided over men's work: for agriculture Hou-chi, Sovereign Millet, the God of Cereals; the inventor of coals, or perhaps the spark itself, *kuan*;[11] the Ancestor of the Fields, T'ien-tsu; the First Husbandman, Hsien-nung, who was perhaps the same as Shen-nung, the Divine Husbandman. Still others concerned themselves with women's work: weaving, the Heavenly Weaving Maiden, Chih-nü; cooking, the First Cook, Hsien-ch'ui. There were gods of occupational groupings: the God of Blind Musicians,[12] K'uei, the one-legged dragon whose voice resounded like thunder, whose skin the Yellow Emperor had used to make the first drum, which he beat with a bone of the thunder-animal, the same that the *Yao tien* euhemerized into Director of Music at the court of Shun, the one who charmed the wild animals and made them dance by striking musical stones. Metal founders had the God of the Furnace.[13] Then there were the gods of animals, such as the Ancestor of Horses, *ma-tsu*, to whom sacrifices were offered up before departure for war or for hunting.[14] Finally, there was a whole host of demons and evil spirits, *kuei*: the eight brothers, will-o'-the-wisps, *yu-kuang*; the echoes, *wang-liang*, like little children with long hair who imitated the human voice to lead travellers astray; the *wang-hsiang* of rocks, who devoured people; the headless demons, *ch'iu-k'uang*; the *ch'ih-mei*, who lived in the mountains; the *fang-liang* and *wei-t'o* of the swamps; the *k'uei* and *hsü* of trees and stones;[15] the Goddess of Drought, the Lady Pa, daughter of the Yellow Emperor, Huang-ti;[16] the demons of epidemics who obeyed the Queen Mother of the West, Hsi-wang-mu;[17] and all the lost souls, *li*, who no longer received sacrifices and who, starving, took revenge for their suffering upon the living; and so on.

At the head of this pantheon stood the three great objects of the official worship: the Lord on High, Shang-ti, God of the Heavens; the Earth Sovereign, Hou-t'u, God of the Soil for the empire; and the royal ancestors. The first two were not a pair: the idea of a divine couple was completely foreign to the mythology of ancient China; both were male gods.[18]

The Lord on High, Shang-ti, or to give him his ritual title, the Lord on High of the Vast Heaven, Hao-t'ien Shang-ti,[19] was the chief of all the gods and of all the spirits, the ruler of men and of gods. He was a giant in human form who usually dwelt in heaven; but when he came down to walk on earth, he sometimes left imprints of his colossal footsteps.[20] Moreover, he had residences here below: certain groups of rocks were the terraces on which he gave banquets, and freshwater springs yielded the liqueur he provided for his guests.[21] Yet his real palace was in the centre of heaven, in the Great Bear, on the highest of the nine celestial circles, the approach to which was guarded by the Celestial Wolf, T'ien-lang (the star Sirius). There he lived with his family, for although his wife played no part, several of his daughters, *t'ien-chih-mei*,[22] had descended to earth and become goddesses there. The most famous was the Queen Mother of the West, Hsi-wang-mu,[23] with tiger fangs and the tail of a panther, who lived in the land of the setting sun and presided over epidemics. Another daughter was the Sorceress Yang, Wu-yang. Yet a third, 'the younger daughter of the Lord', called Yao-chi, died on Mount Wu and there became the magic herb *yao*.[24] Two others were the goddesses of the Hsiang River[25] in Hunan; and the last was the one who ordered Yi-ti to take wine to Yü the Great, at the same time putting him on his guard against the dangers of this new beverage.[26]

Shang-ti had his court in heaven, where his subjects, the souls of the dead, were given their proper place according to their clan, family, and social rank on earth, ranging from the souls of kings, themselves apotheosized and become *ti*, to those of their subjects — at least their noble subjects. Life went on there as at the courts of earthly kings, with feasts accompanied by music; and Chien-tzu of Chao, who spent a time there while living, enjoyed himself greatly.

Not only was Shang-ti the Lord of Heaven and King of the Dead; he was also the great master of terrestrial affairs, observing everything in all the four directions. He made the states and their kings, he bestowed the empire upon royal families, he gave princes their able ministers. In all things he was the master of man below, and he watched from on high.[27] Also, when taking a very solemn oath, one swore by his name, lifting up one's face so that the oath ascended direct to his residence in heaven, after having offered up a sacrificial victim.[28] He punished the guilty, no matter what their rank. In 655, having decided to chastise the Duke of Kuo, he sent his Minister of Punishments, who appeared in a dream. The prince was in the ancestral temple and, frightened by the apparition, wanted to flee, but it said to him: 'Do not flee! The Lord has ordered that I say to you: "I shall bring it to pass that Chin will seize your gate!" '[29]

It was therefore to him that the souls of the innocent who had been unjustly put to death made appeal. In 581 Prince Ching of Chin, after massacring the entire family of Chao, had a dream in which he beheld a great spectre with hair all in disorder, falling to the ground, beating its breast and capering (these were ritual gestures at funerals), and it cried to him: 'You have slain my grandsons unjustly! The Lord on High has heard my plaints.' About a century earlier, in this same land of Chin, Prince Hui on ascending the throne had removed the tomb of his brother, Shen-sheng, whom court intrigue had forced to commit suicide some years before. Thereupon the latter's soul, full of rage at this removal, appeared on a road in broad daylight to his former charioteer, T'u of Hu, and said to him: 'Yi-wu [the personal name of the reigning prince] is behaving contrary to the rites. The Lord on High has granted the appeal I have made to him: he will deliver Chin over to Ch'in, and it is they who will offer up sacrifices to me.' Only through the urging of his friend was he persuaded to 'address a plaint' anew to the Lord on High, who then let the punishment fall on the guilty prince himself: five years later, in 645, he was defeated and taken prisoner by the Count of Ch'in at the battle of Han.[30]

On the other hand, Shang-ti rewarded the virtuous. Thus, he sent one of his gods to announce to Count Mu of Ch'in in his ancestral temple that he would be granted an extra nineteen years of life.[31] For this reason everyone sought by every possible means to gain his favour. In the sixth century a Ch'i prince, fallen ill, wanted to offer up his chief priest as a sacrifice, so that he might plead with the Lord on High on his prince's behalf.[32]

Often, before chastising princes, he sent them warnings. Great disasters which occurred, such as epidemics, fires, comets, mountains collapsing, were so many warnings to kings to change their conduct. If they persisted, he punished them personally; and if the Virtue of the dynasty were exhausted, he deprived them of the Mandate of Heaven, *t'ien-ming*, or Mandate of the Lord, *ti-ming*, the real source for the authority of sovereigns, so as to give it to a better prince.

To help him in his task, he had a whole array of auxiliaries, who like him were called *ti*. Some were the souls of former sovereigns who, aided by the souls of their ministers, helped him to govern the world over-which they had ruled in their lifetimes.

Others were divine personages, though inferior to him. There
were five, one for each region of the world:[33] the Blue Lord,
Ts'ang-ti, or Green Lord, Ch'ing-ti, for the East; the White Lord,
Pai-ti, for the West; the Red Lord, Ch'ih-ti, or Flame-coloured
Lord, Yen-ti, for the South; the Dark Lord, Hsüan-ti, or Black
Lord, Hei-ti, for the North; and the Yellow Lord, Huang-ti, for
the Centre.

The religious role of these divine personages is certainly
ancient. Several of them appear in the oldest mythological
legends; but one of them changed more than the others in the
course of Chou history. Originally each of them was charged
with presiding over one of the five regions; and it is for this
reason that the White Lord (West) received the sacrifices of the
Ch'in counts,[34] whose domain lay to the west of the capital. But
the traditional correlation of the four cardinal directions with the
four seasons led, quite naturally, to their presiding over the
seasons as well and to the inclusion within their worship of
ceremonies which had originally nothing to do with them: those
of 'going to meet the seasons' in the outskirts of the capital.
Ultimately, in the last centuries of the Chou when, under the
influence of astrological theories, the cult of the Five Ti
developed greatly, they became the gods presiding over the five
elements; and, as these already had their own regents, *cheng*, the
efforts made to combine the two bodies of data resulted in a
highly artificial system. This became still further complicated:
the euhemerizing historians, having created human emperors
and given them a place in ancient history — either directly, like
Huang-ti, or by assimilating them to heroes already
euhemerized, as in identifying Yen-ti with Shen-nung — had
made it necessary to take account of these notions in the overall
system.[35]

Besides the Five Lords, other less important gods seem to have
been subordinates of the Lord on High: Ju-shou, his Minister of
Punishments;[36] Kou-mang, his Minister of Rewards;[37] probably
also the gods of the thunder, the rain, the wind, and so on; and
finally a whole hierarchy of celestial messengers, *t'ien-shih*, or
simply *t'ien*, who carried his messages to men.

Corresponding to the gods of heaven, the Lord on High and his
Five Lords, were the gods of the soil: Sovereign Earth, Hou-t'u,
Great God of the Soil for the empire, *ta-she*, and his underlings,
the local or regional gods of the soil, *she*.[38] They are not Earth
personified any more than Shang-ti is Heaven personified; the
functions of all, even the highest of them, are strictly territorial.

They govern and protect a limited domain; and it is only because in theory the Royal Domain extends to the 'Four Seas' that the Great God of the Soil governs the whole inhabited world, the territory 'under heaven', *t'ien-hsia*. They form as clear a hierarchy as do earthly rulers themselves: in principalities there are the princely gods of the soil, vassals of the Great God of the Soil; under them are those of the vassal domains and of administrative districts, down to the lowest level, the hamlet gods of the soil, set up for each hamlet of twenty-five families.

The Great God of the Soil was said to be Kou-lung, son of the monster Kung-kung, who, having helped to put the nine provinces in order after his father's death, became Sovereign Earth and was worshipped as God of the Soil, *she*.[39] But he never acquired a distinct personality of his own: he was too close to the small local gods of the soil who lived much more vividly than he in the worship of the people and were not identified with any legendary hero.

Every god of the soil was originally a tree planted on a mound in the midst of a sacred grove.[40] The type of tree changed according to the region: in the centre a pine; in the north an acacia; in the east a thuya; in the west a chestnut; and in the south a catalpa.[41] That is why certain trees were associated with the three ancient dynasties: the Hsia dynasty had a pine; the Yin, whose capital lay in the east, a thuya, which remained the tree of the state of Sung; and the Chou, whose first capital was at Hao in the west, a chestnut.[42] There was, however, less uniformity than would have been expected. Sometimes the tree was also an oak or a white elm, but in general it was a large, old tree. The god himself, however, was represented from the oldest times by an unpolished stone set up to the north of the tree, which served as the sacrificial slab.[43]

The God of the Soil was, above all, the god of a territory. Thus investitures were announced to him when a clod of earth was taken from his mound to become the foundation of the vassal god's altar in a new fief. The principality being his domain, he watched over the prosperity of all, people and overlord; in consequence the lord, in sacrificing to him, asked good harvests for his people (not as to a god of the soil in his creative capacity, but as to a protector), and for himself, long life. All great initiatives affecting the general life of the principality, such as hunting or war, had to be announced to him and had to start out from near his altar. He was called upon to decide especially difficult disputes. The two parties offered up a sheep to him, read their statements out loud, and then took an oath. This was a very solemn test, and cases are recorded where a perjurer fell dead on the spot, before he had even finished reading out his evidence.[44]

The God of the Soil was thus regarded as the guarantor of oaths. In the case of a particular solemn oath, the most powerful of these gods, the God of the Imperial Soil, was appealed to at the same time as the Lord on High. For instance, Count Mu of Ch'in, having defeated and taken prisoner Prince Hui of Chin at the battle of Han (645), swore by 'August Heaven and Sovereign Earth' that he would not put his captive to death.[45] The oath to the God of the Soil in this case was all the more appropriate since it was to him that prisoners were sacrificed on the return from military expeditions.

For this was a fierce and cruel god, one who loved blood, and the sacrifices offered to him commenced with the anointing of his stone tablet with the victim's fresh blood. The sacrifice was usually of an ox, though human sacrifices did not displease him. He even demanded one, according to tradition, at the beginning of the reign of T'ang the Victorious, when a drought had lasted five years; but when King T'ang offered himself as victim, the rain came.[46] A poet in the beginning of the third century B.C. describes the god under the name of 'Count of the Earth', as a monster 'with nine coils and pointed horns', with a body as large as an ox and the head of a tiger with three eyes, who devoured human beings.[47] In 641 the Duke of Sung had the Viscount of Tseng, who had arrived late, offered up as a sacrifice to the God of the Soil at Tz'u-sui, the place where the duke was presiding over the assembly of the nobles.[48] This seems to have been an exceptional case and one which was much criticized. But human sacrifices on return from war were more or less customary.

The God of the Soil, though not actually a god of war, played an important part in it, probably as lord and protector of the territory. When armies departed on campaign, a sacrifice, *yi*, was offered to him; the drums were presented to him by passing the troops in review, and it was probably at this moment that the drums were smeared with blood. Throughout the expedition he accompanied the army, borne in the Chariot of Purity by the Grand Praying Priest; and offenders were sacrificed to him.[49] Upon returning, the Controller of Horses, *ssu-ma*, minister of war, 'made the offering to the God of the Soil' after the triumphal entry into the capital;[50] and this offering was of prisoners sacrificed to him.[51] As folkways softened, these sacrifices must have been less frequent, yet they continued until quite late. In 532 the men of Lu, returning from an expedition, immolated a prisoner to the God of the Soil of Po. Nor was the memory of the custom ever forgotten. The generals of Ch'in, taken prisoner at the battle of Hsiao (627) and then released, expressed thanks by saying: 'By his kindness to us prisoners, your lord has not anointed his drums with our blood. ...' In 588 an exchanged prisoner returning to his homeland declared: 'I am a prisoner, one whose head is to be cut off. That your men have not anointed your drums with my blood ... is through your mercy, sire.'[52]

At his capital each prince had not merely one god of the soil but two: one for the whole principality and the other for his own family domain. They were the God of the Private Soil, *ssu-she*, as against the God of the Communal Soil, that of the principality, *kung-she*. When a dynasty was overthrown, the God of the Private Soil had to be removed to make room for that of the newcomers. For this he was killed by building a roof over his mound. The new dynasty continued, however, to worship the dead god, but only in accordance with the ritual offerings to the dead among whom he had now been placed. Thus it was that the Chou kings had at their court a dead God of the Soil of the Yin who was called the God of the Soil of Po, *Po-she*, after the name of the ancient capital of the Yin dynasty. Thus too the dukes of Sung had a dead God of the Soil of Hsia. Gradually this cult of dead gods of the soil acquired a symbolic value: one tended to see in such a god a 'warning' god, whose worship was supposed to remind kings and princes of the fate awaiting their dynasty if they 'lost Virtue'.

To what extent were local gods — those of mountains, rivers, and seas — subject to Sovereign Earth and local gods of the soil? It is by no means easy to tell. In any case, most of them seem to have had little enough real existence, being little more than names in the lists of annual sacrifices. Only one of them had in olden times acquired an individuality of his own: this was the God of the Yellow River, the Count of the River, Ho-po, the senior among all terrestrial waters ('for the Yellow River is the chief of the waters',[53] and even the seas are ritually inferior to it).[54] For his domain he had the waters and for people the fishes. He was portrayed sometimes as an enormous fish[55] — this was evidently the primitive form — sometimes with a human head,[56] sometimes as a god 'with human features and mounted on a dragon'.[57]

Towards the end of the Chou dynasty his appearance was fixed in popular imagination. 'As I crossed the River in the prince's suite,' says one writer of the period,[58] 'a turtle seized the left-hand horse [of my chariot] in its beak and started to drag me down into the arms of Chih-chu. I was young at that time and could not swim. I struggled against the current for a hundred paces and then I was swept away for a distance of nine *li*. Then, catching up with the turtle, I killed it. With my left hand I hung on to the horse's tail and, brandishing the turtle's head in my right, leaped out at the ford. Everyone cried out: "That is the Count of the River!" ' About the same period the poet Yüan of Ch'ü describes the god 'mounted on his water chariot with a canopy of water lilies, drawn by two horned dragons in the shafts and a dragon without horns on the right, while shoals of fish accompanied us.'[59] There was a whole legendary story about him, of which we know only a few scraps. He was known as P'ing-yi and dwelt in the whirlpool of Tsung-chi or Chung-chi at the foot of Mount Yang-ou,[60] close to the spot where the Yellow River, just after receiving the waters of the Lo and the Wei, strikes the Hua-shan massif, which throws it back eastwards, and makes an abrupt turn. Here rose his watery palace, 'The Hall of Fish-scales and the Hall of Dragons / the Porch of Purple Shells and Palace of Pearls'.[61] He was the hero of a whole cycle of adventures: his struggle with his neighbour, the god of the Lo River, his defeat by Yi the Excellent Archer who had put out one of his eyes, and so forth.

These legends became mixed up with those of the ancestors of the Yin, one of whom, Ming of Shang, was drowned in those waters and became Regent of the Waters, Shui-cheng, under the name of Hsüan-ming. His son Hai married the daughter of the Count of the River; but the Lord of Yi with whom he lived carried off the young wife after having killed the husband; and later the god helped Hai's son to kill the murderer.[62] The legend of the River God is related to several others. It is on Mount Yang-ou that Yü dedicated himself before undertaking the great task of making the waters flow;[63] there, also, Fu-hsi beheld the horse-dragon appearing to bring him the divinatory trigrams.

The Count of the River had two important sanctuaries: one at Lin-chin near his residence at Tsung-chi, opposite the junction of the Wei and the Lo with the Yellow River (Shensi); the other at Yeh in Wey, near modern Lin-chang (Honan). The latter spot is today quite far from the river but quite close to the next-to-last capital of the Yin dynasty, a fact which explains why the two legends have contaminated one another. Each place was served by a college of sorceresses, *wu*. At Yeh there were about ten of them, called 'disciples', *ti-tzu*, presided over by an old woman of about seventy, the Grand Sorceress, *ta-wu*. The annual sacrifice at both sanctuaries consisted in offering a young girl in marriage to the god. At Yeh the ceremony took place with great pomp on the river bank in the presence of the Grand Sorceress, behind whom were drawn up her disciples, all dressed in embroidered robes.

> As the date of the festival drew near, the Grand Sorceress sought out the most beautiful maiden among the families and said: 'Let this one be the bride of the Count of the River!' Thereupon the betrothal was celebrated, the girl was bathed, she was dressed in a new robe of silk and satin, she was made to fast in the retiring-room of a 'fasting-palace' constructed for her, a tent set up on the river bank, where she lived. An ox was prepared, as were wine and food. After another ten days, painted and bedecked with jewels, she was placed upon the nuptial bed made for her and it was launched upon the river: it floated about ten *li* and then it sank.[64]

At the beginning of the fourth century B.C. this ceremony was suppressed by Hsi-men Pao, a governor of Yeh. But at the sanctuary of Lin-chin, the custom of 'marrying a maiden to the Count of the River' continued. It was even given official recognition about this time. To assure himself the protection of the god, Count Ling of Ch'in decided in 417 that each year before the festival he would adopt the young girl who was to be sacrificed, by conferring upon her the title of princess, *chün-chu*. There too she was cast into the river at the end of the ceremony.[65]

The Count of the River was one of the most feared of deities: every time the river was crossed, men took care to offer up a jade ring. The god punished offences by sending illnesses. At the beginning of the fifth century divination indicated him as responsible for the illness of King Chao of Ch'u; and the diviner advised a sacrifice to him, whereupon the king responded: 'It is not against the River that I have committed an offence!'[66] People called on him to witness oaths, either by throwing the sworn agreement into the river or simply by invoking his name. Yet in spite of his importance he remained a local deity, strictly bound to his river. It was chiefly the river people who worshipped him; and it was because he was not a god of Ch'u that the king of that land refused him sacrifice. Thus too the southward extension of the Chinese Empire was to be fatal to him; and he disappeared almost entirely from religious concerns as the world of ancient China ended.

The Ancestors

Each noble family had its own particular guardians, the souls of its dead ancestors. The ancient Chinese believed that man had several souls which came together in the living individual but separated again after death to follow different destinies. They were the *kuei* and the *shen* or, to be more accurate, the *p'o* and the *hun*.[67] The *p'o* was first to appear, at the moment of conception, the *hun* joined it at the moment of birth. Afterwards both were strengthened by the use of things from which they distilled the subtle essences, *ching*. It was not only these nutritious elements that were consumed: it was also the posts a man had filled, the blood of the family to which he belonged, and so forth. For this reason, the souls of a prince, of a minister, and of their descendants had more strength than those of common people.[68] During life the *hun* sometimes left the body and wandered abroad on its own: this was in dreams during sleep; but such separations from the body could not be long-lasting, or it was death indeed.

After death the *hun* and the *p'o* each led a separate existence, the latter remaining with the body, while the former separated from it at once. The *hun* mounted to heaven, to the domain of the Lord on High. Here everyone retained his rank, the kings being to the right and to the left of the Lord, Shang-ti;[69] they were his guests,[70] themselves deified and become *ti*, and their dead ministers continued to serve them as ministers in the other world.[71] Their vassals likewise were to right and left of the deceased kings, and all together, kings and princes, served the Lord on High.[72] At this heavenly court life passed in festivities similar to those of courts on earth. 'I visited the residence of the Lord on High, and passed a very pleasant time there,' said Chien-tzu of Chao, on awaking from a five-days' cataleptic fit (501). 'Together with the Hundred Genii I strolled about in the central region of Heaven. The music of Space has nine tunes and ten thousand positions of the dance. It is not like that of the three dynasties, its melodies are so moving. ...'.[73]

The way to heaven was complicated and fraught with dangers. At all four points of the compass the soul had to avoid monsters who would devour it: on earth was the Count of the Earth, T'u-po, who would eat it; and in heaven the Celestial Wolf, who would kill it. It also had to know the passwords which obliged the Gatemen of the Nine Levels to open their gates, without which they would not allow passage. Then again, the soul required a guide: this might be the funeral priest who read the prayers before and after burial. In certain cases or in certain countries it had to be a sorcerer or sorceress, *wu*, who was in the habit of mounting into the heavens and so knew the way; during the prayer his soul accompanied the soul of the deceased and, walking ahead, showed him the way. 'The skilful prayeress signs to you: going backwards she walks before you,' was reiterated in the prayer.[74]

The *p'o* remained with the body in the tomb, living on the offerings. By the same token, when those ceased, it was tortured by hunger and became dangerous: then it was that, returning among the living, it became a ghost, *kuei*. 'If the *kuei* should need sustenance, may those belonging to the Jo-ao family not be starved,' cried out one of that family, foreseeing that they were to be massacred (604). These starving ghosts were sometimes content to appear in a dream and claim their offerings, as did Princess Chiang of Ch'i, who appeared to her husband, Hsien of Chin, in 656.[75] But these ghosts were often wicked: then they were called *li* and caused diseases to revenge themselves upon the living for having neglected them. Also (at least in certain regions) regular offerings were made to them at the four seasons to flesh out those they ought to have received, and a special priest was entrusted with their sacrifices.[76] These *kuei* were the more dangerous if the deceased was a rather important personage, since his souls would have acquired the more power during his lifetime. Thus Po-yu, assassinated in 543 in the marketplace of the capital of Cheng and deprived of his sacrifices, came back for several successive years and terrified the inhabitants. Twice he appeared to announce the death of his murderers, and he was pacified only when his son, reinstated in his office, was enabled to make a sacrifice to him.[77] Similarly, the Count of Tu, put to death by King Hsüan, appeared to him at an assembly of the princes, shot him with an arrow, and killed him.

But the *p'o* did not live long: attached to the corpse, it had to die with it. Ancient notions gave the *p'o* an existence of three years, precisely the period of mourning, the time also that it took for the flesh to come away from the skeleton. This did not prevent the *p'o* of very powerful persons, such as kings or princes, from surviving much longer. The soul of King Hsiang of Hsia, deprived of sacrifices, in the seventh century B.C. (more than a thousand years after his death) was still appropriating the offerings made by Prince Ch'eng of Wei to his own ancestors.[78]

Before long popular imagination seems to have created for the *p'o* an underworld kingdom of the dead, the counterpart of the celestial kingdom of the *hun*, presided over by the King of the Ghosts, *kuei-wang*,[79] just as the ruler of the other kingdom was the Lord on High. This underworld was called the 'Yellow Springs', *huang-ch'üan*, or 'Nine Springs', *chiu-ch'üan*. This was not the name of the tomb itself: it was the place where the souls could meet, could rediscover themselves, could all live together, and this is why Count Chuang of Cheng, alienated from his mother, vowed not to see her again before meeting her at the Yellow Springs.[80]

In this world of the *p'o*, as among the *hun*, life was similar to our own: differences of rank were strictly observed, Princes were still princes; they had with them their wives, ministers, and servants, who remained subordinate to them. They were even fearful of falling sick there. Thus, after the death of a high official of Ch'i, Ch'en Chieh (Tzu-chü), his wife and his chamberlain consulted together: 'If His Highness is ill, there will be none to take care of him.' Whereupon they proposed to send someone after him to wait on him in the next world.[81]

In fact, in order to ensure that in the next world, wherever that might be, they should enjoy the same way of life as in this, the dead not only took with them their arms and personal belongings, but also had women, servants, and horses follow them.[82] The funeral of a prince or other important person was accompanied by hecatombs of men and women, who were buried alive in his grave, *hsün*.[83] 'For the [funeral of the] Son of Heaven hundreds, or at least dozens, of people were buried alive; for princes and great officers of state there were dozens or, at least, several people.'[84]

In 678, at the funeral of Count Wu of Ch'in, there were sixty-six human victims; at that of one of his descendants, Count Mu (621), there were 166, among them three of his courtesans, favourite table-companions whom Mu himself had designated; at the funeral of Prince Huan of Ch'i (643), the number of victims was so large that, when the tomb was violated in A.D. 312, bones were found lying scattered all about;[85] at that of Duke Wen of Sung (586) the number was also very large; even a minor prince like Ch'uan of Chu had five persons follow him (507).[86] Grand officers of state did the same. Ch'ou of Wei (Wu-tzu), one of those faithful to Prince Wen of Chin during his exile, ordered his son to bury his favourite concubine with him,[87] and Kan-hsi of Ch'en, a high officer of Ch'i, gave orders for two of his slaves to be placed in his coffin, one on either side of his body.[88] Even women made similar demands: thus the Princess-Dowager Hsüan of Ch'in at the end of the fourth century wanted her lover to be buried with her.[89] Families of lesser rank or wealth had to be content with figures of straw, *ch'u-ling*, or wood, *hsiang-jen*, which were treated exactly like the living persons whose places they took.

The heavenly world of the *hun*, the underground world of the *p'o*, the *kuei* who continued alive in the tomb, and yet other conceptions[90] were clumped together into such a confused mass in the Chinese mind that any description must falsify if it tries to define them precisely. In any case, it was less important to know where souls dwelt after death than to know how to establish them in the array of ancestors, and thus to make them into protectors. Only nobles had this power of creating personal gods for themselves in each generation; the common people had no ancestors. For this purpose, a whole series of special ceremonies had to be performed for the dead. The *hun* had to be helped on its way by providing it with a guide on its journey to the next world.

For the *p'o*, in order to ensure that the corpse should last as long as possible, small pieces of jade (supposed to delay corruption) were placed in all the openings of the body: eyes, nostrils, ears, mouth (under the tongue, on the teeth), under the armpits, and so forth. Food, too, was placed in the tomb next to the body, also clothing and a mirror to provide light. At the same time the family had to be protected against the evil influence emanating from the corpse. However it could not escape entirely, suffering from ritual impurity, which lasted for a longer or shorter period according to the degree of relationship and which obliged it to keep more or less strictly apart from society. This was the period of mourning, *sang*, which usually lasted three years — actually twenty-eight months for father or mother, a lesser time for other relatives. Great care was taken to prevent pollution of the family hearth: the water to be used for washing the body and hair of the deceased was not heated there but over a pit especially dug in the courtyard.

As soon as a noble had died (funeral ceremonies, like all the rites, were not for the common people),[91] the entire family, men as well as women, gave themselves over to uttering loud cries, each according to his degree of relationship: children wailed, brothers and cousins wept, women wept and threw themselves about. This first outburst of grief announced the demise to the neighbours, who made their necessary preparations. At the same time a last effort was made to call the deceased back to life: a man holding the official robe he had worn at the sacrifices to his ancestors climbed up to the roof, and, turning towards the north, the region of the dead, *kuei-fang*, called to the soul (*chao-hun*) using its childhood name, crying out three times: 'I am calling you, so-and-so. Come back!' After that, having established that the soul refused to return, they turned to the funeral rites. The body itself was laid out; the eyes were closed; the jaws were separated so as to keep the mouth open; the feet were tied to a wooden stool to keep them straight. Next the ablutions took place, first of the body and then of the hair, and at the same time fingernails and toenails were cut. After that the corpse was dressed in a special costume, the funeral robe, *ming-yi*, and over that were placed his three ceremonial robes. Finally, a piece of jade was placed in his mouth, together with other small ritual articles. During all this travail (lasting all the first day) and indeed until the interment, lamentations continued without cease, relatives taking turns day and night.

Thus prepared, the body was laid out on a display-bed in the great hall, and from the roof of that hall was hung a great banner, *ming-ching*, inscribed simply with the name of the deceased. Before the body was placed in the coffin, there then remained only one ostentatious ceremony, one intended to show the importance and wealth of the family. This was the exhibition of garments, and it was divided in two: the Small Exhibition, *hsiao-lien*, on one day, and the Grand Exhibition, *ta-lien*, on the next. The two were similar: in an adjoining room a collection of complete costumes was hung, nineteen on the first day, and a much greater number — up to a hundred for princes — on the second day. It was on these two days that relatives and outsiders came to make visits of condolence. The sons of the deceased, clad in white linen, received and greeted the guests; the daughters-in-law received and greeted their womenfolk.

On the evening of the Great Exposition — for kings and princes this could only be after seven days — the body was placed in a coffin lined with black silk. At the four corners were placed small cloth bags containing the parings of his fingernails and toenails, and of his hair, whether it had been cut off or had fallen out, carefully collected throughout his life, so that the deceased could go complete into the next world. Then (relic of an ancient rite of provisional interment, originally no doubt lasting through the period of mourning, for the purpose of letting the flesh fall away from the bones)[92] the coffin, enclosed in a catafalque, was put into a hole with only the lid above ground, concealed by a curtain, with an offering of parched grain and of dried fish and meat; and it was kept thus until the burial-place was ready. When the deceased was thus definitively separated from the living, the children's lamentations redoubled. They could no longer hold themselves upright: the next day they would take the staff of mourning to support them in walking.

Burial (it was done at once only for ordinary commoners, the time between death and interment increasing with rank) was a grand procession in which all relatives and friends took part. The coffin was covered with white linen (the colour of mourning) and a white awning was suspended over it by loops of black silk. It was placed upon a four-wheeled cart with its awning decorated with silk, garlands of red and black silk holding it before and behind. The banner bearing the name of the deceased and his chariots (if he had the right to possess them) carrying the victims followed. At the head marched a sorcerer, the *fang-hsiang*, shaking a halberd in the four directions to ward off evil influences from the road. Howling all the time, the procession moved slowly towards the burial-ground, where the crowd was waiting. While the coffin was being lowered into the ground, with its head towards the north, all lamentations were forbidden. At this moment the Official in Charge of the Tombs went to fetch the victims — men and women, or their substitutes — who descended into the vault, where they were buried alive.

When all was over, the family returned home, and the son proceeded to the ancestral temple, where he set up a temporary tablet beside that of the deceased's grandfather; and for the first time he made an offering to his father as to an ancestor. For the first time, too, a representative of the deceased, *shih*, came to the meal. Followed by another mourner, who wailed, he entered, sat down, took several mouthfuls of the offerings and several draughts of wine, and then withdrew. Before his departure the lamentations ceased, and the outsiders withdrew and took off the mourning vestments. The ceremony was ended. Nothing remained but to raise the earthen mound which covered the tomb, a long and costly task which was often not done until later.

But the deceased had not yet become an ancestor. The time of mourning was a transitional period for him. His temporary tablet was not left in the ancestral temple, but was taken into the room that had been his while living; and it was there that sacrifices to him were conducted at festival times, while the other ancestors received their offerings in the temple. It was only after the sacrifice at the end of mourning that the recently-deceased finally became an ancestor. The tablet of his grandfather was then carried into the next shrine, making that of his own grandfather move on in its turn, and leaving his shrine free. There the permanent tablet, of fresh chestnut, was placed.[93]

From that time on the new ancestor was endowed with a particular power of protection for his family and, if he had been a prince, for the whole territory of his fief. From then on he had his place in the world of ancestors, and regular offerings were made to him. But this power diminished little by little as the generations succeeded one another: after five generations for kings, three for princes, and only one for mere nobles, the ancestor, retiring from position to position within the temple, ended by being cast out among the throng of those to whom no personal offerings were made and who were called *kuei*, likening them to the poor souls deprived of offerings in their tombs. Only a few, endowed with a singular Virtue — the original founder of the clan or of the family, or the original possessor of the fief — always received offerings, never passing into the ranks of the *kuei*. In order to compensate for this decline of the ancestors, special temples were built for them, at least in princely families: thus their offerings never ceased, and their ancestral life had no limit as long as their line continued.

3
Clergy, Places of Worship, and Ceremonies

The Clergy

To enter into communication with these gods was neither easy nor free from danger. Some of them were cruel and took revenge for the slightest offence, even if involuntary. Every patrician was naturally in touch with one or more, thanks to his birth or his position (his own ancestors, the gods of his fief, or those of his office). To them he had the right and duty to offer up sacrifices at the prescribed times. Yet, with the exception of the Son of Heaven, each patrician was thus linked to only a very small number. As for divinities with whom no natural relationship existed, 'to sacrifice to one to whom one has no right to sacrifice, this is an illegitimate sacrifice, *yin-ssu*, and such illegitimate sacrifices are ill-omened, *wu-fu*.' If the need were pressing — if, for example, one of the gods were the cause of an illness and had to be propitiated — then recourse had to be made to persons who possessed the power of conjuring up the gods or the souls of the dead. Moreover, for those very ones with whom personal links existed, the link did nothing to furnish the awareness of the rites and of formulas, lacking which any approach to the spirits was dangerous. Therefore official worship had a numerous clergy of priests familiar with the ritual gestures and the forms of prayer. Kings, princes, officers of state, and even ordinary nobles had their own priests in their residences.

Thus there were two clergies of very different kinds. On the one hand were the priests of the official cult.[2] They were not, properly speaking, servants of the gods, who had neither chosen nor initiated them. Their role was limited to knowing the prayers, the text of which was passed on from father to son or from teacher to pupil, and to reciting them correctly at the religious ceremonies. It was, however, not they but the Virtue of the person performing the sacrifice that induced the gods to come down to earth. But they did invite the gods down, talk to them, and act as intermediaries.[3] They were prayer-readers of all kinds, augurs, diviners, and so forth. The second group were the sorcerers and sorceresses: these were the persons actually 'possessed', *ling-pao*, who by their incantations made a god, who had no personal connection with the sacrificing person, descend into themselves at the time of the ceremony.

In historical times these two classes of clergy were differentiated not only by their religious functions but also by their social status. The sorcerers and sorceresses, suffering from the discredit into which their practices had increasingly fallen, were not esteemed very highly. The priests, on the other hand, had come under the influence of the official world much more than had the sorcerers. To become a priest, all any patrician need do was learn the rites and formulas; it was unnecessary for his person to be certified by the seal of a special initiation. But only a patrician had the Virtue adequate to carrying out the functions of priesthood. By contrast, sorcerers, chosen by the same spirit that possessed them, were much more often commoners than nobles.

As in all ancient religions, the priesthood was very numerous. Each of the different processes by which they entered into communication with the gods had its specialists who made it their job to know the correct rites and formulas. They were divided into different categories: there were firstly all classes of praying priests, *chu*. Each of the great sacrifices had its own, completely specialized: there were, for example, families of priests of the *chiao* sacrifice to the Lord on High.[4] There was a Priest of the Hunt, *tien-chu*, who knew the rites for the *ma* sacrifices at departure for war or the chase; and the Priest for Treaties, *tsu-chu*, who recited the sacrificial prayers for treaties and for the assemblies of princes, who knew the formulas for oaths, covenants and contracts. Then there were all those who officiated at funerals, *sang-chu*, who read the prayers for the dead and superintended all the funeral ceremonies, and who moreover, at the court of the Chou, conducted the ceremonies to the God of the Soil of Po; the Priest of Shang, *Shang-chu*, who looked after everything to do with funeral robes; and the Priest of Hsia, *Hsia-chu*, who was concerned with offerings made to the dead during funerals. And there were many others. At court the priests were legion; their chief was called *ta-chu*, Grand Priest.[5]

The augurs were hardly less numerous or less important. Their role consisted in receiving and interpreting the ancestors' response when they were queried in consulting the fates. It was a very serious business. Their counsel was asked on all kinds of questions: forecasts of the harvest, the consequences of a military expedition or a voyage. Recourse was had to them in difficult situations, when the king and his council did not agree, or when the prince hesitated to make a decision. In Chou times two methods of divination were in use: the tortoise-shell and the milfoil stalks. The first was very ancient, having been used already in Yin times. The shell of a tortoise was pierced with a number of holes at fixed points and then, to consult the fates, was brought near the fire for a moment, then taken away and rubbed with ink. The cracks produced by the heat indicated the answer by their position, their form and their direction.[6]

The Head Augur, *pu-shih*, or Director of Auguries, *ssu-pu* — probably a hereditary office[7] — was charged with all the externals of the consultation: he provided the formulas for putting questions to the shell, verified that it was properly oriented, and lit the fire to the east of it at the moment the ceremony commenced. Under his orders were men responsible for preparing the shells and storing them, for providing the special kinds of wood which were used for heating them, and so on.[8] But it was not he who explained the oracle: it was the Diviner, *chan-jen*, who interpreted the lines and gave the answer.

Divination by the milfoil was considered the less important. If the answers by tortoise-shell and by milfoil did not agree, the judgement of the former prevailed. The milfoil method consisted in manipulating fifty of the stalks so as to obtain one of the sixty-four divinatory hexagrams — that is to say, patterns of six lines, some full and some broken, traditionally preserved in the manuals of divination.[9] These hexagrams had a supernatural origin, having been copied by the first of the diviners, the mythical emperor Fu-hsi or Pao-hsi, from the markings seen on the back of a 'horse-dragon' that in mythological times had come out of the waters of the Yellow River. The milfoil diviners, *shih-jen*, who conducted the ceremony and gave the interpretation at the same time,[10] started by dividing the fifty stalks into two small bundles, each of which necessarily contained either an even or an odd number of stalks. One stalk was then removed from the right-hand bundle, so as to make one even and one uneven, and the diviner placed this stalk between the fourth and fifth fingers of his left hand. Then, leaving one bundle aside, he divided the other by counting out the stalks in fours, the remainder of this division giving him the answer: even signified a broken line, uneven a solid one.[11] The operation was repeated three times for each of the six lines, or altogether eighteen times for the whole hexagram. Depending upon the circumstances, a single hexagram was derived and was interpreted directly, or two were derived in succession and the difference was interpreted, the second being taken as having emerged from the first by transformation.

The interpreters of dreams, *chan-meng*, were responsible for drawing portents out of dreams, but also for making — each year, at the end of winter — offerings to the bad dreams. The interpreters of extraordinary phenomena, *shih-chin*, read omens in the appearance of the sun, moon, rainbow, haloes, mists and so on.[12] In the later years of the Chou dynasty, when Western influence had imported astrological notions, together with more exact knowledge of astronomy, all kinds of astrologers put in an appearance, claiming to draw predictions from the stars, the winds, the clouds, etc.

Then, too, there were many people who had roles in carrying out the ceremonies (since the priests were only scholars and not initiates, the difference between them and assistants is difficult to define). There were blind musicians: flute-players, strikers of bells or sounding stones, drummers. Under the orders of a Director of Music, *ssu-yüeh*, himself blind, they played airs which induced the various categories of gods to come down — airs which varied according to whether it was the gods of the heavens or of earth or the spirits of the dead who were involved. And each college of musicians also rendered worship, at the same time as to the First Musician, to K'uei, the monster with one paw who first taught mankind to call the gods and spirits by striking the sounding stones, the one who had in Chou times been made into Master of Music for the mythical emperor Shun. There were likewise the Masters of the Sacrifices, *ssu-shih*, whose task it was to make the material arrangements for the festivals; and the scribes, who recorded in writing the events of the court or merely of the family, registering them and announcing them to the ancestors. And finally, there were servants and employees of all kinds, each with his own function, attached to each of the categories of priests or assistants.

All these made their living out of the sacred things, and probably each of them guarded his knowledge jealously, transmitted as it was from father to son within priestly families, as Shih Chüeh's descendants passed on the knowledge of the *chiao* sacrifice in the principality of Lu.

For the knowledge of the complicated formulas and rites of the great festivals was not easy to acquire. Those of simpler ceremonies seem to have been scarcely better known, and the numerous priests who appeared in the ordinary ceremonies of the family worship, even among commoners, were clearly professionals. If most educated men seem to have been able to interpret divinations, this was because all the philosophical speculations that grew up around this science appear to have formed part of the general education of a courtier. But this was an exceptional achievement. Needless to say, priestly functions at the courts, whether those of kings or those of princes, were carefully controlled. At that of the Chou, religious affairs formed an important ministry, within which the priests were swamped in the mass of functionaries and servants, all equally under the control of the Count of Religious Affairs.

The life of these priests appears to have been in no way different from that of other patricians. But for the fact that the approach of the big ceremonies bound them to a purification equal to that of the person presiding at the sacrifice, no special duty, taboo or other form of abstinence seems to have been imposed upon them. Perhaps for some of them, as for those sacrificing, a bodily defect posed an absolute bar to the exercise of priestly functions;[13] but one cannot observe any mode of life which distinguishes them from other patricians. If there were special rules for them, it does not seem to have prevented them from occupying the highest official posts. Ts'ung of Kuan, for example, was a son of that Ch'i of Kuan who had been torn to pieces for lying when his patron, Prince Chui-shu (Tzu-nan), first minister of Ch'u, had been disgraced and put to death (551). Tsung, who had been forced to go and seek his fortune in the land of Ts'ai, a dependency of Ch'u, was from a family of diviners by the tortoise-shell; and he took up this function again in 529, when Tzu-nan's son, Ch'i-chi, having mounted the throne of Ch'u, offered to grant him any post he chose.[14] The only incompatibility which bore upon them was a purely religious one: nobody could be at the same time priest and sacrificer in his own ceremonies[15]; so that, even in the families of simple commoners, the presence of priests was necessary at funerals and at ceremonies honouring ancestors, at the side of the 'pious son' and of the grandson who during the sacrifices had to bear in his person the soul of the deceased. The lack of any special rites that could create a feeling of solidarity among the different types of priests accounted for the fact that, although there did exist priestly families in ancient China, there was, in historical times at any rate, no priestly class.

The other clergy, that of the sorcerers, *hsi*, and sorceresses, *wu*,[16] differed markedly from the official, aristocratic, and administrative clergy.[17] Chosen by their own special god, its members belonged to all classes of the population, patrician and commoner alike. Some were connected with a particular deity, as for instance, the colleges of priestesses of the Count of the River at Yeh or at Lin-chin. Most of them, however, seem to have been able to commune with several deities or, above all, with the souls of the dead. They were, it seems, distinguished less by their divinity than by the power they possessed. There were the simple mediums, *chu-tzu*,[18] the commonest of all; the doctors, *yi*; the rain-makers; the exorcists, *fang-hsiang*, who warded off evil influences; and so on.

It is probable that the Ten Immortal Sorcerers who gathered herbs on the Mount of Sorcerers, Wu-shan, beyond the Four Seas (sorcerer Hsien, sorcerer Chi, sorcerer Fen, sorcerer P'eng, etc.) were the founders of the various branches of sorcery, and that each of those categories rendered worship to one of them. Hsien, indeed, was supposed to have been the first of all the sorcerers, and P'eng the inventor of medicine; Yang was the patroness of the sorceresses who communicated with the spirits in dreams.[19] Moreover, the names of the familiar spirits of the sorcerers seem to have varied in form from place to place: in Chin it was the Ancestors of the Sorceresses, Wu-tsu-jen, in Ch'in the Protectress of Sorceresses, Wu-pao, in Ch'u the First of the Sorceresses, Wu-hsien.[20] But these were only protectors or protectresses in their dangerous ceremonies, who aided them to seek out and get into contact with the gods and spirits.

Sorcerers and sorceresses entered into relations with the spirits by a real possession; and thus they were often called 'the possessed', *ling-pao*.[21] When the spirit entered them, 'the body was that of the sorceress, but the heart was that of the god', who spoke through her mouth. For instance, at its first appearance the soul of a deceased prince announced to his former charioteer: 'In seven days, on the west side of the new wall (of Ch'ü-wu) there will be a sorceress and you will have an interview with me.'[22] Sometimes the spirit was not content merely with speaking, but acted through its sorcerer, as is witnessed by that famished spirit, *li*, which — infuriated with the negligence with which Ku of Kuan, the priest responsible for offerings to souls without posterity, discharged his task — suddenly seized upon a medium and made him fell the priest upon the altar with blows from a bludgeon.[23] Between the sorceresses and the gods, relations seem to have been complicated by a genuine love interest: it was the beauty of the sorceress which attracted the god and made him choose her.

Calling the spirits was a rather lengthy business. The sorceress first purified herself by washing her face with water in which orchids had been boiled, and her body with water perfumed with iris; and she then donned magnificent robes, probably those of the deity she was calling.[24] When the sacrificial offerings were ready, she sent her soul to find the god and bring him back with her to take part in the sacrifices, miming this voyage in a dance accompanied by music and songs:

> On this great day, at this auspicious hour,
> it is my respectful wish to please the Supreme Ruler;
> I am wearing the long sword with its jade hilt,
> my pendants go tinkling *lin-lang* [as I walk],
> my hair is plaited with jewels, my ornaments are of jade,
> I shall use the perfume of *ch'iung*,
> a mixture seasoned with wild orchids on a mat of orchids,
> I offer up a cup of spiced wine and broth seasoned with pepper.
> Raise your drumsticks and beat the drums;
> cease beating time with them and play a quiet air instead;
> prepare the lutes and flutes to sing nobly.
> The sorceress dances decked out in her finery;
> marvellous is the great hall filled with guests;
> the five tones blend harmoniously;
> the lord is happy, the music delights him.[25]

These ceremonies were of a disorderly character which more and more displeased the literati, who admired the strict order of the official worship. The sorceresses needed the racket of the drums and flutes, which prepared them to fall into a trance. Their assistants beat the drums and played the flutes faster and faster, until one of them, stimulated by the music, gave herself to the dance, holding in her hand the blossom of either orchid or chrysanthemum, according to the season. When, exhausted, she fell back into her place, she passed the blossom to another who, seized by the excitement, succeeded her.

> While the rites are being performed, beat the drums with rapid strokes;
> hand the blossom to your successor in the dance,
> let pretty girls sing in time;

> holding in their hands an orchid in spring,
> a chrysanthemum in autumn,
> [thus it was] always, since the days of old, without end.[26]

The dance was fast and furious:

> Strike the lutes, beat the drums,
> [let] the bells in their jade-ornamented stands [resound] to the notes of
> the trumpets, let the flutes sing! blow the hautboys!
> This sorceress is clever and beautiful, like a kingfisher in her whirling
> flight, she rises up
> her dance follows the rhythm of the verse,
> her steps respond to the notes.[27]

The spirit thus evoked came down, accepted the offerings, took part in the dances, sometimes even spoke through the mouth of a sorceress, and then returned to its home at the end of the ceremony. Then, the god having departed, the exhausted sorceresses hailed their own souls, *li-hun*,[28] in order to summon back any who 'had forgotten to return'[29] and get them to re-enter the body by breaking in upon their ecstasy.

All this excitement, this noise, these dances with their movements rapid and improvised on the spur of the moment, aroused a kind of contempt among the patricians, whose well-ordered ceremonies were conducted with more pomp. They regarded the sorceresses as nothing but 'stupid women',[30] declared that these rites were quite useless, consisting of 'a continual dance in the Palace', and that, although 'the dancers fly around and the flutes sound high and clear, the Lord is not favourably inclined ... and sends down all calamities.'[31] The role of the sorceresses in the official ceremonies was therefore strictly limited.

Their power was utilized to see, to feel, and to get to know the gods and spirits. Thus at ceremonies for the more distant deities *ssu-wang*, they were given the task of calling to them by name and of making signs to them by waving reeds.[32] But what was chiefly asked of their power was to dissipate malign influences, personal or impersonal. Three times a year exorcists, *fang-hsiang*, drove away baneful emanations, in the countryside or in the houses according to the season of the year.[33] They were employed especially in funeral ceremonies. A prince, when paying an official visit to the body of some important officer lying in state, had a sorcerer go before him armed with the branch of a peach tree and he, assisted by a funeral priest carrying a broom, swept away the malign emanations from the deceased.[34] In funeral processions an armed exorcist marched before the coffin brandishing his halberd to the four corners of the grave before the coffin was lowered into it.[35]

But even in everyday life, men had to have recourse to sorcerers. A prince travelling outside his own borders would not budge without his sorcerer, who was responsible for seeing that nothing harmful came near him.[36] The gradual softening of manners brought to an end, for the official worship, a practice still quite common although frowned upon, that of either making the sorcerers and sorceresses dance in the sun or even of burning them alive, in case of a prolonged drought.[37]

Although they were allowed only a small part in the official worship, that of the patricians, sorcerers and sorceresses played a considerable role in the religious life of the people. For the common people who were deprived of the *sacra*, they were the indispensable intermediaries with the world of gods and spirits. According to Chuang-tzu, a sorcerer from the land of Cheng healed the sick, differentiated between good and bad luck, and could predict almost to a day the span of life of those who consulted him. As a result the people of Cheng, fearful, fled out of his way when they met him. But they went to consult him.[38]

There were sorcerers and sorceresses everywhere. They were in the suburbs of the towns, like the one in Ch'ü-wu whom the soul of the assassinated crown prince used to communicate with one of his friends.[39] They were in the countryside, like the one who interpreted the dream of Yang of Chao (Chien-tzu) and who, refusing to say his name, called himself simply 'a man of the fields'.[40] The Yellow River had a college of sorceresses. In the land of Ch'in Sorcerer Hsien was worshipped officially.[41]

On the other hand, innumerable different forms of sorcery, the wholly personal character of which compensated a little for the aridity of the official worship, must have been widespread among all classes of the population. One of these, that of the Sorceress of the Bell, Chung-wu, had penetrated into one of the great families of Cheng, the Yin family, at the end of the eighth century; and a prince of Lu attached himself to her when he was a prisoner in that principality and residing with that family. He sacrificed to Chung-wu each year in the eleventh month, after having fasted.[42] Unfortunately, on this point, as upon everything else regarding the life of the people and concerning usages which the orthodoxy of the Confucian school disapproved at the end of Chou, the texts are virtually silent.

Places of Worship

This whole world of priests, sorcerers, sorceresses, without actually forming a priestly caste, constituted at the least a considerable number of persons occupied with religious matters. But the lack of any common grouping and of initiation which left them without cohesion always prevented them from playing any political role except as individuals; and it also denied them any deep influence in other areas, even that of religious art. Therefore the ancient Chinese, though they had among them gods and priests as numerous as among any other people of antiquity, left no temples comparable to those of the Mediterranean world. They built in wood and in clay, which do not last, and divine dwellings were no more solidly built than human.

In any case, the gods did not like to be served in closed buildings: open air was necessary if they were to condescend to come to take the offerings made to them. It was only for the souls of the dead, who wished to be treated as in their lifetimes, that palaces like those for men, the funerary temples, were built; or, failing those, they were worshipped in a room of the dwelling. This is why a dead god, the God of the Soil of a defunct dynasty, the warning God of the Soil whom the Chou called the God of the Soil of Po, had a funeral temple raised above his mound, the tree of which had been cut down. Although the autumn sacrifice to the Lord on High was held in a room of the Sacred Palace, it seems to have been one without walls and open to all winds.

With this one exception, the worship of the gods always took place in the open. Each god had his preferences; or rather, every category of gods was subject to unalterable laws as regards the position, shape, and arrangement of their places of worship. For the gods of heaven the altars were round, for those of the earth square, recalling the shape of sky and earth. The former had piles of firewood on which to burn the victims; the latter, pits in which to bury them.

A few of the gods, however, had permanent places of worship. The God of the Soil had his mound in the palace grounds facing the Ancestral Temple; the Lord on High had a circular hillock in the southern outskirts of the capital; the First Husbandman had his altar in the royal ploughing field; the Sun had a mound in the so-called 'Royal Palace', Wang-kung, in the eastern suburbs and symmetrically, the Moon, a pit in the place called 'Night Brightness', Yeh-ming, in the western suburbs.[43] But the Five Lords of the five heavenly regions had only temporary round altars which were erected for their ceremonies, each in the suburb corresponding to its direction. Similarly, the gods of the mountains and forests, of rivers and lakes, had only square and round mounds respectively, which were prepared before each sacrifice.[44] Some gods had no fixed place at all. The God of the Road, to whom a dog was offered up whenever the king left the palace, was invoked on the road itself so that he might seize the victim, which was crushed under the wheels of the royal chariot.

The most important permanent places of worship were those of the Lord on High and of the God of the Soil. The first was an artificial circular mound of three terraces standing on the southern outskirts of the capital. The circle represented the shape of heaven. As for the three terraces, these were explained at the end of Chou by the fact that three is the quintessential *yang* number, and heaven is *yang*. There was no tablet: the Lord on High was the only deity not represented by anything. Thus in the books of ritual, systematizing and later as they were, this exception is explained by declaring that, in the sacrifice to heaven in the southern suburb, 'the sun is considered as a tablet.' In theory, only the king could have an altar to the Lord on High, since he was the sole sovereign on earth, as the Lord was in heaven. In practice, however, the princes of Lu had one, as did the dukes of Sung, and perhaps other princes as well. The exceptions to the rites were explained in Lu as a favour specially granted to the Duke of Chou, and in Sung as the traditional maintenance of the royal rites of the dukes' ancestors, the kings of the Yin dynasty.

The altar of the God of the Soil was square, since earth is square. Each prince, each fief-holder, each district had one, the size of which decreased as did the god's importance. That of the king, who oversaw the entire empire, had each of its sides a different colour, each corresponding to the cardinal direction in Chinese theory: green for the east, red for the south, white for the west, black for the north, yellow for the top (the centre). Those of princes were entirely of a single colour, that of the region where the fief lay in relation to the royal capital. Upon the altar stood a large tree, which was originally the God of the Soil himself. In front of the tree on the north side, the god was represented by a square stone tablet without any inscription, set into the earth. This is the tablet which was smeared with blood during sacrifices. Near the mound was a large square pit in which victims were buried, for those sacrificed to the Earth had to be buried in the earth.

The altars to other deities followed the same pattern: round altars for the Five Lords, who were heavenly gods; square altars with pits for the gods of mountains, forests, and so on, who were terrestrial gods. They were constructed according to exact rules before each ceremony, and as soon as it was over were abandoned and quickly disappeared, being simple mounds of earth which the rain soon washed away.

In contrast to this diversity in the treatment of the gods, there was such complete uniformity in everything connected with the souls of the dead that even between one country and another there were probably only differences of detail. The ancestral temple always stood within the dwelling, on the east side of the court, so that the master of the house, sitting with his face to the south, had it on his left. It was a large enclosure surrounded by a wall with the main gate on the south side. Immediately behind the gate was a large court, in the middle of which stood the stele, *pei*, a sort of stone column, to which the principal victim was tied at the moment of sacrifice. To right and left, two lateral buildings served probably as utility rooms; for example, it was in one of them that those who represented the dead dressed for the ceremonies. At the back, facing south, was the Grand Temple itself, *T'ai-miao*, on a raised platform, *t'ang*, to which one ascended by two sets of steps in front of the façade, the eastern one for the master of the house, the other on the west for guests. This was a large columned hall with light walls of brick or perhaps of clay, the construction and ornamentation of which were subject to rules fixed according to rank. For the Son of Heaven the columns were squared, then polished, and finally pumiced; for a prince they did not have the final pumicing; and in the house of a grand officer, they had to be simply squared without being polished. Otherwise, the columns and the beams supporting the roof had to be neither carved nor painted.[45]

The interior of this hall was divided into small separate chapels, as many as there were ancestors to whom worship was obligatory; and an old tradition fixed the number to which each patrician was entitled according to his rank in the hierarchy — seven for the king, five for the princes, three for the grand officers, *tai-fu*, and only one for simple commoners. The chapels were arranged symmetrically; one in the middle, and the others to right and left. This division of the ancestral temple had led to a special classification of the ancestors for worship. Those who had ranks of uneven number counting from the First Ancestor were always placed on the left-hand side of the temple and were called *chao*; and those with even-numbered ranks, who always occupied the chapels on the right-hand side, were called *mu*.[46] The meanings of these terms have been lost.[47] The middle chapel was reserved for the most ancient of the ancestors to whom sacrifices were offered. For the remainder, however, the detailed arrangement of the temple varied somewhat according to the rank of the family and the number of chapels, and also by region: in this, as in many other items, the rites of Sung, for example, differed from those of Chou.

In the ancestral temple of Chou the central chapel was dedicated to the First Ancestor of the clan, Hou-chi. On either side were the chapels of the three *chao* and the three *mu*. Four of these — two on either side — were called *miao* and were allotted to the more closely related ancestors, who were entitled to monthly sacrifices: father, grandfather, great-grandfather, and great-great-grandfather (each with his lawful wife). The two other chapels, those nearest that of Hou-chi, were called *t'iao*[48] and were reserved for the two most remote ancestors, who were no longer entitled to monthly but only to seasonal sacrifices. These were probably the 'perpetual homes', *shih-shih*, of kings Wen and Wu, the founders of the dynasty. Finally, there was another altar, *t'an*, and an open space, *shan*, without a chapel — intermediate places of worship, one might call them, for ancestors of the fifth and sixth generation until they should be placed definitively in the *t'iao* with their predecessors.[49]

The ancestral temples of princes — at least of those who belonged to the royal house — were arranged in the same way, except that they had only five chapels: two for the nearer ancestors, *miao*, two for more distant ones, *t'iao*, and one for the First Ancestor, *t'ai-miao*. In the state of Wey the central chapel was dedicated to Hou-chi, and the two adjoining ones to King Wen and his son K'ang-shu, the first prince of Wey; the grandfather and father of the reigning prince had the last two.[50] In Lu they did not go back so far as Hou-chi: the central chapel was dedicated to the Duke of Chou, the father of the founder of the principality; the chapel on the left to his son, Po-ch'in, the first Prince of Lu; that on the right to Prince Wu (825–815), though no one knows just why he was chosen; and the last two chapels were for the father and grandfather of the reigning prince.[51] It was the same for the Sung: the central chapel dedicated to Ti-yi, the penultimate Yin king and father of the first duke of Sung (Ch'i, Lord of Wey), and not to Hsieh, the First Ancestor.[52]

In each generation, a series of tablets was displaced from one rank to allow for the new tablet of the just-deceased to be installed: the *mu* series if the newcomer had to be classified among the *mu*, the *chao* series if he had to be classed there. The other series remained unchanged, since a *mu* never became a *chao*, nor, on the other hand, could a *chao* become a *mu*. After having passed — at whatever pace the new generations pushed it back — through the two chapels of its side, where it had received monthly worship, the tablet was carried, securely closed in its box, to the chapel of the First Ancestor, the *t'ai-miao*, where it was ranged with those of its predecessors, along the north wall. It was still taken out at certain sacrifices, to be carried initially onto the altar, then a generation later into the open space (no attention was then paid to whether it belonged to a *chao* or a *mu*, and all the tablets, whichever series they came from, passed successively onto the altar and into the open space) to receive offerings. Finally, after six generations had passed, the tablet attained its definitive place, in the chapel of the First Ancestor, leaving it again only when, lost among all the others, it took part in the collective sacrifices.

Internally, each chapel was arranged the same way. It contained, enclosed in a stone casket, the wooden tablet, *chu*, which served as the abode of the spirit. From there it was brought out only at the time of the ceremonies. Usually, there were two tablets for each ancestor, one remaining always in residence at the temple, while the other was carried on campaign in the army's train. Towards the end of the Chou dynasty, however, the ritualists claimed that only one was the genuine tablet, for 'as in heaven there were not two suns, nor on earth two kings', so there could not be two spirit tablets at the sacrifices. They attributed the origin of this innovation to Prince Huan of Ch'i in the seventh century;[53] but, whatever its true origin may have been, the custom was current at the end of Chou. In the chapel was also kept the collection of the deceased's garments which had been exhibited at the time of the funeral. During the sacrifices, the mourning clothes in which the impersonator of the deceased was dressed were obtained from this collection. Finally, there was the divinatory tortoise-shell consecrated to each ancestor; and there were all the sacrificial utensils, instruments, vases, and so forth.[54]

In their general lines, the temples of the patricians were quite similar to the royal temple, which differed from them mainly in its splendour, size, and importance. Grand officers of state had only three chapels: one for the father, one for the grandfather, and the third for the great-grandfather. For the great-great-grandfather and the ancestor who had first attained the rank of *tai-fu*, sacrifices were offered up on temporary altars specially erected for each occasion. Petty officials had only two chapels, or even one, according to their rank. Private persons had to be content with a temporary altar erected in a room of their private quarters; they had neither temple nor chapel specially dedicated to their ancestors.[55]

Finally, the ancient Sacred Palace, *Ming-t'ang*, to which the kings had been relegated in primitive times, outside the enclosure of their capital, had become a place of worship since the definitive breakdown of the old royal taboos before historic times. But by its very origins, it was not a place of worship reserved to certain particular gods: rather, it was a place where the king continued to exercise his general religious activity. The old arrangement of four buildings placed symmetrically at the four points of the compass around a central building had remained unchanged. For in each of them the king had to perform the monthly ceremony of donning the robes of the right colour for the season, of eating the proper dishes of the season, and of sleeping in the chamber of the month. The Central Temple, *Ch'ing-miao*, the only one in which the king never slept, was dedicated to the ancestor of the dynasty, King Wen. Tradition imposed an antique simplicity upon it. It appears in all ages to have had two storeys,[56] or at least two superposed roofs; but these were of thatch,[57] and its few decorations were rigorously fixed. Here is a description of the *t'ai-miao* of Lu, which had been constructed on the model of a royal *ming-t'ang*: 'Capitals ornamented with seaweed pattern, a second storey with a second roof, polished columns, windows exactly opposite each other, a lattice-work partition screen (outside the entrance gate).'[58]

This was the scene of the great sacrifices which the king had to perform in his own residence: the sacrifice to King Wen in the sixth month of the royal calendar (usually about May); and the sacrifice to the Lord on High in the ninth month, held in the interior of the house to usher in the winter season — a sacrifice with which King Wen was associated. Here too, at least towards the end of the dynasty, was the winter worship of the Yellow Lord, Huang-ti, he of the Five Lords who presided over the central region of heaven. The four other buildings of the Sacred Palace were also used in the same period for the worship of the other four of the Five Lords. The eastern building, Ch'ing-yang, was consecrated to the Green Lord, who presided over the eastern heavens; the western building, Tsung-chang, to the White Lord; the northern building, Hsüan-t'ang, to the Dark

Lord, the southern building, Ming-t'ang, to the Red Lord. And in these the king performed the ceremonies proper to each of them.[59]

Furthermore, every centre of regular activity was at the same time a place of worship: for example, every dwelling place was used for worshipping the household gods. The most important of these places of worship were the schools. There worship was offered to former schoolmasters, *hsien-shih*, to whom sacrifices were made in spring and autumn before the beginning of each term. The school at the capital, which the kings called Pi-yung and the princes P'an-kung, was also consecrated to the ancestor of the reigning family: Hsieh in Sung, 'Sovereign Millet' Hou-chi in Chou and in the principalities of the Chi clan, such as Lu, Cheng, Chin, and Wey. People went there to make offerings on the eve of the *chiao* sacrifices, so as to warn the ancestor that the ceremony was approaching; and they went there also to offer him the head of a prisoner sacrificed upon return from a victorious expedition. There too the great archery contest was conducted; there the king 'entertained the old men' at a banquet; and so on.

The altars and temples became truly places of worship only after a ceremony of consecration with the blood of a victim, *hsin*. The detail of the ceremony is known only for the ancestral temples.[60] The descendant, founder of the temple, proceeded to the newly finished building in person (only princes had the right to send a representative instead), accompanied by his priest and his butcher. All three wore black ceremonial costume, with a skin bonnet the colour of a sparrow's head. The sovereign placed himself in the courtyard facing north, to the south of the block of stone to which the sacrificial victims were tied. The butcher, having washed the sacrificial lamb, led it into the courtyard and tied it to the post; and the priest recited a prayer over it. The butcher then went up into the temple by the middle stairway and, turning to face south, cut the lamb's throat in such a way that the blood, trickling to the ground, consecrated the temple. Then, he descended again and proceeded to consecrate, one after the other, the main entry gate of the court and the side buildings by cutting the throat of a chicken in the centre of each. During this time, the person sacrificing and his priest remained standing in their place near the victim's post, merely turning, successively, to face the gate and each of the buildings. When the blood had thus been sprinkled in each of the four directions, the priest announced to the principal in the sacrifice: 'The consecration by blood of such-and-such a temple has been completed.' After the buildings themselves, the different utensils of worship, vases and the like, had to be consecrated: these were smeared with the blood of a sucking pig.[61] The tortoise-shells for divination, reserved to each ancestor, were also smeared with blood; but for them the ceremony had to be renewed each year in the first month of winter, as it had to be for the divinatory milfoil stalks as well.[62]

Worship

The ceremonies of worship were carried out in these diverse places, but the general pattern remained much the same, despite surface variations: it consisted of offerings, prayers and dances, all accompanied by music, though sometimes one or another of the elements was omitted.

The offerings differed according to the deity and occasion: for the Lord on High, for the Great God of the Soil — Sovereign Earth — and for the royal ancestors, there were the Great Offerings, *t'ai-lao*, each of three victims — bull, ram, and pig (the Roman *suovetaurile*). The offerings to the three were differentiated: for the first, the bull was red; for the second, black; for the third, white. To the gods of the mountains and the rivers a foal was offered; to the God of the Roads, when the king went out of the palace, a dog was crushed under the chariot wheels. Ordinary patricians offered to their ancestors only one victim, a ram. The pieces of jade offered up to the Lord on High were round and blue, as was the sky; those for Sovereign Earth were square and yellow. The Lord on High drank only water, whereas various kinds of wine were offered up to the ancestors, such as unfermented sweet wine, undecanted red wine, clarified greenish-white wine, and so forth. Human victims were frequently sacrificed, but in connection with certain special rites. In Ch'in and Wey a young girl was sacrificed once a year as bride to the Count of the River; the same was done by the people of Shu for the God of the Yangtze. During a campaign the throat of a prisoner was cut and the war drums smeared with his blood. Upon the return from a warlike expedition, prisoners were sacrificed to the ancestors or to the God of the Soil, and their heads or ears buried before the entrance to the ancestral temple, together with those of the enemy dead.[63] Sorcerers or cripples were tortured to death in the sun, to bring rain in summer. Several of a deceased lord's wives and servants were forced to follow him and were buried with him.

The way offerings were made differed no less than the offerings themselves. For the Lord on High, sacrificial victims, fabrics, and pieces of jade were burnt on a pile of faggots in the open, so that the smoke of the offerings could ascend to him in heaven, his dwelling. For the gods of the soil the offerings were buried so that they reached their destination, the earth. For the river gods, they were immersed; for the ancestors a complete banquet was provided. Whatever the kind of offerings, and however they were presented, they had to conform to certain conditions of ritual purity. 'Oxen with a white mark on the forehead, pigs with turned-up snouts, and men suffering from piles are not acceptable to the God of the River. Sorceresses and priests who recognize these defects consider such beings to be unlucky.'[64] The bull (the principal victim of the *t'ai-lao*) to be offered up to the Lord on High in the southern suburbs or to the ancestors at the great quarterly sacrifices, having been carefully selected, was separated from the herd and kept shut up for three months in the stable. The millet to be offered up, like that used in making the various kinds of wine, had to come from the Sacred Field in which the king himself had laboured; the silk had to be that of the queen's silkworms; the water was 'pure water' — dew gathered on a cup at sunrise; the fire was 'pure fire' obtained directly from the sun by means of a parabolic mirror, *sui*, or by drilling a piece of dry wood, *tsan*. The terms used to designate ordinary objects were replaced by ritual expressions when they became offerings: a bull became 'large feet'; a pig, 'stiff bristles'; a sheep, 'soft-wool'; water was 'the divine liquor'; and wine, 'pure beverage'.[65]

The prayers, *chou*, seem often to have been incantations possessing a virtue, a potency (*ling*) of their own, independent of any outside divine action. Thus there were formulas for 'going to meet the sun' at the solstices and equinoxes, those of establishing the seasons, and also that of the great Harvest Festival. The reading of the right prayers at the right time and with the correct ceremonies sufficed to bring about the desired effect, without any god intervening, either to be prayed to or to grant the request. To utter them ceremonially at the wrong season would naturally bring down cataclysms. Besides these incantations in archaic style, however, another form of prayer had been developed. When addressing the Lord on High, the gods of the soil or the ancestors, this was by supplication, requests for good fortune or protection, which they were free to grant or reject.

The great pantomime-dances with which almost all the great religious ceremonies finished were a kind of symbolic representation of what people wished to see happen or continue, and assured fulfillment of this by their own Virtue. At the quarterly sacrifices to the ancestors of the Chou dynasty, the victory of King Wu over Tsou of the Shang was performed and, by thus repeating their ancestor's victory every year, his successors directly acquired his Virtue, thus each time reconfirming for themselves the Mandate of Heaven. In the same way the dukes of Sung, performing the *sang-lin* dance, acquired for themselves the Virtue of their ancestor, T'ang the Victorious, founder of the Yin dynasty, who had sacrificed himself to put an end to a drought. When at the summer solstice the ballet of the Hsien Pool, *Hsien-ch'ih*, was danced to the accompaniment of the *k'ung-sang* lutes, this performance symbolic of the sun's heavenly course ensured its regular continuation.

As for the music, its purpose was above all to make the gods and spirits come. Every act of every ceremony was performed to instrumental music and chants, and precise rules laid down the pieces to be played in each case. The entrances and exits of the king, of divine and human guests, and of victims each took place to the sound of a special march played on gongs and musical stones: the marches *wang-hsia*, *ssu-hsia*, and *chao-hsia* respectively.[66] Then, when all had taken their places, a choir began singing an ode appropriate to the ceremony, supported by stringed instruments (lutes and violins) and by flutes, each phrase punctuated by the beat of a drum. Then the mouth-organs and flutes played the music accompanying a little dance, *hsiang*, or the whole orchestra played airs from the great ballets, *Ta-wu*, *Ta-hsia*, and so on, of the sacrifices; or, if the ceremony were simply a banquet followed by an archery contest, the dance of the bow and the arrows.[67]

All important ceremonies demanded a certain degree of ritual purity, not only for the victims but for all those taking part: the person offering the sacrifice, praying priests, those attending, those representing the deceased, and sorcerers. All had to prepare themselves beforehand by a more or less lengthy and severe period of abstinence, which varied according to the importance of the ceremony and their own rank. Before the sacrifices in the suburbs, as well as before the quarterly sacrifices to the ancestors, the king had to purify himself for ten days, by easy-going rules for the first seven, but very strict ones for the last three. He had to leave his own quarters and go to live in the great reception hall near the Gate of the Lu Chariot. He had to obey certain prohibitions: all relations with women and the use of certain foods were forbidden. The regimen was the same for princes. Grand officers and all patricians had to observe less lengthy but equally strict rules. Priests had to do and to avoid the same things as their patrons. Nor was that all. Those who merely attended were chosen from among the courtiers, several days before the ceremony, at a solemn archery contest in the Pi-yung Palace — that is to say, in the royal college — over which the king presided; and they, too, had to purify themselves. Then, on the eve of the sacrifice, the altars and temples were cleaned, swept, restored and repaired, if necessary, so that they, too, were immaculate.

Although constituent elements of the ceremonies remained always about the same, the festivals did not assume too monotonous a character on that account. On the contrary, they were quite varied and of quite diverse effect. In particular, the difference between the worship of the ancestors and that of the gods was very clear.

When a sacrifice was offered to the ancestors, they came down for the duration of the ceremony, each entering a living person chosen beforehand, just as in the practices of sorcery. Such a person was not simply a representative of the ancestor, responsible for performing his part like an actor in a play: he was the actual bearer of the ancestor's soul, by whom he was truly possessed for some moments. That is why he was called 'possessed by the soul', *shen-pao* (as the sorceresses were called 'possessed by the spirit', *ling-pao*), or again they were called by the word *shih*, the proper meaning of which is 'corpse'.[68] This Corpse was not possessed continually. The soul remained in its tablet when it had nothing to do; and then the Corpse remained standing, motionless. But when the soul had to eat or drink, he invited it by an offering or a libation and when it had occupied him he sat down.[69] When it had to speak, towards the end of the ceremony, to thank the principal at the sacrifice and to promise him good fortune, it used the mouth of the Corpse. Naturally, the soul could use only the body of one of its descendants, but this could never be one of its sons, having to be one of its grandsons, or, if none were available, a nephew — and the agreement of the ancestor was ascertained by divination.[70] It was this obligation to choose a descendant which forced Prince P'ing of Chin to ask the Count of Tung to act as Corpse, when Prince P'ing sacrificed to Kun, father of Yü the Great and a remote ancestor of the Ssu clan, to which the Count of Tung belonged.[71]

The use of a Corpse was strictly reserved to the worship of the dead: no god would allow himself to be represented by a living person. There was, however, one solitary exception: in the sacrifices to the Warning God of the Soil there was a corpse. This was because that god of the soil — the god of a fallen dynasty — was a dead god to whom the funeral priest presented offerings with rites proper to the dead. The Corpse in this case was not the descendant, but the executioner, *shih-shih*, for this was not only a dead god, but a god who had been executed as well.[72]

In itself, worship of the gods was singularly complicated by the fact that one could directly address only those spirits with whom there was a direct relation, either personal (ancestors) or functional (the local gods of the fief). But when deities too high had to be approached — say the Lord on High by the Son of Heaven, or the Count of the River by riverside princes, or the God of the Eastern Peak by princes in his region — a go-between was needed. This had to be a spirit with whom the party offering up sacrifices had direct personal relations — that is to say an ancestor or a local god. Thus, for the sacrifice to the Lord on High in the southern suburbs, *nan-chiao*, the Chou kings used as intermediary their first ancestor, Hou-chi, and the dukes of Sung used theirs, Hsieh.

4
The Annual Cycle of Religious Festivals

The whole religious life of ancient China was dependent upon agricultural life; so, for the one as for the other, the year was divided into two unequal periods. There was the time of nature's great labour, which it was the aim of religion to help and sustain, and there was the time of her great repose, when — work in the fields ended and agricultural life suspended — nothing remained but to give thanks for harvests past and to pray for harvests to come. The festivals were linked once and for all to the proper season. Displacing them would have meant disordering the whole universe, thus bringing about unprecedented cataclysms:

> If, in the second month of spring, the rules for summer were to be observed, rains would fall out of season; grasses and other plants would wither prematurely; and terror would reign constantly in the principalities. If the autumn rules were to be observed then, there would be great epidemics among the people; a violent wind and torrential rains would arise suddenly; all the weeds — puncture weed, darnel, fescue, and artemisia — would run riot. If the rules of winter were used, overflowing rivers would wreak havoc, snow and white frost would appear, and the first sowings would not come up.[1]

And comparable catastrophes would ensue for inappropriate sacrifices in each of the twelve months.

So firmly were the religious festivals tied to the agricultural seasons that when, for reasons we do now know, the Chou kings advanced the beginning of their year, setting the start of spring officially at the winter solstice, the feasts were not thereby displaced.

The ancient Chinese, like those of today, used a luni-solar calendar. Their year was divided into solar months, and it restored the agreement between the abbreviated period of the twelve lunar months and the solar year by intercalating an extra lunar month from time to time. In Chou times the inadequacy of astronomical and mathematical knowledge had not yet allowed them to determine the correct period for inserting the intercalary months; they believed wrongly that it would serve well enough if they added two months in each five-year period.[2] But this theoretical calendar was so untrue and led so rapidly to obvious imprecision that it could not be applied regularly. Between the seventh and fifth centuries the beginning of the royal year, which people continued traditionally to call spring, however much ahead or behind it might be, varied from the month of November to February, according to whether the intercalary corrections had been made more or less frequently than twice for each five-year period.

More than that, different regions had different calendars. In addition to the Royal Domain, the principalities of Lu, Cheng, and Wey adopted the royal calendar. But in Sung a special calendar was used which was supposed to be that of the Yin dynasty and which, about the end of feudal times — when the relationship of the different calendars was definitely fixed — set the beginning of the year a month later than in Chou. Still another calendar was in use in Chin; this was said to date back to the Hsia dynasty (the Chin capital was supposed to occupy the site of the first Hsia capital), and it set the beginning of spring two months later than in Chou. It is abundantly clear that the peasants could not possibly rely upon these official calendars, and in fact a famous passage in the *Shih ching*, recounting the work of the months, dates them in two ways: by the royal calendar and by the agricultural calendar. Still further, official calendars were not used for religious worship, and the ceremonies were carried out at the necessary time for cultivation, thus conforming to the actual seasons, no matter what the calendrical date was.[3] The religious year, like the agricultural, began in the true spring, which is to say in about our month of February, since the Chinese set the equinoxes and the solstices in the middle of the seasons, and not at the beginning as we do.

The whole purpose of worship was not to benefit individuals, but to promote the ordered movement of the world and especially the regular progress of the seasons. Therefore individuals as such had no part in it. It was the exclusive business of those whose position, giving them a share in public administration, gave them responsibility for the proper advance of the world's affairs.

Ruling princes, feudal lords, officials carried out all the necessary ceremonies, each on behalf of his domain or his function, and private persons had nothing to add to what they did. But above all, the king, the sacred personage, unique in the world, had a role in religious life that was pre-eminent and absolutely separate, since every one of his movements, even the most trivial — eating, dressing, choosing a place to sleep or that one of his women who would share his bed, and so on — was replete with a sacred Virtue and contributed to the functioning of the universe. And by that same Virtue, he had to be the first to perform the various acts of life: first to eat the fruits of the season, to wear warm or cool clothing, to perform agricultural work, to go hunting, and especially first to carry out every religious ceremony, for it was he who had the power to establish or to break all taboos.

The royal worship, like that of princes and officials, followed a twofold rhythm, in which phases were superimposed upon one another without intermixing. First, there was the rhythm of peasant life with its two seasons of unequal length: the work in the fields and the seclusion in the home, according to which the whole cycle of festivals in honour of the gods succeeded one another in a cycle of worship that was primarily agricultural and peasant (the sacrifices to the Lord on High, to the God of the Soil, etc.). Second was the regular rhythm of the year with its four astronomical seasons, by which the cycle of feasts for ancestor-worship was arranged. So, too, were other festivals connected essentially with certain astronomical phases: feasts at the beginning of seasons, feasts of the solstices or equinoxes, and so forth. Occasional ceremonies for wars, for epidemics, for floods, for drought, for eclipses, and so on, were interspersed among these regular religious cycles without interrupting them. Only the death of the king upset this orderly arrangement, by requiring the omission of some feasts during the period of mourning.

The Agrarian Cycle

Thus for most of the actions, and the most important ones, of religious life, the year was divided into two unequal periods: one of about eight months (spring, summer and the beginning of autumn), the other of four months (the end of autumn and winter). Each was a distinct unit containing its own series of great feasts, at which the king, in almost the same order, addressed all the deities in succession, so that each of them had his own feast in each period.

The religious year began in spring with a series of important ceremonies, descending by steps from king to common people, which shattered the restrictions of winter and started the work of the fields off again. First of all, the king sacrificed to the Lord on High, Shang-ti, upon the round hillock consecrated to him in the southern suburbs of the capital. Hence the name by which it was usually known: *nan-chiao* (Sacrifice in the) Southern Suburb, or more simply *chiao* (Sacrifice in the) Suburb.[4]

This was the first religious act of the new year, and only the king had sufficient Virtue to perform so serious and so dangerous an act. He was also required to take certain precautions: in a way he prepared the Sacrifice of the Suburbs several days beforehand, by an offering to the 'Four Distant Ones', *ssu-wang*, of which we know nothing except that only sorcerers, *wu*, took part in it, and that it was they who summoned these distant divinities, calling them by name and making signs to them with long reed-stalks which they shook in all four cardinal directions,[5] while the *ta-shao* dance was done.[6] A little later, the ancestor associated with the Lord on High (this was always the First Ancestor: among the Chou, it was Sovereign Millet, Hou-chi; in Sung, it was Hsieh) had to be warned so that in his turn, serving as intermediary, he could go and warn the Lord on High. It was the same in Lu, where they followed the royal rituals. Also, on the eve of the ceremony, the king himself went to make an offering to him at Pi-yung, which is to say at the great college in the northeastern suburb of the capital.

This was one of the most important sacrifices in the religious life of the king, and everything connected with it was carefully laid down.[7] The date had to be a *hsin* day (the eighth day of the denary cycle) in the month preceding the spring equinox,[8] which in theory was the third month of the civil year by the Chou calendar, but which often varied in practice. There were three ten-day periods in a month and thus three *hsin* days, so the ancestors were asked by tortoise-shell divinations to set the auspicious day. It was, moreover, necessary to make preparations long in advance. The victim, a red bull, had to be ritually pure; so three months before, towards the end of autumn, the king went personally to the pasture to choose it, at the same time choosing one designated for the associated ancestor. Bulls with twisted horns were rejected. Once the choice was made, the animal reserved for heaven was put in the stable (that for the ancestor remained in the pasture), and he was kept there in order to avoid all contamination until the day of the sacrifice.

On their side, the king and all those taking part in the ceremony had to prepare themselves by abstinence for ten days, as for all the great sacrifices. At dawn on the appointed day, when the Cocks, *Chi-jen* (this was the name of the officials whose duty it was to announce the rising of the sun) called the awakening, the king, in ordinary garb and wearing a skin cap, first heard the announcement of the ceremony. From that moment on, for the rest of the day, people in mourning had to cease their lamentations, no funeral rites could be performed, and nobody dressed in mourning attire was allowed to enter the gates of the capital. In the morning the king, dressed in a robe ornamented with patterns of the sun, moon, and similar motifs, and wearing a hat with twelve pear-shaped pendants of precious stone, mounted a plain chariot, holding a 'Standard with Twelve Flames' on which were pictured dragons, the sun, and the moon (so that his chariot imitated heaven, which suspends the constellations over our heads), and proceeded to the mound in the southern suburb. All along the way that the cortège followed the road had been swept and sprinkled; and the peasants stood at the edge of the fields, carrying lighted torches to illuminate it. Having arrived at the sacred mound, the king took his place standing to the southeast with his face to the west, while the musicians played to signalize his entry as well as that of the spirits, who descended at this moment. A large pyre was then made on top of the mound, on the bare ground, with no altar. In the meantime the Boundary-men, *feng-jen* — officials responsible for building the embankments of earth which, at the capital, separated the fields consecrated to the God of the Soil from common fields and, away from the capital, separated fiefs from one another — had prepared the victim. This was a young red bull[9] chosen for its purity and kept isolated for three months. They had placed between its horns a piece of wood to prevent it from striking, and they had attached a guide-rope to lead it. The Grand Chamberlain took the cord and led the victim in, to the sound of gongs and sounding stones, while the Boundary-men followed it, dancing and singing its praise. The Grand Chamberlain stopped the victim before the king and invited him to kill it, and he did so with arrows. The blood was collected and was presented to Heaven as the first offering.

Then after the whole body had been placed upon the pyre, together with a bolt of silk eighteen feet long, the king went up and left upon it circular pieces of blue jade. The Chief Priest lit

the fire by using a burning-mirror and, at a signal from the
Count of Religious Affairs, recited a prayer that the year should
be a good one.[10] Afterwards, probably after the prayer, the Chief
Priest gave his orders to the Master of Music, and the choir of the
blind sang the ode *Sheng-min*, which recalled the origin of the
chiao sacrifice founded by Hou-chi, Sovereign Millet, and — after
having recited at length the ancestor's legend — finished with a
short description of the sacrifice itself:

> We fill the wooden cups with offerings,
> the cups of wood and vases of earthenware;
> as soon as its aroma has gone up,
> the Lord on High commences to eat;
> how fine the odour and how precise its timing!
> Hou-chi founded the sacrifice,
> all have carried it out without error or omission,
> from then until this day.

When everything had been burned, the top of the mound was
swept and the king ascended it to the sound of the *Wang-hsia*
march. Then the representative of Sovereign Millet, the ancestor
associated with the Lord on High, went up on it, dressed in the
same costume as the king's, to the sound of the *Ssu-hsia* march;
and the offering of a bull to Sovereign Millet was carried out,
following the rites of the ancestral worship. During this time the
Chief Priest recited a prayer to Hou-chi, and the choir of the
blind sang the ode *Ssu-wen*:

> Oh, perfect Sovereign Millet,
> you have become the associate of Heaven;
> you have given grain to all our people,
> a marvellous gift and without equal;
> you have given us wheat and millet,
> the Lord has made you father to us all, without limit or boundary,
> you have spread grain over all of China.

The ceremony ended with a grand dance, perhaps that called
Gate of Clouds, *Yün-men*, in which the king himself seems to have
taken part.[11]

In a general way the great *chiao* sacrifice marked the reopening of
the new season. Yet before even the most ordinary tasks and
activities could be carried out, a series of ceremonies was
necessary to commence each one in particular: work in the
fields, marriages, silkworm breeding, and so forth.

First of all, the king performed the ploughing ceremony in the
Field of the Lord on High, *Ti-chi*, known also as the Thousand

Acres, *Ch'ien-mou*, which lay in the southern suburb. The actual day was not established, but was selected by divination every year, immediately after the *chiao* sacrifice. The Grand Scribe notified the king of the date nine days beforehand with the words: 'In nine days from now the earth will be turned. Let the king respectfully purify himself and direct the ploughing without the slightest change.'

The Minister of Works had an altar set up in the sacred field, and ordered the grand officer responsible for agriculture to prepare all the necessary utensils. Five days before the ceremony the Director of Music, who controlled the blind musicians, announced that the wind had arrived. On the following day the king, accompanied by his ministers and his court, proceeded to the Palace of Purification and all underwent a preparatory abstinence of three days.

When the day came, the king offered up, on the altar in the Field of the Lord, a sacrifice of three victims — bull, sheep, and pig — to T'ien-tsu, the Ancestor of Agriculture, as the first who had cultivated a field. Then, under the instructions of the Grand Scribe, who cried out in a high voice the movements to be performed, the king guided the plough with his own hands and traced three furrows. His ministers did nine, then the officers of state, the nobles, and finally the peasants completed the ploughing of the thousand acres. Then the Chamberlain, assisted by the Officer of the Table, prepared a ritual banquet on the spot. Under his guidance the king carried out first the ceremony of Feeding upon the Three Victims, and after him the ministers and grand officers, each according to rank; then the ordinary officers and the people partook of the banquet. Finally, when it was finished, a granary was constructed in the southeast corner of the sacred field so that the future crop could be stored there, to furnish the necessary grains for the entire year's worship.[12]

From this day on the ban which had been imposed on the earth throughout the winter months was lifted, and the peasants were given the order to start work again. The ploughing ceremony was carried out everywhere: by princes in their fiefs, where they had a hundred-acre field,[13] by vassals in their domains, and even in the cantons and villages, the rite of 'turning the earth' was performed. That was not all. Before work in the fields and life in the open became possible, the cold weather had to come to an end. Therefore, on a day in the second month of spring, the king offered up to the Master of the Cold, *Ssu-han*, a black victim and black millet, and then, to ward off the calamity of unseasonable cold, he fired blackthorn arrows from a peachwood bow. After that, he opened the storehouse where the cold had been shut in with the ice during the winter, and he ushered it out to the sound of earthenware drums.[14]

Thus, with the earth turned and the cold ushered out, cultivation could resume. But spring was not only the beginning of vegetation: in social life as well, it marked the beginning of a new period when peasant families, each of which had lived separate in its own house all winter, gathered in small groups in their communal summer huts and when marriages, forbidden in winter, were arranged. To open the matrimonial period, the king in the second month chose the 'day of the swallows' return' — that is, the day of the vernal equinox — to sacrifice to the Intermediary, Kao-mei, or Chiao-mei, the God of Marriage and of Fertility, sacrificing three ordinary victims: bull, sheep, and pig. When the sacrifices had been made and the prayers said, the queen and the royal concubines appeared. The Chief Priest handed to those of the women who were pregnant a cup of sacrificial wine 'so as to manifest the favour' which the god had shown by granting them fecundity, and afterwards a bow and arrow, ritual present at the birth of boys, so that the child might be a son. This ceremony lifted the ban which had hitherto obstructed marriage; and the go-between, *mei-shih*, the official in charge of marriages, passed through the countryside and 'commanded the men and women to assemble'.[15]

Gradually social life, which had been interrupted by winter, was resumed in all its forms; but each manifestation of this resumption called for a religious ceremony which the king had to perform first. When it was completely re-established, the gods of the soil had to be informed — not in order to ask their permission to cultivate the land, for they were not the gods of vegetation, but to let them know what was going on in their territory. For this reason, it was only after the sacred field had been ploughed that 'orders were given to sacrifice to the God of the Soil.' These sacrifices did not always take place immediately, moreover, since 'the God of the Soil will not drink stale water', so that in the villages they awaited the first rainfall before sacrificing to him.

It was not enough just to re-establish social life anew; the impurities of winter had to be cleared away. Winter life had been one of reclusion, when the working of the sacramentalized land had been forbidden; that of spring and summer was a life in the open air, of activity and of work in the fields. At this moment of change a hostile influence — not actually evil, but contrary to the season — had to be driven out. This necessitated a number of religious acts which the king, as usual, had to commence. At the beginning of the third month the *no* ceremony took place in the capital.[16] A sorcerer endowed with the power to see spirits, *fang-hsiang*, directed it. His head covered by a bearskin with four golden eyes and clad in a black jacket and red skirt, a halberd in one hand and a shield in the other, he took up position at the head of his assistants to drive out the pestilences. He threw clods of earth at them, fired arrows at them from beechwood bows, threw red pellets at them, and chased them thus through the palace buildings and out of the city, near the gates of which were placed dismembered parts of sacrificial victims as an offering to these spirits. In the meantime, sorceresses had begun the same kind of dancing in the women's quarters. Thereafter, the queen and the princesses went to bathe in and drink from the water of a stream that made a right-angle turn and then flowed eastwards, so that the current would carry away all the contaminations of winter.[17]

In this same month, after the official ceremonies of the king and the princes, the townspeople and villagers everywhere performed rites of the same kind. In the state of Lu a feast was held in about the third month on the banks of the Yi River, near the sacred ground where the ceremonies for rain took place. Two troops, one of adults and one of young boys, went into the stream and performed the dance of 'the dragon emerging from the waters'; and they then proceeded singing to the field, where a sacrifice and banquet terminated proceedings. In Cheng, at the confluence of the rivers Chen and Wei, at the time of thawing and the first rains, youths and maidens performed the ceremony of driving away evil influences, especially that of sterility. The young girls went on the rivers, 'calling the *hun* so as to reunite it with the *p'o*,[18] orchid in hand, they drive away the evil influences.' In Ch'en, when the weaving work was finished, about the second month of spring, youths and maidens danced upon the Yüan mound to the sound of the earthen drum, waving fans and egret plumes.[19] In Ch'i it was the sacrifice to the God of the Soil that signalled the beginning of these festivities among youths and maidens, near the mound, perhaps in the square wood which stood beside it.

Finally, so that everything should be new in the season, the 'fire was renewed', *pien-huo* or *kai-huo*, in all houses, from the royal palace to peasant huts, and it was 'taken out' of the houses, *ch'u-huo*, at the end of spring. The old fire was extinguished and for three days no other fire could be lit. Then a new fire was lit, a pure fire taken directly from the sun by means of a burning-mirror[20] or by rubbing two sticks together. But this new fire was not lit in the houses. It was started in the open on great hearths prepared on each *ching*, for with the end of spring the open-air season began, when the peasants went to live far from their villages in large huts amidst the fields.

In this way the spring months formed a kind of transition period from the winter life to the summer life, which were so different for the peasants. The king opened the new period with sacrifices and ceremonies which licensed the resumption of each kind of activity. Then, at the time of thawing, of thunder, and of the rains, which really marked the visible beginning of the new year, a great purification dispelled the adverse influence of winter, and the new life truly began for a new year. All these ceremonies, which followed one another in a regular order, ended up for the countryfolk by intermingling in a period of great feasts and complete licence, when the young men and girls at the first peal of thunder, 'the elder son of heaven' at his awakening,[21] gathered together, sang together, and mated freely in the fields. At certain places which tradition had consecrated in each region they arrived in bands, dressed in their best clothes, and carried out the rites, dancing, singing, and drinking. Youths and maidens made assignations to meet there again, and they courted, the maidens sometimes making the first advances to the young men. Couples formed to sing together the songs of love that had been transmitted from generation to generation, responding one to another with songs ever more ardent and then mating in the open air. When they parted, the young man gave the girl a fragrant flower.[22]

When the spring period of transition was over, the ceremony of the Establishment of Summer, *li-hsia*, marked the beginning of this season when the open-air life indeed commenced for the peasants. At this time, after renewing the fire and the ceremony of 'carrying the fire out' of the houses,[23] they had to leave their houses and go to live in a hut amid the fields. There the *ssu-t'u* ordered them to 'work with all their might and not remain idle in the villages'.[24] At this point, amid the continual effort of agricultural labour, religious life slacked off. It resumed some activity only in the middle of summer, in the month of the solstice, when there was a whole series of festivals and sacrifices. Apart from the offerings which the Son of Heaven caused to be made locally to mountains, to rivers, and to springs during the second month of summer (as during the second month of each season), the period of the solstice was signalized by a great religious ceremony in which the king went to the great school of the capital, the Pi-yung,[25] to offer a sacrifice to the terrestrial spirits. This school formed a square mound rising in the middle of a lake, an image of the world itself — square and surrounded by the four seas. There the dance of Hsien-ch'ih was performed to the sound of *k'ung-sang* lutes. 'All the terrestrial spirits emerged; one could joy in their presence and pay sacred homage to them.'[26]

But above all, this was the moment when people were concerned with what was for them, in the dry country of northern China, the chief problem of summer: getting rain. In the second month of summer (in the fourth century, it was the appearance of the constellation of the Dragon, *Lung*, which regulated this), the king offered to the Lord on High a sacrifice for rain, *yü*, on a temporary mound built next to the Grand Mound of Heaven in the southern suburbs. Of all the ceremonies of the royal worship, this was the one in which the connections between the personal conduct of the sovereign and the working of the universe appeared most clearly. Not only did he offer up victims, indeed, but he also accused himself for his failings: that his government was bad, that his officials performed their duties poorly, that his palace was too costly, that his women were too numerous, that his table was too well supplied, that flatterers had been given responsibilities. Next, two troops, each of eight children, eight boys and eight girls, performed the *huang* dance, waving white plumes and crying out, 'I want rain!'[27] If rain did not come and the drought were prolonged, sacrifices were offered to a particular mountain, or to mountains and forests generally, as producers of rain,[28] or to the Count of the River, sovereign of the waters.[29] Or again a winged dragon, *ying-lung*, was made out of clay; for the dragon too could bring rain.[30] Or yet again, the *yü* ceremony was repeated with even more pomp. Sometimes sorcerers and sorceresses were made to dance in the sun, or were exposed in the sun until they died; or they were even burned alive in bright sunshine. At other times, in place of sorcerers and sorceresses it was hunchbacks or cripples who were tortured; but these were proceedings which, towards the end of the dynasty, enlightened people strongly condemned.[31]

Once the rain had fallen, religious life faded away during the end of summer and the beginning of autumn. Indeed, all time was taken up by the work in the fields — weeding, guarding crops, harvesting, storing, sowing wheat. As the end of the summer season approached, the series of ceremonies for the transition to the winter season began. This was a sequence of which the elements almost exactly mirrored those of the analogous sequence in springtime. There were the sacrifice to the Lord on High, corresponding to the *chiao*; the festival of the harvest and of the end of field-work, corresponding to the ploughing of the sacred field; the offering to the God of the Soil to inform him that the mode of life in his territory was changing, as in spring; the solemn return into the village houses of the fire which had been taken out in the third month; the expulsion of malign influences, which were driven from the houses which were to be lived in, just as in spring they had been driven from the fields where people were to establish themselves; and so on. The order was not precisely the same as in springtime: the ceremonies described in the ritual books are a division into separate and specialized rites of what were originally grand groupings having a more general religious application. So it is not surprising that, in being dissected into discrete elements, the corresponding festivals are not always apportioned according to the same order within the two series, which were analogous but not identical.

The beginning of the renewal of religious activity was marked by two feasts in the eighth month: a ceremony of ritual purification, *no*, to dispel the adverse influences of summer;[32] and the feast for the return of the cold, wherein the king brought back the cold, which he had ushered out in spring, by offering up — on a night in the second month of autumn, near the equinox — a black ram and black millet to the Master of the Cold, *Ssu-han*.[33]

It was then that the winter period truly began, in the third month of autumn, with the great sacrifice which the king offered to the Lord on High. This was exactly the reverse of the *chiao* in spring. Just as that had preceded the peasants' abandonment of the villages and their life in the huts amid the fields, so the winter sacrifice prepared re-entry into the village and establishment in the houses. This difference was shown by the choice of location: it was carried out, not in the countryside of the outer suburbs, on a mound in the open air, but near the capital in the inner suburbs, inside the Sacred Palace — the temple which had been the true royal palace in the time when the king had been too sacred to dwell within the urban complex, and which had remained the scene of his entire religious life. Thus even the location of the worship in each festival reflected the mode of life in the season being opened. As always, it was necessary for a deceased ancestor to introduce the sacrificer into the presence of this exalted divinity. In this case, however, it was not the ancestor of the entire race, but the founder of the dynasty, the prince who had first received 'the Mandate of Heaven'. For the Chou kings, it was King Wen; for the dukes of Sung, it was T'ang the Victorious; for the princes of Lu, who claimed to have been granted the privilege of carrying out the royal rites, it was also King Wen; for those of Cheng, who are said to have imitated the rites of Lu, it was King Li, father of the first count. The details of the ceremony are unknown. All we know is that at the royal court there was sung the ode 'I have brought' in honour of King Wen associated with the Lord on High:

I have brought my offerings, a ram, a bull.
May Heaven accept them.
I have imitated, I have followed, I have observed the rules of King Wen,
daily pacifying the four regions;
[also] the blessed King Wen,
comes to the right [of the offerings] and accepts them.
Day and night, I,
I fear the majesty of Heaven
thus preserving [the Mandate of Heaven].[34]

With the winter season thus opened, the Establishment of Winter, *li-tung*, took place. The king went solemnly to meet winter in the northern suburb, accompanied by his ministers and grand officers. Then he proclaimed this edict from the Sacred Palace: 'The emanations of heaven rise up, those of the earth sink down, heaven and earth are no longer in touch. Shut and barred [is the passage between], and established is winter!' Then the order was given for peasants to leave the huts in the fields,[35] and return to the village; and the ceremony of renewing the fire and bringing it into the houses, precisely the reverse of the renewing of fire in spring, took place.

The preparations, as much religious as secular, for winter life thus set in motion, and the return to the village completed, big festivals — one after another in the first month of winter — marked the end of work in the fields. First there was the royal sacrifice to the Great God of the Soil, then that to the ancestors, and finally the Harvest Festival.

The king offered a suovetaurile, *t'ai-lao*, to the Great God of the Soil. The bull was black, the day was a *chia* day — that is, the first of the denary cycle. The king, dressed in a tunic of fine dolic linen and wearing a bonnet decorated with twelve pear-shaped pendant gems, walked to the mound. The Count of Religious Affairs, Ta-tsung-po, smeared the plain stone tablet of the god with blood so as to warn and summon the god; and he then offered the victim, its flesh uncooked, together with a roll of silk and a square piece of jade, yellow in colour (the colour of the earth). Small morsels of rare meat were placed on shells and given to the king and to his assistants, who ate with all due respect; and others were set aside to be conveyed to the nobles of the royal clan and also, to do them honour, to the nobles of other clans. The ceremony was carried out before troops of armed men, and it ended — at least in certain states — with an impressive military review. Probably just after the sacrifice to the God of the Soil himself, there was offered — according to the rites of the ancestor worship — a bull to his associate the God of Harvests, who in Chou as well as in Cheng, Wey, Lu, and Sung was Sovereign Millet, Hou-chi, but in Chin — where rites dating back to the Hsia dynasty were followed — was called Chu, and was considered to be the son of the mythical emperor Shen-nung.[36]

The Harvest Festival marked the time after which agricultural work was completely forbidden; the sacralized soil was not to be turned again — as the ploughing ceremony had turned it in the spring month, breaking the winter prohibition. This was called 'the Grand [Festival in honour of the spirits] who are to be sought out', *Ta-cha*, or alternatively '[the festival in honour of the] eight [classes of spirits] whom one seeks', *Pa-cha*. All sorts of offerings were presented — agricultural products, products of the hunt and so on: 'All the ten thousand things, to make an offering of them to the spirits who are to be sought'. Princes took part in it, sending to the Son of Heaven presents of grain, precious objects, game, eggs, women, and so forth, though this did not hinder them from having their own festival in turn within their own domains. This was primarily a harvest festival: its institution was attributed to the Divine Husbandman, Shen-nung; the principal spirit was the First Harvester, Hsien-she. In addition, homage was paid to the first husbandman, to the first builder of dikes, to the first digger of canals, and to the first builder of watchmen's huts on the edges of fields. And the spirits of cats — rat-killers — were called upon, as were those of tigers — wild boar eaters. In a word, all the spirits were included who, by protecting cultivation at any stage, helped to make the harvest abundant;[37] and the sacrifice was accompanied by formulas designed to put all in order so that the next harvest might be prepared: 'May the lands return in their places, may the waters return to their channels, may the insects not be produced, may the harmful weeds return to their marshes!'

The festival seems to have had the character of a vast masquerade: the spirits of cats and of tigers had their representatives, who were men or children masked and costumed. In Chou it was merged with the festival of 'ushering out the dead year' because, with the royal calendar usually placing the new year at the winter solstice, the first month of winter in the agricultural year was the last month of the official year. Thus the person making the sacrifice bore himself as if in mourning: on his head he wore a skin cap and he dressed in white robes with a girdle of hemp, carrying a hazelwood staff in his hand. But at the end of the festival, when the sacrifice was finished and the feast took place, he wore a yellow straw hat and country garb, as everybody did, and the offerings were distributed among the people. An immense orgy then began, during which all the offerings were consumed and in which the old men — in honour of the year's old age — took the leading part.

This was perhaps the greatest festival of the year, one in which the entire populace participated. For not only did the king and the princes in their capitals carry out the ceremonies, but everywhere, in each canton, the patrician charged with being the head of the canton conducted a similar ceremony — sacrificing to the eight classes of spirits who were to be sought and, dressed like a peasant, presiding at a banquet. The Harvest Festival marked the absolute end of work in the fields. From then on the earth was no more to be troubled: it was under an interdict.

Just at the point where the peasants, having already returned to the village at the beginning of winter, after the ceremony of relighting and returning the fire, were about to shut themselves in at home, the king performed a great ceremony for the winter solstice, honouring all the celestial spirits. He offered up to them victims on a round altar — the image of heaven — and he had the Yün-men dance performed to the sound of the Yün-ho lutes.[38] This was the precise counterpart of the festival of the summer solstice in honour of the terrestrial spirits.

After the winter solstice, all the people truly shut themselves up in their houses, the doors being sealed with earth. As always, the king set the example, having the gates of the palace courts plastered shut; and after him, the great officers at court, the princes in their fiefs, and all down to the peasants in their villages closed up their houses and sealed the doors. Life was suspended for about a month, after which, in the last month of the year, the order was given for the peasants to prepare the seed-grain and tools for the next year; and the doors were reopened.[39] The Great Purification drove away hostile emanations.[40]

As in spring, it was the *fang-hsiang* who managed the ceremony in the palace. It began with an imprecation, sung by children, against evil things and beings, threatening them with twelve spirits who would destroy them: 'May the Twelve Spirits drive away ye Evil, ye Unlucky! May they break your spine and your joints! May they cut your flesh into pieces! May they rip out your lungs and your entrails! If you do not hasten to go, those who stay behind will serve the Twelve Spirits as food!' Then the *fang-hsiang* and his assistants, followed by twelve men masked and disguised as animals to portray the Twelve Spirits, pursued the pestilences with loud cries. In their dance they went three times around the palace, waving lighted torches, and ended by expelling the pestilences through the main gate. Horsemen carrying torches then rode straightway to cast them into the River Lo, which ran quite close to the capital. This was already in preparation for the new season which was beginning.

Thus there unfolded perpetually the cycle of the summer and winter seasons, in which natural phenomena, religious acts, and the life of man being in harmony with one another, the secure course of the world was assured.

The Ancestral Cycle

Within this agrarian cycle were interspersed festivals which took no account of the unequal agricultural periods, but recurred at regular intervals throughout the calendar according to the normal order of the four seasons. Almost all were festivals linked by their nature to a fixed period, such as the beginning or the middle of a season. There were the four ceremonies for the establishment of the seasons: the Establishment of Spring, *li-ch'un*; the Establishment of Summer, *li-hsia*; the Establishment of Autumn, *li-ch'iu*; the Establishment of Winter, *li-tung*. The king 'went out to meet' each season and ushered it in. At the beginning of spring this took place on a temporary mound set up in the eastern suburb of the capital; at the beginning of summer, on a temporary mound set up not far from the altar of the Lord on High, in the southern suburb of the capital; and so on.

Then there were the festivals of the solstices and of the equinoxes, when the king 'went out to meet the sun' in the middle of each season: 'In the ——— year, the ——— month, the first day. [Sun, who] illuminates both high and low, who zealously spreads [your benefits] abroad to every part of the four

regions, who displays your majesty in every place, here am I, the
Solitary Man, so and so; and I go out to meet the sun in the
suburb.' So said the king in his prayer at the spring equinox.[41]
The two solstices were celebrated with great sacrifices followed
by dances. In some cases the link with the calendar is difficult to
grasp: for example, the local sacrifices which the king ordered
performed to the mountains and the rivers took place in the
second month of each of the four seasons, though one cannot see
what attached them specially to that particular month. But above
all the cycle of the four seasons was that of the ceremonies of the
ancestral temple.

In fact, the worship of the ancestors was a concern of every day
and every moment, filling out daily life with detailed practices.
Before each meal, the father of the family made a libation,
offering a mouthful to the ancestors. If he had received — from
his patron, from his prince, or from the king — the gift of a dish
or a morsel from their table, the ancestors had to have their
share first. He did not taste the new products of the season —
grain, game, fish, and so on — until the first fruits had been
offered at the monthly sacrifice: in the fourth month, the still
unripe grain with pork; in the seventh month, millet; in the
ninth month, rice; in the twelfth month, fish. But aside from
these ongoing minor ceremonies, each of the four seasons
brought a great festival, at the ancestral temple for those who
had one, or before the ancestral altar for others. These were the
yüeh in spring, the *tz'u* in summer, the *ch'ang* in autumn, and the
cheng in winter.[42] These were sacrifices offered to all the ancestors,
mu and *chao*, who were entitled to special offerings, the number
of which varied according to the rank of the person making the
sacrifice. Princes performed only three, omitting the one for the
season corresponding to the direction in which their fief lay from
the capital, since they were supposed to go to the court at that
season. Ordinary patricians had four sacrifices, one for each
season.

In addition, the king and the princes — but not ordinary
patricians — had a great collective sacrifice to all their ancestors
since the beginning of the family, which was called *hsia*. This as a
regular, but not an annual, sacrifice, remaining always
dependant upon the calendrical rhythm: for it followed the five-
year period which was, in theory, that of the intercalation of
months intended to bring the movements of the sun and moon
into agreement; and it was performed once in that period, in the
ancestral temple. Although this sacrifice could not have
pertained to persons lesser than fief-holding princes, it was

sometimes bestowed upon grand officers in reward for services rendered (from this came the name *kan-hsia*: 'collective sacrifice granted as reward'). That did not license them to go back as far as their First Ancestor, who had no chapel in their temple, but simply gave them the right to use the solemn *hsia* ritual in sacrifice to their ancestors as far back as the fourth generation.

Finally, the king alone, together with the descendants of the ancient dynasties and the Prince of Lu, had another grand five-yearly sacrifice to all his ancestors since the First Ancestor. This was called *ti*, and it was the grandest and most important of all ceremonies performed in the ancestral temple. It too depended upon the quinquennial intercalation, and it was linked with the *hsia*, which occurred in the third year of this five-year cycle, while the *ti* took place in the fifth year, although the two sacrifices seem not to have been put into relation with the intercalation itself. Indeed, in Lu (the usage of the royal court is not known, but the princes of Lu claimed to follow it exactly), it would appear that the cycle of *hsia* and *ti* depended strictly upon the date of the preceding sovereign's death. When the mourning period was finished, the *hsia* was performed for the first time, and the *ti* in the spring of the following year. Thereafter they succeeded one another regularly at five-year intervals till the end of the reign, when a new death altered the regular course of their cycle.[43]

The *hsia* was the sacrifice by which the ancestor was 'reunited' for the first time with the whole line of his ancestors; the *ti* was that through which the deceased king was set among the ranks of the *ti*, Lords, 'to the right and to the left of the Lord on High'. This was, at least, the significance of the first *hsia* and the first *ti* of each series, those connected with the end of the mourning period. The others were simple renewals of the ritual.[44]

No matter how many ancestors they were offered to, the main sacrifices to them were of two kinds. One consisted of collective offerings made at one time to all the ancestors whose tablets and whose *shih* were gathered together at the abode of the First Ancestor. The other was the same offerings made separately to each ancestor in his chapel, the tablets of the most ancient (those who no longer had a chapel) being gathered together in that of the First Ancestor. Among the quarterly sacrifices to the seven ancestors who had chapels, those of summer, autumn, and winter were collective sacrifices, those of spring were individual. Among the five-yearly sacrifices to all the ancestors, the *hsia* were of the first type and the *ti* of the second.

At the beginning of the *hsia* sacrifice, the priest solemnly escorted the four tablets of the *chao* and the *mu*, each from its own chapel to that of the First Ancestor where 'they were assembled to eat'. As they passed, all had to give way. The tablets of ancestors who no longer had their own chapels were also ceremonially taken out of their caskets by the Guardian of the Displaced Tablets, *shou-t'iao* and set in their places at the banquet. The seating was entirely genealogical: The First Ancestor was at the top, facing east; his son at his left, facing south; his grandson at his right, facing north; and all the descendants were thus arranged in two rows, the *chao* to the left and the *mu* to the right following the son and grandson respectively, the distance from the First Ancestor increasing with each generation. The Seven Corpses — there were never more than seven: that of the First Ancestor, those of kings Wen and Wu, and those of the four *chao* and *mu*, the ancestors who had become *kuei* having none — stood by the tablet of the ancestor they represented, on the left side. At the end of the festival, the tablets were taken back to their chapels with the same ceremonial as at the beginning.

In the *ti* sacrifice each tablet was left in its own chapel, with its Corpse next to it, and each had its private banquet at home. Those who no longer had a chapel had a place at the banquet of the ancestor in whose chapel they were kept. The *shou-t'iao* took them out of their caskets and arranged them in genealogical order, all the *mu* descendants of King Wen in one line to his left, all the *chao* descendants of King Wu in a line to his right, and all the *mu* and the *chao* previous to these two kings (that is to say, all those who had not possessed the Mandate of Heaven but had been mere vassal princes) in two rows to left and to right of the First Ancestor, Hou-chi, precisely as in the *hsia* sacrifice. In the quarterly sacrifices, collective and individual, the ceremonial was the same, though naturally the ancestors who had become *kuei* — so that they no longer had a chapel — were excluded.[45]

Aside from these differences in the number of ancestors to whom one sacrificed, in the disposal of the offerings, and so forth, all these ceremonies were nearly the same.[46] Naturally, all those who took part had to be pure (sacrificer, priests, victims) just as in all great sacrifices, whatever they were. The Corpses 'impersonators of the spirits', had to have been approved by the ancestors through divination, and they had to purify themselves as the sacrificer did. The day had to be an auspicious one, and this was ascertained by the milfoil. During the ten days of purification, the final preparations were made: the walls and the roofs of the temples were repaired, the chapels and the platform were swept; the tablets were taken out of their stone coffers and set up in their places; and finally, on the eve of the festival, there was a grand display of vases and offerings.

When the day came, the king donned the dragon robe and the black cap, the queen put on the pheasant dress and her ceremonial wig, and each proceeded separately to the temple, followed respectively by the ministers and grand officers, and by their women. They entered to the sound of the *wang-hsia* march and took their places, he on the external platform of the temple next to the eastern stairway, she within and on the west side. Then all the Corpses, who on arrival had gone to the western lateral building to dress themselves in the ceremonial vestments of the deceased persons they represented, made their solemn entry to the sound of the *ssu-hsia* march. The praying-priest went forward to meet them and accompanied them — he had to act as go-between throughout the ceremony, since the dead and the living could not communicate directly. They washed their hands, then ascended to the temple by the western stairway, while the king, having awaited them in his place, went to greet and invite them (through the priest) to be seated. Without a word, they returned his greeting and sat down, each to the left of his tablet. When they had taken their places, there began the preliminary ceremony of inviting the spirits of the dead to come to the sacrifice and take their share of the offerings. First there was a libation: the king went to the western steps to fill his cup from a wine-vase shaped like an ox which had been placed there; and he offered this to the Corpses, who poured several drops on the ground as invitation to the souls living underground, the *p'o*, and they drank the rest. This was the first of the nine offerings which made up the whole of the sacrifice. Immediately afterwards, the queen, who had gone to fill her cup at the wine-vase decorated with thunderbolts placed next to the eastern steps, offered it to the Corpses, who — without making a libation — drank it. This was the second of the offerings. When the queen had returned to her place, the Corpses left the temple and went to seat themselves west of the gate, facing south, with the tablets placed upon mats nearby, to their right and facing east. They remained sitting there throughout all the morning ceremony, the immolation of the victims, and the preparations for the banquet.

The king went down into the court and, left arm uncovered, went before the main victim, a young bull designated for Hou-chi, the First Ancestor. He led it by a rope, followed by the ministers and grand officers carrying pieces of silk and lesser officers carrying armfuls of straw to place under the victim, and all singing its praises and proclaiming its beauty. The animal was tied to the stone slab set up in the middle of the court. The king, using a knife with its handle ornamented with little bells, cut off some hairs from near the ears and gathered several drops of blood, and gave these to the priest, who then went and offered them in the temple before the tablet of the First Ancestor, to show that the victim was perfect without and within. Thereupon the king killed it with arrows, with the same ceremony as at the *chiao*. It was undoubtedly then that the victims for the other ancestors were brought in and immolated, though without the king taking part directly and without offering the hair and the blood to the tablets.

When the killing was over the king opened up the principal victim with the belled knife, took out the liver, and then passed the knife to the ministers and the grand officers, who did the cutting-up. Some of the fat was taken and smeared upon stalks of artemisia, which were taken to the Corpses, who burned them so that the smoke might rise and invite the souls in heaven, the *hun*. Then the king, after having washed the principal victim's liver in wine, had it cooked and offered it to the Corpse of Hou-chi. The victim's head was taken into the temple, to the north wall, as an invitation to the soul residing in the tablet. Finally, the priest went to make a last invitation, for those souls who were far off, by an offering near the great gate of the temple. Nobody knew where the spirits were, so they were sought everywhere and great exertions were made to attract them though offerings in various places (in the chapel, in the court, near the gate), and cries of 'Are you there? Are you here?'[47]

While the souls of the dead were being invited, the cooks had been preparing the flesh of the victims. Once that was done, the king and queen, with assistants, set out the offerings. As a rule, in the ceremonies of the ancestral temple, the sacrificer was supposed to show respect by doing everything himself; so he took a direct part in all the preparations: 'He set out the cooked meat in wooden bowls; the raw meat, boned or not, on little tables; the meat roasted on hot stones or on a spit, in bowls covered with rushes or coarse cloth.' The variety of dishes allowed the spirits to choose, since 'how could one know what they prefer?' The priest went to present the offerings before the tablets, while the king bowed down twice, prostrating himself.[48] The morning ceremony finished in this way with the preparations for the banquet.

When all the offerings had been set out in order, the second part of the ceremony, the sacrifice itself, began. The Corpses were arranged in the order of the chapels in the ancestral temple, to right and to left of the Corpse of the First Ancestor.[49] They took the lungs of the victim and some millet, then some wine, and each offered some of these to the spirit he represented — who, thus summoned, came down into them for a moment. After that they sat down and ate in place of and on behalf of the spirit. When the Corpse had eaten the first three courses, he declared himself satisfied. The priest, seated next to the king, invited him in the king's name to eat more: 'The noble Corpse is not yet satisfied. I invite him to continue.' He was offered another course, which he tasted and then declared himself again to be satisfied. The king, saying nothing, kneeled and greeted him, inviting him to eat more, and he again took some of another course for the last time.

Then offerings of liquor were brought: the king and queen in turn offered him water, sweet wine, clarified wine, red wine. Each time he rose, poured out several drops as a libation to make the spirit come into him, then sat down again and drank. The sacrificer and all those present took part in the ceremony: when the king and the queen offered the cup to the Corpse, he thanked them by offering it to them in turn. When he had drunk five times, the king had the cup passed to his ministers; the seventh time, to the grand officers; the ninth time, among all the lesser officers.[50] At this moment, when 'hosts and guests, / offered the cup to one another, drinking around the circle',[51] six of the Corpses, those of the most recent ancestors, mingled with the crowd, proffering drinks and accepting them. Only the seventh, the one which bore the soul of the First Ancestor, Hou-chi, remained unmoving, too majestic to give himself over to such merriment.

When the feast was ended, the *shih* expressed his satisfaction and made the king promises of good fortune, which the priest immediately passed on:

> The skilful priest receives the declaration [of the spirits],
> he will pass it on to the pious descendant:
> 'The pious sacrifice is pleasing in odour,
> the spirits are satisfied with drink and with dishes;
> they grant you good fortune a hundredfold:
> such are your desires, such are their realizations;
> you have been precise, you have been diligent,
> you have been correct, you have been careful,
> for evermore they grant you the highest favours,
> by tens of thousands, by hundreds of thousands!'[52]

Then the bells and the drums sounded, the king returned to his place, and the priest announced: 'The spirits are completely drunk!' The Corpses then arose and retired solemnly to the accompaniment of music.[53]

The sacrifice was completed by a kind of communion banquet in which the remains of the offerings were consumed.[54] The Corpses (now no longer possessed by the spirits) ate what had been left over by the ancestors, the king ate what the Corpses had left, the three ministers ate what the king had left, the six grand officers what the ministers had left, the eight lesser officers what the grand officers had left. When these eight had finished, they rose and carried what remained down the steps to the temple court, where the others present ate them in the order of their hierarchical rank, finishing with the humblest — the butchers, the 'pheasants' (that is to say, the dancing-masters), and the gate-keepers,[55] who as men who had been condemned came last. The princes of the royal clan who had been unable to come and attend the sacrifice received their share of the meat, which was borne to them with all dispatch by carriers, *hsing-jen*, and which they ate after having themselves performed a ceremony to their own ancestors.

With the banquet the second part of the ceremony ended, but not all was finished. At this point commenced a third part, at least as important as the others, consisting of dignified dances accompanied by music and song in the courtyard of the ancestral temple: first the Great Warrior (Dance), *ta-wu*, then the Dance of Peace, *ta-hsia*. The first portrayed King Wu's expedition against Tsou of the Yin, his victory, and the pacification of the empire.[56] It consisted of six successive scenes, each with its own particular music, with song, a piece of poetry, and finally a detailed prose libretto explaining the facts represented and the evolutions of the ballet. This was a pantomime played by sixty-four dancers,[57] arranged in eight rows of eight men, the sons of great families attending the *Pi-yung kung* college. These came in, each dressed in a tunic embroidered with dragons, wearing a bonnet with a jade pendant, carrying in the right hand a jade hatchet and with a red shield on the left arm. The king, dressed in the same way, took his place on the east side; he gave orders, directing the dance, and played the role of King Wu, with the dancers representing his army.

The beginning was signalled by a drum-roll: this was the first scene, the departure of King Wu for his expedition. The dancers first took three steps forward to symbolize the opening of hostilities; then they stood motionless, shield on arm, to show the king meditating and awaiting the arrival of the feudatory chiefs,[58] then refusing to continue his march and withdrawing his army to the rear; and the scene ended with the dance of the army's departure: 'Forward, the troops beat the drums and shout; the troops unsheath their swords; those in front sing and those behind dance.'[59] In the meantime the blind musicians directed by the Master of Music sang the ode 'King Wu night and day', the words being:

> Majestic Heaven has settled its mandate;
> the two sovereigns have received it;
> now that he has become king, [Ch'eng] dare not rest;
> night and day he confirms the mandate [upon himself] profoundly,
> silently.
> Ah! he continues to make it gleam,
> he devotes his heart to it,
> so as to assure it for himself![60]

The second scene was the defeat of the tyrant Tsou of the Yin dynasty, and his execution with his two concubines. For a second time the drum was beaten to indicate that the fight was about to start. The king, or whoever was taking his place, 'holding the yellow hatchet in his left hand, brandishing a white pennant in his right hand to give a signal',[61] performed his steps and his movements. To represent the battle, the dancers leaped, struck the earth violently with their feet, and shook their arms; two men equipped with little bells and positioned at the ends of each rank urged them to the assault four times — that is to say, they had them advance several steps and then stopped to reform the lines. 'Today, advance no more than six or seven paces, then halt and set your ranks in order again! Courage, men!'[62] During this time the blind musicians chanted the ode of King Wu:

> O majestic King Wu
> naught equals your glory!
> Truly accomplished was King Wen,
> who opened the way for his descendant [Wu].
> Succeeding him, Wu, you receive [the heritage],
> you defeat Yin, you rebuke their cruelties,
> you bring your work to solidity.[63]

The third scene represented the 'march to the south', i.e., the return to Chou.[64] The dancers, divided into groups, advanced by simply marching, without leaping, so as to indicate that the task had been done, while the *Cho* ode was sung:

> Oh! powerful is the king's army,
> which he nurtures, obedient [to Heaven], in the night-time;
> when the day dawned,
> he took his great weaponry.

> We who, by the [celestial] favour, have received
> the work which the martial king accomplished,
> to use our heritage well,
> truly we will follow your example![65]

The fourth scene showed 'the king fixing the southern frontier', which does not suggest any precise episode of the legend, and the *Huan* ode was sung:

> At peace are the myriad countries,
> one prosperous year follows another,
> the Mandate of Heaven is not exhausted.
> How martial is King Wu,
> how his nobles trust him,
> he employs them in the four directions,
> and assures the establishment of his family.
> Oh! glorious before Heaven,
> who made him sovereign in place of Shang![66]

In the fifth scene, 'the division of government between the Duke of Chou and the Duke of Shao', the dancers spread out their rows and advanced, while the *Lai* ode was sung:

> King Wu laboured with zeal,
> and we have received [the celestial mandate] from him;
> we will spread it abroad by bearing it constantly in mind,
> henceforward we will seek to establish it firmly,
> this mandate of Chou;
> Oh! let us think of it constantly![67]

Finally, the sixth and last scene symbolized the return of peace: the dancers returned and arranged themselves at the point from which they had departed at the beginning of the first scene, and there they remained, putting one knee to the ground.[68] During this time, the *Pan* ode was sung:

> Oh! sovereign is Chou!
> He has scaled the high mountains,
> the steep mountains, the precipitous peaks;
> thus truly he has crossed the subjugated River;
> all under heaven
> he reunites under his dominion;
> Such is the mandate of Chou![69]

When the great martial dance *ta-wu* had finished, a dance of a peaceful character, the *ta-hsia*, was performed. Its invention was attributed to Yü the Great, and since it represented good government and universal peace, it was supposed to contribute to producing order and tranquillity in the empire. The various scenes of this dance are not known in detail; but each dancer was dressed in a robe of tight-fitting white silk, with an open tunic over that, and a skin cap. When the *ta-hsia* was finished, less important dances were probably performed in honour of various princes of the royal house: in Lu the Jen dance of the southern barbarians was done, and the Mei dance of the eastern barbarians; but these were dances peculiar to that country, designed to recall the submission of the neighbouring barbarian tribes.[70]

The ceremonies of the Ancestral Temple, though the most important, were not the only ones in honour of the ancestors. To some among them who had no tablet in the temple, the piety of a descendant had raised a special temple. To begin with, at the Chou court there was (and by imitation, there also was at the court of Lu) the Closed Palace, *Pi-kung*, raised to Chiang Yüan, the First Mother, Hsien-pi, the mother of the First Ancestor, Hou-chi.[71] 'As she had no husband at whose side she might receive offerings as a spouse' — since she had become a mother by walking over the footprint of the Lord on High — a special temple had been raised to her. It remained always closed, since the women's quarters were closed. On festival days, sacrifices were offered there and the *ta-hu* dance was performed in her honour, the origin of this dance being attributed to T'ang the Victorious, the founder of the Yin dynasty.

This sort of precedent allowed the worship of personages who had no place in the Ancestral Temple. Thus in Lu, in 718, a special temple was erected to the mother of Prince Huan (she was the secondary wife of Prince Hui, and in the Ancestral Temple only the legitimate wife had her tablet next to her husband's), and sacrifices were made to her, with dances.[72] But ceremonies of this kind always remained secondary in importance; the only official ancestral worship was that offered in the Ancestral Temple.

Ordinary patricians naturally did not have ceremonies this complicated: they did not have so many ancestors to sacrifice to, they offered fewer victims, they had no dancing. But in its general pattern the ritual remained the same, with women playing an important part throughout the whole ceremony, and with the obligation that the person making the sacrifice must himself serve the souls of his ancestors — servants could not replace him. If the sacrificer were a very young child and could not perform the ceremonies, he was not let off entirely on that account but was made to follow along, carried in the arms of his nurse, and he was thus deemed to have performed them. Those who had no ancestral temple erected a temporary altar in the principal room of the house, and there they set up the tablet of the deceased. A grandson of that ancestor served as the Corpse, and the sacrifice proceeded almost identically to those of kings, except that the number of presentations of wine and of dishes was much less. It ended likewise, with a sort of communion meal of all the family members, after which the Corpse declared that he had eaten his fill and was satisfied, and retired. The worship of ancestors was the cult of all patricians. Every noble family, great or small, had its ancestors who protected it; and the royal ritual had nothing special about it, being distinguished only by its magnificence.

Ceremonies for Special Occasions

Neither the cycle of seasonal festivals nor that of the festivals of the ancestral temple constituted the entire religious life of the king and the lords. Apart from everyday religious observances, every important action was surrounded with numerous ceremonies. Marriage was not complete until after a ceremony to the ancestors. When they had a son, they had to present him to the ancestors in his third month, by giving him a name, and a *suovetaurile* was offered at that time. The taking of the cap of manhood was also carried out in the presence of the ancestors, in their temple.

War, a serious business and one which put the whole state in danger, could not be conducted without a whole series of ceremonies.[73] The prince announced the declaration of war in the ancestral temple, and he gave orders to the commanding general in these terms: 'The trust of the God of the Soil and the God of the Harvest are placed in the general. At this moment the state is imperilled. I hope and pray that you will rise [to this peril].' The commission thus conferred, the auguries were consulted so as to set a fortunate day for the ceremonies of handing over drum and standard and the swearing-in of the general. When the day came, he went to the Ancestral Temple and then, after having received from the prince's hand the halberd and battle-axe and having had the commission for command of the army repeated, he cut his nails, dressed himself in funeral attire, and thus dedicated himself to death if that were required to bring victory. Then they proceeded to the mound of the God of the Soil, and the prince offered up a victim, the blood of which anointed the god's stone tablet, and he offered to the general a piece of the raw meat from the sacrifice. Then there was a grand review of the troops by the mound of the God of the Soil. It was probably at this moment that the drum, which was kept in the Ancestral Temple in peacetime, was given to the general after having been smeared with blood, often the blood of a human victim.

At the time of departure, the Count of Religious Affairs went to the Ancestral Temple to bring out the latest tablet, that of the reigning prince's father, and the Grand Priest went also to take the tablet of the God of the Soil. Each was placed in a chariot, for both had to accompany the army on campaign.[74] The God of the Soil and the Ancestor took an active part in the expedition: it was before the former that punishments were administered and before the latter that rewards were bestowed.[75] But the distinction was not always that clear, and punishments were also carried out before the Ancestor. Thus Ying of Chih, a grand officer of Chin who had been taken prisoner by the men of Ch'u, declared — when he was sent back to his country after ten years' captivity (588) — that he returned to be executed by his father in the ancestral temple.[76]

During the campaign, camp was never set up without making offerings to the God of the Soil of that locality; and every time the king entered the territory of a principality, he notified the Lord on High of this by a *lei* sacrifice — that is to say, by lighting a great bonfire.[77]

On returning, the Director of Horses, minister of war, led the triumphal entry of the victorious army into the capital: 'Holding in his right hand the flute with which he directed the songs of triumph, and in his left hand the battle-axe, he marched before the musicians. He made the offering to the God of the Soil.'[78] This often consisted of one or several prisoners whom he immolated and whose blood sprinkled the tablet, which he had just put back in its place. Others were offered up to the ancestors in their temple, or at the least they were shown off there. Thus in 569 Prince Tao of Chin sacrificed the Lord of Pi-yang in the chapel of his ancestor Prince Wu, when he returned to his capital after destroying the principality of Pi-yang. But from that time on human sacrifice was disfavoured, especially when the victim was a Chinese prince, so that an odd device was used to bring tradition and attitude into accord: the victim was presented as a barbarian prisoner, *yi-fu*.[79]

A great review was held outside the south gate of the Ancestral Temple. Every man brought there the heads of the enemies he had killed or led the prisoners he had taken, and these were arranged in order. The prince drank a cup of wine and offered wine to the troops; and when the scribes had counted the heads taken, he handed out rewards.[80] The heads were carried to the ancestors within the temple and there burned in their honour. Thus, it is said, King Wu had presented to his father Wen the head of the tyrant Tsou of the Yin. 'King Wu before the tablet, the Grand Master [of Music] brought [the corpse of] Tsou, King of Shang. He hung the head by the White Standard, and the heads of Tsou's two wives by the Red Standard. Then, having thus exposed the severed heads, he entered the Ancestral Temple of Chou to burn them.'[81] After that were presented yet other offerings — bullocks, sheep, pigs, and so on — to the God of the Soil and to the ancestors. But if the army had suffered a defeat, it sufficed to announce this to the ancestors and to the God of the Soil by carrying the tablets each to its place with an offering, and the Director of Horses donned mourning vestments to perform the ceremony.[82]

That was not all. An army departing on campaign did not set out until a sacrifice had been offered to the Ancestor of Horses. Again, a city which was besieged, or feared that it might be, prepared itself with numerous ceremonies. It was necessary to make sacrifices to the four cardinal points of the compass. If the enemy came from the east, a cock was offered on an altar erected at the eastern gate; if he came from the south, a dog near the south gate; if from the west, the victim was a sheep; if from the north, a pig. The sorcerers mounted the wall and drew auguries from the wind and from the emanations.[83]

War was not the only unforeseeable event which was the occasion for religious ceremonies. If an eclipse of the sun occurred, it was necessary to go to the sun's assistance. The king went in haste to the mound of the God of the Soil and tied it with a red cord, which he wrapped three times around the tree of the god. Followed by his grand officers, he arranged them in battle formation, had the drum beaten, and himself loosed arrows with 'the bow which aids the sun'. At the same time a victim was sacrificed to the God of the Soil, in the same way as was done whenever arms were taken up near him. Princes, for their part also had the drum beaten, but only in the court of the palace and they were not allowed to offend the God of the Soil by binding him.[84]

In case of flood, the same sort of ceremony was performed they had to protect themselves with arms in hand against the invading waters, just as they had struggled to save the sun, so the drum was beaten and a victim was immolated to the God of the

Soil.[85] After a prolonged drought, when the ordinary sacrifices had been carried out in vain, the sorceresses were made to dance, or some of them were even burned, to get rain.[86]

Was the king ill? Priests, diviners, sorcerers sought to find which offended deity might have visited this malady upon him, so as to appease him by a sacrifice and obtain recovery from him.[87] Sometimes ceremonies were lavished upon even the least happening which was extraordinary. In the second half of the seventh century, a gust of wind blew a strange seabird against the east gate of the Lu capital. The Prince of Lu had it taken at once to the Ancestral Temple, and for three days he offered sacrifices accompanied by music.[88]

In these circumstances, kings and princes only followed the example of common patricians who similarly called in sorcerers or diviners for each illness, each discomfort, each strange occurrence, and sacrificed according to their prescriptions.

5
Religious Feeling

In this religion which was above all social and official, not individual, and which ritualism invaded and desiccated day by day, what place remained for religious feeling? This seems to have varied under the influence of the philosophical schools of the middle and end of the Chou dynasty.

Religious sentiment in antiquity, corresponding precisely to the actual practices of the religion — and from which that faith disengaged itself only to perish — consisted above all in a strict and constant conformity between public and personal acts and the overall shape of the periods of the religious cycle.[1] Sacrifices and great festivals did not indeed constitute all of religious life; it was far from being as limited as that. It ordered all personal life and all social relations by its peculiar observances and its seasonal taboos. That was the very fount of religious life; and the sacrifices, however important, were only marking-posts at particularly critical moments of the periodic cycle. This profound feeling was all the more important because only through it was the great mass of the population — most patricians (those who had no responsible function) and all plebeians — in communion. Only through it did they take part in the general religious life.

In summer, when the village chiefs opened the village gates and the chiefs of families the doors of their houses, when the tolls were suppressed, when all — people and animals — left the houses of the village to go and live in the huts of the fields, when the strict family ties were loosened and families grouped themselves by threes in the same hut, everybody knew that this was because — in the season of open air and universal openness

— it was essential for everything to be positively open; and they felt that, by fulfilling the 'summer laws', every person in his sphere contributed towards assuring the working of the world. By the same token, when in winter the gates of villages and the doors of houses were closed and plastered over to seal them more tightly, when all — men and beasts — had to go back into the house and the stable (so much so that any wandering animal belonged to anybody who took it and shut it in), they knew that 'by this they assisted in the closing and securing of heaven and earth',[2] and were thus participating in the continuation of the universal order.

Upon this general view, however, there had been superposed an idea among the privileged classes who carried out the sacrifices that those ceremonies ought to bring them personal and immediate advantages. The ritual itself contributed to this, since at the end of the ceremonies to the ancestors, the Corpse promised good fortune in giving thanks for the offerings which had been made to him. This feeling, natural though contrary to the fundamental ideas of the official religion, was criticized. Thus the Internal Scribe Kuo, who had been present at the sacrifice which the Duke of Kuo offered to the spirit of Chu of Tan (the son of the mythical emperor Yao) and had observed that the duke was asking an increase in his territory, declared that this self-centredness would irritate the spirit and bring misfortune — a prediction which the conquest of Kuo by the Prince of Chin proved true several years later, in 658. This idea of personal gain, *ch'iu-li*, was contradictory to that pursuit of the general interest which should have been the main object of religious ceremonies; and it was perhaps this opposition which led to the classification of sacrifices by value, holding as evil those which were carried out for any egoistic purpose, quite apart from any defect of ritual. This was an idea current in the fourth century: it was expressed often in that period by the author of the *Tso chuan*. Several schools which then adopted this notion extended it, attaching the greatest significance to the intention, and in general to the spiritual condition, of the sacrificer in the sacrifice. The school of Mo-tzu attributes to the Master a comparison between the man who serves the spirits well and the good servant who does his duty even when his master is not watching, which implies the absence of any egoistic intention.

The Confucian school interpreted a saying of Confucius thus: 'In sacrificing [to the souls of the ancestors] it is necessary to act as though the ancestors [themselves] were present; in sacrificing to the gods, it is necessary to act as though the gods were present.'

The school took a very clear position on this point. 'On the days of sacrifice, [King Wen] was half joyous and half sad: during the offering he was joyous [for the presence of his relatives]; when it was ended he was sad [at their departure].' And again, 'the filial son is totally zealous, totally sincere, totally respectful'; and the ritual acts must be only the externalization of private feelings, though without the slightest innovation — whether of restraint or of addition — being allowed. Thus one arrived at a justification of ritualism: a simple formulation of outward movements inspired by internal sentiments.

If the Chinese of that time sought to rectify his intentions so that his sacrifice might be good, it was not always because he believed that the spirits were really present. Among certain circles of the literati, influenced by the school of the Diviners and their theory of the *yin* and the *yang*, as well as that of the Taoist school, there were doubts as to the existence of gods and spirits. Such ideas were widespread enough so that Mo-tzu, in the second half of the fifth century, devoted a section of his work to demonstrating their existence.

In fact, the world could be explained by the theory of *yin* and *yang*, without the intervention of any god or personal spirit, by the reciprocal interaction of the two primordial substances which, in their transformations, produced all things. Before these grand cosmic laws, universal and immutable, the divinities of the official pantheon cut a poor figure. The Lord on High could still save himself by becoming more and more depersonalized,[3] to become simply Heaven, *T'ien* — which is to say, the first and most general materialization of the *yang*, just as Sovereign Earth and, in general, all the gods of the soil became the materialization of the *yin*. But there was no place for the others. And as for the Lord on High himself, there was doubt that he could intervene in particular cases. When Prince Ching of Ch'i was ill and thought to immolate his praying-priest so as to send him to Shang-ti to eulogize his lord, the minister Yen-tzu dissuaded him by saying: 'If the Lord on High is all-powerful, [your priest] will be unable to deceive him. If he is not all-powerful, the priest will serve no purpose!'[4]

Likewise, with regard to the souls of the dead, although nothing was said flatly as to their existence, doubts were expressed about whether they had retained full consciousness; and the phrase 'if the dead possess consciousness'[5] recurs frequently in the writings of the end of Chou. This trend of thought resulted in a tendency to restrain, not the sacrifices and religious festivals themselves, but the conception people had of the role, always rather vague, which the gods and the spirits played in the ceremonies of worship; and it tended to eliminate them from the philosophical interpretations regarding the efficacy of the sacrifice.

The two currents of thought should have been mutually exclusive — since the one inclined towards the belief that the spirits were actually present at the ceremonies carried out in their honour, while the other tended to deny their existence. Yet they were united without much trouble, probably because they brought out two different faces of the religious act. The one directed attention to the person making the sacrifice and to the state of his soul, holding to the notion that the sacrificer must achieve a particular spiritual condition, concentrate his entire attention upon the actual ceremony, and moreover prepare himself for it by cultivating his Virtue and his morality. The other explained the efficacy of the entire ceremony rationally, and that gave the general coloration to the mixture.

On the other hand, the old ideas regarding the importance of conformity to the regular rhythm of the cyclical periods had lost none of their force. From them sprang a particular theory regarding the religious festivals: they were conceived as procedures designed to harmonize the Celestial Norm, *t'ien-tao* (that is to say, the action of the *yin* and the *yang* through the Five Elements in the physical world), and the Human Norm, *jen-tao* (that is, actions in the moral world, on the one hand by performing them at precisely the right time, and on the other by rectifying one's intentions at that moment, without the intervention of any personal divinity). In this way it became possible to explain all the ceremonies rationally and in detail.[6]

For example, an eclipse of the sun or moon provided the occasion for a military ceremony by the mound of the God of the Soil, which would effect the rescue of the heavenly body and its delivery from the monster which was devouring it. For this mythological explanation another, philosophical, one was substituted: light — the sun — being *yang*, and darkness *yin*, the eclipse is the triumph of *yin* over *yang*. But the earth is *yin* and consequently so is the God of the Soil; and this is why one goes to the aid of the *yang* by struggling against the *yin*, to that end attacking the God of the Soil, the representative of the *yin*. This new explanation completely altered the meaning of the ceremony, but the meaning of religious acts alters from generation to generation, though the rituals remain unchanged.

If life contracted in winter, if one was not to work in the fields, it was because that was the time dominated by the *yin*, repose; if life expanded in summer, if all was opened in that season, if one laboured in the fields, it was because that was the time when the *yang*, activity, was predominant. The *yang* was indeed in the ascendant and the *yin* on the decline until the summer solstice, after which they waxed and waned inversely until the winter solstice. The equinoxes were their times of equality. If the Son of Heaven had to dwell each season in a different pavilion of the Sacred Palace, he did this in order to follow the movements of the *yin* and the *yang* across the seasons: he punished in autumn (*yin*) and rewarded in spring (*yang*), and moreover, each of the five halls of the palace was connected to one of the Five Elements.

On the other hand, *yin* was admittedly inferior to *yang* and had to be treated differently: one commanded *yin*, one attacked it, while one beseeched *yang*. This is why, in time of flood, it was sufficient to reinforce the *yin* by moving the marketplace. The market, established by the wife of the sovereign and situated to the north, was *yin*. By moving it, with ceremonies over which the lord's wife again presided, the *yin* was reinforced and put in position to triumph over the *yang*. In time of drought, however, the *yin* was compelled to manifest itself by making sorceresses dance in the sun: they were *yin*, as were the spirits by which they were possessed, while the sun was *yang*. Thus the ancient dance ritual of the sorcerers and sorceresses, rain-makers, which had originally been sufficient by itself to produce rain, had changed its meaning to become no more than one of the particular instances of the alternation of the *yin* and the *yang*. The offering to the dead included a libation to the subterranean *p'o* and smoke addressed to the celestial *hun*; and it was explained that man, like all things, was composed of the *yin* and the *yang*. Nothing escaped this interpretation, the simplicity of which had a seeming rationality quite seductive to the scholars of the day.

They even managed to justify all sorts of religious innovations by this. Astrology, which Mediterranean influences introduced into China in about the fourth century B.C., found itself accepted, thanks to the assimilation of the Virtues of the Five Planets into those of the Five Elements; and with it came a whole mythology and a worship of the stars which was foreign in origin. Old cults were transformed: that of the Five Lords, for example, into which the theory of the Five Elements and of astrology penetrated together. And it was under the influence of analogous ideas that, towards the end of the Chou period, there arose the theory of the sacrifices *feng* and *shan*, which were to play so great a role in the dynastic worship of subsequent centuries. For, if these were perhaps extremely ancient sacrifices, their reappearance in this era was a true creation. Into it, besides the notions of establishing a new order by the transmission of the line of former sovereigns and the enthronement of a new line — ideas which were undoubtedly traditional — were imported ideas of personal longevity acquired by the sovereign who carried out the rite, and new ideas borrowed from the astrological, numerical, and other speculations of the time.

In the highly special situation of scholarly circles at the end of the Chou period were thus formed the religious theories which, surviving the ancient religion itself, had to serve as the basis for the official orthodoxy of the scholars in Han times and which, developing from century to century, have lasted until our time. But these ideas, destined to have so grand an expansion later, were at the end of Chou times only those of an élite. It was, however, a rather numerous élite, of patricians learned in the various schools of philosophy, who gradually influenced the patrons they followed — sometimes even certain princes, such as King Hui-ch'eng of Wei at the end of the fourth century.

Among all of those from high to low in the social scale who had not felt the influence of the philosophers, religious feeling remained at the same time more simple and more crude. They continued to believe in the gods, to whom were ascribed a personal and often arbitrary will. Thus the defeat suffered in 632 by Te-ch'en of Ch'eng (Tzu-yü), a general of Ch'u, at Ch'eng-p'u on the bank of the Yellow River — the first defeat Ch'u had suffered after years of uninterrupted success — was attributed to the ill will of the Count of the River. Te-ch'en had refused to present him with a deerskin cap ornamented with jade, which the count had asked of him in a dream just before the battle.[7] And despite the protestations of the scholars declaring that 'one does not buy the gods',[8] many remained persuaded that the abundance of sacrifices was pleasing to them and inclined them to grant good fortune, and similarly that stinginess in offerings brought bad luck, even when it was not punished immediately by the famished and discontented spirit.[9]

Sometimes a superstitious terror would seize an entire city: in 543, Po-yu, a former minister driven out of the principality of Cheng, had been killed right in the marketplace when, having re-entered the capital by surprise, he tried to retake power; and a real terror weighed upon the city for several years. His soul lurked around the place of his death; often, without reason, suddenly panic-stricken people would flee, crying out, 'Po-yu is here!' Fear was at its height when he appeared in a dream to a citizen to announce the imminent death of his two assassins on a set day (536). The people were calmed only after his office had been given to his son (535), so that it was permissible to make regular sacrifices to him and thus appease the irritated soul.[10]

Altogether, from Chou times on, one sees manifested the characteristic attitude of the Chinese towards religious ideas and acts. Both were accepted (belief in the power of spirits and in the vengeance of ghosts, on the one hand, ritual acts and gestures, on the other) on the condition that they could be given a philosophical and rationalistic explanation, bringing no religious agency into play. This attitude, in which various superstitious practices and a theoretical rationalism were mixed in various degrees, has remained that of cultivated Chinese to our own day; and it has hardly altered, even though the content of the religion itself has been transformed in the course of the centuries.

Book III
The Hegemonies[1]

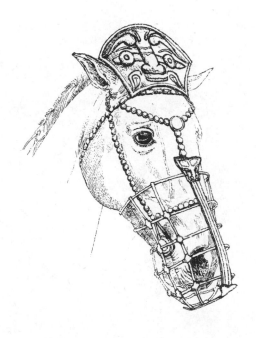

1

The Territorial Formation of the Great Principalities

The death of King Yu of Chou and the sack of the capital had struck a severe blow at the monarchy. When the barbarians departed, one of the nobles, Han, Duke of Kuo, placed one of the King's sons, Prince Yü-ch'en, upon the throne; and the new King, unable to remain in the ruined palace, went and set himself up nearby at Hui. But the Count of Shen and his partisans for their part had nominated Yi-chiu, the Prince Royal (and later King P'ing), who had taken refuge near them; and almost all the lords acknowledged him. At the same time, they dared not go and attack the King of Hui in his western lands, and it was to the capital Lo-yi (near modern Ho-nan fu, on the Lo River) that P'ing was led and solemnly enthroned (770). The royal domain was thus divided into two halves, the western portion — the valley of the Wei, with its ancient capital, Hao — belonging to the King of Hui, and the eastern portion — the valley of the Lo — alone remaining to King P'ing. Only some twenty years later were the two segments reunited again, when the Prince of Chin vanquished and killed the King of Hui (750).

The royal power never succeeded in recovering, as it had once been able to do after the exile of Li. The loss of the capital and of the old hereditary domain was a serious blow: in the country where he was established, the new king was going to be quite isolated. He was very weak: seven great lords alone had followed him and, in order to bind them to him, he had to guarantee, by a solemn oath upon a red bull, that their functions would remain hereditary within their families.[2] Abroad, however, he still retained his prestige and maintained a genuine authority over the feudatories, at least the nearest of them — the princes of

Chin, of Yü, of Kuo, of Wey, of Cheng, of Ts'ai, of Ch'en, and of Shen. Several of these eagerly contested for high offices at court, and in 750 neither the Prince of Chin, after having destroyed the kingdom of Hui, nor the Count of Ch'in, after having defeated the barbarians, dared to appropriate for himself the domains of the vanquished, but restored them to the king.[3]

Moreover, the king still mixed actively in the affairs of the feudatories and let them feel his authority: twice in the last years of the eighth century, in 716 and 708, Huan, P'ing's successor, sent an army to re-establish order in Chin, where a too-well-endowed younger son and his descendants, the counts of Ch'ü-wu, had dethroned their sovereigns to set themselves up instead. But during three-quarters of a century, under P'ing and Huan, power remained in the hands of the counts of Cheng, who succeeded one another from father to son in the post of first minister and who, in this long and uninterrupted exercise of the court's highest dignity, saw nothing but a means of most easily satisfying their personal ambitions and aggrandizing their fief at the expense of their neighbours.

This clan were quite closely related to the king — since they were descended from a younger brother of King Hsüan who, after having held the post of *ssu-t'u* under his nephew, King Yu, had in 773 received a small fief not far from present-day K'ai-feng and, remaining himself at court, had sent his son to take up the fief. There, the son had joined hands with Yi-chiu, then heir apparent, and his maternal grandfather, the Prince of Shen, whose daughter he would later marry.[4] With the Prince of Shen, the Count of Wey, and other lords of the area, he participated in placing this Yi-chiu upon the throne as King P'ing and installing him at Lo-yi. He was rewarded for this by the post of *ssu-t'u* which his father had held,[5] and soon afterwards by a new dignity (768), probably that of count.[6] This represented a political application of the tradition according to which, at the beginning of the dynasty, power had been divided between two counts, the dukes of Shao and of Chou. Count Wu of Cheng took advantage of this to molest his neighbours and augment his own domain: in 767, he seized Eastern Kuo, at the junction of the River Lo with the Yellow River, and little by little made for himself quite an important principality.

At his death (744) his son Chuang succeeded him both as Count of Cheng and as minister, and continued to advance his own affairs under the cover of his public post. Already he was too powerful for the king to shake off the yoke. He tried to do so unsuccessfully towards the end of his reign, seeking to diminish the authority of Cheng by having it shared with the Duke of Southern Kuo. The circumstances seemed favourable, for Chuang was occupied in struggling against his younger brother , who had just rebelled with the aid of his mother (722). But the revolt was quickly snuffed out and the king had to abandon his project; he even had — humiliatingly enough — to ally himself to Chuang definitively by an exchange of hostages.

At P'ing's death (720), his grandson Huan tried once more to rid himself of this inconvenient guardianship; he named the Duke of Kuo minister. Chuang revenged himself by refusing homage and ravaging the royal lands: it was only in 717 that he decided to go to court. The king committed the error of giving this too-powerful vassal an unfavourable reception: he went away furious and returned no more.

Count Chuang did not distress himself overmuch at his disgrace: he considered himself now strong enough to continue his course alone. His ambition was to achieve a great principality in the plain at the elbow of the Yellow River, by subduing or annihilating all the seigniories of the region, and probably end by overthrowing the king and setting himself in his place. All the threatened neighbours formed a league and enlisted King Huan, who had scarcely less to fear than they did and who moreover had to punish this vassal for never appearing at court for ten years. In the autumn of 707, he set himself at the head of an expedition against Cheng; it was disastrous. At the first encounter the troops of the lords scattered, leaving the royal army alone; the king, hard pressed, succeeded nevertheless in effecting a retreat, but during the fighting he was himself wounded in the shoulder by an arrow.[7] This defeat at Hsü-ko marked the final downfall of the monarchy; from that moment it was clear that the king no longer had any real power at all.

In the meantime, if the Count of Cheng was thus rid of all concern in that quarter, he was still far from having attained his purpose. Indeed, in expanding, his lands had come to butt against two long-established principalities, Wey on the north and Sung on the east. These were two fragments of the ancient domain of the Yin kings, dismembered after the conquest: Wey had been formed from the capital and lands situated north of the Yellow River, while the dukes of Sung were reduced to retaining only the southern part, around Po, one of the first capitals of their family, southeast of the Yellow River, in the vicinity of modern Kuei-te fu. These two principalities, with Cheng the newcomer, found themselves nearly equal in power, so much so that none of them succeeded in gaining the upper hand, and so that the great state of which Chuang had dreamed could never be established.

On the contrary, the mutual fears and jealousies began to develop a long rivalry which would be ended only with the termination of their very existence. A little later, Wey was put out of the contest by the repeated incursions of the Ti, the barbarians of the mountains separating Shansi from Honan, incursions which ruined her completely in the first half of the seventh century; but the rivalry between Cheng and Sung lasted for centuries, neither of them being strong enough to secure a definitive success. In the beginning Cheng failed to get supremacy; at that time, in the last years of the eighth century, Chuang, profiting by the troubles which the assassination of Duke Shang had unleashed in Sung, succeeded in placing one of his followers on the throne of that principality (710). When, however, Chuang himself died ten years later, the Duke of Sung escaped from this tutelage by aiding a pretender, T'u, whose mother belonged to a great family of Sung, to overthrow his brother Count Chao and put himself in his place (701). From then on the middle region of the Yellow River remained decisively divided into a series of petty territories of small extent — the Royal Domain, Cheng, Wey, Sung — none of which was ever strong enough to subdue the others. On the other hand, in the regions farther away from the capital, where the central power was less able to convert itself, the scatter of small domains was compacted into several great principalities: Chin in the north, Ch'in in the west, Ch'i in the northeast, Ch'u in the south. The way in which this consolidation occurred varied greatly from case to case.

On the lower River Chi, the principality of Ch'i seems to have been formed very early: inscriptions of Yin times already include the name. From the most ancient times it seems to have been established in its almost definitive boundaries, between the Yellow River and the sea, on the borders of the present-day provinces, Hopei and Shantung, and on both banks of the Chi, to the south of which the capital Lin-tzu was erected.[8] The princes of Ch'i would later claim that they owed their authority in the east to the Duke of Chou, who had sent the Duke of Shao to bring them this charge: 'East to the sea, west to the River, south to Mu-ling, north to Wu-ti, the lords of the five degrees and the chiefs of nine provinces, in truth you will have the right to punish them'[9] — which corresponds to the mandate of a territorial count, *fang-po*. This document is evidently not authentic; but at least it underlines a precise fact, the antiquity of the unity of Ch'i.

On the other hand, in the north and west, Chin and Ch'in had to establish themselves painfully by war and diplomacy during the eighth and seventh centuries. Chin had originally been a small territory a hundred *li* in area, situated in southwestern Shansi between the lower River Fen to the north and the Yellow River on the west, with the city of Yi as capital: it is supposed to have been the ancient T'ang seized by King Wu from the descendants of the Emperor Yao. It was a small domain, like its neighbours; it was even on the point of breaking up for a moment during a civil war when — Prince Chao having committed the imprudence of giving his uncle Ch'eng-shih the important territory of Ch'ü-wu[10] as a fief suzerains (745) — the counts of Ch'ü-wu, more powerful than their suzerains, sought to supplant them and were in constant revolt and war against them for sixty years. The princes of Chin became so feeble that they had to call the royal authority to their aid for defence against their turbulent vassal.[11] But in 678 Wu of Ch'ü-wu finally succeeded, after having assassinated Prince Min, in having himself recognized by King Hsi, through sending him all the treasure of Chin.

Unity was thus re-established and the principality developed rapidly. Wu, already very old, reigned only two years; but his son Hsien was an energetic prince who, during his quarter century of reign (676–651), knew how first to establish his authority firmly over his vassals, and then to aquire primacy in the region. The civil wars between the princes of Chin and the counts of Ch'ü-wu had not been without profit to their vassals. The return of peace could hardly please them and, among them, the uncles and cousins of Hsien were the most turbulent, especially because the prince had taken for chief minister, outside them and his own family, Wei of the Shih, a refugee at his court and a descendant of the Count of Tu who had earlier been assassinated by King Hsüan. Some of them were exiled, others put to death, an ill-conceived revolt of the last allowed the prince to rid himself of them by general massacre (669). Then, since he saw those opponents as retaining too many partisans at the capital, he abandoned it and went to establish himself at Chiang, which he fortified.[12]

Thus secure within the state, he began to expand at the expense of his neighbours. His territory was still quite small: to the west, Keng and Wei, to the southwest Jui and Hsün, to the south Yü and Kuo were immediate vassals of the king and had taken part in the campaigns against Ch'ü-wu. To the north it was the same with Huo, since the lords of Chao had given themselves to Chin, probably in order to have its aid against the Ti barbarians; and Su of Chao was then Prince Hsien's charioteer. The whole triangle contained within the two branches of the River was conquered (661). Soon even crossing the River, Hsien seized Han to the west and Kuo to the south; then he achieved the unification of his territory by the conquest of Yü on the way back from his expedition against Kuo (655).

The conquered fiefs were distributed to those loyal to Chin: Su of Chao, the charioteer, received Keng; Wan of Pi, the halberdier in the chariot, received Wei; Wu-tzu, the prince's uncle, received Han. Elsewhere, Hsien extended his authority eastward and gradually subdued the country of the Red Ti, *Ch'ih Ti*: in 660 the heir apparent, Shen-sheng, led a great expedition against the Kao-lo of the eastern mountains,[13] and subdued them. Thus in a few years the entire organization of the territories north of the Yellow River had completely changed: in the place of numerous fiefs directly answerable to the king and unsubdued territories peopled by barbarians, a great principality had been formed which had subjugated all its old neighbours, removing them from the royal power. 'At that time' (652), says Ssu-ma Ch'ien, 'Chin was powerful: to the west it possessed Ho-hsi and its territory bordered Ch'in; to the north it bordered upon the Ti; to the east, it reached to Ho-nei.'[14]

During this time, on the other side of the Yellow River, in the Wei Valley, events of the same kind concentrated power in the hands of the counts of Ch'in. Their ancestor was a younger son of the family of Ta-lo on the River Ch'ien, who had become the favourite of King Hsiao to the point where the latter had wished for a time to declare him heir of Ta-lo at the expense of his brother. He must have renounced this project for fear of alienating his minister, the Count of Shen, whose daughter was the mother of the legitimate heir whom the king wished to dispossess; and in exchange he had given to his favourite in fief the territory of Ch'in on the upper River Wei. About a century later, the Lord of Ch'in covered himself with glory by winning a brilliant victory over the Jung, who came back to pillage the capital and put King Yu to death; then, when a son of King Yu proclaimed himself king at Hui, in the upper valley of the Wei, the Lord of Ch'in refused him allegiance and acknowledged himself vassal to King P'ing, who was the farther away. The latter rewarded him by bestowing the territory of Ch'i and naming him count, which is to say by conferring upon him the government of the province of Yung, where the eastern capital was (770).[15]

It was for the time being a somewhat illusory title, since the province was partly in the hands of barbarians and partly in the hands of the King of Hui, both still dangerous, as the experience of Prince Hsiang showed (he was killed in the course of a victorious expedition against the Jung, in 766). But when Count Wen had gained new successes over them, and when the King of Hui had been put to death by the Prince of Chin (750), it was possible to make something of the title. It is true that Wen kept none of the territories situated east of Ch'i,[16] which he had just reconquered, restoring them to the king. But the king was far off, at Lo-yi, while the counts had their residence quite close by, at modern Ch'in-ch'eng (in Kansu, near the Shensi border), where they had been established since 762; and with the gradual weakening of the royal power the entire countryside was soon to fall into their hands. They had first to rid themselves of the Jung barbarians, who held not only the mountains north and south but also the outlets to the plain, and whose constant incursions made life impossible for the Chinese settlers in the Wei Valley. Ch'in waged war against them unceasingly. Wen's grandson, Ning, subdued the nearest, those who had been hemmed in amid Chinese territories, the Tang-she,[17] in the hills which separate the River Ching from the River Wei, towards San-yüan (713). Then his son Wu subjugated the P'eng-hsi of Po-shui on the River Lo, [18] and his victory brought him to the foot of Hua-shan and the banks of the Huang Ho (697).

He immediately took advantage of this success to annihilate the unresisting fiefs of the region. The most important of them were Cheng — the old domain which had given their title to the counts of Cheng before they followed King P'ing to his new capital, Lo-yi — and Kuo,[19] situated near modern Pao-chi. These he annexed in 687, and the king, too far away, could not save them. The counts of Ch'in, wiser than their neighbours of Chin, did not creat fiefs in the conquered territories but placed them under their own direct administration and established small districts, *hsien,* there.[20]

Meanwhile the lords from the banks of the Yellow River found themselves in an awkward position between the rival ambitions of Chin and Ch'in, against which the royal power was no longer in condition to protect them. The counts of Jui and of Liang, whose domains were located between Lung-men and the confluence of the River Lo, did not wait to be attacked and, in 677, came to give homage to Ch'in.[21] This humiliation did not protect them long: in 640 both were dispossessed by Ch'in, scarcely fifteen years after their neighbour, the Prince of Han, who had not imitated them, had been subdued by Chin.

Thus, in the same period as Chin managed to organize itself north of the Yellow River, Ch'in unified the valley of the Wei to its own advantage. The two principalities arrived together at the banks of the Yellow River and went on to commence their long rivalry for the territory of Ho-hsi (the west of the River), situated between the River Lo and the River. The first clash took place in 645, at the battle of Han, where Prince Hui of Chin was defeated and taken prisoner;[22] but with the reign of Wen, Chin became too powerful for any successes won over her from time to time to be lasting, and the frontier hardly changed for three centuries. Ch'in at the same time pushed southwards, into the upper valley of the River Han, where her progress would soon bring her into collision with the advance which the princes of Ch'u were making in the opposite direction, driving up the same river.

Indeed, while great states were thus being formed in the north, it happened that in the extreme south of the Chinese world, even beyond the limits of the 'central kingdoms', the barbarian tribes who occupied the great plain formed by the confluence of the Yangtze and the Han began to organize themselves under Chinese influence; and a line of petty chiefs from the region immediately downstream from the Yangtze rapids at I-ch'ang, around modern Chiang-ling, established there the powerful kingdom of Ch'u.[23] King Chao of Chou had already made an expedition thither, it was said, but on the way back he was drowned in the River Han. It seems, at the same time, that this area had been a part of the Western Chou empire, since it is included within the limits of the *Yü kung*, under the name of the province of Ching; but, being very distant, it undoubtedly split off as soon as the royal power began to weaken, and at the end of the eighth century its sovereigns, to whom the royal court refused any title superior to that of sire, *tzu*, had taken that of king to show that they considered themselves entirely independent. Yet their organization, still altogether barbarian, remained rudimentary.

Tradition credits King Wu, who reigned for the whole second half of the seventh century (740–690), with the first military organization of Ch'u; for the first time he planned the arrangement and disposition of his troops, at the same time changing their weapons by giving them the large Chinese pike-with-hooks, the *chieh,* following his first conquests in China (690). Naturally the rich lands of the north excited the greed of these princes and their barbarian subjects; in the ninth century King Hsüan must have established a kind of frontier borderland with fortified cities, which he gave to lords of his court, Hsieh to the Count of Shen, and so on. At the end of the eighth century, with the decline of the royal authority, the petty seignories of the frontiers (Yün, Shen, Hsieh, Chen, and Sui), thrown back upon their own resources, saw their territories constantly raided by their turbulent southern neighbours. If their fortresses resisted siege well enough, the countryside was pillaged and ravaged by the barbarians, who retired as soon as they had struck. In 704 the kingdom of Ch'u reached the southern foot of the Huai Mountains when, following several expeditions against the Lord of Sui, the most important ruler of the region, King Wu imposed his suzerainty upon that state as well as its neighbours, Erh, Chen, Yun (701), and Chiao (700), and obliged them all to recognize him as king. This was only a beginning: in 688 his son King Wen attacked Shen, a little to the northwest, near present-day Nan-yang fu; and ten years later, in 678, he conquered the seigniory of Teng. In a few years he had subdued all the petty states south of the mountains which mark the northern border of the Yangtze Valley, annexing the territory of some and contenting himself with reducing others to vassalage. Master of the passes, he had thenceforward a solid frontier which enabled him to resist any aggression coming from the north, while he could himself raid and pillage the Chinese plains of the north at his will: he took advantage of this in 684, when he took the Prince of Ts'ai prisoner. At the same time, he drew within his influence the savage tribes of the west and the south: in 703, the chief of the people of Pa, who occupied the narrow plain and the mountainous regions of what is now eastern Szechuan, on the banks of the Yangtze River upstream from the Yi-ch'ang rapids, asked for his aid and became his ally.

Thus within a few years, while the royal power weakened more and more under incompetent kings and lost its moral prestige through the selfish and shabby struggles into which the policies of the counts of Cheng led it, new powers grew up in the various parts of the Chinese world: real power slipped out of the weakened hands of the Chou kings, passing to others more vigorous.

2

The Hegemony of Ch'i

When the great newly-formed states began to confront one
another in the first half of the seventh century, the most
powerful and best organized was that of Ch'i.[1] Local tradition
some centuries later attributed to Prince Huan (685–643) and to
his wise minister Kuan Chung the credit for an organization to
which they perhaps put the finishing touches, but which was
probably the work of several generations.

A plains state, Ch'i had been quite easily brought under an
administration tending towards centralization and, although
feudal tenure was the very basis of organization there, as
throughout ancient China, Ch'i had not accepted with that
system so complete an autonomy of vassals as in the hill states.
Even outside the prince's own domain, *kuo*, those of the vassals,
pi, were redivided into regular districts, which allowed for them
to be supervised and for their lords to be kept in hand, and at the
same time effected the proper staffing of the regular armed
forces and avoided the confusion of conscripted masses.

The prince's own domain, *kuo*,[2] was divided into fifteen
districts, *hsiang*, each administered by a noble, *lang-jen*; each
district into ten marches, *lien*, each administered by a chief, *chang*;
each march into four boroughs, *li*, each theoretically containing
fifty families divided into tens, *kuei*. These fifteen districts
comprised only the population attached to the soil: that is to say,
the nobles, *shih*, who had property or enjoyed the use of the land,
with their peasants. But outside these fifteen territorial districts
were formed six fictitious 'districts' where were assigned all those
who had no connection with the land: that is to say the artisans
and the merchants, of whom no military service was demanded.

This administrative organization served as a framework for the army; and every chief of a territorial subdivision was at the same time the leader of his own contingent in time of war. Each group of ten families furnished a squad of five men, *wu*; each borough, a section to accompany a chariot, *hsiao jung*, under the orders of the borough director; the four sections of each march were reassembled into a company, *tsu*, of 200 men; and finally the ten companies of each district made up a regiment, *lü*, of 2,000 men under a nobleman's order. The five regiments were assembled by fives to form three armies, *chün*, of 10,000 men each, commanded, the first by the prince in person, the second by the crown prince, and the third by another of the prince's sons.

The domains of the vassals were arranged into territories, *shu*, divided into circuits, subdivided in their turn into districts, *hsiang*. At the head of each *shu* a grand officer was set; moreover, in each of them, as in the circuits and districts, to control the lord who commanded them, the prince had placed residents called rectifiers, *cheng*, in the *shu*; *mu-cheng* in the circuits; and subordinate rectifiers, *hsia-cheng*, in the districts.[3]

The army was composed of 800 war chariots: that is to say, with the infantry troops accompanying them, some 40,000 men. This is why an ancient writer declares, rounding the numbers, 'Duke Huan got the hegemony with 50,000 men.' It is clear that the figures must be understood to include the entire military organization, and that the prince sent only a portion of his forces into the field: another ancient writer gives him an army of 10,000 men for an expedition.[4] It was the largest and best organized army of its time. The princes of Ch'i trained it carefully, and a solemn review was held each summer on the occasion of the sacrifice to the God of the Soil.

In order to make his principality the leading one of the empire, however, it would not have been enough for Huan to have an army; he had to have dependable financial resources. The state, situated in the great eastern plain, was rich; but by the nature of its revenues, payments in grain by the peasants of the princely domain, these were necessarily variable according to each year's crop. A kind of salt monopoly furnished more stable income: the prince had sea-water boiled for him in the Ch'ü-chan salt marches, and he sold the salt, adding a 50 per cent tax. Even towards the end of the Chou dynasty, the salt of Ch'i was still sold throughout eastern China and served to bring the prince considerable moneys. Iron seems likewise to have been the subject of a monopoly.

Thus, thanks to the head start she had over all her neighbours, in terms of administration, finance, and military power, Ch'i was, in the first half of the seventh century B.C., the most powerful of the feudal states. At that time the situation was grave for the small 'central states', Wey, Cheng, Sung, and so on, immersed in their constant quarrels. An enemy from outside had arisen, the barbarian kingdom of Ch'u, and, taking advantage of their struggles and their impotence, this adversary threatened to absorb them all.

The King of Ch'u seems to have been attracted into this region by the civil wars in Cheng, when its sovereign Li, who had been driven from his capital by his chief minister Chung of Chai (697) and taken refuge in Li, apparently accepted the suzerainty of Ch'u in exchange for help against his rival, Count Chao.[5] The influence Ch'u thus gained frightened the states which it menaced; and several of them (Sung, Ch'en, Ts'ai, Chu-lü) conceived the notion of asking protection from Prince Huan of Ch'i. A meeting was held at Pei-hsing and a treaty signed (681). This was the initial nucleus of the alliance over which Huan was to preside for almost forty years and which, even after the decline of Ch'i, was to remain for over two centuries one of the fundamental elements of the Chinese political scene. Meanwhile Count Li, having succeeded in driving his brother out and in re-entering his capital (680), wished to have himself recognized by Ch'i as he was by Ch'u. He broke with the latter and entered the alliance, soon followed by all the states which had hitherto been hesitant (Wey, Hsu, Ts'ai, and Lu), at the assembly of Chüan (680), which was presided over by a royal emissary, the Count of Shan. The princes soon found that the undertakings accepted in these assemblies had to be scrupulously maintained: when the old rivalry of Cheng against Sung led it to invade that state (679), Huan came to the aid of Sung (678) and Cheng, after a brief struggle, had to submit.

From that moment the League was definitively established under the Prince of Ch'i's presidency. All the eastern states participated; Huan's power was at its apogee; he was hegemon, *pa*; and the presence of the king's representative at the Chüan assembly (680) marked the official recognition of this situation. Just as had happened several years earlier, in the case of Count Chuang of Cheng, justification for Huan's hegemony was found in the legend that in King Wu's time the empire had been divided between two ministers, the two counts, the one from the west residing at the capital and the one from the east having all the outer provinces. Just like the Duke of Chou in days of yore, Huan was the exterior minister, not residing at the capital.[6] At the first attempt his power had attained its greatest extent. It was extended no further afterwards and it never had any influence outside the region of the lower Yellow River; no count of Ch'in ever attended the gatherings over which Huan presided during his long reign; nor did any prince of Chin, despite an intervention he made to re-establish peace in that principality.[7]

The League never held regular sessions, and the great assemblies of princes, *hui chu-hou*, were convened only in case of need. The twelve assemblies over which Huan presided were spread at very unequal intervals: for the first four years, one was held each year — one at Pei-hsing (681), two successively at Chüan (680–679), one at Yu (678). Then in twenty years only two were convoked, about one every ten years, that of Yu (667) and that of Cheng (659). They became a bit more frequent in the last years of his reign, but without ever becoming regular. The extremely serious business of the expedition against Ch'u seems to have been decided following the Yang-ku (657) assembly; the settlement of King Hui's succession brought about the meeting of Shou-chih (655), and after the king's death another was held at T'ao (652).

The princes attended the assemblies in person, accompanied by their ministers. There were two sorts of meeting: one, assemblies in arms for an expedition, being indeed merely the concentration of troops before the campaign, and each prince brought his contingent. These were relatively infrequent: Prince Huan held only three during his long reign. The other sort, ordinary meetings, were peaceful assemblies to which the princes brought only a few guards.

For the one kind as for the other each prince had his own private camp, placed in a direction corresponding to the position of his fief in the empire. Each camp was encircled by a hedgerow; in the middle of each was set the prince's tent, often richly decorated.[8] Protocol governed everything; the order of precedence was fixed carefully, and once for all: the Prince of Ch'i, president, at the head, then the Duke of Sung, in third place the Duke of Ch'en, then the Prince of Wey, the Count of Cheng, the Lord of Hsu, the Count of Ts'ao. Later, during the hegemony of Chin, it was naturally the Prince of Chin who led; and just after him, during the brief periods when he extended his power over Ch'i, that state probably — as former president — came second; for the rest the ancient order stood, Sung, Ch'en, Wey, Cheng, Hsu, Ts'ao, and after them the small, less important states in an order which seems likewise to have been fixed. The only attempt at a different classification is that of the Chien-t'u assembly, over which Prince Wen of Chin presided in 632, when he gave Ts'ai the place of Ch'en, just after Sung, and inverted the order of Wey and Cheng; but from 624 on the former precedences were restored.[9]

Religious reasons probably combined with political grounds for this classification: the descendants of ancient emperors — descendants of Yin (Sung), descendants of Shun (Ch'en) — came at the head; then the princes of the royal family in order of precedence — Lu, Wey, and Cheng; then princes who were not associated with any royal ancestor — such as those of Hsu, descended from Lu-chung, those of Ts'ao from the Chi clan but not of royal lineage, and so on.[10]

The centre of the ceremony was an altar raised to the God of the Soil of the place where the assembly was held, and the lords established their camps all about it. To open the meeting, they performed the rite of mutually offering each other a goblet of wine. It was at this moment that a royal emissary sometimes came to bring the president meat from the sacrifices to the king's ancestors, and an admonition. 'The king says, "Uncle, carry out reverently the king's orders, so as to bestow tranquillity upon the states of the four regions and to cast out all those who are ill-intentioned towards the king!" ' (the Chien-t'u meeting, 632).

Then when the meeting had been opened by these ceremonies the work commenced: the president guided the discussions, seated upon a platform, surrounded by counsellors at the foot of the steps, the other princes in the places which the code of precedence allotted them. Expeditions to be carried out to punish the barbarians or lords who refused to submit were discussed; or disputes between members of the League were adjudicated; or on occasion lords who had committed some offence were judged.

When the deliberations were ended the solemn oath took place. This was conducted on the promenade with three stairs, near the altar of the God of the Soil; nearby was dug a rectangular pit at the bottom of which a victim was sacrificed. This was generally an ox; at least once, in 641, it was a man, when the Duke of Sung ordained that the Lord of Tseng should be immolated after he had shown himself guilty of negligence and had arrived late. The president of the assembly himself presided at the sacrifice and charged one of his grand officers to slay the victim. The left ear was cut off and placed upon a dish ornamented with jade; the blood was gathered in a basin; with this blood were written, on the slips of bamboo which at that time served as material for writing, the articles agreed upon by treaty; then the president, standing upright on the promenade of the three stairs with his face to the north, bore witness as his minister, standing before the altar of the God of the Soil, read in a high voice the articles of agreement. This was the moment when intimidation by one party or another could take place. One might seek to introduce supplementary articles into the treaty, or, on the other hand, a grand officer could profit by the fact that the president was alone and might compel him by threat to grant more advantageous conditions to his own prince. When the reading was finished the president rubbed his lips with the blood of the sacrificial victim, and each of the princes in his turn read and did the same. Then the tablets bearing the treaty were deposited upon the victim in the pit, and the whole was covered over with earth.

The most significant of the undertakings made at the assemblies were probably the princes' engaging to pay to the president, *meng-chu*, regular contributions, the rate of which was bitterly disputed by both sides,[11] and the president's promise of immediate assistance against external enemies, a promise which gained weight from the power of Ch'i. This aid was never wanting. In 668 Huan of Ch'i sent an expedition against the Hsü barbarians to protect the neighbouring principalities of Sung, Lu, and Cheng from their depredations. In 664, at the request of the Prince of Yen, he marched to the defence of that state against the Jung barbarians of the mountains, who raided its territory unceasingly. He defeated them and slew the chiefs of the Ling-chih and the Ku-chu in the mountains which divide the present-day province of Hopei from Manchuria (in the region where Shan-hai-kuan is today). In 659 he defended the princes of Wey and Hsing against the Ti barbarians and constructed fortified walls for the capitals of those states. In 644, on the eve of his death, he sent aid to King Hsiang, who had been attacked by the Jung.

Precisely at the moment when Ch'i thus achieved the highest point of her power, Ch'u on the other hand was undergoing a crisis. The country of Pa, which had submitted a short while before, rebelled in 676; then the death of King Wen during a campaign in 675 had been followed by a civil war which ended only in 671, with the accession of King Ch'eng. Such difficulties were always the more serious for Ch'u since the country, with its enormous extent and its still barbarian population, was not easily administered.

The organization of the purely Chinese principalities was

naturally what had served Ch'u as a model. The king had about
him a chief minister, the Chief of Commands (*ling-yin*), often
assisted by a Chief of the Left (*tso-yin*) and a Chief of the Right (*yu-
yin*). Then there were the directors of ministries in the Chinese
style: Grand Director of the Horses (*ta-ssu-ma*), Minister of War;
Director of the Multitude (*ssu-t'u*), Minister of the Interior, the
indigenous name for which seems to have been *mo-ao*;[12] Director
of Public Works (*ssu-k'ung*); Grand Chamberlain (*ta-tsai*), Minister
of Finance; Director of the Condemned (*ssu-pai*), Minister of
Criminal Law. And there were yet more high functionaries,
some for the king, the palace, the royal family, such as the chief
eunuch, called Director of the Palace Police, *ssu-kung*; the Chief of
the King's Household, *wang-yin*; the Administrator of the Royal
Stables, *wang-ma-chih-shu*; the Grand Officer of the Three Branches
of the Royal Family, *san-lü-tai-fu* who was also called *san-tsu* or *san-
kung* and was charged with surveillance over the three families of
Ch'ü, Ching, and Chao, descendants of former kings. Other
officers were for public affairs: the Grand Scribe, *t'ai-shih*; the
Grand Gateman, *ta-hun*, charged with defending the gates of the
capital; the *lan-yin* and *ling-yin*, who shared the management and
supervision of mountains and lakes; the Chief of Crafts, *kung-yin*,
who supervised artisans; and so on.

All this organization was fine in appearance but of little
efficacy. It was not that Chinese influence was not substantial
and profound, at least among the upper classes: those had
adopted Chinese clothing and Chinese rites, made the Chinese
language the language of administration, and moreover read
and wrote it so well that the greatest poet of China in the third
century B.C. was produced from that milieu. Furthermore,
outside the great chiefs of powerful tribes who had kept their
states after having submitted — the lords of Pa and Shu in
Szechuan, of Kou-wu on the Yangtze River, and of Yü-yüeh in
Chekiang — there did not seem to be, in Ch'u itself, any feudal
nobility possessing particular importance. The country was
divided into districts, *hsien*, commanded by chiefs, *yin*, named by
the king. But what threw the whole apparatus out was the too
powerful court aristocracy. All power was monopolized by the
branches of the royal family, particularly the Tou and the
Ch'eng, descendants of King Jo-ao, who held all the highest posts,
despite the rivalry of other families. On the other hand, with its
population scattered, except in places, across a country so vast,
its difficult communications as soon as one left the Yangtze
River, the state of Ch'u was in no condition to sustain a
prolonged effort, either military or financial.

The first years of the new reign had to be employed in repairing the ravages of the preceding years, and since military expeditions were not possible, Ch'eng tried to replace them with diplomatic negotiations. He was the first king of Ch'u to enter into relations with the Chou court. He announced his accession by sending presents to that court. 'The Son of Heaven gives him some sacrificial meat and says to him: "Maintain order in your southern country, troubled by the [barbarians] Yi and Yüeh; but do not invade the central states!" '[13] The state began to recover, although its sovereign — induced to some prudence by the power of Ch'i and the bloc which comprised the League — dared not intervene again in the states lying south of the Yellow River. He contented himself with maintaining a certain influence in the nearer principalities, especially Cheng and Ch'en. Peace lasted thus for several years, until in 667, viewing himself as menaced (even though he remained in the background) by the defeat of his ally, he felt it necessary to act.

That year, indeed, Cheng and Ch'en 'submitted' to Ch'i — that is to say, feeling reassured by her power, the princes renounced the prudent but costly policy of double allegiance which they had followed for ten years, and definitively rejected the suzerainty of Ch'u. The latter state interposed at once: in the following year its chief minister, Tzu-yüan, the king's uncle, fell upon Cheng without warning, arriving before the capital without a blow having been struck. Fortunately, the city was well fortified, and since the Ch'u troops were not well fitted for a regular siege, the campaign begun so auspiciously dragged out for a long time. The troops of Ch'i arrived in time to save Cheng. The principality remained within the clientele of Ch'i for a dozen years, despite several aggressions which the League aided her to repulse; but by 657, after three successive wars, the count desired to return to the alliance with Ch'u, which was closer than Ch'i and able to make its unhappiness felt so harshly. His minister, K'ung Shu,[14] dedicated to Ch'i, dissuaded him from this project. Nevertheless, it became evident that, if Huan wished to retain his influence in that region, he had to strike a decisive blow against Ch'u.

He quickly realized the situation; but, not wishing to risk anything, he wanted to give himself the advantage of surprise. According to a more or less fanciful tradition, he took the pretext of a personal affair with one of the small neighbours of Ch'u to approach that country's territory without putting it on guard. Among his women he had a daughter of the Prince of Ts'ai, and he wished, for a trifling reason, to return her to her father's house without repudiating her (657); and the father, furious at this affront, had pretended to consider the return as a divorce and had forthwith married her off again. Huan in turn took umbrage at this and, assembling the contingents of the League, organized an expedition against Ts'ai. Thus he was able to bring his troops to the very frontier of Ch'u, which he immediately crossed.

Whatever substance there is to this anecdote, King Ch'eng seems not to have expected this aggression, and he sent an emissary to ask the reason for it, since there was no issue outstanding between the two states. Huan responded in a way which stressed that it was not a matter of his title as Prince of Ch'i but as prince-hegemon representing the king, reproaching Ch'u for not having sent tribute to the Chou court, and demanding of her explanations for the death of King Chao two and a half centuries earlier, during his southern expedition. This was declaring that he wished to break off relations; and the Ch'u ambassador did not deceive himself on that point. His only response was to invite Prince Huan to go himself and make an enquiry at the banks of the Han River, where King Chao had been drowned.

Perhaps a forced march would have enabled the Ch'i army to breach the Huai hills by surprise, for they were not yet guarded; but it advanced slowly instead and stopped prudently at the foot of Mount Hsing, not daring to try and force the passes. It was the Ch'u army which debouched onto the plain; the Chinese troops retreated about two days' march and then halted again. But neither of the adversaries cared to commit itself to battle: each perceived both the futility of a victory and the dangers of a defeat. There was no fighting, and a treaty was concluded. Ch'u promised to send tribute regularly to the Chou court, and Prince Huan withdrew (656).

The only result of this expedition was the definitive destruction of those small Chinese states which remained on the Ch'u border. The coming of the Prince of Ch'i had probably led them to hope for the destruction of Ch'u, and their princes had defected as a body.[15] The departure of the League armies left them defenceless at King Ch'eng's mercy, and he took advantage of this at once: In 655 he annexed Hsien; in 654 he seized Hsu and secured the submission of its prince; in 648 he destroyed Huang; in 646, he annihilated Ying; in 645, he invaded the country of Hsü.

The equivocal success of this expedition did not, in appearance, detract from Huan's prestige. That seemed even to grow the following year, when the Prince Royal of Chou came and gave him the occasion to intervene in the affairs of the royal family, since he sought to have Huan convoke the lords so as to prevent his father from degrading him. In reality, however, the expedition had shown the limits of Huan's power, and that one state at least could hold up its head against him. The lesson bore fruit almost at once.

When the Shou-chih assembly was engaged in recognizing Crown Prince Cheng as heir, to King Hui's great displeasure (655), the latter thought at once of relying upon Ch'u against Ch'i, since the guardianship of Ch'i had become onerous to him. Even before the assembly had been convened, he had pressed Count Wen of Cheng to abandon the League and ally himself to Ch'u; and the prince, thus encouraged, had refused to attend the Shou-chih meeting. The following year, Huan led the lords against him. Needing to win a victory, he had to hasten to the aid of Count Hsi of Hsu, one of his allies, whose capital was besieged by a band from Ch'u. The army of the League rescued the city of Hsu; but as soon as it retired, Count Hsi, feeling himself at the mercy of a new aggression, went to make his submission to the King of Ch'u, who accepted it. The count presented himself in the guise of a vanquished prisoner, prepared for immolation, half-naked, arms tied behind his back, with a piece of jade in his mouth, followed by his officers in mourning dress and bearing his coffin (654).

All considered, Huan had suffered a defeat, and all the area south of the Yellow River — the Royal Domain, Cheng, and the small states bordering Ch'u (Hsu, Ts'ai, and Ch'en) — slipped from his hands for a moment. It was not for long: King Hui was old and his death was expected soon; but the young crown prince had been linked to Ch'i since the Shou-chih agreement. Count Wen of Cheng feared to find himself isolated and, at the news of an expedition preparing against him, submitted once again (652). As before, he was probably admitted among the clients of Ch'i without abandoning allegiance to Ch'u.

When, at the end of the year, King Hui died and Prince Cheng succeeded him without opposition, as had been agreed (he was King Hsiang), Huan's triumph was complete. This was obvious at the next assembly of the lords, at K'uei-ch'iu during the summer of 651, when the new King Hsiang sent his chief minister, K'ung, Duke of Chou, to present meat from the sacrifices to kings Wen and Wu, a red bow (symbol of authority) with its arrows, and a ceremonial chariot, inviting Huan at the same time not to prostrate himself when receiving these gifts. The prince-hegemon, intoxicated with success, wished to acquiesce in this invitation. His minister Chung of Kuan had some difficulty in keeping him from this ritual error, which would have demonstrated rather too clearly whither his ambitions were tending.[16] For it seems indeed that in this period he had ideas of overturning the Chou dynasty and establishing himself in their place. Time was lacking for him to achieve this: he was already very old and his long reign approached its end. His ministers, Chung of Kuan and P'eng of Hsi both died soon afterwards.[17] Huan presided once more over the lords' assembly at Huai (644) and then died himself in the forty-third year of his reign, in 643, being over eighty years old.[18]

His death was the signal of a complete debacle for his states and for the League. He left ten sons, six of them the offspring of six favourites to whom — contrary to the rites — he had given the rank of princesses. On Kuan Chung's advice, he had entrusted the crown prince to the Duke of Sung, the oldest of his allies; but as soon as the firm hand of that minister had disappeared, even before Huan had died, the princes began to contest for power. As soon as he fell ill, each of them armed his servants and his clients and gave themselves to battle. The fighting lasted two months, with nobody minding that Huan had died, his corpse remaining abandoned on his bed. Finally the minister Yi-ya got into the palace, thanks to information sources he had in the harem, and proclaimed as king Prince Wu-kuei, son of the Princess Chi of Wey, who took power just sixty days after his father's death. Only then were the funeral ceremonies attended to: the maggots came out of the door of the bedchamber, and the sight was so horrible that the corpse was prepared during the night, and not the body but the coffin was exhibited.

The crown prince fled to Sung, the duke of which, making good his promise, organized an expedition to help him. In the third month of the following year he gathered up the troops of the League and brought the prince back to Lin-tzu. Wu-kuei and his brothers were defeated, despite their appeal to the Ti barbarians, who arrived too late; and in the fifth month the prince mounted the throne.

These troubles had brought ruin to Ch'i, already exhausted by the glorious but wearing reign of Huan; hegemony slipped away from her at once. Duke Hsiang of Sung tried to take it; but the League broke up; all those small states bordering the Yellow River, pretty much equal in impotence, were indisposed to submit with a good will to one among them. At the assembly which Hsiang convoked at Ts'ao in the sixth month of 641, except for two petty princelings neighbouring Sung, the lords of Chu and Tseng,[19] nobody came, not even the Count of Ts'ao, who was represented by one of his officers; and the following winter, all the neighbours of Sung (Ch'en, Ts'ai, Cheng) formed a league to which Ch'u adhered 'so that good harmony might be cultivated among the lords, and so that the virtue of Huan of Ch'i should not be forgotten', and this was probably directed chiefly against Sung. A new effort by Hsiang in 639 was even less happy; he convoked the lords at Yü. This time, but for Hsiao of Ch'i, almost all the members of the League — the lords of Ch'en, Ts'ai, Cheng, Hsu, and Ts'ao — were present, and even King Ch'eng of Ch'u attended. Hsiang's impotence was displayed for the eyes of all: he was removed in full assembly by Ch'eng's order, without protest by the allies, either because they were afraid or because they were not grieved to see this humiliation visited upon him. When he was released, several months later, the League was splintered. Cheng had returned its allegiance to the King of Ch'u, which had no more to fear in seeing the small central states form a compact bloc against it.

The Duke of Sung meanwhile showed himself inveterate in his efforts. The following year he gathered the allies who had remained faithful to him (Wey, Teng, Hsu, and Ch'en) and made up an expedition with them against Cheng to force it to re-enter the alliance. Unfortunately for him, he was in no condition to win quickly. The campaign dragged on, even continuing into the eleventh month, and then the troops of Ch'u arrived and destroyed his army and those of his allies on the banks of the River Hung. Hsiang received a hand wound in combat, and he died of this in the fifth month of the following year (637).

3

The Hegemony of Chin

The Duke of Sung's abortive effort had demonstrated that the central states were incapable of uniting under one leader from amongst themselves: Neither Cheng nor Sung would yield the leading position, and they lacked the power to seize it. Their rivalry set the stage for the King of Ch'u, who profited by it to oblige them all, one after the other, to accept his supremacy willy-nilly. A brief expedition by Te-ch'en of Ch'eng (his appellation: Tzu-yü) sufficed to bring a general submission: Cheng first re-entered the alliance, then Ch'en (636). Vanquished and impotent, Sung also had to sign a treaty. The authority of Ch'u seemed certain to stop there, however, for farther north Wey and Lu had formed an alliance.

The imprudence of Ch'i opened the way for Ch'u: Prince Hsiao, who had succeeded Huan, fearing that this latter alliance was directed against him, immediately attacked Lu, which had to ask aid from Ch'u. Delighted with this pretext for intervening, Tzu-yü sent a column against Ch'i (634). One of the sons of Huan who had taken refuge in Ch'u accompanied the army, and after the victory he was given the city of Ku,[1] which had just been conquered, but not without there being a garrison on its borders to keep an eye on him. The entire plain as far as Mount T'ai had thus passed under the domination of Ch'u, and at the end of the following year, Ch'en, Ts'ai, Cheng, Hsu, and Lu had to conclude a formal treaty. The triumph of Tzu-yü was complete. King Ch'eng of Ch'u, who until then seems to have been a little fearful of his minister's active policy, was converted by its success, and he dismissed his chief minister, Nou-wu-t'u or Tou (Tzu-wen), and replaced him with the victorious general.

But already in Sung the Duke of Ch'eng, son of Duke Hsiang, made clairvoyant by the fear of Cheng, had seen how to find an external support capable of counterbalancing the power of Ch'u and re-establishing the equilibrium that the downfall of Ch'i had upset. He had appealed to Prince Wen of Chin, who had just come to the fore through a fortunate intervention on behalf of King Hsiang of Chou, who had been driven from his capital by his rebel brother.

Wen had just mounted the throne of Chin, following a revolution, finally re-entering his homeland after an exile of nineteen years. He was a son of Prince Hsien and brother of Hsien's successor, Hui. At the news of the latter's death, Ch'ung-erh (that was Wen's personal name) returned hastily from Ch'in, to which, after numerous adventures, he had withdrawn. He was very warmly received, entered the capital, while his nephew Huai (the son of Hui) fled, and seized the throne. For a moment the hostile faction came near winning again: a plot was laid to assassinate him by burning the palace. Forewarned in time, he fled to Ch'in, whence he soon returned at the head of 3,000 bodyguards furnished by Count Mu of Ch'in, and he was established definitively on the throne (636).[2]

Barely installed, he found himself obliged to respond to the call of his suzerain, King Hsiang of Chou, who — driven out a second time by his brother Prince Tai, *ta-shu Tai* — appealed to the vassals, especially the lords of Chin and Ch'in, whose ancestors had protected his own ancestor P'ing. The king had taken refuge at Fan, a small city in the principality of Cheng, while Tai, not daring to remain at the capital, which seemed hardly safe to him, was settled in his apanage of Wen, on the right bank of the Yellow River. Count Mu of Ch'in and Prince Wen of Chin responded at first rather languidly: the former dispatched a body of troops which stopped at the Chin frontier and returned in a short time without having gone further. As for Wen, newly seated on the throne by force, he hesitated to leave his capital. He put it to divination; but, the tortoise-shell having returned a favourable response — recalling the victory of the Yellow Emperor, Huang-ti, over the rebel Ch'ih-yu — he rejected it on the pretext that 'the augury was too grand for him,' — and put it to the milfoil. The responses being once more good, he allowed himself to be persuaded. He formed two armies, one of which besieged the usurper at Wen, took him and put him to death, while the other went to Fan to seek out the king and return him to Lo-yi (635). The king, thus reinstalled upon his throne, showed his recognition of Wen's aid by bestowing upon him the cities of Wen, Yang-fan, Yüan, and others, which constituted the territory north of the River retrieved from the rebel. Thereafter Prince Wen returned to his principality, the internal state of which demanded all his attention.

The country of Chin had indeed been exhausted by long years of troubles, by successive famines and by wars which had almost ruined it. Hsien, towards the end of his life, urged on by his favourite Chi of the (barbarian) Li, had wished to nominate her son Hsi-ch'i as heir apparent. Following a court intrigue, Crown Prince Shen-sheng, son of Chiang of Ch'i (a wife of Wu, the father of Hsien, whom Hsien had — contrary to the rites — caused to enter his own harem) was accused of having tried to poison his father and had committed suicide (656); then two other princes, Ch'ung-erh and Yi-wu, on the point of being put to death, had had to flee. Hsien had then proclaimed Hsi-ch'i as heir apparent; but the exiled princes retained numerous partisans. Scarcely had Hsien died when Hsi-ch'i was slaughtered before the coffin; his brother Cho-tzu, proclaimed in turn, was himself killed a few days later, the princess flogged and put to death, and their principal partisan, Hsi of Hsün, obliged to commit suicide.

Yi-wu, who was then in Ch'in, promised Count Mu of Ch'in to cede all the territories on the right bank of the River (that is, the west, in present-day Shensi, and the south, in Honan) and even Chieh, on the left bank, in the southwestern corner of Shansi, in exchange for his aid. Hardly was Yi-wu on the throne (650) than he made haste to forget his promise, and delayed matters so much that Count Mu, weary of this, attacked, completely defeated him, and made him prisoner at Han (645). Mu released him (644) only under promise that he would send his son as hostage; Ho-tung (that is to say, southwestern Shansi) remained occupied by Ch'in pending the arrival of the prince, which took place the following year (643). The reign of Hui (this was Yi-wu's posthumous name) had been too short for the principality to recover entirely; and after him the revolution which in 636 brought his brother Ch'ung-erh to the throne had cast it into disorder again.

The country of Chin did not lend itself to so rapid and complete a unification as did Ch'i or even Ch'in. Communications were difficult among the various valleys; and the loess plateaus with their sunken roads favoured guerrillas and brigandage. Also the great vassals there guarded their independence jealously, aided in this by the numerous civil wars which enlarged their influence. Since he was incapable of subsuming them within a regular organization which could keep them in order, it seems that Prince Wen was always forced to establish a sort of equilibrium among the great families, which numbered about fifteen, so as to neutralize one by another and thus to maintain authority. It was a dangerous system and one which, under masters less energetic than he, would surely have had the worst consequences, yet one which, at the start, was not without advantages.

Wen gave Chin an entirely new organization. Before him, the principality had an administration paralleling that of the Royal Domain and the other principalities, with its three ministers (*ssu-t'u,*[3] *ssu-k'ung, ssu-ma*). At the same time on many points of detail the state had its own particular usages — ceremonial vestments, calendar, and so on — which were explained in Chou times by saying that they were following the rites of Hsia, the capital of the Great Yü having been in that territory; and like the rites, the administration must have differed in minor ways from that of the other feudal principalities. Wen put military organization first, making it the pivot of his entire administration. At the beginning of the seventh century Chin had but a single army. It was due to that restriction, it is said, that King Hsi in 678 had recognized the usurpation of the Count of Ch'ü-wu; but already in 661, at the moment of the conquests which had established the territory, Prince Hsien had created a second army. Wen established a third, when he resolved to intervene in the affairs of the empire (633). Then in the following year he raised another three more for a campaign against the Ti barbarians, though he did not presume to call them armies, *chün* (for to have six armies was a privilege of the Son of Heaven), styling them simply columns, *hang*. He seems moreover to have disbanded them when the expedition returned. In 629, on the occasion of a new expedition against the barbarians, he created two 'new armies', *hsin-chün*, which were to last a longer time than the three columns, being abolished by his son Hsiang at the end of his reign, in 621. In 588, political necessities again brought about the creation of three 'new armies', *hsin-chün*, which were retained until 559. At that time the alliance with Wu allowed Chin to reduce its military forces.

Each army comprised 200 war chariots, each mounting three men and accompanied by a section of 75 foot soldiers, making 15,000 infantrymen in all. This was, we can see, very nearly the same figure as that we came to for the army of Huan of Ch'i,

45,000 foot soldiers for the three armies. The number was doubled, when the situation required, by forming six armies. Although these numbers must refer rather to recruitment than to troops actually raised for each expedition,[4] one can understand how Chin, with this considerable military power, could retain the hegemony so long.

The armies had been commanded at first, in the time of Hsien, by the prince himself and the heir apparent. Wen, however, conferred in fief both command-in-chief and secondary command upon the families of the great vassals: Chao, Wei, Han, Hsi, Fan (also called Shih), Luan, Hsien, Hsü, Hsün (of which a branch bore the name Chung-hang, since its ancestors had commanded the centre column), Chih (another collateral branch of the Hsün), Yüan and Hu. The armies themselves, at least in the beginning, did not belong to these families, and it was the command within an army of the prince's choice which alone constituted the fief of that family.[5] The great lords moved from one army to another at the will of the prince and in pursuit of promotion.[6] In effect, there was a hierarchy among the armies: the three original armies ranked above the three new armies and, within each of these groups, the centre army, *chung-chün*, was the first; then came the upper army, *shang-chün*; and finally the lower army, *hsia-chün*. The chiefs of the armies, *chiang*, and lieutenants, *tso*, were administrators, ministers of the principality. The chief of the centre army handled matters which in earlier times had fallen to the *ssu-t'u* and was also chief minister; he and the other chiefs and lieutenants of the army comprised the prince's council. Their precedence was governed by that of the armies which they led, the chief and lieutenant of the central army coming at the head, then the chief and lieutenant of the upper army, and so forth.[7]

Below them were only personages bearing pompous but empty titles borrowed from the royal court — the Grand Master, *t'ai-shih*; the Grand Guardian, *t'ai-fu* — often themselves old ministers whom age had obliged to retire (like Hui of the Shih, former commander of the centre army, who was named *t'ai-fu* in 592 after an embassy to the royal court) or favourites belonging to the families which had no access to military commands, like Hsi of Yang-she (Shu-hsiang), who received the title of *fu* in 557. The most lasting and least happy result of Prince Wen's reorganization was in fact to divide the aristocracy of Chin into two classes, the nobles who had the right of command, and those who had not that right, and to establish for the former a privilege which would become fatal for the princely family and the country itself when, with time, the number of the privileged was reduced to the point which placed the entire principality in the hands of several families.

Thus the entire administration of Chin was strongly militarized. Administration of the peasantry was put under the direction of the chief of the centre army, who must have viewed this above all as a sphere for the recruitment of troops. Also Chin was the first country where the complicated old system of the *ching* disappeared, replaced by a simpler system of allocating land by family rather than by a group of eight families. If this system did not quite vest landed property in the peasants, it was at least quite clearly a step forward. The Director of Works, *ssu-k'ung*, kept his title but ceased to be a minister and became a simple grand officer, his responsibilities consisting chiefly of military works, fortifications and roads. The Director of Criminals, *ssu-k'ou*, or *li*, also reduced to the rank of grand officer, seems to have retained only the management of prisons and was the chief of the executioners.

The weak point of this entire organization, as in all the principalities of ancient China, was its financial structure. The revenues of the prince's own domain had to constitute its principal resource, to which the contributions of the vassals must have been joined somehow; but we do not know completely how it worked. We know only that in Chin, as in all the principalities, the system of paying functionaries by allocations of land had been kept and that these were valued according to the military organization. A minister was given a domain with a population sufficient to raise a battalion of 500 men; a grand officer received a domain whose population allowed a company of 100 men to be raised; and so on.[8]

Prince Wen spent two years in consolidating his throne and reorganizing his principality. It was an appeal from the Duke of Sung which made him send out his reserve (634): Duke Wen concluded an alliance with him, promising him protection. It was needed almost immediately, for, at the news of this defection, the King of Ch'u summoned his allies to an expedition against Sung, and the Chief of Commands, Te-ch'en of Ch'eng (Tzu-yü), besieged its capital, (633–632). Not daring to attack the army of that alliance directly, Wen invaded the two small principalities of Ts'ao and Wey, neighbouring his territory; he made the Count of Ts'ao prisoner and drove the Prince of Wey out of his state (spring, 632). Tzu-yü sent troops to their aid, without raising the siege of Sung, the resistance of which was beginning to flag.

The Chin army was at the shores of the Yellow River, Wen was undecided about crossing, fearing that, if he should be defeated, his neighbours Ch'i and Ch'in might take advantage of the dangerous and risky position of his army isolated on the right bank of the River, the former by blocking his crossing and the other by invading his territory. As for Ch'i, he had some guarantee from a treaty at Lien-yü, but Ch'in remained an uncertainty. The Duke of Sung seems to have succeeded in gaining the good will of both states' generals by rich gifts and thus in reassuring Wen who, in the fourth month, resolved to undertake the campaign. The commander-in-chief was Chen of Hsien, who had just conducted the campaign into Ts'ao and Wey brilliantly. He marched straight to the help of the besieged city. Chief of Commands Tzu-yü pleaded in vain for reinforcements from his king, who sent him only an absurdly inadequate contingent. He then offered to raise the siege of Sung if the Prince of Chin would reinstate the Count of Ts'ao and the prince of Wey; and when Wen refused and continued to advance, Tzu-yü did not wait but marched to meet him.

Prince Wen, still uncertain about risking battle, beat a retreat to Ch'eng-p'u (not far from modern Ts'ao-chou fu, Shantung), three days' march back from his furthest advance. The tale of Prince Wen of Chin, of which the *Tso chuan* has preserved a summary for us, later explained this retreat (like all the events of his reign) by remembrances from his time of exile. Previously, when the exiled Ch'ung-erh had lived in Ch'u, he had promised the king that if ever, after returning to his state, he was at war with Ch'u, when the armies met on the field of battle, he would retreat three day-stages, after which — if the troops of Ch'u persisted in attacking — he would fight with all his forces. Whatever we think of this anecdote, it seems clear that Wen, like Huan before him, would have preferred not to engage in combat.

It was Tzu-yü, whose constant success during six years had persuaded him that his soldiers were superior to all Chinese troops, who wished to give battle. He perceived quite clearly that a victory was needed to banish this new intrusion from the political scene in central China and to stabilize the position he had just acquired there. He followed the army of Chin to Ch'eng-p'u, where he set himself up in a strong position, and then he waited quietly, since a new retreat by his enemy would have been in fact the equivalent of a victory. He contented himself with having a challenge carried to the Prince of Chin. Wen did not know what to do and could not make up his mind, despite the advice of all his officers, who urged him to attack. Various auguries decided the issue, especially a dream in which he saw himself boxing with the Lord of Ch'u, who, having thrown Wen down, suddenly knelt down and sucked his brain — a dream which, contrary to appearances, was interpreted as favourable.[9]

The Chin army is said to have included 700 chariots, which is to say some 52,000 men, divided into three corps, the prince being with the centre army. There were in addition the auxiliary troops of Sung and Ch'i. The soldiers of Ch'u must have been roughly equivalent; the generalissimo also commanded the centre army; the right wing was composed of the auxiliaries from Ch'en and Ts'ai, and the left wing by a second Ch'u army. The auxiliaries could not stand up to the shock of the Chin chariots. They were scattered and put to flight from the onset. At the same time the left wing was put into disorder by a ruse: the commander of the Chin first (right) army, to draw his adversaries out of position, feigned disorganization with the first attack but gathered his troops and destroyed the enemy, who were disordered in pursuit. The centre army sought in vain to reassemble the fugitives; all that Te-ch'en could do was to beat a retreat himself in good order without allowing himself to be cut off. The Chin army plundered the enemy encampment for three days; but they dared not pursue the retreating general and themselves retired northwards. The King of Ch'u was enraged at the news of this defeat and had word sent to the Chief of Commands: 'If you come here, how will you reply to the elders of Shen and Hsi [regarding the loss of their sons]?' Tzu-yü committed suicide (632). Upon hearing of his death, it is said, Prince Wen cried, 'There is nothing more to poison my joy!' Tzu-yü was indeed Ch'u's finest general, the one who had for five years given that state the mastery of central China; and thus he disappeared from the scene.

Wen's victory had an enormous impact. All the allies of Ch'u abandoned her immediately. King Hsiang came in person to see Wen, then camped at Chien-t'u, about seventy-five kilometres from present-day Kaifeng, to congratulate him. The king was presented with a portion of the loot, a thousand prisoners, a hundred war chariots, and so on; and for his part he gave splendid gifts, robes to wear in the grand ceremonial chariot for sacrifices, robes to wear in the war chariot, a red bow and a hundred red arrows, a black bow and a thousand arrows, a jar of spiced wine, and 300 of his own bodyguards, *hu-pen*, to serve as a personal guard for Wen. Above all, he conferred upon Wen the charge as Count of the Sovereign Lords, *hou-po* 'The terms of the charge were: "The king says: Uncle, be obedient to the king's orders, so as to give tranquillity to the states of the four regions and to drive away all those who are ill-disposed towards the king." The prince refused three times, but finally accepted, saying: "I, Chung-erh, venture to do obeisance twice, my forehead touching the earth. I accept the great, distinguished, excellent charge of the Son of Heaven." Then he received the tablet and went out.'[10] Several days later he held an assembly of the lords at Chien-t'u itself. The king had departed but had left his brother to preside over the ceremony: the princes agreed to aid the royal house and to refrain from mutual transgression. With this meeting the period of Chin hegemony commences in China, a period which was to last more than a century, until that principality, exhausted by the exertions required to maintain this position, broke up through internal troubles.

The Prince of Chin appears to have determined to profit from his victory by immediately getting rid of several sovereigns too closely tied to Ch'u. Ch'u retained within its clientele the princes of Hsu, Cheng, and Wey, states constituting a salient from the frontier of Ch'u to north of the Yellow River and completely separating Chin from the states of the League, not allowing free communication between them. This was the situation which Wen wished to end, by replacing the hostile princes of these states with clients of his own.

In the winter of that year (632), he called a meeting at Wen to decide upon punishing the princes of Hsu and Wey, traitors during the campaign against Ch'u. The Prince of Wey, who came, was not admitted by Wen, who had him and his ministers arrested and cast into prison to await judgement, which the king had to pronounce. The prince was released only two years later. As for Hsu, an expedition was sent against it, but without success, since Wen had fallen ill. The following year it was Cheng's turn. The armies of Chin and Ch'in came to lay siege to its capital, bringing with them one of the reigning count's sons, who had gone into exile and taken refuge in Chin, which had promised him succession to the principality.

Prince Wen wished to replace — with a client of his own — the chief minister of Cheng, Shu Chan. The younger brother of the count, Shu had governed for over twenty years and since the hegemony of Ch'i had always been a convinced partisan of the Ch'u alliance. Shu Chan committed suicide, and his body was carried to Wen. The siege continued nevertheless; but the army of Ch'in grew weary and went off after having made a separate peace. Wen could not take the city and had to content himself with exacting the recognition of his protégé as heir apparent (630). In short, he had not succeeded in his plans; but he had made his power sufficiently felt among his enemies that they decided to submit. Count Wen of Cheng, and after him his son, Count Mu (the same count whom Wen of Chin had just had designated to the succession), became faithful allies of Chin for more than twelve years. Ch'u itself gave up the struggle for a time and asked for peace (628).

Order seemed to have been restored again within the empire, but the situation was precarious. Prince Wen of Chin was sixty-one years old; he could not be expected to live very long, and the uncertainty of the future made his accomplishments quite unstable. Besides, it was clear that from then on he and his successors would have to struggle to preserve the order they built, not only in the south against Ch'u but also in the west against Ch'in. The defection of that principality during the campaign against Cheng was only the first manifestation of a fear that the years could only cause to grow.

For about half a century since they had managed to unify the Wei Valley for themselves, the ambition of the lords of Ch'in had been to validate their claim to the title of count by reunifying all of the old province of Yung, subduing the barbarians in one part of it and in the other pushing eastward to the Yellow River, which they wished to make their frontier. The first of these ambitions seemed to have been realized: Count Mu, who reigned from 659 on, had by a kind of peaceful penetration brought a dozen or so petty chiefs of barbarian tribes, who tenanted the mountains from which the Wei and Ching rivers descend, to recognize his suzerainty; and even though these successes were bound to be ephemeral, they had been sufficiently striking that the Son of Heaven had been willing to congratulate Count Mu, sending him a bronze drum (623). As for the second, having gained a section of territory after the victory at Han (645), Count Mu had to let it go at the peace treaty; and the power which Prince Wen acquired several years later not only postponed any chance of his succeeding in his purposes but also, by its own consolidation, threatened to create a real danger for the counts of Ch'in.

The death of Wen, at the end of 628, seemed to offer Count Mu a chance to defeat his eastern neighbour, taking advantage of the fumbling and uncertain period at the beginning of a reign. In 627 his troops, returning from a fruitless expedition against Cheng, attacked Hua, a dependency of Chin, and destroyed it.

The new Prince of Chin, Hsiang, immediately put his armies into the field and even summoned the Chiang Jung. He went out himself at the head of his troops in mourning garments, which he had simply spotted with black to avoid the evil omen of the colour white. He went to await the Ch'in army at the Hsiao gorge, leading his troops through the hills which separate the River Lo from the Yellow River. The Ch'in force was destroyed and its three generals taken prisoner (627). The struggle between Ch'in and Chin, broken off for several years during the preceding reign, resumed with even greater intensity. Less fortunate than his father or Huan of Ch'i, who had had only the one adversary (Ch'u) in their efforts to take control over the riverine states of the Yellow River, Hsiang and his successors had henceforth to deal also with Ch'in. Luckily Ch'in, the neighbour of Ch'u, was also constantly at war in that quarter, first over possession of the River Han and later over domination of the barbarians in the region which today constitutes Szechuan.

The geographical configuration and the political situation imposed a special character upon the struggle among these three great Chinese states. Chin and Ch'u, far from one another, contested the supremacy of central China, which they controlled from their almost inaccessible mountains, the one in the north and the other to the south. Ch'in, however — since its rivals denied it all routes eastward, the one being on both banks of the Yellow River and the other on the Han and Yangtze rivers — was obliged to take no further interest in the politics of the empire at large, merely seeking to seize from its two strong neighbours, city by city and district by district, a route towards the wealthy principalities of the centre, the conquest of which conferred hegemony.

The breach of friendly relations between Chin and Ch'in made its effects felt at once. King Ch'eng of Ch'u took advantage of it to tear up the treaty signed the previous year: he sent his chief minister, Chief of Commands P'o of Tou (Tzu-shang), to lead an expedition which, after subduing Ts'ai and then Ch'en, dashed itself against the walls of the Cheng capital. A show of force by Chin had no effect, for the two armies did not care to engage one another, and both retired without fighting (627). The assassination of King Ch'eng by the heir apparent who, fearing to be reduced in rank, attacked his father and forced him to commit suicide, was an incident so sudden that it did not weaken the state even briefly. Nevertheless, fear of future trouble drove the Prince of Ch'en into alliance with Chin; Wey alone remained faithful to Ch'u though isolated amidst hostile principalities, a situation which could not last long.

In 626, Ch'ü-chü of Hsien, son of the former minister Chen of Hsien, led a Chin army against Wey, without any clear success. The effort was renewed the following year at an assembly of the lords held at Ch'ui-lung; but Chin's allies were little inclined to help her, either because they were tired of war or because they feared to bring yet greater power to Chin: they interceded for the Prince of Wey, gaining his acceptance within the League (625). Pardon was granted all the more easily since Prince Hsiang was at that moment required to consider his own security, which was menaced by Count Mu of Ch'in, eager to revenge his recent defeat. Prince Hsiang had to despatch Generalissimo Ch'ü-chü of Hsien to the right bank of the Yellow River, which Ch'in had invaded; he met the Ch'in forces at P'eng-ya, not far from the River Lo which they had just left and defeated them utterly, though he did not succeed in expelling all the garrisons which they had installed in frontier cities early in the campaign. Also Hsiang, more concerned to insure his own success than to revenge himself upon the Prince of Wey, readily pardoned the latter in order to get contributions of League troops for a planned expedition against Ch'in the following winter. Thus he was able to retake the fortresses of Wang and P'eng-ya, and for a time to relieve himself of all fears on his western quarter. But scarcely was he freed there than he had to hasten southwards to the aid of allies menaced anew by Ch'u. The expedition, furthermore, had no result: once more, when the two armies confronted each other, they did not dare engage. An agreement was reached and each retired to its own side (624).[11]

The troubles which followed the death of Prince Hsiang (621) began to check the development of Chin power. The heir apparent, Yi-kao, was a child, and the nobles wanted to replace him with his uncle, *kung-tzu* Yung, younger brother of the dead sovereign, hoping that, because he had taken refuge in Ch'in and married a princess of that country, he could bring about a reconciliation between the two states. Yi-kao's mother succeeded in winning over the most senior counsellor, chief minister and commander of the centre army, Tun of Chao (Hsüan-tzu), the son of Ts'ui of Chao, who had been one of those faithful to Prince Wen, and the grandson of Su of Chao, who had been one of Prince Hsien's generals and had received from him the fief of Keng. Tun immediately proclaimed Yi-kao as Prince Ling, and drove away the partisans of Yung, who fled to their leader. He soon came with a Ch'in army: Tun marched to meet him and defeated him completely at Ling-hu. The prince being very young, it was the chief minister who took over government. As soon as possible he called the lords together at Hu: all were present, the princes of Ch'i, Sung, Wey, Ch'en, Cheng, Hsu, and Ts'ao, and they recognized Ling, renewing the pact of alliance.

Thus the position of Chin as leader of the League seemed to have survived all these changes; but this was only in appearance. The situation was made difficult on the one hand by the hostility of Ch'in, which continued to support the ousted pretender, and on the other by the enmity of Ch'i, which sought to take advantage of the circumstances and retake the topmost position. Moreover, internal difficulties abetted the external. The pretender had numerous partisans within the state, and Tun was not really sure even of his own army. In 618, following the assassination of K'o of Hsien, lieutenant of the centre army, Tun had to put to death the chief and lieutenant of the lower army, Cheng-fu of Chi and Tu of Hsien, as well as the Director of Works, Hu of the Shih, whose nephew Hui was in Ch'in and was Yung's principal partisan. The pretender's party began to decline little by little after these executions, all the more because successive defeats of the Ch'in armies had already hit them hard. Yet it was only in 614 that Hui, judging the cause to be hopeless, finally gave up and returned to his country. This whole period was thus marked by a decline in Chin's influence, and there were numerous defections from the League, which disbanded step by step.

To the north the Prince of Ch'i menaced his neighbours, Lu, Chü, Chu, and Ts'ao, seizing territory from them; and, wearied of appealing in vain to the leader of the League for help, they concluded an alliance with Ch'i as insurance. To the south, first Ts'ai and then Cheng and Ch'en passed into the clientele of Ch'u (618); and an expedition forced Duke Chao of Sung, who had alone remained loyal, to submit (617). Thus all of central China in fact slipped from Chin's grasp, and Tun, having to protect himself against Ch'in, could do nothing to stop it. He could only maintain the alliance of Wey and Ts'ao by returning to them territories which Chin had won from them earlier.

Just at this moment, however, the death of King Mu (614) was the signal of very serious troubles in Ch'u. Since his son, King Chuang, was very young, the nobles contested the regency with arms; and a great famine added horror to the civil war. The mountain people of the west, dying of hunger, rushed into the plain and in numerous bands threatened Ying, the capital. In a panic the court thought of fleeing to the upper reaches of the River Han (611); the remonstrances of the Regulator of Crafts, *kung-cheng*, Chia of Weiy, succeeded in deterring them. Moreover disorder soon appeared among the famished and ill-led gangs. The king personally took command of what troops remained to him; two other units were entrusted to generals Chiao of Tou (Tzu-yüeh) and Tzu-pei. The Viscount of Pa, the only one of the barbarian vassals to remain loyal, brought an army; even the Count of Ch'in, who was disquieted by these movements of barbarians on his southern frontier, sent help; and they succeeded in throwing the rebels back into their mountains (611).

It required several years of peace to rebuild what had been ruined in these few months, and there could be no question of Ch'u's intervening in Chinese affairs. During this time all of her allies naturally defected and submitted to Chin. It was only in 608 that King Chuang felt himself strong enough to resume the external policy of his predecessors and once more accepted the alliance of the Count of Cheng, who came to ask his protection and who took advantage of it to attack Ch'en and Sung. Tun of Chao came quickly to their aid but, beaten at Fei-lin by Chia of Weiy, then Minister of War, he had to retreat, and soon afterwards the army of Sung in its turn was completely destroyed (607).

Success seemed to have returned solidly to Ch'u; the quarrels of the nobles snatched it away. For over a century power had almost always been in the hands of the two branches descended from King Jo-ao (709–673): the branch of the counts of Tou and that of the lords of Ch'eng, who had contributed almost all of the chief ministers.[12] Their power drew upon them the hatred of all the other families. In 612 Chief of Commands Pan of Tou (Tzu-yang), son of Nou-wu-t'u of Tou (Tzu-wen) — who himself had held this position for twenty-seven years and had turned it over, in 637, to his cousin Te-ch'en of Ch'eng (Tzu-yü) — had been put to death after scarcely a year of governing. This followed a cabal brought about by the Regulator of Crafts, Chia of Weiy, the chief of another branch of the royal family descended from King Fen-mao (754–741), which bore the name of his fief of Weiy. Chia was the son of Lü-ch'en, who had been *ling-yin* in 632, and he had hoped that the position of *ling-yin* would revert to him; but it was given to a cousin of Tzu-yang, Chiao of Tou (Tzu-yüeh), then Minister of War.[13] Tzu-yüeh dreamed only of avenging his relative. In 605, taking advantage of a favourable occasion, he summoned his clan to arms, abducted Chia of Weiy, and put him to death.

Frightened, King Chuang offered him pardon, and even hostages. Tzu-yüeh refused and, managing to arm his partisans, revolted openly; he just missed shooting the king dead at the

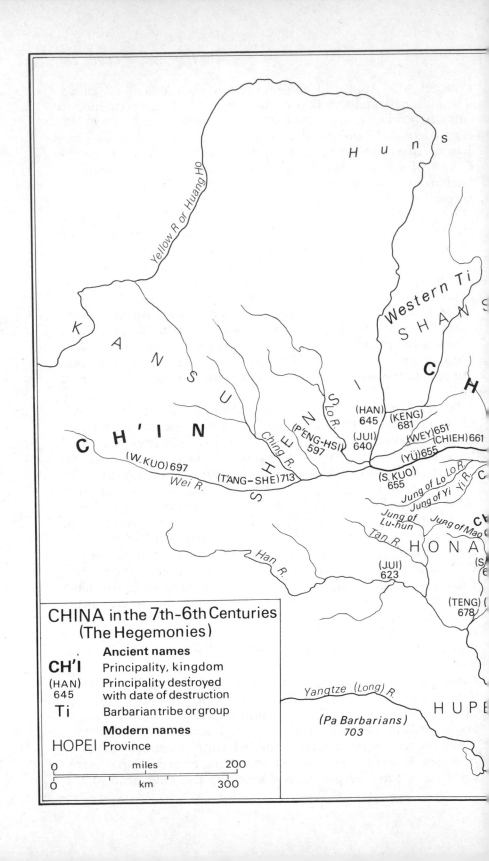

H u n s

Yellow R or Huang Ho

Western Ti

S H A N S

K A N S U

C H'I N

C

H

S. Lo R.

(HAN) 645

(KENG) 681

(JUI) 640

(WEY) 651

(CHIEH) 661

(P'ENG-HSI) 597

Ching R.

(YÜ) 655

(W. KUO) 697

S H E N S I

(T'ANG-SHE) 713

(S. KUO) 655

Jung of Lo Lo R.

Wei R.

Jung of Yi Yi R. C

Jung of Lu-hun

Jung of Mao Ch

Tan R.

H O N A

Han R.

(JUI) 623

(S E

(TENG) 678

CHINA in the 7th-6th Centuries
(The Hegemonies)

Ancient names

CH'I — Principality, kingdom

(HAN) 645 — Principality destroyed with date of destruction

Ti — Barbarian tribe or group

Modern names

HOPEI — Province

Yangtze (Long) R.

H U P E

(Pa Barbarians) 703

| 0 | miles | 200 |
| 0 | km | 300 |

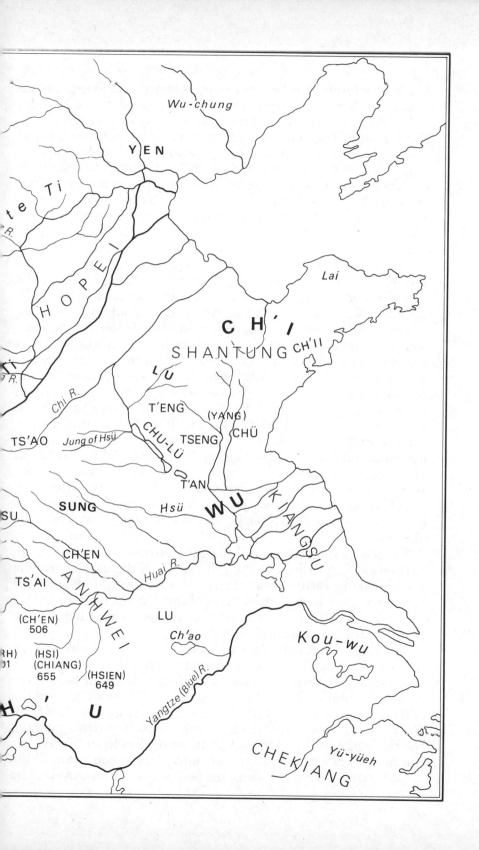

Wu-chung

YEN

te Ti

HOPEI

Lai

CH'I

SHANTUNG CH'II

LU

T'ENG   (YANG)

Chi R.

TS'AO   Jung of Hsü   CHU-LÜ TSENG   CHÜ

T'AN

SUNG   Hsü   WU
SU   KIANGSU

CH'EN

TS'AI   Huai R.

ANHWEI

LU

(CH'EN)
506   Ch'ao   Kou-wu

RH)   (HSI)
01   (CHIANG)
655   (HSIEN)
649

H'U   Yangtze (Blue) R.

CHEKIANG   Yü-yüeh

battle of Kao-hu; but he was finally defeated and killed, and his entire family was exterminated. Of the descendants of King Jo-ao, of the Tou branch as of the Ch'eng, only one was spared — K'o-huang of Tou, Tzu-wen's grandson, who was on embassy to Ch'i at the time of the massacre but who nevertheless came back to report upon his mission and to whom the king showed mercy in remembrance of his ancestor. And some escaped, such as Fen-huang of Tou, who fled to Chin, where he received a fief at Miao, and Hsiung of Ch'eng the grandson of Chief Minister Ta-hsin (Ta-sun-po), who was put to death later in 530.

This temblor had shaken the kingdom of Ch'u, and her allies again abandoned her. The efforts made to compel their submission were of little success, and they brought about the victorious intervention of Chin in 600 and 599; this led to little, since that state was also shaken by internal troubles.

Tun of Chao, who had governed in Chin under Prince Ling, had gone on to assassinate that sovereign following an attempt on the part of the prince to rid himself of the minister (607); and he had replaced the ruler with his uncle, who was Prince Ch'eng. But he could not run this prince, who was already mature, as easily as his predecessor, and had been forced to retire about 603. K'o of Hsü, who replaced him as chief minister, went mad after some months; and Ch'üeh of Hsi, his successor, died or was disgraced after a brief time (597) and was replaced by old Lin-fu of Hsün, former chief of the centre column in the time of Prince Wen (631) — he had been lieutenant of the centre army since 615. This series of old men and madmen at the head of government had produced a policy that was at once weak and little obeyed.

For ten years, each year brought into the central states an expedition from Chin and one from Ch'u, the armies retiring after pillaging, bearing with them treaties destined to be violated as soon as they were concluded, without any positive success on one side or the other. This state of things, harrassing for the people, came to an end only in 597.

In spring of that year, King Chuang, who had come to lay siege to the capital of Cheng, managed things so quickly that, despite the resistance of the inhabitants, the city was taken before the army of assistance from Chin could arrive. This news reached the chief of the centre army (that is to say, Generalissimo Lin-fu of Hsün) just as he was preparing to cross the Yellow River. Judging the campaign now useless and perilous, he decided to turn back; but his generals refused to follow him, and the lieutenant of the centre army, Hu of Hsien, himself crossed the River. The generalissimo was weak enough to follow him. On his side, moreover, the King of Ch'u was undecided whether or not to fight: the chief minister, Yi-lieh of Weiy (Sun-shu-ao), thought that they should beat a retreat; a favourite of the prince, Wu San, rather urged combat, and in the end he won the day.[14] The victory of Ch'u was complete. The Chin army, surprised before it was in battle formation, was scattered and barely managed to recross the River in disorderly fashion, leaving war chariots and arms in great number on the battle-field of Pi.

That defeat eliminated Chin for a while from the region. Her faithful ally, the Duke of Sung, felt the effects of it at once: in 596 a Ch'u army came to camp before his capital. After a siege of two years, during which Prince Ching of Chin dared not send help, he had to submit (594). This time the triumph of Ch'u was definitive: all the states south of the Yellow River recognized her hegemony. King Chuang held it from then on without contest; even at his death, in 591, it survived, despite the fact that his son, King Kung, was a minor aged only ten. The Prince of Wey alone thought himself able to take advantage of the circumstances and re-ally himself to Chin. An expedition, in which the small prince wished to take part, was decided upon. It was in actuality a triumphal parade: as soon as it approached a principality, the army received its submission. In the meantime the troops of Chin, on the other side of the River, followed the Ch'u movements from afar (589). But just at the moment when it seemed most solidly established, the hegemony of Ch'u collapsed, almost as suddenly as it had been born.

It was distant and apparently irrelevant events that ruined her and returned supremacy to Chin. The momentary eclipse of Chin had reawakened the ambitions of Prince Hui of Ch'i, who wished to take advantage of it and take Chin's place, or at least to extend his influence over his immediate neighbours. Already for twenty years Ch'i had dominated the state of Lu. Since 609 she had placed it under a sort of protectorate, first aiding the minister Hsiang-chung to enthrone (despite the opposition of the nobility) Prince Hsüan, the son of a favourite, rather than the son of the principal wife, and later by supporting him in the struggle he waged against the three great families descended from Prince Huan — the families Chi, Meng, and Shu-sun, which had become almost all-powerful. At Hsüan's death (591), the chief of the Chi family, Wen-tzu, banished the son of Hsiang-chung and retook the hereditary position of his family, that of chief minister, under Prince Ch'eng of Lu. In Ch'i, Prince Ch'ing, who had succeeded Hui during 598, feared that he might lose all influence in Lu and attacked her, seizing the city of Lung. Wen-tzu appealed to Chin, the protector of his family.

Prince Ching of Chin immediately sent K'o of Hsi with an army of 800 chariots against Ch'i, which was completely defeated at An (589). Ch'ing escaped being taken prisoner, owing his safety completely to the devotion of his charioteer, who pretended to be his master. The victorious army advanced rapidly towards the capital without meeting any resistance. The Prince of Ch'i obtained peace only on condition that he cede to Lu the territory he had seized. This was a true renewal of Chin power: internally, Ching had just subdued the Red Ti Tribes living in the valleys of southeastern Shansi (593);[15] externally, Ch'ing of Ch'i paid homage to him (588), at the same time as Cheng, in the centre, submitted; the League was completely reconstituted; Ch'u, despite its triumph of the year before, made a treaty and exchanged prisoners. The power of Prince Ching seemed so great that Ch'ing of Ch'i went to him and proposed that he take the title of king. He refused. He had no need of the title, since the hegemony, which had passed for an instant into the hands of Ch'u, had returned to his house.

4

The Alliance of Chin and Wu

The suddenness with which these hegemonies arose and collapsed shows how fragile they were. In fact, by the beginning of the sixth century Chin and Ch'u were about equal in strength, and neither of the two was capable of winning the definitive success which would destroy its rival and force it to renounce completely all further intervention in the affairs of central China. The two states seemed destined to wear one another out through incessant and sterile struggles pursuing a hegemony which they were quite able to seize for the moment but could not retain. Then it was that a former minister of Ch'u — Wu-ch'en of Ch'ü, whose appellation was Tzu-ling — who had taken refuge with Prince Ching of Chin after having abducted the beautiful Hsia Chi, gave Chin the idea of creating a diversion against Ch'u by organizing the barbarians of the lower Yangtze River and making allies of them; and he proposed to perform this delicate and dangerous mission himself.[1]

The barbarians of Kou-wu, who inhabited the rich plain situated at the mouths of the Yangtze and the Huai rivers, were made up of small communities governed by hereditary chiefs under the suzerainty of the Ch'u kings. Since the seventh century, those kings had in fact extended their influence over all the barbarian tribes of the Yangtze River, from what is now Szechuan in the west as far as the sea. The people of Kou-wu lived principally by agriculture and fishing; they differed from the Chinese in that they cultivated rice and perhaps a little wheat, rather than millet; moreover, they tattooed their bodies and wore their hair short. Otherwise, they must have been rather like the Chinese, since they seem to have been a backward and 'barbarian' branch of the great Chinese family. The influence of civilization, which reached them at the same time directly from the states of the middle Yellow River and indirectly by way of their masters in Ch'u, made itself felt little by little among them. When Wu-ch'en arrived at the residence of King Shou-meng of Wu in 584, he was probably not the first adventurer from the central states who had sought to make himself a career in these barbarian lands. Shou-meng received him warmly, letting himself be persuaded without too much trouble to conclude an alliance with Chin against Ch'u. Wu-ch'en organized an army for him in Chinese style: he taught the local people to handle chariots and the art of drawing an army up in battle order. When he thought his soldiers sufficiently trained, Shou-meng took advantage of a moment when the troops of Ch'u were occupied in an expedition against Cheng and he revolted, while from its side the army of Chin went to the aid of Cheng.

Shou-meng, who had taken the title King of Kou-wu (or more simply of Wu) to show that he considered himself the equal of his former suzerain, Ch'u, gained quick successes: he subdued the barbarians of Ch'ao, who lived on the shore of Lake Ch'ao, between the lake and the Yangtze River, as well as those of Hsü, who lived north of the Huai River near the Hung-tse Lake. The first minister of Ch'u, Prince Ying-ch'i (Tzu-ch'ung), the uncle of King Kung, had to hasten there with all speed from Cheng, where he had been carrying on a campaign, and then left again hastily, without having achieved anything, at the news that the Minister of War, his brother Prince Tse (Tzu-fan), who had remained in the north, had just been defeated by Chin (584). The year passed thus in marches and countermarches, exhausting for the Ch'u armies, which were obliged to confront enemies suddenly and unexpectedly on two fronts. Tzu-ch'ung and Tzu-fan journeyed from one front to the other seven times in a single year. Shou-meng took advantage of this to subdue the barbarians of the east who had hitherto recognized the supremacy of Ch'u and, driving again up the Huai River, he advanced as far as Chou-lai (near Shou-chou in modern Anhwei). All the land which today comprises Kiangsu and the northern half of Anhwei had fallen clearly within the domain of the new kingdom of Wu.

During this time Chin seized Ts'ai and Ch'en, at the very frontier of Ch'u (583). The authority of Prince Ching of Chin became extensive: to the southeast, the kingdom of Wu made an alliance with him and, by way of reward for services rendered, was admitted to the assembly of princes (582); to the east, Ch'i became his ally, in recompense for which he made Lu return the territories reconquered after the victory of An; in the centre, all the states of the League, except Cheng, submitted, and Ch'u, which had not only lost all influence among the states of the centre but was even obliged to defend itself within its own boundaries, soon decided to send an embassy to Chin, asking that the two states henceforth maintain a firm friendship and establish a lasting peace (582). In all of China, only Ch'in remained hostile; and it did not remain so for long. The peace between Chin and Ch'u was the longest China had seen. It lasted eight years, without the death of Prince Ching (581) shaking it: the two states exchanged embassies virtually every year.

Prince Li, continuing his father's work, took advantage of this to turn all his forces against Ch'in to put an end to a war which had lasted for years. In 580, things seemed near to being settled. It was decided that the two princes should meet at Ling-hu and make a treaty; but at the last moment Count Huan of Ch'in refused to cross the Yellow River to go and meet Li, sent one of his officers instead of himself, and then soon — returning to his capital — broke the treaty and prepared to resume campaigning. But he sought in vain to ally himself with the Ti and with Ch'u, who refused and remained loyal to Chin. In 578, he found himself attacked by all the troops of the League, whom Li had persuaded, under the pretext of the broken treaty and vow, to march against Ch'in with the King of Chou's sanction. Ch'in sustained a grave defeat at Ma-sui. This was the peak of Chin's power: at that moment she exercised virtually sovereign power within the empire.

Once more it was Cheng which brought about the rupture between Chin and Ch'u. She had not ceased raiding the small state of Hsu, her neighbour, a vassal of Ch'u; in 577 she obliged Hsu to cede her a large strip of territory. The following year, King Kung of Ch'u, probably to revenge Hsu, decided to break the peace, though he had not been directly attacked. As the ministers discussed the opportunity of the expedition, his uncle Tse (Tzu-fan) declared: 'If we can take advantage of an enemy, we must make the expedition. What is the importance of treaties?' The king allowed himself to be convinced and sent Tzu-fan to invade Cheng and Wey (576). The Prince of Chin had attached no importance to the matter so, emboldened by this impunity, he then proposed to Count Ch'eng of Cheng that he should abandon the League and ally himself to Ch'u, in exchange for which he would cede to Cheng the territory of Ju-yin, on their common frontier. Ch'eng accepted at once and went to attack Sung. This time Li was disturbed and organized an expedition. The army of Ch'u, having come to the aid of its ally, crossed the Yellow River and went to Yen-ling (575). The battle was hotly fought, lasting all day and into the evening. The princes participated in person: King Kung had an eye gouged out by an arrow, the Count of Cheng twice missed being taken prisoner. By evening the fight was undecided, and when night forced the combatants to separate each party expected to resume combat on the morrow and made preparations. But the Ch'u Commander-in-Chief, Prince Tse, got so drunk when the fighting was over that he could not respond to the king's call when summoned to a council; and the king, not understanding the situation, believed that he had been defeated and gave the order to withdraw immediately. In the morning the men of Chin found the camp abandoned but dared not undertake pursuit. During this time, Tse, finally aroused, committed suicide despite the remonstrances of the king, who told him that he was not considered in any way responsible for the defeat.

The incursions of Ch'u were halted for a time, but peace had become precarious: Furthermore, these continuous wars began to weary Chin; this hegemony which had to be constantly reconquered through ruinous expeditions ended by costing more than it could repay. The great lords especially, who undoubtedly saw in it expenditures without personal profit to themselves, were in large number opposed to it. Before the Battle of Yen-ling,[2] some of them did not scruple to hope for a defeat which, by detaching the League from the prince, would force him to retire to his states and live there in peace. It even seems that a certain group wished to take advantage of the prince's absence with the army to seek a revolution in the capital and put a distant relative, Chou, upon the throne. The victory prevented them from carrying their project through, and Li, who had got wind of it, took revenge by massacring the Hsi family at the end of 573; but he dared not carry through to the end and visit the same fate upon the Luan and the Chung-hang. He even recalled them to the court and returned their honours to them. It was giving himself up to death: Shu of Luan and Yen of the Chung-hang succeeded in surprising him and casting him into prison, where he died after six days. Then they had Chou come to succeed him, as Prince Tao.[3]

The assassination of Li marked the end of the Chin princes' real power. Henceforeward none of them made any further effort to rid themselves of the guardianship of the great vassals. Tao, forty years old at his accession, began the series of weak sovereigns who were mere playthings in the hands of their ministers, the chiefs of great families, who contended for power among themselves. For almost all of his reign he suffered the arrogance of Chiang of Wei, who went so far as to insult the king's brother but who could not be dismissed.

Otherwise, externally, nothing of the traditional polity had changed: the prince continued to call the lords together and to head the League; Cheng, which had sought to profit from the change of reign by leaving that League, was beaten and forced to submit (571); and in the following year Hsu suffered the same fate. The power of Chin seemed great enough to urge Ch'en, a state which had long previously withdrawn from the League to accept the suzerainty of her powerful southern neighbour, to abandon that loyalty (570). But that power could not function effectively in so distant a region and could not defend Ch'en several years later, when its capital was besieged (566).

Nearer home, on the other hand, Chin remained great. She was able to promptly break up the alliance concluded in 561 between Ch'u and Ch'in, which might have had serious consequences. Chiang of Wei, leading the troops of the League against Ch'in and penetrating to the heartland of enemy territory, gained a great victory and passed the River Ching at Yü-lin (559), after which the Count of Ch'in, seized with fear, broke off the alliance with Ch'u and made peace. In eleven years Tao had called the lords together nine times; under his son, Prince P'ing (556–531), the situation seemed no less happy. A triumphal expedition against Ch'i contributed again to the heightening of Chin's prestige: Ch'i's troops were crushed at P'ing-yin and dispersed; her capital, Lin-tzu, was blockaded and its suburbs burned; and the entire countryside was sacked (555).

But an incident showed how unstable this power was. In 550 a grand officer, Ying of Luan,[4] who had been accused of conspiracy against the Prime Minister, Kai of the Shih, and had been forced to fly first to Ch'u and then to Ch'i, returned at the head of an army from Ch'i. He summoned his vassals to arms, seized the city of Chiang with the aid of Shu of Wei (Hsien-tzu), and — concealed by him and the lord of Hsi — succeeded in entering the capital. The revolt was so unexpected that Prince P'ing, taken at court, wished to kill himself, and his minister, Kai of the Shih (Hsüan-tzu of Fan), prepared to flee; they were saved by the intervention of the families of Han, Chao, Chih, and Chung-hang, who had vendettas against the Luan family; and also by the personal energy of Yang, Kai's son. He surprised Shu of Wei at the moment when, with those loyal to him, he was going to rejoin Ying of Luan, and — not leaving him enough time to recover — hustled him before the prince, where he was put beyond any chance of doing harm. Ying, abandoned by all, was forced to take flight. The rescued prince revenged himself by putting all the Luan family to death. Then two years later he took advantage of troubles in Ch'i, where Prince Chuang had been assassinated, to invade it, defeating its army at Kao-t'ang. Despite this prompt repression, the fundamental vice of Chin government had just shown itself naked: the impotence of the prince, who, unable to impose his will upon the great vassals, was reduced to playing one off against the others and counting upon mutual greed and hate to preserve an authority over them that became more and more precarious.

This anomaly — the omnipotence of the princes externally and their impotence internally — could not last. The kings of Ch'u took advantage of it to regain, little by little, the lands they had lost. In 546 a minister of Sung, the Master of the Left (*tso-shih*) Hsü of Hsiang, hoping to put off the inevitable conflict, conceived the idea of making the two states accept a sort of shared hegemony. An assembly was held at Po, the capital of Sung; twelve states sent ministers there — Chin, Ch'u, Ts'ai, Wey, Ch'en, Cheng, Hsu, Ts'ao, Sung, Lu, Ch'in, and Ch'i (though the last two were not parties to the agreement). It very nearly ended in a slaughter, for the *ling-yin*, Chien of Ch'ü (Tzu-mu) wanted to take the Chin army by surprise and massacre them. It was possible to persuade him that this ambush would be impolitic; and it was agreed that the two rival leagues would unite in a vast confederation of which the two states of Chin and Ch'u would have the joint leadership, and that all the princes would send embassies regularly to Chin and Ch'u simultaneously.[5] The treaty, renewed at Kuo in 541,[6] was solemnized several times but, with the power of Chin declining steadily, her rival soon felt strong enough to oust her completely.

In 538 King Ling of Ch'u, who three years earlier had taken the place of his nephew, King Chia-ao, after having strangled him,[7] 'sent an embassy to Chin to announce there his wish to call the lords together'. This was a polite way for him to indicate that he had succeeded in setting up a counter-league opposed to Chin's, and that he had broken off relations with Chin. This is indeed how it must be understood. At the meeting of Shen, over which King Ling presided, Chin and her allies (Sung, Lu, Wey, and Wu) were not present: and an expedition was decided upon against the most powerful of them, the kingdom of Wu. The following years were marked by Ch'u's victories and expansion without Chin daring to respond; the war against Wu, to be sure, lasted several years with varying success on the one side and on the other; but to the north, the lands of Ch'en and Ts'ai were conquered and established as a fief for Prince Ch'i-chi, the brother of King Ling.

At this moment, all the states menaced by the incursions of Wu, which is to say all the principalities situated near her borders or on the seacoast (Ch'i, Lu, Weiy, Chü and Chu) sought the protection of the King of Ch'u and recognized his hegemony. Fortifications were raised around the capitals of Ch'en and Ts'ai to protect the northern frontier; King Ling prepared to conquer Cheng on the pretext that Hsu, the original domain of the ancestors of his house, had been there. Still more, he dreamed of dislodging the dynasty of the Chou and replacing it upon the throne. It is said that one day he put a question to the tortoise-shell augury, asking whether he could make himself master of the empire, and the response being unfavourable he violently disavowed the shell and reviled Heaven, saying, 'You do not wish to grant me this petty thing? Then I shall take it all by myself.' But all these great projects did not go on without exhausting the population. Between military expeditions and construction, the people were overwhelmed with corvées.[8] One whole faction of malcontents were grouped about the king's brothers — Prince Ch'i-chi, Duke of Ch'en, and Prince Pi of Ts'ai. In 529, taking advantage of the fact that the king had personally accompanied the army in a new expedition against Wu, they attacked the capital with the troops of Ch'en and Ts'ai. The heir apparent, Prince Lu, was killed, Pi was named king and Ch'i-chi became Minister of War.

At the news of this *coup d'état*, the entire army of King Ling dispersed. Furthermore the king, distraught over the death of his son, lost his head and gave way entirely to distress: on hearing of the death, he cast himself down from his chariot, saying, 'Do men love their sons as I loved mine?' 'Far more deeply,' replied one of his attendants. The king resumed, 'I have slain many sons of other men; could it fail to be visited upon me as well?' And he gave way to grief with such abandon that he discouraged the last of those loyal to him. The Master of the Right proposed at first that the king should go himself to the capital, where his return would probably be enough to re-establish order, then that he should get troops in the neighbouring fortresses, and finally that he ask help from one of the northern princes. King Ling turned all these counsels aside without deciding upon any. To the last he replied, 'The great opportunity comes only once. I should only be bringing a rebuff upon myself!' Then he embarked upon the River Han to go to Yen, the secondary capital of the kingdom.

Little by little, seeing him incapable of making any plan and fearing to perish with him, everyone abandoned him. He wandered alone in the mountains; no peasant dared to take him in, and he went three days without eating. A former sweeper from the palace whom he met told him that all who gave him anything to eat would be put to death with all their kin. Not daring to spurn him, however, the fellow followed for a while but then took advantage of a time when the king was sleeping to flee. When the king awoke, he was too weak to get up. The son of a former official, Shen Hai, hearing of his distress, went to seek him out, and found him dying at the pool of Li; he gave him food and took him in. In the fifth month, the king committed suicide in Shen Hai's house, and that worthy, in order to inter his master fittingly, slew his own daughters and buried both of them with the king, so as to accompany him in the next world (529).[9]

While King Ling died thus, abandoned by all, at the very moment when he envisioned himself already master of the entire empire, the conspirators at the capital, jealous of one another, did not know what to do, fearing lest they might see him suddenly reappear. The brother of the new king, Ch'i-chi, took advantage of this terror to provoke a panic by announcing the arrival of Ling. The new king committed suicide and Ch'i-chi mounted the throne: he was King P'ing. In order to be accepted among the lords after his double murder he restored their states to the princes of Ch'en and Ts'ai, whom Ling had dethroned, and he also returned to Cheng the territories which had been conquered earlier (528).

By this, moreover, he inaugurated a policy of peace abroad, necessary for returning prosperity to the country which Ling's constant warfare had exhausted. He rounded this out by marrying the daughter of the Count of Ch'in, thus safeguarding himself in that quarter.

It seemed that, after the ten years of Ch'u supremacy under King Ling, power would return to Chin as in the past. Prince Ch'ing of Chin resumed the presidency of the League; he re-established order in the royal house of Chou and brought back to the capital King Tao (520), whom his brother Chao had driven away right after the death of their father, King Ching. Then, Tao dying soon afterwards and Chao having tried once more, with the help of Ch'u,[10] to take power, Prince Ch'ing charged his troops in the lands south of the River (formerly Kuo) to enthrone another brother of King Tao, King Ching (519–516). This was the

Prince of Chin to whom Prince Chao of Lu — driven from his state (517) by Yi-ju (P'ing-tzu) of the Chi clan, the father of Confucius's protector, and by the nobles of the principality — appealed for reinstatement three years later, though without success. Even after Ch'ing died (512), the king appealed to his successor, Ting, as chief of the lords in order to get the subsidy needed to restore a wall girdling his capital; and when Prince Ting called the lords together to discuss this at Ti-ch'üan, there was not a single failure to respond (510). Finally, he presided over the assembly at Shao-ling (506), in which eighteen states took part, several of them loyal vassals of Ch'u, but where they discussed the opportunity of an expedition against Ch'u, which was openly protecting Chao, the pretender to the Chou throne.

The time was right for the decisive destruction of Ch'u. The incessant and ever-victorious campaigns of the Wu armies had exhausted her; her allies, who knew this, sought only to abandon her, and her intrusion into the affairs of the royal house had given them an excellent pretext. Success was certain, as the King of Wu's crushing victory a few months later proved. Prince Ting did not dare seize the occasion, the meeting at Shao-ling displaying his weakness to all eyes. He was seen as tossed about among the hands of his various ministers, not knowing what he wanted; and they, corrupted, were openly up for sale. He ended by refusing the expedition, on the pretext that the northern barbarians had aroused his fears; a mere military demonstration of no import was decided upon.

That was the weakness of the Chin hegemony. Only the lack of another sufficiently strong power prevented most of the princes from abandoning the League; but Cheng re-established relations with Ch'u (505), and Wey and Lu did the same with Ch'i. The long civil war among the great families which, from 497 on, would trouble the entire end of Ting's reign, with its various alternatives and with the intervention of Prince Ching of Ch'i, who furnished troops and subsidies to the rebels constantly, served to weaken the League. One by one, the members resumed their independence. Once the civil war in Chin was ended, a brilliant campaign against Ch'i, which had aided the rebels so long and had given them refuge after their defeat, retrieved some prestige for Chin (485). Yet she was felt to be incapable of the energetic and sustained policy which the empire needed; and these victories, which they knew would certainly have no repercussions, no longer had any effect upon the princes. They all realized that, drained by the civil wars, Chin no longer had any real power; her hegemony was no longer any more than a habit tolerated for want of a better one, and the least incident could demonstrate its emptiness. The incident occurred in 482, when the old ally of the Chin princes, the King of Wu, drunk with his successes, claimed and at Huang-ch'ih got the presidency of the assembly of lords, which Prince Ting of Chin contested with him in vain.

In the course of a century, indeed, the kingdom of Wu had become extremely powerful. She accepted and gave high responsibilities to all those banished from Ch'u, thus assuring herself of a valuable aid against that country. She succeeded in pushing Ch'u back completely west of the Huai hills and, on the Yangtze, drove her back farther still, conquering the area of the Po-yang Lake. In vain the men of Ch'u had tried to organize the barbarians of Yü-yüeh or Yüeh (in Chekiang) against her; having imprudently assaulted her in 510, they had been easily beaten and obliged to submit.[11] Nevertheless, until this time she had been a faithful ally of Chin and had never interposed in matters proper to the kingdoms of the centre. Towards the end of the sixth century the policy of Wu became more independent.

King Ho-lü, who had mounted the throne in 510 by assassinating his nephew, King Liao, had as his counsellor and first minister Yüan of Wu (Tzu-hsü), a noble of Ch'u, whose father and elder brother had been put to death by King P'ing and who urged war out of desire for vengeance. In 506 the time seemed right: the land of Ch'u was exhausted, the grand officers hated one another. Thanks to the treason of the vassals, T'ang and Ts'ai, surprise was complete and success overwhelming. Ho-lü traversed half the kingdom of Ch'u from east to west and advanced to the Han without encountering any resistance. There, finding the enemy forces drawn up for battle to oppose his crossing, he dared not engage them. But then his younger brother, Fu-kai, at the head of 5,000 men, succeeded in crossing the river and surprising the enemy, who were vanquished and beat a retreat, pursued by the troops of Wu, in the direction of Ying, the capital. There were five fights, all victories for the soldiers of Wu, who entered Ying in triumph, while King Chao fled to Sui. The victorious generals, Wu Tzu-hsü and Po P'i, two exiles from Ch'u, disinterred the corpse of King P'ing and flayed it to avenge their fathers.

But the triumph of Wu was so complete that it frightened everybody. Count Ai of Ch'in hastened to send troops to the aid of Ch'u, and the men of Wu were defeated. At the same time, the King of Yüeh took advantage of the fact that Wu had been stripped of troops to attack her and gain easy victories. King Ho-lü, however, refused to recognize that his conquest was escaping him. Obstinately he remained in Ch'u, not seeing that the situation was becoming more critical every day. His eyes were opened at last when his brother Fu-kai, believing the king was finished, hastened to return to Wu and take the title for himself. Ho-lü then hurriedly returned and defeated his brother, while King Chao re-entered Ying, his liberated capital (505). It was not for long. Scarcely had order been re-established in the two states than Ho-lü organized a new expedition against Ch'u. At this news, Chao left Ying without waiting for the enemy to arrive. He went and set himself up at the mountain gateway to the north, on the Han River, at a place called Jo, because the inhabitants of the old principality of Jo, situated up-river from there, had settled there after the sack of their country by Ch'in in 623. King Chao gave this city the name of Yen-ying, in memory of his former capital (504). Fortune had also turned for Ho-lü, who was beaten in 496 by King Kou-chien of Yüeh at Tsui-li and, wounded in the foot during the fight, died soon afterwards of his wound.

Three years later his son, King Fu-ch'ai, revenged him by a brilliant defeat of Yüeh: Kou-chien, who had taken refuge on the Kuei-chi Mountain south of his capital and had been reduced to the final extremity, offered his total submission. It was accepted, despite the counsels of Wu Tzu-hsü, who wished to slay Kou-chien and reduce his country to a province, thus bringing the struggle to an end; and the country of Yüeh became a vassal of Wu (494).

Thus King Fu-ch'ai felt himself freed of all anxiety both on the west, where Ch'in had been rendered innocuous, and on the south, where Yüeh had been completely subdued. And, against the advice of his minister Wu Tzu-hsü, who — more clear-sighted than his sovereign — saw that their enemies had not been disarmed, he turned his ambitions northward. In 489 he took advantage of the troubles which followed the death of old Prince Ching in Ch'i and attacked that country; he vanquished it and subdued the small principalities on Ch'i's southern frontier which recognized its supremacy (Lu, Chu, and so on); but in spite of these victories, the war continued for several years with no decisive success. In 485, an attack by sea directed against Lin-tzu, the capital of Ch'i — on the pretext of avenging Prince Tao, who had been assassinated by Mu of Pao — failed completely; and from that moment on the attacks against Ch'i ceased.

Despite this failure, the King of Wu was at that instant the most powerful sovereign in all China: the rapidity of his victories over Ch'u, Yüeh, and Ch'i had given him the real supremacy of which the Prince of Chin had enjoyed only the appearance. He soon desired to take that very appearance for himself: he convoked the lords at Huang-ch'ih so as to make them grant him the hegemony. Between Prince Ting of Chin and King Fu-ch'ai the dispute was very lively; at one point Yang of Chao proposed to settle the issue with arms. It seems that they arrived at a compromise: the Prince of Chin retained the honorary presidency and precedence, but the actual leadership belonged to the King of Wu (482).[12]

At the very moment when that worthy thus attained the peak of his power the period of disasters had commenced for him. It is said that his minister Wu Tzu-hsü had foreseen that the ambitions of his master within China would be the ruin of the country and had turned himself over to the enemy in Yüeh, and that, having received the order to commit suicide in 485, he cried, at the point of death, 'Plant a catalpa on my tomb; when it can serve as the haft of a tool, tear out my eyes and place them on the eastern gate of Wu so that I can behold the annihilation of Wu by Yüeh!'[13]

The facts did not contradict his forecast: while the king was far away to preside over the assembly of Huang-ch'ih, a band of 5,000 men from Yüeh attacked Wu, pillaged the capital, and seized the heir apparent; then they retired. Upon receiving this news, Fu-ch'ai, to insure that it should not be noised about among the assembled princes, himself decapitated seven men in his tent. Furthermore, he could take no revenge for the affair; his army was weakened by lengthy campaigns in the north, his son a prisoner, his land wearied with war. Upon his return he could only purchase peace with valuable gifts offered to Kou-chien. But this was only a moment of respite: six years later, Kou-chien attacked anew, defeated him, and laid siege to his capital; he resisted for two years but finally, in about the last months of 473, he had to surrender. His adversary did not make the same mistake that Fu-ch'ai had with him before, but annexed the entire country. As for the old king, Kou-chien wanted to give him a little fief at Yung-tung in the Chusan Islands. He refused: 'I am old,' he said, 'and cannot serve Your Majesty. I regret not having followed Wu Tzu-hsü's counsels. It is I myself that am the cause of my downfall!'[14] Then he covered his face and said, 'I do not wish to have a face to look upon Wu Tzu-hsü!' for he feared the reproaches of his former counsellor's spirit in the other world; and he cut his throat.[15]

The kingdom had lasted scarcely a century, but this brief space of time had sufficed for it to destroy the prestige of two states which had until then seemed the most powerful in China, Ch'u and Chin.

The period of the hegemonies was thus suddenly ended. The new victor, the King of Yüeh, had not the stature to hold the prime role in China. Chin, without its ally in Wu, was no longer in condition to impose its will upon the other principalities, and moreover it was soon to disappear, destroyed by internal dissensions. After its downfall, Ch'in and Ch'i, freed of their fears, would be capable of preventing Ch'u from gathering in the succession. An era of unstable equilibrium was beginning, that of the 'Warring States', *chan kuo*.

Book IV
The Warring Kingdoms

1
The Ruin of Chin

The Huang-ch'ih affair had brutally highlighted the basic weakness of Chin, though this was still cloaked by the prestige of her past power; but that weakness was not enough in itself to bring about her downfall. About twelve years later the principality seemed to revive and to regain her status abroad. This was due to the victories of the Count of Chih: first over Ch'i, the army of which he destroyed at Li-ch'iu after a short and brilliant campaign (472) to punish her for the aid she had given to rebels over the years; and then over Cheng, which was first saved when help came from Ch'i, but was finally defeated and forced into submission in 463. Unfortunately there were deeper causes for the ruin of Chin. In actuality, she destroyed herself through the quarrels which rose incessantly among the great vassals and among which the authority of the reigning house finally foundered.

This evil dated almost from the beginnings of the state. The princes of Chin had freely bestowed lands upon their favourites — either portions of their own domain or, especially after the seventh century, newly conquered territories. Thus they had nourished the growth around them of a powerful aristocracy of great vassals whom the very configuration of the country, mountainous and difficult, cut up by narrow valleys and tight gorges, allowed to take on more and more independence in their domains. This was a turbulent aristocracy of great families whose chiefs, secure in the loyalty of their junior branches, constantly struggled among themselves to expand their fiefs or for new posts at court.

An initial nucleus had been formed by the descendants of loyal followers of the counts of Ch'ü-wu, who had helped them overthrow the senior branch at the beginning of the seventh century. These were the lords of Han, descended from a brother of Prince Wu who had been the prince's charioteer in his march upon the capital; the lords of Liang, descended from the halberdier of his chariot; the overlords of Luan, and so on. There were also the descendants of Prince Hsien's favourites who had assisted him in his conquests — Su of Chao, who had received the territory of Keng; Wan of Pi, who had received Wei; and the descendants of Prince Wen's companions who had followed him faithfully during his exile — Ch'en of Hsü (Chiu-chi); Lin-fu of Hsün, his charioteer during the expedition against Ch'u; his cousins on his mother's side, Mao of Hu and Yen of Hu. All these formed powerful houses, not to mention Ts'ui of Chao and Ch'ou of Wei, who placed theirs, already important, within the first rank. Aside from these, there were the collateral branches of the princely house, such as the Luan family, descended from Prince Ching (858–841); that of Yang-she, descended from Prince Hsien (822–812); the Chi family (so named after their ancestor, who had been *chi*, Chief of the Archives), descended from Prince Wen (780–746); the family of Han, whose ancestor had been the uncle of the Count of Ch'ü-wu. And finally there were families of various origins, such as the Ch'i and the Fan,[1] who claimed descent from a son of the Count of Tu (killed by King Hsüan in 730) who had taken refuge in Chin, and thus descent from the ancient overlords of T'ang, which is to say of the land where the Chin capital had been before the Chou dispossessed them. There were great barbarian chiefs who had adopted Chinese civilization, like the Hu family of the T'ai-yüan region, whose daughter was Prince Wen's mother, and so on.

All these families were jealous of one another and quarrelled with one another, going to the brink of real war. The creation of two supplementary armies and of three so-called columns after the three new armies gave a preponderant influence to some of these, since their commands became veritable fiefs which, though not absolutely hereditary, remained in the families of Chao, of Han, of Wei, of Fan, of Luan, of Hsien, and of two branches of the Hsün, one of which took its distinctive name from its military post, being named Chung-hang (centre column).

At the end of the seventh century, the Chao family was most powerful, under Tun, the son of Ts'ui and nephew of Prince Wen on the maternal side. As regent during the minority of Prince Ling, he had had the prince assassinated (607) and had retained power under the prince's uncle, Prince Ch'eng, whom Tun placed on the throne. This continued under Tun's son Shuo, who had married Prince Ch'eng's elder sister. But Shuo, having in turn become too powerful, offended the other nobles, who attacked and massacred him, together with his whole family (583). The Chao family thus found its power broken for nearly half a century. Its property and its official posts, initially confiscated and given by the prince to Hsi of Ch'i, were later restored to a son of Shuo's who had escaped the massacre.[2]

During the entire first quarter of the sixth century it was the Hsi family to whom the greatest importance attached. Under Prince Li (580–573), three of its members were ministers and five others were grand officers.[3] Li tried to rid himself of them by relying upon their enemies, the Hsü. He had 'the three Hsi' and all their relatives massacred, and the corpses of the three ministers were exposed in the palace courtyard (574); but his heart failed him when his favourites also wished to take the chief and the lieutenant of the centre army, Shu of Luan and Yen of Chung-hang (Hsien-Tzu of Hsün), and slay them before his eyes. He had them released and immediately paid with his life for this moment of weakness (573).

After him the authority of the princes could scarcely be maintained any longer except by the jealousies of the great families, who kept a wary eye on one another. This showed clearly in 550, when Ying of Luan made a surprise attack on the capital, which failed only because families inimical to the Luan opposed it.[4] But from generation to generation, these great families disappeared. If that of Chao had the good luck to avoid extermination, that of Hsi was massacred in 574, that of Luan was put to death in the aftermath of the 550 affair, those of Yang-she and Ch'i were destroyed in 514; and in 506 it was the turn of the Po, whose chief fled to Wu.

In 497 a long civil war started between Chao, Wei, Han, and Chih (a branch of the Hsün family) on the one side and on the other the Lord of Fan and the chief of the Chung-hang family, supported by the Prince of Ch'i and — of little real effect, but lending a certain measure of legitimacy to the rebellion — by the Chou king. The conflict ended only in 490 after all the holdings of the rebel families had been conquered, their chiefs forced to flee to Ch'i, and their territories first returned to the Prince of Chin and then, in 458, divided among the four victors.

Among the four surviving great families, the overlords of Chao and the counts of Chih were then the most powerful, but they neutralized one another by their mutual enmity. Only after the death of Yang of Chao did the chief of the Chih, Yao of Hsün, having managed to succeed Yang as chief of the centre army — that is to say, as prime minister — feel himself freed and give full play to his ambition to set himself upon the Chin throne. He nearly succeeded in 457, when he expelled Prince Ch'u, who had tried appealing to Ch'i and Lu for aid in getting rid of Yao, and had replaced him with an infant, Prince Ai.

Wishing to subdue his former allies, Yao pressed them to hand over their share of the properties of the Chung-hang and Fan families. The lords of Han and Wei submitted. Only Wu-hsü of Chao, the son of Yang, felt himself strong enough to refuse: he left the court and went off to entrench himself in his fief of Chin-yang (near the present-day prefecture of T'ai-yüan). The Count of Chih marched against him, together with the lords of Han and Wei (455). A quick victory would probably have insured Yao's definitive success; but the siege dragged on and his allies, who had followed him only reluctantly, secretly betrayed him to come to an understanding with Wu-hsü of Chao. Yao was assassinated, his family destroyed, and his properties divided among the families of Chao, Han, and Wei (453).

According to the story, it was the arrogance and imprudence of the Count of Chih which brought him low. In the course of the siege, he had had a branch of the Chin River diverted to flood the city. One day when he was inspecting the work, going by in a chariot with his charioteer Chü of Wei (Huan-tzu) and his halberdier Hu of Han (K'ang-tzu), he suddenly said, 'I never knew that one could destroy a man's kingdom, but now I do. The River Fen could be used against An-yi and the River Chiang against P'ing-yang.' The two lords nudged one another, for it was their own capitals that he had mentioned. Soon afterwards they reached an agreement with Wu-hsü. Yao was killed, his head cut off, and his skull coated with varnish to serve as a drinking-cup for the Lord of Chao.[5]

The next thirty years were the most troubled that the state of Chin had ever experienced.[6] The death of the Count of Chih had completed the dissolution of the central power: the three *tai-fu* of Chao, Han, and Wei were too fearful from then on to accept the power of the prime minister. They preferred to refuse it, passing it from one to another. About 424, they recognized their mutual independence, while the descendants of their former sovereigns, Prince Ching and then his son Prince Yu, reduced to the cities of Chiang and Ch'ü-wu, were obliged to pay homage to their too-powerful vassals. In 420, Wen of Wei took advantage of the troubles caused by the death of Yu, who was assassinated by his wife, to place upon the throne one of his followers, Prince Lieh.[7] The latter and his two successors were from then on subject to the princes of Wei, until the day when the last of them, Prince Ching, was deported and reduced to the rank of an ordinary commoner (376). The Son of Heaven, King Wei-lieh, recognized the situation officially in 403 by granting the three lords of Wei, Han, and Chao the title of princes.

The boundaries of the three new principalities were extremely confused. At the beginning of the fifth century, Chao comprised all the north of the former state of Chin. The prince's own domain was the basin in which T'ai-yüan stands today. To the south, it is difficult to know whether or not the old familial fief of Chao, on the lower reaches of the Fen, from which the family had taken its name, still belonged to it; the fiefs of the family and of its vassals extended well beyond its limits. To the west, Chao probably reached to the Yellow River. To the east, it was certainly the former course of this river (roughly represented today by that of the River Hu-t'o or of the Chang) which served as its border with the principality of Ch'i, in the region where today we find the prefectures of Kuang-p'ing and Shun-te in Hopei province, and where a collateral branch of the reigning family held the fief of Han-tan. To the north, the Keng of the barbarian Tai kingdom, in the region of the modern prefectures Ning-wu and Ta-t'ung, soon followed by the submission of the Huns of Tan-lin and of Lin-hu, which were on the two banks of the Yellow River, almost doubled the area of the principality and made a compact bloc of all these scattered fiefs. It was from there that the princes of Chao would draw the levies of horsemen and mounted archers who would provide the mainstay of their armies in the fourth century. In the eastern sector lay the capitals: first Chung-mou (424) and later Han-tan, after 386.[8] This eastern section seems to have been separated from the western and northern parts by territories belonging to Han and to Wei.

The principality of Han was much smaller. The lords of Han belonged to the Chi clan, the first of whom, Wu-tzu, had received the fief of Han on the right bank of the Yellow River. But they seem not to have long retained this fief, which was conquered by Ch'in; and at the beginning of the fifth century they set up their residence in a less dangerous region, on the River Fen, near present-day P'ing-yang fu. In this period the importance of the family was already well established, and from 587 on Ch'üeh of Han was one of the six dignitaries of Chin, the hereditary commander of one of the six armies. At his death the domains of his family must have expanded far to the east, since his son moved his residence to the lower course of the Ch'in-ho, at Chou, which is today Wu-she. In 514 Han aggrandized herself with the spoils of the Yang-she and Ch'i families, which had been wiped out, and then in 453 by those of Chih-po.

At the end of the fifth century there were numerous fiefs changing hands, so that they are difficult to follow. For example, P'ing-yang belonged to the Han family and it was there that Ch'üeh of Han resided. At some point it passed to the Yang-she family; when this was exterminated and its goods confiscated, in 514, that fief was given to Ch'ao of Chao — at least three changes of hand in a hundred years. Nevertheless, the territory of Han at this time generally included the whole basin of the River Ch'in, with the mountainous region to the east of it, where the two rivers Chang rise (this region then formed the country of Shang-tang, where the Red Ti barbarians dwelt), the whole of present-day southeastern Shansi and, in Honan, the western portion of Huai-ch'ing prefecture. Han was thus bounded upon the north by Chao, and on the south by Cheng, from which the Yellow River divided it. It conquered this latter state a little later (375), thus expanding throughout the whole central part of modern Honan, between what remained of the domain which the Chou kings ruled, on the west, the Ch'u kingdom on the south, and the principality of Sung on the east.

Finally, the principality of Wei had inherited almost all of the ancient Chin domain in the bend of the Yellow River. This principality increased little by little around its original domain, the fief of Wei (nowadays, Jui-ch'eng in Chieh-chou, in the southwestern corner of Shansi), which had been given in 661 to Wan of Pi, who had been the right-hand man in the chariot of a Marquis of Chin and had accompanied him on his victorious campaigns. The family was originally one of the families of the Chi clan, country squires who had in all times — with the Ssu clan and others — formed the local petty nobility on the two banks of the Yellow River, from the mouth of the Fen to that of the Lo. Ever since one of them had succeeded in founding the Chou dynasty, the families of this clan had claimed that their genealogy reached back to various members of the royal family.

Wan of Pi claimed that his family had begun by playing an important role in the state of Chin. The genealogists had no difficulty in finding an ancestor for him: the Duke of Pi. The traditions concerning the founding of the Chou dynasty associated this personage with the Duke of Chou and the Duke of Shao, as one of those who had helped confirm the new dynasty.

His name fitted so well in explicating their own surname of Pi that the Wei readily accepted him as an ancestor.[9] But the true fortunes of the family did not begin until about a century later.

In the middle of the seventh century the Lord of Wei, Wu-tzu, and after his death his son Tao-tzu attached themselves to the fortunes of Ch'ung-erh; and when he finally returned to his state after fifteen years of exile to become Prince Wen of Chin, he rewarded Tao by restoring his fief of Wei and bestowing upon him that of Huo, in the north of Chin, together with the title of *tai-fu*. Tao-tzu's son Chiang was the favourite of Marquis Tao of Chin and was a minister for eight years (569–562). From that time on the house of Wei was counted as one of the 'six dignitaries' among whom power was shared in Chin. At the end of the sixth century Hsien-tzu, Chiang's grandson, again became minister.

It is scarcely possible to follow the territorial growth of the Wei *tai-fu* in the course of the fifth century. All we know is that they took over important segments of the properties of the proscribed families: Ch'i and Yang-she in 514, Fan and Chung-hang in 490, and Chih in 453. At the end of the fifth century, when it had become definitively independent, the principality of Wei comprised all the original territory of Chin between the two branches of the Yellow River in the southwest corner of present-day Shansi. There she possessed the ancient capitals of Chin, and there also was her own, An-yi to start with, until 365. In addition she held territory on the right bank of the River which had once belonged to Chin, both in the south (in the northwest of modern Honan) and in the west: in the triangle situated between the Yellow River and the River Lo, Ho-hsi, reconquered from Ch'in in the last years of the fifth century.[10]

Aside from this compact domain on the two banks of the River, southwest of ancient Chin, Wei held the eastern portion of the ancient principality of Wey and also all of Ts'ao — that is to say the two banks of the Yellow River at its great eastern bend, on the borders of the modern provinces of Hopei, Honan, and Shantung, around the city of Ta-liang (approximately the present-day K'ai-feng prefecture, capital of Honan province), which became her capital in 365[11] and remained so until the end of her independent existence.

But these two territories, separated by the principality of Han, had no communications between them. Finally the principality of Chung-shan, conquered in 408 (in the region of Ting-chou, in Hopei), enclosed in Chao territory, remained always separated from both the western and the southern domains of Wei. It seems to have formed the apanage of a prince of the reigning family: first of the heir apparent Chi, then after his accession (as Prince Wu, 386) of his brother Chih, then of other princes,[12] until it was conquered by Chao in 300, and its prince deported (296). This conquest was facilitated by the isolation of the Chung-shan principality, separated from the rest of Wei.

This intermingling of their territories created recurring rivalries without end among the three principalities, each seeking to unify itself. But every attempt, no matter whence it came, remained unsuccessful. In 386 Prince Wu of Wei tried in vain to seize Han-tan, when trouble broke out over the succession of Prince Wu of Chao, by sustaining the claim of Wu's son against that of Prince Ching — whom the Chao nobles had placed on the throne — and by aiding him to besiege the city. Several years later, in 370, when Wu of Wei himself died, the princes of Han and Chao took advantage of the ensuing troubles to invade his country. Prince Ch'eng of Chao wished to profit from the occasion to obliterate the principality and divide it up. Prince Yi of Han, no doubt fearing to find his ally's strength growing beyond control, opposed this. In this period, moreover, the strengths of the three principalities, which had initially been very disparate, had been equalized little by little until in 375 the smallest, Han, had conquered and annexed the old principality of Cheng. Any chance of ever having a powerful state reconstituted in the north was thus definitively ruled out.

2
The Chinese World at the End of the Fifth Century

Chin perished from not having known how to change according to the times, from having remained a feudal state on the old basis at a time when the entire Chinese world began to break away from that basis. Indeed, from the end of the sixth century and during the fifth century, new tendencies had appeared, under the great philosophers and theoreticians of politics of that time, such as Confucius and, after him and more successfully, Mo-tzu, and others. Under the appearance of traditionalism and of wishing to return to the principles of antiquity, these thinkers basically ended up in modifying the state of things in their time and in actually overturning the contemporary establishment from the ground up.

The end of the fifth century and the beginning of the fourth was a period of intense ferment. Then the old feudal forms finally disappeared; new ideas were introduced everywhere in legislation, administration, and even religion; and, amidst the disarray and disequilibrium which prevailed within the old society, new principles were shaped which, developing over the course of the centuries, were to become sovereign patterns for the Chinese world.

The collapse of Chin had brought about a sort of lull. The surviving great states — Ch'i, Ch'in, and Ch'u — eyed one another rather uncomfortably, but none of them dared try to retake the hegemony for itself. They used the time in reorganizing themselves internally as best they could.

The principality of Ch'i, after the brilliant period of Prince Huan in the seventh century, had suffered a long eclipse during the time when Chin was hegemon. It was necessary for her to recover from the exhaustion caused by the ambitious policy of Huan and his minister I-wu of Kuan. She stood aside for a long time, while Prince Ch'ing, after his defeats at An and Ma-ling, had had to recognize the hegemony of his powerful neighbour, to whom he had even proposed that he should take the title of king (587). Ch'i had to renounce seeking the topmost rank in the empire, contenting herself with expansion at the expense of her small neighbours, whom she conquered one after the other.

During the entire sixth century she exhausted her strength in the rivalries of the great vassal families, for the descendants of the successive ruling princes formed a feudal group within the state, recent in origin but extremely turbulent. There were the Kao, descendants of Prince Wu of the ninth century; the lords of Ts'ui, who claimed descent from Prince Ting (tenth century ?); those of Tung-kuo and those of Ch'ing, who were descended from Prince Huan (685–643); those of Luan,[1] descendants of Prince Hui (608–599); and finally the T'ien, descendants of Wan, the son of Prince Li of Ch'en (706–700), who had taken refuge in Ch'i in 672 and had been well received at the court. These last would soon rise to the topmost rank.

All the sixth century was occupied with the struggles of the Kao against the various other families to seize and retain power. The assassination of Hou of Kao in 554 ushered in a brief triumph of the Ts'ui under Chu of Ts'ui. After having assassinated Prince Chuang and replaced him with his younger brother Ching, Chu came to an understanding with his rival Feng of Ch'ing to share power, himself remaining prime minister, with the title Minister of the Right. Feng received the title Minister of the Left, and all the officers of state were forced to take an oath to both of them (548). In 546, however, Feng took advantage of dissensions within the Ts'ui family and exterminated them completely. Chu of Ts'ui committed suicide, and Feng of Ch'ing remained the sole minister. He did not enjoy his success for long. In the following year the families of T'ien, Pao, Luan, and Kao formed an alliance against him. One day when he was hunting they attacked his palace and massacred his family, and Feng had to flee to Wu (545).

It was the T'ien who triumphed. Their chief Ch'i became prime minister, showing himself energetic enough to control the turbulent vassals during all the long reign of Prince Ching (547–489), the more easily since the weakening of Chin gave him the means to divert the great families' ambitions to external affairs. He intervened in all the troubles of Chin, supporting the rebel families of Fan and Chung-hang. At the same time he made a great effort to become absolute master of the entire plain of the lower Yellow River and to subjugate the petty principalities of that region, especially Lu, the strongest of them, with which he began a struggle which was never to end. This policy brought him into conflict with Wu, then at the height of its power after King Ho-lü's victories over Ch'u; but he did not hesitate to stand up to her. After having defeated the Wu fleet several times, he succeeded without difficulty in reducing all his nearer southern neighbours — Lu, Chu-lü, T'an, and so on — to a sort of vassalage (487).

Already at this moment, however, the death of Prince Ching (489) brought the usual troubles in its train. Very aged, 'he did not like to discuss anything concerning the succession'; moreover, he hesitated which of his numerous sons to choose and 'feared to speak his mind'. Only on his death-bed did he name as heir presumptive T'u, the son of his favourite and still an infant, confiding this choice to Hsia of Kuo and Chang of Kao. T'u was assassinated almost immediately by Ch'i of T'ien, who enthroned another of Ching's sons — Yang-sheng, who became Prince Tao — and seized power himself.

At Ch'i's death (485), Mu of Pao assassinated Tao and replaced him with his son, Prince Chien, who tried to throw off the T'ien yoke. As his minister he took K'an Chih, a man whose origin is uncertain but one whom Chien had known while exiled in Lu; yet despite K'an Chih's advice, he could not bring himself to make away with Heng of T'ien, Ch'i's son, whom instead he named Minister of the Left. Heng would not be satisfied with this favour: he armed his family, attacked and killed K'an Chih, and put Chien to death. Then he replaced Chien by his younger brother, as Prince P'ing (481); and he exterminated all his adversaries — Mu of Pao, Yü of Yen, and the members of the princely family.

Heng's power was now solidly established, all the more in that his family no longer had any rival; nevertheless he set himself to consolidating it as best he could. He divided the principality into two sections, taking the larger, that of the east (the Shantung peninsula) for himself, and leaving only Lin-tzu, the capital, with the western lands (the plain between the foot of T'ai-shan and the Yellow River) to Prince P'ing. When Heng died, his son P'an, who succeeded him as minister, named his brothers (he had seventy of them) and his relatives as governors for all the towns and cities of Ch'i, thus fastening his hold upon the entire country and 'making preparations to take possession of the principality'.[2]

But it was not he who dared take the decisive step: it was only his grandson, Ho, who in 391 transported Prince K'ang, P'ing's grandson, to the seacoast, giving him as apanage only a single town. K'ang died there in 379, leaving no descendant; and the Lü family of the Chiang clan, which had governed Ch'i since its beginnings, died out, being definitively replaced by the T'ien family of the Kuei clan.

Ho had not even awaited K'ang's death to spell out this downfall. In 387, he had obtained the intermediacy of Wen of Wei with King An of Chou to assist in getting him recognized as among the princes, and the Son of Heaven had agreed. He became Prince of Ch'i (386), and is known in history by his posthumous title of T'ai-kung.

Thus Ch'i had escaped partition and dissolution. The destruction of the other great families by the T'ien had allowed them to reconstitute the unity of the principality to their own advantage. The large vassal holdings were not restored. Except for the members of their own very numerous family, the princes of the T'ien family, probably having little faith in the loyalty of their subjects, employed few Ch'i people. They seem to have been the first to devise the system of employing political adventurers, literati or soldiers, who had come from outside the state, who owed all their fortune to the prince who had taken them in, and who were consequently docile instruments — the system which was to become pervasive in the Chinese principalities during the fourth century.

While the eastern part of the empire seemed thus to be organizing itself under Ch'i hegemony within the old framework of leagues of sovereign princes, in the west Ch'in became a power of the first rank under Count Hsiao and his minister Yang of Wey. But this was not done without difficulty: the country had just passed through one of those internal crises which periodically shook Chinese principalities and it had emerged half-ruined.

For almost fifty years, since the assassination of Huai, besieged and massacred in his palace by his grand officers (425), the throne had scarcely been occupied except by children. These successive minorities, with the intrigues to which they gave rise and the struggles between princes and grand officers, had made civil war a permanent way of life. The son of Count Huai had died before his father, and the heir was a child, Count Ling, who reigned for ten years and then died, barely an adult, leaving behind him only a young infant (415). The latter was set aside, and his great-uncle,

Count Chien — a younger brother of Huai — was summoned to the throne. He seems himself to have been quite young, and at his death had only a youth or barely an adult, Hui, to succeed him; and Hui too died quite early, leaving as heir a baby one year old (387).

With that the succession reverted to the legitimate heir, Ling's son, who had grown up in Ho-hsi, in the principality of Wei, where he had taken refuge. The young prince was drowned, together with his mother, and Count Hsien, who seems to have been about thirty years old, ascended the throne.[3] He held it for twenty-four years, and all his efforts during his long reign were directed towards restoring prosperity to his ruined domains by keeping the peace as much as possible both at home and abroad. Under him and under his son Hsiao, the principality of Ch'in was profoundly altered in political structure, administration, and finances. From the archaic system of the antiquated feudal states, she changed into an organization less rudimentary and more orderly.

The main role in this veritable revolution seems to have been played by a minister of Count Hsiao, Yang of Wey, the Lord of Shang.[4] Chinese historians nevertheless surely exaggerate in attributing to him alone what must have been the work of several generations. Like many of the great personages of that period, he was an adventurer whom chance had brought to Ch'in. He belonged to the princely family of Wey and bore the family name Kung-sun, which was given to the grandsons of reigning princes. He had begun his career in Wei (of which his country of birth, Wey, was then a dependency) in the service of Kung-shu Tso, who esteemed him and, when he was dying, recommended Yang to King Hui.

The tale says that, when the king refused to employ him, the minister advised the king to put him to death to prevent his serving another prince. The minister then warned Kung-sun Yang to flee, since they had become friendly; but the young man refused, saying: 'This king was incapable of following your advice to give me a post. How can he be capable of following advice to kill me?' And he remained in Wei.

Later, when Count Hsiao, at the beginning of his reign, 'summoned the wise men' (361), Yang proceeded to the audience and was presented to the sovereign by a counsellor, Chien of Ching, another adventurer, who belonged to a collateral branch of the Ch'u royal family. The count welcomed him and admitted him to his circle of friends. But when Yang proposed his first reforms he ran into the opposition of the counsellors Kan Lung and Tu Chih. Nevertheless he succeeded in convincing the prince, who gave him the rank of *tso-shu-chang* (356), and then that of *ta-liang-tsao* (352), one of the highest in the Ch'in court, in the sixteenth degree of a hierarchy which included only eighteen levels (352); and Count Hsiao continued to support him steadfastly. His fortunes were at their zenith in 340, when the prince set up the small domain of Wu, in the Ch'in-ling Mountains, as a fief under the name of Shang and bestowed this upon his minister, who took from that the title Lord of Shang, *Shang-chün.*

But when Hsiao died, his son disgraced Yang. There is said to have been an old quarrel between them: when the prince was not yet heir apparent, he had refused to follow certain of the minister's regulations, whereupon the latter had ordered the nose of one of the prince's tutors to be cut off and the other to be branded — a humiliation which had never been forgiven. Thus, when this prince acceded, Yang became alarmed and fled to Wei, which sent him back and gave him over to Ch'in. He managed to escape and took refuge in his apanage of Shang, where he armed his people; but he was defeated and seized. The count had him torn asunder by chariots, and his entire family was massacred (338).

Yang of Wey's reforms were very extensive, covering all sorts of questions, as can be seen by the way he grew bolder: the success of his first measures encouraged him to dare more. The first steps were police regulations designed to suppress brigandage, from which Ch'in, like all the Chinese principalities, suffered. The population was divided into groups of five or ten families jointly responsible for one another. When a member of one of these committed a crime, unless the guilty party was handed over, the whole group was tried. Anybody who knew of a criminal and did not denounce him was cut in half at the waist. Whoever sheltered one suffered the same punishment as soldiers who deserted to the enemy: he was put to death, and his wife and children were reduced to slavery. On the other hand, anyone who denounced a criminal was rewarded.

Next, vagabondage was put down: every traveller had to have a certificate, and if he did not, he was tried. These measures, vigorously applied, restored some measure of security in the principality. At the end of ten years with this regime 'there were no longer brigands in the mountains' and the people did not 'pick up lost objects lying in the road'. An administrative reorganization added to its efficacy. The principality was divided into thirty-one districts, *hsien*, with a chief, *chang*, placed at the head of each. The reform seems to have served especially to provide cohesion, by putting the areas of peasant villages, *hsiang*, and the petty feudal domains, *yi*, under the same authority.[5]

At the same time, Yang tried energetically to increase the general prosperity by more positive measures designed to make the people work harder. A first series, penalties and rewards for agriculture and forced labour for the idle, seems to have had little effect. The standardization of weights and measures, with Draconian punishments for transgressors, was more successful but had only a limited impact. Repair of the roads and regulations for their maintenance were already initiatives of a more general character.

In 350, no doubt feeling the results achieved inadequate, Yang ventured a complete reform of the landholding system. Until then, in Ch'in as in all of China, landed property was an essentially religious affair. Only the fiefs were truly the property of the lords, but outside of that patricians were not owners of domains granted them by right of emolument or apanage, nor were the people owners of their fields, lots of which had been assigned to them according to the *ching* system. Yang of Wey did away with this system entirely and probably distributed a part of the old common lands among the peasants, leaving to each the whole disposition of all or part of what he possessed. The sale of commoners' land, forbidden until then, was allowed. This reform brought along another, of a financial kind.

Up to that time a prince's revenues had consisted of the tithed product in kind of the *ching*. After this system was abolished, Yang introduced a system of land taxes in kind, proportioned to the extent of the field.[6] This had the advantage of assuring to the state a fixed revenue, without having to take account of the variations of harvests (348). These various measures had a clear success: 'at the end of five years the people of Ch'in were rich and powerful.'

A great work carried out at this time brought wealth to the principality. This was the drainage of the marshes which covered its northern portion, at the foot of the mountains, by means of a canal connecting the rivers Ching and Lo. And as a symbol of this enrichment, Count Hsiao had a great capital built for himself in 350, one worthy of his new importance, at Hsien-yang.[7] Abandoning the small citadel of Yo-yang, which his father Hsien had constructed in 383 after having left Yung, the capital of his predecessors, Hsiao erected palaces which his successors added to, down to the end of the dynasty; and to commemorate his victories over Wei he set up the Pillars of Chi, *Chi-ch'üeh*, there.[8]

Aside from these internal reforms, there was another reason for the growth of Ch'in power. In the fourth century the long efforts against the Jung barbarians who surrounded the principality on all sides began to bear fruit; and the principal tribes were finally subdued. The struggle against the Jung had for centuries been the principal occupation of the counts of Ch'in. It was that which had used up all their resources; it was certainly the most important of the reasons why they had so long kept apart from the affairs of the rest of the empire, and why they were hampered in following any continuing external policy. The Chinese of the Wei Valley were only lately arrived colonists who, a little before the beginnings of the historic era, had occupied the plains, subjugating and apparently assimilating the indigenous populations, but without making any inroads upon the nearby mountains which dominated the plain.

When the Chou kings had maintained their capital of Hao in this area, they had already had to fight the mountain tribes, whose incursions had been not least among the motives for abandoning the too-exposed western capital. The counts of Ch'in inherited this difficult situation, and on them fell the task of protecting the Chinese population against the barbarians. It was this necessity of struggling without rest against the semi-barbarians which gave the men of Ch'in that tough and cruel quality which would be seen in them later, and which at the same time imposed a prudent policy upon their princes.

The barbarians, divided into a great number of tribes, felt the influence of Chinese civilization more and more; but they defended their independence from it with no less ruggedness. At the end of the seventh century, Count Mu had indeed defeated the Jung kings, annexed twelve kingdoms, and opened a thousand *li* of territory, becoming then the chief of the Western Jung.[9] He had subjugated the Jung of Mien-chu and of Ti-huan on the upper Wei River, the Wu-chih of the upper Ching River, the Yi-ch'ü of Mount Ch'i-liang to the north of the Wu-chih, and on the other slope of that mountain chain the Hsü-yen, who perhaps spread to the Yellow River around Ling-chou — that is to say, all the mountainous massif where the Ching and Wei rivers had their source and which separated them from the upper course of the Yellow River. And the Son of Heaven had sent him a metal drum (623). But these brilliant conquests had been ephemeral, and the submission of the barbarians had been more apparent than real.

The struggle resumed under Mu's successors. For centuries they had to carry on a very tough war against these same tribes, which put up a fierce resistance, aided by the nature of the country, cut by ravines and covered with forests. It was necessary to conquer it foot by foot, opening roads and building forts to match, in a very slow progress. The most powerful tribe, the Yi-ch'ü, held off the Ch'in armies for over a century (444–315) and the neighbouring kingdom of Huan, on the headwaters of the Wei, was still independent in 361, when its king was defeated and killed.

Long before the conquest was finished, however, the barbarians were at least contained everywhere. Their incursions into Chinese lands, though not entirely ended, became less frequent and were no longer a cause for serious alarm. Their complete subjugation thrust the people of Ch'in abruptly into touch with the farthest West. Before the end of the fourth century, the definitive conquest of the Yi-ch'ü country gave the Ta-lung Mountains into the hands of the Ch'in counts. Since on the west side this separated the upper Wei and the upper Ching from the Yellow River, it allowed them access to the River around present-day Lan-chou fu, where their military district of Lung-hsi existed from 280 on. They probably found a Chinese colony already installed at this point, which was at once the uppermost port for small-boat shipping on the river and also the point of arrival for caravans from central Asia. The influence and fame of Ch'in spread from there towards the West: it is likely that Westerners adopted that name to designate the civilized populations of the Far East, the Cîna or Mahâcîna of the Indian epic poems, the Σîναι or Θîναι of the Greek geographies.

Ch'in did not expand westwards only: her expansion also reached countries to the south. After 475 the barbarian chiefs of Shu (the vast and rich Ch'eng-tu basin in Szechuan), unsettled at the advance of Ch'u and perhaps fearing even more their neighbours of Pa, vassals of Ch'u (on the upper Yangtze River, in the area of modern Sui-fu or Hsü-chou fu in Szechuan), had come to beg protection of Count Li (Li-kung) of Ch'in. But this was merely an episode without immediate consequences, and it was only a century and a half later, in 316, that the country was conquered by the General Ssu-ma Ts'o. Even then, because of its remoteness, it was not at first transformed into a province but was set up as apanage for a prince of the Ch'in house. Only after some forty years of this arrangement was it made into a commandery.

All these conquests, which absorbed many barbarian tribes, had put the counts of Ch'in in direct contact with the nomads of the north and northwest, Huns and Yüeh-chih; and it is perhaps to this fact that the great reform of their armies in the course of the fourth century must be attributed.[10] Until then the Ch'in armies had been like those of the other Chinese princes, made up of chariots supported by infantry. It is said that Count Mu had three hundred war chariots. Ch'in was first, together with the princes of Chao (likewise in contact with the Huns on their northern frontier), to substitute cavalry corps for these unwieldy masses of chariots, which no general could manoeuvre as he liked. Unfortunately, their organization is little known, but we do know that in the fourth and third centuries cavalry constituted the main strength of their armies. It seems likely that the counts of Ch'in owed their uninterrupted series of victories to the ease with which these light troops handled the clumsy chariot armies of their adversaries.

Thus there arose in the west a state which was powerful, well organized, wealthy, and provided with dependable resources. Her sole weakness was the difficulty of communication among the various parts of the state, separated by enormous mountain chains; but she was compensated by the protection which these same mountains provided against her adversaries, leaving her vulnerable only to an enemy descending from the Shansi plateau. But the downfall of Chin had assured her against any serious danger from that quarter.

During this time the kingdom of Ch'u was recovering slowly from the exhaustion of the wars in the preceding century. To her more than to any other state the beginning of the fifth century had brought deliverance, rather more by the downfall of Wu (473) than by that of Chin. The kings of Yüeh, the conquerors of Wu, were too weak to be a danger; and moreover they were using their strength to the north, struggling with Ch'i for suzerainty over the petty Chinese principalities of the eastern plain.

Almost all the half-century of King Hui (488–432), as well as the reigns of his successors Chien (431–408) and Sheng (407–402), passed thus in a healing peace. The annexation of small Chinese principalities of the northern frontier (Ch'en in 479, Ts'ai in 447, and so on) and lands on the upper Huai River — ceded by King Kou-chien of Yüeh after the destruction of Wu (473) — did nothing to trouble that peace.

The Ch'u kings seem to have devoted themselves to a process of reorganization which was rendered particularly difficult by the immensity of the country, the vast extent of forest and swamp which covered the greater part of it, the still-savage state of the barbarian tribes which made up the base of the population, the fact that even in the richest areas the population was probably very sparse, and finally the growing disharmony between the increasingly sinicized court and the still half-savage people. A tradition of little reliability[11] ascribes especially to King Tao (401–381) a complete reform of administration, of justice, of the army. It is likely indeed that efforts of this kind were made during the fifth century, though it is impossible to say what they amounted to.

While large states, very nearly equal in strength, grew up in the northeast, the west, and the south, the small states of the centre were becoming extinct. Neither Chou, nor Cheng, nor Wey, nor Sung, nor Lu was ever again to play any important role; and their complete disappearance was no more than a matter of time.

The kings of Chou had fallen indeed since the sixth century. In the time of the Chin hegemony they had still cut a great figure, though they no longer had any effective authority; and first Prince Wen and then Prince Hsiang had repeatedly evidenced their respect publicly by official acts. But the collapse of Chin had been disastrous for what remained of the royal prestige. The external marks of deference, long maintained, themselves disappeared little by little. True enough, it was still the Chou king of whom the lords of Wei, Han, and Chao (403) and later the chief of the T'ien family (386) asked the legitimization of their usurpations. But this was merely asking his assent to an accomplished fact; it was a sort of negotiation that merely emphasized the impotence of the royal house. The Royal Domain too was diminishing constantly, nibbled at by Ch'u on the south, by Wei on the north, by Ch'in on the west; and in no great time it was reduced to the immediate surroundings of the capital.

In the middle of the fifth century, King K'ao diminished it still further by dividing it with his younger brother Chieh. Having ascended the throne by murdering his brother, King Ssu — who had himself seized the throne through the murder of their elder brother King Ai (441) — he feared that he might suffer the same fate in turn. He offered Chieh half of his domain, reviving for him the old title of Duke of Chou, which had been extinct since the Duke Ch'u had fled to Chin (580), driven out by the descendants of King Hui — the Kan, great-grandsons of the rebel Prince Shu Tai — and by those of King Hsiang.[12] For himself

K'ao kept the eastern portion, with the new royal residence founded by King Ching three-quarters of a century earlier (512), known by its old name of Ch'eng-chou. To his brother he gave the western part, Ho-nan, yielding him the former capital, still called the Royal City, Wang-ch'eng, the founding of which was attributed to the Duke of Chou, brother of King Wu, in the first years of the dynasty and which had been the royal residence from P'ing to Ching (770–512).

Duke Huan of Ho-nan was nominally a dependent of the king's, but in fact he enjoyed from the first the same independence as the other sovereign princes. For this reason his successors took the title of Western Chou, Hsi-chou. Furthermore, in 367,[13] the second year of King Hsien, Duke Hui, Huan's grandson, ordered his younger son Pan to take power in the eastern city, with the title 'Deputy to the King', *feng-wang*; and he gave Pan as apanage the city of Kung. This prince utilized the order to seize the entire royal territory and founded the principality of Eastern Chou, Tung-chou, of which he was Duke Hui.

From this moment on, the kings no longer possessed any territory of their own, and their minuscule domain found itself divided between two rival principalities which exhausted their strength in petty local quarrels — over the allotment of irrigation water in their valley, for example.[14] The political role of the Chou was finished for good.

Quite near Chou, the principality of Cheng had already been reduced to semi-vassalage by Prince Lieh of Han, despite ten years of bitter struggle (408–398), thanks to its own internal dissensions which had followed the assassination of the minister Tzu-yang of Ssu at Prince Hsü's order. The prince had been assassinated by the minister's partisans (396), who set Prince Hsü's brother on the throne as Prince K'ang (395). But Cheng was to disappear completely soon enough, conquered by Prince Ai of Han (375).

Though the state of Wey continued to exist nominally, its territory was steadily reduced through the encroachments of Wei, whose suzerainty her prince also had to recognize. In the south, Ch'u had successively annexed Ch'en (478) and Ts'ai (447), as well as Ch'ii (445) and Chü (431), the latter two of which Ch'i was later to take away; and Sung remained independent, resisting Ch'u with great difficulty.

Farther to the east, the struggle of the Lu princes with their all-powerful hereditary ministers, the Chi, caused the state to fall gradually under the control of its powerful neighbours, Chin,

Ch'i, and Ch'u. The princes of Ch'i supported those of Lu. At the beginning of the sixth century Chin had to intervene to insure that the chief of the Chi family, Wen-tzu, would return to power; the Battle of An (589) set Lu among the allies of Chin for half a century.[15] The accession of a pusillanimous prince, Chao, to the Lu throne (541) allowed Ch'i to take a hand again, probably by giving aid to the numerous enemies of the Chi. Those enemies relied upon Ch'i in the name of Prince Chao, who had been insulted by Chin and was angry with that principality and with the Lu Prime Minister whom Chin supported. They attacked the chiefs of the three great families descended from the younger brothers of Prince Chuang (693–662): the Meng-sun, the Shu-sun, and the Chi-sun,[16] families which had divided up the country and reduced the prince to impotence, while leaving him the semblance of power. But Prince Chao, after an abortive attempt to rid himself of Yi-ju of the Chi (P'ing-tzu), chief of the Chi family and hereditary Prime Minister of Lu, had been expelled by the coalition of three families and compelled to flee (514). He never succeeded in returning to his country and died in exile (510). During his absence, Yi-ju exercised sovereign power, relying upon Chin for support against Ch'i. Even under the new Prince Ting he kept power, until his death in 505.

At this point Yi-ju's steward, Yang Hu, knowing himself to be out of favour with the Chi family heir, Ssu of the Chi (Huan-tzu), had the latter arrested and usurped the title of Prime Minister. He set out to humble the three great families, especially the Chi, and to rally around himself noble families who were not of their party. Thus it was that the young Confucius received a post from him. But finally the interests menaced by Yang Hu grouped themselves against him, and he had to flee (503), leaving his post to Ssu of the Chi, who became prime minister. Despite all this, he had gravely weakened the house of the Chi;[17] and the constant squabbling of the three families brought the principality to ruin and depression, although its position between Ch'i and Wu (and later Yüeh) allowed it to maintain a show of independence, thanks to the rivalry of its powerful neighbours.

In sum, the Chinese world at the end of the fifth century displayed four great and strong states on the periphery — Ch'i, Ch'in, Ch'u, and Yüeh — and filling in the intervals, in the centre and the north, numerous small principalities — Yen, Chao, Wei, Han, Sung, Lu, and so on — whose weakness rendered them powerless, and whose rivalries and jealousies tended to make them the prey of their powerful neighbours.

The fall of Chin had not meant merely the disappearance of one of the great states. Also lost was an ideal of political organization formed by a sort of confederation which in some measure respected the rights of local princes. After the fifth century the old system of the hegemonies was indeed dead: the struggles among the great states were not aimed at reviving it for their own advantage, but merely at aggrandizing themselves directly at the expense of the weakest among their neighbours, until the final victory of one state should realize for the first time the absolute unity of the whole Chinese world.

3
The Warring Kingdoms

The large states, set at the four corners of the empire, lay far enough apart so that for a long time it seemed likely that they would not be brought into conflict. Nevertheless, they shared a common interest: not to allow a powerful state to reconstitute itself in the north. It was this which seems to have led them to intervention in the affairs of the 'three Chin' (Wei, Chao, Han). In addition, they jealously watched each other's policies towards the states of the centre, each determined not to allow another to regain for himself the influence which Chin had wielded so long over these petty principalities, and which had been a part of its strength. Thus, despite distance, conflicts were sooner or later inevitable.

The immediate cause of these conflicts was the imprudence of the princes of Wei, and their policy, which was too daring for the real strength of their country. Thanks to the troubles that racked Ch'in at the end of the fifth century, Prince Wen (423–387) had been able to reconquer from her all the territories on the right bank of the Yellow River — Ho-hsi, as far as the River Lo (419–409). His son, Prince Wu (386–371), considered himself strong enough to require that the princes of Chao and Han submit to him, and to re-establish for his own advantage, if not the unity that Chin had once imposed, at least a sort of hegemony of northern states.

The Prince of Han, knowing how weak he was, seems to have submitted willingly enough; but the Prince of Chao, less docile, sought help from the princes of Ch'i, who were thoroughly determined not to allow the restoration of a power so dangerous to their own country. In 386 Wu almost succeeded in getting his hands on Chao by supporting one of the pretenders to the succession of Prince Wu. He laid siege to the capital, Han-tan; but it was well fortified and resisted all his attacks. He had to retire, but not before he had made the new prince — whom he had been unable to expel — conclude a new alliance with him and against Ch'i, designed to exclude the latter from intervening in the affairs of the 'three Chin'.

This alliance lasted through the reign of Wu, despite several defections which were quickly punished; and the efforts which the princes of Ch'i made to intervene were immediately stopped by a series of victorious campaigns — Lin-ch'iu (384), Sang-ch'iu (380), and finally Ling-ch'iu (378) — which stripped Ch'i of any wish to interfere in the affairs of the 'three Chin'. In fact Wei, in this first half of the fourth century, seemed in the process of becoming a very important state, especially after the victory of Lu-yang over the Ch'u army (371), when it seemed for a moment that she might take over the protection of the central principalities, so long held by Chin.

Wu's death, the civil war, and the invasion by a Han-Chao coalition which followed (370) weakened Wei only for a time; and Prince Hui at the beginning of his reign could still be considered the most powerful prince in north China. His prestige was so great that not only Han but Chao as well believed it essential to maintain the alliance. It sufficed also to group the princes of Han, Wey, Lu, and Sung[1] around him and to form under his presidency a league against Ch'i, which solemnized the treaty of the Fan Terrace, Fan-t'ai (356). It thus seemed that he had established a sufficiently stable power in the north.

That did not suit his neighbours, however. Alarmed that the former power of Chin might be re-established in a new form, they were constant in their efforts at enticing one or another of the allies to quit the League. It was moreover not very difficult to achieve this: leagues and counter-leagues overlapped like treaties of insurance and of counter-insurance. In the very year of the Fan-t'ai meeting, Ch'eng of Chao concluded an alliance with Ch'i at P'ing-lu, and Sung joined in. But this did not imply breaking off good relations with Wei, for in that same year Hui of Wei managed to effect a reconciliation between the princes of Chao and Yen during a meeting at An-yi, his former capital; and in the following year Ch'eng of Chao sent him rich presents.

In 354, however, an ill-starred war with Ch'in, ending in the defeat at Yüan-li, lost Wei the territory of Shao-liang, between the Lo and Yellow rivers. Prince Ch'eng of Chao thought he had found in this the opportunity to burst the bonds that held him.

He had miscalculated his rival's strength: hardly was the campaign in the west finished when the Wei army turned back to the east, defeated the Chao army, and went on to besiege his capital, Han-tan. The occasion was too good for their neighbours to resist taking advantage of it. First the King of Ch'u and then the Prince of Ch'i intervened immediately, and Wei had to raise the siege. This defection by Chao threatened to break up the League altogether. Also, the Prince of Wei returned to the attack the following year, and this time he took Han-tan before any help could come (353). The situation was even more serious than before: Wei was clearly on the way to reconstituting the former unity of Chin, to her own advantage. Ch'i, Ch'u, and even Ch'in felt themselves menaced and sent troops: it took two years of war to persuade Hui to relinquish his conquest and to force him into signing a peace ratified by an agreement sworn to on the banks of the River Chang (351).

These defeats destroyed Wei's prestige. Only Han remained faithful, perhaps for fear of Ch'u, which had become her neighbour since the conquest of Cheng and over which the two allies gained a brilliant victory in 346.[2] But the dissolution of the League had made it very difficult for them to carry on the struggle against the influence of Ch'i; and, reduced to relying upon Ch'in for this, they concluded a treaty with her at T'ung (350). In the following year they allowed Ch'in troops to pass through their territory for a campaign against Ch'i; and in 342 they attended the Feng-tse assembly, where Count Hsiao of Ch'in had himself acknowledged prince-hegemon. It was probably there that the Prince of Han came to realize Wei's weakness and the uselessness of her protection; for upon his return, in that same year, he broke off the alliance.

When Hui determined to chastise him and bring him to heel, what had occurred ten years before happened all over again. The Ch'i court was the first to send aid to Han: an army commanded by Sun Pin, a general to whose name is credited a little tract on the art of war.[3] The army of Wei was destroyed at the Ma-ling pass;[4] the commanding general committed suicide; and the heir apparent, who had accompanied him, was taken prisoner (341). This defeat signalled the kill. Chao entered the campaign. Then in the following year Yang of Wey, at the head of a Ch'in army, gained a victory and granted peace only after a portion of Ho-hsi, the territory on the right bank of the Yellow River, was ceded to Ch'in. The principality of Wei was saved only by the intervention of a Ch'u army which invaded Ch'i from the south.

Wei never recovered from this disaster, in which its power had

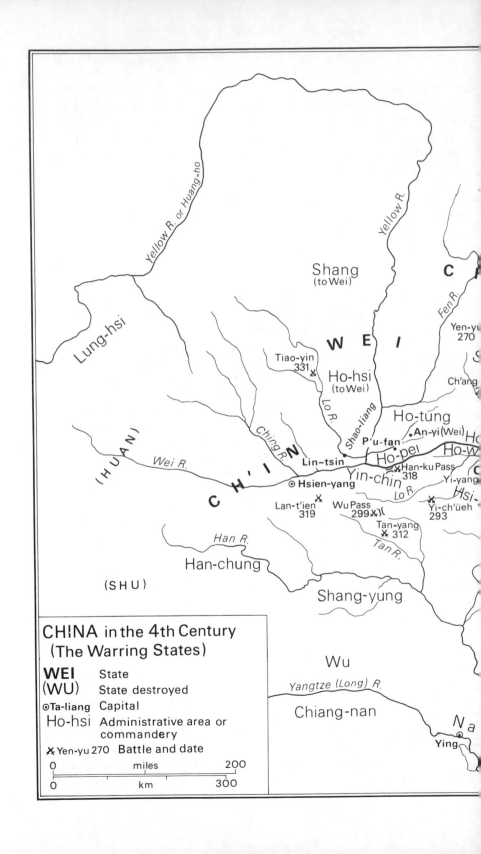

Yellow R. or Huang-ho

Yellow R.

Shang
(to Wei)

C

Fen R.

Lung-hsi

W E I

Yen-yü
270

Tiao-yin
331

Ho-hsi
(to Wei)

Ch'ang

Lo R.

Shao-liang

Ho-tung

(HUAN)

Wei R.

Ching R.

N

An-yi (Wei) Ho

P'u-fan

Ho-w

Lin-tsin

Ho-pei

Han-ku Pass

Hsien-yang

Yin-chin

318

Yi-yang

Lo R.

Hsi

Lan-t'ien
319

Wu Pass
299

Yi-ch'üeh
293

Han R.

Tan-yang
312

Tan R.

Han-chung

(SHU)

Shang-yung

Wu

Yangtze (Long) R.

Chiang-nan

N a

Ying

CHINA in the 4th Century
(The Warring States)

WEI   State
(WU)   State destroyed
⊙Ta-liang   Capital
Ho-hsi   Administrative area or
            commandery
✕Yen-yu 270 Battle and date

0   miles   200

0   km   300

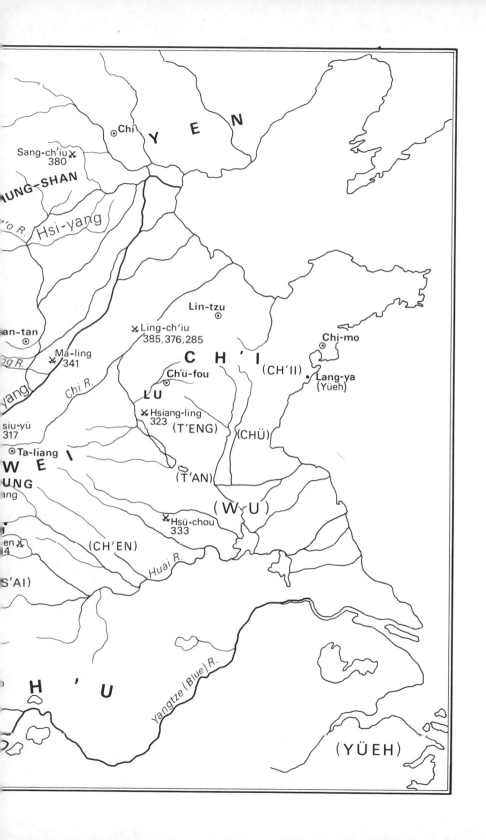

Chi

Y E N

Sang-ch'iu ✕
380

UNG-SHAN

o R. Hsi-yang

an-tan ⊙

Ma-ling ✕
/341

ng R.

Chi R.

yang

Lin-tzu
⊙

✕ Ling-ch'iu
385, 376, 285

C H ' I

(CH'II)

Chi-mo
⊙

Ch'ü-fou ⊙

LU

• Lang-ya
(Yüeh)

siu-yü
317

✕ Hsiang-ling
323

(T'ENG)

(CHÜ)

⊙ Ta-liang

W E I

(T'AN)

UNG

ang

(W · U)

✕ Hsü-chou
333

en ✕
4

(CH'EN)

Huai R.

S'AI)

H ' U

Yangtze (Blue) R.

(YÜEH)

been decisively broken. The luck of the way in which the territory of Chin had been divided had established Wei on both banks of the Yellow River, both at its eastward bend as it leaves Shansi and at its northward bend as it leaves Honan. Thus Wei was made to hold the keys to the west and the east, barring the way to Ch'in or to Ch'i when they wished to intervene in Shansi. This was, however, a very difficult role to play, since the hinterland belonged, not to Wei, but to Chao and Han. The enmity of these two states from the middle of the fourth century on rendered Wei's task impossible, at the same time that successive defeats exhausted her.

All the later years of King Hui's reign were taken up with attempts to buy peace through all sorts of concessions to his neighbours, so that he might spend those declining years among the scholars and philosophers whom his reputation for liberality attracted. They were welcomed and given titles and emoluments, though they played no active role; and the old sovereign gladly gave them audience to carry on discussions with them, or he set them to vying with one another and had them debate before him. His court thus became the meeting-place for all the intelligentsia of the period. Chuang-tzu was there, and he is said to have refused a position which was offered to him (333); Hui-tzu was a counsellor there; and so was Yang-tsu, with whom Chuang-tzu and Hui-tzu often argued. Later on there came Kung-sun Lung, the favourite of the Prime Minister, the lord of Chung-shan. Mencius passed that way in the last years of the reign; and Tsou Yen also came there.[5]

Resigned to doing anything to gain peace, Hui easily came to an understanding with Hsüan of Ch'i. The latter, satisfied to have nothing to fear from the west, did not dream of pushing his advantage too far, but was content with the influence his victories had won him throughout the countries of the north and the centre. The two princes met at Hsü-chou and reciprocally recognized the other's title of king, *wang* (335), thus openly proclaiming for the first time what had been a fact, but until then an unavowed one: the downfall of the Chou king.[6] This act was perhaps a protest against the hegemony granted to the Count of Ch'in some years earlier. They remained allies, having friendly meetings almost every year.

But Hui could not carry things off the same way with Ch'in, where Count Hsiao was determined to take advantage of the situation to satisfy the old ambitions of his family, finally pushing his frontier to the Yellow River. Thus every effort, every concession Hui made to establish a lasting peace was useless:

every year saw fresh incursions. The lands west and south of the River had been stoutly fortified and were bitterly defended; but they were left to their own resources after Hui removed his capital from An-yi, near the Fen River, to Ta-liang in his eastern domain (near K'ai-feng fu), and they inevitably had to succumb. The first to be conquered was the country south of the Yellow River, the territory of Yin-chin at the foot of Mount Hua (332). Then it was the turn of the western commanderies, Ho-hsi, of which the defeat at Tiao-yin (331) forced the cession in the following year, and Shang, north of Ho-hsi, which had to be handed over to get a treaty of peace (328), following an expedition by the Ch'in army on the left bank of the Yellow River (329).

When Count Hui-wen of Ch'in in his turn took the title of king (325), he had just brought to fruition the traditional policy of his ancestors by giving his state a frontier on the Yellow River, since the entire right bank belonged to him. At the end of his reign, victory over the barbarians of the upper Wei River and the rapid conquest of the land of Shu (316) made him the uncontested master of all the west of the Chinese world. But this last conquest, in giving him the rich Szechuan basin and the countries of the upper Yangtze, brought him into conflict with Ch'u, since that kingdom, which held the lower and middle valley of the Han, blocked the best route leading from Ch'in to Shu.

King Wei of Ch'u (339–329) had just achieved a considerable success, in destroying the kingdom of Yüeh and annexing the northern part of her territory, which had previously formed the kingdom of Wu. After the victories of Kou-chien, which had set him for a moment at the head of the Chinese world, the kings of Yüeh had squandered their forces in wars, which were fruitless (and of which little is known), against their northern neighbours, whose wealth excited their barbarian greed and which they went to pillage regularly. Thus in 415 King Chu-kou had seized the principality of T'eng; and in 414 that of T'an, both situated in southern Shantung. In 379 the capital which Kou-chien had established at Lang-ya (Shantung), near present-day Chiao-chou, was for some unknown reason moved back to the former capital of Wu (in Kiangsu) by King Yi. This transfer did not bring him good luck: he was assassinated soon afterwards by his older brother Chu-chiu (376). The new sovereign scarcely had time to enjoy his power, since he was put to death after a few months and replaced by a prince who was in turn assassinated soon afterwards (375). That was not the end of the troubles. King

Mang-an, whom a grand officer of Yüeh then placed on the throne, was killed ten years later (365), and his successor, Wu-chuan, reigned for only a few years (364–357).[7]

Only then did King Wu-chiang succeed in restoring peace. The beginning of his reign had to be devoted to restoring order in the land, exhausted by this lengthy crisis. Only in his last years did he resume the external policy of his predecessors and enter into conflict with Ch'i. King Wei of Ch'i managed to turn this initiative away towards Ch'u, against whom the two states seem to have formed an alliance (335). After quite a long war with no decisive success, the Ch'u army went to besiege Hsü-chou, which was defended by a garrison from Ch'i. King Wu-chiang himself marched to the aid of the city. In the fight that ensued, he was killed, his troops were scattered, and the Ch'u army, unexpectedly victorious found itself master of all the lands north of Chekiang — that is, all of what had formerly been the state of Wu (333). The remnants of Wu-chiang's army withdrew to the original territory of Yüeh, where all the various princes fought among themselves for power and ended up by founding separate petty kingdoms in their apanages, under the suzerainty of Ch'u.[8] All the valley of the Yangtze, from where it leaves Szechuan to the sea, was unified once more under the sceptre of the King of Ch'u.

Thus the events of the end of the fourth century made Ch'u border upon Ch'in in the west and upon Ch'i in the northeast; and this association was to renew their rivalries. War broke out first between Ch'u and Ch'i. It lasted some ten years, without any very clear success on either side, while Ch'in took advantage of the fact that her rivals were engaged against one another and so could do nothing against her, and she seized the western provinces of Wei. In 323 the fates seemed to have decided: the army of Wei, allied to Ch'i, was destroyed at Hsiang-ling by the Ch'u general Chao Yang, and he took advantage of this victory to threaten Ch'i.

King Wei of Ch'i,[9] alarmed, asked for and received the mediation of Ch'in. A meeting took place at Yeh-sang between the ministers of Ch'u and Ch'i, in the presence of Chang Yi, Prime Minister of Ch'in. Since the ministers of all the principalities had been called there as well, this became a sort of peace convention, where the treaty between Ch'u and Ch'i was signed (323). The belligerents were so exhausted by this long war that the peace was more enduring than anybody would have believed possible. Furthermore, a rather egregious manifestation of Ch'in's ambitions served to unite the former rivals in an alliance against the principality. Immediately after the Yeh-sang meeting, she had openly installed a veritable protectorate in Wei, where her minister Chang Yi became a sort of resident-general, with the title of minister, *hsiang*, of Wei. The appearance of the country's independence was still respected, but it became in reality a mere vassal.[10]

The fear which this growing power inspired brought the former enemies ever closer together. Their relations became quite cordial: in 321, Wen of T'ien, Lord of Meng-ch'ang (son of Ying of T'ien, Lord of Ching-kuo), minister of Ch'i, was sent as an envoy to Ch'u, where he was welcomed warmly and received very handsome gifts. The alliance against Ch'in was probably decided upon then in principle, with the reservation that they should await a suitable occasion. In 319, the death of King Hui of Wei offered one: his successor, Hsiang,[11] barely mounted upon the throne, threw off the Ch'in yoke and sent Chang Yi away. Immediately Ch'u and Ch'i, to bring him aid, brought all the kingdoms of the north — Han, Chao, and Yen — together into a league against Ch'in, even including the Hun barbarians from the borders of modern Mongolia, since they had for about a century and a half recognized the suzerainty of the Chao princes more or less formally.[12]

Hardly had this league been formed, however, than the rivalry of Ch'i and Ch'u reappeared over a question of precedence. They disputed over the presidency of the League, and when this was given to Ch'u, who was designated its chief, this wounded the King of Ch'i: without withdrawing positively, he took no part in the campaign.

The expedition so inauspiciously begun had no success. The Ch'in army was dug in at the Han-ku Pass, which the allies attacked in vain; and they had to retire without having been able to force a passage (318). The only result of the affair was to give Ch'in a pretext for invading her neighbours, Wei and Han. The latter suffered most severely, her armies sustaining a great defeat at Hsiu-yü and her generalissimo, Shou Shen-ch'a, being taken prisoner (317). Negotiations were initiated but then were broken off after Ch'u offered assistance; but the resumption of the campaign was again unfavourable for Han, which sustained a new defeat at An-men, near Hsü-chou (Honan), and in order to secure peace, had to hand over her heir apparent as a hostage (314). At the same time, farther to the north, the armies of Ch'in crossed the Yellow River without difficulty and plundered the lower Fen Valley as far as Ch'ü-wu, which was taken by storm (314), while the troops of Wei were put to flight. King Hsiang of

Wei had a meeting with Hui-wen of Ch'in at Lin-chin and sued for peace. He was able to get it only by ceding all that remained to him of the right bank of the Yellow River, so long disputed (312); and this time the conquest was final. The losers had begged help in vain from Ch'u, which had promised it but had not fulfilled the promise, and from the King of Ch'i as well; but he, still nursing the wound to his pride inflicted when his rival of Ch'u was designated as chief of the League, had not budged. Thus neither Han nor Wei hesitated to leave the League or to ally themselves to Ch'in — which is to say, to become her vassals.

But if King Hsüan of Ch'i did not come to the aid of his allies, Wei and Han, it was mainly because he was absorbed in keeping an eye on his northern frontier, where the affairs of the principality of Yen were then troubled by the minister Tzu Chih's attempt at usurpation. The princes of Yen had not previously played any part in the general politics of the Chinese world. Lying in the extreme north of the empire, they were too involved in protecting themselves against the attacks of the northern barbarians, Tungusic tribes who several centuries earlier had subdued the Chinese populations of southern Manchuria, and against whom Yen had had to appeal for aid, in 664, to Prince Huan of Ch'i.

At the end of the fourth century, King Wu-ling of Chao seems to have reduced the northern barbarians, Hun and Tungus, to vassalage; and he seems also to have made Yen acknowledge a sort of protectorate. It is probably for this reason that King K'uai of that country found himself involved in the coalition of 318 against Ch'in. This very aged prince had left the conduct of all business to his minister Tzu Chih, who also had enough influence over the king to persuade him to name the minister as his successor, against the claim of the Prince Royal, P'ing — in the same way that 'Po Yi was presented to Heaven as successor by the Great Yü, denying Ch'i's claim'. P'ing turned to the King of Ch'i, who promised his aid and sent an expedition (314) but took advantage of this to seize the country for himself, occupying the capital and maintaining a garrison there. Only after two years did a general revolt of the people of Yen drive out the Ch'i soldiery and permit P'ing to ascend the throne as King Chao.[13]

While King Hsüan of Ch'i was wasting his time in this way, Ch'u became an easy victim to the vengeance of Ch'in.[14] In the spring of 312 the Ch'u general Kai of Ch'ü was beaten and taken prisoner with his whole army at Tan-yang, on the River Tan (Honan). The king hastily called up a general levy and, crossing the passes of the Ch'in-ling with this new army, sought to carry the war right into the land of Ch'in. At the same time he sent a relative of his, the poet Yüan of Ch'ü, on an embassy to Ch'i, trying to renew the broken alliance. Unfortunately for the King of Ch'u, his levies lacked discipline: they were beaten where the road emerges from the mountains onto the plain of the Wei, at Lan-t'ien, southeast of Hsi-an fu (Shensi).

The news of this second defeat did nothing to make the task of his ambassador easier, and he got no satisfaction. King Huai managed, indeed, to collect the remnants of his army; but it was impossible to continue the struggle, all the more since Han and Wei, Ch'in's allies, seized the chance to attack him from the north. He was reduced to buying peace by ceding the commandery of Han-chung on the upper Han River (311). This was a very serious loss: hitherto the mountain barrier had protected Ch'u on the west better than all her armies, but from this point on it was breached. The forces of Ch'in could at their leisure concentrate at Han-chung; and from there they could drive down the river without encountering any natural obstacles, direct to the Ch'u capital, Ying.

4

The Triumph of Ch'in
(Third Century)

The double conquest of Ho-hsi and Han-chung by Ch'in during the last years of the fourth century was an event which was certain to have the gravest of consequences. In effect it gave her the keys to all the roads of China, those to the east as well as those to the south. The high mountains which surrounded her, hitherto obstacles to her development because the exits from them were in the hands of her enemies, had become her ramparts, protecting her against any attack from outside. At the same time her armies, masters of the passes, needed only descend the Yellow River or the River Han to threaten the neighbours of Ch'in whenever her rulers wished to do so.

This situation imposed a special character upon the rivalries of the three great states, Ch'u, Ch'i, and Ch'in. The first two, about equal in strength (the one in the north, the other in the south), sought during their long struggle to gain the adherence of the petty states of the north and the centre and to form leagues with themselves as presidents. Ch'in, on the other hand, well protected in her far western domain, advanced slowly along the Yellow River, seizing and annexing cities and provinces. Like a tentacle it extended a long strip of conquered territories from west to east, thus applying the policy of expansion which the Chinese politicians styled 'transverse', *heng*. When Ch'i and Ch'u, momentarily interrupting their quarrels, united against her, the league formed from north to south by these states and their clients was the 'longitudinal', *tsung*, league.[1] But these coalitions were rare, and it is rather the story of Ch'in's uninterrupted conquests than that of her adversaries' spasmodic efforts which gives unity to the history of this period.

His victories over Ch'u had made King Hui-wen of Ch'in the arbiter of all China. He had scarcely time to take advantage of it, since he died soon afterwards, in 311. His son Wu, who succeeded him, reigned only three years, dying from the effort he had exerted in sport, trying to raise too heavy a tripod (307). His unexpected death might have signalled a grave crisis, since he left no children. This was averted thanks to the energy of the mother of the nearest heir (a younger brother of the deceased king) and of her brother Wei Jan, Prince of Jang. They seized power and put to death all who opposed them; then they sent for the young prince, who was at the time a hostage at the Yen court. Soon afterwards, a plot inspired by the dowager queen, Wu's mother, was foiled, and the old queen was put to death, together with the rebel princes (305).

Although security had been disturbed only very slightly and had been so quickly re-established, this brief crisis was enough to rouse hope in Wei and Han, who once more renounced their allegiance to Ch'in and turned to the side of Ch'i after King Wu's death. To prevent the King of Ch'u from joining this league, the King of Ch'in signed a treaty with him at Huang-chi: the territory of Shang-yung (Hupei) was returned to Ch'u, and the two states concluded an alliance. The princely heir apparent of Ch'u was sent as a hostage to Hsien-yang, the capital of Ch'in; and a Ch'in princess was given in marriage to King Huai. It would seem that the Prime Minister, Chi of Ch'u-li, who was the younger brother of King Hui-wen (337–311), who had held this post since 309 and who was to keep it until he died in 300, sought above all to consolidate the position Ch'in had gained, without involving the obviously exhausted country in new wars. In 302 he managed to re-establish relations with Wei and Han: a treaty was signed at Lin-chin and, in exchange for the return of several cities which Ch'in had seized previously, an alliance was concluded. Negotiations were also undertaken with Ch'i, and these seem to have ended in a treaty of alliance and an exchange of hostages. King Chao-hsiang, who was still childless, sent his brother K'uei to Ch'i, while King Hsüan of Ch'i sent his nephew Wen of T'ien, the son of his brother, the former minister Ying of T'ien, to the Ch'in court, where he received the title of minister.

At this moment when a series of treaties stabilized the position of each, it seemed that after a century of incessant struggles the Chinese world was tending to divide itself up among the three great states of Ch'i, Ch'u, and Ch'in, whose respective zones of influence included the less important principalities. In the northeast, the King of Ch'i had reduced the petty princes of his southern border (Lu, Chü, Tsou, and so on) to a sort of vassalage; but the unfortunate expedition of 314 had permanently alienated the northern state of Yen, whose King Chao was Ch'i's most implacable enemy. In the south, the successive ruin of Wu and Yüeh had relieved the Ch'u kings of all fear from the east; and for a moment Ch'u had succeeded, at the start of the fourth century, in bringing under her influence all the lands south of the Yellow River which the downfall of Chin had left defenceless. The kings of Ch'u had lost their old ally Cheng, conquered by Prince Ai of Han (375); but this loss had been balanced by the alliance with Sung, which fear of Han and an unfortunate war, followed by the partial loss of the Huai territories, had driven into their arms; and they had taken the dukes of Sung, as well as the kings of Chou, under their protection. Finally, Ch'in had just imposed a sort of protectorate over the kings of Wei and Han, and she had concluded a close alliance with Yen, the enemy of Ch'i. Only Chao, thanks to her geographic situation, remained independent.

The relations of the princes among one another were governed by a sort of protocol which, by keeping up appearances, humoured the sensitivities of the weaker states. There were various degrees of relationship. The most flexible were conventions providing for marriage and the exchange of hostages, such as those of Ch'i with Yen in 331 or of Ch'in with Ch'i in 301, which left the contracting parties in principle on an equal footing, while their relative power alone determined their real position. But sometimes, in order to assure a clearer domination, the protector state would set up one of its own officers as minister for the protected prince, thus instituting a real protectorate, with a sort of resident-general. Such was the case with Wei and Han: Ch'in sent Chang Yi as resident to the former (322–317), and Chi of Ch'u-li (308–306) to the latter. Thus it seems that during the last years of the fourth century the three great states, satisfied with the domination they exerted, sought to establish their hegemony definitively over their neighbours simply through a system of treaties and alliances, without resorting to new conquests.

But events did not allow them the time to complete this diplomatic consolidation, out of which a kind of equilibrium might have emerged; and they were thrown back into a warlike policy. In 302 the heir apparent of Ch'u, then a hostage in Ch'in, quarrelled with a courtier and killed him, after which he fled. Ch'in prepared an expedition at once, and for this she asked assistance from her new allies — Ch'i, Han, and Wei. King Huai of Ch'u, having been defeated in every encounter and having had two of his generals killed, sought safety in breaking up the coalition. He sent the heir apparent to Lin-tzu, offering to leave him there to obtain peace (300). Chao-hsiang revenged himself with a veritable ambush: he invited Huai to a personal meeting at the Wu Pass, to negotiate peace directly. In the course of the meeting he seized Huai and carried him off as a prisoner (297). The result was not what he had counted on: Huai refused to cede the territories of Wu and Chiang-nan (upstream from present-day Yi-chang) in exchange for his liberty. The grand officers of Ch'u, for their part, placed the crown prince, then a hostage in Ch'i, upon the throne, and the war resumed at full scale. It was, moreover, disastrous for Ch'u; and when in 292 the new king, Ch'ing-hsiang, had to plead for peace, he had lost the entire valley of the Han. Ch'u did not recover from this series of defeats, and for ten years she kept herself aloof from the general politics of the Chinese world.

In the meantime Wen of T'ien, Lord of Meng-ch'ang, who felt himself suspect at the Ch'in court, had taken flight after several months. Returning to his homeland of Ch'i, he became minister to King Min, who had just succeeded his father, Hsüan. He broke off the alliance with Ch'in, concluded barely a year before (299). Then, taking advantage of the fact that Ch'in was involved in the war with Ch'u, he had won over the states of the north and the centre to himself. In 296 he thus formed a league of which he was the chief, comprising Wei, Han, Chao, Chung-shan, and Sung — that is to say, all of what then made up China, apart from Ch'in and Ch'u.

The moment seemed to him well chosen for an expedition against Ch'in, all the forces of which were engaged in the war with Ch'u. He advanced to the Han-ku Pass and achieved a brilliant victory; but he could not breach the passes, and the campaign dragged on without result. King Chao-hsiang had nothing to offer but some restitutions of territory to Wei and Han to buy peace. To the former he returned Ho-pei, in the southwest corner of Shansi, and to the latter Ho-wai — that is, the territory lying south of the Yellow River, where the Lo joins it (Honan). Although this was no great matter, it sufficed to cause the Prime Minister of Ch'in to be dismissed in disgrace. Lou Huan was of alien origin (he was from Chao and had long served that country before settling down in Ch'in), which made him suspect. He had to retire and, under the influence of the Queen Mother, power was given back to the king's uncle, Wei Jan, who would carry on the external policy of Ch'in with great vigour for thirty years.

When Wei Jan took the government of the principality in hand, the repeated defeats which had been inflicted upon Ch'u gave him greater freedom of action. He took advantage of this to recall one of the armies, which he entrusted to a loyal follower of his own, Po Ch'i, one of the finest generals Ch'in had ever had, who also received the rank of Guardian of the Left, *tso-keng*, the twelfth level in the Ch'in hierarchy. Po Ch'i commenced by winning a great victory over Han and Wei at Yi-ch'üeh (293). Then, in 289, he seized from Wei alone 'sixty-one cities and towns'; and in the preceding year he had forced her to cede Ch'in the whole territory of Ho-tung, the triangle situated where the Fen enters the Yellow River in southwestern Shansi.

There the effort of the Ch'in soldiers dashed itself against the stubborn resistance of those who dwelt in the former land of Chin, whom centuries of war had schooled in hatred for the men of Ch'in. The Ho-tung triangle was taken, lost, and retaken over and over again. P'u-fan (today P'u-chou), taken in 303, was restored to Wei the following year, retaken almost immediately, only to be lost again in 296, then reconquered in 292 and definitively annexed in 290. But once this area was occupied it formed a solid base of operations for expansion north of the Yellow River, which was rapid. Yüan and Ho-yung on the banks of the River (near Chi-yüan, in Huai-ch'ing fu, Honan), were taken in 289, giving Ch'in possession of a gateway onto the great eastern plain, at the place where the Yellow River exits from its long defile.

On the south bank this outlet had been acquired several years earlier, for progress there had been more rapid, the Han resistance being obstructed by the total impotence of the Chou kings, who had the last remnants of their domain there. In 308 the Ch'in armies had taken Yi-yang from Han; then in 295, skirting the southern foot of Sung-shan, they had taken from Wei the city of Hsiang-ch'eng (which still bears that name today), where the River Ju enters the plain. From there they could mount incursions against the Wei capital, Ta-liang, near present-day K'ai-feng fu, and against the Han capital, Cheng.

In 288 the kings of Ch'in and Ch'i signed an agreement delimiting their respective spheres of influence: Ch'i in the great eastern plain, Ch'in in the mountainous region of present-day Shansi. And to signalize their sovereignty over the local kings, they granted themselves the ancient religious title of emperor, *ti*, which legends attributed to the sovereigns of high antiquity. The

King of Ch'in was the Emperor of the West, Hsi-ti, and the King of Ch'i, the Emperor of the East, Tung-ti. They had to give up these titles almost immediately due to the reproaches that were aroused; but they did not abandon their claims upon their neighbours, and these they began at once to realize. Wei Jan was satisfied with making the King of Wei cede him the territory of An-yi, the ancient capital of the Wei ancestors (near Chieh-chou in Shansi). King Min of Ch'i seemed at first to have drawn the better portion of the treaty: almost without striking a blow, he annexed the duchy of Sung (286).

This principality[2] had passed through very difficult times since the fall of Chin had left her defenceless against her enemies, Cheng and Ch'u. In the fourth century, after Cheng was conquered by Han and disappeared, Sung saw herself threatened by neighbours too powerful for her, so she tied herself to the fortunes of Ch'u, becoming as faithful an ally of that state as she had been of Chin in previous centuries. This naturally brought down upon her the enmity of Ch'i, with which she had often been at war. At the end of the fourth century, however, the kings of Ch'in, Ch'u, and Ch'i were too much occupied in the struggle among themselves to bother about the affairs of central China. Duke K'ang, who ascended the Sung throne in 329, had been able to take advantage of their indifference and expand in all directions. He had seized T'eng, a small state on the southern border of Lu; he had conquered from Ch'u the lands of northern Kiangsu as far as the seacoast; from Wei and Ch'i he had taken several scraps of territory east of the Yellow River; and from Han he had retaken the territories along the Huai which he had previously lost. Having thus succeeded in carving out a very extensive kingdom for himself in the southern part of the great eastern plain, he had taken the title of king (318). Unfortunately, these expeditions had worn his people out; and the festivals he gave after his victories and the public works he undertook completed their exhaustion. When Ch'i, Wei, and Ch'u attacked him in order to retrieve the territories he had seized earlier from them, their armies encountered no resistance. The king fled, and died soon afterwards in Wei; his state was divided into three portions, the largest of which was annexed by Ch'i (286). Thus disappeared the last scrap of the domain belonging to the ancient sovereigns of the Yin dynasty which had ruled over China before the Chou.

The conquest of Sung had confirmed Ch'i's power in the east. Lu and Tsou, and the twelve little principalities on the banks of the River Ssu declared themselves her vassals; Ch'u allowed her, without protest, to take all the territory north of the River Huai. For a moment it seemed possible that a powerful kingdom would arise in the eastern Chinese plain; but the triumph was ephemeral. The very rapidity of his successes turned the head of King Min, who was very old by now: he saw himself as soon the master of all China, ascending the throne of the Chou.

Min attacked the 'three Chin' (286), thus breaking the agreement with Ch'in; and she, alarmed by these too-rapid successes, responded at once to the call for help, sending an expedition which seized several cities from Ch'i (285). At the same time, moreover, Ch'in found an ally near at hand in Yen, whose King Chao burned to avenge Ch'i's treachery in 314. He immediately called up all his troops and gave command to his best general, Yo Yi, who crossed the Yellow River, attacked the northern border of Ch'i, and won a great victory west of the River Chi, advancing to the city of Ling-ch'iu and taking it (285). All of Ch'i's neighbours formed a coalition against her, and their troops invaded her from all sides. While the Yen army continued to march from the north, Chao, Wei, and Han sent forces to operate in the west, a Ch'in army invaded the southwest, and finally a Ch'u army on the south penetrated into the basin of the Huai.

King Min was frantic. A veritable terror reigned in the capital: anybody who had criticized him was decapitated without trial; but at the same time he put to death his minister, whom he judged to have been unquestionably responsible for the disaster. A favourite, Hsiang-tzu, received command of Min's last army. He was unable to prevent the enemies from effecting a junction west of the River Chi and, forced to accept an unequal engagement, he was utterly defeated, his armies scattered, and he himself fled with but a single chariot.

This victory was enough to satisfy all the allies except the Prince of Yen, and they wished to stop there. Unable to sway them, the Prince of Yen ordered his general Yo Yi to continue the campaign alone. But the debate had undoubtedly given a respite to the men of Ch'i. A general, Ta-tzu, had managed to gather up the fleeing men and to form an army, with which he several times held up the troops of Yen, reduced now to only their own strength. But Ta-tzu received little encouragement from the king, who undoubtedly thought the peril past since the coalition had broken up and who refused him any reward; so he ceased resistance; and his soldiers, the only ones who were protecting the capital, dispersed. Yo Yi entered Lin-tzu unopposed, and it was given over to pillage, the temples and palaces being burned. The treasures of Ch'i were loaded on carts and sent off to Yen; and then the country was systematically occupied.

King Min, who had managed to escape in time, took refuge in Wei, where the prince received him warmly; but his arrogance soon caused him to be expelled from there. He then sought to take shelter with the princes of Lu and of Tsou; but they, who two years before had declared themselves his vassals, refused to receive him (284). He took up his abode in Chü, the only city of his, except for Chi-mo and Liao, which had not surrendered. From there he managed without much difficulty to detach the King of Ch'u from the coalition, since the latter had been alarmed by this sudden collapse. But everything turned against the unhappy King Min. General Nao Ch'ih, sent from Ch'u to his aid, preferred to come to an understanding with Yo Yi; and he had barely arrived in Chü when he assassinated King Min — thus sharing part of the Lin-tzu booty (284).

The heir apparent had to hide for some time as a domestic servant in a house at Chü. Only after Nao Ch'ih departed did he venture to reappear and take the title of king. But his kingdom no longer existed. Yo Yi had organized his conquest as a territory of Yen, dividing it into commanderies and districts, and installing garrisons in them. To make the new regime popular, he reduced taxes and promised to respect local laws and customs. He was, in fact, able to administer the country without resistance for six years, but this was essentially a personal achievement. Hardly had he fallen into disgrace than General Tan of T'ien, who held the city of Chi-mo for King Hsiang (Min's son) launched a surprise attack, took the capital, and drove the troops of Yen out (279). Within a few days the entire principality of Ch'i was reconstituted within its former boundaries, and King Hsiang re-entered his capital.[3] But from then on the state remained too weak to take up and play the leading role in the east ever again. King Hsiang, and perhaps even more his wife, Queen Hou, realized this very well; and they concluded an alliance with Ch'in. This continued under their son, King Chien, and, except for a few brief episodes, was not breached until the end of the principality.

The real victor in this campaign had been Ch'in rather than Yen; and the allied states could quickly see that, in helping to overcome Ch'i, they were bearing arms against themselves. Ch'u was the first to feel it. King Ch'ing-hsiang had, through the victory over Ch'i, retaken the territories north of the Huai and had added to that the former territory of Sung (283). He had forced Prince Wen of Lu, previously a vassal of Ch'i, to recognize his suzerainty; and he did the same for the Lu successor, Ch'ing, from whom he would take his state and annex it in 249. He had imposed an alliance upon the King of Han (281) and prepared to occupy the Royal Domain of Chou. He was, in sum, master of all China south of the Yellow River.

Wei Jan, after a more or less voluntary retirement of one year, had resumed the post of Prime Minister of Ch'in. No doubt he feared to leave the King of Ch'u the time to organize his conquests and preferred to take the offensive against him. In 280, Ssu-ma Ts'o, governor of Shu, made an expedition the length of the Yangtze and took the territories of Wu and Chiang-nan. In the following year, Po Ch'i, who had only recently been elevated to the rank of *ta-liang-tsao*, drove down the Han and advanced to the Ch'u capital, Ying. This he took in 278, while King Ch'ing-hsiang retreated with the remnants of his army into the Huai Valley, where he remained until his death (263). The displacement of the capital put the kings of Ch'u out of reach of their enemies for a moment; but, by forcing them north, it made them abandon their hold on the Yangtze Valley as well as that of the Han. To get peace, they had to cede the territory of Ying — which became for Ch'in the commandery of the South, *nan-chün* — as well as the territories situated upstream, which became the commandery of Ch'ien-chung (277). An effort to recover the lost lands, in 276, was only partly successful: the province of Yang-tzu South, around the T'ung-t'ing Lake, was reoccupied, but the capital remained in the hands of Ch'in.

Peace was finally concluded, the King of Ch'u sending his son, Prince Wan, as a hostage to Hsien-yang (272); and this peace lasted till the death of Ch'ing-hsiang (263). His successor, K'ao-lieh (262–238), who had spent ten years as a hostage in Ch'in, took Hsieh of Huang as his Chief of Commands. Hsieh had accompanied and served him during that period; and the king gave him — in addition to the chief ministry — a considerable fief on the banks of the Huai, with the title Lord of Ch'un-shen. Both king and minister undoubtedly understood the true power of their formidable neighbour, and they tried to keep the peace. Hsieh could buy it only by abandoning the region where the River Han flows into the Yangtze, the country of Chou (nowadays Mien-yang, west of Han-yang), the last remnant of the royal family's ancestral domain (262).

The war against Ch'u had for a time diminished Ch'in activity in the north. Wei Jan took it up again with renewed vigour, now that Ch'i and Ch'u, the two states strong enough to oppose

Ch'in, had been put out of action. Wei, his most threatened neighbour, knew that she was incapable of defending herself and thought she could find safety in actual recognition of Ch'in sovereignty, under the usual form of an alliance (283). But treaties with Ch'in lasted only so long as that state thought it advantageous to observe them. As early as 276, having just made peace with Ch'u, Wei Jan broke off relations with Wei to take advantage of the mourning following the death of King Chao, whose successor was An-hsi; and the conquest of the north bank of the Yellow River recommenced. Within ten years Ch'in had taken the quadrilateral between the River Ch'in to the north and east, and the Yellow River to the south. In 275 an expedition led by Wei Jan himself brought the Ch'in army under the walls of Ta-liang, the capital of Wei, which was saved only by aid sent from Han; but the town of Wen had to be ceded.

An alliance of the 'three Chin' was ill-starred. Their armies were completely defeated by Po Ch'i at Hua-yang, losing 150,000 men (274). A victory won under the walls of Yen-yü by the allied troops of Chao and Han (269) did not even interrupt the Ch'in advance for a moment. In 268 her armies seized Huai (which is today Wu-chih) and soon afterwards Hsing-ch'iu nearby (266), thus reaching the River Ch'in and the Han frontier. Soon afterwards, they crossed the river and took Yüan-yung (nowadays Yüan-wu) in Han (259).

Wei Jan's prudent but tenacious policy bore fruit. When the death of the Queen Mother, in 265, forced him to retire, nothing could any longer stop the advance of Ch'in. Ch'i's adherence to the coalition of the 'three Chin' did not affect the course of events. In 263 an army led by Po Ch'i seized from Han, in addition to the territory of Nan-yang, the long, narrow pass through the T'ai-hang Mountains which led from the Yellow River plain into the region of Shang-tang, the former domain of the Red Ti (in southeastern Shansi). This was a success of the first order: from then on the kingdom of Han, cut into two fragments — one north of the T'ai-hang, the other south of the Yellow River — was rendered impotent for the future. After having struggled vainly for a year to try and recover the defile, and having already lost what remained to him of the left bank of the River, the King of Han found himself in no position to aid Shang-tang. The governor of that territory, reduced to his own resources, offered the province to Chao, which accepted (262).

It was a dangerous move to step between the wolf of Ch'in and the prey which it considered already in its grasp. Almost immediately Chao was invaded. Her general, Chao K'uo, allowed himself to be surrounded by Po Ch'i in the Ch'ang-p'ing gorge (southwest of Lu-an fu). Unable to break through the enemy lines, he defended himself stoutly despite lack of food, awaiting an army of rescue which King Hsiang was hastily raising. But the levy was delayed for want of rations which the King of Ch'i, against the advice of his ministers who were more clear-sighted than he, obstinately refused to furnish. After forty-six days, Chao K'uo was killed in a skirmish, and the leaderless army surrendered under a promise that their lives would be spared. Regardless of his given word, Po Ch'i had them massacred to the last man: it is said that 400,000 heads were counted. Then Po Ch'i moved on to besiege Han-tan, the capital of Chao, at the same time detaching two units to take Shang-tang, one to the northeast, the other to the centre of that territory (259). The King of Chao offered six cities of the province in return for peace; but before the treaty was signed he succeeded in persuading the King of Ch'i to conclude an alliance, and the negotiations were broken off.

The war resumed at once, the army of Ch'in coming in the eighth month to lay siege to the Chao capital, Han-tan. The city was very strongly fortified and able to hold out for a long time: in the preceding century the army of Wei had besieged it for two years. This time the siege was again difficult. Po Ch'i, who had been disgraced owing to a court intrigue, considered the effort badly conceived, and steadfastly refused to take command, finally committing suicide (258). It seemed to the Ch'in army that the siege might go on indefinitely.

The king's uncle, Sheng of Chao, Lord of P'ing-yüan, who was Prime Minister, asked aid from King An-hsi of Wei, whose sister he had married. That king, torn between fear of Ch'in reprisals if he yielded to the plea and fear of a definitive Ch'in victory if he did nothing, ended up by sending General Chin Pi to the frontier with an army to keep an eye on what happened. But then his brother, Wu-chi, lord of Hsin-ling, who was more intelligent and saw what a disaster for Wei the destruction of Chao would be, carried out an audacious coup. He armed his personal followers, thus forming a bodyguard of 100 chariots, with which he proceeded to Chin Pi's camp, assassinated the general, took his command, and fell upon the troops of Ch'in, which were crushed by this unexpected attack.

The kingdom of Chao was saved, but that of Wei paid dearly for this success. Even though the Lord of Hsin-ling remained in Chao after his victory to show clearly that he had not had the sanction of his brother, Ch'in now turned her whole effort against Wei. The policy of making conquests along the Yellow River had so absorbed her energies that she had not taken the time to complete the conquest of the eastern portion of Wei by taking the cities of the lower Fen. She now turned to this and succeeded without great difficulty (255).

In the meantime Chao had to defend herself against her neighbour on the northeast, Ch'in's ally Yen, whose army had taken part in the campaign against Han-tan and which continued the war on its own hook. In 251, negotiations were begun; but the Prime Minister of Yen, Li Fu, and his general Yo Chien — the son of Yo Yi, conqueror of Ch'i — who had gone to the Chao court to conduct these talks, returned from them convinced that Chao had been so worn down that she was incapable of resistance, and they urged that the war be continued. A double expedition was organized, ending in the total defeat of the Yen armies, whose generals were taken prisoner. The victorious Chao general, Lien P'o, came before the walls of the Yen capital, and King Hsi sued for peace (250). But this was only a truce. Strong in the support of Ch'in, King Hsi returned to the campaign almost immediately. In 248 Chao had to ask help from Wei against him, and during that time the Ch'in army seized the opportunity to launch an expedition against both of them. One force advanced up the Fen Valley, and into the T'ai-yüan basin, taking thirty-seven cities (248). Another attacked Wei on the north bank of the Yellow River, but it was stopped by the king's brother, Wu-chi, Lord of Hsin-ling, who in this extremity had been hastily recalled from his exile and put at the head of an army (247). Peace was signed, but it was a precarious peace which could not last very long.

Amidst all these events, the disappearance of what remained of Chou, which was wiped out by Ch'in in 249, passed unnoticed. Since 367 the kings of Chou had possessed neither territory nor power. Kings Hsien and Shen-ching had been in the hands of the lords of Eastern Chou; King Nan was in the hands of Duke Wu of Western Chou. Wu hastened the end by an unfortunate initiative: terrified by the greed of Ch'in, he thought that it would be prudent to guarantee himself a protector, and he appealed to the princes of Wei, Han, and Chao. He was engulfed in their ruin. In 256 a Ch'in army occupied his domain, the king and he being exiled to the village of Tan-hu, where they soon died. The Chou dynasty had ceased to exist. Wu's cousin, who had taken no part in his initiative towards the 'three Chin', kept his domain of Kung several years more, but he did not assume the title of king. He was merely the Lord of Eastern Chou, Tung-Chou-chün, and he too was dethroned in turn, in 249.

The end was coming for all. In 230 Ch'in without difficulty finished off the conquest of Han, which had been begun in the preceding year. In 229 Chao was attacked. The resistance was bitter; but two columns invaded from the west and the south, while a third invested the capital. The king, who strove to continue the struggle in the Tung-yang area, was taken prisoner; and after a siege of one year, Han-tan fell (228). The King of Ch'in insisted upon making a triumphal entry into the city; and he took vengeance for its long resistance by having part of the population massacred. In 226, General Wang Chien, the victor of Chao, destroyed Yen. The capital, Chi, near present-day Peking, was taken; the heir apparent, who a little before this had sought to have the King of Ch'in assassinated, was beheaded; and his father, King Hsi, was obliged to flee into Manchuria, to Liao-tung, the farthest east of his domains. In 225, Wang Pen, Wang Chien's son, took Ta-liang, the capital of Wei, and annexed that state. In 223, old Wang Chien, who had retired after his victorious campaign in Yen, was again put at the head of an army and sent against Ch'u, which he destroyed in a campaign lasting two years. King Fu-ch'u was taken prisoner: he had reigned for five years after having assassinated his brother, King Ai, in 228. In 222 the last remnant of Yen, in Liao-tung, was conquered by Wang Pen, while his father, pursuing his successes in the south, marched triumphantly down the Yangtze Valley and secured the submission of the princes of Yüeh. Finally, in 221, he was sent against Ch'i: King Chien surrendered with his entire army. All of China was unified under the sceptre of the King of Ch'in.

In that same year, in order to manifest the new order of things, the King of Ch'in took a new title. He had himself called August Lord, *Huang-ti*, a title which remained that of the Chinese sovereigns until the revolution of 1912, and which we translate as 'emperor'. The old China had disappeared for good, and a new world was beginning to organize itself on the ruins.

Book V
Ancient Literature and Philosophy

1
The Origins of Literature

The first fumbling beginnings of ancient Chinese literature appeared in the last period of the Western Chou empire. At this time, in the brilliant court of kings Hsüan and Yu, were created the first literary forms in verse and prose, at the same time as the first, still rather childish, attempts at philosophic thought. The origins of literature were religious: the most ancient works were in fact all of a ritual character — sacrificial verse hymns designed for the regular festivals or for occasional ceremonies, or ritualistic pieces in prose, libretti to the great pantomines in the ancestral ceremonies, or official minutes of the king's solemn charges to the great dignitaries, documents intended for the Grand Scribe's archives, or fictional pieces in imitation of them.

We still have a certain number of fragments from this very remote period (they precede the time of Mo-tzu and that when the Confucian school compiled the *Lun yü*, since both of those quote these documents). In the Chou period they were called the 'Odes', *Shih*, and the 'Documents', *Shang shu*, and are today ordinarily called *Shih ching* and *Shu ching*.

Poetry

The religious odes make up the last three parts of the *Shih ching*, called since antiquity *Hsiao ya*, *Ta ya*, and *Sung*. The most ancient appear to be hymns intended for chanting to accompany the dancing and music of the festivals in honour of the royal Chou ancestors. They probably went back to the great epoch of the monarchy — that is, to about the ninth century.[1] They served as models for pieces composed later, as much at the Chou court itself as at the courts of the principalities. In Sung, certain pieces of evidence seem to show, the odes which have come down to us were composed towards the middle of the sixth century; in Lu, according to tradition, it was Prince Hsi (659–626) who had them composed. Naturally there existed a great number of them; but those not collected in the *Shih ching* have disappeared today. There remain hardly more than the fragments of a versified legend about Yü, which seems to have been made up for the sacrifices to that emperor. These pieces were not all designed for the ceremonies of the ancestral temple. Some were composed, perhaps in imitation of those, for all the ritual festivals of the court, for banquets, for archery contests, for receptions; and not only for those which occurred regularly, but sometimes also for those which seemed to celebrate particular occasions. Thus King Hsüan had the account of his military expeditions written up in verse, probably for his triumphs.

Whatever was the purpose, or the subject, of these odes, they were always constructed along the same lines. They are in regular stanzas, though the number of lines varies from piece to piece; and the lines are always very short, formed of only four words. That is, since Chinese is monosyllabic, they are in four-foot lines, with a verse of five words being introduced very rarely. The rhythm of the dance which they accompanied probably imposed upon the poet both this basic monotony and the few departures from that general rule.[2] Some of these poems are unrhymed, but most are rhymed, though often in quite an irregular fashion. Different combinations of rhymes — couplet rhymes, rhymes of two and two lines separated by unrhymed lines, and so on — are to be found mixed in the same piece.

To tell the truth, the poetic value of these odes is not very high. The authors were probably restricted by the demands of the music and the dance, and by the monotony of the rhythm. Furthermore, it is probable that the expression of wishes and vows, of requests to the spirits, and of thanks had to be couched in terms hallowed by usage, which they could hardly change; and the strictly religious parts are banal in the extreme. The narrative passages are better, some of them quite lively little scenes.[3]

The poetry did not, however, long remain purely religious, the form thus created being used to treat secular subjects. There was, for example, a satire by a court grandee (a Lord of Su, whose family held high posts under the Western Chou, according to the preface to the work) against one of his enemies, the Lord of Pao.[4]

There were satires of a more general sort, against slanderers and flatterers;[5] or against bad government so extreme that the sun went into eclipse;[6] or again a sort of elegy on parents' love for their children;[7] the complaints of soldiers against the general who had led them to defeat;[8] a widow's lament;[9] and so on. These poems, in which the authors are no longer restrained by the required rhythm of the dances, as they were in the religious pieces, are better, though a little short on invention and a little monotonous in style. They belong to the last years of the Western Chou; and one of them, which is precisely dated by the eclipse of 735 B.C., provides us with an important bench-mark.[10]

At about this time a very different poetic genre made its appearance: the poetry of popular imitation. Using the rhythms and themes of the young people at the great spring festivals,[11] an elegant form of court poetry sprang up in the eighth and seventh centuries, a form which had a very rapid and great success, spreading throughout the Chinese world. The most ancient pieces are found in the first section of the *Shih ching*, the *Kuo feng*; the *Shu ching* contains one; others, of a later period, are quoted in the *Tso chuan*, the *Kuo yü*, and so on.

These are freer than the religious pieces. The stanzas are not always regular; the four-word rhythm is still the most frequent, but the lines also show different measures, not only of five words, but also longer ones, of six, seven or eight words, and shorter ones too, of three, two or even a single word, intermingling with the regular four-word lines or combined with them. Rhymes are arranged much as in the religious pieces.

The distinctive feature of this poetry was its borrowing of popular themes and refrains, and using these as allusions to the events of contemporary court life. They are not themselves folk-poetry: the simple fact that they are all written in the same dialect, no matter which principality they come from, proves this. But they imitate it very closely.

The weakness of this kind of literature is that it becomes incomprehensible as soon as the event which gave rise to it is forgotten; and that happens quickly. The commentators who have sought to recover the original significance have wasted their time and achieved nothing. The history of the period is too little known, and in any case what one would have to know is not so much history as the court gossip of the moment. Certain pieces may have been meant to serve political ends; but the greatest number are obviously love poems about assignations, reproaches, estrangements, the sorrows of love,[12] regrets, complaints, sketches of young men and women;[13] and the popular themes are merely a transparent veil covering the author's sentiments. The mannered poetry of England and France shows a similar pattern.

Other poems seem to be little occasional pieces for the marriage of a princess or for the birth of a child, eulogies of a princess or a prince, of a great deed in the hunt, of a military victory.[14] And finally there were pieces of all kinds: there are verses celebrating the tree under which the Duke of Shao is said to have sat when he dispensed justice, in the golden age of King Wu; some explicate a proverb; there are little scenes from everyday life; and so forth.[15]

Prose

The School of the Scribes

At about the same period, Chinese prose was being shaped within a closed and very special field, that of the court scribes. I have already described the role of the scribes, charged on the one hand with setting down and on the other with keeping official documents, with preparing the programme for ceremonies and festivals, and so on. They had to adapt the language to the precise expression of precise facts — administration, ritual law — and it is from this effort that Chinese prose was born, with all its qualities of precision and exactness, but also with a dryness that always reveals its documentary origin a bit. And it was from the varying requirements of their tasks that the diversity of styles emerged.

From the beginning, indeed, the variety of the official papers they were required to draw up obliged them to create quite different forms. To direct the great pantomimes which accompanied the sacrifices honouring the ancestors of the dynasty, they had to write scenarios recounting the legend in detail and in such a way that every scene which the dancers mimed would be explained in the libretto. Thus they created the narrative style. The necessity for remaining constantly in touch with the movements of the dancers imposed both restraint and concision. About half of one of these libretti, that of the great *Ta-wu* dance, celebrating the great victory of King Wu over the last sovereign of the Yin dynasty, made its way into that compilation of ancient texts, the *Shu ching*, making up several chapters of it: the *T'ai shih*, the *Mu shih*, the *Wu ch'eng*, and the *Fen ch'i*.[16] Fragments of another libretto for the sacrificial dances of Sung to T'ang the Victorious,[17] are certainly among the opening chapters of the Books of Shang in the *Shu ching*, from the *T'ang cheng* to the *T'ang kao*. Furthermore, the *Kan shih* of the Books of Hsia is certainly a fragment of another libretto for the sacrifices to Yü.

The necessity of explaining the movements of the dancers is seen in the precision of certain descriptions. 'At dawn on the day *chia-tzu*, the king arrived in the Mu plain in the suburb of Shang; then he delivered an address. Holding the yellow battle-axe in his left hand, and in his right hand waving the white pennon to make a signal, he said: "You have come far, men of the western lands!" '18 Again it is a description of a dance (the last of the first scene, according to the *Li chi*) which we find in a passage of the *T'ai shih*:

> Eight hundred princes, without being summoned, came on their own; without the date's having been fixed, they came at the same time; without consulting one another, they departed together. All of them said, 'Shang must be attacked!' The king said, 'You do not know the mandate which Heaven [has given me]. He must not be attacked yet.' But on the day *ping-wu* he assembled his army; those before the army beat the drums and cried out, and the army unsheathed its weapons; those in front sang and those behind danced; [their shouts] reached high, even to heaven, and low, even to the earth, as they said: 'Be at ease, without care; Heaven is going to raise up one who will be our father and mother; the people will have a government, will have peace.'19

These passages suffice to show what this genre of literature was, in which the precise and minute description of ritual movements by dancers alternates with discourses designed to let the spectator follow the hero's thought.

But this is not all that ancient literature owes to the scribes. The most important of their duties, the composition of official documents, led them to create the documentary style. Besides administrative correspondence — reports, letters, and so on, of which no examples have survived — there were documents of a more solemn character, such as those conferring an official post or a fief. In these pieces, besides the traditional and unalterable sacred formula, the scribes had to set down a form of words, indicating the date, the witnesses (ministers or high officials who were present), describing the ceremonies succinctly and reporting the king's words. The original was kept in the Chief Scribe's archive, and a copy was given to the beneficiary, who often had it engraved on a ritual bronze vase cast for the occasion. The task was the more difficult when it was necessary to set down a judgement, together with a summary of the proceedings, of intervening acts, and of the sentence or final decision. In all these documents the style was necessarily simple, going straight to the point, without ornament, a little dry, but perfectly clear.[20]

A true literary genre was born from this; it consisted of composing fictitious documents in the administrative style, in which the writer's imagination gave itself free rein, developing some of the themes in the document to a greater or lesser degree. Some, choosing the frame of an especially solemn ceremony, composed pieces in which the principal element of interest consisted in the detailed recitation of the ceremony itself, thus mixing the narrative style of the pantomime libretti with the purely documentary style.

We have several works belonging to this genre: the *Ku-ming*, for example, in which an unknown scribe narrates in detail the ceremony of the king's accession under the fiction that he is describing that of King K'ang of Chou.[21] But most often it was less the whole ceremony than the address given there which interested the authors, since that gave them the opportunity to offer political, religious, or moral descants in which the author could express his personal opinions as he pleased. Thus were born several literary genres, among which that of the discussion between a king and his ministers was the simplest and the most widely utilized, since it lent itself best to developments of all kinds. Addresses by emperors of antiquity to their ministers were composed, or of ministers to their sovereign: the *Kao-yao mo* and the *Yi chi* take the venerated names of the saints and sages of the time when Yao and Shun lived, and attach to them the ideas of some unknown Chou-period scribe regarding the conduct of kings. In these tracts were developed the first elements of philosophy, and Chinese thought began to be aware of itself. It is difficult indeed to date them. They seem to go back to the period when the Chou kings, established in their new eastern capital, still held to the illusion of wielding a power which slipped from their grasp more and more during the seventh and sixth centuries.[22]

At a date difficult to fix precisely — tradition attributes this work to Confucius — a certain number of these literary pieces were brought together in a collection, of which a small portion has survived, known as the *Shang shu*, or more commonly the *Shu ching*. The collection is said to have included a hundred pieces, a list of which was drawn up in about the fourth century B.C. (it constitutes the preface today); but more than half of them were already lost in Han times, and, of those which were then recovered, again about a half were lost again quite soon and were replaced, about the middle of the third century B.C., by spurious texts.[23] These were clumsy efforts to reconstitute the 'text in the ancient script'; so of the *Shu ching* as published today, only about half is authentic.

It was in their little treatises in the form of administrative records that the scribes gradually worked out a complete political doctrine, especially a theory of kingship, which guided the political development of China right down to the Revolution of 1912.

They started from the religious ideas of their own time regarding the king, to fix the meaning of his relations with Heaven and with the people. The king and the dynasty owe their power to the Lord on High, who has given them the Mandate of Heaven. Its maintenance does not depend upon the king or upon his ministers, but only upon Heaven; and 'the Mandate of Heaven is not easy to keep', since 'one cannot put one's trust in Heaven'.[24] Sovereigns who, counting upon the mandate, do not take care to deserve it, lose it. Thus it was with the last princes of the Hsia and the Yin: it was not that Heaven had premeditated their removal, but they themselves, by their excesses, believing themselves secure in the mandate, took no heed of warnings. The mandate was taken from them, and bestowed upon T'ang and upon Wu. To keep the mandate, it is necessary to apply oneself to imitating the founding princes of dynasties;[25] there can be no doubt that Heaven was satisfied with them, since it raised them up. In sum, kings are always responsible before the Lord on High, who punishes them with the loss of the mandate if he is dissatisfied with them. Moreover, there is nothing arbitrary about the working of Heaven, nor is there any predestination: it is the conduct of the kings at every moment which determines Heaven's action.

The principles for the conduct of kings are set down precisely in a text, the *Kao-yao mo*. The most important rule is 'to know how to evaluate men, so as employ the best and thus give peace to the people', declares Kao-yao. And when Yü retorts that 'to achieve that completely is a difficult thing even for the Lord on High', it goes on to explain through examples. Men are evaluated by examining them according to the Nine Virtues. Whoever practises three of these is capable of managing his family, whoever practises six is capable of ruling a state. To give the people peace, all one must do is adhere strictly to the rules Heaven has given us. The Five Duties, *wu tien*, regulate relations among men; the Five Rites, *wu-li*, regulate relations with the gods; and for those who contravene these two series of rules, there are the Five Punishments, *wu hsing*. But these are questions of detailed application: the main thing is for the king to perfect himself.[26] His influence (his Virtue) is in fact sovereign. It was only necessary for Ch'ih-yu first to create disorder, and the whole people became brigands, assassins, thieves, and so on.[27] And the author of the *Yao tien*,[28] in portraying the sage-emperors of antiquity, Yao and Shun, shows the former diffusing his Virtue and transforming the world by it alone. He shows the latter's scrupulousness in doing things at the opportune time and place so as to 'conform to Heaven' — that is, to allow no contradiction between his acts and the phenomena of the physical world.[29]

Thus was created a theory of the royal power, of the king's Virtue, as much from a political as from a supernatural point of view. All these ideas, still somewhat diffuse, were taken up and systematized, probably in the eighth century, in a remarkable treatise, the 'Great Principle', *Hung fan*.[30] In this an anonymous author seeks to order and classify the different values into numerical categories, and to define for man, and especially for the king, his proper place in the world.

The theory expounded there is placed under the patronage of the Great Yü. It is said to have been derived from 'the Great Plan with its nine divisions' which Heaven presented to that sage-emperor when he made the flood-waters flow away; and to have been handed down by him to his descendants the Hsia, then by them to the Yin; and to have been expounded by the Viscount of Chi, brother of the last king of that dynasty, to King Wu, founder of the Chou dynasty. Its basic principles seem to have been, on the one hand, the opposition between man and the universe, and on the other, their precise correspondence. The universe, the perceptible world, is a product of the Five Elements, *wu hsing*: water, fire, wood, metal, earth.[31] These are not metaphysical entities, nor are they influences or powers: they are quite simply the five actual substances which bear those names, and they have the physical properties of them. 'Water flows and descends, fire burns and ascends, wood is crooked and straight, metal is malleable, the earth allows sowing and harvests.' These properties produce the appropriate flavours: 'that which flows and descends produces saltiness; that which burns and ascends produces bitterness'; and so on.

The action of the Five Elements is not explained. From this period on there must have been a number of theories on this subject: a text from that time seems to allude to a theory according to which they work by successively triumphing, one over another.[32] The *Hung fan* enumerates them in another order, arranging them two by two, according to the cardinal points of the compass to which they correspond: north (water), south (fire), east (wood), west (metal), ending at the centre (earth). Their action seems consequently to have been conceived as due to their alternating succession in an unending motion.[33] In none of these theories do they ever penetrate one another or intermix.

As opposed to the material world, man (the moral world) also depends upon five principles, probably to correspond to the Five Elements. These are the Five Activities, *wu shih*: gesture, speech, sight, hearing, thought. Like each of the elements, each of the activities has its properties: 'gesture is respectful, speech is reasonable, sight is clear, hearing is delicate, thought is penetrating.' And the activities in their turn produce results: 'What is respectful produces dignity; what is reasonable produces good order; what is clear produces discernment; what is delicate produces prudence; what is penetrating produces sanctity.'

To develop the Five Activities in conformity with the regular order of the Five Elements is the duty of the prince, and to that end he has the Eight Methods of Government, *pa cheng*. First there are the three great occupations of man in general: (1) nourishment, that is, agriculture; (2) goods, that is, the product of artisans: clothes, implements, and so on; (3) the sacrifices, by which one keeps in touch with the gods and the ancestors and assures oneself of their protection. Then there are the three ministers through whom the king controls human affairs: (4) the Minister of Public Works, who sets the boundaries of fiefs and apanages, oversees irrigation and roads, and so on; (5) the *ssu-t'u*, who controls the peasants' husbandry, teaches men their duties, and directs their whole life and activity; (6) the Minister of Justice, who acts against criminals. Finally there are the two relations of the prince with his vassals: (7) the receiving of guests, that is, peace; (8) the army, that is, war.

As the two worlds correspond perfectly to one another, the harmonious working of the Eight Methods of Government (the moral world) echoes the regular progress of the Five Regulators, *wu chi*, in the material world: the year, the month, the day, the constellations, the calendar. This agreement is made possible by the August Perfection, *huang chi*, that is, the royal power, which is like the centre upon which the universe and man converge simultaneously; and the centrality of the king in the world, as well as his transcendental relations above and below, are expressed in a striking formula: 'The Son of Heaven is the Father and the Mother of the People.'[34] This formula gives unity and coherence to the structure of the world by establishing the necessary hierarchy between its two constituent elements.

The king's methods of action are the Three Manifestations of Activity, *san te*: equity, severity, mildness. By these he governs — by the first in peace, by the second in troubled times, by the third in times of order and harmony — according to the character of his subjects; severe with slack and weak people, mild with the intelligent. If any difficulties arise, the 'examining of what is doubtful', *chi-yi*, through divination by means of the tortoise-shell and the milfoil can resolve them all.

And since there is an absolute congruence between the perceptible world and the moral world, between the universe and man, the latter will always know, thanks to the Eight Verifications, whether things are going well or ill. These are the examination of natural phenomena — rain, sun, heat, cold, wind — which, depending upon whether they come in season or out, tell whether the government is good or bad. To this end the king examines the whole year, the nobles one month, the ordinary officers one day. Rain at the right time shows that the king is earnest, continual rain that he is unjust; heat at the right time shows that he is wise, constant heat that he is lazy; cold at the right time shows that he is considerate, and so on.

If all goes well, the final result is the Five Happinesses, *wu-fu*: longevity, wealth, health, love of virtue, and a fitting end to one's life. If things go badly, there are the Six Calamities, *liu-chi*: violent and premature death, illness, suffering, poverty, misfortune, weakness. These come from Heaven to the people through the intermediacy of the king, who 'concentrates in himself the Five Happinesses to dispense them among the people', as of course he also does the Six Calamities.

It was not only philosophy which the scribes fathered. Another of their activities, the classification of the archives, led to another literary genre — to history. It was probably at about the turn of the ninth to the eighth century that the Grand Scribe, responsible for the custody and maintenance of the archives, began to compile a catalogue, in the shape of a chronological list of short notes, succinct summaries of what the documents contained. This was the origin of the official chronicles, and they always retained on the one hand a valuable precision and exactness in dates and names, and on the other hand an extremely dry style and a lack of satisfactory linking between the various notes.

Nothing has survived from the official chronicle of the Chou kings; but a portion from that of the principality of Lu, the *Ch'un ch'iu,* has been preserved. It was this that Confucius is said to have had in his hands and that his school used in teaching the science of government. It extends from 722 to 480. The chronicle of the counts of Ch'in has also survived, having been incorporated by Ssu-ma Ch'ien, the great historian of the second century B.C., in his *Historical Records.* Finally, by chance, the looting of tombs in A.D. 281 brought to light the chronicle of the principality of Liang, or Wei: compiled in the third century B.C., this has unfortunately been transmitted to us only after many emendations. These documents suffice to show that, once the genre had been created, it hardly changed, and that official history retained, in the hands of the Grand Scribe, the same precise, dry style that it had had in the beginning.

The School of the Diviners

Not all prose, however, was born through the work of the scribes. During this period, indeed, the college of court diviners by the milfoil, *shih-jen,*[35] created what might be called the scientific style, by attempting to compile the rules for divination by milfoil. Their work is preserved in the *Yi-ching,*[36] and one can see from the outset that everything — inspiration, method, habits of style — differs from the scribes and their writings. The diviners use a language which is concise to the point of obscurity, crammed with technical terms and with short little phrases having no connection between them.

The work was based upon a series of sixty-four hexagrams, figures of six lines. Some of these were unbroken lines, and their technical name was determined by the positions of the numbers nine and seven; and others, broken lines, were named by six or eight.[37] Each hexagram was given a name. The origin of this series evidently goes back very far, as far as milfoil divination itself. It was the same, and had the same names, throughout all of China, in Sung and Chin as well as in Ch'u and Lu, though the divination manual differed.

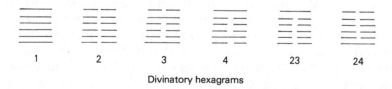

Divinatory hexagrams

The order of arrangement in those manuals was not arbitrary. Except for the first two hexagrams, one composed entirely of full lines and the other entirely of broken ones, and the six which could not be reversed because of their specific symmetrical order (28–31, 61–62), all the others were arranged in pairs in which the second pair is produced by reversing the first, the lower line of one becoming the upper line of the next: for example, the third and the fourth, and so on.[38]

The first task consisted of setting down in a few words the new rules for interpreting each figure: these were called the *T'uan*. These rules were based upon a long tradition, the origins of which are difficult to discover. Sometimes it is the exterior form of the hexagram which determines the entire interpretation: thus hexagrams in which the lines are arranged symmetrically are particularly lucky. Or again it is the relative position of the lines: the single broken line under five full lines of number 44, *kou*, suggests the interpretation 'a violent and powerful woman'. The hexagrams of a pair sometimes have inverse meanings when reversed, as numbers 23 and 24 do; but this by no means occurs regularly. Ordinarily, the general meaning is derived from the very name of the hexagram. For example, the seventh is called *shih*, which means 'army', and consequently represents armies on the march; the tenth is called *lü*, meaning 'to place the foot on something': that is why the hexagram represents 'a man who puts his foot on a tiger's tail'; and so on. But the hexagram was not a symbolic representation of the thing, it was the thing itself, in reality,[39] and this is why the divination was 'divine'. It was not the more or less happy interpretation of symbols; it was the verification of actual facts, producing real objects in the hexagrams. Man was incapable of altering anything in this 'divine' reality, which lay beyond him.

All that the diviners could do was to get as close as possible to the significance. This is what they tried to do a little later, by using a new procedure, the line-by-line analysis of each figure, in a second work, the *Yao*. This procedure came quite naturally out of the methods of divination, since — each line being obtained by a series of distinct operations[40] — it was easy to concede that the spirits of the ancestors who presided over them attached a special meaning to each, and that it was the recombination of these particular meanings which made up the sense of the whole, rather than having that arise suddenly out of the juxtaposition of lines having no significance of their own. The difficulty lay in finding rules for passing from the general interpretation of the figure, the only data given by tradition and verified by experience, to the separate interpretation of the lines.

Certain of the six positions which the lines could occupy seem to have been considered more important than others; and also the fact that broken lines appeared in even-numbered rows (counting the rows from the bottom of the hexagram) and that uneven-numbered rows had full lines[41] seem to have been given a certain importance. But no attempt was ever made to give a general fixed meaning, either to the lines themselves because of their form, or to the positions, or to the lines according to their place, and to deduce an explanation by reconciling that meaning with the meaning associated with the figure in general. Each hexagram was treated by itself, independently of others. Furthermore, attempts were often made to give a somewhat artificial unity to the whole combination by repeating the name of the hexagram, or merely making allusion to it, in each paragraph. Thus each of the six paragraphs treating each of the six lines of hexagrams 19, *lin* (to approach), and 20, *kuan* (to observe), contain a word having this meaning, but with various qualifications.[42] The *T'uan* and the *Yao*, which probably date from the end of Western Chou,[43] soon became a sort of established canon, with which nobody dared to meddle. This was the manual of the diviners at the royal court, and its compilation was ascribed to the sainted founders of the dynasty, King Wen and the Duke of Chou.[44]

The conciseness and difficulty of this work soon led to the need for commentaries. There are two of them, one for the *T'uan*, called *T'uan chuan*, and the other for the *Yao*, entitled *Hsiang chuan*; and these explain the texts to which they apply, phrase by phrase. But they were not literal commentaries alone: they contained also a new interpretation of the general meaning of the hexagrams made according to a new principle, which sought to eliminate the arbitrariness of an interpretation in which the same line in the same place has not the same meaning in the different hexagrams. Those were considered no longer as each an indivisible whole, but rather as a composite made up of two figures of three lines — two trigrams — the number of figures thus being reduced to eight elementary trigrams, which received the name and the meaning of the hexagrams made up by their reduplication. These two trigrams were considered to be either in repose or in motion.

In repose, a simple comparison of them served to explain the general meaning of the hexagram which they made up. For example, hexagram 30, *Li*, is composed of two similar trigrams which have the meaning of 'light'. The author understands from this the two chief luminaries, the sun and the moon; and as the word *li* means 'to adhere to', the entire figure is interpreted, '*Li* is to adhere to; the sun and moon are adherents to heaven.' Or again, hexagram 36 bears the name *Ming-yi*, which means 'light obscured'; it is decomposed into two trigrams, earth above, and light below; and thence comes the interpretation: 'The light penetrating into the earth, that is light obscured.'[45]

In motion, the upper trigram forms the lower one by 'mutation', *yi*, introducing its own lines there in place of those which the rules of correct correspondence would have required. These rules, for example, demanded that the second and fifth lines of the hexagram — particularly important, since they are the central lines of the trigrams — should be, the first strong (a full line), and the second weak (a broken line), or vice versa.[46] Thus, hexagram 6, *Sung*, having two strong lines, it is said that 'a strong line [central in the upper trigram] has come and taken the central place [in the lower trigram]'; from this comes the idea of 'opposition and obstruction.'[47]

The diviners had thus arrived at a rational and scientific theory of divination by the milfoil and the hexagrams: it allowed them to interpret everything that had to do with their science and seemed to them justified by their constant experience in the practice of divination.

After having been long content with this purely technical task, they in their turn began — influenced by the work of the scribes — to try to establish the rules for good government which their science had been designed to assist, and above all to frame a definition of the sage-king. There has survived to us a small tract of theirs on this subject, the cut-up fragments of which are scattered within another work, the *Hsiang chuan*, where they form the first paragraph of the chapter devoted to each hexagram. The diviners' responsibility at the court seems to have led them to an interest in these questions, which moreover the authors of the *T'uan* and especially those of the *Yao* had already touched upon. Divination was, after all, one of the means which kings employed to 'resolve doubts' and consequently to guide their conduct; so the study of it should provide sure principles capable of bringing back the Government of the Sages.

Besides the sages whom Heaven had appointed and whose Virtue was therefore innate, they also marvelled that men who gave themselves to the study of divination and achieved a perfect knowledge of its principles came at length to understand through their labour what the sage knew naturally, and thus acquired a Virtue analogous to his, though of a lesser kind. They had created for their own use a special terminology, calling the first the Great Men, *ta-jen*, and the second the Superior Men, *chün-tzu*. These persons did not have the same impact, as we see from a passage in the *Yao* which sets forth how they transform people and lead them to the right path:[48] 'The changes which the Great Man [makes] are as [clearly apparent as] the tiger's stripes: before having inquired about him through divination, one has confidence. The changes which the Superior Man [effects] are [vaguely visible] like the leopard's spots.' Below these two classes were the common run of people, the Small Men, *hsiao-jen*, made to be led.

Since the Superior Man is he who has accurately grasped the principles of divination, it is possible to become one by education. The author of the very brief tract incorporated into the *Hsiang chuan* tried to develop this idea by showing what, in his opinion, each hexagram teaches when taken as a rule of conduct.

> The movement of Heaven is force: the Superior Man must, in accordance with this, make incessant efforts. The power of the earth is denoted by [the hexagram] *k'un*: the Superior Man, in accordance with this, should support things by the breadth of his Virtue [as the earth does]. Above is Heaven; below, the Marsh, that is [the hexagram] *lü*: the Superior Man must, in accordance with this, distinguish between superiors and inferiors so as to settle the desires of the people. Heaven and earth communicating, that is [the hexagram] *t'ai*: the sovereign must, in accordance with this, achieve the way of Heaven and earth, manage to put Heaven and earth in order, so as to benefit the people. ... Fire above Heaven, this is [the hexagram] *ta-yu*: the Superior Man must, in accordance with this, repress evil, cherish good, in conformity to the mandate bestowed by Heaven.

Thus they arrived at a portrait of the Superior Man, studying the sayings and the actions of the ancients (hexagram 36), seeing to the integrity of his conduct and busying himself with the instruction of others (hexagram 29), capable of retiring from the world without regret (hexagram 28), cultivating his Virtue so as to diffuse it throughout the world (hexagram 30), never taking a step except in conformity to the rites (hexagram 34), correcting his own faults (hexagram 42, and compare hexagram 51), prepared to sacrifice his life to attain his purposes (hexagram 47). This Superior Man is necessarily a king, who regulates the calendar and retains the Mandate of Heaven (49, 50, and compare 22, and so on). Thus the terms sovereign, king, and Superior Man alternate freely in the various paragraphs of the text.

Since it is from the investigation of the hexagrams that one thus derives the nomenclature for all the virtues of the sage-king, it is by the ever deeper study of them and the perfect knowledge of divination that sanctity can be attained — or at least that lesser state of sagehood that can be acquired and is not conferred directly by Heaven. Thus the Superior Man developed in this way will be able to give the world the good government for which it waits.

Such were the ideas of the school of Scribes grafted upon the science of the school of Diviners. Various notions, still somewhat confused in the first, became clarified. Sanctity remained always attached to the royal dignity, but two degrees were distinguished, according to whether it was natural or acquired. Still more, a procedure was set down for acquiring sanctity. Finally the portrait of the saint was definitively established.

All these ideas, obscurely worked out by anonymous generations of men, were to dominate the thought of Confucius and through that, despite the mutations of centuries, all of Chinese thought.

2

Confucius, Mo-tzu, and the Metaphysicians

Confucius

It was upon the old ideas of the ancient schools of the Scribes and the Diviners that Confucius, at the turn of the sixth to fifth century, erected his sytem of morality and political ethics.

What is known of the true historical Confucius amounts to very little: a few names, a few dates, the place of his death; beyond that, anecdotes of doubtful authenticity. K'ung Ch'iu (his appellation was Chung-ni) was born about the middle of the sixth century B.C.[1] at Tsou, a small fortified place of which his father was governor. His family claimed to represent the elder branch of the dukes of Sung, and thereby they claimed descent from the ancient kings of the Yin dynasty. Their first ancestor had abandoned to his younger brother his rights to the throne, so that he would not have to avenge the assassination of an uncle who had usurped power. One of his descendants, driven from his country by the hatred of an all-powerful minister, had taken refuge in Lu, where he had been welcomed and given an official post: he was Confucius's great-grandfather.

Young Ch'iu, born to a very aged father who had married at the age of seventy, had been raised by his mother in poverty. This was the common lot for widows of functionaries who had no personal fortune and were thus reduced to making the best of the small piece of land granted them in lieu of pension. He later attributed the variety of his practical knowledge to this poverty: 'When I was young, I was very poor. That is why I acquired many skills, but they are things of no importance.'[2] We know nothing about him before the last years of the sixth century.[3] He seems then to have accepted, after some hesitation, a position with Yang Hu, an officer of the Chi-sun family, who had taken

advantage of the death of his master, Prime Minister Yi-ju of the
Chi (P'ing-tzu), to imprison the latter's son Ssu and seize for
himself the family position of Prime Minister (505). He was no
doubt trying to rally about him the noble families who were
outside the clientele of the Chi.

After the defeat and flight of this usurper (502), Confucius —
no doubt feeling himself compromised — considered for a
moment turning to the usurper's successor, Fu-jao of Kung-
shan, who still held Pei, the principal fief of the Chi, and who
summoned him. His friend Chung Yu (Tzu-lu), a client of the
Chi, dissuaded him and probably reconciled him with Ssu (Huan-
tzu), who had just taken on the hereditary position of the Chi as
Prime Minister; and he entered the service of the Chi.[4] A
tradition depicts him as commencing as administrator of Chung-
tu, one of their cities, and then receiving a position at court.[5] He
was entrusted with a mission to Ch'i; and he seems to have
enjoyed high favour with the minister, if one may judge by the
rank which Prince Ching of Ch'i assigned him when he was
received.

It was probably the death of Ssu (492) which interrupted his
career. Ssu's son and successor Fei (K'ang-tzu) did not continue to
show him favour; and Confucius, for some unknown reason,
had to resign his posts and even to leave Lu. Later on, the
Confucian school would not reconcile itself to confessing that
they did not know the cause of this disgrace and, taking up once
more the oft-repeated theme that women had a baleful influence
on government, they told how the Prince of Ch'i and his
ministers, fearing that under the benign management of
Confucius the state of Lu might become first in the empire and
they might have to suffer for this, sent Prince Ting twenty-
four female musicians and dancers. He accepted them, and for
three days he did not hold audience, so that public affairs were
not dealt with. Thereupon Confucius quit his post.

He left Lu, accompanied by several followers who had joined
their fortunes to his, Chung Yu (Tzu-lu), Yen Hui, and others,
who later formed the nucleus of his disciples. He seems to have
spent his life in wandering endlessly from one to another of the
little courts of Wey, Ch'en, and Sung, according to his moods or
those of the princes who received him. In these journeys, various
misadventures (a rather brief list of them seems to have been
compiled quite early) gave him the opportunity to display the
Virtue of a sage.[6] It was in this period, no doubt, that he
definitively set his views on the science of government and on the
turning-back to the modes of the ancient sages — views that

were to be the basis of his doctrine. It was probably also then that he began to conduct a true school in the various places where he sojourned. Finally the favour which his disciple, Tzu-yu, attained with Fei of the Chi got him permission to return to his country. He set himself up in the capital and, having no hope of any public position, gave himself over to organizing his school and his teaching for the numerous disciples whom his renown, and the celebrity acquired during his travels, attracted. He died there several years later.

One would like to reconstruct the moral portrait of a man who played so considerable a role in developing Chinese thought — to understand his character, his conduct in everyday life. The rapid idealization of the Master unfortunately makes this impossible. The chapter in the *Lun yü* devoted to this subject is indeed nothing but a description of the ideal man, the *chün-tzu*, not that of a real and living person.[7] Certain traits, however, emerge here and there which throw a remarkable light upon him. Like Socrates, Confucius believed that he had a sort of 'familiar spirit': this was the Duke of Chou, sanctified brother of King Wen and ancestor of the princes of Lu, who appeared to him in a dream and advised him, no doubt conveying to him the wisdom of the ancients.[8]

Confucius left no writings behind. To discover his ideas, one must seek them in what his school has passed on. This was a school in the strictest sense of the term. Like those of all the teachers of that day, it was held in the second courtyard — that attached to the principal hall of the household — at the back of which opened the door leading to the private apartments.[9] One must no doubt picture the Master seated with his face to the south in this hall, looking down the few steps from the platform to the courtyard where his disciples were assembled and giving his teaching as a prince might give instructions to vassals, while at other moments he would mix with them in familiar conversation.

The disciples who came to study with him paid a fee; but he accepted all who came, however meagre the sum was.[10] He demanded of his pupils, above everything, thoughtfulness in their studies; he wished them to be capable of finishing their lessons by themselves.[11] He seems to have followed the framework of teaching derived from the official schools,[12] though leaving out the dancing, archery, and charioteering — that is, the curriculum of summer — and following that of winter: rites, music, and literature. He made them study the *Shu ching* and the *Shih ching*, especially the latter. He gave real courses on the rites; and, although the *Li chi* is evidently much more recent, certain chapters of it offer us at least an echo of his manner. Moreover, the idea of using the official chronicle of the state of Lu, the *Ch'un ch'iu*, as a manual of politics and of the philosophy of government is credited to him; and several collections of what is supposed to be his teaching on these questions have come down to us.[13] Finally, the *Yi ching* also formed a part of the Confucian teaching, either because the Master himself — who, at least towards the end of his life, seems to have taken a liking to it — placed it among the properly classical books, or because disciples of his had composed one of the appendices to this work and introduced notes and comments into another.

It was a complete cycle of studies which Confucius directed in his school, and these studies had a clearly traditionalist character. He did not teach a fixed philosophical doctrine. He gave lessons on the books of antiquity, on rites, and on politics. When by chance in teaching he developed some point of doctrine for his disciples, it was not presented as a novel idea, but as the natural product of the old texts. Thus it is understandable that he rejected any originality for his own thought: 'I transmit and do not invent,' he declared. The system which he constructed, despite all the new ideas it contained, was never in his eyes anything but a correct interpretation of the thought of the ancient masters, and he himself remained unaware of his own personal contribution to it.

The aim of Confucius[14] was the good government of the people. He followed in the train of the old masters of the school of Scribes and of their doctrine of government. The individual as such remained as completely a stranger to his researches as to theirs; the concept of perfecting the individual never even entered his head. It is the Virtue of the sovereign, the supernatural influence which he derives from his position, from the Mandate of Heaven, which produces the good or evil conduct of the people. 'To govern is to behave correctly. If you lead the people by being correct, who will dare not to behave correctly?'[15] This theme reappears in various forms: 'If the prince is correct personally, he will rule without having to make laws; if he is personally incorrect, though he make laws, they will not be followed.'[16] To each of the prince's qualities there corresponded an inverse quality of the people: 'K'ang of the Chi asked what had to be done so that the people should be respectful and loyal and should strive for virtue. The Master said: "Let the prince be dignified in approaching them, and the people will be respectful. Let the prince be filial and compassionate, and the people will be loyal. Let the prince promote the good and instruct the incapable, and the people will do their best." '[17]

In the same way, however, the prince's vices correspond to those of his subjects, so that he is responsible for their evil conduct: 'If you are without greed, the people will not steal, even if they are rewarded for it.' The influence of superiors over inferiors is as inescapable as a natural law: 'The Virtue of the sovereign is like the wind, that of the small people is like the grass: the grass must bend when the wind passes over it.'[18] It is not the prince's example which will guide the people to well-being,[19] it is his Virtue which transforms them: 'He who governs through his Virtue is like the polestar which remains fixed in its place, while all the stars pay homage to it.'[20]

This Virtue was perfect only among the sages; but if, in the degenerate times when Confucius lived, sages were not produced, it was at least possible to approach that ideal by becoming the sort of second-degree saint which the school of the Diviners had defined — the Superior Man, *chün-tzu*. No obstacle opposed this. 'By their innate qualities, *hsing*, men are nearly alike. It is by their practices, *hsi*, that they become different.' Every man can change himself: 'It is only the greatest of wise men and the worst of fools who never change!'[21] The first thing to do is devote oneself to study, as the school of Diviners, from whom Confucius borrowed this idea, had already affirmed; but he understood study in quite a different way, divination no longer playing the primary role: 'Let [him who would become] a Superior Man study all the books thoroughly and let him be guided by the rites, and he will not be able to set his foot wrong.'[22] But one must know what should be studied, for 'to devote oneself to eccentric doctrines is dangerous indeed!'[23] The literature which must be studied is the writings which the sages of antiquity left behind, above all the *Shih ching*;[24] and there are also the rites and the music to complete one's education.[25]

Study is not everything. To become a Superior Man, one must strive to attain a moral perfection, the purpose of which is to attain the cardinal virtue of Confucian doctrine, Altruism, *jen*, and which consists in 'loving others'.[26] In this virtue all the perfection of the Superior Man can be summed up. 'If the Superior Man neglects Altruism, how can he fulfil the demands of the name? The *chün-tzu* cannot be adverse to Altruism, even for the time of a single meal!'[27] It is this virtue which is the basis for the maxim which regulates the mutual relations of men: 'Do not do unto others what you would not wish them to do to you!'[28] Thus filial piety, *hsiao*, and brotherly love, *t'i*, are its bases;[29] for by practising Altruism in one's duties towards the closest relatives one understands its practice towards other men. Altruism is not undifferentiated; it is not a love encompassing all humankind, without distinction between those closely related and those quite unconnected to us. (In this it is distinguished from the universal love which Mo-tzu was to preach a little later.) On the contrary, the Altruist, *jen-che*, must have strongly marked sympathies for the good and antipathies for the wicked: 'The Master says: Only the Altruist is capable of loving anyone, or of hating anyone!'[30]

The way of attaining this Altruism consists essentially in 'conquering oneself and returning to the rites'.[31] Conquering oneself means suppressing in oneself the love of superiority over others, boasting, resentment, and greed — and even this, though very difficult, is perhaps not enough.[32] It is in morality, as it is codified by the rites, that a sure guide can be found. One must neither look at, nor listen to, nor say, nor do anything contrary to the rites.[33] From that comes the extreme importance of the rites in Confucianism: they are merely practical rules for applying Altruism in particular cases of human relations; but since these rules go back to the sages of antiquity, they bring from their origin the force of commandments.

A double effort, in learning and in morality, is thus necessary for him who wishes to become a Superior Man. Learning alone is not enough: 'For a man without Altruism, what good are the rites? For a man without Altruism, what good is music?'[34] And the wise man perceives very well in what respects he is lacking: 'The Altruist trusts Altruism; the wise man desires Altruism.'[35] Thus it is the moral effort which must be made first: 'A disciple must practise filial piety at home and brotherly love outside it, must be zealous and sincere, overflowing with love for all men, and a friend to the altruists. And if, after having done all this, he still has time, let him study literature!'[36] It is this double effort which Confucius calls by a general term, 'self-cultivation', *hsiu chi*.[37] Once this 'cultivation' is accomplished, the Superior Man, having attained his goal, will be almost like what the sage is by nature. Not quite, however: 'Those who are born possessing wisdom are the highest; those who acquire it by study come next.'[38] The first are the sages, the second the Superior Men.

Yet this cultivation of the individual self is not an end, but simply a means.

Tzu-lu asked about the Superior Man. The Master replied, 'He cultivates himself with all reverence.'

Tzu-lu asked, 'Is that all?'

The Master replied, 'He cultivates himself so as to settle all the people. It was to this that Yao and Shun applied themselves.'[39]

It is consequently not for his own benefit, but for that of the entire people, that a man seeks to perfect himself (this conforms to the virtue of Altruism). And this benefit to the people is not to be sought through individual conversions which imperceptibly and by degrees achieve a general reform. There is, in fact, no intelligent effort to be expected from the people: 'The common people can be made to follow [a course of action]; they cannot be made to understand it.'[40] They can therefore not be relied upon. Conversion can only come from above, from the governing powers, thanks to this marvellous power with which the sage is endowed, and which Confucius attributes equally to the Superior Man. If one of those who govern the people, prince or minister, is a *chün-tzu*, he will re-establish universal order by his Virtue at a single blow: 'If a [real] king were to arise, in one generation Altruism would prevail.'[41]

Thus the moral teachings of Confucius were not designed for the common herd. Basically aristocratic, like the world of his time, they were addressed only to the masters of the people; and all the effort expended could produce a useful effect only if the Superior Man became one of them: if he remained an ordinary person, he would be completely useless. This did not mean that regular functionaries, or indeed ordinary patricians, were released from making this effort. Any noble might be summoned by the sovereign to receive a ministerial post: he had to hold himself ready for this eventuality, and to 'cultivate' himself to that end.

Such, in broad outline, is the Confucian system — if not the way he conceived it himself, at least as it was taught in his school about a century after his death. Aside from the considerable influence which the almost religious notion of the sage and his Virtue had in it, the principal characteristic is that of being a system of social rather than personal ethics. Man is never considered in himself here, but always in his relations with society, as master (prince or minister) or as subject. The perfecting of each individual appears in it only secondarily, as one of the processes by which the Superior Man is produced — who, at a single blow, by his mysterious Virtue, can make order and universal harmony prevail in the world.

It is just here, however, that Confucian doctrine is original: to start with, it perceived for the first time in China that science and morality were distinct entities; and moreover it sketched, without meaning to, in the course of its search for the Superior Man, some lines of a real individual morality which shows through the distortions imposed upon it by the system. From certain points of view (and especially in his attachment to the old theory of the sage's Virtue), Confucius clings too closely to those ancient scribes whom he loved so much. In other respects, however, he touches upon and even foreshadows more original philosophers who would come after him. With Confucius, Chinese philosophy emerges from its childhood.

Mo-tzu

The work of Confucius was continued in the fifth century by a more original genius, Mo Ti, or — as he is politely called — Master Mo, Mo-tzu. His life is even less well known than that of Confucius. The only points that seem to be established, though not beyond question, are that he too was originally from Lu[42] and that he lived during the second half of the fifth century. He founded a school, nobody knows when or where, and it was his renown as a teacher that made his fortune: one of his disciples, Wen-tzu, of Lu-yang, was a grandson of King P'ing of Ch'u (528–515) and a son of Tzu-ch'i, Minister of War in that state (died in 478), and was himself counsellor to King Hui (487–430).[43] This prince was infatuated with the doctrines of the Master, whom he caused to accompany him to his apanage, finally taking him along to court. In the end he even presented Mo-tzu to King Hui, towards the end of that monarch's reign.[44] But the meeting led to nothing, and Mo-tzu returned to Lu in the last years of the fifth century.[45] It was probably there that he definitively established his school and spent the last years of his life, in the first years of the fourth century.[46]

Mo-tzu was not so fond of the things of the past as Confucius had been.[47] He loved books, though several tirades against them are ascribed to him; and it is said that, when sent on an embassy to Wei, he loaded the chariot down with them. But he cherished a hatred for music, which he considered the source of all the corruption and immorality of his time. One of his characteristic traits was a great piety: he believed in the power of the Lord on High, whom he called by that name more often than by the less personal name 'Heaven'. He believed that the dead had souls, and he was convinced that their constant intervention in the affairs of the world was beneficent.

Outward ritual demonstrations, on the other hand, displeased him. He condemned the lengthy mourning of three years, which he would have wished to replace with a three-month mourning period; he condemned over-complicated and over-long ceremonies; and above all he condemned music. His religion was an entirely personal one, consisting primarily in conforming to the will of Heaven, and by its individual quality it was opposed to the totally social religion of ancient China. It was at this point that he most clearly opposed the Confucians, for whom the rites had a value in themselves and who loved to carry them out, not caring to whom the worship was addressed. He was religious, and they were ritualists.

From the literary point of view, Mo-tzu was above all a dialectician, a logician: he was the first to take care concerning the logical sequence of ideas. Before him, books had been series of unconnected paragraphs, with ideas tossed in pell-mell at random, never set forth as a whole. This is, for example, the appearance of the *Hsi tz'u*, a work scarcely older than himself. Mo-tzu, on the other hand, arranged his ideas into lectures of a kind, in which he explained successively the cardinal points of his doctrine. In each chapter he endeavoured to discuss some particular point in full, by defining his terms and facing up to all the objections. He was not satisfied to assert, he wished to prove; and that was something absolutely new in China. It was certainly one of the great reasons for the success of his school.

It was a school in the true sense of the word, where the students came to learn the art of debating. They learned this rapidly, and almost too well. Mo-tzu died at the beginning of the century and, almost immediately after him, first his school and then rival schools poured out upon the Chinese world floods of sophists, for whom the art of debate was all in all, and thought was merely incidental. But if they abused the tool which their master had created, that did not make his service to the Chinese any the less: he taught them to organize their thought logically.

A vast collection of fifty-three sections divided into fifteen chapters exists under the name of *Mo-tzu*.[48] The nucleus of it consists of ten chapters (sections 8 to 37), which present the doctrine in the guise of personal instruction by the Master. They are so clearly of the same style, from the same hand, and this style is so individual, that it is impossible not to concede that they represent the writings of Mo-tzu himself.[49] There is a curious feature to them, in that they exist in three different versions, though they are often quite similar to one another. One senses the same hand throughout all three. They must evidently be viewed as the dissimilar editions belonging to the three schools among which the disciples of Mo-tzu divided themselves in the third century.[50]

The chapters are in a clearly oratorical style: for the written version of his lectures Mo-tzu retained the oral mode in which he excelled. That often gives them a somewhat slow and even hesitant tempo, with repetitions and tedious passages which the style imposed.

Aside from these ten chapters, which are the work of the master himself, composed by him during his life, his disciples after his death gathered up a series of small, very brief teachings, conversations, discussions with disciples, with princes, with various personages, in the style of the *Lun yü* of Confucius: that constitutes sections 46 to 48 of the modern book.[51] Anecdotes of the same sort, but compiled later (like those about Confucius which were gathered in the *Li chi*), make up sections 49 and 50. Small manuals on logic, attributed to the master but considerably later, together with a commentary, make up sections 40 to 45. Finally various other products of the school have been added at the beginning and the end of the work. All the activity of the Mo-tzu school is thus represented, during about two centuries, until near the end of the Chou dynasty.

Mo-tzu's system is basically a logical development of that of Confucius, whom he follows very closely despite all the divergences. The principal difference lies in the fact that Mo-tzu does not seek to justify his theory by the authority of the ancient sages, rather looking for justification to reasoning and logic. The old conceptions of the scribes and diviners concerning the sage, the Superior Man, and their Virtue, which Confucius had piously preserved, are abandoned completely. Mo-tzu borrows from him only the idea which Confucius had himself originated — that notion of Altruism out of which he had made the fundamental virtue of the *chün-tzu*. Mo-tzu developed this. He pushed it to an extreme point, making it into Universal Love, *chien-ai*, and giving this abstract concept the Virtue, the effective influence, which his predecessor attributed to the sage's supernatural power. It is this, properly applied, which will make all go well.

But this Universal Love goes infinitely farther than Confucius's Altruism. It is no longer a matter of loving men more or less by rank and by class, and less and less as they recede from the centre — that is, from oneself and one's family. In this Universal Love all, near and distant, are mixed without distinction. The love that makes distinctions, *pieh-ai*, is not a virtue; quite the contrary, it is the cause of all the ills of the world. It is the love which makes no distinctions which will alone save the world.

> It is the sage's business to regulate the world: he must [thus] know whence disorder comes in order to be capable of regulating it. It is like a doctor who wishes to struggle against an illness: he must know whence the illness comes to be able to struggle against it. ... Thus, if the origin of the trouble is examined, that origin is the lack of mutual love. ...
>
> If there are thieves in the world, it is for this reason: the thief cherishes his own household and does not cherish those of others. This is why he robs others' houses to benefit his own. The thief loves himself alone and does not love others; this is why he robs others' houses to benefit himself. What is the cause of all this? It is the lack of mutual love. If there are grand officers who cause disorder among neighbouring families, who attack their neighbours' principalities, it is also for this reason. ...
>
> All the disorders of the world have this cause and this alone: if one examines the causes, they arise from the lack of mutual love. ... If mutual love prevailed universally throughout the world, no state would attack another state; no family would trouble another family; thieves and brigands would not exist; princes and subjects, fathers and sons would all be filial and good. Thus the world would be well governed. ... This is why our master, Master Mo, says: 'We have only to arouse the love of others.' ... Some replied: 'Yes, this Universal Love would be excellent, but it is the most difficult thing in the world.' Our master, Master Mo, said, 'This is simply because you do not comprehend its advantages. To attack a fortified town, to fight in the cropped fields, to sacrifice one's life for glory, that is the most difficult thing in the world for people to do; but if the prince orders it, nobles and commoners alike are capable of doing it. How much more reasonably would they be capable of loving one another universally and helping one another, for that is a much easier thing. ...
>
> 'Where do [these ills] come from? Do they come from loving others, from advantages to others? Clearly not: they come from hatred of others, from violence towards others. And in the world, do hate and violence come from Universal [Love] or from [the love which makes] distinctions among persons? Clearly, from the love which makes distinctions among persons. Thus it is the love which makes distinctions among persons which causes all the ills of the world; and it is therefore bad. ...'[52]
>
> Our master, Master Mo, also says: 'Universal [Love] must replace that which makes distinctions among persons.' ... Others say: 'This Universal Love is good, it is just; but it cannot be put into practice! ... We all desire this Universal Love, but it is an impracticable thing.' But this Universal Love is very advantageous, and far more easy to practise than you imagine. I believe that, if it is not put into practice,

that is because the rulers take no pleasure in it. If the rulers took pleasure in it ..., I believe that men would throw themselves into it, as fire throws itself upwards, as water throws itself downwards. Nothing on earth could stop them ...[53]

This principle of Universal Love must be pushed to its logical end, to the sacrifice of oneself: 'To kill a man to save the world is not to act for the good of the world. To kill oneself to save the world: that is acting for the good of the world.'

This abstract principle of Universal Love is the centre of Mo-tzu's doctrine. It is from this viewpoint that he judges princes and their way of governing, that he attacks their inflated expenditures, their festivals which impoverish the people, and the lengthy period of mourning which they impose upon their subjects.[54] He would have them revert to the simple ways of the ancient sages, who were content with rough clothing and crude fare. He would wish them to simplify their ceremonies by suppressing music, that useless luxury. By the same principles he also condemns war as 'the worst injustice'.

To kill a man is called an unjust thing: it is a crime deserving death. To kill ten men is ten times more unjust, a crime deserving ten deaths; to kill a hundred men is a hundred times more unjust, a crime deserving a hundred deaths. Today every prince in the world knows that this must be punished, they declare it unjust. Yet the greatest of injustices, the making of war, they do not punish. On the contrary, they glorify it and declare it just! Truly they do not know how unjust they are....[55]

Only the practice of Universal Love will cause all to go well in the world. The sages governed the world well, because they practised it; to it alone were due their influence and their good government. In the beginning all men had their own ideas, which they sought to make prevail; egoism reigned alone. Fathers and sons, older and younger brothers strove for their personal advantage; they were like savage beasts. To put this right, the wisest man must be chosen — the best, the most saintlike in the world — and he must be established as Son of Heaven, and then he must be given other sages as assistants. Thus order will begin to replace anarchy.[56]

But it is not necessary that one reign or be a minister for the practice of Universal Love to create good fortune for the world. It has its influence, its own Virtue, and has no need to be carried by the Virtue of a sovereign — like the Altruism of Confucius. 'If one considered his son, his younger brother, or his subjects as he considers himself, would he be inimical towards them? If there were no more hatred or enmity, would thieves still exist? If another's house were considered as one's own, who would steal?'[57] It is thus everybody's duty to practise Universal Love to assist in the coming of universal happiness.

How does one achieve this? For that, it is necessary to practise Altruism, *jen*, and Justice, *yi*. As with Confucius, the practice of Altruism and Justice presupposes a moral perfection: 'One must rid oneself of good humour and anger, pleasure and sorrow, love and hate' — that is, all of the passions. 'It is necessary to put hands, feet, mouth, nose, ears, and eyes at the service of Justice.' But not everyone who would serve Justice can do it: it is necessary to know the true method. 'Master Mo-tzu says: "The man who wishes to practise Justice but is not in condition to do so has surely not found the true method. He is like a carpenter who wishes to cut wood but cannot do it because he does not know the true use of the chalk-line." ' In this difficult quest, one must not refuse the aid of others: 'Master Mo-tzu says: "The *chün-tzu* of our time wish to practise Justice; but when one helps them to perfect themselves, they are unhappy. It is precisely like somebody who wants to build a wall and, when somebody tries to help him build it, is unhappy. Isn't that unreasonable?" '[58]

Mo-tzu does not look for the true method of moral perfection, as Confucius had, in the pure and simple study of antiquity, either in the books which constitute its written remains or in the rites which are the remains endorsed by tradition. For him, morality rests upon something more profound: men must 'take Heaven for their model, do whatever is pleasing to Heaven and avoid whatever displeases it'.[59] But, he adds, what is it that pleases Heaven, and what displeases it? 'Heaven loves equity and hates wickedness. When I urge people to act with equity, I do what Heaven wants, I fulfil Heaven's desire, and Heaven in its turn will fulfil my desires.'[60]

But for Mo-tzu Heaven is the Lord on High, a personal god, omnipotent and omniscient. His eye is the sun, which sees all, illuminates all, so that 'for Heaven there is no shadowy gorge, no hiding-place, no desert into which his light does not see.'[61] An entire chapter is devoted to this theory of submission to the will of Heaven, showing that it is necessary to interpret that will correctly and to conform to it.[62] That is where one must study, that is where one must know, that is the true method which one must discover. And this is why he declares that science consists in the adoration of Heaven and the gods, and in the love of men.[63] The adoration of Heaven and of the gods, for him, is not a matter of accomplishing the regular rites punctually, but of submitting to their will and conforming to it, just as loving men is universal love.

In sum, Mo-tzu did no more than follow in the way opened by Confucius, but with more awareness of its originality and with less devotion to the ancients. His thought, more profound than that of his predecessor, sought to reach farther, even to the primary principle of all social relation, which he believed he had found in Universal Love. By placing the foundation of morality there, Mo-tzu succeeded in bringing into unity, into one absolutely single and logical doctrine, the various elements which Confucius had left separate. Mo-tzu had sought the basis of morality outside the awareness of the rites, and on the other hand had sought that of social relations in the inner awareness, in Altruism.

The Metaphysicians

While Confucius was taking up the work of the ancient scribes and developing it in his fashion, that of the ancient diviners was taken up for its part by a school which continued it, developed it, and carried it far forward, deriving a metaphysical theory from it. The work of this school is to be found complete in a brief treatise, the *Hsi tz'u*, which is nowadays preserved among the appendices to the *Yi ching*. This was not a dogmatic exposition, and in its present-day form it is extremely confused. It is basically composed of very brief little texts, between which fragments of commentaries have come to be inserted. The task of working them out lasted quite a long time, but it must have been finished about the end of the fifth century B.C.[64] Thereafter it was used as a classical book for the Confucian school of Tzu-ssu, who gave the *Yi ching* its definitive form; and the notes and interpolations made by the masters of that school served to produce its present disparate and incoherent aspect.

The ancient diviners had always regarded the hexagrams as having a real existence like that of tangible things: this is why an absolute correspondence between them and the world was possible. But they had not explained either the connections between the divinatory objects (hexagrams) and tangible things, nor the way in which the correspondence was established. The authors of the *Hsi tz'u* likewise accepted the reality of the hexagrams; but, observing that this reality could not be exactly the same as that of ordinary objects, they conceived the idea of setting them apart and making from them an ideal world of which they constituted the fundamental elements. Thus, against the visible world of material things, the authors of the *Hsi tz'u* set up the ideal world of divination. The universe was conceived as existing somehow on two planes, the material plane where men and ordinary things were — the 11,520 Things[65] or, as they said less precisely, the Ten Thousand Things — and the ideal place of divination, where the sixty-four hexagrams were. These two worlds were equally real, equally true, and they also corresponded to one another exactly. Divination proved this, since it allowed constant passage from one to the other.

Moreover, the theory of the trigrams had been completed. They had been arranged originally in an order such that, when they were written in a single column, the two trigrams whose form and meaning were exactly opposite were found by taking alternately the one at the top and the one at the bottom of the column. For example, the first hexagram was *ch'ien* and the eighth *k'un* (three full lines, three broken lines: Heaven, earth); the second was *tui* and the seventh *ken* (one broken and two complete lines, one complete and two broken lines: pit filled with water, mountain). They were then arranged so as to form a family, in which *ch'ien* (Heaven) was the father and *k'un* (earth) the mother, with the others becoming sons and daughters, according to their forms. In this way the trigrams and, even more so, the hexagrams were all derived ultimately from *ch'ien* and *k'un*, being produced by the reciprocal action of those two.

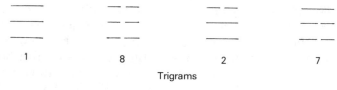

Trigrams

The authors of the *Hsi tz'u* started from this point. But since the world was double, it was not possible simply to say that all things derived from the trigrams *ch'ien* and *k'un*, since that was true for the ideal world of divination, but not for the tangible world. Furthermore, if *ch'ien* and *k'un* corresponded to Heaven and earth, a distinction had to be made between the hexagrams so named, which corresponded to the material earth and heaven, and the trigrams so named, which were in a way the prototypes of heaven and earth. It was therefore necessary to look beyond Heaven and earth. The authors contented themselves with applying to the perceptible world this notion of prototype which the two trigrams represented, and with giving to the thus enlarged concepts the names, new in philosophy, of *yin* and *yang*.[66]

Yin (corresponding to *k'un*) and *yang* (corresponding to *ch'ien*) were two substances,[67] each possessing its own Virtue, *te*, and each producing the other. '[*Yin*] gives birth [to *yang*], [*yang*] gives birth [to *yin*]; and this is what is called a transformation, *yi*.'[68] By their transformations they produce all the things of the perceptible world. 'The perpetual to and fro [of *yin* and *yang*] is what is called penetration, *t'ung*; when that becomes visible, it is what is called the Figures, *hsiang*.'[69] This is to and fro moreover received a special name: 'A succession of *yin* and *yang* is what is called Tao.'[70] That allows the sequence of transformations to be described in more precise terms: 'That which is antecedent to the form is called *tao*; that which is subsequent to the form is called Body, *ch'i*.'[71] Thus there is an uninterrupted continuity of Tao in all things. It is a transformation which carries on in successive phases, from *tao* which is formless to things having form, by passing through that which, though formless, is visible. Material things are made of *tao* to the degree of ultimate transformation; and *yin* and *yang* are not forces presiding over this transformation, since they are *tao* itself. In fact, in the *Hsi tz'u*, *tao* is never defined in itself, but always in relation to *yin* and *yang*, of which it is merely the sum.[72]

Correlatively, the things of the ideal world are produced by transformations of the same kind. In that world where all is line, what corresponds to the two primordial substances, *yin* and *yang*, are the two elementary lines, the broken and the full, or, as they are called, weak (*jou*) lines and strong (*kang*) lines; these are the two *yi*. To the first phase of transformation — the passage from what is formless to that which is visible, *hsiang* — correspond the first groups of lines which do not yet have a defined form, those of only two lines, the four *hsiang*. To the second phase — that of bodies which have form, *ch'i* — correspond the groups of three lines, the eight trigrams, *kua*, the first divinatory signs established. To the third phase — that of beings and things which are specifically distinct, *wan wu* — correspond the definitive patterns, the sixty-four hexagrams, *kua*. And the universe with its two levels can be summed up thus in a sort of table:

The Perceptible World	The Ideal World
Invisible and formless: the two substances *yin* and *yang*, the sum of which forms *tao*	The two lines, strong and weak, *kang* and *jou*, the sum of which forms the Great Absolute, *T'ai chi*
Visible, formless: ideas, *hsiang*	The four groups of two lines, *hsiang*
Visible, having form: bodies, *ch'i*	The eight trigrams, *kua*
Specifically distinct things: all the kinds of beings and things, *wan-wu*, to the number of 11,520	The definitive figures, hexagrams, *kua*, numbering sixty-four

Since the two worlds correspond exactly to each other, it is always possible to act upon one by means of the other. And since it is hardly possible, as experience readily shows, to obtain a result by acting upon each of the 11,520 things of the perceptible world, the sixty-four hexagrams of the ideal world offer a more restricted field. He who knows how to produce the transformation of the hexagrams will be able to act upon the ideal world, and from that his action will have repercussions upon the perceptible world.

This was the way the masters of the *Hsi tz'u* developed the theory of their predecessors in the school of Diviners, that the sage is the man who knows the principles of divination. For them, this was the man who, by his perfect knowledge of the ideal world of the hexagrams, is capable of acting upon them, and through them upon the tangible world. He is the perfect wise man who by his science is capable of aiding Heaven in its action:

> The sage, gazing upwards, contemplates the celestial figures; gazing downwards, he examines the terrestrial forms; and thus he knows the cause of that which is obscure and that which is clear. He retraces things to their origin, follows them to their end, thus knowing what may be said about life and death. ... There is a similitude between him and Heaven and earth and consequently there is no opposition between them and him. His science embraces all things and his activity is useful throughout the whole world, and consequently he is never mistaken.[73]

The authors of the *Hsi tz'u* thus succeeded in creating a complete metaphysical synthesis, in which all the theories of divinatory technique as well as the moral and ethical doctrines of their predecessors found their place. If one part of their doctrine — according to which the sage must begin his action upon the physical world by way of the ideal world of the hexagrams, good government following necessarily thanks to the harmony of the universe — if this rapidly fell into disuse, their theory of the *yin* and the *yang* spread rapidly. By the end of the fifth century, it was generally adopted by all the philosophers. It has governed Chinese thought down to our own day.

3
The Taoist School

The unknown author of a small work entitled *Lao-tzu* must probably be placed around Mo-tzu's last years. In that book there appeared for the first time the principles of a school which was to shine so brilliantly at the end of the fourth and the beginning of the third centuries, and was even to survive — the only one besides the school of Confucius — the collapse of the ancient world, to play an important role in the religious life of the Han period. This was the Taoist school.

In what period was it founded? Its own claim was that it had always existed, had been the doctrine of all the sages of antiquity — to one of whom, the Yellow Emperor, Huang-ti, the composition of the *Lao-tzu* is even attributed sometimes. We can only say that about the end of the fifth century a mystical teacher established a coherent system, taking as its base the metaphysical system of the school of Diviners, which had begun to find universal acceptance, and modifying that only in a few points. He used it as the philosophical basis for practices of asceticism and auto-suggestion, probably borrowed to a great extent from those of certain sorcerers and sorceresses.[1] The first exposition of this system appears in the *Lao-tzu*, or — as it is commonly called today — the *Tao te ching*.

Neither the name, nor the origin, nor the precise date[2] of the author is known. About a century later, the school which claimed derivation from him gave him the name Lao Tan and told how, after having long been keeper of the royal archives at the capital of the Chou, he had retired to P'ei (in the southern part of present-day Shantung) and had founded a school there. There Confucius is said to have gone to pay him a visit. However meagre and uncertain the biographical information is regarding him, his personal character emerges clearly enough, thanks to his own self-portrait, which shows him in the light of the melancholy mystic:

> Others are happy when they are taking part in a banquet or climbing a tower in spring. I alone am unmoved and display no desires. I am like a child that has never smiled; I am sad and downcast, as though I had no place of refuge. Others have more than they need; I alone seem to have lost everything. My mind is that of an idiot — what a muddle! Others have an intelligent air; I alone seem a simpleton. Others seem full of perception; I alone am stupid. I seem to be carried along by the currents, as if I had no place to rest. Others all have their tasks; I alone am as narrow as a savage. I alone, I differ from the others in esteeming the Nurse-Mother [the Tao].

The writer who best expounded the doctrines of the school was Chuang-tzu, who lived in the second half of the fourth century. His proper name was Chuang Chou and he is said to have been born in the eastern part of the state of Wei. Several anecdotes connect him with King Hui (370–318) of that country, and with a prince of Chung-shan, probably the one who was minister of Wei in 343. He seems to have journeyed to the land of Ch'u.[3] The book which bears his name does not seem to be entirely by him; the last four chapters must have been composed within his school about the middle of the third century. Others, such as the nineteenth, seem to have been lost early and replaced or fleshed out with fragments taken from other works, in particular the *Lieh-tzu*. The greatest part, however, is certainly authentic.[4] Chuang-tzu is the finest writer of ancient China. His style is brilliant, he has a marvellous sense of rhythm, and his wonderfully supple language lends itself to all sorts of nuances.[5] His lively imagination gives to all the anecdotes with which he embroiders his tales an extraordinary colour and life. At the same time, he was probably the most profound thinker of his time.

Chuang-tzu seems to have had a number of disciples and to have founded an important school. This was not scattered by his death, lasting at least until the middle of the third century B.C. About that time all the writings that circulated within the school were assembled for publication. They were very diverse. Some were mere variants of texts which Chuang-tzu had already published, others were the work of his disciples. Several chapters were made of these, some of which were added to the authentic works of the master, while others made up a little separate work under the name of *Lieh-tzu*, taken from that of a real or imaginary hero of Chuang-tzu's anecdotes.[6] The work thus composed is disconcertingly uneven in both style and thought. Certain passages are excellent and others worse than second-rate. There was also composed a sort of general explanation of the doctrines of various contemporary philosophical schools, probably as a sort of apologetic for Taoism, a fragment of which remains to us.[7]

Other Taoist mystics besides Chuang-tzu claim Lao-tzu as their inspiration, and one of these, whose name is unknown, composed a small treatise towards the end of the fourth century. This is in a rather dogmatic style, under the names of Lao-tzu himself and a claimed disciple of his, Yin Hsi, or, as he styles it, Master Yin of the Pass, *Kuan Yin tzu*, who had accompanied Lao-tzu on his voyage to the West. The work soon became famous. Its principles, in so far as one can judge from the brief fragment which remains,[8] were the same as Chuang-tzu's.

What is peculiar to the school of Lao-tzu and Chuang-tzu[9] is that, instead of being purely intellectual like that of Confucius, or that of Mo-tzu, it is based principally upon the practice of mysticism.[10] Its aim, as with all the schools of the day, was to acquire sagehood, but science was inadequate to lead to it, and so was the discussion of philosophical ideas. 'The Yellow Emperor once went for a stroll north of the Red Lake and ascended the K'un-lun mountain. On his way back he lost his black pearl. He sent Science to look for it, but without success. He sent Discernment to look for it, but without success. He sent Discussion to look for it, but without success. He sent Abstraction to look for it, and Abstraction found it. "Strange indeed," said the Yellow Emperor, "that it had to be Abstraction that found it!" '[11]

One must not rely upon books: they are 'the dregs and refuse of the ancients.'[12] Reasoning must itself be abandoned, for it obscures the true knowledge which is intuitive.[13] Indeed, true science is not the knowledge of perceptible things, those unstable products of *yin* and *yang*, as the school of the Diviners had shown, but lies in the understanding of the supreme reality which is beyond perceptible things, the Absolute which the school called Tao. And this knowledge cannot be acquired by science and study. 'Those who seek to obtain Tao by study are seeking what study does not give. Those who would obtain it by effort are seeking what effort does not give.' The mystical life alone allows of laying hold upon the Tao, after one has passed through those great stages which mystics have described in all times and all countries: the period of detachment from the exterior world; the period of renunciation, more or less extended, corresponding to the *via purgativa* of Christian writers; then ecstasies, sometimes defined by the popular expression designating the trances of the sorcerers — 'a spirit, *kuei*, has entered me' — and sometimes by the vision itself; and finally the mystical union which is 'the Great Mystery'. And the mystical life includes, in addition to meditation, all sorts of regular exercises — breathing exercises, for example, which preserve youth, and others of the same kind such as 'the nourishing of the vital [principle]', *yang-shen*, which gives longevity.[14]

Thus adherence to the Taoist school was not a simple act of intellectual acquiescence, as in the other schools. It implied a whole way of life; it required a genuine conversion, an illumination, in which the neophyte felt himself truly changed: the psychological equilibrium which had been normal previously was upset, giving way to a totally new condition.[15] 'Yen Hui cried out: the Yen Hui who has not yet obtained this is I, Yen Hui. When I have obtained it, I shall be a Yen Hui who never existed before.' This conversion is followed by a long phase of purification [*via purgativa*] which Chuang-tzu calls the fasting of the heart, *hsin chai*: 'Concentrate your mind. Do not hear [what] the ear [hears], but hear [what] the heart, *hsin* [hears]. Do not hear [what] the heart [hears], but hear [what] the soul, *ch'i* [hears]. Let what you hear stop at your ears; let your heart concentrate. Then the soul will be empty, *hsü*, and it will grasp reality. Union with the Principle, *Tao-chi*, can only be attained through the void. It is this void that is the fasting of the heart.'[16]

In sum, as with all mysticisms, it demands renunciation and detachment from external things, simplification, unification, and concentration of the mind so that the soul 'emptied' of all external influence can grasp reality and enter into an immediate and direct unity with the Absolute. This effort at detachment cannot be carried through without struggle. We get an impression of internal combat between the personality awakened by the conversion, which Lao-tzu calls 'the Heavenly One', and the ordinary personality, 'the Human One', which defends itself and must be overcome. This struggle displays itself in varying ways in different individuals: some abandon everything and give themselves over to the hermit life;[17] others do not believe it necessary to go and live in the desert, but give themselves over to purification at home, among their family.[18] For all, however, this is the period when the neophyte detaches himself from the artificial so as to return to primitive simplicity, *p'u*, by 'controlling the human and by obeying the Heavenly'.[19]

Once this is done, when he has achieved the 'void', ecstasy is the first reward of his long and painful effort. He gains 'a piercing vision, clear as the morning light' and 'sees That which is Unique'. At this moment his breathing grows weak, he is as if detached from his body, as if his body had lost its companion:[20] 'His body is like the stump of a dead tree, / his heart is like a dead cinder.'[21] All clear perceptions vanish or are confused:

> What was inside and what was outside [of me] were intermixed. I had the same sensations through the eyes as through the ears, through the ears as through the nose, through the nose as through the mouth. All sensations were alike. My heart was concentrated; my body was scattered; my bones and flesh turned to water. I no longer knew what supported my body or on what my feet were set. At the wind's will I went from east to west, like the leaf of a tree, like a piece of dried straw, so that in the end I knew not whether it was the wind that bore me or I who bore the wind.[22]

This period of ecstasies leads on imperceptibly to the 'Perfect Union', 'The Great Mystery', when the spirit is 'absorbed into That which pervades all things', when it has 'penetrated the Divine', when in fact it is in 'union with mysterious Heaven'. Then it is that one has 'attained Tao': that is, has managed to unite it to himself, not in fugitive ecstasies, but in a definitive fashion. This is not to say that one knows it, for it remains unknowable: 'The Tao that can be named is not the true Tao.' At best one may try to define it through a number of comparisons:

> O great square without corners,
> great vessel never finished,
> great voice which forms no words,
> great apparition without form.[23]

Or, as Chuang-tzu exclaims:

> O master! master! Thou destroyest all things and art not cruel, thou givest bounty to ten thousand generations and art not good! Thou art more aged than remotest antiquity and art not old! Thou coverest the heaven, supportest the earth; thou shapest every form and art not clever! It is thou who art called Celestial Joy![24]

He who 'knows Celestial Joy' is called sage, *sheng-jen*, by the Taoists, or more often called by a term they invented, the Man Made Real, *chen-jen*. United with and identified with the Tao, he is eternal and all-powerful, as it is.

Perhaps not all the masters of the Taoist school managed to

achieve union with the Tao, but at least they had taken the first steps along the way: conversion, 'the fasting of the heart', ecstasy. Thus the mystical experience dominated their entire philosophy. From it they derived what was original in their metaphysics, from it they got their psychology, and finally it furnished the principles for their philosophy of government.

The mystical experience had taught them to consider the world, and consequently the problem of man, under two different aspects which are violently opposed to one another: on the one hand, what is perceived by the senses; on the other, what is known intuitively through the mystical ecstasy. They might have been able to discover in this, as Westerners did, the beginnings of a theory setting mind off against matter. But that was a distinction absolutely unknown to the Chinese of the time, and they were content to adapt the doctrines of the school of the Diviners to their own experience.[25] The things perceived by the senses, the things of the external world, remained for them just about what they had been for the diviners (except that the hexagrams no longer played any part at all in the Taoist doctrine); and they were able to accept the idea that things were produced unceasingly by the succession and interaction of the *yin* and *yang*. Yet the object of intuitive knowledge gave them an impression of uniqueness so clear and vivid that they were obliged to look beyond the dualism of the diviners' school, seeking a primordial Unity which they grasped directly in ecstacy.

They did not have to invent this Unity, for the school of Diviners had provided them with at least the name, in its Great Absolute, *t'ai-chi*, or — as the Taoists called it, with a name their predecessors had sometimes used — the Principle, *tao*. For the diviners this term had been merely a handy expression to designate the simplest of the combinations of the two primary substances, a single succession of *yin* and of *yang*. It had not designated any proper metaphysical entity and had been placed in the first rank, above *yin* and *yang*, owing to the monistic tendency which their mystical experience had imposed upon them. Initially composed of *yin* and *yang*, their first product, it became on the contrary their source, their principle, of which they were considered products.

The Tao was thus the supreme Principle which ecstacy and mystical union revealed. It was that absolute Reality, immutable and unchanging, which was set off in opposition to the various and changing perceptible world. It was unique Substance as against multiple Modes. The *yin* and the *yang* lost all concrete reality and were no more than two modalities of the Tao, which by their reciprocal action and reaction produced the diversity of the tangible world: 'that which is without form' equally with 'that which has form'.

The theory is already set up as early as the *Lao-tzu*: 'One produces Two, Two produces Three, Three produces all things. All things come from the *yin* and go to the *yang*. They are put in harmony by the Breath of the Void' (One is the Tao, Two — even — is the *yin*, Three — uneven — is the *yang*).[26] A little later Chuang-tzu describes it thus:

> Heaven and earth are the immensity of that which has form, *hsing*, the *yin* and the *yang* are the immensity of that which is without form, *ch'i*. Tao is common to both. ... The *yin* and the *yang* illuminate one another, control one another; [and in consequence] the four seasons succeed each other, produce each other, and destroy each other. Attractions and repulsions, movements towards each other and movements apart then arise in their distinctive characteristics. The separation and the union of that which is male and that which is female exist from this moment on.[27]

In sum, creation (which is not an act accomplished once and for all, but which is reproduced indefinitely) comes out of the Tao's passing from the state — or rather the aspect — of repose, *yin*, to the aspect of movement, *yang*. These are, moreover, nothing but aspects, appearances, since in reality the Tao remains immobile.

Thus the Tao is the first origin of everything: it is 'fathomless and like the ancestor of all things', says Lao-tzu. And again: 'There is something indefinite and complete which precedes the birth of Heaven and earth. O immutable! O formless! Who alone is unchanging! Who pervades all without being changed! It may be considered as the mother of the world!'[28] Yet it is a present source, the action of which continues unceasingly. 'The great Tao pervades all, it is found to right and to left; all things depend upon it for their existence, and it does not refuse them; and when its work is done, it asks no praise.'[29] It is the Essence of things.

> The Master of Tung-kuo asked Master Chuang: 'Where is this thing you call Tao?'
> Master Chuang replied: 'There is no place where it is not.'
> The Master of Tung-kuo said: 'Be clearer, so that I may understand!'
> Master Chuang said: 'It is in this ant.'
> 'Where is it, lower still?'
> 'It is in this blade of grass.'
> 'Where is it, lower yet?'
> 'It is in this tile!'

'Where is it as low as possible?'
'It is in this excrement!'
To this the Master of Tung-kuo made no further reply. ... There is not a single thing without Tao.[30]

It is from the Tao that the sage, or the Man Made Real, *chen-jen*, derives the supernatural powers with which he is endowed. United with the Tao and sharing its nature, he is like it in all things, pervades all, and is consequently capable of modifying the appearance — that is to say, modifying tangible things — by his action upon their real nature, which is the Tao. There is continuity, *chün*,[31] between Tao and all things.

In sum, what the school of Diviners had believed concerning the *yin* and the *yang* — that all the things of this world, those with and those without form, were fundamentally made up of the *yin* and the *yang* at a more or less advanced stage in their transformation — is transferred to the Tao by the school of Lao-tzu. All things are essentially undifferentiated Tao and are diversified in appearance only by the illusory transformations of the *yin* and *yang*. Considered in itself, the Tao is the unique Substance, and the *yin* and the *yang* are its Modes. Considered in every being and every thing, the Tao is their Essence, and what one may know by the senses is the Accident.

That the world is merely illusion is expressed quite explicitly in the book called by the name of *Lieh-tzu*, which describes it by the word used to designate conjuring tricks, *huan*.[32] And it is a constantly moving phantasmagoria, in which the appearance of everything changes continually.

Of all these changes the most obvious to man, and the one which interests him most personally, is that from life to death. Man is thus no more than an appearance, having no real existence at all. Each of these terms presents one face of the transformation of the *yin* and the *yang*, no more. 'That which has life returns to that which does not, that which has form returns to that which has not. ... Life must of necessity cease, cessation cannot not cease.'[33] Life and death are thus successive and inevitable phases of the perpetual change. 'Death and life are a going and a returning. How do I know that dying here is not being born there?'[34] Or again: 'The ancients called the dead "those who have returned". Ah! If they say that the dead are the returned, then the living are the departed.'[35] Or, as Chuang-tzu says in a magnificent comparison: 'The life of man between heaven and earth is like the leap of a white colt as seen through the crack in a wall beyond which it passes and suddenly disappears. As he comes with effort, he goes again quickly and easily. By one transformation he lives, by one he dies. ...'[36] Or finally, expressing the same idea by a popular proverb: 'The ancients said [about life and death]: the Lord hangs up and he takes down.'[37]

But these are merely unimportant phases in this universal phantasmagoria which is the world. Even while living, do we know what we are? 'How do we know whether the Ego is what we call Me?'[38] Chuang-tzu illustrates this with a charming anecdote: 'Once upon a time I, Chuang Chou, dreamed that I was a butterfly, a butterfly that fluttered about, and I was happy, I didn't know that I was Chou. Suddenly I awoke and I was myself, the real Chou. And I did not know whether I was Chou dreaming that he was a butterfly, or a butterfly dreaming that he was Chou.'[39] If a man is unhappy awake and happy in dreams, which condition can be called real?[40]

To all these variations, life or death, waking or dreaming, the Man Made Real attaches no importance. 'He knows neither the love of life, nor hate for death: the entry into life gives him no joy, the departure from it arouses no resistance in him.'[41] Lieh-tzu, showing a skull picked up by the roadside, says to one of his disciples: 'I and this skull, we know that there is really no such thing as life, and no such thing as death.'[42] The elements which made up the living being make up something else after its death. 'If the Creator [the Tao] transforms my left arm into a cockerel, I shall use it to tell the hour of night. If he makes my right arm into a crossbow, I shall use it to shoot crows for roasting. If he makes my torso a chariot and my mind a horse, I shall ride them,'[43] declares a dying man in the *Chuang-tzu*. It is necessary to resign oneself entirely to the Tao, not fretting about what occurs to oneself: 'When the smelter works his metal, if the metal were to jump about and say, "I want to be a sword like Mo-yeh," the smelter would consider the metal ill-omened. If I were to usurp human form and cry out, "I want to be a man," the Creator would consider me ill-omened. When we have understood that heaven and earth are a great smelting-pot and the Creator a great smelter, where could we go that would not be good for us?'[44]

The mystical experience, which had given the Taoist masters the elements of their metaphysics, also furnished them with the foundations of their psychology. With the help of this experience they became aware of the Ego, which earlier schools had accepted as a simple matter of fact not requiring any definition. They delimited it on the one hand by relation to other things, as distinct from every other Ego (the They, *pi*, as Chuang-tzu says[45]), and on the other hand by relation to the Absolute, as something distinct from that Absolute. But the Ego thus determined was a rather confused item, being at the same time the product of the transformations of the *yin* and the *yang*, and hence differentiated, and also a partaker in the nature of the Principle, and hence capable of being united with it.[46] The mystical experience allowed some clarification of this double nature of the Me by showing two distinct elements in it: the one which sought to unite itself with the Tao, and the other which resisted the Union. They gave names to these two constituent elements of the Ego: the first the Celestial, the second the Human.[47] Chuang-tzu defined them by a comparison: 'Horses and oxen have four hooves, that is the Celestial. Horses have harness on their heads and oxen have their noses pierced, that is the Human.'[48] The Celestial is the very essence of man, his real nature, the Tao that is in him. The Human is the sum of the appearances that mask Reality; it is what civilization, education, rites, and morality have made of him, transforming him and making him lose his 'nature of a little child'.

The primary origin of this perversion is the five senses: 'Ah! the loss of original nature has five causes: first is the five colours which have so confused the eyes that the eyes do not see; second is the five sounds, which have so confused the ears that the ears do not hear; the third is the five odours, which have so confused the nose that it does not smell; the fourth is the five flavours, which have so confused the mouth that it does not taste; the fifth is love and hate [that is, the passions], which have so confused the mind that original nature has fled. From these five causes come all ills.'[49] The senses are the origin of evil because, perceiving differences, they lead on to differentiation and thus estrangement from the Tao; and the passions, *ch'ing*, when all is considered, are nothing but differentiations.

These passions have been classified into four series of six each. There are those that excite desire (pursuit of honours or wealth, of distinction or respect; of renown or profit); those that trouble the mind (over-niceness in behaviour or movement, sensuality and morality, excitability and reflection); those that hamper the influence (of the Principle), *te* (hatred and desire, contentment and anger, pain and pleasure); those that interpose a direct obstacle to the Principle (antipathy and sympathy, charity and egoism, intelligence and ability).[50] But all can be summed up in a fundamental pair, love and hate, *hao wu*: to love or to hate is to choose, and thus to move away from the Tao. Thus the passions belong to the Human and are among the things one must forsake in order to attain sagehood.

This explains why Taoist psychology, already limited enough, comes immediately to a halt: the analysis of the Human did not interest the Taoists. They preferred to try and analyze the stages of the mystical life — that is, the return to nature. But the lack of a sufficient knowledge of normal psychology, that of the non-mystical man, reduced them to merely noting the most important stages of the progress, without being able to analyse the states of consciousness, as the Christian, Muslim, and Hindu mystics have done.

No philosophical school in ancient China could do without a doctrine of government: that of the Taoists follows logically from their system. The government of the Taoist sage, of the Man Made Real, must be modelled upon the Tao itself, since the Man Made Real is in union with it. Thus the Tao remains immobile and everything is produced: 'The Principle is always non-active and yet everything is done by it. If princes and kings would keep to it, all beings would become perfect by themselves.' Thus the Man Made Real must himself 'be non-active', *wu-wei*, and must avoid utilizing his supernatural powers on the pretext of helping or being useful in the world. 'The sage contemplates Heaven and does not assist it; he is aware of the non-worldly Influence, *te*, without interfering; he conforms to the Tao without making any plan.'

Chuang-tzu, by an example, shows very clearly the difference between the Man Made Real of the Taoists and the Superior Man of Confucius and Mo-tzu.

> The Yellow Emperor had reigned for nineteen years and his laws were in force throughout the empire when, hearing that Kuang-ch'eng-tzu was at the summit of Mount K'ung-t'ung, he went to see him. 'I have heard,' said he, 'that you have attained the Perfect Principle. Allow me to ask you about the essence of the Perfect Principle. I wish to grasp the essence of Heaven and earth, to utilize this in helping to grow cereals so as to nourish the people. I wish to control the *yin* and the *yang*, so as to assure the well-being of all living creatures. How should I proceed?' Kuang-ch'eng-tzu replied: 'What you are asking me about is the primordial integrity of matter. What you wish to control is the diversity of things. If you were to govern the world in accordance with your wish, the vapours of the clouds would fall as rain even before they had come together; the grasses and the trees would lose their leaves before they had yellowed; the light of the sun and moon would quickly be extinguished!'[51]

The Yellow Emperor wished to act, as the Confucian sage would:

the Taoist sage replies that he will throw everything into disorder and that, if he wishes the world to be in order, he should do just the opposite — nothing at all.

To act is bad. It is necessary to leave man to himself, and then, thanks to his fundamental simplicity, *p'u*, he will let things happen in conformity with the Tao, he will abandon the Human and revert quite naturally to the Celestial. Consequently all teaching, which diverts man from this primitive simplicity, is bad. 'The sage, in the practice of government, empties the minds and fills the bellies, weakens the wills and strengthens the bones. His constant purpose is that the people know nothing, desire nothing; and he sees to it that those who know dare not act. By the practice of Non-action, there is nothing that will not be well regulated.'[52] And the ideal society is described thus: 'In the time of the Emperor Ho-hsü, men remained in their dwellings without knowing what they were doing and went abroad without knowing where they were going. When, the mouth well stuffed, they were content, they tapped their stomachs to show it. Such was their only ability.'[53]

The system of the Taoist school was certainly the most complete and coherent of all the ancient Chinese philosophical systems. Thus its influence was considerable in all directions: not only did it have numerous initiates among all those whom the active life of that troubled period frightened, or those whom it had injured (like the poet Yüan of Ch'ü), but it also reacted on the other systems, even those which accepted neither its mystical practices nor its fundamental theories. It furnished a metaphysical base to schools whose tendencies were more practical, such as those of Yang-tzu and the Legalists, upon whom it exerted a considerable influence. Moreover, even the Confucian school of the fourth and third centuries, especially Mencius and Hsün-tzu, borrowed a great deal from them.

4

Schools Derived from Taoism: Yang-tzu and the Legalists

From the somewhat abstruse theories of the old school of the Diviners, the Taoist mystics had developed a broader metaphysics which could in its turn be detached from the mystical practices of the sect. Adopted for itself, this could serve as a foundation for doctrines which were often very different indeed. The philosophers of the fourth and third centuries had indeed a tendency to seek a metaphysical basis for their systems, so that they might be presented as a whole which was not only coherent but also complete; and the Taoist theory furnished this basis. Two schools in particular felt the influence of Taoism and of its metaphysics very clearly, though they were influenced in quite different directions. These were the schools of Yang-tzu and of the Legalists, *fa-chia*.

Yang-tzu

The doctrine of Yang-tzu is both very close to Taoism and very distant from it.[1] The fragments which remain from him give the impression of a rather gloomy spirit who, having tried the mystical experience in vain, getting no response to his efforts, had retained a profound bitterness at his failure. Yang Chu lived about the middle of the fourth century, a little later than Mo-tzu, whom he quotes, but before Mencius, who did not know him personally and only met disciples of his, and also before Chuang-tzu, who mentions his name frequently. His life seems to have been passed at the small courts of eastern China (Lu, Sung, Wei), where various anecdotes depict him conversing with princes or ministers.² His works have been lost, except for a rather short fragment.³

Yang-tzu's philosophy, as far as one can judge it from the bits and pieces that remain, is a mixture of pessimism and fatalism, far more personal in its character than Mo-tzu's. He does not hide his profound disgust with life: 'A hundred years are the extreme limit of life; and of a thousand men, not one attains a hundred years. Suppose there were one: his infancy, carried in somebody's arms, and his decrepit dotage make up almost half of his time. Illness and sorrow, sadness and pain, loss and ruin, fears and alarms take up nearly half as well. And of the ten or more years remaining, there is not an hour completely without care. What then is the life of man? Where is the pleasure in it? ...'⁴ Life is so miserable that it is not worth the trouble of seeking to prolong it:

> What would eternal life be?⁵ The five feelings, with their alternations of love and hate, today as always before; the four limbs, with their alternations of health and illness, today as always before; successive sorrows and joys, today as always before; order and disorder, today as always before. All this has been understood, all this has been seen, all this has been repeated! A hundred years of it would be too much: how much worse would be the pain of an eternity!

Yet life must not be shortened, and Yang-tzu expressly condemns suicide. What then should man do? Take life as Heaven has given it and live it out even to the end of his destiny. Take death when it comes accepting it in its hour. 'Life must be borne with unconcern, fulfilling one's desires so as to await death; death must be borne with unconcern, fulfilling its coming so as to abandon oneself to annihilation. Both must be accepted with unconcern, both must be endured. Then, for such affairs, why trouble oneself about a little earlier or a little later?'⁶ There one catches an echo of Taoist doctrines, though the Tao is excluded from it.

Not only must man do nothing to shorten his life, but his duty is to conserve it with meticulous care, to keep it from any damage. From this comes the anecdote, famous in Chinese literature, of the refusal to sacrifice a single hair to save the world. 'Ch'in-tzu asked Yang Chu: "If by parting with a single hair from your body you could save the world, would you do it?" Yang Chu replied: "The world surely cannot be saved by a hair!" Ch'in-tzu said: "But if it could, would you do it?" Yang Chu did not reply.'⁷

Thus to sacrifice nothing of one's own, no matter for what

purpose, is the duty of man Why? Because in Yang-tzu's opinion, life has no compensations. For life does not belong to man: it comes to him by destiny, as death does too, and as do all the qualities which differentiate the living from one another. 'That in which beings differ is life; that in which they are the same is death. During life they are wise or stupid, rich or poor, that is how they differ. Dead, they are a stinking mess, and that is how they are the same. All live and all die, the wise and the stupid, the rich and the poor. Some die at ten years of age, some at a hundred; the good and the sagelike, the wicked and the stupid die. Living, they are Yao and Shun, dead they are rotten bones. The rotten bones are all alike: who could see a difference in them? So let us hasten to take advantage of living: what is the use of worrying about what will happen after death?'[8]

The best way to preserve oneself is to fend off any external constraint, and to give oneself up to the passions. Again, this is a Taoist theory which Yang-tzu has borrowed. But he has moved it to the top rank, since for the Taoists the greatest good was to abstain from all passion. Yang-tzu, who had no fear of paradox, took advantage of this to eulogize the notorious tyrants of Chinese legend — Chieh, the last sovereign of the Hsia dynasty, and Tsou, the last king of the Yin; and he also made fun of the sages — Yao, Shun, Yü, and Confucius.

> Yang-tzu says: 'Those whom the world holds admirable are Shun, Yü, the Duke of Chou, and Confucius. Those whom the world sees as villainous are Chieh and Tsou. Yet Shun cultivated the land north of the River [*ho-yang*] and was a potter on Lake Lei. His four limbs had never a moment of repose. For his mouth and his belly he never found pleasant food or warm clothing. He did not have the love of his parents, he did not have the affection of his brothers and sisters. At the age of thirty, he had not yet obtained his parents' permission to marry. When he received Yao's abdication, he was old and his intelligence had decayed. His son Shang-chün was incapable and he had to abdicate in favour of Yü. He was miserable to the day of his death. Of all men he was the most unhappy!'

He continues thus to describe all the misfortunes of Yü, and the tortured life of the Duke of Chou, and finally that of Confucius, setting against them the lives of the villainous tyrants Chieh of the Hsia and Tsou of the Yin.

> Chieh inherited the wealth of successive generations; he maintained himself on the honourable seat which faces south [the imperial throne]; his intelligence was able to keep him supreme over his multitudes of subjects; his power was sufficient to preserve all within

the Four Seas. He gave himself over to every pleasure to which his eyes and ears attracted him. He did whatever he had a mind to do. He enjoyed life right till his death. Of all men he was the least constrained and the freest.

And he concludes:

These four sages had not a single day of pleasure during their lives. Since their death they have had a reputation that will last for a myriad generations. But this reputation is a thing that nobody values if he cares for what is real. ... These two villains, during their lives, had the joy of satisfying all their desires. Since their death they have a reputation for folly and tyranny. But the reality of their pleasures is something that no reputation can give. Insult them, they don't know about it; praise them, they don't know about it. All of that affects them no more than it does the trunk of a tree or a clump of earth.⁹

For all of them, death has been the common lot.

But if the life of the sage and that of the fool both end alike in death, it does not follow that the two are alike. Shun, Yü, and Confucius are fools who wasted their lives doing good, and Chieh and Tsou are fools who wasted theirs doing evil. The wise man should imitate neither the one nor the other:

There are four things that prevent men from obtaining peace. The first is the desire for longevity, the second the desire for fame, the third the desire for rank, the fourth the desire for wealth. Because of these four, they fear the spirits, they fear men, they fear power, they fear punishments. These are what may be called fools: they may be killed or allowed to live, but their destiny is fixed outside themselves. On the other hand, if anybody does not rebel against his destiny, what does longevity matter to him? If he does not care for high rank, what does reputation matter to him? If he does not wish for power, what does rank matter to him? If he does not desire fortune, what does wealth matter to him? These are what may be called the people who accept [events]. In the whole world there is nobody who can stand up to them: their destiny is fixed, within themselves.¹⁰

This is the ideal for Yang-tzu. His sage is the man who is sufficiently detached from the things of this world so that nothing can touch him, and so that — life and death being all one to him, mere facts accepted as they come — he is always master of his fate, always dominating whatever external events bring him. Even more than the Taoists, Yang-tzu is individualistic. What he seeks is not a precept by which to govern the world, but a precept by which to govern himself. He is preoccupied with the individual, not with society.

Nevertheless, he too had elaborated a political theory which, though the logical product of his ideas, is still permeated with Taoism. The prince should not concern himself with anything, but — leaving all to fate — should let everybody give himself over to his passions: everything will go just right. It is the same conclusion as that of the Taoist school. 'Yang-tzu says: "Have you ever seen a shepherd with his sheep? A herd of a hundred sheep? Picture a little boy five feet tall marching behind them with his whip. If they want to go east, they go east; if they want to go west, they go west. Picture Yao dragging a single sheep and Shun behind with a whip, and they will not be able to make it go forward!" '[11]

Yang-tzu's system was by no means the Epicureanism that is ordinarily attributed to him. On the contrary, it is a pessimistic fatalism pushed to the extreme, considering life as an evil and death as another evil, both of which must be borne with indifference, since they are ordained by destiny. The pleasures which destiny places in our path must be taken as they come, and suffering as well, without rebelling against it; and for that same reason it is necessary to give oneself over totally to the passions, which are sent by fate. It is fate which rules all, and the man who knows this is truly a sage, upon whom external things have no hold. Strongly influenced by Taoism, this system was far removed from the Taoism of Lao-tzu which Chuang-tzu was soon to develop, in that it left out all mystical inquiry. Its individualistic position was too remote from contemporary tendencies to influence them deeply. It remained an isolated phenomenon in Chinese philosophy.

The Legalists, *Fa chia*

The great upheavals of the fourth century, especially the efforts at internal reform and reconstruction which the great states undertook in this period, encouraged a number of contemporary thinkers to seek for the bases of good government no longer in fixed principles (like the teachings of the ancients for Confucius, or abstract principles such as Universal Love for Mo-tzu, or a metaphysical entity such as the First Principle of the Taoists) but rather in a constantly changing evolution which could be modified according to circumstance. It was the Law itself which they made into the principle of good government. Indeed, since the world goes from worse to worse, is corrupted every day, and draws farther and farther away from the golden age when, according to all the schools, everything was perfect, it is absurd to try and govern the corrupted men of today as the uncorrupted men of old were governed. It is indeed that very effort which engenders disorder. It is necessary, on the contrary, to modify the method of governing constantly to suit conditions which are new every day. It is necessary to replace the ancient laws with new ones as the old become obsolete.

The Legalists, *fa chia*, the name given them because they attached so much importance to the Law, came from all the schools. Among them can be found Taoists such as Yin Wen tzu and Han Fei tzu, a Confucian leaning towards the doctrines of Mo-tzu's school such as Shih-tzu, disciples of Mo-tzu such as Sung K'eng, and so on. Thus the Legalists were not, strictly speaking, a school deriving its principles from a founder. They were thinkers who tended to conceive of government in a certain way and sought to make their empirical view of the world fit in with the principles of the school to which they belonged.

The fundamental principles seem to have been set forth by the scholars of the Chi gate at Lin-tzu, the capital of Ch'i, in the second half of the fourth century. This was a sort of academy, the Association of Mount Hua, *Hua-shan hui*, whose members had adopted a special bonnet, flat on top and bottom, as a head-dress by which they could be distinguished. King Hsüan had established there the scholars of all the schools whom he attracted to his court and to whom he granted large salaries. There were Yen of Chou, a master of the *yin-yang* school; Sung K'eng,[12] a disciple of Mo-tzu; T'ien P'ien, nicknamed T'ien of the Divine Tongue; and P'eng Meng and Yin Wen, who were Taoists. Mencius was one of them for some time and perhaps Chuang-tzu as well. It was probably in this setting, in about the third quarter of the fourth century, that the *Kuan-tzu*, one of the most ancient works that can be assigned to the Legalists, was composed. This was a sort of historical utopia, philosophical and romantic, based partly upon the institutions of Ch'i and set forth under the name of Kuan Yi-wu, the great minister of Duke Huan in the seventh century. The fragments of it which remain are too insignificant to allow any determination of its principal doctrines.[13]

An anecdote involving T'ien P'ien, Sung K'eng, and P'eng Meng shows us how they formulated their theory. 'T'ien-tzu, reading the *Shu* [*ching*], said: "The time of Yao was the Great Peace." Sung-tzu said: "Was this due to the government of the Sage?" P'eng Meng replied: "It was due to the government of sagacious laws and not to that of the sage!" ' And this remark is attributed to T'ien Pien: 'Men act in their own interest and cannot act in the interest of others. This is why a Prince ruling over them makes it appear that they are acting in their own interest, and not in his.'[14]

A somewhat later writer, Yin Wen, who lived in Ch'i during the last years of the fourth century,[15] expounded similar ideas in a small work which has come down to us, unfortunately in a rather suspect form.[16] He too had Taoist leanings, though he did not belong to the mystical school, which rather looked down upon him. He derived everything from the Tao, the sole reality. The ideal would be to govern by the Tao, since that would be the rule of Non-action, and all would be well in the world. But since, in the present state of the world, government by the Tao is impossible, it is necessary to utilize the eight 'Political Methods', *shu*, instituted by the sages of antiquity: altruism, justice, rites, music, names, laws, punishments, and rewards. These are irresistible, and when they are put into practice government is necessarily good, whether the sovereign is a sage or a fool, since good government derives from them and not from the sovereign.

How are they put into practice? For Yin Wen names, *ming*, possessed the same mysterious power which they had had for the generation which attributed this famous saying to Confucius: 'To establish good government, the first thing to do is to "rectify names", *cheng ming*.'[17] Among them had been founded a school of Names, *ming chia*, which made this rectification its fundamental principle. Thus for the laws to be correct, they insisted above all that the names must be correct and must correspond precisely to things. It was thus essential to begin by rectifying names and verifying their application to things, distinguishing between those which applied to forms and those which applied to formless qualities, between those which applied to the subject and those which applied to the object: hence the importance of the dialectic. The correction of names puts all things, good and bad, in their places; and what results is order, not by the suppression of evil things (the Tao, indeed, is neutral, and moreover good and bad are relative notions), but by their correct classification, each being assigned to its right place. It must be noted, however, that if the eight Political Methods had produced, as the sages foresaw, all of the human virtues, they had at the same time produced the contrary defects and vices. 'Altruism is the great source of benevolence towards beings, but also the source of egoism. The rites bring about the practice of respect, but they are also the source of all irreverence. ...' Thus it is essential to bear in mind that these are only means of governing, designed to lead on to government by the Principle.

In the third century the doctrine of laws enjoyed a great vogue, and a whole series of writings appeared, usually attributed to great men of ancient times. A work on the Political Methods was published under the name of Shen Pu-hai, a minister of Prince Chao of Han (358–333); another was attributed to Teng Hsi, minister of Cheng who came into conflict with Tzu-ch'an, who put him to death at the end of the sixth century. In one, Li K'uei explained at length to Prince Wen of Wei (424–385) the ways of enriching his principality and making it strong. Still another was set under the indirect patronage of Yang of Wey, the great minister of Hsiao of Ch'in, and attributed to a fictitious personality, Shih Chiao, who is represented as one of those who inspired Yang. About the same time or a little later, an unknown writer of the third century attributed his own ideas directly to Yang himself, giving his work the title of *Shang-tzu*, and thus borrowing the title of the Lord of Shang, Shang-chün, which Yang of Wey had received.[18] Like the *Kuan-tzu*, this was a semi-historical and semi-philosophical work, in which the author took the theory that a prince must govern through punishments and rewards and used it to justify the laws actually existing in Ch'in, some of which really went back to Yang of Wey or were attributed to him. All of these works are lost today or have been replaced by modern forgeries.[19]

Of all the Legalist school, only a single work has been preserved nearly complete. This is the *Han tzu*, or, as it has been called since the tenth century A.D., the *Han Fei tzu*. Its author, Fei of Han, belonged to the royal family of Han; he is said to have been a disciple of Hsün-tzu, the most famed of the Confucian masters after the death of Mencius. In 234 he went as ambassador from King An of Han to the King of Ch'in, the future First Emperor. He remained at the Ch'in court but, soon coming under suspicion because of his foreign origin, was thrown into prison and committed suicide (233). It is said that the jealousy and calumnies of his former co-disciple, the all-powerful minister Li Ssu, had brought about his disgrace, but that the King of Ch'in, regretting his action at the last moment, had granted him pardon and sent a messenger, who arrived too late.[20]

Han Fei's work is a sort of summing-up of the Legalists' theories on the eve of their ephemeral triumph in the internal politics of China, with the victory of the kings of Ch'in and the unification of the Chinese world.[21] Like Yin Wen and like the author of the *Teng Hsi tzu*, he borrows the metaphysical and psychological foundation of his theory from Taoist doctrines. Their influence is so strong that two sections of the work are devoted to explaining their terms and justifying their ideas by citations from the *Lao-tzu*.

The Tao is the origin of all things, from which come names and things which have form. And when names and things are in agreement, the prince has no difficulty in governing. On the other hand, the mind of man is divided between the Celestial — that is, simple sensations — and the Human — that is, reflection, judgement, and the passions. Good government consists in moderating the passions and diminishing the use of reflection. But human passions are produced by two moving principles: the desire for goods (wealth, high rank, long life, and so on) and the fear of ills (poverty, premature death, and so on). By acting alternately upon these two motivations one arrives at good government; and such action is produced by the employment of punishments and rewards, the two 'handles', *ping*, of government. 'The way in which the enlightened prince manages his officials is by these two handles alone. The two handles are Punishments and Virtue, *hsing te*. What do Punishments and Virtue mean? Killing the guilty is called Punishment, rewarding the meritorious is called Virtue. Functionaries fear to be punished by death and seek to profit by rewards. This is why, when a prince utilizes Punishments and Virtue, all his functionaries fear his majesty and enjoy his bounty.'

But he must rely upon himself and himself alone in allotting punishments and rewards. 'If a prince does not act so that the fear and the hope of punishments and rewards come from himself, if he listens to his ministers in using punishments and rewards, all of his subjects will turn towards the functionaries and away from their prince; this prince will have the misfortune of losing the punishments and rewards. What allows tigers to conquer dogs is their claws and teeth. If the tigers lost their claws and their teeth, and if dogs had them, it would be the dogs that would conquer the tigers. As for princes, they control their officials through Punishments and Virtue. If they divest themselves of Punishments and Virtue and allow them to be used by their officials, it will be the ministers who will control the princes.' This would be the ruin of government. 'Power must not be entrusted by the prince to the ministers ... [otherwise] the interests of the prince and of the ministers will become different, and the ministers will no longer be loyal. And the interests of the ministers will be strengthened, while the interests of the prince will be destroyed.'[22]

Punishments and rewards must be precisely proportioned to the deed. This follows from the general rule which demands that names and things be in agreement so that government will be good. Thus the man who is too modest and conceals his merits, and in consequence does not receive from the prince the reward to which he is entitled, should be punished like the man who, by his boasting, receives too great a reward. In both cases, what is punished is the fault of designating a meritorious act by a name which does not belong to it; and since the fault of bringing about disagreement between names and things is greater than the greatest of meritorious deeds, it must be punished. In all this the prince is merely the guardian of the regular order of things: he should have no personal initiative or passion in punishments or rewards. He must be as impartial as the Tao itself.

Besides, the respective duties of the prince and his functionaries are clearly laid out. The prince, like the Tao, must practise Non-action, *wu-wei*: that is, he must not act on his own but must make his ministers act. 'Above, the enlightened prince takes no action; below, the ministers are zealous and fearful.' The glory for what they do redounds to the prince: 'the ministers have their tasks, the prince has the merit,' and he disavows those who do not succeed.[23] The prince controls his ministers from above by the 'political methods', *shu*; the ministers control the people under the prince's direction by the laws, *fa*. Both of these, the political methods of the prince and the laws applied by the ministers, are equally necessary to good government. It was the error of Shen-tzu (Shen Pu-hai) to concern himself only with the political methods and not to care about the laws, just as it was the error of Shang-tzu (Yang of Wey) to concern himself only with the laws and not to care about the political methods.[24]

The laws, being impersonal and impartial, control the people without any clash. 'As for the application of the laws, the wise cannot criticize them, the violent cannot oppose them, punishments do not spare high functionaries, rewards do not forget the common people. ...' It is indeed the characteristic of the laws that they are applied to all, high and low, so that all are equally bound by them, and none can even think of escaping them. 'The laws: when the decrees and ordinances have been posted on the buildings of public administration, punishments weigh on men's hearts. Reward conduces to the observation of the laws, punishment is the consequence of violating them. They are the rule of the ministers.'[25] Even the prince, though in some measure above them since he makes them, must constrain himself carefully to applying them, from the moment they have been properly promulgated 'If the prince violates the Law and follows his personal [passions], superiors and inferiors are no longer distinguishable.' That is disorder.

Yet the prince must abolish or modify the laws when they are bad. For they are not immutable: they are not the examples of the ancients, to be followed blindly. 'If someone had built a nest in a tree, if someone had taken a tinder-box in the times of the Hsia sovereigns, Kun and Yü would have roared with laughter at it. If someone had channeled the rivers [like Yü] in the times of the Yin and the Chou, T'ang and King Wu would have roared with laughter at it. When today the principles of Yao, Shun, Yü, T'ang, and Wu are praised, it is something for a modern sage to laugh at.'[26] The laws must change with the times. 'The government of the people has no immutable rule; it is the laws which make the government. If the laws change with the times, [the people] are governed; when the government suits the times, it is good. ... If the times change but the laws are not modified, that is disorder.'[27]

In ancient times men, few in number, found a plentiful living without the need of working. It is different in the present age, in which families have at least five children, population is excessive, and even with the most exhausting labour, they do not get enough. The men of other times, being able to satisfy their needs without difficulty, were calm and peaceable, and there was no need for a very strict system of punishments and rewards. Nowadays, on the other hand, since they must struggle among themselves in order to live, they are constantly disturbed, and it is necessary to increase both punishments and rewards in order to govern well. To imitate the ancient sages' methods of government without regard to the change in circumstances could only produce disorder.[28] This is precisely the reverse of the theories of Confucius and Mo-tzu, and it is easy to see why Han Fei-tzu does not spare them his jibes.

Since the Law is not founded upon any stable authority, how can it be justified? By its efficacy, *kung-yung*: if anything has a good result, it is necessarily good. But on the other hand, efficacy considered thus as a principle allows of no contradiction. The greatest efficacy rules out lesser efficacies which are incompatible with it. 'Incompatible things must not be established at the same time. To give rewards to those who have beheaded enemies and to praise acts of piety and kindness highly; to grant promotion to those who have seized a city and to place credence in a discourse on Universal Love; ... when one acts this way, the government cannot be strong. When the state is at peace, it cherishes scholars; but when troubles come, it uses soldiers. Those whom it cherishes are not those it uses; those whom it uses are not those it cherishes. ... That is why our time is a troubled one.'[29]

The doctrine of Han Fei, and that of the Legalists in general, tended to lower still further the position of the individual life, so little developed in ancient China and so constantly sacrificed to the life of society. On the other hand, it had the defect of sacrificing morality to Law, just as Confucius sacrificed it to the Rites, Mo-tzu to Universal Love, and the Taoists to the Mystical Union. It would seem that the ancient Chinese philosophers, bounced about among extreme theories and also little impressed by individualistic tendencies, had for a long time been incapable of founding a morality, and even of recognizing the existence of a morality outside of social relationships and governmental ethics. The theories of the Legalists, applied by the Ch'in dynasty to the government of the empire, had a great influence — despite the brevity of that dynasty — upon the formation of the modern Chinese mind.

5

The School of Mo-tzu and the Sophists

The school of Mo-tzu had remained very powerful and brilliant after the Master's death; it was large and well organized, with a very strict discipline.[1] After his death, Mo-tzu had been replaced as head of the school by one of his disciples, perhaps Ch'in Ch'ü-li,[2] and he directed it with the same absolute authority as the dead master. Meng Sheng succeeded him and established himself at Yang-ch'eng in Ch'u, where he died in 381, after having handed the leadership over to his disciple T'ien Hsiang-tzu, a native of Sung. Towards the end of the fourth century the supreme leadership was in the hands of Fu T'un, who lived in Ch'in under King Hui (337–311). These chiefs of the school received the title of Grand Master, *chü-tzu*; they were considered as sages and, consulted on all important questions, were strictly obeyed.

This period of the school's unity under a Grand Master seems to have lasted throughout the fourth century. But the expansion of the doctrine all across China, in a troubled period as well, was hardly favourable to maintaining unity of authority and doctrine. Local schools were formed, it seems, towards the end of the fourth or the beginning of the third century. There was that of Master Hsiang-fu, Hsiang-fu-tzu; that of the Master of Hsiang-li, Hsiang-li-tzu; that of the Master of Ten-ling, Teng-ling-tzu.[3] This last seems to have been a reformed branch and took the title of Pieh-Mo, separated school of Mo-tzu. These continued during part of the third century, and then they seem to have been reunited again, while at the same time their influence waned; for the group whose fundamental texts survived and were published under the Han carefully preserved, as the works of the Master himself, the three versions of all three schools.

Yet beside these disciples who thus followed Mo-tzu and were content to teach his doctrine, there appeared others who, probably by comparison with the perfectly ordered Taoist metaphysics, considered the Master's fundamental theories — Universal Love, and so on — as simply assertions without any foundation. Mo-tzu had indeed succeeded in establishing a coherent system by developing several fundamental principles; but he had never dreamed of seeking out a basis for the principles themselves, which were left hanging unsupported in mid air.

The first man who attempted to set Mo-tzu's theory upon a metaphysical base seems to have been Hui-tzu. He was named Hui Shih and was a native of the state of Wei, where he spent his life. He was a minister of King Hui (370–319) and is said to have been one of the counsellors at the Hsü-chou interview of 336, where the prince and Hsüan of Ch'i recognized each other's title as king. Hui Shih was still at the court when Hui died (319); but he himself probably died soon afterwards.[4] Very open-minded, he had studied the science of his day deeply — astronomy, astrology, the science of the *yin* and *yang*, the numbers, and so on. Thus, 'when Hui-tzu was asked why the sky did not fall and the earth did not break up, or the causes of the wind, of rain, of thunder, and of lightning, he replied without hesitation, he answered without reflecting. He discoursed at length on all things, without leaving off, voluminously and without pause.'[5] His eloquence was famous. '[To hear] Hui-tzu [speak], leaning up against a stool' was one of the things which Chuang-tzu classed as a wonder of the time.[6] His very numerous works would have filled five wagons.[7] Nothing of them at all remains, and we are reduced to judging them by a few anecdotes from Chuang-tzu and a list of paradoxes which are attributed to him.[8]

Hui-tzu sought to justify the principle of Universal Love by the theory, Taoist in origin, that all things and beings are essentially identical, differing only in appearance. But in his view this essential identity did not lie in the immutable Tao: he sought a physical origin for it in the material world, which he considered real — in this being quite different from the Taoists. He based his metaphysics upon the notions of space and time, conceived of as limitless.

Space is limitless: 'South is both limitless and limited'; or again: 'I know the centre of the world. It is north of Yen [the northernmost principality] and south of Yüeh [the southernmost principality].'[9] Since space is limitless, the relations of length, size, height, are meaningless: 'That which has no thickness can have no size, yet it may be big enough to cover a thousand *li*.' And another paradox: 'The heavens are as low as the earth, the mountains on the same level as the lakes.' Thus the notion of spatial measure appears as a purely human notion, true only in relation to man, but without reality in itself. It is the same with time: since that is limitless, all the small divisions which we introduce into it — yesterday and today, birth and death — are equally unreal, an idea which Hui-tzu presents in the form of paradoxes: 'The sun shines obliquely at noon. A thing dies the moment it is born.' And: 'I leave for Yüeh today and I arrive there yesterday.'

But if the notions of measure, both in time and in space, are non-existent, how can there be differences or resemblances among things? This is because things display identities and differences only when they are considered in relation to man. Considered against limitless space and time, things are both different and identical. '[To say that] what has many points of identity is different from what has few points of identity is what is called the lesser Identity-and-Dissimilarity. [To say that] all things are entirely identical [to one another] and entirely different [from one another] is what is called the greater Identity-and-Dissimilarity.' In these conditions any distinctions are illusory, and on this is founded Mo-tzu's principle of Universal Love without distinction: 'Love all things equally, the world is one.'[10]

Hui-tzu's system is thus a metaphysics of Mo-tzu's doctrine. It is in fact the only system of metaphysics which a Chinese has tried to build up entirely outside of Taoism. But oddly enough — due in great measure, it seems, to the very manner in which Hui-tzu presented his ideas — it was not the metaphysical part of his work that his contemporaries noticed and admired. Logician and dialectician above all, Hui-tzu insisted upon the classification of things. Rather than contenting himself, as the Taoists had, merely with reiterating the fundamental principle upon which he founded his doctrine of the identity of contraries, he seems to have taken pleasure in discussing particular cases. From that comes the paradoxical manner in which his theories were set forth, a manner which aroused the listener's attention, though not without some danger of obscuring substance by its form. With Hui-tzu, and perhaps still more after him, paradox became a scholastic technique. At this time commenced a succession of dialecticians and sophists, *pien-che*, who in their principles belonged to all the schools but who, disputing over names, *ming*, rather than ideas, held forth on definitions and distinctions, and are known as the Nominalish school, *ming-chia*.

Hui-tzu had already felt the influence of Taoist metaphysics to some extent. In his discussion of Identity and Dissimilarity, he had presented the latter as subjective and unreal, in fact as an illusion of the human mind, and the former as the sole reality; and he ascribed the difference between them to a difference of viewpoint, according to whether they were related to the finite (man) or to the infinite (space and time). The masters of the generation which followed, Huan T'uan (also called Han T'an), Ti Chien, and Kung-sun Lung, sought to free themselves from this Taoist influence and to give a real foundation to this distinction of Identity and Dissimilarity, which they accepted. Of these three personages, the first two are scarcely more than names.[11] The third, however, is known through a small fragment from his works, and by quotations in the *Chuang-tzu* and the *Lieh-tzu*.

Kung-sun Lung lived in the last years of the fourth century in Wei, where he had a warm partisan in the person of Prince Mou of Chung-shan. Later he visited the court of King Chao of Yen (312–279), and he was there during the conquest of the kingdom of Ch'i (284). He went next to the court of Hui of Chao (298–266). He remained a long time in that country and was at the side of the Lord of P'ing-yüan in 259–258, during the long and fruitless siege of the capital, Han-tan, by the Ch'in armies.[12] He belonged to the school of Mo-tzu; but he also adopted, not without modifying them, some of Hui-tzu's ideas, and a rather confused tradition places him in contact with Hui-tzu.

The great difference between Hui-tzu and Kung-sun Lung bears on the relative value of Identity and of Dissimilarity. While preserving the fundamental theory of the essential identity of things, Kung-sun Lung rejected Hui-tzu's semi-Taoist explanation and substituted one that was also borrowed from the physical world. For the theory that space and time are immeasurable he substituted that of their infinite divisibility.[13] 'If a ruler one foot long is cut in half every day, after ten thousand generations something will remain.' This division of things to an infinite degree reduces complex entities into simple elements. At the same time, since the correct name corresponds to the thing, the definition — if it is to be precise — must also consist of a more and more precise division, in a separation of the constituent elements. From this comes the formula, 'A white horse is not a horse,' since 'white horse' is in fact 'horse' plus 'white'. And if it is admitted that 'horse' and 'white horse' are identical terms, one will be forced to allow the same identity between 'horse' and 'black horse' or 'yellow horse,' which leads on to the absurd conclusion that 'white horse' and 'black horse' are identical terms.[14]

But this distinction of elements must be made with caution. Thus: [In] a white, hard stone, there are two [elements].' In fact, since whiteness is perceived by the eyes and hardness by the hands, it is impossible to perceive whiteness and hardness simultaneously. In reality one perceives only complexes of the two elements successively: white stone (sight) and hard stone (touch). It is the mind which, 'applying' to one another what is known by sight and what is not, what is known by touch and what is not, makes the synthesis, *li*, of these discrete perceptions and thus arrives at knowledge.[15] For an analogous reason one can say, 'Fire is not hot.' Upon this distinction of elements Kung-sun Lung founded the distinction between individuals, as against their combination in generic types.[16]

But if this division, carried to a certain point, seemed to give a fundamental reality to individual distinctions, when pushed to an extreme it showed on the contrary the identity of those very things which had initially appeared distinct. And this is the way, it seems, that he managed to demonstrate the identity of contraries. Rest and motion are identical: 'The rapid motion of an arrow is [the succession of] moments in which it is neither stopped nor in motion.'[17] It is in motion if one takes as a unity the space through which it travels from the bow to the target; it is at rest if one takes as a unity the space which the arrow occupies, and if one considers, not the whole trajectory, but each of these unities taken separately. Or again: 'The shadow of a flying bird does not move.' By taking as a unity the space which a bird's shadow occupies at a given moment, one obtains a series of shadows, each different from the one preceding and all motionless, rather than a single shadow in motion. Motion and rest are thus identical terms. In this way the identity of all things can be demonstrated: 'A dog is a sheep.'

The Sophists had demonstrated, and were demonstrating every day, the importance of dialectic and the art of disputation; and in this Hui-tzu and his successors were continuing the work of Mo-tzu. He had owed part of his success to the greater precision he had brought to methods of reasoning. He had even created a form of reasoning which was both more supple and less loose than that of his predecessors, especially Confucius, and which endeavoured to push proof nearer to certainty. Mo-tzu had known how to argue with adversaries who were less clever than he, and he had recognized the value of a dialectic, in which he took some pride.

From the beginning, instruction in dialectic thus played a considerable role in the studies of his school. For this they used small treatises, which have been preserved, though they are difficult to interpret. The first two (chapters 40–41) are collections of very brief aphorisms,[18] entitled the 'Canon', *ching*. These seem to have been attributed to Mo-tzu himself, but they are much later than that. The following two (chapters 42–43) are explanations, *shuo*, still exceedingly brief, of the first two. This is not a commentary composed later, but a simple method of committing the Canon aphorisms to memory. The whole thing probably dates from the middle of the third century B.C. A reference to coinage in one of them forces us to date it quite late.[19] Moreover, it is clear that the authors have gathered here in a concentrated form the entire logical and dialectical work of the Sophist school. Certain of the paradoxes of Kung-sun Lung are here, sometimes being accepted, sometimes — it seems to me — being refuted or being explained in a different way than Kung-sun Lung's.[20]

These works are not dogmatic expositions, yet certain general principles are expressed in them. For example, the principle of causality: 'There must be a cause for there to be an effect';[21] and there is a clear distinction between universal causes, *ta ku*, and partial causes, *hsiao ku*.[22] Likewise, the principle of contradiction: 'All that is ox is distinct from what is non-ox: there is nothing which does not belong in these two [categories]. In argument, [a thing] is designated as ox, or it is designated as non-ox: the one excludes the other. ...'[23] Discussion is in fact concerned as much as possible with these definitions, and the definitions are concerned with the authentication of resemblances and differences.[24]

All sorts of things are also found in these little tracts, from geometrical definitions[25] to moral and metaphysical aphorisms, mixed up with rules of logic or dialectics. They show the entire range of the activity of Mo-tzu's school during the period which preceded their composition, though in a rather chaotic fashion.

Only one of them seems to be a didactic treatise composed in a coherent way: this is the *Hsiao ch'ü p'ien*,[26] from the same period as the preceding ones. In it the author does not examine the theoretical problems of analyzing the reasoning process or the theory of logic. Rather, he poses the quite practical question of dialectics: how to show that one's adversary in a discussion is wrong. And, since he finds that the best method is to make evident whatever errors in reasoning that adversary has made, he devotes himself to the empirical task of drawing up a classification of correct propositions and of incorrect ones, using an empirical method. He does not seek fundamental rules, but provides series of examples which can serve as models by analogy. This failure to elaborate upon theoretical notions also hampers him in his task, to the point where it makes certain of the difficulties he encounters insurmountable.[27]

At the moment when the reformed school of Mo-tzu, Pieh-Mo, was seeking to classify judgements, propositions, and arguments and was attempting to set up a system of logic which would be formal if not theoretical, at least as a practical method of dialectics, its time was running out. For this was one of the schools which did not survive the persecutions of the literati at the end of the third century. Confucianism and Taoism began to flourish again when peace was restored at the beginning of the Han, but all the branches of the school of Mo-tzu perished in that troubled time. Everything vanished, men and ideas. Only the processes of logic and of dialectic survived, were developed and, having become in a way the common property of all thinkers, exercised a lasting influence upon the Chinese mind and upon the way in which it viewed philosophical and scientific problems.

6

The School of Confucius in the Fourth and Third Centuries

Although the death of Confucius was a serious blow to his school, that did not put an end to its activity. Organized as a teaching institution, it continued to give instruction under the Master's disciples and to produce students brought up in his doctrine. But while its role in the intellectual shaping of patrician youth was thus a considerable one, it was not very obvious. No Confucian master seems to have taken part in the development of ideas for more than a century. This was perhaps because they remained too faithful to the founder's tradition. Confucius had never dreamed of being a philosopher. He believed himself to be a man of action, an administrator and politician capable of leading the world back on to the true path. His dream was not to write his ideas down but to make them come to fruition in the government of a principality which a sovereign had entrusted to him. What his disciples came to seek of him was not a philosophical system, but the science of government. It took them a long time to realize that they could not make antiquity live again, and to resign themselves to being handlers of ideas, when they had wished to be handlers of men.

The First Generation of Disciples

Almost all the first generation of Confucius's disciples were to be found in the small courts of the princes in eastern China, if we credit a tradition which, despite some uncertainty in detail, seems nevertheless to be true on the whole.[1] Tzu-wo took service in Ch'i; Tzu-kung in Lu, then in Wey, and finally in Ch'i; Tzu-kao and Tzu-lu in Wey; Tzu-yu in Lu; Tzu-hsia became the teacher of Prince Wen of Wei; and so on.[2]

Between times they may have tried to spread their master's teaching, founding schools and training students; but the main centre always remained in Lu, near Confucius's home and his tomb, where the most faithful of his disciples were settled, making up a village of perhaps a hundred dwellings, the village of K'ung, *K'ung-li*. According to Ssu-ma Ch'ien, writing in the second century B.C., three thousand students had come there to attend his lectures; sixty-four disciples had received his complete course of instruction. When he died, the latter went into mourning and lived by his tomb for three years, as though he had been their father. 'When the three years of mourning were over, they packed their baggage and prepared to return home. When they went in to say farewell to Tzu-kung [one of them], they looked at one another and broke out into lamentations until they lost their voices. Then they went home. Tzu-kung came back to build himself a dwelling on the platform [which was by the tomb]; and he spent three years there before going home.'[3]

The Master's family preserved the relics: his official vestments, his ceremonial bonnet, his lute, his chariot, and his writings. All were arranged in the hall where he had done his teaching.[4] It had been turned into a funerary temple, where the Prince of Lu offered sacrifice each year. At the end of the second century B.C. all these relics still existed,[5] and Ssu-ma Ch'ien saw them: 'When I went to Lu and beheld the funerary hall in the temple of Confucius — his chariot, his vestments, his ritual utensils — I went back in, filled with respect, and lingered there. I could not tear myself away.'

What kept the school of Confucius going was not the importance of any of its representatives in themselves (it did not have a single writer of genius before Mencius) but that of the instruction in the ancient literature which was given there. Confucius had based his teaching upon the 'Odes' (*Shih ching*), the ancient 'Documents' (*Shu ching*), the rites and the music. His disciples continued piously in the same path. Beside Taoists who set their inner life upon the highest level, and disciples of Mo-tzu who turned more and more towards a pure dialectic, the Confucians were masters of ritualism and antiquity. They were neither brilliant nor famous; but they trained so many students that they would survive all the upheavals that would destroy their rivals.

This rather thankless role as educators seems to have sufficed them for a long time. Aside from the parent school in Lu, run by the Master's descendants (the most famous of whom, Chi, also called Tzu-ssu, set himself up in Lu after having lived in Wey), a certain number of branches were founded under the patronage of his principal disciples: that of Tseng-tzu, that of Tzu-hsia at Hsi-ho, that of Tzu-yu, and that of Tzu-kung seem to have been particularly important about a century after the Master's death.[6] They quarrelled bitterly among themselves over petty details of the rites, which they interpreted differently.[7] It was probably about the beginning of the fourth century[8] that they came to an agreement to publish a selection of the traditions preserved within the family and the school of Confucius and his immediate disciples, so as to establish definitively what had been his true doctrine. This work has come down to us as the 'Analects', *Lun yü*.[9]

For the task of compiling this, they had at hand more ancient collections,[10] which their own caused to disappear, though slowly enough for some traces to have been preserved for us in the *Tso chuan* and perhaps in the *Li chi*.[11] The editors of the *Lun yü* seem to have been content to set them side by side without modifying them otherwise, except to eliminate repetitions and anecdotes which seemed to them to display Confucius in a somewhat unfavourable light. No effort was made to classify the conversations or arrange them according to subject matter. The entire work remained a collection of little disconnected pieces, scrappy and disjointed.

The style of it presents a totally new character: in their desire to reproduce as much as possible the Master's own words, they did not recast them into the written language, after the example of the works just composed by Mo-tzu and Lao-tzu, but kept in some measure the forms of the spoken language, or at least some of its more striking forms. From this we have rather free phrase structures, and a wealth of particles and auxiliaries, which give it a peculiar appearance. On the other hand, the introductory phrases and in general everything that is not put into the mouths of speakers is set out in the written language. Only the *Lun yü* and, in imitation of it, the compilation of the *Mencius* have adopted this style.

About the time when they published the conversations of Confucius in this pell-mell fashion, a fraction of the school was trying to give his theories a systematic form. This seems to have been partly the work of K'ung Chi, better known under his appellation Tzu-ssu, or at any rate of his disciples. At least, the composition of one of the small texts which have survived is attributed to him. These are the 'Invariable Mean', *Chung yung*, and the 'Great Learning', *Ta hsüeh*.[12] Tradition makes Tzu-ssu the

Master's grandson; but this hardly fits in with what Mencius says about him, and he was probably at least one step further removed.[13] All that is known of him[14] is that he was a minister in Lu under Prince Mu (407–377) and that he also had a post in Wey.[15] He seems also to have taught, for a school which was still flourishing in Lu in the third century B.C. claimed descent from him.[16] Its characteristic trait seems to have been the importance which its teachings gave to the *Yi ching* and in general to divination, besides the 'Odes' and the 'Documents'.[17]

The 'Invariable Mean', *Chung yung*, as it appears today, is made up of two sections, each of which is a separate work, though they belong to the same school. The first section, the older of them, is a very brief (no more than several lines) dogmatic exposition, in rhythmic but unrhymed prose, followed by explanations of fundamental terms in it and haphazard development of certain points, mixed with quotations from Confucius and the 'Odes'. The second, and more recent, section is a small treatise on the Virtue of the sage, set in the form of a discourse by Confucius to Prince Ai of Lu. It has been strongly influenced by the *Wen yen* (the fourth of the appendices to the *Yi ching*), certain passages of which it imitates, as well as by the *Mencius*. The whole thing is perhaps, in conformity with the tradition, the remains of what was taught in the school of Tzu-ssu.

The doctrine as laid down in the first part of the *Chung yung* is simple enough: it is a question of determining the perfect mode of action of the sovereign sage, which will as a matter of course bring about the re-establishment of universal order. That is a Confucian theory, though starting with this first effort to elaborate it systematically the disciples of Confucius had come under the influence of Taoist ideas.[18]

At his birth man receives from Heaven a nature, *hsing*, to which he must conform; and it is in conforming to this nature (and thus obeying Heaven) that the Principle lies, the study of which leads on to sagehood.[19] This, though transposed into the Confucian system, is basically a Taoist idea. The Superior Man, *chün-tzu*, must cultivate 'that which is unique in him' — that is, what has been given him by Heaven, his Ego.[20] When the spirit which has attained peace through conformity with Heaven is at rest, when the emotions are not aroused, he is in the state of equilibrium, *chung*. When the emotions are aroused, he is in the state of harmony, *ho*. But 'when the states of harmony and of equilibrium are perfect, all things will thrive'. The development illustrates these ideas by means of examples, so as to complete the portrait of the Superior Man.

The 'Great Learning', *Ta hsüeh*, must be — at least its oldest portion — of nearly the same period as the 'Invariable Mean', but it probably does not belong to the same school.[21] Not very long, the work is made up of two parts, a very brief and rather old text, and a much more recent commentary, which systematically repeats each phrase of the original text, together with a short explanation. The original text seems to have been preserved in full, but the greater part of the commentary (the beginning and end) is lost today,[22] only a few of the passages in the middle remaining.[23] The 'Great Learning' was certainly a more complete summary of the Confucian doctrine than the *Chung yung*. However, it is no more concerned than the latter, with the individual as such: it looks always to the sovereign or minister.

It taught how 'to shed light upon Virtue, to love the people, and to rest in the highest excellence'.[24] It is always the Virtue of the Superior Man which by itself must produce the total transformation of the people. If the prince, or whoever is entrusted with the government, has indeed accomplished that self-cultivation of which Confucius spoke, his Virtue will suffice to regulate his family. With the family well regulated, his Virtue will grow with all the accumulated power of the Virtues proper to each of its members, and the State will be well-governed. It is not their example, any more than it was for Confucius, but their Virtue which will produce the transformation supernaturally.

As for the way of self-cultivation, that is briefly explained: 'The ancients ... desiring to cultivate themselves, began by rectifying their hearts; in order to rectify their hearts, they began by making their thoughts sincere; in order to make their thoughts sincere, they began by extending their knowledge; the extension of knowledge consists in getting to the reality of things.'[25] Here in a few words we have all the elements of Confucian doctrine: study and moral reform, nothing more. This is the systematization of Confucius's doctrine, but not its development.

Mencius

The Confucian school dragged along thus in mediocrity, without much spark though not without influence, until Mencius came along in the second part of the fourth century. He gave it some distinction, at the same time refurbishing the doctrine by introducing new ideas to make it suit the taste of the times.

Like Confucius, Mencius was a native of the state of Lu.[26] He belonged to an unimportant branch of that Meng family which was descended from Duke Huan and which, together with the Shu-sun and the Chi, had usurped power at the expense of the princes. His parents had settled in Tsou, where he was born in the second quarter of the fourth century.[27] Again like Confucius, he had been brought up by his mother who had been widowed very early. It is said that 'she changed her lodging three times for him', in order not to expose him to unsuitable surroundings.

At this time, a century after the Master's death, Confucian influence seems to have been preponderant among the literati of Lu, who had all taken more or less of their studies under one or another of his disciples. Mencius seems to have sought instruction at the source, in the very family of Confucius, if one believes the tradition on this point, which connects him with the school of Tzu-ssu.[28] Then, returning to Tsou, he founded a school in order to earn a living; and from the very first he attracted to it some of his best pupils. But this seems not to have made his fortune, for at about the age of forty,[29] he allowed himself to be tempted by the reputation for generosity which King Wei of Ch'i (357–320) enjoyed. The king had richly entertained a series of learned men: Yen and Chi of Tsou, Chieh-tzu, the Legalist Shen-tzu, the Taoist T'ien P'ien (nicknamed P'ien of the Divine Tongue), and many others as well, who are called 'the masters of the Chi Gate', *Chi-hsia hsien-sheng.*[30]

Well received initially by this prince, Mencius had a number of interviews with him, but the relationship soured quite rapidly. He refused substantial presents offered to him — a hundred ingots of copper, each of twenty-four ounces [31] — and he finally left the court. He proceeded to Po, the capital of Sung, where he had probably been invited by friends, lived there for some time, and was presented to the duke, who gave him seventy ingots. From there he returned to his native village of Tsou, where he very likely resumed the management of his school.

But he soon left it again. During his stay at Po, the hereditary Prince of T'eng, who had been one of his disciples and had been passing through on a mission to the court of Ch'u, had paid him a visit, and had invited him to go to his father's court. When his father died, in about 323,[32] he reiterated the invitation, which was accepted this time. Mencius did not remain long in T'eng. No doubt the courtiers, not anxious to see this stranger gain power, succeeded in working on the prince's mind; for Mencius had to leave the country almost immediately. From there he went to Liang, the capital of King Hui of Wei. The king was very old, and after a brilliant period at the beginning of his reign he had experienced nothing but reverses. Now he was relaxing from the cares of state among learned men and philosophers. Mencius was well received but had scarcely time to enjoy his favour, since Hui died in 319, and his son showed himself less well disposed. Mencius returned to Ch'i, where King Hsüan,[33] Wei's successor, received him very warmly. The king gave him an honorific post,[34] and employed him in various missions, especially sending him to bear official condolences to the Prince of T'eng, his former protector. The death of his mother recalled Mencius to Lu, where he gave her a splendid funeral; but at the end of the mourning period he returned to Ch'i and resumed his duties. In 314 he persuaded the king to undertake an expedition against Yen; but when, two years later, the revolt of the newly conquered country forced the troops of Ch'i to retire, he fell into disgrace.

With that Mencius left Ch'i for good, to return to his native village. Soon afterwards his disciple Yüeh-cheng, who was a minister of Prince P'ing of Lu (316–297), came to invite him to the court; but the prince did not come to pay him a visit on his arrival and Mencius, considering himself insulted, returned immediately to Tsou. He lived there amid his disciples until his death, the exact date of which is unknown.

Mencius considered the doctrine of Confucius to be a happy medium between that of Mo-tzu, whose altruism he found excessive, taking no account of family ties, and that of Yang-tzu, which he found too egoistic.

> The words of Yang Chu and of Mo-tzu fill the world. Anything people say that is not Yang's is Mo's. If the principles of Yang and Mo are not brought to a stop, if the principles of Confucius are not published, these evil discourses will pervert the people and destroy Altruism and Justice. ... I dread these things; I defend the principles of the ancient sages, and I oppose Yang and Mo. ... Whoever is able to resist Yang and Mo is a disciple of the sages.[35]

At the same time, while he took up the theories of Confucius again, he modified them. To start with, he discarded all that was out of date, such as the superhuman action of the sage and of his Virtue, which was no longer believed in his day. Moreover, he was strongly influenced by Taoist psychology, and also that of Yang-tzu. True enough, he did not dare go as far as Yang-tzu and set up the individual development of man as his goal; he retained the old Confucian notion that the individual is improved through good government. For he was as convinced as

Confucius had been that the people could only be led, and that, though it was the sovereign's duty to govern them well, he had no reason to expect that they would behave well by themselves. 'Not to have a secure means of living and yet to be secure in their minds, this is something of which nobles alone are capable. If the people have no secure means of existence, their minds will be unstable. If their minds are unstable, then moral laxity, depravity, corruption, licence — there is nothing to which they will not give themselves.'[36]

For this reason he did not attempt, any more than Confucius had, to convert men individually. Like his master, he believed that good government would succeed in transforming them *en masse*, or at least in bringing them up to the highest level they could attain. The reason he gave was not half-metaphysical, as Confucius's was, but was above all economic and practical. Not for nothing had Mencius lived so long at the Ch'i court, at the time when the first masters of the Legalist school were establishing the principles of their doctrines. Although he had not accepted all their theories, he had been deeply influenced by them. 'When an Altruist is upon the throne, can he set snares for the people? An enlightened prince will regulate the people's means of existence so that these will suffice to let them, on the one hand, serve their parents and, on the other, nourish their wife and their children, so that in good years they will be completely satisfied and in bad years they will escape death. After that he will stimulate them towards good, and the people will follow him readily.'[37]

As for the best way to assure the people's means of existence, he sought these as Confucius had, in antiquity, advocating return to the system of agriculture in common which is known by the name of *ching*,[38] together with various encouragements to commerce, especially suppression of customs duties.[39] After that, when the people had become rich, he advised — again like Confucius — that they should be instructed, though he restricted the substance of this precept only to teaching the people 'the relations among men,' *jen-lun*, within the state and within the family, that is, their duties towards those who governed them. 'Establish [colleges] — *hsiang, hsü, hsüeh*, and *hsiao* — for the instruction [of the people]. ... Their whole object is to make clear the relations among men. When relations among men are made clear by the superiors, the common people will be filled with kindly feelings.'[40]

Actually, while preserving the external forms of Confucian doctrine,[41] he repeats — with less cynicism but with equal force

— the Taoist theory of ideal government which the *Lao-tzu* had summed up in the formula: 'Fill the bellies and weaken the wills.' All these philosophical theories of ancient China were equally aristocratic; all the masters, whatever school they belonged to — Taoists, Confucians, disciples of Mo-Tzu, Sophists, Legalists — were equally convinced of the basic superiority of their class, the noble class, over the common people and peasants who surrounded them; and on this point at least their doctrines are all in agreement.

This is not to say that Mencius despised the people; on the contrary, he conceded them a great importance within the State. 'The people are the most important element; after them come the gods of the soil and of the harvests; the prince is the least important.'[42] But this importance attaches only to the people *en masse*, since they are what make known the Mandate of Heaven: 'Heaven does not speak. ... Heaven sees as the people see, Heaven hears as the people hear.'[43] This he says, quoting for his purpose a passage from the 'Great Harangue', *T'ai shih*, a chapter of the *Shu ching*.[44]

The reciprocal relations of Heaven, people, and sovereign are well defined in this passage:

'Is it true that Yao gave the empire to Shun?'

Mencius replied: 'No, The Son of Heaven cannot give the empire to anyone.'

'Yes, but Shun possessed the empire. Who gave it to him?'

'Heaven gave it to him.'

'When Heaven gave it to him, did it confer charge of it with detailed instructions?'

'No, Heaven does not speak. ... The Son of Heaven can present a man to Heaven, but he cannot make Heaven give the empire to that man, just as a prince can present a man to the king but cannot make the king give a principality to that man. Yao presented Shun to Heaven, and the people accepted him.'

'How is it that when Yao presented Shun to Heaven, Heaven accepted him, and when he presented him to the people, the people accepted him?'

'He had him preside over the sacrifices, and the gods were content: thus Heaven accepted him. He had him preside over the conduct of affairs, and the affairs were well managed: thus the people accepted him.'[45]

Since the people's acceptance is the visible sign of the Mandate of Heaven, the loss of the people is the sign that the mandate has been lost. From then on the prince who has lost the people is no longer a true sovereign; and when he is killed, it is not a king who has been put to death, but a malefactor.

King Hsüan of Ch'i asked: 'Is it true that T'ang banished Chieh, and that King Wu overthrew Tsou?'

Mencius replied: 'That is in the history.'

'May a minister kill his prince?'

'The man who outrages Altruism is a brigand; the man who outrages Justice is a malefactor. A brigand or a malefactor is called a mere low-class fellow. I have heard it said that the fellow Tsou had been put to death, but I have never heard that a prince had been killed!'[46]

Nevertheless, it is not up to the people to overthrow him; this is for his ministers to do. It is, in fact, a matter within the ruling class: the governed manifest by their disaffection that the Mandate of Heaven has been lost, but they have no right to take action; it is for the ruling class to settle things among themselves. 'If the prince has great faults [the ministers who are of his family] should address remonstrances to him. And if, after they have done this repeatedly, he does not heed them, they should dethrone him.'[47]

Thus Mencius had preserved some of Confucius's illusions about good government, from which he expected the conversion of the people *en bloc*. But he differed from Confucius and followed the example of Mo-tzu in that he attributed this conversion, not to the supernatural Virtue of the sage but to the underlying principles which guided it. However, for the principle of Universal Love he substituted the Confucian principle of Altruism, *jen*, to which he joined Justice, *yi*. Altruism and Justice became for him the supreme virtues, those which characterized the Good; and he set the former against opposite exaggerations — Mo-tzu's Universal Love and Yang-tzu's Egoism. Both of those suppressed all due distinction in relations between men: Altruism and Justice, on the contrary, gave them meaning, for Filial Piety is 'the fruit of Altruism' and obedience to the elder brother is 'the fruit of Justice'.[48] The latter, Justice, he opposed to Utility, *li*, by which the school of Mo-tzu had come to characterize the Good.[49] Thus he also gained a cheap success, by giving the term its popular meaning rather than the particular significance that the school of Mo-tzu seems to have given it.

How does man acquire these fundamental principles? Confucius had said 'by conquering oneself' and had set forth several principles for a morality which drew its line of conduct exclusively from an external rule — the totality of the ritual principles handed down by the sages.[50] Mencius, on the contrary, sought a principle which was 'internal'[51] — that is, innate. For him, human nature is originally good: at birth the heart of the infant is pure, and it is corrupted only little by little. This theory, which he claimed to have rediscovered in Confucius, by interpreting certain not-very-conclusive passages in this way, came to him from Taoist psychology,[52] though perhaps indirectly, through the intermediacy of the *Chung yung* and the school of Tzu-ssu. It naturally had to be transformed to fit in with Confucian doctrine. For the Taoists, thus, the nature of man was the Tao itself, neither good nor bad but neutral; but for Mencius it is what Heaven has 'put into us', and which is necessarily good since Heaven cannot have given us anything evil. Thus the Great Man, *ta-jen*, is he who has preserved 'his heart of a child' — that is, his original simplicity and natural goodness. Mencius goes on to specify that Heaven has put four innate virtues into us, to guide us: Altruism, *jen*, Justice, *yi* (a sense for relations with men), Religious Sentiment, *li*, and the knowledge of Good and Evil, *chih*. 'Man has these four virtues as he has four limbs'. It is they which preside over ethics, which is no longer reduced, as it is for Confucius, to seeking its foundations externally in the teachings of the rites handed down by the sages. Instead it has its solid basis in the heart of every man, the heart being the receptacle into which Heaven put the four innate virtues.

If a man has not preserved his heart of a child, it is thus necessary to work to recover it. 'The body has its noble parts and its base parts, its large parts and small parts. What is large should not be made to suffer for what is small, nor what is noble for what is base. He who develops what is small [in himself] is a small man, *hsiao-jen*; he who develops what is great [in himself] is a great man, *ta-jen*.' Here again the influence of Taoist psychology can be noted: it was the school of Lao-tzu and Chuang-tzu which introduced this notion, that the human mind is dualistic in character, into Chinese philosophy. The result is that — although Mencius distinguishes, as Confucius had, between the man who is a sage by nature (like Yao and Shun) and the man who becomes that way by study (like T'ang the Victorious and King Wen), and although he places the first above the second — he nevertheless admits that 'anyone can become a Yao or a Shun'. Yet, always like his master, he is unwilling for this moral transformation of the individual to be for his personal advantage: Mencius would have regarded that as retrogressing into the egoistic doctrine of Yang-tzu. It was designed to allow the influencing of a prince, and thus the realization of good government. Indeed, 'Only the Great Man can rectify what is evil in the mind of a sovereign. Let the prince be altruistic, and all his acts will be altruistic; let him be just, and all his acts will be just; let him be correct and all his acts will be correct. And if the ruler's conduct is correct, the State will be regulated.'[53]

Thus Mencius remained a good Confucian through the primary importance he accorded to good government. The moral development of the individual had interest for him only insofar as it prepared him to be a good counsellor for princes. As against the Taoist school, for whom the preoccupation with government took second place, and that of Yang-tzu, which discarded them entirely in favour of the interests of the individual himself — as against these, Mencius took up again the Confucian conception of a philosophy of government, the morality of which was above all a morality of those who govern, an aristocratic morality, with very clear distinctions between the duties of the various classes of society.

Mencius was too much outside the mainstream of the Confucian school to exercise a great influence upon it. He had a school of his own, which survived him and even subdivided after his death, his disciple Yüeh-cheng K'o having founded a branch in his turn. But it had little effect upon the old, well-established schools, those of Tzu-chang, of Yen Hui, and so on, which scarcely concerned themselves with anything but ritual questions. Indeed, even though he undoubtedly had some fame outside the school, in the courts where he spent time, the Confucian literature of the third century took very little from him.

Hsün-tzu

It was the same, in the following century, with Hsün-tzu, who also, though in a more systematic fashion than Mencius, tried to formulate a general philosophical theory upon the basis of Confucianism.

Hsün K'uang (who is ordinarily called Hsün the Minister, Hsün-ch'ing, from the title given him, as to Mencius, in Ch'i) was a descendant of that Hsün family, long one of the greatest in Chin, but fallen from its high estate since the assassination of the Count of Chih, its chief, in 453. The branch to which he belonged was settled in Chao, where he was born and where he passed the first part of his life. Then, towards the age of fifty, it is said,[54] he went to Ch'i to study there among the famed scholars of the Chi Gate.[55]

But the school was decaying: it was by then the epoch of King

Hsiang (283–265), and all the disciples of the great dialectician T'ien P'ien were already dead. Hsün-tzu nevertheless remained for some time at Lin-tzu, well received by the king, who conferred upon him the honorific post of Distinguished Grand Officer, *lieh tai-fu*, a title King Hsüan had created earlier for illustrious scholars. From there he seems to have travelled twice to Ch'in, where he knew the minister Sui of Fan and was given an audience with King Chao,[56] though he was offered no employment. He went then to his native state of Chao, but had no more success there.[57]

Upon returning to Ch'i, he was slandered to the king and therefore accepted the invitation of the Chief of Commands of Ch'u, the Lord of Ch'un-shen, who entrusted him with the government of the city of Lan-ling. He kept this post until the death of his protector; but he was ruined in the reaction against his patron's clientele after Li Yüan assassinated that worthy (238).[58] Being very old, he did not leave Lan-ling, where he remained as a private citizen, and where his school, famous especially for its treatment of the rites, attracted a great number of disciples — among others, the philosopher Fei of Han, and the future prime minister of Ch'in, Li Ssu.[59] There he died, probably not long afterwards. One work of his has survived, which seems originally to have borne the title 'The New Writings of Minister Hsün', *Hsün-ch'ing hsin shu*,[60] but since the ninth century called simply *Hsün-tzu*.[61]

Hsün-tzu, like Mencius, like all those who belonged to the Confucian school, was mainly concerned with the problem of good government and put forward the principle that this should be the government of a sage. He did not, however, believe with Confucius that good government would come of itself through the Virtue of a sage, nor with Mo-tzu that it would be the spontaneous product of Universal Love practised with the sage. Like all those of his time, he sought to realize it by applying more immediate principles — with the Nominalists, the 'rectification of names'; with the Legalists, the use of punishments and rewards.

If, with the Nominalists, Hsün-tzu conceded that the sage's first concern must be to 'rectify names', *cheng ming*, according to the formula attributed to Confucius himself, this was not necessarily because he believed — as the Nominalists did — in the Virtue of names. On the contrary although, for Yin Wen, good names designate what is good and bad names designate what is bad — so that 'what is good has good names and what is evil has bad names'[62] — for Hsün-tzu, 'names are not by nature congruent; it is by convention that they are used to designate things. Those which are conventionally fixed and established by custom are called congruent; those which vary from the convention are called non-congruent. Names are not applied to [such-and-such] a real thing by their nature; they designate real things through convention. Those which are conventionally fixed and established by usage are called names applying to reality. Names are not by nature good; those which [are] easily [applied] are called good names'.[63] But the rectification of names, by establishing — conventionally but definitively — the relations between names and things, by fixing the correct designations and definitions for the people, avoids disputes and disorders.

Again, although like the Legalists he wishes to have severe laws, this is not because he believes with them in the Virtue of the Law itself. 'Sung-tzu,' he says, 'was deceived in seeing good government as derived from the Law, and he did not know [that it came] from the sages.' It is rather because he believes, contrary to what Mencius thought, that human nature is basically evil. 'Human nature is evil; what is good in it is artificial. From birth human nature has in it the love of gain. Because it clings to this, strife and rapacity are born, and self-effacement and charity do not exist. From birth it has envy and hate; and because it clings to this violence and injustice are born, and loyalty and faith do not exist. From birth it has the desires which come through eyes and ears, it has the love of sounds and beauty and because it clings to these luxury and disorder arise, and Rites and Justice do not exist.... If human nature is evil, where do the Rites and Justice come from? Rites and Justice come as an artificial production of the sages; it is not the nature with which man was born originally.'

By this original evil of human nature he justifies the need for a severe government, to teach men the good of which they are ignorant by nature. But, although by this roundabout route he reaches the conclusions of the Legalist school, he does not accept the ideas of Sung-tzu or the Legalists with Taoist tendencies (the only ones whose theories he seems to have known) concerning the ineluctability of the Law in itself, as derived immutably from the immutable Tao. Like them, he sought in the Law a fundamental principle which explains its value; but this principle, rather than strengthening it, relegates it to a lower level. It is Rites and Justice which are considered the source of all morality and all ethics. 'A straight piece of wood has no need of the press to be straight; it is straight by nature. A curved piece of wood must be softened and reshaped in order to become straight, for by nature it is not straight. Since human nature is evil, it must be subject to the patterns of the sages and transformation by the Rites and Justice, in order to become perfectly submissive to the Law and accommodated to the good.'[64]

Rites and Justice, *li-yi*: by these we see that Hsün-tzu is influenced by Mencius; but he goes much farther than his predecessor.

> What is the origin of the Rites? From birth men have desires. These they cannot satisfy, but no more can they not seek to satisfy them. When they seek [to satisfy them], since there is no fixed limit to divisions [among individuals], they cannot avoid disputing among themselves; and the dispute produces disorder. The disorder produces limitation [in the satisfaction of desires]. The former kings hated disorder: that is why they established the Rites and Justice, so as to fix individual shares, to satisfy man's desires, to give him what he seeks, and to insure that his desires are not limited by things nor things subjected to his desires, [so] that [real things and man's desires] mutually sustain each other directly. That is the origin of the Rites.[65]

Justice is the very origin of society, without which society would go under:

> Water and fire have breath but not life; herbs and trees have life, but not knowledge; birds and beasts have knowledge but not a sense of Justice. Man has breath, life, knowledge, and the sense of Justice. This is why he is the noblest being on earth. His strength is not equal to that of an ox, nor his speed to that of a horse; yet ox and horse are at his service. Why? Because men are capable of organizing themselves into society and [oxen and horses] are not. How is it that men are capable of organizing themselves into society? By division [among individuals]. How can this division be practised? By Justice. Thus Justice in making divisions brings men into agreement; being in agreement, they form a unity; forming a unity, they have great power; having great power, they are strong; being strong, they have a mastery over things. This is why they can have palaces and houses to live in; this is why they can order the four seasons, control all things, and do good universally throughout the world. This has no other cause, but that man has the Rites and Justice. In consequence, from birth on, men are bound to organize themselves in society; if they organize themselves into society and do not make divisions, they will dispute among themselves; disputation will produce disorder, disorder will produce disunity; disunited, men are weak; weak, they will not have mastery over things. For that reason they will not have palaces to live in. This shows that the Rites and Justice cannot be left aside for a single moment.[66]

Thus society emerged entirely through the will of the sages, desirous of establishing order among men; and it is by the Rites and Justice that society has been set up and that it is able to last.

In sum, good government will be assured by the sage, who, by rectifying names so that all can understand his commands and then by educating the people through the rites, will bring order into the world, and will maintain that order by severely punishing those who stray from the right path, either by discourse contrary to the rectification of names or by acts contrary to the Rites.

But Hsün-tzu does not think, as Confucius and Mencius do, that the sage's government must be modelled upon that of the sages of antiquity, such as Yao and Shun. On this point again the Legalists have influenced him more strongly than Mencius has, though the ideas he borrowed have been greatly modified. The reason why the sage's government is no longer suitable is not, as the Legalists thought, because the world of today is different from the world of old. Quite to the contrary, it is just the same, the men of today being like those of times past. But the sage-kings of antiquity are so remote that nothing is known about them. Thus it will be much better to imitate more modern sage-kings, who can be much better known.[67]

Moreover, the sage, by the very fact that he is a sage, can form judgements without needing to imitate others. Thus he can distinguish truth from falsehood and, by his own mental effort, between good and evil. But, since human nature is evil, how can man choose the good?

All men are basically the same, Yü the Sage like Chieh the Tyrant: 'All men are alike in some things. When they are hungry, they wish to eat. When they are cold, they wish to warm themselves. When they are tired, they wish to rest. They love what is advantageous to them and detest what is hurtful. That is what men possess from birth; that is what they are immediately. That is wherein Yü and Chieh are alike.'[68] That, 'wherein men are men', is their nature, *hsing*;[69] and it is evil.

Thus, in order to be able to recognize what is good and what is evil and to choose that which is good, the sage, whose nature inclines rather towards evil, requires an effort of the mind — of the 'heart', by the Chinese terminology. Yet (and it is here that Hsün-tzu comes closest to Taoism), this effort is not purely intellectual; it is not expressed as mere reasoning. Hsün-tzu has borrowed from the mystical school certain of its techniques, and seeks to attain truth not by reasoning (by that one risks 'by being wrong on a single point, being in the dark with relation to the

Great Doctrine', the sole truth,[70] as happened to Mo-tzu, Sung-tzu, and so many others), but by a meditation pushed very far, to the point where the spirit, freed from all surface phenomena, grasps the very nature of things directly and becomes capable of knowing them and naming them without mistake. He comes thus, if not into what may properly be called an ecstasy, at least into a state of trance, in which the spirit is transported outside itself. This is what he calls the Great Pure Clarity, *ta-ch'ing-ming*, and he describes this state in terms which recall Chuang-tzu and his school. Whoever is in this condition, 'of the ten thousand things he might discourse upon, there would not be one whose classification he would not know. Seated in his dwelling he sees the whole world; living in the present, he discourses upon the remote past. He sees through all things and knows their true nature, he studies order and disorder and comprehends their names, he governs Heaven and earth and governs the ten thousand things.'[71]

The procedure by which this state is arrived at also shows, even in its technical terms, the Taoist influence.

'How can the principle, *tao* [of good government] be known?'
'By the heart.'
'How does the heart know it?'
'The heart must be at rest, in emptiness and concentration.'
There we recognize the Taoist 'emptiness'. As in mystical practices, indeed, for meditation the mind must entirely eliminate that which encumbers it ordinarily.

> Man has knowledge from birth; having knowledge, he has intentions; these intentions are what is contained. At the same time [despite this 'content', the mind] has what is called the void; not to allow what is contained to harm what is to be received, that is called the void. From birth the mind has knowledge; having knowledge, it differentiates; to differentiate means to know several things at the same time; to know several things at the same time is to scatter oneself. [In spite of this scattering, the mind] has what is called concentration: not to let one [idea] be harmed by an [-other idea] is what is called concentration. When one sleeps, the mind dreams, when one neglects it, acts by itself, when one uses it, reflects. This is why it is not untroubled. [At the same time] it has what is called calmness: if it does not trouble knowledge by the illusions of the dream, this is what is called calmness.[72]

Hsün-tzu, like Mencius, believed every man could aspire to this saintly way, which was the very condition of good government. It would suffice for him to make the same personal effort that all the sages must have done, and he could thus become a sage, *sheng*, or at least a Superior Man, *chün-tzu*, or Great Man, *ta-jen*. This evolution of a sage was one of the questions which most engrossed Hsün-tzu. Like Mencius, he accepted the distinction (Taoist in origin, it had become a commonplace of the psychology of the time) between two elements in the mind of man: that which he called Nature, *hsing*, and the Artificial, *wei*. 'What is characteristic of man from birth is called Nature, *hsing*'; this is what is granted by Heaven, 'what can be neither learned nor served'; it is 'what one is incapable of making, but which is produced naturally'. The Artificial, on the contrary, is the product of reflection: 'When the mind reflects and is capable of being moved thereby, this is what is called the Artificial. When the reflections accumulate, one can acquire habits and in consequence perfect oneself. This is what is called the Artificial: it is what can be acquired by study, what can be perfected by serving it.'

Nature includes the natural faculties (sight, hearing, and so on), but also the primordial instincts (to eat when hungry, to warm oneself when cold), and finally the passsions, *ch'ing*, 'love and hate, contentment and anger, pain and pleasure', which are their reactions to contact with external things. The Artificial includes the Rites and Justice, morality, and so on. It is the passions which lead one from the Natural to the Artificial, for they partake in some way of both, being not innate but acquired, and on the other hand evolving by themselves rather than by re-flective and voluntary study. 'They are not something which I possess, but something produced of themselves.' It is they which serve as a substratum for the Artificial: 'the mind chooses among them, and this is what is called reflection';[73] and it is the accumu-lation of reflection which little by little forms the Artificial.

But Nature is evil, and all that is good in man is artificial. The sage's effort, far from consisting in reverting to a natural simplicity, as the Taoists would have it, or recovering his 'heart of a little child', as Mencius counsels, must on the contrary be devoted to removing himself as far as possible from evil nature by developing the Artificial. The sage is he who has accumulated good ideas through continued study. Sagehood can thus be acquired: 'every man, if he accumulates the good to fulfilment, is what is called a sage.' And this accumulation can be accomplished through education, for education is all-powerful: 'The children of the people of Yü-yüeh and the Mo barbarians utter the same cries when they are born; but when they are grown up, they have different customs: it is education which has made them that way.'[74]

But it is not necessary that this education should include everything taught in the Confucian schools: the 'Documents' (*Shu ching*), 'Odes' (*Shih ching*), and 'Chronicle' (*Ch'un ch'iu*) are useless indeed; the sole important study is that of the Rites. And again, 'the Rites and the music give examples, but they do not speak.' Nothing is so important as to put oneself under the direction of a master who is a Superior Man. 'In studying, nothing is so expeditious as to be in friendly relations with one's master. Conforming to the Rites comes next. If one can neither be in friendly relations with his master nor conform to the Rites, what is the use of setting oneself to studying the various sciences? Merely to practise the 'Odes' and the 'Documents' is to be one's whole life long a mere marginal scholar.'[75] As to the dialectical subtleties dear to the Sophists, the Superior Man, *chün-tzu*, attaches no importance to them and spends no time on them.

Understood thus, study leads on to a complete transformation: 'When the Superior Man studies, it enters by the ears, fixes itself in the mind, spreads into the four limbs, and shows itself in action and repose. He speaks correctly, he moves with dignity. In every situation he may be a model.' But, wrongly directed, studies serve no purpose. 'When the small man, *hsiao-jen*, studies, what goes in by the ear comes out by the mouth. From mouth to ear is four inches: how can that be enough to improve a body seven feet long?'[76]

A powerful intellect, Hsün-tzu succeeded in creating a coherent and original system which revivified Confucianism. His influence upon his contemporaries seems to have been considerable. It lasted into the second century and left a clear mark upon the literati of the Han period until the time when the rediscovery of Mencius began to diminish Hsün-tzu's prestige.

The Ritualists

Beside the schools of Meng-tzu and Hsün-tzu, the most brilliant in the Confucianism of the third century, great if quiet work was being accomplished within the ritual schools. Those of Tzu-yu and Tzu-kung, so important a century earlier — when the *Lun yü* had been compiled — seem to have disappeared; but those stemming from Tzu-chang, Tzu-ssu, Yen Hui, Tseng-tzu, and Ch'i-tiao Ch'i, more or less illustrious disciples of Confucius, were still flourishing,[77] as was that of Tzu-hsia.[78] The traditional Confucian teaching continued in these: that is, one studied the

'Documents' (*Shu ching*), the 'Odes', the *Ch'un ch'iu*, the rites, and music,[79] and also the *Yi ching*, at least in the school of Tzu-ssu. Their masters were reproached for their dry and superficial ritualism, as well as for being too anxious not to commit themselves.[80]

They worked hard. To one of the schools, that of Tzu-ssu, is owed the definitive ordering of the *Yi ching*,[81] about the middle of the third century, as well as the composition of the last appendices of that work — the *Wen yen* (fourth appendix) and three other less important ones (fifth to seventh) — and also the interpolation of Confucian commentaries in the *Hsi-tz'u* (third appendix). At the same time the members of this school edited a number of ritual treatises, mostly lost, though some of them are preserved in the *Li chi*. The second section of the *Chung yung* must have been one of their last works, on the eve of the persecution of scholars by the First Emperor of Ch'in; that work had been strongly influenced by Mencius and by the *Wen yen*.

The rivals of that school showed an activity no less remarkable, and a number of small Confucian works of the third century are owed to them. Some of these appeared under the form of ritual and political commentaries to the *Ch'un ch'iu*: such were the *Kung-yang chuan*, the *Ku-liang chuan* and others, lost today.[82] These were supposed to be the oral teaching of Confucius, but seem rather to have been compilations of the traditional teaching in each branch, retrospectively set under the Master's name. They were, moreover, only compiled quite late,[83] between the middle of the fourth and the end of the third century. The *Kung-yang chuan* is probably from Ch'i, since it bears the marks of that culture, and in its turn it exercised some influence upon Mencius there; the *Ku-liang chuan*, more recent, was perhaps from the south, having felt the influence of Hsün-tzu and his school.

Others of these works were true treatises on the rites: some were given out as the work of Confucius, such as the *San ch'ao chi*, in seven sections, which claimed to reproduce Confucius's conversations with Prince Ai of Lu during three audiences which the prince had given him.[84] But the greatest number were attributed to the most famous disciples: there was a collection under the name of Tseng-tzu, who was also supposed to be the author of a small work on filial piety, the *Hsiao ching*, probably composed in the state of Wei in the third century;[85] others were connected with Tzu-ssu. It is probable that each branch of the school placed the doctrines it taught under the patronage of its founder; and there are echoes of the lively disputes that occurred between them regarding ceremonial details.

Several of these works are complete rituals of certain ceremonies: for exchanges of ambassadors between principalities, for the taking of the bonnet of manhood, for marriage, and for archery contests — and especially there are a number of tracts on funerals. Attempts were thus made to adapt the Confucian doctrines to the theories in vogue: the *Wu ti te* and the *Ti hsi*[86] show the influence of Tsou Yen and his ideas about the action of the *yin* and the *yang* and that of the Five Elements in the development of human affairs, and their application to history. Another such treatise, the title of which has been lost, but which reports the colloquy of Confucius with an unnamed prince,[87] tries to establish some agreement with the doctrines of the Legalists. In it Confucius is made to say that the government of the ancient dynasties, though it could serve as a model, could not be applied to the present age[88] — which was one of the principles of that school.

Many of these works must have disappeared in antiquity. Those among them which survived into Han times were then published in various ways, according to the chance of how the ancient texts had been found. Some, discovered together, constituted a special work, the *Yi li*; others, hardly different, but discovered in other conditions, have been incorporated in the *Li chi* and the *Ta Tai li chi*, large compilations in which pieces of every date and every sort of origin are included;[89] and others finally, remaining separate, have disappeared altogether or partly, like the *San ch'ao chi*.

Though Mencius and Hsün-tzu were the most illustrious representatives of the Confucian school in the fourth and third centuries, it was not to them that the school owed its vitality and the strength to survive the great crisis of the third century and emerge from that crisis more vigorous than before. This was due chiefly to those less brilliant and less celebrated ritualists who had carried on the role of educators which Confucius had created. The doctrines themselves seem to have played only a minor role in the survival of the philosophical schools; it was the practical disciplines they taught which saved them.

The school of Mo-tzu perished because it had been devoted to dialectic, the taste for which was only a passing fashion, and this died with the society which had given rise to it. On the contrary, the teaching of the rites among the Confucians and that of the mystical practices among the Taoists responded, in varying degrees, to the deep needs which social and political upheavals did not change. That was the salvation of those two schools and, of course, of the doctrines to which they were connected.

7
Historical Romance and History

Besides the official chronicles of the Grand Scribe, dry and cold, which in general do not seem to have been published, there arose, about the fifth century, a genre less forbidding for public consumption. In it, by mixing true historical facts with the products of pure imagination, writers produced real romances. They included all possible forms, from the adventure romance in which the events themselves, romantic embroidery upon a legendary or historic theme, are the main element to the political or philosophical romance, an actual treatise put into the form of a discourse attributed to a more or less authentic person, and in which the historical or romantic happenings serve only as a framework for the exposition of the ideas.

Of the adventure romances, there remain hardly more than fragments of one, the 'History of Mu, the Son of Heaven', *Mu t'ien-tzu chuan*.[1] For its hero this has King Mu, whose military expeditions, hunts, voyages and love-affairs it relates. What remains of it deals chiefly with two episodes. One of these is a grand journey to the west of the world, to the sources of the Yellow River, during which, the River God having given his grandson as guide, King Mu goes to the place where the sun sleeps and to the land of the Queen Mother of the West, Hsi-wang-mu, daughter of the Lord on High and Goddess of Epidemics, who receives him well and exchanges verses with him. The other is a hunting expedition in the south, where he meets the beautiful Chi of Sheng, with whom he falls in love and whom he marries, but who dies soon afterwards and for whom he gives a magnificent funeral. This work, which seems to date from the fifth or the fourth century, is probably one of the most ancient of its kind. The adventures are barely sketched; the stages of the journeys are laid out almost day by day with a monotonous dryness. Only a few episodes — that of the interview with the Queen Mother of the West, and that of the funeral of Chi of Sheng — are treated at somewhat greater length, but still very briefly. The author has been inspired by the official chronicles to try and produce in their image a chronological recital of a sequence of events; and his style smacks of his model.

Another biographical romance, probably composed around the middle of the fourth century, that of Prince Wen of Chin, seems (in so far as the fragments which have been preserved allow us to judge) to show a great advance. The hero is that Ch'ung-erh, the son of Prince Hsien, who is driven from Chin by a court intrigue, leads an adventurous life for twenty-odd years, wanders from principality to principality and is received more or less well, finally succeeds in seizing the throne at an advanced age, and soon becomes hegemon. This dramatic life inspired a writer. In order to give his subject interior unity, he pitched on the idea of linking the two parts of his hero's life — his time as a pretender and his time as reigning prince — by interpreting all the events of the second period as consequences of events in the first, and by inventing the details of episodes in that first part which would justify the second. The treaty with Ch'i and the expedition to the aid of the Duke of Sung thus became the reward for the courteous reception he got from the princes of those two countries. On the other hand, the dethronement of the Prince of Wey and the Count of Ts'ao in 632 are the results of ill-treatment suffered in those principalities. The most famous of these episodes, the retreat of three day-stages before the Ch'u army preceding the Battle of Ch'eng-p'u, is explained by a promise which the exiled pretender had made to King Ch'eng of Ch'u several years earlier, in gratitude for the good treatment he had received there.

From the brief summary which is all that has survived,[2] this romance seems to have been very well composed; but it is difficult to say how much the philosophical and political discourses may have detracted from the interest of the original.

A whole romantic literature sprang up around the *Shu ching* and its heroes. An echo of this can still be found in the fragments of a collection of traditions regarding that work, the *Shang shu ta chuan*, which was compiled towards the beginning of the second century B.C., and in which the materials have been reworked historically.[3] On the other hand, the romance regarding the origins of the Chou dynasty exists almost complete in the *Yi Chou shu*.⁴ This is a sort of recasting of the chapters from the *Shu ching* dealing with the first Chou kings. It is in the same style and spirit as the original, but it recounts systematically and consecutively the struggle between Chou and Shang, the reigns of kings Wen and Wu and the regency of the Duke of Chou. It also contains narratives imitating the libretti of the royal dances and discourses imitating the small treatises of the scribes. The work has no great literary value; its lengthy and muddled narratives trail on at wearisome length. Even the best, that of the victory over King Tsou of Yin, of his suicide and the offering of his head to the ancestral tablets, is dry and dull, without any dramatic *character*.⁵ It is difficult to fix the date when this work was composed; but it probably goes back to the middle of the fourth century.

Around that period, besides the adventure romances, the philosophical romance also started to appear, through an enlargement of the little treatises which the school of the Scribes produced. The actual history of the hero lost its importance steadily, and the main interest lay in the ideas which he was made to present. A great number of illustrious men became heroes of romances of this type.

The *Kuan-tzu*,⁶ which was probably composed in the second half of the fourth century,⁷ was an administrative utopia attributed to Yi-wu of Kuan, the minister of Prince Huan of Ch'i in the seventh century. His adventures, his long ministry, his administration, his political theories, his discourses to his sovereign, the treaties from the assemblies of the princes, all were set forth in detail. And truth and fiction seem to have been mixed unceasingly in this work, where the constitution of Ch'i on the one hand and the history of Prince Huan on the other seem to be the real models which the author idealized.

It is hardly possible to judge its literary merit by the few fragments which are all that has survived, and which are probably merely summaries of certain parts; but certainly it was a great success in its day, for all the authors of the fourth and third centuries know and quote it.

Another minister of Ch'i, Yen Ying, who lived in the century after Chung of Kuan and died in 493 B.C. after having served three generations of princes in his country, also, in about the same period, became the hero of a similar romance, the *Yen-tzu ch'un ch'iu*.⁸ The author seems to have been a writer from Ch'i, about the middle of the fourth century B.C., whose philosophical tendencies, contrary to those of the *Kuan-tzu* author, seem to

have leaned rather towards the school of Mo-tzu than towards
that of Confucius.⁹ In any case, his ideas are not particularly
interesting, showing the same banality as those of most
romancers of that period. The general plan of the work is not
very felicitous, historical tidbits being arranged by subject: first
came the remonstrances, then questions, and finally varied
anecdotes.¹⁰ What puts this work in a class by itself is the
liveliness with which the scenes, or some of them at least, are
described, whether it is an orgy at the court of Prince Ching; or
the crossing of the Yellow River where Ku-yeh-tzu — not
knowing how to swim — nearly drowns;¹¹ or the famous scene
in which Ching views his capital from afar and weeps at the idea
that he will one day have to leave it by dying;¹² or the
assassination of Prince Chuang by his minister Chu of Ts'ui and
Yen-tzu's visit, where he weeps over the body.¹³ The author
knows how to make his characters come alive, how to give them
appropriate bearing and ways of speaking. In other things he is
less able: the taste of the time unfortunately demanded that he
overload his work with dissertations on government, morality,
and so on; and his philosophical ideas are thoroughly
commonplace.

There is hardly a single well-known person of the Chou period
who has not become the hero of a romance. Imagination being
given free rein, imaginary episodes were invented when the real
biography seemed insufficient. This happened for Wu Ch'i, a
general from the state of Wei and author of the *Wu-tzu*, to whom
were ascribed extraordinary adventures, followed by a tragic
death in Ch'u.¹⁴

Sometimes the hero himself was imaginary, like Ch'in of Su in
the *Su-tzu*, a political romance of the middle of the third century.
This shows Su Ch'in, a poor scholar but intelligent and eloquent,
who is mocked by his family and then rebuffed by the King of
Ch'in, to whom he had first gone to offer his talents. To revenge
himself for this, he has the idea of organizing a league of all the
other Chinese states. Driven from Chao by a minister's jealousy,
he is well received in Yen, whose prince gives him the means to
return to Chao as soon as he hears of his enemy's death. He
persuades the King of Chao to adopt his plan and, commencing
a round of embassies through the principalities, creates the
league against Ch'in, and is named prime minister by each of the
confederated princes. He returns then in triumph to his village to
show himself off to his family before going to settle in the state of
Chao. There he governs the federation for fifteen years, during
which the Prince of Ch'in dares not attack it; but at the end of

that time Ch'in gets the better of him thanks to Chang Yi, a personal enemy who for vengeance succeeds in breaking up the confederation. Su Ch'in then flees to the state of Yen, whence his love-affair with the king's mother soon obliges him to depart, and he goes and settles in Ch'i. There he is again well received and quickly gains the prince's favour; but in the end he is assassinated. This romance had so great a success that a sequel to it was produced almost at once, relating the adventures of Su Ch'in's brothers.[15]

The popularity of the romance had not entirely killed true historical works. Official chronicles became common first. Not only did a new country such as Wei have its *Chi nien*, but even an older state like Ch'in apparently began to keep regular annals, the *Ch'in chi*, before the fourth century. But these seem to have inspired a taste for a new genre, rather similar to history as the ancient Greeks and Romans understood it, in which the detailed and lively narrative patterned on that of the romances replaced the dryness of the official chronicles, while it retained their precision and accuracy.

Besides the *Ch'un ch'iu* of Lu, Mencius knew the annals of two great states, those of Chin, the *Sheng*, and those of Ch'u, the *T'ao-wu*.[16] It was not a matter of chance that the only two complete chronicles which Mencius's contemporary, the author of the *Tso chuan*, used, combining them to make the frame for his work, were precisely those of Chin and Ch'u. It is very probable that these were the works of which Mencius spoke. One was a great chronicle of the state of Chin from the time when the younger branch of the royal house, the counts of Ch'ü-wu, came to power, down to the end of that principality and its division into three states, or perhaps only until the assassination of the Count of Chih. The other was the chronicle of the state of Ch'u from its beginnings down to an uncertain date. Both are lost, but the *Tso chuan* used both constantly, and in addition significant fragments have been rediscovered in a sort of collection of extracts compiled about the middle of the third century, the *Kuo yü*. In the same genre, but with less precision and more a flavour of romance, a chronicle of the principality of Chao seems to have been composed, also in the third century, and the *Shih chi* contains a résumé of it.

Yet again, biographies of famous men became a fashionable genre. Their origin was probably to be found in the funeral eulogies given at the burial services for princes and noblemen, of which the *Tso chuan* has preserved several specimens. Ssu-ma Ch'ien has given summaries of the biographies of the 'four heroes', *ssu hsiung*, of the third century.[17] These were Wen of T'ien, Lord of Meng-ch'ang, minister to King Min of Ch'i (326–284); Prince Sheng, Lord of P'ing-yüan, younger brother of King Hui-wen of Chao and minister of Hsiao-ch'eng (265–245), who died in 252; Prince Wu-chi, Lord of Hsin-ling, younger brother and minister to King An-hsi of Wei (276–243), who died in 243; and finally Hsieh of Huang, Lord of Ch'un-shen, minister of King K'ao-lieh of Ch'u (262–238), who died in 238.

Biographies of personages from even older times were produced. Chung of Chai, the minister of the princes of Cheng at the turn of the eighth to the seventh century, had his, in which the founding of the principality of Cheng was recounted. Even ancient legends were searched for former heroes, and there seems to have been a romance of Yi Yin, the minister of T'ang the Victorious, and of his becoming a cook after his flight from the Hsia court.[18]

The distinction between romance and history was not very clear. If the *Su-tzu* was a work of the imagination, the romance of Ch'ung-erh (Prince Wen of Chin) seems to have mixed romantic tales with historical narratives. The biography of Chung of Chai: was this a romance or history? To what extent did the *Kuan-tzu* mix utopia with reality in describing the administration of the state of Ch'i? Even contemporaries were not very sure about it and were deceived. Purely documentary works were not exempt from the romantic contamination. The *Chou li* sets out the administrative ritual of the Chou, compiled at the turn of the fourth to the third century, when the kings, reduced to their strictly religious role, had seen the last scraps of their power usurped by the two branches of the new dukes of Chou, descendants of a brother of King K'ao. Yet this *Chou li* sometimes gives place to the administrative utopias which were fashionable in that period, and of which the author of the *Kuan-tzu* and Mencius have provided other examples.[19] And as for the historians, the author of the *Tso chuan* utilized romance and history with an even hand as sources of his great chronicle.

The *Tso chuan*[20] is the sole great historical work of the end of the Chou dynasty which has come down to us. But it is not complete and, what is worse, was much revised in Han times. As it is nowadays, it is a composite work made up of two parts which were originally distinct: a small commentary on the *Ch'un ch'iu* of the standard kind (that is to say, mainly treating ritual questions), and a voluminous chronicle which has been cut up (probably in the second century B.C.) in such a way that its narratives, brought in after the phrases of the *Ch'un ch'iu*, serve as a historical commentary to this little chronicle of Lu, which it has become a matter of habit to consider the work of Confucius. The authors of these two originally independent works are both unknown. The traditional attribution credits the whole work to a certain Tso-ch'iu Ming, or Tso Ch'iu-ming (for the precise form of his family name is not clear), who had been a disciple of Confucius and who, having become blind towards the end of his life, had composed this work to serve as a commentary to the work of his master. In reality, they are of far more recent date, and neither the one nor the other can be set farther back than the end of the fourth or the beginning of the third century.[21]

The chronicle which forms the greater part of the *Tso chuan* as we have it today[22] seems to have been in origin a real attempt to compose a history of China in the chronological framework of the history of Chin from the usurpation of Count Wu of Ch'ü-wu, in 678, to the assassination of the Count of Chih in 453, with an introduction summarizing the history of the counts of Ch'ü-wu starting from the time when their fief was established in the middle of the eighth century. As his base, the author took the chronicle of Chin, which I have mentioned, supplemented this with the chronicle of Ch'u, and added résumés or extracts from most of the historical or romantic works dealing with this period. He does not seem to have known the *Ch'un ch'iu*, since he knows very little about the state of Lu; and at times he contradicts it.

Two romances served as his sources for the principality of Ch'i: the *Kuan-tzu* and the *Yen-tzu ch'un ch'iu*. Two others were for Cheng: a biography, more or less romantic, of Chung of Chai, the minister of counts Chuang, Li, Chao, and Cheng from 743 to his death in 682; and a collection of philosophical and political anecdotes about Prince Tzu-ch'an, minister of that state in the middle of the sixth century. Yet another two seem to have covered the country of Wu: one on Wu Ch'en, recounting the amorous intrigues of this great lord of Ch'u, his flight to Chin and his journey to the land of Wu, which he organized against his former homeland; and the other on Wu Tzu-hsü, the minister of the last kings of Wu, recounting the struggles between that land and its neighbour, Yüeh. He utilized the chronicle of the principality of Wei and that of the princes of Ch'i who were of the T'ien family, though only the older portions of them, those in which the ancestors of these princely families were grand officers of Chin and Ch'i. He drew upon part of the *Shih ch'un*,[23] a collection of astrological anecdotes, the heroes of which were Pei Ts'ao of Cheng and Tzu Shen, and especially the scribe Mo of

Ts'ai. And he also took parts from a collection of ritual anecdotes, very famous in its day, attributed to the scribe Yin Yi, one of the ministers of King Ch'eng of Chou.

All these elements and others as well were blended in a whole which, despite the alterations of Han times, constitutes a truly remarkable work. It is perhaps better from the literary point of view than from the historical. The style is simple, the narrative lively and fresh; the speeches are neither too long, nor too full of vague commonplaces; the author had a feeling for dramatic situations, and knew how to hold and guide the reader's attention. What was most lacking was a psychological sense: his characters, even the most important, are always portrayed in a superficial way. They are seen to move, but not really to live. From the historical point of view, the indiscriminate use of romances and of properly historical works gives the work a very uneven value, depending upon the sources used. Despite all this, it is nonetheless an admirable depiction of Chinese life in antiquity.

Some of the sources which the author of the *Tso chuan* used have been exploited, though in a different way, by another writer — likewise unknown — who must have been a contemporary, or have lived at most a half-century afterwards. This was only a compiler, who collected historical anecdotes and discourses and classified them by country, without troubling to link them with a connected chronological narrative. He thus preserved lengthy fragments from the *Kuan-tzu* and various other works. His book, which has borne the title of *Kuo yü* since the Han dynasty, is devoid of either originality or unity. One has only to glance through the chapters on Wen of Chin, on the country of Cheng, on the struggle between Wu and Yüeh, to realize the considerable differences in the way the narratives are composed, and above all in the style. In sum, it is a collection of selected pieces, often of bare summaries.

This formula was successful, for it was imitated in the second half of the third century by yet another unknown writer, who made a collection of discourses by politicians of the recent past, entitled 'Documents of the Warring Kingdoms', *Chan-kuo ts'e*. Elements originating with romances unfortunately occupy rather more space in it than in earlier works. We must assume that this sort of work, which picked out the most interesting pieces, a sort of guide to the voluminous literature of the time, was pleasing to the Chinese; for it survived revolutions and still had successful imitators in Han times.

The historians at the end of the Chou dynasty seem to have

been groping for a formula which, lacking a critical sense, they were unable to create. History remained for them, in some degree, either a dry annalistic chronicle or a work of the imagination. It was not until Han times that the genius of Ssu-ma Ch'ien was able to perceive (in theory, if not always in practice) how to keep separate those elements which had hitherto been confused — romance and history.

8

The New Chinese Poetry of the Fourth and Third Centuries: Ch'ü Yüan

While all the literary genres were developed and regenerated from century to century, the poets of the fifth and fourth centuries continued to compose pieces in verse similar to those of the *Shih ching*: short little pieces modelled on popular songs or large pieces modelled on the religious odes. The great odes composed in about the fourth century, honouring the Count of Ch'in and engraved upon stone, which are commonly called 'The Stone Drums', are in the style of the religious pieces; and they also imitate certain portions of the *Shih ching* quite closely.[1] Light poems of the popular type fill the *Tso chuan* and the *Kuo yü*; several chapters of the *Lao-tzu* are in this sort of verse; Chuang-tzu also has several passages in verse, though he ordinarily prefers prose; and verse is to be found in romances such as the *Mu t'ien-tzu chuan*.

It was a poet of barbarian origin who seems, about the end of the fourth century, to have transformed Chinese poetry, not only in its inspiration but also in its subject matter and its form. Yüan of Ch'ü (also called P'ing of Ch'ü), who was also called Cheng-tse and Ling-chün, belonged to one of the great families of the kingdom of Ch'u, one which was descended from King Wu (740–690) and which took its name from the fief of Ch'ü. He was born about the middle of the fourth century.[2] His family's rank made him eligible for the highest posts at court: he was Left Director of the Multitude[3] under King Huai (328–299). Due to the intrigues of one of the courtiers, the Grand Officer Shang-kuan, who denounced him to the king, he was removed from his post and, as Ch'u was then engaged in a disastrous war with its neighbour Ch'in, he was sent on an embassy to the King of Ch'i to persuade that monarch to conclude an alliance against the western enemy. But the news of the defeat at Lan-t'ien (312), which arrived while he was at Lin-tzu, deprived him of any chance of success, if indeed there had ever been any. He returned to his homeland without having been able to achieve anything (311).

He apparently continued to live at the court where, even though he had been discharged from his official post, his family's power still left him an important position. In 299 he tried vainly to prevent King Huai from going to the fatal meeting at the Wu Pass, where the King of Ch'in had him kidnapped. Only a short time afterwards, a satire which he wrote against kings Huai and Ch'ing-hsiang, and especially against the latter's brother, Chief of Commands Tzu-lan, caused his banishment from the court (297). He seems to have retired south of the Yangtze River, near the River Hsiang on the bank of the River Mi-lo, in an area which was probably one of his family's domains. There he lived for about ten years,[4] sighing the regrets of the courtier exiled in the wilds; and he died there, probably very old[5] and in obscurity, in about 285,[6] without having been allowed to return to the court despite his ardent wish to do so.

Except for a collection of religious pieces, the *Chiu ko*, which seem to have had an official purpose, his works all date from the end of his life, in the time of his disgrace. His longest poem, the *Li sao*, seems to belong to the beginning of his exile;[7] the *Yüan yu* and the *Chiu chang* are from his last years.[8]

A man of Ch'u, Yüan of Ch'ü was a barbarian. Chinese was not his mother tongue, and from that perhaps comes a certain awkwardness of expression which Chinese have since noticed. From that also may come the pedantry, the desire to show off his knowledge of antiquity, in which we should probably see the slightly puerile vanity of the good student proud of his painfully acquired erudition.[9] But leaving aside these formal defects, he is one of the greatest poets the Chinese have known. He created a new genre, long poems in verse with a very free rhythm, in which the caesura is marked artificially by a sort of exclamation, *hsi*, which does not count in the metre.

This form, which appeared for the first time with him, differed completely from that of contemporary poets in the north, who carried on the prosodic patterns of the *Shih ching* more or less successfully. Perhaps Yüan imitated the rhythm of the popular poetry in the indigenous language of his homeland.[10] His earliest collection, the 'Nine Hymns', *Chiu ko*, is already in this genre. It is a series of religious pieces (eleven, to be exact) for ceremonies addressed, through the intermediacy of the sorceresses, to various divinities: the Greater and Lesser Directors of Destiny; the Princess of the East, goddess of the sun; the Count of the River; the goddesses of the River Hsiang (one of the tributaries of the Yangtze); and so on. These pieces differ widely in character, for the poet, having the sorceress speak, describes her voyages in search of the divinity and her visit at the goddess's abode in verse which is sometimes majestically calm (as in 'The Count of the River', *Ho-po*, or 'The Princess of the East', *Tung-chün*) and sometimes by contrast breathless and wild (in 'The Greater Director of Destiny', *Ta-ssu-ming*), like the very sensations of the sorceress in a trance.

Far more than in the form, however, his originality is shown in the subject matter of his poems. Ch'ü Yüan was the first in China to produce a personal lyricism, and this is the reason why, despite the interest of the *Chiu ko*, his other works are far more famous. He is himself the subject of all his work: these are his feelings, his sorrows, his regrets that he sings of, above all his despairs in exile. And he does it quite openly, without concealing his feelings under any veil of allegory, putting himself squarely on stage with a constant 'I'. He is inconsolable at having lost the royal favour, at having had to leave the court. One of his poems is entitled 'Regret for Past Days', *Hsi wang jih*, another 'Alas! Ying!', *Ai Ying*, and so on. All of his work is a long lament on the same theme.

> When I was young I loved this strange costume, grown
>   old I cannot console myself [to have left it behind].
> I wore the long sword that swung right and left, my cap
>   was tall enough to part the clouds,
> from my shoulders, like the resplendent moon, precious
>   pendants.
> This envious world knew me not: in my pride, I did not
>   cast my eyes [upon it];
> I mounted my chariot yoked to green dragons, drawn by
>   white dragons,
> I departed on a journey with Chung-hua [the mythical
>   emperor Shun] to the garden of the jewels [in the
>   K'un-lun Mountains],
> I crossed the K'un-lun, I ate of the flower of jade;
> I shall live as long as heaven and earth, my splendour
>   is like that of sun and moon.
> Alas! among the barbarians of the south, none has known me![11]

The theme which recurs most frequently in these verses is that of the voyage, whether in search of a sage or with the sage himself. This is the subject of his chief work, the *Li sao*, it is also the subject

of a little poem, the *Yüan yu*, and suggestions of it at least are to
be found in the *Hsi wang jih* and in the *Huai sha* of the *Chiu chang*.[12]
It is a clearly Taoist theme, and Ch'ü Yüan does no more than
give a poetic amplification to this passage from the *Chuang-tzu*:
'[The Perfect Man] mounts the wind and the clouds, he rides the
sun and the moon, he roams beyond the universe.'[13]

The *Li sao* is a true biography of the poet, often in allegorical
form, recounting his childhood, his first successes at court, then
his disgrace, his retirement and apparently his first attraction
towards the Taoist philosophy, his fruitless efforts to regain
favour with King Huai and his successor Ch'ing-hsiang, and at
the end his definitive withdrawal into seclusion. He had been
disgraced because he had believed he could speak too candidly:

> That crowd sought nothing but their own amusement,
> the path was dark and dangerous,
> how could I have stepped back out of fear for myself,
> when I dreaded lest the Illustrious Chariot [the
>   sovereign] suffer harm!
> Suddenly, I fell to running before, behind,
>   to make him follow in the footsteps of the former kings;
> the [prince, like an] iris flower, took no heed of my loyalty,
> he trusted the flatterers and fell into a rage.
> I well knew that firm and honest speech would put me
>   in the wrong,
> but I could not keep myself [from speaking out];
> I appealed to the Nine Heavens to set him right;
> Ah! it was only for [the prince's] vast and
>   transcendent Virtue![14]

Despite his sister's counsels, he was unwilling to be more
accommodating and had to leave the court. From this point on,
allegory gains the upper hand in the poem, and it is not always
easy to understand.[15] Grieving at his disgrace not for his own
sake, but for the prince, the poet pours out his complaints by the
tomb of the Sage-emperor Shun. At once a chariot drawn by
dragons comes to fetch him and bears him off to Mount K'un-
lun. With the chariot of the sun he roams about the world and
then seeks to penetrate to the abode of the Lord on High, but the
Lord's gatekeeper disdainfully refuses him entry. (This seems to
refer to his conversion to Taoism and his entry into the mystical
life, although this time he did not succeed in achieving Union
with the Principle.) Repulsed there, he returns then to earth and
tries successively to win the hand of two princesses of mythical
times; the Lady Fu, daughter of Fu-hsi, and the daughter of the
Prince of Sung, ancestress of the kings of the Yin dynasty. He

gives up the first because she is haughty and licentious; he is turned away from the second by the bad advice of his intermediaries and moreover because he understands that the Emperor Kao-hsin has preceded him, so that the beauty is no longer free.

From the way this tale is told, it seems to me that this rather bizarre allegory relates his relations with kings Huai and Ch'ing-hsiang and with Kao-hsin representing his enemy, the minister Tzu-lan, King Ch'ing-hsiang's brother, who succeeded in gaining the royal favour before he could himself. He thereupon renounces the court finally and, laying aside his regrets, withdraws into solitude, where he meditates upon the principles of the mystical life.

In his exile and isolation, indeed, Ch'ü Yüan fell back upon Taoism. He had recognized that 'Heaven and earth alone are free from trouble, / — alas! the life of man is one long misery,' and to lighten his sorrows, he had turned to mystical practices. His 'Distant Voyage', *Yüan yu*, is no longer, like the *Li sao*, the search for a prince, but the search for that Unity, for that First Principle, with which he wishes to unite himself: 'I pass through Non-Action, and I arrive at Purity, / — I am approaching the Sublime Beginning',[16] that is to say, the Tao. The *Yüan yu* is clearly a mystical reworking of the *Li sao*; and the better to mark his progress in the Way, the door of the celestial palace which the Lord's gatekeeper had kept disdainfully closed before him on his first voyage[17] is opened to him this time by the same personage. Preceded by the God of Thunder, Feng-lung, as courier before his chariot, he proceeds as far as the T'ai-wei Palace, is received at the court of the Lord on High, and beholds his Pure Capital, Ch'ing-tu. Before his departure, his guide describes the Tao[18] for him, and here one finds phrases taken word for word from Lao-tzu and Chuang-tzu.[19]

Yüan of Ch'ü was the leader of a small group of poets who were also great lords of Ch'u — his relatives, disciples, and friends — who composed works in the same style and form as his own. There is his nephew Sung Yü,[20] to whom is attributed a curious poem about Yüan's death, 'The Summons to the Soul', *Chao hun*,[21] as well as several less well known little pieces — 'Words of Advice', *Feng*, to the King of Ch'u; 'The Dance', *Wu*; and so on. And there is Ching Ch'a, who is sometimes considered the author of the 'Great Summons [to the Soul]', *Ta chao*, and of several other works.

Ch'ü Yüan's personal fame does not seem to have gone beyond the borders of Ch'u. He is not quoted during the third century except by Hsün-tzu, who passed all the end of his life in that country. However, the verse form that he had created, the *fu*, spread gradually. In the second half of the third century, at least two out of the five little *fu* which remained out of ten that Hsün-tzu had composed were clearly trying to imitate this rhythm.[22] At about the same time, there is mentioned a *fu* by King Yu of Chao, who was dethroned by the armies of Ch'in in 228. A little later a collection could be made of nine pieces in this genre composed by poets of the Ch'in dynasty.[23] But above all it was especially in the following century that Ch'ü Yüan became celebrated, when Ssu-ma Hsiang-ju, the great poet from the land of Shu, made him fashionable at the court of the emperors of the Han dynasty. From that time on, not only has his personal fame never been eclipsed, despite the difficulty of his works, but also the type of poem[24] of which his works give the first examplar, the *fu*, has always remained one of the most popular literary forms in all ages and to our own day.

9
The Scientific Movement and Foreign Influences

If the fourth and third centuries were marked by an intense zest for life and an originality which China scarcely knew thereafter, this was due in part to the new ideas brought in then by the first contacts, distant and limited though they were, with the Mediterranean civilizations. Spreading little by little, these finally succeeded in overthrowing the scientific ideas of the Chinese.

The Chinese seem to have come into direct contact with the Western world first in about the fifth century. The Persians had absorbed all the neighbouring older empires and, pushing their arms far to the east, they had unified all the Iranian tribes under their rule. Darius had conquered the great plains which formed the eastern and northern slopes of the Iranian plateau, eastwards to the Punjab in India and northwards to Bactriana and Sogdiana. In the relative order and safety which the new regime imposed, ongoing and regular relations could be set up. And across the countries of the Tarim Basin, with their Indo-European languages, caravans began to carry merchandise, and also ideas — very simple ones, at least — from the West towards the Far East. Curiously enough, it seems to have been Hindus, and not Iranians, who carried on this Far Eastern link. The Hindu traders, however, probably did not go so far as China itself: they seem to have stopped around Lan-chou, where they found the terminus of Chinese shipping on the Yellow River. According to the *Yü kung*,[1] Chinese shipping went further up, as far as Chi-shih, which is said to have been near modern Ho-chou (Kansu). That must have been where the princes of Ch'in established the Commandery of Lung-hsi, after the barbarian lands were conquered in the third century.

What China received thus were initially quite simple ideas. The foreigners who came there were not philosophers, and they were concerned above all with their business dealings; and in addition the Chinese they encountered were equally uncultivated. To start with, they brought geographical knowledge. The Chinese suddenly learned of an unknown world to the west, of which they had had no inkling and to which they had never gone. They took in all that the travellers told them, items of genuine geography and of mythical geography at the same time (their informants made virtually no distinction between the two). They learned that in the west lay the sacred mountain of the Indians, Meru, with its four rivers which, after circling the mountain, went and emptied into the ocean, each towards one of the cardinal directions. They even believed that this could be identified with a place in their own geography, the K'un-lun, which had nothing in common with it, but which superficial similarities caused them to confuse with it. In fact, Meru was made to serve a double purpose when it came to China: as a simple geographical fact it became the K'un-lun; but as the mountain of the gods, set in the midst of the ocean and resting upon a tortoise, it became the Isles of the Immortals, situated in the middle of the sea upon tortoises, and it was placed in the only ocean the Chinese knew, the Eastern Ocean. At the end of the third century, expeditions seem to have been sent to sea to look for them, as Chang Ch'ien, a century later, seems to have looked in vain for the K'un-lun in central Asia.

The Chinese learned from the foreigners things that they had not known before; but they had for several centuries been able to construct the elements of a sort of geography, into which they had already put almost all that they have demanded of that science in any age: administrative descriptions and lists of rivers and mountains. These two classes of documents were also of differing origins and were certainly considered as works of entirely different kinds.

It was the needs of government which had created political geography. In Western Chou times, the scribes seem to have drawn up various reports in administrative style on the general situation of the empire, province by province, especially as regards taxes, the yield of the land, and so on. It is one of these reports — or more likely a literary essay in that genre — which constitutes the prose portion of the *Yü kung*, one of the chapters of the *Shu ching*, which seems to date from the eighth century B.C. In that work each of the nine provinces is briefly covered: its mountains and rivers, the class of its land, that of its taxes, and finally the route for tribute to the capital of the mythical emperor Yao. The territory described in it seems to be that of the Chou Empire at its greatest extent. Another small work, similar but probably later, and corresponding to another arrangement of the provinces, is to be found in the *Chou li*.

Besides these documents of an administrative kind, the catalogues of rivers and mountains were, by contrast, drawn up to meet religious requirements. It was necessary to establish the list of those to which, four times a year, the Son of Heaven sent envoys to carry out official sacrifices on the spot. The first such lists seem to have been compiled in very ancient times. One of them from the end of the Eastern Chou has been preserved: the *Wu tsang ching*, which today makes up the first of the treatises in the small collection called *Shan hai ching*.[2] This clearly shows the impact of foreign influences in its description of the mountains of the Far West.

The *Wu tsang ching* describes twenty-six mountain chains: three in the south, four in the west, three in the north, four in the east, twelve in the centre. The author was certainly a man of Lo-yi, as is shown by the importance he gives to describing the environs of that city and of the private domain of the Chou kings;[3] and he seems to have lived about the end of the fourth century.[4] His geographical horizon is not very broad: to the north he gets almost to the edges of the desert, and he places the Northern Sea, the Moving Sands, *liu-sha*, some hundreds of *li* farther on; to the south he is well acquainted with the mountains which hem in the small northern coastal plains of Chekiang in the land of Yüeh, those which form the southern border of the T'ung-t'ing Lake basin, and finally those of Shu, the Ch'eng-tu region in Szechuan. Yet farther on he places two very vaguely defined chains of mountains well spaced out, which begin in the west at the Western Sea and end in the east at the Eastern Sea and which symbolize — in their eastern portion — the mountains which define the southern edge of the Yangtze basin, beyond which nothing is known. To the west, beyond the sources of the Wei, he knows only a single mountain, Yen-tzu, where the sun sets, on the shore of the Western Sea. He locates this 360 *li* from the headwaters of the Wei but near the sources of the Yellow River; and beyond that to the west he sets an immense chain which also ends at the shore of the Western Sea.

In the description of this western region, all the elements imported from abroad are mixed with Chinese traditions. In particular, the author has sought to systematize the data from a romance of the period, the *Mu t'ien-tzu chuan*. There, in the fabulous lands where the Queen Mother of the West, *Hsi wang mu*, dwells on the Jade Mountain, is Mount K'un-lun, from which spring four rivers, one from each face. One of these is the Yellow River which, after circling the mountain and traversing the Bottomless Water, *Wu-ta shui*, emerges from there towards the southwest, through the Stone Gate at the Mountain of Heaped-up Stones, *Chi-shih shan* (an ancient name from the *Yü kung*, but shifted very far to the west); it then flows eastward across the Lands of the West as far as Lake Yu (Lob Nor?), into which it flows, and from which a course, first subterranean but soon above ground, leads it to China. Throughout this region stretches the desert, 'the Shifting Sands', *liu-sha*, which the author rather seems to have imagined as a sort of river of liquid sand, and which it is necessary to cross to reach the Jade Mountain.

About the same period annotated maps of the world began to appear. These were supposed to be reproductions of the patterns which Yü the Great had engraved upon the Nine Tripods,[5] and they had been affected, even more than the *Wu tsang ching*, by foreign influences. The maps seem to have represented the world as square, surrounded by the four seas, with sketches portraying the gods, the foreign peoples, and the monsters who inhabit the borders of the world, and the name of each one written next to the drawing. The maps are lost, only the written notes being preserved in several different texts: the *Hai wai ching* ('Classic of the World beyond the Seas') and the *Ta-mang ching* ('Classic of the Great Peaks') of the *Shan hai ching*; and the *Hai wai san shih liu kuo* ('Thirty-six Lands beyond the Seas') of the *Huai-nan-tzu*. In these notes the old Chinese legends are mixed in rather random fashion with elements of Hindu, and even Greek, folklore, all in an extremely concise form.[6] All of these works are totally lacking in any literary value, and even more in geographic value; but they let us see one of the curious aspects of the influence of foreigners upon the Chinese mind in this period.

This enlargement of their geographic horizon, however inaccurate it may have been, had obliged the Chinese to modify the childish conception of the world they had produced. From the Hindus they had already learned that the world is made up of seven continents, great islands surrounded by water, arranged around Meru, the great central mountain about which the sun and the moon revolve, and that their country did not constitute the entire world, *t'ien-hsia*, but only one of the continents, just as the land of the Hindus was another. These ideas broke new ground and, at the end of the fourth century, Tsou Yen,[7] joining them to the ancient Chinese tradition that the (Chinese) world was divided into nine *chou*, taught that around K'un-lun, the centre of the world, were disposed nine continents, *chou*, each surrounded by a girdle of seas which prevented them from communicating with one another, with the ocean, *ta-ying-hai*, surrounding the whole. He taught that China, which scholars called 'the Kingdoms of the Centre', was itself only a ninth of one of these continents, the southeastern one; that the sun and the moon made the round of heaven incessantly without ever descending below the horizon, passing over the nine continents, above which they appeared to rise and set successively; and that the phenomena of day and night were in reality due only to distance, the sun being visible when it was near and invisible when it was far away.

He introduced this description into a general system of the world which was in other respects purely Chinese. He tried to fit into it the theory of the *yin* and the *yang* and that of the Five Elements, by conceiving of these as arranged so as to succeed one another in the order in which the one triumphed over another. He also extended this influence of *yin* and *yang*, as well as that of the Five Elements, to human affairs, by bringing the succession of dynasties into relation with that of the Five Elements. Each dynasty reigned by the Virtue of one of the elements (Shun by the earth, the Hsia by wood, the Yin by metal, the Chou by fire) and triumphed over its predecessor as its element triumphed over the preceding element.

This theory aroused all the more attention and had all the more success since in this period the Chinese were remodelling their astronomy under Western influence. Until that time they had had only the vaguest notions about this science, no more than they needed to establish a rather fictitious correlation between the celestial movements and their own inexact calendar. Certain brilliant stars, certain figures traced in the sky by popular imagination, had been given names and these served as markers for the seasons. By making observations a little after sundown, when the stars begin to be visible — so that Antares, or the Pleiades, or Aquarius[8] was passing over a point which they considered as marking precisely the south of their observatory — they believed that they could determine the precise days for the solstices and the equinoxes, which they knew to be approaching by the lengthening or shortening of the days and nights. But the rough way they divided the day into unequal periods and their lack of instruments for measuring time precluded their knowing exactly which day was the longest, or the shortest.

Their observations seem, moreover, to have been mediocre,

for they were able to determine the length of the solar year only approximately, reckoning it as 366 whole days.⁹ The period of time between new moons had been better calculated, though not well enough so that eclipses of the sun did not sometimes fall outside its first day.

As for the day, they divided it roughly into five periods of unequal length, depending upon the seasons: dawn, *mei-chuang*, or cock-crow, *chi-ming*; morning, *chao*; noon, *jih-chung*; afternoon, *jih-tse*; and twilight, *hun*, or sunset, *jih-ju*. Following these came the five watches of the night, which were also unequal.

On these foundations they had established a luni-solar calendar which was quite inexact, in which as a rule two supplementary months were to be intercalated for every five-year period.¹⁰ This kind of five-year calendar was in theory the one used during all of the Chou dynasty. It goes without saying that it could not be followed in practice. Even if it had been tried to start with, it had been abandoned by the end of the eighth century; and the *Ch'un ch'iu*, as well as the *Tso chuan*, show highly irregular intercalations. People consoled themselves at the impossibility of bringing theory and practice into agreement by saying that it was the corruption of the times and the evil governance of the world which caused the difficulty. It was not the calendar that had to be changed, it was the government: if a sage-king had returned into the world, the theoretical calendar would have found itself in accord with the reality.

It was foreigners who gave the Chinese the first scientific notions of astronomy. They acquainted them with the rudimentary instruments of ancient astronomy, the gnomon and probably also the water clock. They taught them the difference between stars and planets and showed them the movements of those heavenly bodies. There seem to have been two great waves of foreign influence, the first coinciding roughly, though not without some lag, to the period of Darius's conquests and the second to those of Alexander in India and central Asia.

The first wave probably brought in the division of the horizon by means of the twenty-eight mansions, *hsü*. Foreign astrologers searched the Chinese sky for most of the star-groups they were habituated to examining at home; but they were forced to take account of groupings of stars which the Chinese had already conceptualized. After some hesitation, it seems, they reached a definitive accommodation.¹¹ They also taught the Chinese to distinguish between planets and stars by demonstrating their movements — those of Jupiter, at least: they showed how that planet made the circuit of the heavens in twelve years and taught them how to derive from that the elements of a cycle, first astrological, and later chronological, in the first half of the fourth century B.C.[12]

The second wave brought notions which were more precise and more mathematical. The Chinese learned to measure the celestial sphere in degrees equal to the sun's daily progression through the twenty-eight *hsü*, in the course of its apparent annual motion across the sky, and to calculate the exact day of the winter solstice with the aid of certain stars. They adopted the Babylonian division of the day into twelve double-hours. They drew up their first catalogues of the stars, about the middle of the fourth century: that of Kan Te in the state of Ch'i, that of Shih Shen in Wei, and that which is attributed to the mythical Wu Hsien.[13] They began to observe the retrograde movements of Venus and Mars.[14] Finally, towards the end of the fourth century, the foreign astrologers taught them to determine the beginning of the year scientifically according to the vernal equinox, and also to apply the Babylonian embolismic method of intercalating months, a nineteen-year cycle in which the intercalary month was regularly placed after the autumnal equinox.

It was upon these principles that the most ancient Chinese astronomical calendar was based, the one which is called 'the calendar of Chuan-hsü'. In it, to accommodate to the Chinese custom of solstices and equinoxes in the middle of the seasons, the calculations have been carried back to an arbitrary date, the Establishment of Spring, *li-ch'un*, forty-five days before the equinox. A reform of this calendar, probably designed to simplify calculations by making them start from a real date, but also due in large measure to astrological considerations, received the name of the Yin calendar.[15] In it, the calculations were carried back to the date of the winter solstice, which remained the basis of all Chinese calendrical calculations until the introduction of European theories. The calendar of Chuan-hsü was officially adopted in the state of Ch'in during the first half of the third century,[16] and it remained in use until the reform of 104 B.C., under the Han.

At the same time that they brought astronomy, foreigners had brought the principles of astrology to China. The *Tso chuan*, and perhaps the *Kuo yü* even more, are filled with astrological observations. The heavens were divided into nine sectors, *fen-yeh*, to each of which corresponded one of the nine terrestrial regions. There were also divisions into twelve sectors (with twelve terrestrial provinces) and even into thirteen; but these seem to have been less widely accepted. Observations were made of the movements of the planets, their retrogressions and their conjunctions, and of the changes in the brilliance and the colour of certain stars, and so on. Everything that occurred in the heavenly sector allowed prognostication of coming events in the corresponding terrestrial region. The observation of haloes around the sun or moon, of the wind, of clouds, of rainbows, and so forth completed the system. These ideas corresponded so well to the ancient ideas regarding the reciprocal influence of good government and the physical world that they had an immense and lasting success. By the end of the fourth century they were accepted everywhere.

This astronomy and astrology with their scientific tendencies demanded some knowledge of geometry, and in fact it was in this period that the first rudimentary notions of mathematics were introduced into China. Foreigners taught Chinese the properties of geometric figures, particularly those of the circle ('the circle has a single centre with equal radii') and of the square. They also taught the identity of these properties, regardless of size or material: 'the figure of a small circle is like that of a large circle', and 'all squares have exactly the same shape: they all come from the same model, though they are distinct; whether they are made of wood or stone makes no difference to the identity of squares.' And the foreigners also brought the elementary mathematical instruments: the set-square for making right angles, the compass for drawing curves, and so on.[17]

Above all, foreigners thus introduced a whole structure of new sciences and technical methods. For some time China must have been a place full of possibilities for exploitation by astrologers, by alchemists, by doctors, by augurers of all sorts who came from India or Iran to seek their fortune. Then indigenous schools were formed, which sought to force all these new doctrines into the frameworks of indigenous theories, that of the Five Elements, that of the *yin* and the *yang*, and so on, claiming to stem from ancient sages: Shen-nung, Chuan-hsü, Yao, Shun, and above all Huang-ti. Gradually they invaded the older schools, which usually made room for them: at the end of the fourth century the astrologers had their official rank at the royal court, alongside the diviners by the tortoise-shell and the milfoil, and the interpreters of dreams. Thus little by little disciplines of foreign origin became acclimatized and naturalized, and a certain number of Western ideas penetrated into indigenous sciences. The unification of the empire at the end of the third century and direct contact with strangers from the West could only accelerate this process.

From the point of view of ideas as well as institutions, the third century witnessed the final break-up of the ancient world. A new China was about to be born.

Notes

Page references to the text are given at the head of each page of notes. Numbers in parentheses indicate the point in *La Chine antique* (1965) where the first note on the page appears.

Common Abbreviations

BEFEO	*Bulletin de l'Ecole française d'Extrême-Orient*
Ch. Cl.	Legge's *Chinese Classics*
J. As.	*Journal Asiatique*
J. Roy. As. Soc.	*Journal of the Royal Asiatic Society*
ch.	*chüan* (chapter)
TP	*T'oung Pao*
Var. Sin.	*Variétés sinologiques*

In Chinese books, pagination is done by chapters (*chüan*). Moreover, pages have only a single number for obverse and reverse, which are indicated here by the letters *a* and *b*.

Book I: The Beginnings

Chapter 1. The Primitive Chinese World

1 Andersson, *An Early Chinese Culture* (Peking, 1923), has pointed out the similarities between Chinese pottery of the transition period from the Stone Age to the Bronze Age and that of certain localities of central Asia, especially Susa (Persia), Tripolje (Caucasus) and Anau (Turkestan). Arne, *Painted Stone Age Pottery from the Province of Honan, China* (Peking, 1925), has revived the question and extended the circle of comparison. He has proposed dating the Chinese pieces from about 3000 B.C. It is not necessary to suppose, as Arne does, that this pottery was introduced into China by civilizing invaders from the west. The more cautious Andersson mentions only the migration of art and technique, the ordinary flow of exchange and attempts at imitation suffice to explain these facts. Cf. Pelliot, *Jades archaïques de la Chine* (1925), p. 9.

2   For a geographical description of China, see *Histoire du Monde* (E. Cavaignac, ed.), I, p. 209 ff.

3   In ancient China there were two small states whose names, written with different characters, and formerly pronounced differently, are now, in the Peking Mandarin which serves as a standard for sinologists, exact homophones even in their tone. To distinguish them without inserting the characters, I use an arbitrary procedure which should not suggest any difference in pronunciation. [Wey is to be taken as the smaller, ancient state to which this note is appended; and Wei denotes the greater, later state, one of the 'Three Chin' produced when the state of Chin broke up in 453 B.C. The River Wei, a name which recurs often and also has the same sound, is written with yet a third character; but as there is no possibility of confusing it, I make no distinction for it. See also Ch'ii on p. 8 below, designating another small state, a close neighbour of the great Ch'i, and specifying it by this variant romanization.]

4   Henri Maspero, 'Les Origines de la civilization chinoise' (*Annales de Géographie*, 1926, pp. 138–42). Ku Tung-kao has collected the references to the various barbarian tribes scattered through the *Ch'un ch'iu* and its commentaries into a series of tables forming chapter 39 of his *Ch'un ch'iu ta shih piao* (*Huang Ch'ing ching chieh hsü pien, ch.* 118). These have been summarized by Legge, *Ch. Cl.*, V, 1, *Prolegomena*, p. 122 ff. The fullest note on this question is by Plath, 'Die fremden barbarischen Stämme in alten China' (*Sitz. b. Philos. Cl. Ak. Wissensch. München*, 1874), but it is uncritical. The ancient Chinese had no general term expressing the idea of 'barbarians'. They distinguished the Ti, the Jung, the Man, and the Yi, terms now taken to mean barbarians of the north, of the west, of the south, and of the east. This signification is no more than very roughly accurate for the ancient Chinese. Only the terms Ti and Yi have a specific meaning: the Ti are a distinct group of tribes making up confederations in what is now Shansi, and the Yi are barbarians of the Shantung peninsula. Jung and Man seem to have been general terms, the former for all the barbarians west and south of the Yellow River, the latter for the peoples of the Yangtze.

5   The *Li chi*, trans. Couvreur, I, 295 (cf. Plath, op. cit., p. 452) declares that they lived in caves, wore skins, and did not cook rice, exactly opposite to the Chinese way of life. No importance should be attached to this passage, which is found in the *Wang chih* chapter, one of the latest in the *Li chi* compilation. It dates from the middle of the second century B.C., a period when the Ti had already long been assimilated. It is moreover not a geographic and ethnographic but a theoretical description of the barbarians of the four regions, in which traits opposite to the customs of the Chinese are arbitrarily assigned to them.

6   For all modern names, I give that in use prior to the administrative reform of 1914, as this is the only one to be found on the maps. However, the names of some districts were changed in this reform.

Prefectures of the first class, *fu*, were replaced by circuits, *tao*, and prefectures of the second and third classes, *chou* and *t'ing*, were abolished leaving only the sub-prefectures, *hsien*. To describe all these names as modern is not therefore absolutely correct.

7 For the San Hu see the *Shih chi, ch.* 110, 2*b*; for the autumn assembly of the Huns, ibid., 4*b*; for the Mo, see Mencius, trans. Legge, p. 442.

8 There are two rivers with the name Lo, both tributaries of the Yellow River. One in Honan passes Ho-nan-fu and the other in Shensi flows into the Yellow River at the same place as the Wei. The word Lo is written by the same character for both, and there is no way of distinguishing between them. As they are far apart, however, there is little likelihood of confusing them.

9 I cannot understand why most European historians have insisted that all the peoples who were called barbarians were of a totally different origin from the Chinese. F. Hirth, *The Ancient History of China*, p. 168, is so thoroughly convinced that Ti and Jung are 'Tartars' that he inserts this word on his own authority in a text of Ssu-ma Ch'ien which does not contain it. Likewise A. Tschepe in his *Histoire du pays de Tsin* regularly renders the words Ti and Jung as Tartars. Recently De Groot, *Die Hunnen der vorchristlichen Zeit* (1921), p. 5, proposes taking the word Ti, to which he wrongly attributes an ancient pronunciation Tik, as a transcription of Turk. The main reason for all this appears to be that Ssu-ma Ch'ien, in his *Shih chi, ch.* 110, makes the Jung and the Ti the ancestors of the Hsiung-nu (Huns). This simply proves, however, that in his time these peoples had been assimilated, and barbarians were no longer considered foreigners.

10 *Tso chuan*, trans. Legge, p. 464, year 560.

11 Henri Maspero, 'Légendes mythologiques dans le Chou king, I: La légende de Hi et Ho', pp. 29–37, *J. As.*, 1924, p. 204, contains all the references to the Chinese texts from which the above is taken.

12 In my article (op. cit., p. 33) I placed these eight pillars beneath the earth, but this is wrong. The context in the *T'ien Wen* shows that they were imagined as above the earth, upholding the sky, placed symmetrically at the four cardinal points and at the four intermediary points. The *Huai-nan tzu, ch.* 4, 27*b*, reckons them in this way, cf. Erkes' translation, 'Das Weltbild des Huai-nan tze', *Ostasiatische Zeitschrift*, V, 1916–1917, pp. 53–54. However, the *Ho t'u k'o ti hsiang*, a work which appears to date from former Han times, places them beneath the earth under the K'un-lun Mountains: 'The K'un-lun Mountain is the pillar of the sky. ... The K'un-lun is the centre of the earth; under the earth there are eight pillars 100,000 *li* long,' etc. (*Ch'u hsüeh chi, ch.* 5; *Tai-p'ing yü-lan, ch.* 35; *Ku wei shu, ch.* 32, 4*a*; *Shou shan ko ts'ung shu* edition.)

13 *Huai-nan-tzu, ch.* 3, 2*a* (*ch'i-lin*); *ch.* 17, 1*b* (*tan-chu*).

14 *Shan hai ching*, sec. 8, 42*a*; sec. 17, 83*a*.

15 By the Neolithic Age, the inhabitants of North China were, in anthropological type, almost the same as today. See Black, 'The

human skeleton remains from Sha kuo t'un' and 'A note on the physical characters of the prehistoric Kansu race' (Peking, 1925).

Cf. Biot, 'Recherches sur les moeurs des anciens Chinois d'après le Chi-king', in *J. As.*, IV, ii (1843), p. 310 (English translation by Legge, *Ch. Cl.*, IV, *Prolegomena*, p. 144). For portraits of women see *Shih ching*, Legge, *She King*, pp. 95, 77, 102. Of the portraits of men, the first is taken from the *Tung-kuan Han chi* (first century A.D.), the second from the *Chin ch'i chü chu* (fourth century A.D.), works which have been lost but are quoted in the *T'ai-p'ing yü lan*; the third is the portrait of Lao-tzu in the *Shen hsien chuan*.

The dragon's nose is not prominent and does not stand out at the bridge.

16 *Shih shuo hsin yü*, ch. 3B, 7*b*.

17 A complete review of the theories on the origins of the Chinese is in Cordier, *Histoire générale de la Chine*, I, pp. 5–37.

18 Conrady, who clearly saw the impossibility of establishing a relationship between Chinese and the families to which Mongols, Manchus, Japanese, Koreans, etc., belong, set up a vast group of languages in which he lumped together Chinese, Thai, Tibeto-Burman languages, Himalayan languages, Malay and Austronesian languages, Mon-Khmer languages, Nicobarese, etc. ('Neue austrisch-indochinesische Parallelen', in *Asia Major*, Hirth Anniversary Volume (1923), p. 23 ff.). The theory, if not improbable, is at least premature; moreover, the comparisons are often too superficial to be convincing.

19 Tones, as with other phonetic elements in kindred words of Chinese and the Thai languages, show regular patterns. It is, therefore, not a matter of an independent development within each family, but of an element which goes back to their common period. Edkins's theory ('The Evolution of Chinese Language', *J. Peking Oriental Soc.*, II (1887), pp. 1–91; and also numerous articles in the *China Review*), which he believed could establish the chronology of Chinese tone-formation, and Conrady's (*Causativ-denominativ Bildung in den indochinesischen Sprachen*), which did the same for Siamese, must thus be rejected altogether.

20 Karlgren in 'Le proto-chinois, langue flexionnelle', *J. As.*, 1920, pp. 205–32, has recently tried to rediscover traces of inflexion in the way personal pronouns were used in some ancient Chinese texts. But to me his conclusions go far beyond his premises.

21 An excellent and very clear account of the elements in the formation of the Chinese language and writing is to be found in B. Karlgren, *Sound and Symbol in Chinese* (1923).

22 This is a matter only of cultural, not of ethnic, relations. In the present state of our knowledge, nobody can have even an approximate idea what races, anthropologically speaking, lie concealed under the purely geographical, linguistic, social and political denominations of Chinese, Lolo, Miao-tzu, Tibetans, Burmese, Thai, Vietnamese, etc.

23 Chinese civilization is generally supposed to have been born in the west, in the Wei Valley and southern Shansi, and to have moved eastward from there into the great plain. This is a quite improbable theory, although sanctioned by long use. It has had the good fortune that all the prejudices which have been successively applied to the study of ancient China favoured it. Conrady, *China*, p. 522, was the first to abandon it, placing the origin of Chinese civilization astride the middle course of the Yellow River between southern Shansi and northern Honan, from which it spread east and west. This theory is, however, counter to the fact that some centuries before the time of Christ all the mountains of this region were still in the hands of the barbarians, who thus cut in two the domain which it would regard as proper to the Chinese. Cf. H. Maspero, 'Les Origines de la civilisation chinoise' (*Annales de Géographie*, 1926, pp. 135–54).

24 Fujita, 'The River Huang in the Reign of Yü' (*Shinagaku*, I, xii (1921), pp. 1–32), exaggerates the pace at which deposits from the Yellow River on the floor of the Gulf of Chihli built up the shoreline. He represents the sea as extending, in the third century B.C., as far as the environs of An-chou and Kao-yang hsien, a few kilometres from Pao-ting fu and about 150 kilometres from the present-day coastline. I believe that in historical times the shore of the gulf must have been at most near Tientsin and that the entire region lying upstream from there was, not a gulf, but an immense marsh, the 'Nine Rivers'. In the *Yü kung* (*Shu ching*, III, I, ii, II, 9–14 Legge, pp. 137–41) the country between the Yellow River and the Chi (which constituted the province of Yen) is a region of bush which the colonists were in the process of making useful by clearing it, and to encourage them the new lands brought into cultivation were exempted from taxes, *fu*, for thirteen years.

25 For the history of the rhinoceros in China, see Laufer, *Chinese Clay Figures*, I, pp. 1–173. There are two Chinese words, *ssu* and *hsi*, both generally translated as 'rhinoceros', and which, according to Laufer, actually designate two varieties of rhinoceros. Laufer's explanation is conclusive for modern times. But the drawing of the character *ssu* on the Yin tortoise-shells, an animal whose head seen from the front has two horns curving backward symmetrically placed on each side of the head, appears to me to exclude the rhinoceros for this word in this remote epoch (see *Yin hsü shu ch'i, ch.* 1, 50*a*, 51*a*, 51*b*, etc.; and cf. Gotō, 'Study on the Chinese Ancient Characters Carved on "Tortoise Shells" ' in *Tōyō Gakuhō*, IV (1914), pp. 38–40). A true rhinoceros is portrayed on a bronze attributed to the Yin period and reproduced from the *Po ku t'u lu* by Laufer (op. cit., p. 130).

There is an account of hunting the wild ox (?), *ssu*, in the *Shih ching*, Legge, p. 292, *Chu shu chi nien*, in Legge, *Shoo King*, p. 149; *Chan kuo ts'e, ch.* 5, 5*a*; and hunting for rhinoceros, *hsi*, is mentioned in *Chu shu chi nien*, p. 153.

26 Henri Maspero, 'Les Origines de la civilisation chinoise', pp. 146–47.

27 *Tso chuan*, p. 5.

28 *Mencius*, p. 208.

29 Ku Tung-kao, *Ch'un ch'iu ta shih piao*, ch. 72 (*Huang Ch'ing ching chieh hsü pien*, ch. 792, 12a; photolithographic edition, ch. 19, *chung*, 6a): southwest of present-day Shang-ch'iu hsien in Kuei-te prefecture is a wall of 300 paces, popularly called the O-t'ai (or Yüeh-t'ai, as it appears in the *Tu shih fang yü chi yao*, ch. 50, 16b, which places it three *li* from the modern sub-prefecture).

30 *Tu shih fang yü chi yao*, ch. 41, 32a: fifteen *li* southeast of the present-day sub-prefecture of Yi-ch'eng hsien is the ancient wall of Yi, the ancient Chiang of the state of Chin; the wall is two *li* around.

31 See the standardized description of the capital in the fourth century B.C. in *Chou li*, ch. 41, 20a–21a, trans. Biot, II, pp. 555–64.

32 *Shih ching*, pp. 600, 368, 373.

33 H. Maspero, '*Légendes mythologiques dans le Chou king*, II: Les légendes dites du Déluge', *J. As.*, 1924, pp. 47–94.

34 For the cycle of the legends of Yü the Great, see Granet, *Danses et légendes de la Chine ancienne* II, pp. 466–572.

35 Granet, *Danses et légendes*, I, p. 376, II, p. 572, etc., endeavours to distinguish two legends, that of Yi the Excellent Archer and that of Yi the Wicked Archer. As a matter of fact, the Chinese historiographers have introduced two successive Yis into their narratives. But for them this is simply a matter of chronological arrangement, and wherever concern for this does not interfere, there is only the one hero to whom the slaughter of all the monsters is attributed. The legend, as contrasted with history, recognizes only one Yi, so that after having established the general distinction, Granet notes in almost every individual case (actually for each of the incidents which have not been construed as history since ancient times) that we do not know which Yi is meant.

36 I deem it sufficient to sum up briefly the legends which comprise what is called the history of the origins of China as constituted in the Chou period, and reject anything that seems to be a later accretion, such as the legend of P'an-ku, etc. For further details, see Cordier, *Histoire générale de la Chine* (1920), I, pp. 102–15; Wieger, *Textes historiques* (1929), I, pp. 23–97; Puini, *Le Origini della civiltà secondo la tradizione e la storia dell' Estremo-Oriente* (1891); Wedemeyer, 'Schauplätze und Vorgänge der altchinesischen Geschichte' (*Asia Major*, prelim. vol.).

37 Chavannes, *Les Mémoires historiques de Se-ma Ts'ien*, I, introd., p. cxl.

38 Granet, *Danses et légendes*, II, pp. 395–590, gives a description of the dynastic dances which is quite different from the above. This is primarily due to the fact that I am speaking of the formal and comparatively late ceremonies in the ancestral temples whereas Granet studied the most primitive characteristics of the dances.

Chapter 2. *The Dawn of History: the Yin Dynasty*

1 In 1898–99, inundations of the Yüan River carried away the soil at the village of Hsiao-t'un near An-yang-hsien, in Chang-te prefecture, in extreme northern Honan north of the Yellow River, and brought to light fragments of inscribed tortoise-shell. The peasants excavated the neighbourhood and unearthed several thousand similar fragments as well as several objects of bronze, ivory, etc. The discovery was purchased by Mr. Wang I-jung, who however lost his life in the Boxer insurrection of 1900, and his collection was sold by his son to Liu O (whose *tzu* was T'ieh-yün), who in 1903 published photographic facsimiles of rubbings of the inscriptions under the title of *T'ieh-yün ts'ang kuei*. Sun I-jang made the first decipherment in his *Ch'i wen chü li* (1904). This work was revised and completed in 1910 by Lo Chen-yü in a work entitled *Yin hsü shu ch'i k'ao shih*. In 1919, Wang Kuo-wei, in the archaeological review *I shu ts'ung pien*, no. 16, made a fresh study of them in his article *Chien-shou t'ang so ts'ang Yin hsü wen tzu k'ao shih*. The discovery was first made known in America by the Rev. Chalfant, 'Early Chinese Writing', in *Memoirs of the Carnegie Museum*, IV, no. 1 (1906); but it was Chavannes, 'La Divination par l'écaille de tortue dans la haute antiquité chinoise d'après un livre de M. Lo Tchen-yu' (*J. As.*, X, xvii (1911), pp. 127–37), who made the first study of it in Europe, soon followed by Hopkins, 'Chinese writing in the Chou dynasty in the light of recent discoveries' (*J. Roy. As. Soc.*, 1911, pp. 1011–38). Since that time Hopkins has published a series of articles relative to the deciphering of these documents. Finally, Jung Keng has lately provided a sort of recapitulated table of the results attained, followed by an excellent Chinese bibliography on the question in an article 'The Discovery of the Bone Inscriptions and Their Deciphering' in *Kuo-hsüeh chi k'an*, I, iv (Oct. 1923), pp. 655–73. See also Tchang Fong, *Recherches sur les os du Honan et quelques caractères de l'écriture ancienne* (Paris, 1925), pp. 3–9; and for later books and articles, Kuo Mo-jo, *Chia ku wen tzu yen chiu* (Shanghai, 1930), introd., pp. 1–3.

Besides inscribed shells, various objects of rhinoceros horn, ivory, jade, bronze, and fragments of pottery have been found and studied by Lo Chen-yü, *Yin hsü ku ch'i wu t'u lu* (*I shu ts'ung pien*, 1916, 4th–6th months), and by Hamada (*Kokka*, 1921, no. 379). Several others are included in Lu's collection, where they are described by Pelliot, *Jades archaïques de Chine appartenant à C. T. Loo* (Paris, 1925). Furthermore, Lo Chen-yü has published his beautiful collection of rubbings of inscriptions on bronze vases attributed to the Yin, under the title of *Yin wen ts'un*, in the *I shu ts'ung pien*, 1917, fourth month. In December 1928, Tung Tso-pin carried out some excavations for a fortnight and found bones and shells. He has published a work with reproductions of the inscriptions, translation, and commentary in *Hsin huo pu tz'u hsieh pen*, and a small pamphlet with maps which is the first scientific account of the excavations at Hsiao-t'un.

2 For the date of these inscriptions, cf. Lo Chen-yü, *Yin hsü shu ch'i k'ao shih*, p. 1 *a–b*, and p. 104*a*; Wang Kuo-wei, *Chien-shou t'ang so ts'ang Yin hsü wen tzu k'ao shih*, p. 10*b* (in *I shu ts'ung pien*, year 1919, eighth month). Over half the kings of Yin are mentioned in the inscriptions, up to the twenty-eighth and twenty-ninth; but the two last do not appear at all. It is therefore likely that the next to last king, Ti-i, was the last to consult the oracle, and that the inscriptions are due to him and his immediate predecessors. This fits in well with the tradition of their descendants, the dukes of Sung, who assigned the removal of the capital to this place to King Wu-i, the twenty-eighth of the dynasty and grandfather of Ti-i, and its abandonment to the last king. The *Chu shu chi nien* gives the reigns of these sovereigns as in the second half of the twelfth century, but such chronology has no more value than any other chronology for this period. Nevertheless, the dukes of Sung preserved the genealogical list of their distant ancestors, the kings of Yin, very exactly, so it is unlikely that they would err in that of their nearer ancestors; thus the time from Ti-i back to Duke Tai (799–765) can be calculated approximately. Depending upon whether one allows an average of fifteen or of twelve years for the eleven intermediary princes (the last King of Yin and the first ten dukes of Sung), the reign of Ti-i may be placed in the second half of the eleventh century or the first half of the tenth. The inscribed bones, which date the reigns of Wu-i, Wen-ting, and Ti-i, thus go back roughly to the twelfth or eleventh century before our era.

3 The exact data which the inscriptions supply about Chinese culture in the Yin era — religion, administration, social organization, and material culture — were brought together for the first time in 1910 by Lo Chen-yu in the last pages of his *Yin hsü shu ch'i k'ao shih*; later by Kuo Mo-jo in the third part of his *Chung kuo ku tai she hui yen chiu* (Shanghai, 1930) pp. 217–93; and also in numerous passages of his *Chia ku wen tzu yen chiu*.

4 The Yin sacrifices were far more numerous and diversified than those of the Chou, so that many characters designating them in the inscriptions have no equivalent in more recent times and have not been identified. The Chou simplified the rituals, less by suppressing feasts than by reducing the diverse ceremonies to certain fundamental types.

It is not impossible that the succession to the throne may have been through the collateral line of elder brother to younger brother. In worship, distinctions seem to have been made between the sacrifices a king made to his direct ancestors and those made to their brothers who had also reigned (cf. Wang Kuo-wei, *Yin Chou chih tu lun*, p. 3*a* ff.; Granet, *Danses et légendes*, II, pp. 423–26.

5 Unfortunately the inscriptions are not sufficiently explicit to tell us whether, as the Chou did later, the kings of Yin had a palace for

residence in the capital, or whether they resided outside in what was later called the *Ming t'ang*.

6   Lo Chen-yü, *Tseng ting Yin hsü shu ch'i k'ao shih, ch.* 3, 59*b*: 'Petition: for the harvest to the God of the Soil of the Country'.

7   Lo Chen-yü has summed up what is known from the tortoise-shells concerning the Yin administration in pages 106–7 of his *Yin hsü shu ch'i k'ao shih*. On the sacrifices of Yi Yin, cf. Wang Kuo-wei, *Chien-shou t'ang so tsang Yin hsü wen tzu k'ao shih*, p. 30*b*. For the passages regarding divination on the subject of the harvest, rain, wind, above translated, and for numerous similar passages, see especially these same two works.

8   The *tsai* is not mentioned in the tortoise-shell inscriptions, but is found in the inscription on a vase dedicated to King Yi, which appears to be contemporary with the inscribed tortoise-shells. Cf. Juan Yüan, *Chi-ku-chai chung ting i ch'i k'uan shih, ch.* 2, 16*a*; Lo Chen-yü, *Yin wen ts'un, ch.* 2, 23*b*. Likewise the *ta-chu*, cf. Takata Tadasuke, *Gakko hatsubon, ch.* 7, 23*a*.

9   Mention is made of 'large bands of domestics' sent on expeditions which shows them employed as soldiers or officers. On the other hand, the king gives his overlords as a reward whole families of domestics, according to numerous bronze inscriptions. Cf. Kuo Mo-jo, who puts the different texts together, in *Chia ku wen tzu yen chiu, ch.* 2, pp. 1–6 (*Shih ch'en tsai*). He calls the *ch'en* slaves, *nu* (a word that is seldom found in Yin inscriptions), wrongly in my opinion. I should be more inclined to regard them rather in the light of the bondsmen, *leudes*, of Frankish chieftains.

10 The hypothesis recently set forth by Niwa, 'Social Revolution from Yin to Chou', *Shinagaku*, III, 9 (Sept. 1924), that the inhabitants of eastern China, subjects of the Yin, were essentially hunters, while those of western China, subjects of the Chou, were herdsmen and agriculturalists, rests simply on a false interpretation of somewhat superficial statistics drawn from both the Yin inscriptions and legends. It has been refuted by Ojima, '*Agriculture and Pasturage in the Yin Dynasty*', *Shinagaku* III, 10 (Feb. 1925).

11 *Yin hsü shu ch'i k'ao shih*, p. 97*a*.

12 *Shu ching*, II, i, 11n. (Legge, p. 38); IV, ii/part 2, 16 (Legge, p. 241).

13 See the reproduction of three Yin halberd blades found at Pao-ting fu (Hopei), *Yi shu ts'ung pien*, 1917, fourth month.

14 Chang Hung-chao, '*Shih-ya*, Lapidarium Sinicum', *Mem. Geolog. Survey of China*, B.2 (Peking, 1921), app. Cf. Demiéville, *BEFEO*, XXIV (1924), pp. 298–99.

15 Laufer, *Jade*, pp. 81, 88, 94, figs. 20–24. A very large halberd blade of jade (from the Tuan-fang collection) is reproduced ibid., pl. 9; cf. Lo Chen-yu, *Ku yü tao mo pen pa* (1919), in *Yün ch'uang man kao*, 31*a*. There are reproductions of three other smaller ones, two from the Eumorfopoulos collection in Pope-Hennessy, *Early Chinese Jades*, pl. 27, and one from the Loo collection in Pelliot, *Jades archaïques de Chine*, pl. 4. While these pieces are much more recent, appearing to

go no farther back than the end of Chou, they can give some idea of implements in remote antiquity.

16   Several inscriptions, at least, mention units of 3,000 men despatched on expeditions. It does not necessarily follow, however, that this figure was that of a regular element in the Yin armies.

17   Lo Chen-yü, *Yin hsü shu ch'i ch'ien p'ien, ch.* 8, 12, no. 6; *ch.* 4, 8, no. 2; Kuo Mo-jo, *Chia ku wen tzu yen chiu,* I, 2 (*Shih ch'en tsai*), 4*b*–5*a*.

18   Lo Chen-yü, *Yin hsü shu ch'i k'ao shih,* p. 97*a*; Wang Kuo-wei, *Chien-shou t'ang so ts'ang Yin hsü wen tzu k'ao shih,* p. 25*a*. I regularly replace this name by a X. Dashes serve for characters lacking or illegible, and brackets mark the words whose translation is doubtful. Takata Tadasuke, *Kochūhen, ch.* 51, 14*b*, suggests reading 图 *hu*.

19   For the reading of this character, which has not been deciphered by Lo Chen-yü, see Wang Kuo-wei, op. cit., p. 2*b*. Kuo Mo-jo in *Chia ku wen tzu yen chiu, ch.* 8, 2*b* (appendix *T'u fang k'ao*) has tried to make use of the data in the inscriptions about this state. He places it northwest of the Yin capital, and therefore in the direction of Shansi, which is plausible but not certain. But he places it too far away when he tries to calculate from various inscriptions that it lay twelve to thirteen days' march from the Yin capital, which he considers equivalent to twelve to thirteen hundred *li*, and is therefore led to make it a tribe of the Huns (Hsien-yün, op. cit., p. 3*b*).

20   Wang Kuo-wei, op. cit., p. 25*b*.

21   The *Chu shu chi nien,* at the end of the Chou, assigns 496 years to the Yin dynasty, which would fix its beginning, at the advent of T'ang the Victorious, in 1558 B.C. The chronology subsequently adopted by Chinese historians, which is based on calculations of Han times, sets its commencement in 1766 B.C. Both dates are equally invalid. For the traditional pseudo-history of the Yin, see the *Chu shu chi nien,* Legge, *Ch. Cl.,* III, vol. i, *Prolegomena,* pp. 128–41; the *Shih chi, ch.* 3, Chavannes, I, pp. 173–208; and cf. Wieger, *Textes historiques,* I, pp. 67–90; Cordier, *Histoire générale de la Chine,* I, pp. 107–15.

22   The discovery of bronze halberd blades which are manifestly in the Yin style near Pao-ting fu in Hopei (*I shu ts'ung pien,* year 1917, fourth month) is insufficient to prove that the kingdom extended so far north; but such extension is not entirely unlikely. It would even appear that the whole of southern Manchuria was part of the Chinese domain at the time, and was occupied by the barbarians only later in Chou times. Cf. Andersson, 'The Cave Deposit at Sha kuo t'un in Feng-t'ien', in *Palaeontologia Sinica,* ser. D, I, i (1923).

23   L. C. Hopkins, 'Metamorphic Stylization and the Sabotage of Significance, a Study in Ancient and Modern Chinese Writing', in *J. Roy. As. Soc.,* 1925, pp. 470–73.

24   These identifications are not absolutely certain, and I give them only with reserve.

25   The *I shu ts'ung pien,* year 1917, tenth month, attributes to the Yin a very beautiful bronze vase found in the region of Hsi-an fu, in

Shensi. This assignment, however, is incorrect. The style of decoration cannot be earlier than Han. Likewise a bronze wine-jar, in the form of an owl, found near T'ai-yuan fu in Shansi and also attributed to the Shang (ibid.) is clearly much more modern.

26 Tung Tso-pin, *Hsin huo pu tz'u hsieh pen*, no. 277: 'The king consults the fates about this question: to give orders to the Prince of Chou that this month there should not be … ;' cf. nos. 248 and 249. The word 'Chou' also appears four times preceded by the word *k'ou*, 'plunderer', which seems to show that tradition was not wrong in showing Yin and Chou in conflict. Cf. Kuo Mo-jo, op. cit., *ch.* 3, 1*a*–3*b*.

27 The genealogy of the ancestors of the Chou kings can provide an approximate chronological indication, if one accepted, as seems likely, that it is as accurate as that for the ancestors of the dukes of Sung. The founding of the family domain on the upper course of the Ching and Wei rivers, at Pin, is attributed by tradition to the twelfth ancestor of King Wu, Duke Liu. According to whether an average of fifteen or of twelve years is granted for the reigns of these twelve lords of Chou, as well as to the first ten kings of the dynasty (the flight of King Li in 842 gives the first reliable date), the establishment of the ancestor of the Chou at Pin can be placed at the beginning or at the end of the twelfth century B.C.

28 On this ancient colonization, see Henri Maspero, *Les Origines de la civilisation chinoise*, pp. 149–53 [English translation by C. W. Bishop in *Smithsonian Report* for 1927, pp. 433–52.]

29 [As earlier in the cases of Ch'i and Wei, Maspero used diacritical marks to distinguish the three variant clans which share the Mandarin romanized form *chi*. Since the Chi clan descended from Hou-chi is much the most important of the three, he used that form unmarked; and we do the same. For the Chi clan descended from Lu-chung we use the romanization Chy, and for the clan descended from Huang-ti, we use Chii.]

30 The ancient Chinese clans were not territorial clans, and they can in no wise be considered, as by Haloun, 'Bieträge zur Siedlungsgeschichte chinesischer Clans' (*Asia Major*, 1923, pp. 165–81), actual small states. They seem to have had, however, certain zones of special authority, not because they were the only ones in such regions, or even because they were necessarily more numerous than the other clans, but their names are not found, or at least seldom found, elsewhere. No clan ever appeared as occupying a strictly delimited domain where it was the sole master, and none of their religious traditions preserves anything to suggest such a thing. Moreover, it is inaccurate to speak of the domain of a clan. There were lords belonging to a clan and possessing domains, but it was solely the descendants of these lords, and not the entire clan, which had rights over such domains. We can therefore speak of the territorial distribution of lords belonging to the same clan, but not the territorial distribution of the clans. Finally, the clans

were essentially patrician. A clan name belonged only to the nobles
descended from a common ancestor, while their plebeian subjects,
who had no ancestors at all, remained entirely outside this pattern.
When I speak of the action of such-and-such a clan in colonization,
the action of the clan in its entirety should accordingly not be
understood. Such a formula designates simply the personal action
of certain individuals of the clan, probably the younger members
of certain seigniorial families, and it is solely the impossibility of
designating precisely the principality from which these individuals
sprang which obliges me to employ this convenient, but inexact,
formula.

31   The other lords of the Chi clan in this region were the descendants
of various princes of Lu, and are consequently more recent. The
origin of the princes of Lu themselves may give one pause. I grant
the authenticity of the tradition which attaches them to the royal
family and makes their establishment one of the consequences of
the victory over the Yin: see below, p. 34. The lords of Ts'ao also
claimed descent from a brother of King Wu.

32   Schindler, 'The Development of Chinese Conceptions of Supreme
Beings', *Asia Major* (1923), p. 361, places the 'patrie d'origine' of the
Ying clan in 'a region, determined in the east by the districts which
surround T'ai-shan ... and in the west extending as far as Han-tan
(Kuang-p'ing fu and Cheng-ting fu), Fei-lei, Liang-ch'eng', with its
centre near the present Fan-hsien, at 'the ancient city of Ch'in,
which may be regarded as the point of departure for the future
dynasty' (Ch'in). This is because it is in the state of Lu where, so it is
said, was found the fief of the mythical emperor Shao-hao, the
predecessor of Yao, ancestor of the Ying clan, and because the
name Ch'in is found in both Shantung and Shansi. I have just said
what I think of the theory of territorial clans. Here it leads
Schindler to place the origin of the Ying in a country where in
historical times not a single fief of this clan existed. Moreover, the
argument drawn from the location of Shao-hao's fief is weak: we
can easily see that the historians place it near the Lu capital because
the tomb of this personage was found there in historical times, but
we know far too little of his legend to see what links it to this
region. For all we know, it was a mythological legend belonging to
the sun tree, the K'ung-sang, cf. Granet, *Danses et légendes*, II, pp.
436–37. This complete cycle was naturalized in ancient times in the
state of Lu, where we find the names related to it throughout local
topography; but we know neither why nor how this adaptation
occurred. Placing the tomb of Shao-hao in Lu is one consequence
of it and accordingly has no more value than any other
geographical identification of this legend — for example, that of
the K'ung-sang tree with a mountain of the principality. No great
importance should be attached to it. As to the similarity of names,
this has been too frequent in China from ancient times on to
provide any basis for argument. The existence of two Ch'in, one in

the east and the other in the west, only begins to become meaningful if both were fiefs of the same clan. And the example of the two fiefs of Yen, southern Yen, of the Chi clan, descendants of Hou-chi, and northern Yen, of the Chii clan, descendants of Huang-ti, shows clearly that a nominal identity between territories and the clans of princely families does not necessarily mean a connection. A study of the distribution of the seigniories of a clan in the historical period is the sole method which, despite its difficulties, rests on exact data. Any other is necessarily arbitrary. Cf. H. Maspero, 'Légendes mythologiques dans le Chou king', pp. 81–84.

33 This fief of Tung, whose lord belonged to the Ssu clan (*Kuo yü, ch.* 14, 15*a*) differed from the Tung whose lord was of the Chy clan (*Kuo yü, ch.* 13, 3*b*).

34 Though we do not know the actual history of this colonizing movement, we know at least a little of the conception which the Chinese formed of it about the eighth or seventh centuries B.C., through the ritualistic odes of the Chou, certain passages of which I have quoted. These have only the validity of religious hymns composed long after the epoch of which they sing, and are naturally not historical documents.

35 The second line of the stanza signifies: 'He began his journey,' and Legge understands that this means the emigration of Duke Liu, and that the stanza narrates the journey of those emigrants. In actuality it involves only the establishment of the duke at Pin and the clearing of a site favourable for setting up his habitation there.

36 The *Shih ching,* 437 (*Ta ya,* Decade of *Wen-wang,* 3, Ode *Mien*): 'The ancient Duke T'an-fu / — made huts of clay, made caves, / — there were no houses yet.'

37 *Shih ching,* p. 438.

38 *Shih chi, ch.* 3 and *ch.* 4, Chavannes, I, pp. 201–5, 215–22.

Chapter 3.   The Chou Empire (Ninth and Eighth Centuries)

1 *Tso chuan,* Legge, p. 754.

2 Several pieces in the *Shu ching* claim to be documents originating in the chancellery of the early Chou, but are of later date. See below, bk. IV, ch. 1.

3 One of these romances, written in the fifth or fourth century B.C., the 'History of Mu, the Son of Heaven', *Mu t'ien-tzu chuan,* has been partly preserved. See below, p. 357.

4 *Shih chi, ch.* 4, Chavannes, I, p. 250; *Chu shu chi nien,* pp. 149–51.

5 *Kuo yü (Chou yü), ch.* 1, sec. 12, 14*a*. The queen was from Fang, and the lords of Fang were descended from Chu of Tan, who had had his fief at Fang during his exile.

6 The entire *Mu t'ien tzu chuan* was an account of these travels; cf. also *Chu shu chi nien,* p. 150, which gives a summary of this romance; *Tso chuan,* p. 465, but it is difficult to say whether the author was already

acquainted with the *Mu t'ien-tzu chuan* or whether he merely alludes to the source from which the latter book came; *Kuo yü*, *ch.* 1, 1*a* (*Chou yü*).

7   *Chu shu chi nien*, loc. cit.

8   *Mu t'ien-tzu chuan*, *ch.* 6.

9   *Lieh-tzu*, *ch.* 3, Wieger, p. 105.

10   [Where homophonous names threatened confusion, Maspero distinguished them by using tone marks. It is standard in modern sinological work to use variant romanizations to make the same clarification. In this case, where Maspero used Yí and Yî, we use Yi and Yii. For comparable adaptations of other names see notes 3, ch. 1, and 29, ch. 2.]

11   *Shih ching*, p. 549.

12   According to the *Chu shu chi nien*, p. 154 (cf. *Chuang-tzu*, *ch.* 28; *Lu Lien-tzu*, ed. Hung Yi-hsüan, *Ching tien chi lin*, *ch.* 21, 2*a*). Ho, Lord of Kung, took the regency; according to the *Shih chi*, *ch.* 4 (Chavannes, I, p. 275), the Duke of Chou and the Duke of Shao exercised it conjointly; on the discussions to which this divergence has given rise among Chinese scholars, see Chavannes, *Mémoires historiques*, I, Introd., pp. clxxxvi–cxcvi. This is the period which the Chinese historians call *Kung-ho*, and from here on the various chronological systems are nearly in accord, though that does not imply absolutely that they are correct.

13   Nothing in these pieces demands absolutely that they be attributed to King Hsüan, but the tradition of the end of the Chou dynasty is firm on this point, as we see from the *Chu shu chi nien*, the *Tso chuan*, the preface to the *Shih ching*, and so on. All the more clearly, there are fewer reasons to expunge them since after King Hsüan there was no king to whom expeditions of this kind could be attributed.

14   *Shih ching*, pp. 281–83, 287, 555–58.

15   This name, which means 'the thousand acres', is also that of the sacred field where the king conducts the ceremonial of ploughing. A legend explains that, King Hsüan not having carried out this ceremony for long years, Heaven abandoned him and made him sustain this defeat in the very place (or in a place of the same name) where he had committed his offence (*Shih chi*, *ch.* 4, Chavannes, I, 276).

16   *Shih chi*, *ch.* 4, Chavannes, I, p. 284; *Kuo yü*, *ch.* 16, 7*a–b*.

Chapter 4.   The Court and Administration of Western Chou

1   *Shu ching*, pp. 544–45; cf. *Chou li*, I, pp. 476–77.

2   *Shu ching*, pp. 544–65 (*Ku ming* and beginning of *K'ang wang chih kao*). These chapters, both authentic, have been badly cut up by a forger of the third century A.D. in this edition of the *Shu ching*, so that the first three paragraphs in the present-day editions of the *K'ang wang chih kao* are really the end of the *Ku ming*. This text claims to describe the funeral of King Ch'eng.

3 A description of the hunting of wild boar is in the *Shih ching*, pp. 36, 292; of tiger, ibid., p. 129; of wild oxen (?), ibid., p. 292 (Legge translates it 'rhinoceros', cf. note 23 to ch. 1). *Chan kuo ts'e*, *ch*. 5, 5*a*; of wolves, *Shih ching*, p. 152, etc.

4 A description of archery ceremonies occupies all of *ch*. 7 of *Yi li*, trans. Couvreur, pp. 212–83.

5 *Shih ching*, p. 276.

6 *Ibid.*, p. 475.

7 *Ibid.*, p. 373.

8 *Ibid.*, pp. 398–99.

9 *Ibid.*, p. 614.

10 A passage in a lost chapter of the *Shu ching* quoted by Mo-tzu, *ch*. 8, 18*b* (*Fei yo*), Forke, p. 371, describes, while condemning them, the scenes of the sorceress dances, which he attributes to the epoch of the Shang kings.

   This passage has been incorporated into one of the chapters which is not authentic, having been fabricated in the third century A.D., the *I hsün* (*Shu ching*, p. 196), but not without some distortions.

11 *Kuo yü* (*Chou yü*), ch. 1, sec. 3; *Lü shih ch'un ch'iu*, ch. 20, 12*a*; *Chu shu chi nien*, p. 153 (year 846); cf. *Shih chi*, I, p. 275.

   Similarly the Zulu kings of the last century had their sorceresses who 'smelled out' those in the grand royal assemblies who wished evil to the king, and they were forthwith executed.

12 *Chu shu chi nien*, p. 153.

13 The picture which follows differs from what is usually given in accordance with the rituals, because I have attempted to establish it for this period (the most interesting since it is the only one when the Chou administration was actually vigorous and controlled a great empire), by taking the *Shu ching* and the *Shih ching* as a basis. These can only provide a general framework, however, and for everything regarding the detailed way things functioned it has been necessary to flesh them out with the aid of the *Tso chuan* and especially the *Chou li*, which are later documents. Biot, in his 'Recherches sur les moeurs des anciens Chinois, d'après le Chi-king' (*J. As.*, ser. 4, vol. II (1843), pp. 307–430) has unfortunately left out everything which deals with administration, contenting himself with references to the *Chou li*, which he was translating at the time. There is indeed a chapter of the present-day *Shu ching* devoted to this subject, 'The Officers of the Chou', *Chou kuan*; but it is one of those which are not authentic. Likewise the article by C. de Harlez, 'Le *Tcheou-li* et le *Chan hai king*, leur origine et leur valeur historique' (*TP.*, V (1894), 11–42, 107–22) is scarcely usable, for it is a comparison of the names for functions in the *Chou li* and those in the *Chou kuan* chapter of the *Shu ching*. Schindler, *Das Priestertum im alten China*, 61 (Leipzig, 1919), although committing the same fundamental error of not taking into account the unauthenticity of the *Chou kuan* chapter, has performed an incontestably useful task

by assembling a large number of quotations from the classics concerning the titles of ancient functions.

14   The *ch'ing-shih* is outside and above the other ministers, cf. the *Yi Chou shu*, ch. 2, 6*b*, where he is specially mentioned as being aside from and before the San-lao; also in the inscription on the vase of Che, where he is ordered to control them, *yin san shih* (Lo Chen-yü, 'Che yi shih k'ao', in *Shinagaku*, V (1929), pp. 481–85).

15   For the prime ministers of the Chou kings in the *Ch'un ch'iu* period, see Ku Tung-kao, *Ch'un ch'iu ta shih piao*, ch. 20, and the genealogies, ibid., ch. 12, in which the texts of the *Tso chuan* are collected. The arrangement in chronological tables which the author adopted obliges him to be often more precise than the documents warrant, but with this reservation, the work, a conscientious compilation, is useful.

  For the second line of the dukes of Chou, see Chavannes, *Mémoires historiques*, I, p. 301, n. 1.

16   Six ministers are generally attributed to the Chou, as indeed the *Chou li* states. Such must have been the organization at the time that work reflects (fourth century B.C.). The *Shu ching*, however, recognized the expression *liu ch'ing* only in the sense of 'commanders of the six royal armies' (p. 152), while the sense of 'the ministers' only appears in an unauthentic chapter (p. 530).

17   *San-lao*: *I Chou shu*, ch. 2, 11; *san yu shih*: *Shih ching*, p. 323; *san shih*: ibid., p. 326; *Shu ching*, p. 515; *san shih tai-fu*: *Shih ching*, p. 326. The term *san li* (*Tso chuan*, p. 349) possibly designates the three ministers of the second rank, as in the *I Chou shu*, loc. cit.

18   They are enumerated in this order in the *Shu ching*, p. 298 (*T'ai shih*, a reconstituted text); p. 301 (*Mu shih*); p. 414 (*Tzu ts'ai*); p. 516 (*Li cheng*); the *Chiu kao* (p. 411) chapter places the *ssu-ma* first. The chapter *Hung fan* (p. 327) alone employs a different enumeration: *ssu-k'ung, ssu-t'u, ssu-k'ou*, but these names make their appearance in the midst of a list of various things and titles set up on philosophical principles and are not contradictory to the preceding, which are purely administrative forms. Moreover, the list of the three royal ministers is confirmed by that of the three ministers of the feudal princes, which is the same. In this instance, as in many others, the later rituals which attribute six ministers to the king have only systematized a simple accident in the historical development of the royal administration, by according it the force of a general principle.

19   The words in quotation marks here, and after the names Ch'i-fu and Hung-fu below, translate phrases from the *Shu ching*, p. 411.

  The title *ssu-t'u* is found in the *Shu ching*, pp. 327 and 411. Schindler, op. cit., p. 53, n. 3, translates *ssu-t'u* as 'commander of the foot-soldiers', and assumes that his original function was to command the peasant levies who fought on foot.

20   *Tso chuan*, p. 309 (this refers to the *ssu-t'u* of the state of Ch'u).

21   *Chou li*, I, p. 192 ff.

22   *Ssu-ma:* *Shu ching,* p. 397 (*Hung fan*), p. 414 (*Tzu ts'ai*), p. 516 (*Li cheng*), etc.; *ch'i-fu: Shu ching,* p. 411; *Shih ching,* p. 298.

23   The *chi-fu* led an expedition, *Shih ching,* p. 283; cf above, p. 37.

24   *Chou li,* II, pp. 182–83.

25   *Ssu-k'ung: Shu ching,* pp. 43, 301, 327, 414, 516, etc. *hung-fu:* ibid., p. 411.

26   Under this title of *ssu-k'ung* Kun and Yü were made responsible for draining the floods, diking the rivers, dredging the channels, and so on (*Shu ching,* p. 43). The chapters of the *Shu ching* on Yü show sufficiently well how the authors, in the time of the Western Chou, envisaged the duties of an ideal *ssu-k'ung.*

27   *Chou li,* II, pp. 456–600.

28   Except for the expression *san li,* the meaning of which is not clear (cf. above p. 44), I have found no term collectively designating these three personages; and possibly there was none, for they did not comprise a homogeneous group.

29   *Tsai: Shih ching,* p. 322; *Ch'un ch'iu,* pp. 3, 43; *chung-tsai: Shih ching,* p. 533 (in the *Shu ching* this title is found only in two unauthentic chapters); *t'ai-tsai: Chou li,* I, p. 20 is probably only a title of a late period. The *tsai* is clearly distinguished from the *ch'ing-shih* in *Shih ching,* p. 322, and it is in his capacity as comptroller of the palace that drought disturbs him, since this makes provisioning difficult. Similarly the *tsai* despatched to Lu in 722 and 708 (*Ch'un ch'iu,* loc. cit.) are distinct from the prime ministers, *ch'ing-shih.* One was named Hsüan, the other Po-chiu of Ch'ü, while the prime ministers of the time were the Count of Cheng, at first alone, and then with the Duke of Kuo (708).

30   This was the role he still played in Ch'u in the sixth century, without being prime minister. In Lu and Ch'i the prime minister never received the title of Grand Chamberlain; in Sung, on the other hand, at the beginning of the seventh century Tu of Hua was prime minister for thirty years, with that title (*Tso chuan,* pp. 37–39).

31   *T'ai-tsung: Shu ching,* p. 557; *Tsung-po: Chou li,* I, p. 397 (in the *Shu ching,* this title appears only in a non-authentic chapter).

32   *Shu ching (Lü hsing),* p. 605 (commutation of penalties); p. 606 (number of cases). This is the code attributed to King Mu. *Chou li,* II, p. 354 (number of cases in the fourth century). It would appear that the ingot of copper, *wan,* weighed from six to seven ounces.

33   *Shu ching (K'ang kao),* p. 388.

34   *Shih ching,* pp. 322, 533.

35   This description of the local administrative organization is taken almost entirely from the *Chou li,* and consequently belongs to a much later period (fourth century B.C.) than the list of court ministries which I have sought to draw up principally from the *Shu ching* and the *Shih ching.* The chief defect of the *Chou li,* nevertheless, is perhaps not so much its relatively recent date (for the archaic aspect of the administration which it describes guarantees that the alterations therein were made slowly) as its extreme

systematization, carried at times to the point of absurdity. Thus, taken literally, the table of regional divisions with their six districts in which the subdivisions (except one only) are regularly five in number for each rank, down to the group of five families, is calculated to give a *fixed* population of 150,000 families for the Royal Domain, which is nonsense. I believe that it represents a theoretical systematization of the state of affairs existing at the time when it was composed. The description of the officers certainly provides a sufficiently precise idea of their activities. This systematization (which has caused certain Chinese scholars to consider the *Chou li* as a Utopia of Han times) arises from the fact that about this time the mechanism revolved aimlessly, the Royal Domain having been reduced to almost nothing, and yet being unable to simplify itself — as I have indicated above — due to the concepts of the mystic role each function played in the progress of the world.

36 *Chou li*, I, p. 390 (*ts'ang-jen*); p. 357 (*lü-shih*); p. 384 (*lin-jen*); p. 289 (*chün-jen*); p. 361 (*wei-jen*); p. 309 (*ssu-shih*); p. 326 (*ch'üan-fu*).

37 *Chou li*, I, p. 302 (*ssu-chiu*); p. 303 (*t'iao-jen*); II, pp. 327–34 (*shih-shih*); II, pp. 311, 330 (trial and judgement); II, pp. 357–59 (*ssu-yüeh*); II, p. 313 (the Lung-coloured Stone); II, p. 346 (the Kao Drum); II, pp. 336, 342, 364 (criminal trials and executions).

38 According to the *Chou li*, II, p. 302, he who exacted vengeance was not punishable if he had taken pains previously to notify the Deputy for Criminal Affairs.

39 The text of these compacts was frequently engraved upon a bronze vase preserved in the Ancestral Temple. A number of them have thus been preserved: agreement for the restoration of lands with settled boundaries (inscription on a plate of the San family: *Chin shih ts'ui pien*, ch. 2, 3*b*–5*b*); agreement for the division of lands between two brothers (inscription on the tripod of Shu and Tsung of Li, *Chi-ku-chai chung ting k'uan shih*, ch. 4, 31*a*); agreement in the matter of sale of slaves, in the matter of ricks of stolen grain (inscription on the tripod of Hu, ibid., ch. 4, 36*b*, 38*b*). The translations of these texts by P. Wieger, 'Caractères chinois', in *Graphies antiques*, pp. 531, 495, 499, give a sufficient idea of them, though they are somewhat too free.

40 *Chou li*, II, p. 311; according to the commentary of Cheng Hsüan, a bar of copper, *chün*, weighed thirty pounds. Biot, op. cit., translates *chün chin* by 'thirty pounds of gold or metal'. In the ancient Chou descriptions *chin* always signifies 'bronze' (copper), see below, bk. 5, ch. 6, n. 31.

41 All that follows on the military organization is likewise drawn from various passages of the *Chou li*, unless otherwise indicated. Organization: I, p. 222; command by drums and bells, II, pp. 170, 176–77; layout of camps, I, p. 115.

42 It is hard to say whether this description, which dates from a time when the royal army no longer existed, rests upon at least a

theoretical reality or is due merely to juggling with numbers. At any rate it is clear that when King Hsuan led the six armies against the Huai barbarians, in about 821 (*Shih ching*, p. 555, and above, p. 38, he did not have in his train a multitude of 75,000 men with 600 chariots.

43 *Tso chuan*, p. 319, provocations by Ch'u warriors against the army of Chin before the Battle of Pi (597). These methods of provocation are given as traditional customs, and not as individual caprices. Cf. Granet, *Danses et légendes*, I, p. 138.

44 *Tso chuan*, p. 396, description of the preparations made by the Chin army before the Battle of Yen-ling (575).

45 *Tso chuan*, p. 210.

46 *Ibid.*, pp. 397–98. This was the role of the Ch'u commander-in-chief throughout the Battle of Yen-ling.

47 Cowries have been found on the site of the Yin capital, and ancient inscriptions frequently mention gifts of cowries by the king.

48 Under the Han dynasty, *wan* was the name of an ingot of six or seven ounces. On the other hand, the coins of the state of Liang about the fourth century B.C., which were marked *wan*, weigh only thirteen to sixteen grams (to judge by ten pieces in the Tanaka collection, Tokyo, which were weighed in July 1929). Two gold pieces of the Chou period, marked *wan* of Ying, weigh 11.26 and 17.54 grams respectively (Nakamura Collection, Tokyo). That is roughly the weight of a *chin* (cf. n. 51 below). The monetary unit must, therefore, have been the ancient ingot. Payments in copper *wan*: *Shu ching*, p. 605; *Chou li*, p. 311; inscription on the tripod of Hu, *Chi-ku-chai chung ting yi ch'i k'uan shih*, ch. 4, 38a, cf. Wieger, *Graphies antiques*, p. 495.

49 The only specific text relative to coinage of a more ancient time is a passage in the *Kuo yü*, ch. 3, 13a (*Chou yü*) attributing to King Ching the casting of large pieces of money in 524. It appears rather dubious. For this question, see the article of Ojima, 'Money Economy in the Ch'un Ch'iu Age' (*Shinagaku*, 1921, II, pp. 45–51; VIII, pp. 52–67), the general conclusions of which I adopt here. Cf. Lo Chen-yü, *Yung-lu jih cha*, on the discoveries of ancient coins, the mints, and the dates. In Ch'in, the first coins are believed to have been struck in 318, the twentieth year of King Hui-wen (*Ch'in pieh chi*, a lost work, cited in the *Ch'i kuo k'ao* of Tung Shuo, ch. 2, 4b).

50 Some fine castings of sword-shaped coins with the name of the state of Ch'i have been reproduced in the review *Yi shu ts'ung pien*, 1916, by Lo Chen-yü in *ch.* 2 of his *Ku ch'i wu fan t'u lu*. See also Herbert Mueller, 'Numismatische Miszellen', II, 'Zur Geschichte des "Käsch" ' in *Mitteil. d. Semin. f. Orient. Sprachen*, 1919, *Ostas. Studien*, pp. 12–19.

The indications of weight are given above according to the weighing of numerous pieces belonging to the beautiful collections of Chinese coins belonging to Mr. Nakamura Fusetsu and Mr. Tanaka of Tokyo. Taking advantage of this occasion, I thank these collectors for the cordiality with which they allowed me to carry out these weighings and measurings during my stay in Japan in 1929.

51   The monetary unit was the *chin* of about sixteen grams, which weighed half an ounce. This remained the monetary unit of the Ch'in under the new name of 'half-ounce', *pan-liang*, but with the same weight.

52   For the local differences in the tithe and its transformation into a land tax, see below, bk. 2, ch. 1, n. 3.

53   *Chou li*, I, p. 278.

54   *Kuo yü, ch.* 10, 18a.

55   The *Shih ching* mentions fifteen of them, the *Ch'un ch'iu* more than sixty, the *Tso chuan* more than a hundred, without taking the barbarian tribes into account. The *Chu shu chi nien*, the *Kuo yü*, the extant fragments of the *Shih pen*, and the *Shih chi* furnish some further names. The number of a hundred is a rather low limit. See Map 1.

56   At times it was also borne by princes who seem to have been Chinese, though it is not easy to discern the cause for assigning it to them. Possibly their ancestors had been barbarians.

57   In the Chou period only three degrees were counted in the hierarchy, and not five, as the writers of Han times state, and as has been repeated ever since. This is confirmed by the number of brevet titles accorded them (*Chou li*, II, p. 1), and the ceremonial of the court audiences (*ibid.*, II, pp. 400–403), actual ritual facts, which the authors of the *Chou li* could not have mistaken. The passage on the size of the respective principalities (ibid., I, pp. 205, 206) sets up a hierarchy of five degrees, but this is denied by a contemporary text on the same matter (*Mencius*, p. 374) which distinguishes only three degrees (differing, it is true, from those indicated above): (1) *kung* and *hou*; (2) *po*; (3) *tzu* and *nan*. In both works, it is only a matter of theoretical ideas outside all political reality (when, for example, the figures given are compared with the actual extent of the domains of the *hou* of Wei, of the *po* of Ch'in and of the *tzu* of Ch'u), and which possess only a speculative interest. On the other hand, the *Tso chuan*, thirteenth year of Chao, p. 652, distinguishes only two degrees (the passage concerns certain taxes to be paid): (1), *kung* and *hou*; (2) *po* and *nan*. But this is a specific classification established for the payment of taxes to the king (or to the President of the League, prince-hegemon) and that is probably the reason why the last two degrees were not distinguished from one another. Yet the same bipartite division is found in another passage (*Tso chuan*, fourth year of Chao, p. 597) where Hsü of Hsiang, minister of Sung, explains to the King of Ch'u, at the Shen assembly (538), the proper rites of the dukes towards nobles of lesser rank, and Tzu-ch'an of Cheng answers by explaining the rites due by nobles of inferior rank (*po*, *tzu* and *nan*) towards the dukes (*kung*), not mentioning princes (*hou*). These titles are generally translated as duke, marquis, count, viscount, baron. I have partly abandoned this translation which for

the Chou period seems misleading. I translate *hou* as 'prince' (in place of 'marquis') and *tzu* by 'lord' (in place of 'viscount'); thus, first degree, duke (*kung*); second degree, prince (*hou*) and count (*po*); third degree, lord (*tzu*), and baron (*nan*). For the modern era when the hierarchy truly represented five degrees, the usual translation will be resumed. It is to be noted that (except *hou*, which seems to be only a different form of the character *hou*, sovereign), all these titles are actually terms of relationship. *Kung* is an honorific form for 'father'; *po* is 'uncle', elder brother of the father or mother; *tzu* is 'son'.

58 The *Yü kung* is one of the genuine chapters of the *Shu ching*. It comprises a document from the royal archives (or rather a literary imitation of an administrative document), fused rather incongruously with a poem concerning the labours of the great Yü, both retouched so as to conform to the traditions about the capital of Yü, but dating from the end of the Western Chou. It is extremely important for the political geography of the Chou Empire just before its period of decadence. Legge has of course translated the *Yü kung* with the rest of the *Shu ching*, pp. 92–151; similarly, Couvreur, *Le Chou king*, pp. 52–77; a mediocre translation accompanied by excellent geographical notes was made by Richthofen, *China*, I, pp. 277–364. The best translation is that of Chavannes, *Mémoires historiques*, I, 103–49, which distinguishes the portions in prose from the portions in verse, thus providing a fine critical interpretation of this document. See also Kingsmill, 'The Structure of the Yü kong', in *China Review*, XIV, pp. 17–21.

59 *Kung-yang chuan*, fifth year of Yin: 'To the east of Shaan (or Chia) the Duke of Chou was master, to the west of Shaan the Duke of Shao was master.' Chinese commentators and historians usually interpret this tradition by stating that the latter's region included the capital together with Yung, the former's the eight other provinces. Another interpretation considers the division as going back to the time of King Wen, and concedes that it relates to a partition of the former domain of Chou. Another, which has not been accepted by the official historians, but which has left some traces in local popular traditions, presumes a partition of the Lo region. In the eighth century the spot at Yi-yang was still pointed out where the pear-tree stood beneath which the Duke of Shao dispensed justice within his half of the Royal Domain, and during several centuries, the neighbouring sub-prefecture retained the name of 'Pear-tree', *Kan-t'ang hsien*. The 'partition of Chou between the Duke of Chou on the left and the Duke of Shao on the right' formed the fifth scene of the Ballet Ta-wu, at the festival of King Wu, representing the victory over the Yin (*Li ki*, trans. Couvreur, II, p. 97). This is one of the clearest instances of historical tradition drawn from the interpretation of these ritual dances.

60 The *Shu ching* recognizes only the term *mu* (pp. 511, 515, 516, 517); the title of *po* appears in the *Shih ching*, p. 536, where the fact that it

is conferred upon a *prince* of Shen discloses clearly that it refers to a practical function and not to a title of nobility. The term current in the literature of the fourth and third centuries is *fang-po*, local count, *Kung-yang chuan*, ch. 3, 5*a*; *Li chi*, pp. 270, 272, 327, etc.

61 *Tso chuan*, p. 140; cf. *Shih chi*, ch. 32, Chavannes, IV, p. 40.

62 *Shih ching*, p. 536; *Chu shu chi nien*, p. 155, which gives the date of 821.

63 *Shih ching*, p. 551; *Chu shu chi nien*, p. 155; *Shih chi*, ch. 32, Chavannes, IV, p. 105; *Kuo yü*, ch. 1, sec. 8, which appears sufficiently clear as regards the office conferred upon Prince Hsiao of Lu.

64 *Chu shu chi nien*, p. 153.

65 *Kuo yü*, ch. 1, sec. 7; *Shih chi*, ch. 33, Chavannes, IV, pp. 105–6. In these two instances the choice of a brother in place of a son as successor to the guilty party seems to me an aggravation of the penalty: the offender would thus be deprived of worship in the ancestral temple.

66 *Chou li*, II, p. 405.

67 *Chu shu chi nien*, p. 155.

68 Ibid., p. 155.

69 This entire description is taken from the *Yü kung* which, although connected by its author to the era of the Great Yü, employs documents from the end of the Western Chou, and basically describes the organization of the latter.

Book II: Social and Religious Life

Chapter 1.   Society in Ancient China

1 I use the term 'patrician' for *shih* in preference to 'noble' because of the well-known distinction between the person who belonged to the aristocratic class by birth, *shih,* and one who became noble, *kuei,* by training after assuming the hat of manhood *(Li chi,* I, p. 605, *Chiao t'e sheng,* and see also below, p. 78).

2 *Li chi*, I, p. 53 (*Ch'ü li*).

3 *Kung-yang chuan*, ch. 7, 14*b*; *Ku-liang chuan*, ch. 7, 8*b*; *Chou li*, I, pp. 226, 240–241; II, p. 566; *Mencius*, pp. 243–45; *Li chi* I, p. 265 (*Wang chih*); *Han shih wai chuan*, ch. 4, 7*a* (ed. *Ssu-pu ts'ing k'an*). Of these texts the last two are of the Han era, and come from more ancient sources, that of the *Wang chih* probably from Mencius, and that of the *Han shih wai chuan* partly from the *Ku-liang chuan*. As to the others which are spread over the fourth century, that of the *Chou li* is independent (so that it is often considered to be an interpolation); but those of the *Kung-yang chuan*, the *Ku-liang chuan* and *Mencius* appear to be closely related to each other. Contrary to the opinion of Hu Shih, *Ching t'ien pien* in *Hu Shih wen ts'un, ch.* 2, pp. 247–84, who derives the first two, and even the passages from the *Chou li,* from Mencius, it is clear that the latter only sets forth the teachings of the school of Confucius as preserved for us in the two commentaries on the *Ch'un ch'iu.* The three texts, whatever their

date, are not derived from each other, but share a common source.

This entire *ching* organization, described in rather too theoretical a way, has been queried by some Chinese and Japanese scholars, who regard it merely as a Utopian conception and not a real picture. On the contrary, however, the ancient texts, and even the commentaries of the Han era, with their characteristic details, demonstrate clearly that it was an actual social organization, the memory of which remained singularly vivid in Han times, in spite of revolutionary changes. (On this question, see the article by Hashimoto Masukichi, 'On the early Chinese Land Regulations' in *Tōyō gakuhō*, 1922. The *Ching t'ien pien* by Hu, mentioned above, has been excellently summarized by Paul Demiéville, *BEFEO*, XXIII (1923), pp. 494–98.)

Moreover, the *ching* system fits in very well with the history of Chinese agriculture. In prehistoric times the Chinese, like most of the barbarian peoples of south China and northern Indo-China, began by creating temporary fields through burning off patches of brush, but these had to be abandoned after a few years when the soil became exhausted and they had to move on. Even in historical times, when the diking of rivers and digging of irrigation canals would have permitted the establishment of permanent fields, the primitive methods of crop-rotation must have involved frequent moves to let the land lie fallow. In the *Chou li*, I, pp. 206–07, the distinction between 'unchanging lands' (*i.e.*, permanent fields) and lands of one or two changes (*i.e.*, lying fallow for one year in two, or for two years in three) shows how the right of cultivation, though not yet that of ownership, became fixed. The fields of 200 *mou* lying fallow for a year, and those of 300 *mou* lying fallow for two years, are in effect parts of the bush of which a different half or third was cleared every year. In this time, however, each peasant moved on to a piece of ground which was allotted to him once and for all, instead of (as formerly) each group of peasants moving after each allotment to cultivate new land. The stabilization of a peasant family on a fixed terrain paved the way for individual peasant property-holding. This made its appearance towards the end of the Chou period in various parts of China and was probably established by Ch'in and Han times. This stabilization was prepared, or at least facilitated, by fiscal measures. The ancient system of tithes, which was irregular and difficult to fix, was gradually replaced by proper land taxes, no longer fixed in accordance with the harvest, a quantity that varied each year, but by the acreage under cultivation, a set quantity. In the state of Lu, the only one concerning which we have exact information, the land tax was introduced in 594. *Ch'un ch'iu,* fifteenth year of Hsüan, I, pp. 325–27: 'For the first time the tax was fixed by *mou*'. In Ch'in the changeover was wrongly or rightly attributed to the laws of Yang of Wei in the fourth century; it is not known when it took place in Chin; but a land tax, *tsu-fu,* is found from the beginnings of the state of Wei and Prince Wen (436–387) is supposed to have increased it. By Mencius's day (end of fourth century) the *ching* system, from the fiscal point of view, had become so forgotten in eastern China that the Prince of T'eng had to have Mencius explain it to him (*Mencius,* p. 243).

4   For Chou writers The states of Sung and Chin represented the rites and customs of the Yin and Hsia dynasties; so it is in this sense that we must interpret the passage in *Mencius,* p. 241, which associates these areas with the regulations of those dynasties. Cf. also *Ch'ien-Han shu, ch.* 29, 1*b.* The exact relationship between the lots assigned to the peasants in different states is difficult to establish, for the amounts certainly varied from one state to another.

5   *Mencius,* p. 461.

6   *Chou li,* II, p. 556. For the general description of the market, with its sections, the role of functionaries, and so on, see ibid., I, pp. 309–28.

7   Ibid., I, p. 317, sites the sale of 'foodstuffs, men, oxen, and horses, weapons and household goods, rare and valuable objects.'

8   Ibid., I, p. 322 (*ssu-pao*), 323 (*ssu-chi*).

9   Ibid., I, 52, pp. 311 (tallies, *chi,* and deeds of sale, *chih*), 317–18 (guarantors, *chih-jen*).

10   Ibid., I, p. 312.

11   That is to say the soil of the smallest district, Chavannes, *Dieu du Sol,* pp. 439–40.

12   *Li chi,* I, p. 386 (*Yüeh ling*).

13   A *li* was made up of five *lin* of five families each, which makes twenty-five families (*Chou li,* I, p. 337), nearly equal to the number of families for three *ching,* each *ching* having eight families. These numbers are always approximate, as the various descriptions of peasant society in the Chou period have undergone various systematizations which have distorted them. Thus, each *ching* having eight families, the *li* should have exactly twenty-four families. It is probable that the number was rounded off so as to be divisible by five, and so that the five neighbourhoods, *lin,* should be in theory equal. Chavannes, *Dieu du Sol,* p. 439 ff., translates *li* by *canton,* a term which appears to me somewhat excessive for a division of twenty-five families, say two hundred inhabitants, according to the official Chinese computation of eight to a family, a figure already used by the *Mencius,* p. 149. The terminology differed according to the region. Besides the terms *li* and *lin,* we have the grouping, *pi* of five families, and the village, *lü,* of twenty-five families (*Chou li,* I, p. 211). The *Shang shu ta chuan, ch.* 4, 13*b,* a more modern work (second century B.C.) gives still another organization, quite theoretical and based on the numbers of the calendar: in it the neighbourhood, *lin,* is made up by the eight families of a *ching,* and the hamlet, *li,* contains nine

neighbourhoods — that is, seventy-two families (the number of *hou* in a year) — and the *yi* includes five hamlets, *li,* or 5 × 72 = 360 families (the number of days in a year). About the same time (under Emperor Wen-ti of the Han, 179–157 B.C.) Ch'ao Ts'o in a memorial to the emperor describes another 'ancient' organization: five families make one *wu,* with a chief, *chang;* (the families commanded by) ten *chang* make one *li,* with an overlord, *chia-shih* (Commentary of Yen Shih-ku: *chia* 假 = *ta* 大); four *li* make one *lien,* with a *chia-wu-po* (at its head); ten *lien* make one *yi,* with a *chia-hou* (*Ch'ien-han shu,* ch. 49, 7a). Ch'ao Ts'o came from Ying-ch'uan. His account seems to have been taken from the *Kuan-tzu* (fourth century B.C.); see below, p. 180, with only two alterations: the *hsiang* of the *Kuan-tzu* has become *yi,* and the tens, or *kuei,* have become *wu.*

14 *Shih ching,* p. 230.
15 Ibid., p. 232.
16 Ibid., p. 226.
17 *Chou li,* II, pp. 195, 389. The 'fire was brought back in' no less ceremonially in the last month of autumn in returning to the houses of the villages. This was called 'renewing the fire', *kai-huo,* or *pien-hou* (*Chou li,* II, p. 195).
18 The *Shuo wen* defines *lu* as a temporary accommodation, *chi*: 'They live there in spring and summer. They leave it in autumn and winter'; cf. *T'ai-p'ing yü lan,* ch. 182, 2a. A discussion on the value of the word *lu* and its difference from *chai* and *ch'an* (*Wu t'ien chih chai k'ao*) is to be found in Ku Yen-lun, *Ku-ching ching-she chih chi,* which forms a chapter of the *Ching yi ts'ung ch'ao* of Yen Chieh, ch. 17, from *Huang Ch'ing ching chieh,* 178th *chung,* ch. 1387.
19 The *ching,* formed of nine lots, was composed of three rows of three lots. Since the families of each row got together to live in the same hut during the summer, the row of three lots was called a 'residence', *wu* (*Chou li,* I, p. 231). Each hut thus had three families, except that of the middle row (the one where the common field was), which had only two. Cf. *Ch'ien-Han shu,* ch. 24, A, 1b, 2a, and Yen Shih-ku's commentary; but the author supposes that in ancient times, as in his own, the peasants went out from the village each morning, returning each evening.
20 Granet, *La Polygynie sororale et le sororat dans la Chine féodale,* p. 42.
21 On this term, see Granet, *Coutumes matrimoniales de la Chine antique,* in TP, new series XIII (1912), p. 550.
22 Granet, *Polygynie,* p. 42, assumes that the common people possessed clan names, *hsing,* which were the same for all the inhabitants of a hamlet, *li*; and he quotes as an example the father-in-law of the Prince of Han, Kuei-fu (father of Kuei, or chief of Kuei), whose family residence was in the village (*li*) of Kuei (*Shih ching,* p. 549). But this is not a happy example. Kuei is not the clan name, *hsing,* of this person, who belonged to the Chi clan (cf. ibid., p. 550). It was the name of his fief, and Kuei-fu, 'the father of

Kuei', does not mean 'Chief of the Kuei clan', as Granet seems to take it, but the Chief, the Lord, of the Land of Kuei. Moreover, a person whose sister had married King Li of Chou, and whose daughter had married the Prince of Han, was obviously not a commoner.

23 Granet, *Coutumes matrimoniales*, pp. 542, 543, 551, somewhat hesitatingly admits that the young folk must have spent the summer apart. I believe that the separation in summer to which several passages in the *Shih ching* refer was caused by special circumstances, due to the fact that the young man who came from a great distance at the time of the spring festivals was obliged to return home to work in the fields and was thus unable to return before finishing his labours towards the end of autumn. In my opinion such separation was not of a ritual kind.

24 On the marriages of commoners, see Granet, *Coutumes matrimoniales*, pp. 517–53; and *Fêtes et chansons*, the conclusions of which I generally follow. Nevertheless, I believe that these were not basically marriage customs (cf. *BEFEO*, XIX, v (1919), pp. 67–72), but that they tended to become such under the influence of the patricians' ethical code. In placing marriage in the autumn I have adopted the views of Cheng Hsüan (end of second century A.D.) as against that of the school of commentators of Wang Su (third century A.D.), which places it in the spring, with the betrothal in the preceding autumn. On these differences, cf. Granet, *Fêtes*, p. 132, who is of the same opinion and places 'the beginning of housekeeping' in the autumn (ibid., p. 317). The theory that marriages must be delayed even for several years until the girl was pregnant has been suggested to me by the fact that such a custom is still practised among all the southern barbarian tribes. Among some this is the rule (Lolos), among others it is at any rate the practice, though the theory is quite different (the Tai of Upper Tonkin). I have no formal Chinese text bearing on this subject, but we will see that the marriage of a patrician had a rite that was a relic of some analogous custom.

25 Only the nobles possessed a *hsing*: see the commentary of the third century wrongly attributed to K'ung An-kuo in the *Shu ching*, *Yao-tien*, on the expression *po hsing*, the hundred clans. Only those who had an official post had a clan name, *hsing*. Cf. Yang Shen, *Sheng-an ching shuo*, ch. 3 (*Shu ching*), 1a: *Po hsing*; Ku Yen-wu, *Jih chih lu*, ch. 23; Chavannes, *Mémoires historiques*, I, pp. 3–5, n.; Gustav Haloun, 'Constributions to the History of Clan Settlement in Ancient China', I, *Asia Major*, I (1924), p. 76. Granet is in my opinion wrong when in his *Polygynie*, p. 42, he attributes a clan name to commoners. See note 22 above.

26 H. Maspero, 'Légendes mythologiques dans le Chou king', *J. As.*, CCIV (1924), p. 69. I cannot agree with the theory of G. Haloun, op. cit., p. 79, that 'each *hsing* possesses a definite portion of land as its place of original establishment (original habitat)'.

27   As to this hypothesis, see Chavannes, *Mémoires historiques*, I, pp. 3–5, n. 1; Conrady, *China*, p. 485; Granet, *Polygynie*, p. 48, n. 3, *Danses et légendes*, I, p. 13 ff.; II, p. 428.

28   *Li chi*, II, p. 423 (*Fang chi*, attributed to Tzu-ssu); *Tso chuan*, first year of Chao, p. 580, quoting an ancient work, *Ku chih* (identical text).

29   The opposite is generally held, namely that the actual number was much higher, and certainly today the number of *hsing* is much more. But this larger number is due to the confusion, towards the end of the Ch'in, between the clan names, *hsing*, and the family names, *shih*.

30   *Shu yi chi, ch.* 1, 1a.

31   *Shih chi, ch.* 5, Chavannes, II, p. 5.

32   Ibid., *ch.* 43, Chavannes, V, pp. 27–31. He also beheld the ancestor of the grand officers, *tai-fu*, of Fan (clan Ch'i descended from Yao) in the shape of a bear, and the ancestor of Hsün (clan unknown) as a striped bear. The symbolic animal appears in these cases to be the insignia of the family, emblazoned on the standard of the family chief (Granet, *Danses et légendes*, I, pp. 386–90). In this is clearly shown the gradual weakening and transformation of the belief in animal ancestors.

33   There is no point in generalizing this subject by extending these ideas to figures who could never have been regarded in that light. For instance, Schindler in his *Development of Chinese Conceptions of Supreme Beings*, playing on the character for the name of Shun and an almost identical character for the word 'sea-gull', derives from this emperor a 'sea-gull totem'. Belief in ancestors of animal form is part of the common culture baggage of the Chinese, Tai, and other races. Cf. H. Maspero, 'De quelques interdits en relation avec les noms de famille chez les Tai-noirs', in *BEFEO*, XVI, iii, pp. 29–114; Laufer, 'Totemic traces among the Indo-Chinese', *Journal of American Folklore*, 1916. The importance of these 'traces of totemism' should not be exaggerated in historical times. Cf. Matsumoto Nobuhiro, 'Shina no sei to totemizumu' [The Chinese *hsing* and totemism], in *Shigaku*, I, 1921–22; Granet, *Danses et légendes*, II, pp. 602–6.

34   Thus the head of the Shu-sun house in Lu is called simply Shu-sun shih (*Tso chuan*, p. 598).

35   *Tso chuan*, p. 276: an elder brother, head of the family, gives his sister in marriage, then takes her away, whether she likes it or not, from this first husband, and gives her to a second one.

36   *Tso chuan*, p. 599.

37   *Li chi*, I, p. 637.

38   *Tso chuan*, p. 726.

39   *Li chi*, I, p. 74.

40   Ibid., I, p. 637.

41   On patrician marriage, see especially Granet, *Polygynie*.

42   Granet, op. cit., p. 45, adds: 'The ban on marrying outside the allied group to which one belonged', and he supposes that each

family could unite in marriage with only a small number of families connected to it by a king of *jus connubii*. The text of the *Kuo yü, ch.* 2, 1*a*, which is his authority, does not seem to me sufficient as base for a judicial law which, in any case, is confirmed neither in history nor in the romances. Given the late date of this work (middle of the third century B.C.) I see rather an allusion to a collection of precedents concerning matrimonial divination, in which the marriages of kings and princes of antiquity were analysed, to serve as rules.

43   *Shih ching*, p. 240.

44   *Tso chuan*, p. 376.

45   For a description of the rites of patrician marriage, see *Yi li, ch.* 2, pp. 367–71, Couvreur, pp. 25–27; *Li chi,* I, pp. 606–11 (*Chiao t'e sheng*), II, pp. 367–71 (*Ai kung wen*) and all of *ch.* 41 (*Hun yi*), II, pp. 641–51. The role of go-between is described without the words being mentioned in the text of the *Yi li*, and Couvreur has supplied 'messenger'.

46   The *Tso chuan*, p. 298, mentions the sending back of the horses, after the marriage of a daughter of Prince Hsüan of Lu, in Ch'i (604).

47   *Li chi*, I, pp. 429–39.

48   Cf. another explanation of this three-month period in Granet, *Coutumes matrimoniales*, pp. 556–58.

49   *Shih ching*, pp. 306–7.

50   To accept the infant was called 'receiving' it, *chieh* (*Li chi*, I, 663); or 'lifting it up', *chü* (*IIsi ching tsa chi, ch.* 2, 2*b*); to refuse it was 'not lifting it up', *pu chü* (ibid.; *Ch'ien-han shu, ch.* 97B, 5*a*); to expose it was 'abandoning it', *ch'i* (*Tso chuan*, p. 297).

51   Cf. *Kuo yü, ch.* 14, birth of Shu Yü. *Tso chuan*, p. 296: Tzu-wen, chief of the house of Jo-ao in the state of Ch'u, advises that his newly-born nephew be killed immediately, because from its cries he foresees that the child will ruin their house; but the father refuses. (The text does not say whether the uncle had seen the child, but Legge adds the word wrongly in his translation.) On the other hand Pi, Count of Tou, having secretly had a son (Nou-wu-t'u, or Tzu-wen) by the daughter of the Prince of Yün, the latter's wife orders the child, her natural grandson, to be exposed in the wilds, where it is suckled by a tigress (p. 297). Certain times were considered unlucky for birth. The fifth of the fifth month is an example: it was believed that boys born on that day would kill their father, and daughters their mother (*Shih chi, ch.* 75, 1*b*), and they were often abandoned. But there were many other reasons for exposing children. Twins were accepted but, if a woman had three children at one time, they were not 'lifted up'. Then, too, children born in the same month as their father were not accepted, etc. (*Feng su t'ung*, from *T'ai-p'ing yü lan, ch.* 361, 2*a*). See also *Ch'ien-Han shu, ch.* 27, 10*a*, where a child is 'not taken up' because it had cried in its mother's womb two months before

birth. It is buried in an embankment, where for three days passers-by hear it crying, after which the mother digs it up alive.

52 *Li chi*, I, pp. 662–72, II, p. 678; Granet, *Le dépôt de l'enfant sur le sol*, in *Revue archéologique*, 1921, pp. 305–61.

53 Ibid., I, p. 605 (*Chiao t'e sheng*).

54 *Li chi*, I, p. 468 ff.; *Chou li*, II, pp. 27–29; I, pp. 292–93 (the Three Virtues), p. 297 (the Six Sciences). On the school considered as a 'house of men', see Quistorp, *Mannergesellschaft und Altersklassen im alten China*, pp. 20–22.

55 *Yi li*, ch. 1, Couvreur, pp. 1–24 (cf. *Li chi*, ch. 40, Couvreur, II, pp. 636–40; the date of the second month is taken from the *Hsia hsiao cheng*. Quistorp, op. cit., pp. 8–18, has well shown the initiatory character of taking the hat of manhood, and the relation of the school to the primitive house of young men, facts previously noted by Conrady, *China*, p. 448.

56 Chavannes, *Dieu du Sol*, p. 456.

57 *Shih chi*, ch. 41, Chavannes, IV, p. 431.

58 *Li chi*, I, p. 77; *Chou li*, II, p. 455 (*chia*); *Li chi*, I, p. 511 (*ts'ai*).

59 The domains of the grand officers of state had no particular god of the soil (Chavannes, *Dieu du Sol*, pp. 445–46).

60 According to a tradition of the Confucian school King Chao of Ch'u wanted to give the Master 700 hamlets with their gods of the soil and their peasants, but not a fief of 700 hamlets (*Shih chi*, ch. 47, Chavannes, V, p. 371). And Yi-wu of Kuan, according to the *Hsün-tzu*, ch. 3, 22b–23a, had similarly received '300 registered gods of the soil, *shu-she*', which made him the richest man in Ch'i, but nevertheless did not constitute a fief, although it was a hereditary domain.

61 *Mencius*, pp. 162, 242.

62 Ibid., pp. 247–48.

63 Ibid., p. 284.

64 This reform was ascribed to Ch'in, the most progressive state in ancient China. It is placed among the laws that Yang of Wey [i.e. Lord Shang] got Count Hsiao to adopt about 350 B.C.

65 *Tso chuan*, p. 590: the fields of Chou had formerly been part of the fief of Wen which had been ceded by the king to the Prince of Chin, and by him to the Chao family; so they had changed hands at least three times in less than a century.

66 *Lun yü*, p. 188; *Mencius*, p. 335.

67 *Li chi*, II, p. 606. This necessarily refers to a noble, as a common man could not become a scholar, *ju*. Moreover, the description of the dwelling proves this: a peasant had the right to $2^1/_2$ *mou* for house and garden. The material situation of the poor noble was indeed worse than that of a peasant who had the right to a grant of a certain amount of land.

68 Thus, if one accepts the text literally, it was a square hut less than three metres to a side. A structure 17 feet across and 8 feet deep (17 + 17 + 8 + 8 = 50 feet; 4.25 by 2 metres), divided in the Chinese

fashion into three sections of 6 by 8 feet (1.5 by 2 metres) would give tiny partitions indeed. This hut was probably one without internal sectioning; but in that case any ritual ceremonial would be impossible.

69   *Tso chuan*, p. 186 (twelfth year of Hsi).

70   Ibid., p. 448 (tenth year of Hsiang).

71   See for example the influence exercised over Shu-sun P'ao, head of the Shu-sun house in Lu, by his squire, Niu (*Tso chuan* p. 599).

72   Tzu-kao, a disciple of Confucius, was steward, *tsai*, of Pi for the Chi family (*Lun yü*, trans. Legge, p. 246), after another disciple, Min Sun (Tzu-ch'ien) had refused the post (ibid., p. 187). A third disciple, Tzu-hsia, was steward of Chü-fu (*ibid.*, p. 270); etc.

73   *Tso chuan*, pp. 186, 191, etc.

74   Ibid., p. 191. In this passage the lord is the prince.

75   Ibid., p. 501.

76   Ibid., p. 186.

77   Ibid., p. 465.

78   *Li chi*, I, p. 147 (*T'an kung*), literally: 'that [a son] must not permit [himself and the murderer] to be together in the world'. Cf. ibid., I, p. 56 (*Ch'ü li*).

79   *Li chi*, I, p. 148. These counsels about family vengeance are put into Confucius's mouth. Cf. Haenisch, 'Die Rachepflicht, ein Widerstreit zwischen konfuzianischer Ethik und chinesischem Staatsgefühl', in *Deutsche Morgenl. Gesell.*, X (1931), nos. 1–2.

80   *Shih chi*, Chavannes, IV, p. 23.

81   Ts'ung of Kuan, from one of the great Chou families, recalls that one of his ancestors was a diviner by the tortoise-shell (*Tso chuan*, p. 649).

82   *Chou li*, I, 8, pp. 92–98.

83   There were veterinary doctors, *shou-yi* (*Chou li*, I, p. 98); and even horse-sorcerers, *wu-ma* (ibid., II, p. 259).

84   At the royal court the domestic cooks, *nei-yung*, like the public cooks, *wai-yung*, were both nobles of the second rank (*Chou li*, I, 6, p. 79). Other texts show the cooks, *yung-jen*, wearing a black robe and a hat the colour of a sparrow's head (the patrician ceremonial attire) taking part in the consecration of the Ancestral Temple (*Li chi*, II, p. 195, *Tsa chi*).

85   *Chou li*, I, 6, p.76.

86   *Shih-tzu*, in the *Ch'ün shu chih yao*, ch. 36, 8a.

87   *Lü shih ch'un ch'iu*, ch. 4, 6a.

88   *Shih chi*, Chavannes, IV, p. 442.

89   *Tso chuan*, p. 224.

90   Ibid., p. 353.

91   *Shih chi*, Chavannes, IV, pp. 439–48. The adventures of Li of Fan in Ch'i and then in T'ao seem to be a romance; but the story of a patrician, a great lord fallen into disgrace, becoming wealthy through trade remains an interesting morality tale from the general point of view.

92 *Tso chuan*, p. 664.
93 *Mencius*, pp. 340–41.
94 *Yi Chou shu*, Section 48 (*Tso Lo*), ch. 8, 7b; cf. Chavannes, *Le Dieu du Sol*, 456–57.
95 Henri Maspero, 'Le mot *ming*', in *J. As.*, 1927.
96 *Shih ching*, II, vi, 1, Legge, p. 360.
97 The usual expression is Mandate of Heaven, *T'ien-ming*; but *Ti-ming*, 'Mandate of the Lord' is also used (*Shih ching*, 447), or 'Mandate of the Lord on High', *Shang-ti-ming* (*Shu ching*, p. 369; *Yi Chou shu*, ch. 5, 3a).
98 Chang Ping-lin in *Shen-ch'üan shih-tai T'ien-tzu chü shan shuo* [In the theocratic epoch the Son of Heaven lived in the mountains], in *Chang T'ai-yen wen ch'ao*, ed. Chung-hua t'u shu kuan, ch. 4, 37a–39b, has recently put forward the idea that the ancient kings 'dwelled on the high hills so as to be closer to the vault of Heaven', because they were 'servants of Heaven' at a time when 'divine and human affairs were not clearly distinct'. Their ministers, however, remained on the lower slopes. This theory, based on premises that are worse than shaky, is not worth considering.
99 Granet, *La Polygynie sororale*, p. 39.
100 For the translation of this word, cf. H. Maspero, 'Le mot *ming*'. The name Ming-t'ang has been consecrated by the rituals; but it is not certain that it is much older than the fourth century B.C., when it first appears in the literature.
101 *Li chi*, I, pp. 677–78 (*Yü tsao*); *Lun yü*, III, xvii, p. 161; cf. *Tso chuan*, p. 245.
102 *Yi li*, Couvreur, pp. 380–82.
103 *Yi Chou shu*, ch. 5, 8a (section 48, *Tso Lo chieh*). The *Chou li*, Biot, II, p. 555, gives it as nine *li* around, which is nearly the same.
104 A little northeast of the wall at present-day Ho-nan fu.
105 For that reason it did not have to be consecrated after construction, before being lived in. *Li chi*, II, p. 197 (*Tsa chi*).
106 I have generally followed the detailed description (with plans) of the royal palace by Chiao Hsün in *Ch'ün ching kung shih t'u*, ch. 1, 21a, 44a (*Huang Ch'ing ching chieh hsü pien*, ch. 395; ed. photolith., ch. 64), which is well done, though somewhat too precise. It gives an excellent discussion of the ancient texts and commentaries.
107 The ancient writers do not tell us exactly the number of gates, courts, and buildings in the royal palace. Han writers give it an array of five gates, but are not in agreement as to their order. (See the discussion of Cheng Chung's opinion, he being a commentator of the first century A.D., by Cheng Hsüan of the second century in his own commentary to the *Chou li*, II, p. 347, n.) And this was generally accepted up to the eighteenth century when Tai Chen showed, conclusively in my opinion, that the royal palace, like those of the princes, had three gates in succession (*San ch'ao san men k'ao*, in *Tai Tung-yüan chi*, ch. 2, 3a–4b).
108 *Chou li*, II, pp. 347–48.

109   Po was the first capital of the Yin dynasty, conquered by the Chou.

110   *Han Fei tzu, ch.* 13, 13*a*. The anecdote is set in the land of Ch'u.

111   *Tso chuan*, p. 156. The present condition of the mounds around Sian ascribed to the Western Chou affords us no clue on this point: Segalen, 'Premier exposé des résultats archéologiques obtenus dans la Chine occidentale par la mission Gilbert de Voisins, Jean Lartigue et Victor Segalen' (1914), in *J. As.* (1916), pp. 401–5. As to the princely tomb of the land of Wu, described by the same author, its arrangement does not enable us to recognize whether the long underground corridor is a *su* (contrary to the rites) which has been broken off because the burial chamber was not placed at its end, for safety against robbers, or whether, as the author himself suggests, it is the actual burial chamber (Segalen, 'Le Tombeau du fils de Wou, Ve siècle avant notre ère', in *BEFEO*, XXII (1922), pp. 41–54).

112   On the role of this minister see Granet, *Danses et légendes*, II, pp. 405, 422–28.

113   *Shu ching*, pp 557–60 (*Ku ming*); Wang Kuo-wei, *Chou shu Ku ming li cheng*, from *Hsüeh shu ts'ung pien*; Henri Maspero, 'Le mot *ming*'. The *Ku ming* is a small work which describes the ceremonies carried out after the death of King Ch'eng, and the enthronement of his son King K'ang (ninth century?). The mention in it of Prince Chi of Ch'i (p. 549) in my opinion shows it to have been composed at the time Duke Hsüan of Ch'i was hegemon (middle of seventh century), when the author was trying to court favour with Hsüan by giving his ancestor an important place in the ceremony. It is thus the ritual of *Ch'un ch'iu* times which is described in that work.

Chapter 2.   *The Ancient Religion: Mythology*

1   On these divinities, see Henri Maspero, 'Légendes mythologiques dans le Chou king', pp. 8–15.

2   *Shih chi, ch.* 117, 9*a*; *Ch'ien-Han shu, ch.* 57A, 9*b*; *Ch'u tz'u pu chu, ch.* 1, 23*a*; cf. H. Maspero, op. cit., p. 57.

3   *Ch'u tz'u, ch.* 3 (*T'ien wen*), 14*a*. This being seems to have been originally represented as a toad. Cf. H. Maspero, loc. cit..

4   *Shan hai ching, ch.* 14, 8*a*, Kuo P'o's commentary. This had perhaps originally been an owl; cf. Granet, *Danses et légendes*, II, pp. 527–49.

5   Wang Ch'ung, *Lun heng, ch.* 23, tr. Forke, I, 292; Granet, *Danses et légendes*, II, p. 510.

6   *Shan hai ching, ch.* 6, 1*b*; *Huai-nan tzu, ch.* 4, 16*a*; cf. Erkes, *Das Weltbild des Huai-nan-tze*, p. 69.

7   On the gods of the Four Seas, see *Shan hai ching, ch.* 8, 6*a*; *ch.* 14, 5*a*.

8   *Ch'u tz'u, ch.* 2, 12*b*–16*b*; *Li chi*, p. 266.

9   Kao-mei: *Li chi*, I, p. 342 (*Yüeh ling*); Chiao-mei: Mao's Commentary to the *Shih ching, Shang sung, Hsüan niao* (cf. Legge, p. 536). On this divinity, see Granet, *Fêtes et chansons*, p. 165.

10   The *Po hu t'ung, ch.* 1, 3*a*, gives, as the fifth of the domestic gods, the well, while the commentaries to the *Li chi* give that of the street. The first four are mentioned separately in the *Yüeh ling*: *hu*, p. 331; *tsao*, p. 354; *chung-liu*, p. 396; *men*, p. 373. Cf. Chavannes, *Dieu du Sol*, p. 438; Granet, *Danses et légendes*, I, p. 368.

11   *Chou li*, II, p. 195: the *ssu-kuan* sacrificed to the spark before every sacrifice.

12   *Shan hai ching, ch.* 14, 8*a*; Granet, op. cit., I, p. 263, II, pp. 505–15. The Divine Blind Man, Shen-ku, to whom the musicians of the Lu court rendered worship (*Kuo yü, ch.* 3, 20*a*, *Lu yü*), was the first musician and not the God of Music. The distinction is analogous to those existing, for example, between Hsien-nung, the First Husbandman, and Hou-chi, the God of Agriculture, or between Hsien-ch'ui, the First Cook, and Tsao-kung, the God of the Hearth.

13   Granet, op. cit., II, p. 501.

14   *Chou li*, II, p. 99; *Shih ching*, p. 291.

15   *Han chiu yi*, in *Hou-Han shu, ch.* 15, 4*b*; *Chuang-tzu, ch.* 19, tr. Wieger, p. 363; Chang Heng, *Tung ching fu*, in *Wen hsüan, ch.* 3, 7*a*. Cf. Granet, *Danses et légendes*, I, pp. 306–20.

16   *Shan hai ching, ch.* 17, 82*a*; *Shih ching*, p. 532; cf. H. Maspero, op. cit., p. 56.

17   *Shan hai ching, ch.* 2, 24*b*; *ch.* 16, 77*a*.

18   Every time the ancient texts speak of Hou-t'u, they mean the imperial God of the Soil, Kou-lung. The idea of making a goddess of the earth is a recent idea in China, going back no farther than the Han period (Chavannes, *Dieu du Sol*, p. 524). It is so difficult to banish from European minds the notion of the classical Mother Earth that they have repeatedly tried (see. Laufer, *Jade*, p. 144; Schindler, *Supreme Beings*, p. 312) to show that in ancient China as well Hou-t'u was a goddess, impossible though it is to bend the ancient texts to this theory or rather to reintroduce that idea through a slant which is more ingenious than convincing. (Granet, *Le Dépôt de l'enfant*, pp. 358–61; *Danses et légendes* I, p. 17.) Cf. an excellent passage in Grube, *Religion und Kultus der Chinesen*, pp. 35–36.

19   The translation of this expression must be considered extremely tentative, since its precise meaning is really not known. Even the meaning of each of the terms is doubtful: that of *hao* seems to have been lost since Han times, and the traditional gloss is transparently nothing but an amplification of the idea of Heaven; *shang* can mean 'on high' literally, or 'supreme' figuratively. Even the words *t'ien* and *ti* are far from simple: given the antiquity of the expression, the meaning of *t'ien* is doubtful. It has long been noted that the ancient character uses the human form for writing this word, which seems to imply an anthropomorphic conception of Heaven; and the corresponding word in the Tai languages, *t'en*, designates the celestial gods, while the phsyical heaven, the firmament, is designated by the word *fa*. As for the word *ti*, it seems

to be literally a designation of the celestial gods, from which its usual meanings (ritual title of a dead emperor or, in general, emperor) are merely derivatives.

Schindler, *Supreme Beings*, has tried to take this expression apart and to rediscover in it two distinct divinities, one belonging to the Chinese of the west and the other to those of the east; but these hypotheses are quite unsatisfactory.

20   *Shih ching*, Legge, p. 465.

21   For example, the rock of the banner of the Lord's Terrace, *Ti-t'ai chih ch'i*, on Mount Hsiu-yü (*Shan hai ching*, ch. 5, 21*b*); the Liqueur of the Lord's Terrace, *Ti-t'ai chih chiang*, on Mount Kao-ch'ien (ibid., p. 43*b*).

22   *Shih ching*, p. 434.

23   *Shan hai ching*, ch. 2, 24*b*; ch. 16, 7*a*.

24   Sung Yü, *Kao t'ang fu*, in *Wen hsüan*, ch. 19, 1*a*; cf *Shan hai ching*, ch. 5, 22*a*; Granet, *Danses et légendes*, II, pp. 519 n., 524.

25   *Shan hai ching*, ch. 5, 51*a*. The euhemeristic tradition makes them into daughters of a human *ti*, Yao, and identifies them with the wives of Shun.

26   *Chan kuo ts'e*, ch. 7, 7*b*; *Lü shih ch'un ch'iu*, ch. 17, 10*b*.

27   These phrases are all translations or adaptations of passages from the classics: *Shih ching*, pp. 448, 451; *Shu ching*, p. 245; *Shih ching*, pp. 543, 434. Schindler, *The Development of the Chinese Conceptions of Supreme Beings*, pp. 338–39, gathers a great number of ancient quotations on Shang-ti.

28   *Tso chuan*, Legge, p. 514.

29   *Kuo yü*, ch. 8, 5*b* (*Chin yü*).

30   *Tso chuan*, pp. 374 (year 581), 157 (year 650).

31   *Mo-tzu*, ch. 8, 3*a*, Forke, p. 346.

32   *Yen-tzu ch'un ch'iu*, ch. 1, 15*a*.

33   It is not impossible that in reality there were, not five regional Ti under Shang-ti, but five Ti in all, Shang-ti being at the same time the lord of the central region of heaven, the Yellow Lord, Huang-ti. It is quite remarkable that this latter never had a peculiar place of worship. The division of this divinity into two may be laid to the literati of the end of Chou or of Han who, tending to systematize things, so often distorted the old religion through their love of symmetry.

The Five Lords are not a recent mythological creation (end of Chou or beginning of Han), as Wang Su wrongly supposed in the third century A.D., and as scholars of all ages have often repeated since then. They appear already under the name of Lords of the (Heavenly) Regions, *fang ti*, in an inscription from Yin times in which three of them are mentioned — those of the South, the East, and the Centre (*Tseng ting Yin hsü shu ch'i k'ao shih*, ch. 3, 60*a*).

34   *Shih chi*, ch. 5, Chavannes, II, p. 16; IV, p. 420.

35   G. Haloun, *Die Rekonstruktion der chinesischen Urgeschichte durch die Chinesen* in *Japanische-Deutsche Zeitschrift für Wissenschaft und Technik*, III (1925), pp. 243–70.

36 *Kuo yü, ch.* 8, 5*b.*
37 *Mo-tzu, ch.* 8, 3*a,* Forke, p. 347.
38 Generally on the God of the Soil, see Chavannes, *Le Dieu du Sol dans la Chine antique* (appendix to *Le T'ai-chan,* pp. 437–525).
39 Chavannes, op. cit., p. 505, believes that Kou-lung is merely the deity associated with the sacrifices of the God of the Soil, rather than the God of the Soil himself. This is Cheng Hsüan's theory (second century A.D.), but it cannot hold against examination of the ancient texts. Especially the *Tso chuan,* p. 731, and the *Li chi,* II, pp. 268–69, declare explicitly that, in consequence of his fine conduct, the son of Kung-kung, Kou-lung, Sovereign Earth, became God of the Soil, *she.* The *Tso chuan,* naturally euhemerizing, makes Hou-t'u into the title of a functionary and sets his apotheosis in the time of the Emperor Shao-hao; but that should not conceal the mythological nature of the legend. Franke, *Kêng tschi t'u,* p. 7, has correctly observed the identity of Kou-lung, of Sovereign Earth, and of the God of the Soil; and Schindler goes wrong (*The Development of the Chinese Conceptions of Supreme Beings,* p. 312 ff.) in seeking to separate them so as to make Hou-t'u a goddess.
40 *Mo-tzu, ch.* 8, Forke, p. 352. Chavannes, op. cit., p. 473, after having demonstrated that the God of the Soil was originally a tree, has sought to prove that it was even originally the whole sacred forest; for his part, Granet, *Fêtes et chansons,* p. 254, makes the God of the Soil the inheritor, for feudal worship, of the ancient Sacred Place of pre-feudal times.
41 One of the lost chapters of the *Shu ching,* in *Po hu t'ung, ch.* 1, 3*b.* Cf. Chavannes, *Dieu du Sol,* p. 467.
42 *Lun yü,* p. 162; Chavannes, op. cit., p. 468.
43 Chavannes, *Dieu du Sol,* p. 477. Certain Chinese scholars suppose that the tablet was originally of wood, and this hypothesis has been taken up by Schindler, *Supreme Beings,* p. 319; but it does not seem correct to me.
44 *Mo-tzu, ch.* 8, Forke, p. 350.
45 *Tso chuan,* Legge, p. 168.
46 Chavannes, *Dieu du Sol,* p. 475.
47 *Chao hun (Ch'u tz'u, ch.* 9), 4, trans. Erkes, pp. 21–22.
48 *Tso chuan,* pp. 176–77.
49 *Shu ching,* p. 155 *(Kan shih).*
50 *Chou li,* pp. 182–83.
51 Granet, *La Religion des Chinois,* pp. 73–74.
52 *Tso chuan,* pp. 629, 225, 352.
53 *Hsiao ching yüan shen ch'i,* in *Ch'u hsüeh chi, ch.* 6; *T'ai-p'ing yü lan, ch.* 8, 16*a; ch.* 61, 1*b.*
54 *Li chi,* II, p. 44 *(Hsüeh chi).*
55 *Shang shu chung hou,* in *T'ai-p'ing yü lan, ch.* 82, 3*a; ch.* 872, 5*a.*
56 *Han Fei tzu, ch.* 9, 3*b.*
57 *Shan hai ching, ch.* 12, 4*a.* In place of the modern text I adopt that of the ancient citations appearing in the *Wen hsüan, ch.* 12, 5*a; Ch'u tz'u pu chu, ch.* 2, 20*a.*

58   *Yen-tzu ch'un ch'iu*, in *Hou-Han shu*, ch. 90A, 4*b*.
59   *Chiu ko* (*Ch'u tz'u*), ch. 2, 9*a*.
60   *Shan hai ching*, ch. 12, 4*b*; *Mu T'ien-tzu chuan*, ch. 1, 4*a*; *Shui ching chu*, ch. 1, 4*b*.
61   *Chiu ko*, p. 9*a*.
62   *Chu shu chi nien*, *Prolegomena*, pp. 121, 122; *T'ien wen* (*Ch'u tz'u*), ch. 3, 12*b*; *Shan hai ching*, ch. 14, 5*a*.
63   *Huai-nan tzu*, ch. 19, 1*b*; Granet, *Danses et légendes*, II, p. 466 ff.
64   *Shih chi*, ch. 126, 5*b*–6*b*.
65   *T'ung chien kang mu*, *ch'ien pien*, ch. 18, 14*a*.
66   *Tso chuan*, p. 810 (year 488); *Shih chi*, ch. 40, Chavannes, IV, pp. 379–80 (year 489).
67   These four terms are not possible to pair off two by two: *p'o* and *hun* are far the more precise and almost technical in designating human souls (*hun* in this sense is a very ancient word, since we find its cognate, *k'uan*, in the Tai languages). The other two designate all spiritual manifestations, and *kuei*, used by itself, seems to denote particularly the exterior manifestations of the soul remaining in the tomb. These are ideas of very diverse origin and date, which have been more or less well amalgamated to form the classic theory.
68   *Tso chuan*, p. 618 (year 535).
69   *Shih ching*, Legge, p. 428: 'King Wen is up there, / how he gleams in the heaven! / King Wen rises and descends, — he is at the right and the left of the Lord.' Cf. the inscription of the Chou ancestral bell, *Tsung-Chou chung*: 'My late father the king before me, full of majesty, is up there, he is powerful and rich, he makes many blessings descend upon me ...' (Juan Yüan, *Chi ku chai chung ting yi ch'i k'uan shih*, ch. 3, 9*b*; Wu Shih-fen, *Chün ku lu*, ch. 3, 3, 57*b*).
70   *Yi Chou shu*, ch. 9, 6*a*: a crown prince of Chou, foreseeing his death, says, 'In three years I shall go up to be the guest of the Lord on High.'
71   In the *Shu ching*, p. 230, King P'an-keng, speaking of the sacrifices made to dead kings, declares to his ministers: 'When I perform the great sacrifices to the former kings, your ancestors in their retinue delight in them with the kings.' And again (p. 240): 'Your ancestors, your fathers, will abandon you. ... Your ancestors, your fathers, will advise my sovereign [ancestors], saying, "Inflict a great punishment upon our descendants".'
72   Cf. *Tso chuan*, p. 618: King Ching, sending his condolences to Prince Ling of Wey upon the death of his father Prince Hsiang (535), says: 'My uncle is dead; he is at the right and at the left of the kings who preceded me to assist them in serving the Lord on High.'
73   *Shih chi*, Chavannes, V, pp. 26–27.
74   *Chao hun* (*Ch'u tz'u*) ch. 9, 3*a*, trans. Erkes, p. 23.
75   *Tso chuan*, p. 142.
76   *Mo-tzu*, ch. 8, Forke, pp. 348–49 (land of Ch'i).
77   *Tso chuan*, p. 618.
78   *Tso chuan*, p. 219 (year 629).

79 *Chan kuo ts'e, ch.* 5, 6*b*.
80 *Tso chuan*, p. 6.
81 *Li chi*, I, p. 226; for the personal name and the date of this personage, see *Tso chuan*, p. 716 (year 516).
82 The most important texts regarding this custom up to our time have been gathered and translated by De Groot, *The Religious System of China*, II, p. 1, III, pp. 721–35, and by Shigematsu Shunsho, *Shina kodai junsō no fūshū ni tsuite* (Researches on the custom of suttee in ancient China) in *Shiratori hakase kanreki kinen tōyōshi ronsō* (Tokyo, 1925), pp. 481–540.
83 The word *hsün*, designating the human victims interred alive in tombs, is simply a special application of the word *hsün*, 'to follow': 'those who follow the deceased'.
84 *Mo-tzu*, Forke, p. 300.
85 *K'uo ti chih*, citation appearing in *Shih chi cheng yi, Shih chi*, ch. 32, 6*a* (at the end of the *Yung-chia* era, pp. 307–12).
86 *Shih chi*, II, p. 22 ; *Tso chuan*, pp. 244, 347, 747.
87 *Tso chuan*, p. 328. This is not the only case known from Chin: *Tso chuan*, p. 374, contains an anecdote regarding a servant buried with Prince Ching of Chin (581).
88 *Li chi*, I, p. 229.
89 *Chan kuo ts'e, ch.* 3, 50*b*.
90 On the several known cases of the dead conceived of under animal form, and the rare traces of totemism, see above, p. 74.
91 For funeral ceremonies, see especially the *Li chi, ch.* 19 (*Sang ta chi*), Couvreur, II, p. 203; *ch.* 32 (*Wen sang*), p. 552; *ch.* 33 (*Fu wen*), p. 561; *Yi li, ch.* 11–14, Couvreur, pp. 439–540.
92 In neolithic times, the prehistoric ancestors of the Chinese practised double inhumation and after the corpse had lost its flesh, covered the bones over again with a coating of ochre before laying them in the final tomb (Davidson Black, 'A Note on the Physical Characters of the Prehistoric Kansu Race', in Andersson, *Preliminary Report on Archaeological Research in Kansu, Mem. of the Geolog. Survey of China*, Ser. A, no. 5 (June 1925), pp. 55–56. In historical times when the stripping away of the flesh was no longer practised, the various objects of funeral furniture were still coated with a layer of vermilion (Pelliot, *A propos des bronzes de Sin-tcheng, TP* (1924), p. 255).
93 See below, pp. 122–25, for the arrangement of the chapels in the Ancestral Temple.

Chapter 3. Clergy, Places of Worship, and Ceremonies

1 *Li chi*, I, p. 100 (*Ch'ü li*).
2 Schindler, *Das Priestertum im alten China*, p. 35, considers the king and his functionaries, as well as princes and lords, to be priests of the official cult. Clearly the king had a sacred quality (yet it was his alone, and neither princes nor functionaries shared it). But not every person endowed with a sacred character is necessarily a

priest: for example, the Brahmins are always sacred, but not always priests.

3   The rituals show very clearly that the presence of one or several praying-priests by the side of the sacrificer is indispensable, and that nobody can be both at the same time. See below, p. 116, and compare the anecdote regarding the spirit of Chu of Tan which had come down at Kuo: King Hui sent him a descendant to offer sacrifice, because 'the ancestors only eat the offerings of their descendants'; but the ceremony was carried on by the Grand Priest (*Kuo yü, ch.* 1, 14a, *Chou yü*). The same formula is found in the *Tso chuan*, p. 157 (tenth year of Hsi); ibid., p. 219 (thirty-first year of Hsi).

4   The *Chu shu chi nien*, p. 160, notes that in 727, Prince Hui of Lu having asked King P'ing of Chou about the rites of the *chiao* sacrifice and of the Ancestral Temple, the king sent to him Shih Chüeh (or, Chüeh the Scribe) to make him cease these sacrifices. The *Lü-shih ch'un ch'iu, ch.* 2, adds that Hui kept the scribe at his court and that his descendants who remained in Lu continued to manage the *chiao* sacrifices there.

5   On the various kinds of priests, see *Chou li*, pp. 85–101. The Priest of Shang and the Priest of Hsia are mentioned in the *Yi li*, pp. 448 ff.

6   Chavannes, 'La Divination par l'écaille de tortue dans la haute antiquité chinoise, d'après un livre de M. Lo Tchen-yu', in *J. As.*, ser. 10, no. 17 (1911), pp. 127–37.

7   A hereditary post of *ssu-pu* appears in the inscription on the tripod of Hu: 'Thus speaks ... the king ...: Hu, I charge you to continue the services of the director of the Auguries of your grandsire and of your sire!' (*Chi ku chai chung ting yi ch'i k'uan shih, ch.* 4, 35b). Cf. also the Kuan family of Ch'u, *Tso chuan*, p. 649.

8   *Chou li*, II, p. 76: overseer of tortoises, *kuei-jen*; p. 77: overseer of *chui* wood, *chui-shih*.

9   The official manuals of divination varied according to the state: at the Chou court, it was the *Yi ching*; at Sung the *Kuei tsang*; at Chin the *Lien shan*. The list of hexagrams was the same everywhere, though their order varied.

10   *Chou li*, II, p. 80.

11   *Yi ching*, app. 3 (*Hsi tz'u*), Legge, p. 365 (*Sacred Books of the East*, XVI).

12   *Chou li*, II, p. 82 (*chan-meng*); p. 84 (*shih-chin*). Ssu-ma Ch'ien has preserved a summary of a *shih-chin* manual, *Shih chi*, III, pp. 385–96. The king had his dreams interpreted, *chan-meng*, to find out which were auspicious; to dream of a bear foretells the birth of sons, to dream of a serpent the birth of daughters (*Shih ching*, II, iv, 5, sts. 6–7, Legge, p. 306). When the shepherds see men who change into fish, that means that the harvest will be bountiful; when one dreams of little standards which are replaced by great banners, that means that the population will increase (ibid., p. 309).

13   Incapability of sacrificer: *Tso chuan*, p. 619: in the middle of the seventh century, Meng-chih, eldest son of Prince Hsiang of Wey was barred from the throne because, being weak in the legs and

walking with difficulty, he was unfit for the ancestral worship. At about the same time, Ch'eng of Ts'ui (a member of one of the important families of Ch'i) was disqualified because he was a cripple, and his younger brother was designated as head of the family (ibid., p. 535). This was not only because their ailments would have materially hampered or embarrassed them in the course of the ceremonies, since new-born infants managed those, carried in their nurses' arms. There is no special text concerning priests; but it is clear that they must have been subject to similar disqualifications. Certain impurities (mutilation, conviction of an offence) prevented one from even attending ceremonies (*Lun heng*, ch. 23, Forke, II, pp. 378–81).

14   *Tso chuan*, p. 649.

15   This incompatibility is nowhere stated; but it emerges clearly from the rituals, in which priests and sacrificing principals appear always with perfectly separate roles.

16   *Kuo yü*, ch. 18, 1*a–b*. Cf. *Pao p'u tzu*, ch. 2, 9*b*: to see ghosts, *kuei* — called *hsi* if male and *wu* if female — is a natural gift which cannot be learned.

17   De Groot, *The Religious System of China*, VI, ii, pt. 5, 'The Priesthood of Animism', pp. 1187–211.

18   *Mo-tzu*, ch. 8, Forke, p. 349.

19   *Shan hai ching*, ch. 16, 3*a*; cf. *ch.* 7, 3*b*, the land of the sorcerer Hsien, where all the sorcerers live, and *ch.* 11, 6*a*, the six sorcerers who gather the herb of immortality. The legend of the sorcerer Hsien, Wu Hsien, has been mixed with that of the Yin dynasty, and he has become the wise minister of King T'ai-mou (*Shu ching*, p. 478), to whom sacrifices were offered. The *Shuo wen* ascribes to him the invention of sorcery, and to P'eng that of medicine. On the sorceress Yang, besides the *Shan hai ching*, loc. cit., cf. *Chao hun* (*Ch'u tz'u*, ch. 9), 1*b* (Erkes, p. 13, translates in a different way), where she responds to Shang-ti, who orders her to summon up and reunite the souls of Ch'ü Yüan: 'I am responsible for dreams, my lord — your order is difficult to carry out.' Nevertheless, the classical interpretation is that she is concerned with divination. The sorcerers of Fukien still nowadays carry on a special worship of Wu Hsien (De Groot, op. cit., p. 1205).

20   *Shih chi*, ch. 28, Chavannes, III, p. 451. This passage concerns sacrifices established in 201 by Kao-tsu of the Han dynasty to commemorate the sojourns of his ancestors in various principalities. Despite the rather late date, however, it is only the official establishment and the creation of colleges which is specific to the Han. For the cults themselves, it is unlikely that Kao-tsu made any innovation: these spirits must have been those to whom the local sorceresses had sacrificed for a long time.

21   *Chiu ko* (*Ch'u tz'u*, ch. 2), p. 16*b*; cf. H. Maspero, 'Légendes mythologiques dans le Chou king', p. 22.

22   *Tso chuan*, p. 157.

23   *Mo-tzu, ch.* 8, Forke, p. 346.
24   *Chiu ko (Ch'u tz'u, ch.* 2), p. 3*b, Yün chung chün*: purificatory baths. See the description of the sorceress's costumes in several poems: court costume with sword for the *Tung-huang t'ai-yi* (p. 2*a*); robe of variegated colours for the Lord of the Clouds, *Yün-chung chün* (p. 4*a*); pendants of jade for the Grand Director of Fate, *Ta ssu-ming* (p. 16*b*); etc.
25   Ibid., pp. 2*a*–3*b* (*Tung-huang t'ai-yi*).
26   Ibid., pp. 24*a*–*b* (*Li hun*). Pfizmaier, *Das Li sao und die neun Gesänge*, p. 188, by error includes in this piece the last stanza of the preceding one.
27   *Chiu ko (Ch'u tz'u, ch.* 2), p. 17*b* (*Tung chün*).
28   Ibid., pp. 24*a*–*b* (*Li hun*).
29   Ibid., p. 19*a* (*Mo po*); this is the usual expression to designate ecstasy.
30   *Li chi,* I, p. 262 (*T'an kung*).
31   *T'ang chih kuan hsing* (a lost chapter of the *Shu ching*), in *Mo-tzu, ch.* 8, 18*b*, Forke, pp. 371–72, the reading of which I accept.
32   *Chou li,* II, p. 103. Cf. below, p. 135.
33   *Li chi,* I, p. 207; II, pp. 234, 244.
34   *Li chi,* II, p. 236.
35   *Chou li,* II, p. 225.
36   *Tso chuan,* p. 547; *Li chi,* I, p. 235 (*T'an kung*). Prince Hsiang of Lu, who was visiting the Ch'u court in 544 due to the fact the King K'an had died, was obliged to go and clothe the corpse as a sign of his dependence; and he revenged himself for this humiliation by appearing at the ceremony preceded by his sorcerer. The anecdote shows that sorcerers accompanied princes on journeys.
37   *Chou li,* II, p. 102; *Tso chuan,* p. 180; *Li chi,* I, p. 261 (*T'an kung*).
38   *Chuang-tzu,* p. 95; cf. *Lieh-tzu,* p. 265.
39   *Tso chuan,* p. 157.
40   *Shih chi,* Chavannes, V, pp. 29–31.
41   See the inscription of the 'Imprecations against Ch'u of King Hui-wen of Ch'in', undated, but probably from 313 B.C., Chavannes, *Mémoires historiques,* II (app. 1), p. 546.
42   *Tso chuan,* p. 34. The name of Chung-wu signifies literally 'the sorcerer (or sorceress) of the bell'; but it is not clear that it should be translated as such.
43   *Li chi,* II, p. 259 (*Chi fa*).
44   *Chou li,* I, p. 441.
45   *Tso chuan,* pp. 106, 107: *Kung-yang chuan, ch.* 6, 10*b* 11*a*, and the commentary on *ch.* 3, 17*b*.
46   For example, among the Chou, kings Wen, Ch'eng, Chao, Kung, Hsiao, Li, Yu, etc., were *chao*; kings Wu, K'ang, Mu, Yii, Yi, Hsüan, etc., were *mu*. The arrangement of the ancestral temple served as a model for the conception of how the ancestors were classified in the other world: they are spoken of as 'to the right and to the left of the Lord on High' in heaven, as the *chao* and the *mu* were to the right and left of the First Ancestor in the Ancestral Temple.

47 Granet, *Polygynie*, p. 61, sees in this division of dead ancestors into *chao* and *mu* a final vestige of an ancient social division among the living, into alternating classes. Cf. Granet, *La Civilisation chinoise* (1929), p. 373.

48 The word *t'iao* actually designates the tablets which have been displaced and removed from the chapels they occupied, the ancestors they represent having lost the right to regular worship; and also by extension it means the place where these old tablets were kept.

49 *Li chi*, II, p. 262 (*Chi fa*); cf. I, p. 287 (*Wang chih*). The arrangement of the Ancestral Temple of the Chou kings has been the subject of numerous discussions among Chinese scholars. The theory I adopt is close to that of Cheng Hsüan and of the Han commentators.

50 *Kuo yü*, ch. 15, 6*b*. Prince Chuang of Wey, in 492, invokes in prayer 'his august ancestor King Wen, his illustrious ancestor K'ang-shu, his accomplished ancestor Duke Hsiang, his father Duke Ling'. The last two are his father and grandfather. It is clear that he is invoking the entire line of his ancestral temple, except for the First Ancestor, *Shih-tsu*, since otherwise the choice of these ancestors would be incomprehensible. Cf. *Tso chuan*, Legge, p. 799: the same enumeration except for the father.

51 *Li chi*, I, 737 (*Ming-t'ang wei*).

52 *Tso chuan*, second year of Wen, Legge, p. 234.

53 *Li chi*, I, p. 431 (*Tseng-tzu wen*).

54 *Chou li*, II, p. 14.

55 *Li chi*, II, pp. 263–65 (*Chi fa*).

56 Before Chou times, the kings of Yin had had two storeys to the central building of their Sacred Palace, if we may believe the tradition of their descendants, the dukes of Sung. In Sung this two-level construction was so characteristic that it gave its name to the whole palace, the House with Two Storeys, *ch'ung-wu*.

57 *Tso chuan*, p. 40.

58 *Li chi*, I, p. 734 (*Ming-t'ang wei*).

59 The arrangement of the Ming-t'ang has given rise to very confused discussions among Chinese scholars. In the absence of archaeological evidence, only a very summary description seems to me possible. See H. Maspero, 'Le mot *ming*'.

60 *Li chi*, II, p. 195 (*Tsa chi*).

61 *Ibid.*, p. 197.

62 *Li chi*, I, p. 393 (*Yüeh ling*).

63 Or even outside the gate of the capital, as princes Wen of Lu (in 616) and Hui of Ch'i (in 607) did to chiefs who had been taken prisoner (*Tso chuan*, p. 258; *Shih chi*, Chavannes, IV, pp. 63, 115, 116). A feudatory prince who had made an expedition against rebels or barbarians sent prisoners to the king so that he might present them at the Ancestral Temple (*Tso chuan*, pp. 118–19).

64 *Chuang-tzu*, ch. 4, 241.

65 Cf. Granet, *La Religion des Chinois*, p. 82; *Yi li*, p. 596.

66 *Chou li*, II, pp. 36–37.
67 An excellent interpretation of the ancient texts on music has been given by Mr. Wang Kuo-wei: *Yüeh shih k'ao lüeh* in *Kuang-ts'ang hsüeh ch'ün ts'ung shu*, ser. 1, no. 1 (year 1916).
68 *Shen-pao*: *Shih ching*, pp. 370, 372; *shih*: *Shih ching*, pp. 372, 375, 477, etc.; *Li chi*, I, pp. 13, 47, 455, 462, etc. The meaning of the expression *shen-pao* has been established by Chu Hsi, who related it to *ling-pao*; and Legge, loc. cit., is wrong in adopting an interpretation which, although generally accepted, is no less certainly incorrect.
69 *Li chi*, I, pp. 557, 618.
70 *Li chi*, II, p. 335 (*Chi t'ung*); *Yi li*, pp. 543, 584.
71 *Kuo yü*, ch. 14, 15a.
72 *Chou li*, II, p. 332.

Chapter 4. The Annual Cycle of Religious Festivals

1 *Li chi*, ch. 4 (*Yüeh ling*), I, pp. 338–39.
2 *Yi ching*, trans. Legge, p. 365 (app. 3).
3 On the identity between agricultural and religious calendars, see also Granet, *Fêtes et chansons*, p. 179, n. 3.
4 M. Schindler, *On the Travel, Wayside and Wind Offerings in Ancient China*, 633 ff., believed himself able to prove that the *chiao* was originally a sacrifice to the Winds upon departing (on an expedition, etc.). That the *chiao* rite was used as a solemn sacrifice on various occasions is not in doubt; but it seems certain to me that it was originially tied to a seasonal period.
5 *Chou li*, II, p. 103. This ceremony, which seems to have been rather mysterious — since the names of the divinities appear to have been known only by the same sorcerers, *wu*, who summoned them — was poorly understood by the commentators. As early as Han times there were controversies over the nature of the 'Four Distant Ones', which Cheng Chung supposed to be the sun, moon, stars, and oceans, while others considered them the gods of mountains, rivers, seas, and so on.
   The princes of Lu, having only a limited local authority, sacrificed only to the Three Distant Ones, *san-wang* (*Tso chuan*, p. 219; *Kung-yang chuan*, ch. 5, 28a–b), who are no better known. The Distant Ones to whom the kings of Ch'u sacrificed were four rivers, the Yangtze and three of its tributaries, the Han, the Ch'ü, and the Chang (*Tso chuan*, p. 810). One of the Distant Ones to whom worship was rendered in Chin was Mount Liang, near Hsia-yang, in Shansi (*Erh ya*, ch. chung, 13b, ed. *Ssu pu ts'ung k'an*).
6 *Chou li*, II, p. 31.
7 The description of the *chiao* sacrifice is taken principally from the *Chiao t'e sheng* (*Li chi*, I, p. 589 ff.,), fleshed out with the aid of various passages from the *Shih ching*, the *Tso chuan*, the *Chou li*, other chapters of the *Li chi*, and so on. Most of these texts were reassembled in the

eighth century A D by Tu Yu in his *T'ung tien, ch.* 42; and Ma Tuan-lin did it more completely in the thirteenth century in the *Wen hsien t'ung k'ao, ch.* 68.

8   Father Couvreur, *Li chi*, I, p. 589, following the commentators, sets the *chiao* sacrifice at the winter solstice and has his second paragraph begin with these words: '[At the winter solstice], the sacrifice offered to heaven in the countryside. ...' The text has nothing corresponding to the words in brackets. It states simply that 'the *chiao* sacrifice accompanies the coming of the long days', which is far from precise and could designate the time of the spring equinox, after which the days are longer than the nights, as well as it could the winter solstice, after which the days begin to grow longer. The commentators have given the passage a precision which it does not possess.

They take their main argument from the following passage of the *Chiao t'e sheng*, p. 591: 'For the *chiao* sacrifice, a day was chosen [the first cyclical character for which was *hsin*]. When the Chou performed the *chiao* sacrifice for the first time, the *hsin* day fell upon the winter solstice.' But no ancient text gives calendar indications this precise. They are found, indeed, among the authors of Han times, but these were derived by calculation; they thus represent no tradition and have consequently no validity, so that the argument derived from them falls to the ground. (Cf. *Shih chi, ch.* 28, Chavannes, III, p. 417, citing the *Chou kuan*: 'At the winter solstice, a sacrifice was made to Heaven in the southern suburb to accompany the coming of the long days.' Chavannes indicates in a note that this passage does not occur in the *Shu ching*, nor in the *Chou li*.) On the contrary, an ancient text gives the date for the *chiao* sacrifice, offered for the first time by King Wu after his victory over the Shang and his return to Chou. This is a passage in the authentic *Wu ch'eng* (the chapter of the present-day *Shu ching* which bears this name is false), cited by Liu Hsin in a note from the end of the first century B.C. (*Ch'ien-Han shu, ch.* 21B, 12*b*): 'The fourth month ... the day following [the twenty-third of the month] *hsin-hai*, he sacrificed on the altar of Heaven.' The choice of a *hsin* day demonstrates that the author of this passage wished to indicate a *chiao* sacrifice, and that informs us as to the usage of the court in the time when he was writing — which is unfortunately not certain. But the fourth month of the official Chou calendar is the second month of spring according to the agricultural calendar, in which the equinox occurs.

Moreover, the objections which the commentators pose to this date are not historical, but ritual: The *chiao* sacrifice in Lu occurred in the spring, and they wish the royal sacrifice to precede that of the vassal Lu; but on the other hand, the *chiao* had to begin the year, so they wish to set it in the first month, whatever the calendar might be. To attain their ends, any way seemed good to them. According to the legend, King Wu won his victory in the first month (that of the solstice) and he made a sacrifice to Heaven right on the battle-field of Mu-yeh (*Ta-chuan* in *Li chi*, I, p. 776). Since Mu-yeh was in the southern suburb of the Yin capital, this sacrifice — the first he made as a king — was considered as the first *chiao* of the Chou dynasty.

From that come the phrases in the *Chiao t'e sheng*; from that also the fact that the forger who fabricated the text of the present-day *Wu ch'eng*, utilizing the ancient data but arranging them according to his point of view, modified the passage on the sacrifice which King Wu — returned to Chou — offered in the fourth month of the following year (*Ch'ien-Han shu*, ch. 21B, 12b), and made of the 'sacrifice on the altar of Heaven' which characterized the *chiao*, a mere 'offering on a pyre', which might be a sacrifice upon returning from an expedition (*Shu ching*, p. 309). There is no great interest in following the Chinese scholars into this area where questions of ritualistic orthodoxy take precedence over historical criticism; and it seems to me preferable to leave their hypotheses aside and stick to the facts.

The princes of Lu performed their *chiao* sacrifice in spring — the theoretical date being the fortnight *ch'i-chih* 'when the insects swarm' (*Tso chuan*, p. 46), which is to say a fortnight in the month preceding the equinox. For the usage at the royal court we have but a single example: that takes us back to the same period, in the month of the equinox. The tradition according to which the princes of Lu followed the royal practice indeed seems to me to have been confirmed: in consequence, it is around the spring equinox, and not around the winter solstice, that the royal sacrifice must be placed, as well as that of the princes of Lu.

9   In Sung the sacrificial victim's colour was white.

10   *The Wen hsien t'ung k'ao*, ch. 68, 5b (for reasons which I do not know) gives a prayer — that said by the Emperor Chao of Han when he took the cap of manhood — as the ancient formula of the Grand Priest at the *chiao* sacrifice.

11   The odes *Sheng-min* and *Ssu-wen* are preserved in the *Shih ching*, pp. 465 and 580.

12   The *Kuo-yü*, ch. 1, 6b–9a, sec. 6 (*Chou yü*), gives a long description of the Ploughing Festival, but since it is ascribed to high antiquity, its precise validity for certain types of functions is difficult to ascertain. See also *Li chi*, I, 335 (*Yüeh ling*), from which I have borrowed the name of the Field of the Lord, *Ti-chi*. Cf. the inscription of the Ling tripod (Wu Shih-fen, *Chün ku lu*): 'The king performed the Great Ceremony of Ploughing in the field of Chi [the inscription is not dated, either by year or by month; and there is no description of the ceremony]; there was a banquet; the king shot with the bow.'

13   *Li chi*, II, p. 292 (*Chi yi*).

14   *Tso chuan*, pp. 595–96.

15   Granet, *Fêtes et chansons*, p. 164 ff., admits that the sacrifices took

place in the southern suburb. In fact, no text tells us where it was conducted under the Chou. It is only after the last years of the second century B.C. that the Emperor Wu of Han, following the tardy birth of an imperial prince, re-established this neglected worship, which he performed in a temple situated in the southern suburb of the capital. For the ancient period, the repeated assertion by modern Chinese scholars that it was held in the southern suburb seems to be due only to the interpretation of the two characters *chiao-mei* (which are one of the names of the god) as 'the intermediary (to whom one sacrifices) in the suburb'. But is not certain that this interpretation ought to be given to these two words. The god has another name, *Kao-mei*, which, if we take account of the usual sense of the characters, means 'the Exalted Intermediary'. The two characters *kao* and *chiao* were, in antiquity, almost homophones, distinguished only by the vowel (*kâo*, *kào*); and it is likely that they were used only for their pronunciation and not for their meaning, as happens so often with ancient names.

16 *Chou li*, II, p. 225.

17 *Li chi*, I, p. 353 (*Yüeh ling*); *Chou li*, II, p. 225.

18 Since the living man was formed by the *hun* and *p'o* souls united, their reunion by the calls and rituals of this ceremony was supposed to produce children and banish sterility.

19 Granet, *Fêtes et chansons*, pp. 155–64, who was the first to collect and interpret the texts relating to these festivals, admits that it was only much later that they took on the role of purification rites which the Chinese scholars traditionally attribute to them, and that in the beginnings their meaning was quite different, the rites not yet being specialized (p. 172).

20 *Chou li*, II, p. 195. Cf. De Groot, *Les Fêtes célébrées annuellement à Emouï*, I, p. 208 ff. Following the *Chou li*, the fire was renewed four times, at each of the seasons. It is possible that the official religion may have thus regularized a rite which was conducted among the populace only at the two great changes, at the end of spring and of autumn.

21 *Hung fan wu hsing chuan*, in *T'ai-p'ing yü lan*, ch. 13, 14b.

22 Granet, *Fêtes et chansons*, pp. 85–87. Cf. above, p. 72, the role of these festivals in peasant marriage.

23 *Chou li*, II, p. 195. In the era when this work was composed, the 'taking out' and the 'bringing back' of the fire was given a connection with the appearance of the Fire Star (*huo* = Fire), Antares, in the third month, and its disappearance in the ninth month.

24 *Li chi*, I, pp. 356–57 (*Yüeh ling*).

25 The Pi-yung kung is not specified by name, but that is where the ceremonies 'on the lake' ordinarily took place. Cf. *Chiao t'e sheng* (*Li chi*, I, p. 591).

26 *Chou li*, II, p. 36. The fact that the dance bears the name of the Hsien-ch'ih Lake, in which the sun bathes each morning before mounting to heaven (cf. above, p. 10), seems to show that the

Goddess of the Sun played an important role in this festival; but it is hard to see why she is thus classed among the terrestrial spirits. See also Henri Maspero, 'Légendes mythologiques dans le Chou king: I, La légende de Hi et Ho', pp. 26–28. The dance of Hsien-ch'ih is mentioned as one of the great religious dances which 'bring gods and men into accord' in a *fu* of Fu Yi, the *fu* of the dance (*Wen hsüan*, ch. 17, 5a; tr. von Zach, in *Deutsche Wacht* (Batavia), September 1923, p. 41); but Fu Yi lived under the Later Han, and it is unlikely that he really knew this dance.

27   The *yü* ceremony for rain is described by Ho Hsiu, an author of the second century A.D., in his commentary to the *Kung-yang chuan*, ch. 2, 7a, but without giving the name of the dance, which I have taken from the *Chou li*, I, p. 269 (Biot translates: 'dance with vari-coloured plumes'). I think it best to avoid the theory of some commentators, according to whom the *yü* sacrifice was addressed to the Five Lords.

28   This was an occasional sacrifice to obtain rain, different from the regular offerings of the fifth month, which have just been mentioned.

29   *Yen-tzu ch'un ch'iu.*

30   *Shan hai ching*, ch. 14, 66b. On the legend of the Winged Dragon, see above, p. 18.

31   *Tso chuan*, p. 180; *Li chi*, I, p. 261; *Chou li*, II, p. 102.

32   *Li chi*, I, p. 381 (*Yüeh ling*).

33   *Tso chuan*, pp. 595–96.

34   *Shih ching*, pp. 575–76.

35   *Li chi*, I, p. 392 (*Yüeh ling*).

36   *Tso chuan*, p. 731; *Kuo yü*, ch. 4, 7b (sec. 7); *Li chi*, II, pp. 268–69 (*Chi fa*); Chavannes, *Dieu du Sol*, pp. 504–6.

37   What we know of the *Pa-cha* festival comes almost exclusively from the *Li chi*, I, pp. 594–600 (*Chiao t'e sheng*). Cf. Granet, *Fêtes et chansons* (pp. 178–91); I adopt his conclusions (p. 179) on the controversial question of the exact date. The name is obscure: the meaning of the word *cha* is unknown, and that given it in ancient texts ('to seek out') is far from certain.

38   *Chou li*, II, p. 195.

39   Ibid., II, p. 36.

40   *Hou-Han shu*, ch. 15, 4b. Cf. Granet, *Danses et legéndes*, I, pp. 299–320.

41   *Shang shu ta chuan*, ch. 5, 8b (ed. *Ssu pu ts'ung k'an*).

42   The *Shih ching*, p. 257, quotes them in the order *tz'u yüeh cheng ch'ang*, which is not the normal order of the seasons, as Legge wrongly believed in his translation: cf. *Chou li*, I, p. 422. The summer sacrifice is called *ti* in the *Chi t'ung* (*Li chi*, II, pp. 342–43), following the special usage of Lu and dating back to the beginning of the sixth century B.C. (cf. *Tsa chi*, ibid., II, p. 191). The same name is tied to the spring sacrifice in the *Chi yi* (ibid., II, p. 27), since in Lu, an eastern state, the quarterly spring sacrifice (East = spring) was not performed, and consequently the only ancestral sacrifice offered at this season was the five-yearly *ti*.

13 The *Kung-yang chuan, ch. 6, 2b,* says merely: 'In five years the complete sacrifices are made twice' (that is to say, the *hsia* and the *ti*). It was Cheng Hsüan, one of the best Han experts, who (in the second century A.D.) proposed the dates I have set forth above. He had compared this text with various passages of the *Ch'un ch'iu* and the *Tso chuan*, in his *Lu li ti hsia chih* ('Treatise on the *ti* and *hsia* sacrifices according to the rites of the state of Lu'). Chinese scholars have discussed this hypothesis at length; but I still think it offers the best explanation. Liu Hsiang, towards the end of Later Han, gave a similar explanation of this text (cf. *T'ai-p'ing yü lan, ch.* 528). This was the interpretation which was followed when the first *ti* sacrifice was performed in 12 B.C. by Ch'eng-ti. The 3–5 cyclical rotation is indicated, but not the connection to the end of the mourning period. Likewise, Chang Ch'un's memorial on this subject in 50 A.D. fixed the *hsia* in the tenth month (winter) and the *ti* in the fourth month (summer), which was accepted (*Hou-Han shu, ch.* 19, 1*b*). The *Li chi ming cheng*, from the Later Han period, says with more precision (probably following the *Kung-yang chuan*): 'the third year the *hsia*, the fifth year the *ti*' (*Ch'u hsüeh chi, ch.* 13; *T'ai-p'ing yü lan, ch.* 528). The *ti* is known through inscriptions, but not the *hsia*. A *ti* sacrifice is mentioned in the inscription on the Tz'u tripod (Lo Chen-yü, *Chou chin wen ts'un, ch.* 2, 28; Kuo Mo-jo, 'The Origin of the Rules in Giving Posthumous Names' in *Shinagaku*, VI (1932), p. 35): 'The king performed the *ti* sacrifice, he sacrificed an ox to the great one …; he performed the *ti* to king Shao'; and, in a Yin inscription: 'Divination of the day *ting-hai*: the king went to the Ta-yi [temple] for the *ti* sacrifice,' 丁亥卜貞王賓 [= 儐 = 假] 大乙禴 [= 禘]. … A passage from a book on the rites found in the imperial Han library (*Yi li*) defines the *ti* in this way: 'All [the spirits of the dead] ascend to meet at the abode of the [First] Ancestor,' (cited by Liu Hsin, *Ch'un ch'iu Tso shih chuan chang chü* ed. *Yü-han shan-fang chi yi shu*, p. 2*b*).

44 The very names of the sacrifices indicate their meaning clearly. The word *ti*, which I translate 'Lord', is the substantive form of the verb *ti*, 'to offer the sacrifice which makes one become a lord' (one might say, *ti*-ify, as we say 'deify'), with alternate initial voiceless and voiced consonants: the ancient pronunciation of the verb was *dei*, and of the substantive *tei*, with no change of tone (since the normal tone of the derivatives is the *ch'ü-sheng* and the primitive word already has this tone). The word *hsia* (*hap*) derives from the word *ho* (*hap*), 'to assemble, reunite'; so the sense is 'to offer a collective sacrifice to all the ancestors assembled together'. The script has retained the clear trace of these etymologies.

45 *Kung-yang chuan, ch.* 6, 2*b*; *Li chi*, I, p. 435 (*Tseng-tzu wen*); Cheng Hsüan, *Lu li ti hsia chih*, in *T'ung tien, ch.* 49, 7*b*.

46 A royal sacrifice to the ancestors is described in the *Shih ching*, pp. 368–73 (*Ch'u tz'u*): This is the text upon which my description is based, fleshed out with the aid of various chapters from the *Li chi*

(especially the *Li yün*, I, pp. 505–9; the *Li ch'i*, I, pp. 552–669; the *Chiao t'e sheng*, I, pp. 610–17; the *Chi t'ung*, II, pp. 325–51; etc.) and their commentaries, as well as the *Chou li* (the paragraphs dealing with the religious role of each functionary), and even the *Yi li*, even though this refers, not to a royal sacrifice, but to one made by a grand officer.

47 The general order of the preparatory ceremony at the Chou court is given by the *Chiao t'e sheng* (*Li chi*, I, p. 612). In Sung, the music preceded the libation. For the position of the king and queen at the beginning: see *Li ch'i* (*Li chi*, I, p. 563); the ceremony for bringing in the victim: ibid., p. 566; *Chi fa* (II, p. 265); *Chi yi* (II, pp. 285–86); *Chi t'ung* (II, pp. 325–26); the ceremony of shooting it with arrows: *Chou li*, II, p. 207 (commentary of Cheng Hsüan); the offering of hair and blood, and cutting up the victim: *Chiao t'e sheng* (*Li chi*, I, pp. 615–16); the triple invitation to the spirits of the dead: ibid., p. 613; the seeking out and summoning of the souls: *Li ch'i* (I, p. 567).

48 *Li chi*, p. 618; II, pp. 280, 321; cf. *Shih ching*, p. 369. The presentation of tablets is described in *Yi li*, p. 596.

49 *Yi li*, *chs.* 15–16; *Li chi*, II, p. 337. The rituals almost always describe ceremonies in which there is only one *shih*. In consequence, it is difficult to know whether, when there were several, a ceremony was performed for each one separately or for all together.

50 *Li chi*, II, p. 336 (*Chi t'ung*).

51 *Shih ching*, p. 370.

52 *Shih ching*, pp. 371–72. The formula given by *Yi li*, p. 604, is almost identical: 'The august Corpse orders the skilful praying-priest [to say to you]: I promise you abundant good fortune, without limit, filial descendant! Come, filial descendant! I will cause you to receive heavenly grace; I will make the harvest of your fields plentiful; a long life, ten thousand years; forever and ever I will bestow favour upon you!'

53 *Shih ching*, p. 372.

54 This is described in the *Shih ching*, p. 372, as follows:

The august Corpse rises,
drums and things accompany [the departure of] the Corpse,
the Possessed [*shen-pao*] goes home.
The stewards, the women who preside,
take up and carry away [the tables] without delay;
uncles and cousins
all are admitted to the banquet, every one.
The musicians all start to play. ...
The meats are arranged;
there are no regrets, all are satisfied,
they are drunk, they are sated. ...

For the details of the feast, see also *Li chi*, II, pp. 329–30 (*Chi t'ung*).

55 *Li chi*, II, p. 341 (*Chi t'ung*).

56 The *ta-wu* dance is well known: see Wang Kuo-wei's excellent article, *Yüeh shih k'ao lüeh* (Study on Music and the Odes Related to It) in the *Kuang-ts'ang hsüeh ch'ün ts'ung shu*, which has definitively

established the connection between the scenes of this dance and various odes in the *Shih ching*. To begin with, it is described in detail in a chapter of the *Li chi*, II, pp. 94–98 (*Yüeh chi*), see also *Tso chuan*, p. 320; again, the songs for each scene are preserved in the *Shih ching*; and finally, the libretto of the pantomime has also been partly preserved in the *Shu ching*: it forms chapters *T'ai shih*, *Mu shih*, *Wu ch'eng*, and *Fen ch'i*, respectively the first, second, third, and fifth scenes (those of the fourth and sixth seem never to have been part of the *Shu ching*). It is known nowadays that only the *Mu shih* is authentic; the *T'ai shih* and *Wu ch'eng* are forgeries of the third century A.D., though many fragments of the former are genuine. As for the *Fen ch'i*, it has been lost since Han times.

57 *Kung-yang chuan*, ch. 1, 13*a*.

58 *Li chi*, II, p. 97 (*Yüeh chi*). The general description of this dance is taken from this passage, except where I give other references.

59 *T'ai shih*, redaction by Chiang Sheng, *Shang shu chi chu yin shu*, cf. Legge, *Shu ching*, II, p. 298.

60 *Shih ching*, Legge, p. 575. The title I give is that of the *Li chi*, Couvreur, I, p. 328 (Chi t'ung); the modern title is made of the first verse. On the reasons for identifying the portion of the *Shih ching* with that to which the *Li chi* gives this title, see Wang Kuo-wei, op. cit., 14*b*–15*a*.

61 *Mu shih*, in *Shu ching*, p. 300.

62 *Mu shih*, in *Shu ching*, p. 304. This passage of the royal harangue before battle, inspired by the movements of the *ta-wu* dancers, gives a good description of that dance.

63 *Shih ching*, p. 594.

64 The departure was called *Pei-ch'u*, exit towards the north; the return must evidently have been called *Nan*, march to the south. It is noteworthy that these orientations, geographically incorrect if related to the legend, are correct if related to the movements of the dancers in the court of the ancestral temple. That temple was at the back of the court on the north side; and when the dancers faced it, the departure and march to combat of the first and second scenes made them advance northwards, while the return of the third and sixth scenes, bringing them back to the starting point, had them moving south.

65 *Shih ching*, p. 606.

66 Ibid., p. 607. Shang is another name for the Yin dynasty.

67 Ibid., p. 608.

68 *Li chi*, I, p. 95.

69 *Shih ching*, p. 609.

70 *Li chi*, I, pp. 731–32 (*Ming-t'ang wei*).

71 *Chou li*, II, p. 32, and commentary by Cheng Hsüan, from which is taken the quotation which follows; *Shih ching*, p. 620.

72 *Tso chuan*, p. 19.

73 *Huai-nan-tzu*, ch. 15, 16*a*; Granet, *Danses et légendes*, I, p. 324.

74 *Li chi*, I, pp. 433–34 (*Tseng-tzu wen*); Chavannes, *Dieu du Sol*, p. 512.

75   *Shu ching*, I, p. 155 (*Kan shih*).

76   *Tso chuan*, p. 352. In the same way the Lord of Pi-yang was offered as a sacrifice by Prince Tao of Chin, in 569, in the chapel of his ancestor Wu. An ally of Ch'u, this lord had resisted the armies of Chin and the League for a year (see below, bk. 2, ch. 4, n. 79).

77   *Li chi*, I, p. 276 (*Wang chih*).

78   *Chou li*, II, pp. 182–83.

79   *Tso chuan*, p. 446.

80   The *Tso chuan*, p. 210, describes the triumphal entry of Prince Wen of Chin into his capital after his victory over Ch'u (632).

81   *Yi Chou shu*, ch. 4, 11*b* (sec. 40).

82   *Chou li*, II, p. 183.

83   *Mo-tzu*, Forke, pp. 615–16. This passage belongs to ch. 15, which probably dates from the third century B.C.

84   *Kung-yang chuan*, ch. 3, 19*b*, and the commentary of Ho Hsiu (second century A.D.) on this passage. Cf. Chavannes, *Dieu du Sol*, pp. 480–90.

85   *Kung-yang chuan*, ch. 3, 20*a*; the *Tso chuan*, p. 109, considers the ceremony incorrect.

86   *Chou li*, II, p. 102; *Tso chuan*, p. 180; *Li chi*, I, p. 261 (*T'an kung*).

87   *Tso chuan*, p. 810.

88   *Kuo yü*, ch. 4, 7*a* (*Lu yü*); *Chuang-tzu*, p. 353.

Chapter 5.   Religious Feeling

1   De Groot, *Universismus*, ch. 11, pp. 303–30.

2   *Li chi*, I, p. 403 (*Yüeh ling*).

3   The old texts give the impression that an effort was made to give the gods personalities and to construct a mythology (begun despite rather unfavourable conditions and then stopped under the influence of philosophical ideas which tended to depersonalize divinities), rather than to preserve the impersonal or, at most, only semi-personal forms which must have been those of the prehistoric Chinese religion. But those ancient forms were never very far away, either in time or in popular religious sentiment, and this explains why most of the gods never acquired very strong personality and why they lost it very easily.

4   *Yen-tzu ch'un ch'iu*, ch. 1, 4*b* (sec. 12).

5   *Mo-tzu*, ch. 8, Forke, p. 345; *Kuo yü*, ch. 19, 21*a*; *Chan kuo ts'e*, ch. 3, 50*b*.

6   On the influence of the philosophical theory of the *yin* and the *yang*, cf. Granet, *La religion des Chinois*, p. 117 ff.

7   *Tso chuan*, p. 210.

8   Ibid., p. 146.

9   See above, p. 117, the anecdote of the priest killed upon the altar by a spirit furious at his niggardliness in offerings (following *Mo-tzu*, ch. 8, Forke, p. 346).

10   *Tso chuan*, p. 618 (335 B.C.).

Book III: The Hegemonies

Chapter 1. *The Territorial Formation of the Great Principalities*

1 Chinese historians and, following them, European historians speak of this period as that of the 'Five Hegemons', *wu pa*: Huan of Ch'i (685–641); Mu of Ch'in (659–621); Hsiang of Sung (650–637); Wen of Chin (636–626); Chuang of Ch'u (613–591). This is really nothing but an application of the Five Elements with their corresponding Five Cardinal Points. There is no point in retaining this arrangement, which is of no historical validity, and I have left it out altogether.

2 *Tso chuan*, Legge, pp. 448–49.

3 The chronology is uncertain: all the texts agree in placing the expedition of the Chin prince in 750; but for that of the Count of Ch'in, the *Chu shu chi nien*, p. 159, gives 753, and the *Shih chi*, ch. 5 (Chavannes, II, p. 17), gives 750. There is no overriding reason for choosing between them. It can be accepted, as I have done here, that the two expeditions took place at the same time, or one can argue that the defeat of the Jung by the Count of Ch'in made it possible for the Prince of Chin to dethrone the King of Hui.

4 For this marriage and its consequences see *Tso chuan*, p. 5; *Shih chi*, Chavannes, IV, pp. 452–53.

5 *Chu shu chi nien*, Legge, p.158.

6 From this probably came Cheng's title of Count of the Overlords.

7 *Tso chuan*, Legge, pp. 45–46.

8 North of Ch'ing-chou fu in Shantung province.

9 *Shih chi*, IV, p. 40; *Tso chuan*, p. 140. Mu-ling is Mount Ta-hsien, about 115 *li* southeast of Lin-ch'ü in the prefecture of Ch'ing-chou; Wu-ti is near Yen-shan in T'ien-chin fu, Hopei.

10 Ch'ü-wu corresponds to modern Wen-hsi in Chiang-chou, in southern Shansi. Ch'eng-shih was the uncle of Chao, the younger brother of his father Wen, according to the *Shih chi*, IV, pp. 252–53; the younger brother of Chao himself, according to the *Chu shu chi nien*.

11 There is a good account of the struggle between the Chin princes and the counts of Ch'ü-wu in Tschepe, *History of the Kingdom of Chin*, pp. 17–21.

12 South of modern Ch'ü-wu, which is a long way from the ancient city. Chiang was the Chin capital from 669 to 585.

13 For the Red Ti and their tribes, see pp. 5–6 above and Map 1.

14 *Shih chi*, Chavannes, IV, pp. 269–70. Ho-hsi is the territory lying between the Yellow River to the east and the Lo River to the west, in Shensi; Ho-nei (which was the name of a sub-prefecture before the 1914 reforms) is the region of Huai-ch'ing fu in northern Honan.

15 *Chu shu chi nien*, Legge, p. 158; *Shih chi*, II, pp. 14–15. The overlords of Ch'in who 'ranked among the princes' used the title 'count', which implies the former investiture of a local count. The sacrifice to the

White Lord (West) in 769, far from being any kind of usurpation, was only the performance of the religious duties of the Count of Yung. The fact that the Ch'in domain occupied the ancient royal territory is recalled by an inscription on a *kuei* of a Ch'in prince of the sixth century: 'Since my Illustrious August Ancestor received the celestial mandate …, twelve princes in the … imperial have majestically fulfilled the celestial mandate …,' (cf. Kuo Mo-jo, in *Shinagaku*, VI (1932), p. 15.

16 *Shih chi, ch.* 5, Chavannes, II, p. 17, (year 750). The *Chu shu chi nien* sets the event in 753. The chronology is uncertain.

17 *Shih chi, ch.* 5, Chavannes, II, p. 19.

18 *Shih chi, ch.* 5, Chavannes, II, p. 20.

19 It must be remembered that there are three Kuo: an Eastern Kuo, destroyed by Cheng in 767 (see above, p. 172); and two Western Kuo, one, also called Southern Kuo, south of the Yellow River near Ho-nan, destroyed by Chin in 655 (see p. 176), and the other called Small Kuo, Hsiao-Kuo, in Shensi. This last was the one destroyed by Wu of Ch'in in 687.

20 *Shih chi, ch.* 5, Chavannes, II, p. 23.

21 *Shih chi, ch.* 5, Chavannes, II, p. 35.

22 See below, p. 194.

23 The capital Ying was situated on the Yangtze, in the region of the modern sub-prefectures of Sha-shih and Chiang-ling (Hupei province).

Chapter 2. The Hegemony of Ch'i

1 The work that should be our chief source of information about the organization and history of the state of Ch'i is the *Kuan-tzu*, since it is attributed to the Prime Minister of the country in that time. Unfortunately, in its present form it is almost entirely a forgery of the fourth or fifth century A.D., even the few remaining authentic parts of which have been touched up. Its authenticity has often been championed (see Grube, *Geschichte der chinesischen Literatur*, 1902; and recently E. H. Parker, 'Kuan tze', *New China Review*, III (1921), i–ii, pp. 405–513; and also Tucci, *Storia della filosofia cinese antica*); but it cannot stand up to critical examination.
   There existed a *Kuan-tzu* which, though not the work of Kuan Chung himself, must have dated from the fifth century B.C. Chapter 6 of the *Kuo yü* and several passages of the *Tso chuan*, of the *Mencius*, of the *Kung-yang chuan*, of the *Han-fei-tzu*, and so forth (perhaps also of the present-day *Kuan-tzu*) have probably preserved for us fragments of it in resume form. See below, book V, ch. 7, p. 359.

2 *Kuo yü, ch.* 6 (*Ch'i yü*): 'Kuan-tzu thereupon organized the princedom into twenty-one districts: six of artisans and traders, and fifteen of nobles.' The peasants are not mentioned separately, because they belonged to the land of their overlords. Although this

description is very cut and dried, it does seem to be based on the actual organization of the principality of Ch'i in the fourth century, an organization which was attributed to Kuan Chung.

3 *Kuo yü, ch.* 6, 9*b*. How artificial this arrangement is can be clearly seen from the figures: five *chou*, ten *hsien*, and three *hsiang*, so that there were fifteen districts in a prince's domain, and 150 in the Royal Domain, the proportion of one to ten being the correct ritual proportion of king and prince.

In his commentary of the third century A.D., Wei Chao admits that the five *cheng* were special officials, but insists that *mu-cheng* was another title of the *tai-fu* of the governments and *hsien-cheng* of the *shuai* of the districts. This explanation does not seem to agree with the text; but it does agree with a passage in the forged modern version of the *Kuan-tzu*. That also gives a description of the military organization of the vassal domains, and its figures are even less credible.

4 *Kuo yü, ch.* 6, 11*b*; *Wu-tzu, ch.* 1, 1*b*; *Lü shih ch'un ch'iu, ch.* 8, 10*a*. All these figures undoubtedly come from various passages in the lost *Kuan-tzu*. For the revenues of Ch'i in 521, see also the *Tso chuan*, pp. 683–84 (year 521).

5 According to the *Tso chuan*, p. 95, it was because he had accepted the suzerainty of the King of Ch'u that Li was reproached with not conforming to the rites, for not having announced to that prince his return to his capital. Li, the posthumous name of the Count of Cheng, and the name of the town of Li where he took refuge are written with different characters.

6 See above, pp. 171–72.

7 For Huan's policy and his expeditions, as well as the expansion of his power, see G. Haloun, 'Seit wann kannten die Chinesen die Tocharer'. *Asia Major* (1926), p. 47 ff.

8 *Tso chuan*, pp. 533, 648, 650–2. Cf. Granet, *Danses et légendes*, I, p. 172.

9 The order of precedence which the *Ch'un ch'iu* gives in the lists of princes taking part in the Chien-t'u meeting, for the year 632 (Legge, p. 202), does not agree with the fragment of the treaty protocol preserved elsewhere in the *Tso chuan*, under the year 506 (p. 754). In this fragment we read that the authenticating deed of the treaty of Chien-t'u contains the following passage: 'The king speaks thus: Ch'ung [-erh] of Chin, Shen of Lu, Wu of Wey, Chia-wu of Ts'ai, Chieh of Cheng, P'an of Ch'i, Wang-ch'en of Sung, Ch'i of Chü ...' But this passage is cited in a speech by Wey against the order of precedence ascribed to Ts'ai at the assembly of Kao-yu in 506. It is no certain proof, and the order given in the *Ch'un ch'iu* seems to me more reliable.

10 These questions of precedence and protocol played a large part in the relations between the different principalities. See, for example, the discussion as to the order in which the Prince of Lu is to sign the treaties with Chin and Wey in 588 (*Tso chuan*, p. 353). Here it seems that the rank of the ambassador decides precedence, as all the

principalities are considered equal if their princes have the same title (in this case, *hou*). The difficulty had arisen here because both states had sent ambassadors of equal rank. The precedence was given finally to Chin, as the prince was President of the League, *meng-chu*.

11   Cf. *Tso chuan*, p. 652 (thirteenth year of Chao), for the discussion between the delegates of Cheng and Chin (this latter being president) about reducing the contribution of the former, at the assembly of P'ing-ch'iu in 529.

12   *Huai-nan tzu, ch.* 19, 12a.

13   *Shih chi, ch.* 40, Chavannes, IV, p. 346.

14   The K'ung families of Cheng, Wey, and Ch'en had no connection with that of Sung, to which Confucius belonged.

15   This is certain of one of them: Mu of Hsü, who died in the Ch'i army after the return of the expedition (*Ch'un ch'iu*, Legge, p. 140).

16   *Tso chuan*, p. 154; *Kuo yü, ch.* 6 (*Ch'i yü*) 13b; *Shih chi*, Chavannes, IV, p. 54, who follows the *Kuo yü*. Both *Tso chuan* and *Kuo yü* are clearly derived from the same source, the original *Kuan-tzu*; the *Tso chuan* is very concise; the *Kuo yü*, more detailed, perhaps reproduces the original text better.

17   *Shih chi*, IV, p. 57 (Ch'i), gives the date 645; but II, p. 30 (Ch'in) gives 648, which is also that of the *Ku-liang chuan, ch.* 5, 12a.

18   Huan was in his seventies at the assembly of K'uei-ch'iu; see *Tso chuan*, p. 154.

19   The Lord of Tseng, having arrived late, was sacrificed to the God of the Soil of the place where the assembly was held (*Ch'un ch'iu*, p. 176; *Tso chuan*, p. 177).

Chapter 3. The Hegemony of Chin

1   Near Tung-o, on the Chi River, on the southern border of the principality.

2   The adventures of Prince Wen of Chin were made the subject of a historical romance which has been lost. But the *Tso chuan*, p. 186 (twenty-third year of Hsi), has preserved a summary of them, and extracts from the lost original make up chapter 10 of the *Kuo yü*. The theme seems to have been to explain all of the prince's actions during his reign by his adventures in exile: for example, the alliance with Sung was the consequence of the good reception he had enjoyed in that country; the war against the Prince of Ts'ao would be justified by the latter's rudeness when Ch'ung-erh was staying at his court; etc. (See also the anecdote of the famous three days' retreat before the Ch'u army, p. 198 below.) This romance, probably of the fourth century B.C., must of course be considered only a work of imagination and not a historical source.

3   This official must have had a different title, as *ssu-t'u* was forbidden, having been the personal name of Prince Hsi of Chin (840–823). What the other title was is not known.

4   According to the *Tso chuan*, p. 204, at the Battle of Ch'eng-p'u (632) the Chin army had 700 chariots.

5   From the *Tso chuan* a list can be made up of the chiefs of the centre army. It seems complete for certain periods. The names of all the great families will be found intermingled in it.

Chen of Yuan	632
Ch'ü-chü of Hsien	627
I-ku of Hu	621
Tun of Chao	621
K'o of Hsü	603
Ch'üeh of Hsi	601
Lin-fu of Hsün	597
Hui of the Shih (Fan family)	593
K'o of Hsi	592
Shu of Luan	587
Ch'üeh of Han	573
Ying of Chih	566
Yen of Hsün	560
Kai of the Shih	554
Wu of Chao	548
Ch'i of Han	540
Shu of Wei	514
Yang of Fan	509
Yang of Chao	497
Yao of Chih	475–453

6   There was true passage from one command to another. It was not merely a matter of honorary posts, with the same army remaining in the hands of the same chief, and changing its name with his title. This can be seen from a series of postings in the beginning of the sixth century which I give below.

In 597 the commanders and vice-commanders were as follows: Centre army: Lin-fu of Hsün with Hu of Hsien; upper army: Hui of the Shih, with K'o of Hsi; lower army: Shuo of Chao, with Shu of Luan. In 596 Hu of Hsien was put to death and Hui of the Shih took over his post as vice-commander of the centre army. and was himself replaced by K'o of Hsi as commander of the upper army. In 593 Lin-fu of Hsün died and Hui replaced him as commander of the centre army; K'o of Hsi became vice-commander of the centre army. Postings in the upper army are uncertain; but it seems likely that Shui of Hsün replaced K'o of Hsi in 596 and became commander-in-chief in 593 and that Keng of Hsün then became vice-commander. In 592 Hui of the Shih retired on the excuse of age, K'o of Hsi took over as commander of the centre army, and Shui of Hsün probably replaced him as commander of the upper army. Hsieh of the Shih, son of Hui, certainly then became his vice-commander. As for the lower army, in 593 Shu of Luan, vice-commander, replaced the commander, Shuo of Chao, on the latter's death. Shu of Luan was later to become commander of the centre army with Shui of Hsün as his vice-commander, after K'o of Hsi died in 572.

7 The list of transfers and promotions between 597 and 572 shows clearly that the commander of the upper army was considered of lower rank than the vice-commander of the centre army, because he received promotion on changing from the one post to the other. It was the same for the other armies.

8 *Kuo yü, ch.* 14, 13*b*.

9 *Tso chuan,* p. 209.

10 *Tso chuan,* p. 211.

11 There is an inscription on a bronze basin, probably dating from 624, in which Prince Hsiang eulogizes his ancestor and his father. See Wu Shih-fen, *Chün ku lu,* III, pp. 3, 28; Kuo Mo-jo, *Chin wen yün tu pu yi,* in *Shinagaku,* VI, 1 (1932), p. 22.

12 It is possible to make up a rough list of *ling-yin* of Ch'u in the seventh century, from King Hui on; before his reign it would be very incomplete:

Tzu-yüan	(688)–664
Nou-wu-t'u of Tou (Tzu-wen)	664–637
Te-ch'en of Ch'eng (Tzu-yü)	637–632
Lü-ch'en of Weiy (Shu-po)	632
P'o of Tou (Tzu-shang)	631–627
Ta-hsin of Ch'eng (Ta-sun-po)	626–615
Chia of Ch'eng (Tzu-k'ung)	615–613
Pan of Tou (Tzu-yang)	612
Chiao of Tou (Tzu-yüeh)	611–605
Yi-lieh of Weiy (Sun-shu-ao)	604–591
Ying-ch'i (Tzu-ch'ung)	590–570

13 The date of these events is uncertain. The *Tso chuan* mentions them in 605, as if they had happened earlier, but gives no details. Pan of Tou became *ling-yin* 'after the death of his father Tzu-wen' (*Tso chuan,* p. 297), but this set phrase, which would appear to say that he succeeded, does not make sense here; for Tzu-wen gave up his post to Tzu-yü (ibid., p. 201). My reason for adopting the date 612 is that there is no mention of Chia of Ch'eng after 613 and that from 611 on Tzu-yüeh seems to have filled the primary role, although the title *ling-yin* does not actually appear till 605.

14 I agree with the majority of Chinese scholars that *Sun-shu-ao* is the *tzu* of Yi-lieh of Weiy and that they are one person. The *Shih pen* makes Sun-shu-ao — or Ao of Weiy — the brother of Yi-lieh: the latter is supposed to have been *ling-yin* from 604 to 598, and was supposed to have been succeeded by his brother Ao in 597.

15 *Shih chi,* Chavannes, IV, p. 319.

Chapter 4. The Alliance of Chin and Wu

1 *Tso chuan*, pp. 347–48, 364; *Shih chi*, Chavannes, IV, pp. 5, 281–82. These passages are transparently a digest of a romance, the hero of which was Wu-ch'en. It must, however, have a historical basis, for the alliance between Chin and Wu gives weight to its assertion that Chin had helped with the organization of the Wu barbarians.

2 See the speech attributed to Hsieh of Fan (Wen-tzu) on this occasion (*Tso chuan*, p. 395).

3 On these affairs, see below, p. 227.

4 The *Tso chuan* writes the name Ying, the *Shih chi* writes it Ch'eng. The original text must have had a simpler form of the character *ying*, which the *Tso chuan* has fleshed out in the modern text. Ssu-ma Ch'ien read it wrongly as *ch'eng*, a character which is very similar. Cf. also Chavannes, *Mémoires historiques*, V, p. 228, n. 2.

5 *Tso chuan*, pp. 532–35; *Kuo yü*, ch. 14, 8b; Doré, 'Le Congrès de la Paix en Chine en 546 av. J. C.' *Les Etudes*, July 1918, pp. 77–82; Warren, 'The First League of Nations' (*New China Review*), I (1919), 356–67.

6 *Tso chuan*, p. 575; *Kuo yü*, ch. 14, 10a.

7 King Kung (590–560) was succeeded by his son King K'ang (559–545). The latter's son Chia Ao succeeded him and took his uncle, Kung's son, Prince Wei, as his prime minister (542). In the next year the king fell ill, and Wei strangled him on the pretext of inquiring about his health, and seized the throne as King Ling.

8 For public works under King Ling, see *Yen-tzu ch'un ch'iu*, ch. 2, 8a.

9 *Tso chuan*, pp. 648–49; *Shih chi*, IV, p. 364.

10 If the hypothesis of Juan Yüan, *Chi-ku-chai chung ting k'uan chih*, ch. 4, 22a, is correct, the inscription on the tripod of Yün of Chi, which mentions an unnamed king's voyage from Lo-yi to the land of Ch'u, would refer to Prince Chao's assuming the royal title and would contain the report of the Lesser Chamberlain (*Chou li*, Biot, II, 229) responsible for preparing his retreat into the land of Ch'u as the Chin army approached: 'The first month, the king was at Ch'eng-chou; he moved to the forest of Ch'u and ordered the Lesser Chamberlain, Ling, to go ahead and inspect the Ch'u residence. Arriving at his new residence, the king rewarded the Lesser Chamberlain with a gift of cowries and two horses. ...' Cf. Wieger, *Caractères chinois*, app.: 'Graphies Antiques', p. 483.

11 *Shih chi*, IV, p. 22; *Ch'un ch'iu*, p. 740.

12 *Tso chuan*, II, pp. 832–33; *Kuo yü*, ch. 19, 8b–11b; *Shih chi*, IV, p. 31, 334. According to the *Tso chuan*, and the *Shih chi*, p. 31, which follows it closely, the presidency was left to Chin. According to the *Kuo yü* and the *Shih chi*, p. 334, it was given to Wu. The actual account of the meeting shows that the King of Wu had the real presidency. My theory seems to me to reconcile the two conflicting accounts best.

13 *Shih chi*, Chavannes, IV, pp. 29–30.

14 *Shih chi*, IV, p. 32.

15 *Shih chi*, IV, p. 431; cf. *Kuo yü*, ch. 19, 18a.

Book IV: The Warring Kingdoms

Chapter 1. The Ruin of Chin

1   The Fan family also bore the name Shih, which it derived from an official post held by one of its ancestors.

2   This is the story of the 'orphan of the Chao family' which is told so dramatically by Ssu-ma Ch'ien in the *Shih chi*, Chavannes, V, pp. 15–22. The only certain historical facts are the putting to death of the Chao family in 583, reported in the *Ch'un ch'iu* (eighth year of Ch'eng, Legge, p. 366), and the return of its property to the family later on, since that family reappears thirty years afterwards. The rest of the story must come from one of the numerous historical romances with which the literature at the end of Chou teemed. Though their names are written with somewhat similar characters and sounded alike in some contexts, the two families Ch'i and Hsi are completely different as can be seen from the preceding page.

3   *Kuo yü, (Chou yü)*, ch. 3, p. 1.

4   *Tso chuan*, p. 501, sheds light on this situation of the various families. Cf. Tschepe, *Histoire de Tsin*, pp. 273–74. On this subject, see above, pp. 213–14.

5   *Chan kuo ts'e*, ch. 6, 1b (Chao); cf. *Shih chi*, V, p. 174.

6   Those years are also the least known. Between 453 and 424 we know absolutely nothing about what happened in the states of Chin, Chao, Han and Wei. The *Shih chi*, Chavannes, IV, p. 335 (Chin), records only a single fact: the submission of Yu to his powerful vassals. The chapters on Chao, Wei and Han contain nothing about this period. The *Chu shu chi nien* (Ch.Cl., III, pp. 167–68) does not even mention the siege of Chin-yang or the death of the Count of Chih, and only hints at the installation of Duke Wen of Wei in 434 (eighteenth year of Prince Ching, who reigned 451–430; cf. quotation in *Shih chi so yin* [*Shih Chi*, ch. 39, 15b]; the text existing today, which gives the twelfth year, is wrong). These two works are not even in agreement on the posthumous name of the prince who was put on the throne by the Count of Chih: the *Shih chi* calls him Ai and the *Chu shu chi nien* calls him Ching. The reason for this silence would appear to be that, Chin having been rendered powerless, the official chroniclers had nothing to record about the doings of the almost independent great vassals, while these had not yet started keeping regular official annals in their own domains.

7   *Chu shu chi nien*, in *Shih chi so yin* (*Shih chi*, ch. 39, 15b, cf. Chavannes, IV, p. 335). The modern text of the *Chu shu chi nien*, p. 168, writes *Chin tai-fu*, a grand officer of Chin, for *Chin fu-jen*, the Princess of Chin; but the name Ying of Ch'in is a woman's name, which shows up the error.

8   Both are in the same region: the first is near T'ang-yin in Chang-te fu (Honan) and the latter near Kuang-p'ing fu (Hopei).

9   *Shu ching*, XXII, p. 3, XXIII, p. 1, etc., Legge, II, pp. 545, 562, etc.; *Shih chi*, ch. 44, 1a; Chavannes, *Mémoires historiques*, V, p. 223.

10   The *Ch'in chi* (*Shih chi*, Chavannes, II, p. 58) mentions the conquest of
      Ho-hsi about the year 385. But the context shows that this territory
      was not a dependency of Ch'in at that time, and that the mention
      of the victory over Wei is merely an explanatory gloss (either by the
      annalist or by Ssu-ma Ch'ien) in order to make clear that this
      territory, which had been conquered by Ch'in some years
      previously, had been reconquered by Wei. This conquest was prior
      to the death of Prince Wu of Wei (387), because General Wu Ch'i
      governed it on behalf of this prince for several years (*Shih chi, ch.* 65,
      3*a*). Unfortunately Ssu-ma Ch'ien summarizes the *Wu-tzu*, in which
      the life of Wu Ch'i had been embellished with romantic episodes
      by a writer of the third century B.C. who had no knowledge of
      history, and so it is stuffed with anachronisms. The conquest was
      certainly a result of the expedition of 409 (*Shih chi*, Chavannes, V, p.
      138; *Chu shu chi nien*, Legge, p. 169).
11   340 B.C., according to the *Shih chi*, V, p. 157, note 1, citing the *Chu shu
      chi nien*.
12   A lord of Chung-shan, *Chung-shan chün*, became the minister of
      Prince Hui in 343 (*Shih chi*, Chavannes, V, p. 155). He was perhaps
      the same Mou of Chung-shan whom Chuang-tzu mentions, who
      was a philosopher and wit and who complained about his exile in
      the solitude of his half-savage apanage (Chung-shan was inhabited
      by the White Ti tribes) after the brilliant life at court (*Chuang-tzu, ch,*
      28, p. 460; *Lieh-tzu, ch.* 4, p. 127; *Lü shih ch'un ch'iu, ch.* 21, 7*b*). His
      descendants continued to govern the principality (*Lü shih ch'un ch'iu,
      ch.* 2, 9*b*).

Chapter 2. The Chinese World at the End of the Fifth Century

1   The noble family of Luan in Ch'i was in no way related to that in
      Chin. The former belonged to the Chiang clan and was descended
      from Prince Hui of Ch'i (608–599), whereas the Luan family of Chin
      belonged to the Chi clan and was descended from Prince Ching of
      Chin (858–841). As their names were exactly the same (even in the
      Chinese character), their fiefs also bore the same name.
2   *Shih chi*, Chavannes, V, p. 236.
3   On the troubles in Ch'in, see *Shih chi, ch.* 5, Chavannes, II, p. 58: 'In
      these latter years Ch'in often changed its ruler; both princes and
      subjects used all these opportunities to make trouble.' It is not
      explicitly stated that a given prince was only a child on coming to
      power, except for the last one, little Ch'u-tzu, whose birth in 338 is
      mentioned. But that seems to emerge from the genealogy, such as
      we can reconstruct of it from the *Shih chi*.
4   This person's biography is in the *Shih chi, ch.* 68. The work which
      exists nowadays under the title *Shang-tzu* and is attributed to him is
      apocryphal.
5   *Shih chi, ch.* 68, 2*a–b*.
6   This reform is sometimes assigned to a later period, the date of 303
      being given (*Ch'in pieh chi*, in *Ch'i kuo k'ao, ch.* 2, 1*b*; for this lost work

see bk. 1, ch. 4, n. 49 above). None of these dates must be taken too literally. It is probable that in the case of Yang of Wey, like that of Yi-wu of Kuan, the reforms of several generations were lumped together, after the event, under the name of a well-known personage.

7 I have taken the date from the *Shih chi*, II, p. 65. The *Ch'in pieh chi* claims that the construction was started in 349 and took twelve years to finish (349–338). This is probably an echo of a clearly exaggerated local tradition (*Ch'i kuo k'ao, ch.* 3, 2*b*).

Hsien-yang lay quite close to modern Hsi-an fu.

8 Chi was the former capital of Chin, of which Wei was one of the heirs: hence this title (*Ch'i kuo k'ao, ch.* 4, 4*b*). Another explanation of this name may be found in Chavannes, *Mémoires historiques*, II, p. 65, n. 3.

9 *Shih chi, ch.* 5, Chavannes, II, pp. 44–45, and cf. *ch.* 110, 2*b*, from which are taken the details about the subjugated tribes. Terrien de Lacouperie, *Western Origins of the Chinese civilization*, pp. 264–75, and following him, Chavannes, V, pp. 488–89 (app. 2), assumed that Mu's conquests had led him as far as Kucha in central Asia. But, if the number of 'twelve kingdoms' is to be taken literally, the most likely interpretation would be that the reference is not to distant kingdoms in central Asia, but to the seven countries named above in the *Shih chi, ch.* 110, and five others in the same region on the borders of the modern provinces of Shensi and Kansu.

In the name of the barbarian tribe *Wu-chih*, the second character, ordinarily pronounced *shih*, must here be pronounced exceptionally as *chih* (*Ch'ien-Han shu, ch.* 28B, 2*b*). See Map 1.

10 The *Shang-tzu* gives a detailed description of a military reorganization which it ascribes to Wey Yang. But I have ignored this, as the work which bears this name today is a comparatively modern forgery.

11 The biography of General Wu Ch'i who served under princes Wen and Wu of Wei, is full of fabulous details, especially the end, which tells of his flight from Wei and his retirement to Ch'u, where King Tao is said to have made him minister and reformed the whole administration on his advice. He reduced the number of officials, reorganized finances and made economies, reformed the army, and so forth. Then there was his dramatic end, killed by arrows of the jealous nobles, as he tried to seek shelter behind the scarcely cold body of King Tao (*Shih chi, ch.* 65, 3*a–b*). The whole of this part of the biography is simply romance, as is easily shown by a flagrant anachronism: King Tao died in 381 (*Shih chi, ch.* 40, Chavannes, IV, p. 384), but Wu Ch'i was still in Wei in 378, four years later, when he was ordered to lead an expedition against Ch'i, and won a victory at Ling-ch'iu (*Shih chi, ch.* 44 and 46, Chavannes, V, pp. 148–49, 241). Cf. Henri Maspero, 'Le Roman de Sou Ts'in', in *Etudes asiatiques publiées à l'occasion du 25e anniversaire de l'Ecole française d'Extrême-Orient*, II, p. 140. A small work with the title *Wu-tzu* exists

about the art of war, attributed to Wu Ch'i It seems to be merely a fragment, which has been touched up, of the work which Ssu-ma Ch'ien saw and from which he took the materials for his biography.

12 *Tso chuan*, Legge, p. 376.

13 The date 367 is taken from the *Shih chi cheng yi*, a commentary on the *Shih chi*, published in 737 by Chang Shou-chieh, which is generally edited with the text; see *Shih chi, ch.* 4, 13*b*: second year of King Hsien. Chavannes, I, p. 301, n. 1, writes 376, which is obviously only a misprint.

14 *Chan kuo ts'e, ch.* 2, 4*b*. The chronology and history of the houses of the western and eastern dukes of Chou is very confused, and the fact that two princes who reigned in the two duchies in the fourth century bear the same posthumous title, Hui, adds to the confusion.

15 On the battle of An and the events of this period in Lu, see p. 208 above.

16 The first and third of these are also called, more briefly, Meng and Chi.

17 Cf. the anecdote concerning Yang Hu in the *Han Fei tzu, ch.* 16, 17*a*, in which the minister of Prince Ching of Ch'i blames his sovereign for wanting to receive Yang Hu with honour. He argues that Yang Hu, who is seeking refuge, had tried to weaken the 'three Huan', whose quarrels had produced Lu's weakness and Ch'i's strength.

Chapter 3.   The Warring Kingdoms

1 *Shih chi*, Chavannes, V, p. 249: *Chu shu chi nien*, Legge, p. 172 (gives 357 as the date); *Chan kuo ts'e, ch.* 7, 6*b* (gives no date).

2 The only mention of this expedition is found in the *Chu shu chi nien*, Legge, p. 173. The date is not absolutely certain, for it places the Feng-tse assembly of princes under Ch'in presidency in the same year, though that meeting was actually held in 342 (*Shih chi*, Chavannes, II, p. 67).

3 For Sun Pin see *Shih chi, ch.* 65, 1*b*. Tradition connects him with this treatise, known as the *Sun-tzu*, making his distant ancestor the author. The work, if not a complete forgery, must date, at the earliest, from the third century B.C.; and it can therefore have nothing to do either with Sun Pin or with his fabulous ancestor. The *Shih chi, ch.* 44, Chavannes, V, p. 155, is in error when it says the campaign was directed against Chao rather than Han.

4 The *Chu shu chi nien* describes firstly a victory of Wei over Han at Ma-ling in 345, then a defeat inflicted on Wei by Ch'i at the same spot in 343. In view of the geographical position of Ma-ling (near Ta-ming fu in Hopei) two different battles may indeed have taken place here within an interval of a few years. In that case the defection of Han would have to be placed in 344. The chronology of this whole period is ill established. There is from one to three years' difference between the *Shih chi* and the *Chu shu chi nien*. I have

preferred to follow the first, the many alterations in the second making it relatively unreliable.

5 About these persons, see below, pp. 306, 330, 317, 341, 375.

6 Hui, or Hui-ch'eng, when he took the royal title, started counting the years of his reign afresh, as the *Chu shu chi nien* shows. The *Shih chi* has used the second series of years of King Hui's reign as the reign of another king, whom it calls Hsiang. See Chavannes, *Mémoires historiques*, V, p. 158, n. 4. As a result it wrongly places the Hsü-chou meeting in 334, and the battle of Tiao-yin in 330.

7 For the history of Yüeh in this period, see the *Chu shu chi nien*, Legge (*Shu ching*, pp. 170–71). The *Shih chi*, Chavannes, IV, pp. 433–34 gives only a list of kings, and even that is incomplete.

8 One of them, retaining his title of King of Yüeh, sent presents to Wei in 312 (*Chu shu chi nien*, Legge, p. 175). And we shall find the descendants of two of them again as kings in the second century B.C., one in Tung-hai, and the other in Min. There is no document allowing the conjecture that the inhabitants of Yüeh emigrated southward from Chekiang in this period and during the following century peopled the Tonkin delta, where they became the ancestors of the Annamites, as M. Aurousseau has suggested in his 'Note sur les origines de peuple annamite', appendix to 'La Première Conquête chinoise des pays annamites', in *BEFEO*, XXIII (1923), pp. 254–64.

9 The *Shih chi*, Chavannes, V, p. 260, which has King Wei dying in 343 and King Hsüan in 324, places these events as occurring during the mourning, on the day before King Min, Hsüan's son, acceded to the throne; and it has Min reigning from 323 to 284. But this chronology, which is contradicted by all contemporary writers, is wrong. The following must be adopted: Wei 357–320; Hsüan 319 to about 301; Min about 300 to 284. Cf. Henri Maspero, 'La chronologie des rois de Ts'i au IVe siècle a.C.', in *TP* (1927), pp. 367–86. Takeuchi Yoshio, 'Roku koku nempyō teigo' [Rectification of the chronological table of the Six Kingdoms], in *Takase hakase kanreki kinen shinagaku ronsō*, Tokyo, 1929, pp. 89–216.

10 According to the romance version, Chang Yi's coming as minister to Wei was a trick he was playing to deceive the King of Wei. His arrival there is nevertheless an authentic fact, though one might well doubt it, for it is mentioned in the *Ch'in chi* (*Shih chi*, ch. 5, Chavannes, V, p. 161; cf. *Chan kuo ts'e*, ch. 7, 6a, and also 15b, which gives the romance version). Something of the same kind happened in 308 when, after the convention of Lin-chin between Wu of Ch'in and Hsiang of Han, the former sent his uncle, Chi of Ch'u-li, as resident to Han, where he was appointed minister, *hsiang* (*Ch'in chi*, in *Shih chi*, II, p. 75).

11 He is called Ai by Ssu-ma Ch'ien, who makes a whole series of errors there: Hui-ch'eng, having taken the title of king in 335, re-started a new reign-period of years at that time. That is what Ssu-ma Ch'ien attributes to King Hsiang. The evidence of a

contemporary, Mencius, leaves no doubt as to this error. Cf. Chavannes, *Mémoires historiques*, V, pp. 462–63.

12 This is the first definite mention of an incursion by the nomadic barbarians, the Huns, from the northern frontiers of China.

13 Mencius, pp. 222–24; *Shih chi*, IV, pp. 140–44.

14 It is said that King Hui sent his minister Chang Yi to Huai of Ch'u and offered to cede him Shang and Yü in the Ch'in-ling Mountains if he would break off relations with Ch'i. Huai accepted and sent a bravo to Ch'i to insult the king in the presence of his court. But after he had done that, his ambassador to Ch'in could not get the promised territories released. Thereupon, he is said to have declared war against Ch'in in his rage. This anecdote, like the one about Chang Yi surrendering to the King of Ch'u in order to save the country of Ch'in, comes either from the romance of Su Ch'in or from one of its sequels. For the success of that romance gave rise to imitations, the best-known of which is the romance of Su Tai and Su Li, Su Ch'in's brothers.

Indeed, the history of this whole period has been travestied in similar romances. A number of these are about well-known persons, such as the Wei general Wu Ch'i; Yang of Wey, Lord of Shang; and perhaps also Fan Chü, a Ch'in minister. The whole history of Chao seems to have been treated in romance form, traces of which remain in chapter 43 of the *Shih chi* and in the biographies of various persons, as well as in the *Chan kuo ts'e*. I have naturally tried to omit all these romances and anything that critical study of documents has shown me to have them as its source. Yet, if the account of the period has gained in historical reliability through this, it has lost in life and picturesqueness. For the romance-histories of the fourth and third centuries, see the various works of Father Tschepe, *Histoire du royaume de Ts'in, Histoire du royaume de Tch'ou*, etc.

Chang Yi is a real person who was minister in Ch'in from 328 to 312, and, when driven out of there, took refuge in Wei, where he was well received but died after a short time. The author of the romance of Su Ch'in, having portrayed Chang Yi as the enemy of his hero, credited him with a series of more or less true adventures which, collected in the *Chan kuo ts'e*, have passed subsequently into all the histories. He is mentioned by his contemporary Mencius, III, II, 2, Legge, p. 140.

Chapter 4. The Triumph of Ch'in (Third Century)

1 A certain Ch'in of Su, who came originally from the environs of the Chou capital, is said to have been the first to have the idea of forming a league against Ch'in by bringing about a reconciliation between Ch'i and Ch'u and by grouping all the principalities of the north, centre, and east around them. Having conceived this idea, it is said, he first sought to convince his sovereign, King Hsien of

Chou, then Hui-wen of Ch'in, but in vain. He seems to have had more success with the Prince of Chao, who sent him on a mission to visit each of the princes. Su Ch'in having persuaded them by his eloquence, the six states (Chao, Han, Wei, Ch'i, Yen and Ch'u) formed a league against Ch'in, of which he was the head, each of the six states having simultaneously nominated him Prime Minister. It was enough for him to inform the Count of Ch'in of this for the latter not to venture to invade any of his neighbours for the next fifteen years. Only perfidy and treason ruined his work. His personal enemy, Chang Yi, who had become Prime Minister of Ch'in, was able to persuade two of the allies, Ch'i and Han, to attack a third, Chao, where Su Ch'in was living. He was obliged to flee to Yen from the anger of the king, and the league, deprived of its head, broke up.

This anecdote, which has been carefully preserved by Chinese writers, is nothing but a historical romance, composed about the middle of the third century B.C., in which a writer hostile to Ch'in has developed his political ideas. It is full of anachronisms and has no historical basis. See Henri Maspero, 'Le Roman de Sou Ts'in', in *Etudes asiatiques publiées à l'occasion du 25e anniversaire de l'Ecole française d'Extrême-Orient*, BEFEO., XX, pp. 127–41. The original work, now lost, was still extant in Han times. An abridged form has been preserved by Ssu-ma Ch'ien, *Shih chi, ch.* 69, and lengthy fragments of it are to be found in different chapters of the *Chan kuo ts'e*. An excellent summary is to be found in Martin, 'Diplomacy in ancient China', in *Journal of the Peking Or. Soc.*, II (1889), pp. 241–62. See also Tschepe, *Histoire du royaume de Ts'in*, pp. 131–36.

2   For the history of Sung in the fifth and sixth centuries, see *Chan kuo ts'e, ch.* 10 (*Sung ts'e*), which contains almost all that is known about it. The *Shih chi, ch.* 38, Chavannes, V, pp. 239–47, gives almost nothing from this period except the chronological list of the dukes. All the legends about King K'ang are repetitions of those about the wicked Yin kings Wu-yi and Tsou. But the contamination has been reciprocal, for at least one of them, that of the king shooting at heaven, seems to be of Iranian origin, and consequently can hardly have been introduced into China before the last years of the Chou dynasty. Cf. Darmesteter, 'La Flèche de Nemrod, en Perse et en Chine', in *J. As.*, VIII (1885), pp. 220–28. In this he brings out the identity of the Middle Eastern and Chinese legends well, but — relying too confidently upon the authenticity of early Chinese history — falls into the error of assuming transmission in the reverse direction (from China to Iran). Conrady, in 'Indischer Einfluss in China im 4. Jahrh. v. Chr.', in *Zeitschr. der deutsch. morgenl. Gesellschaft*, LX (1906), p. 349, has already pointed out this improbability.

3   *Shih chi*, II, p. 85; IV, pp. 145, 402; V, pp. 96, 169, 219, 272–77; *ch.* 80 (biography of Yo Yi); *ch.* 82 (biography of T'ien Tan); *Chan kuo ts'e, ch.* 13, 1a–4b (ed. *Shih-li-chü ts'ung shu*). Here again many romance

elements seem to have been introduced into the history; but the short summary I have given seems to me admissible.

Book V: Ancient Literature and Philosophy

Chapter 1. The Origins of Literature

1 These are for the most part attributed to the founders of the dynasty, King Wu and the Duke of Chou; these traditional attributions are without foundation. At the end of the dynasty, everything dealing with political, administrative, and religious organization was lumped together as the work of the Duke of Chou.

2 The dances themselves were actually much more ancient than the odes.

3 See for example pp. 42–43 above, the translation of several passages describing a royal feast with drunken courtiers quarrelling.

4 *Shih ching*, Legge, p. 343.

5 Ibid., p. 346.

6 Ibid., p. 320.

7 Ibid., p. 350.

8 Ibid., p. 298.

9 Ibid., p. 411.

10 Ibid., p. 320.

11 On these festivals, see pp. 70–72, 141 above.

12 *Shih ching*, Legge, p. 23.

13 Ibid., p. 136.

14 Ibid., pp. 10, 21; 19; 22, 25; 36, 129; 131.

15 Ibid., pp. 26; 84; 134.

16 It is known that the present-day *T'ai shih* and *Wu ch'eng* of the *Shu ching* are not authentic. It has been possible to reconstruct the *T'ai shih* partly with the help of ancient quotations (Chiang Sheng's reconstruction is to be found in Legge, *Ch. Cl.*, III, pp. 298–99). Of the authentic *Wu ch'eng* nothing remains except a few insufficient quotations. The *Fen ch'i* is one of the chapters of the *Shu ching*, only the name of which is known from the preface, the work having already been lost in pre-Han times.

   The four chapters represent respectively the libretti to scenes I, II, III, and V of the ballet, those of scenes IV and VI not having been included in the collection. Cf. above, pp. 154–57.

17 I do not mean that the whole series of chapters which the preface sets between these two were sections of this libretto; but some of them were. The original texts were separated, as those of the *Ta-wu* were by the intrusion of the *Hung fan* between the *Wu ch'eng* and the *Fen ch'i*. It is impossible to be any more precise regarding the dances of Sung, since we know nothing of them in detail.

18 *Mu shih* (*Shu ching*, Legge, p. 300; cf. Chavannes, *Mémoires historiques*, I, p. 233).

19 *T'ai shih* (ibid., Legge, p. 298).

20   Some ancient inscriptions have preserved specimens for us. Cf. above, bk. 1, ch. 4, n. 39.

21   *Shu ching*, pp. 544–68.

22   Naitō, op. cit., seems to suggest too late a date for these when he attributes their composition to the Confucian school during its gradual rise in the course of the fifth, fourth, and third centuries.

23   Chavannes, *Mémoires historiques*, I, intro., pp. cxiii–cxxxvi.

24   *Shu ching*, pp. 475, 476 (*Chün shih*).

25   Ibid., pp. 497, 498, 499, 500 (*To fang*).

26   Ibid., p. 70 (*Kao-yao mu*). This text takes the form of discussions between Kao-yao, Minister of Justice, and Yü, Prime Minister, before the Emperor Shun. Like all the chapters about Yao and Shun, it seems to be relatively recent.

27   Ibid., p. 590 (*Lü hsing*).

28   The *Yao tien* was a short treatise, probably dating from the end of the Western Chou, which today forms the first two chapters of the *Shu ching* under the titles of *Yao tien* and *Shun tien*. We know, in fact, that the original *Shun tien* was lost and that, at the end of the fifth century, a certain Yao Fang-hsing detached the second half of the old *Yao tien* and added a forged introduction of twenty-eight words to it. This received the title of *Shun tien*, which it has retained to our day (cf. Legge, *Ch. Cl.*, I, 30).

29   On the king's Virtue, see above pp. 86–88.

30   *Shu ching*, Legge, pp. 320–43. An excellent account of the *Hung fan* and the theories it contains is in Wieger, *Histoire des croyances religieuses et des opinions philosophiques en Chine*, reading 6, pp. 57–63. My own account differs only in having set aside all explanations based upon the *yin-yang* theory, which in my opinion was worked out much later (see below), and in having given less importance to the interpretations of the commentaries.

31   I cannot agree with Naitō that the theory of the Five Elements, being a recent invention, is an interpolation in the *Hung fan*; nor with Honda, op. cit., pp. 62, 63, that the composition of this work must therefore be ascribed to around the third or second century; nor even that it should be simply dated back towards the middle of the Warring States period, as Shinjō would have it in 'The *Kan chih wu hsing* theory and the so-called *Chuan hsü* calendar' in *Shinagaku*, II, 516. The theory of Five Elements is certainly ancient; and it is only the use of it in astrology, history, and so on which is of later date.

32   A lost chapter of the *Shu ching*, in the *Tso chuan*, p. 250, gives the enumeration of them in the order (water, fire, metal, wood, earth) which is that of the Triumphs of the Elements. This passage is inserted into one of the non-authentic chapters of the modern *Shu ching*, the *Ta Yü mo* (Legge, p. 56).

33   For the explanation through correspondence with the cardinal directions, see Granet, *Religion des Chinois*, p. 118; but to introduce the numerical passages of the *Hsi tz'u* seems to me anachronistic.

Chavannes, *Mémoires historiques*, IV, p. 219, n. 5, has suggested that the order adopted by the *Hung fan* should be viewed as a copyist's error and that the order of the Triumphs can be retrieved by replacing wood with earth; but the text seems to me certified by a passage in the *Yi Chou shu, ch.* 3, 10*b*, sec. 28) in which the order is the same.

34 *Hung fan* (*Shu ching*, Legge, II, p. 393).

35 At least towards the end of the Chou dynasty, when the ritual works were composed, this was a small college having only two graduates and four scribes, plus some assistants, a store-keeper, and servants (*Chou li*, Biot, I, p. 410).

36 The *Yi ching* today is composed of two parts, the text and seven appendices, which the Chinese, by an arbitrary division, call the 'Ten Wings', *shih yi*. I am concerned here only with the text; on the appendices, see below, pp. 300–304. There are several translations of the *Yi ching*, all bad: by its very character, the work is almost untranslatable. I refer to Legge's, *The Yi king, Sacred Books of the East*, XVI.

37 The terms 9 and 6 are those of Chou and are used in the *Yi ching*; 7 and 8 are those of Sung and are used in the official divination manual of that principality, the *Kuei tsang*. They seem also to have been those used by the Chin diviners and by their book, the *Lien shan*; but this is less certain, for the work had vanished by the Han era, and the fragments that are quoted come from a forgery.

38 This arrangement seems to me to exclude the Chinese theory of forming the hexagrams by superposing two trigrams (see below, pp. 283–84); for if the hexagrams are reversed, two completely different trigrams are formed. If the Chinese theory were correct, the order adopted would have to be that in which, for each hexagram, the displacement of two trigrams would make them come up alternately upper and lower (for example, this sequence: 3–40, 4–39, 5–6, 7–8, 9–44, 10–45, 11–12, 13–14, 15–23, 26–24, 17–54, 18–55, 19–45, 20–46, and so on).

39 This arises from the very language of the *Yi ching*, which never states that a given hexagram represents or symbolizes a given thing but asserts that it is the thing itself. The translators are more often than not responsible for importing this notion, which is borrowed from the commentators of the Sung period. And this appears even more clearly in the appendices: when the *T'uan chuan* declares that 'the principle of *ch'ien* is to change and transform in such a way that each thing has its correct natural destiny', and that '*k'un* is thick and supports things', it is quite obvious that heaven (*ch'ien*) and earth (*k'un*) themselves are meant, and not symbols for them.

40 See above, pp. 113–14.

41 The places were numbered for the whole hexagram, which was regarded as a whole and interpreted as such. There is nothing to show that the interpretation by mutation, *yi*, of the two trigrams into which every hexagram can be separated, goes back to any very

early date. It is true that this is the classical method of interpretation today; but it appears first in the first and second appendices (*T'uan chuan* and *Hsiang chuan*) of the *Yi ching*: and there is no reason to introduce the ideas of these relatively modern commentaries into the interpretation of the ancient text. A single passage alone seems to allude to the trigrams: this is the beginning of the *T'uan* on the hexagram *k'an*: 'doubled pit', *hsi k'an*. But this passage stands quite alone and cannot be regarded as adequate support for a theory which the other sixty-three hexagrams refute. The symmetry of the figure was a sufficient reason for causing one to think of this 'redoubling' (always supposing that, following the commentator, one may take the incomprehensible word *hsi* to have a meaning which it does not normally convey, though that meaning comes close to the technical sense it bears as a term in divination: cf. *Shu ching*, p. 355, and a passage from a lost chapter of the *Tso chuan*, p. 851). See a somewhat unsatisfactory attempt at a different interpretation by Haas, in *Textbuch der Religionsgeschichte*, p. 14.

42 This arrangement led de Harlez to infer that the original basis of the *Yi ching* in earliest times was a fragment of a dictionary with sixty-four words, for which the *T'uan* as known today gave the definitions, while the *Yao* was a series of examples borrowed from the old popular ballads. This theory seems to have been adopted recently by A. Conrady and his students: cf. Erkes, *China*, Perthes kleine Völkerkunde, VII, p. 128; and more recently Hans Haas in the chapter 'China', 3, of Lehmann and H. Haas, *Textbuch zur Religionsgeschichte*, relies upon Erkes's authority when he declares that the *Yi ching* is a 'Stichwörterbuch für Staatslenker' (a book of maxims for leaders of states). The attempt to translate hexagram 29, *k'an*, 'pit', by the *T'uan* and *Yao* (ibid., pp. 16–17) is most baffling but has the value of demonstrating vividly the arbitrariness of the distinction, basic for the author, between the modern 'oracular terms' and the ancient lexicographical portions. For example, Haas considers as an 'oracular term' the passage from the *Yao* on the sixth line of the hexagram: 'For three years he will not succeed,' and he detaches it from the two preceding clauses, which form two lines. But the suspect clause is itself a verse line which rhymes with the two preceding lines, and in consequence cannot be separated from them. Thus the distinction which Haas is trying to make falls to the ground, as does also his interpretation of the two lines he has taken apart, and which he takes to be a description of an ancient funeral custom.

43 The fact that the king still performed the sacrifice to Mount Ch'i, a mountain in the fief of the first lords of Chou (*Yao*, hexagram 46, Legge, p. 160), carries us back in all probability either to times before the western capital was abandoned (771 B.C.) or perhaps to the first years of the eighth century, when Duke Wu of Ch'in conquered the lower valley of the Wei. On the other hand, the

passage relating to the Lord of Chi, who had attained the rectitude of mind denoted by the hexagram *ming-yi* (*Yao*, hexagram 36, Legge, p. 135), seems to show that the *Hung fan*, which alone justifies such admiration, existed in this period. The *Yao* must therefore date from the eighth century B.C., about the end of Western or the beginning of Eastern Chou.

44 This is the text of the present-day *Yi ching* without the appendices.

45 *T'uan chuan*, in *Yi ching*, Legge, pp. 216, 219, 228 (app. 1). It will be noted that the interpretation through the two trigrams descends from the upper to the lower trigram, while the analysis of the lines ascends from the line below to that above.

46 Cf. hexagrams 13, 16, 21, 33, 37, etc.; pp. 225, 227, 230, 240, 242, etc. (*T'uan chuan*).

47 *T'uan chuan*, p. 219.

48 *Yi ching*, p. 168.

Chapter 2.   Confucius, Mo-tzu and the Metaphysicians

1 The dates officially adopted — at least up to the Revolution of 1912 — for the birth and death of Confucius are 551 and 479 respectively. But they are far from being as certain as is generally assumed. For his birth, the sources fluctuate between the tenth month (*Ku-liang chuan, ch. 9, 10a*) and the eleventh month (*Kung-yang chuan, ch. 9, 12a*) in the twenty-first year of Prince Hsiang of Lu (552), and the twenty-second year, roughly 551 (*Shih chi*, V, p. 289). His death, which is mentioned in what is called 'the sequel to the *Ch'un ch'iu*' and, following that, in the *Shih chi*, is set on the *chi-ch'ou* day (twenty-sixth of the cycle) of the fourth month of the sixteenth year of Prince Ai (479). These divergences in the date of birth have greatly worried Chinese scholars. The authority of Chu Hsi caused the dates of the *Shih chi* to be accepted officially; but since the eighteenth century discussions have never ceased. Chiang Yung in *Chün ching pu yi* [Supplementary glosses to all the classics] prefers the dates of the two *chuan*, wherein he is followed by Ti Tzu-chi in his *K'ung-tzu pien nien*. Somewhat later K'ung Kuang-mu in his *Hsien Sheng sheng tsu nien yüeh jih k'ao* [An examination into the day, month, and year of the birth and death of the Ancient Sage] adopts the year of the *Shih chi*, the month of the *Ku-liang chuan*, and the day of the latter and of the *Kung-yang chuan*. Modern scholars, however, generally remain faithful to the *Shih chi* and to Chu Hsi.

   In actual fact none of the dates can be guaranteed. For the death, the day and month only may possibly be correct, as they were perhaps preserved thanks to the annual family sacrifices. It was according to these that the year was later recalculated, and owing to the difference between the incorrect calendar of the fifth century and the mathematical calendars of the fourth and third centuries B.C., when the calculations were made, the cyclical date for the day did not agree with the earlier ones. The reconstruction obtained with the help of the calendars with regular intercalations (see below pp. 375–78) had nothing in common with the true dates of the empirical calendar employed in the fifth century. It is probable that the legend about the capture of a unicorn in 481, which was regarded as predicting the death of the Sage, was responsible for the choice of 479, as it was the first year after 481 in which there was a *chi-ch'ou* day in the eleventh month.

As to his birth, its mention in the two *chuan* seems due to much later interpolations. Thus the *Shih chi so yin* (ch. 47, 11*b*) admits that 'as the *Ch'un ch'iu* and its commentaries do not give the date of the birth of Confucius, the exact age of the Sage is not certain.' This is confirmed by a commentator of the seventh century, Lu Te-ming, who pointed out that even in his day some copies of the *Kung-yang Chuan* did not contain the relevant passage. The cyclical date is impossible. Therefore the interpolator of the *Ku-liang chuan*, better advised, placed it in the tenth month instead of the eleventh. The sole ancient date is the one in the *Shih chi*, but that gives neither day nor month. It seems to have been derived by combining the date of death given in the sequel of the *Ch'un ch'iu* with a tradition which says that Confucius lived seventy-three years.

The dates for Confucius are no more reliable than those for other ancient writers. All that can be said is that he lived in the second half of the sixth century and the first half of the fifth, without being more specific. There appears to me no insurmountable difficulty in making the traditional date later by about a quarter of a century.

2 *Lun yü*, p. 218.

3 I have endeavoured to provide a biography of Confucius solely according to the *Lun yü*, as it is the most ancient collection of traditions concerning him. It goes without saying that no full history of his life could be written from a work of this kind. Nevertheless it has the advantage of never presenting facts merely for their own sake, but only in order to explain and localize conversations on doctrine, so that to a degree it evades the influence of themes from folklore or religion, which would have affected a narrative work more. I believe, moreover, that the life of Confucius (unwritten) did not take shape in this school till long after the composition of the *Lun yü*, in imitation of the philosophical romances which became so popular towards the end of the Chou period.

A good exposition of the traditional biography will be found in Legge, *Ch. Cl.*, I, *Prolegomena*, pp. 56–90, taken from the works of Liang Yung (eighteenth century). This takes into account more modern traditions, which are for the most part assembled in the *Li chi*. The first chronological arrangement is the one attempted by Ssu-ma Ch'ien (*Shih chi*, ch. 47, V, p. 283), which all later works have used as their base. According to tradition, he first took service with the Prince of Lu, then lost his mother and did not take up official work again after the mourning period. Instead he turned for the first time to teaching and founded a school. Tradition also sets in this period a visit to the court of the Chou kings.

4 This fact, which the *Mo-tzu* (*ch.* 9, sec. 39; Forke, p. 409) clearly indicates, and which the tradition concerning his employment as magistrate at Chung-tu corroborated, later seemed inconsistent with the image that had been formed of Confucius. For it became impossible to believe that he had served only his own prince. For this reason all the passages in the *Lun yü* about audiences with the head of the Chi family are interpreted as referring to interviews with the Prince of Lu, sometimes, indeed, contrary to common sense. For the audiences with the Chi family see *Kuo yü* (*Lu yü*) with reference to K'ang-tzu of Chi, and also the arguments of Hu P'ei-hui in his *Yen-liu shih tsa chu* (*Huang Ch'ing ching chieh*, ch. 1302, 1a).

5 The tradition of his school has him filling the high posts of Director of Works and then of Director of Criminals (*Lü shih ch'un ch'iu. ch.* 14, 18b; in the *Tso chuan*, first year of Ting — Legge, p. 745 — it is said that 'when K'ung-tzu was Director of Criminals, he had a ditch dug and the tombs joined up'). This is most unlikely: these posts were hereditary, the first being held by the chief of the Meng family, the second by the chief of the Tsang family. He is also said to have played the chief part in the interview between the princes of Ch'i and Lu at Chia-ku in 500 (*Tso chuan*, pp. 776–77; Granet, *Danses et légendes*, I, pp. 171–213); and an attempt to re-establish princely authority by forcing the heads of the great families to dismantle their fortresses was also attributed to him (*Tso chuan*, p. 781). It is strange that in the *Ch'un ch'iu*, which is the official chronicle of Lu in that period, the name of Confucius is not even mentioned.

6 The four great ordeals of Confucius during his travels (Huan T'ui, in Sung, felling the tree under which he used to sit; his forced departures from Wey; his distressful position between Shang and Chou; and his seven days' siege between Ch'en and Ts'ai) form a series, the order of which had become fixed by the end of the fourth century (*Chuang-tzu*, ch. 20, 373; *Lieh-tzu*, ch. 7, 175). Perhaps this series followed the points of the compass; east (Sung), north (Wey), west (Shang and Chou), south (Ch'en and Ts'ai), the centre not being represented.

7 *Lun yü*, X, pp. 227–36.

8 Ibid., VII, 5, p. 196. 'The Master said: "How I decline! It is a long time since I saw the Duke of Chou in my dreams." '

9 For this reason the disciples are called *men-jen*, 'men of the gate' (*Lun yü*, XI, 14, p. 242) or else 'disciples of the gate', *men-ti-tzu* (ibid., IX, 2, p. 216). The expression has remained current in Chinese.

10 *Lun yü*, VII, 7, p. 197.

11 Ibid., VII, 8, p. 197.

12 For these schools, see above p. 79

13   These are the commentaries called *Kung-yang chuan, Ku-liang chuan*, and the non-narrative portion of the *Tso chuan*.

14   I have constrained myself to setting forth the theories of Confucius as one finds them exhibited in the most ancient book of traditions relating to him, composed in his school, his 'Analects', *Lun yü*, rejecting all that is reported in the *Li chi*, because the texts of the latter work are of a much later time and have been subject to the influence of the fourth century thinkers. Even the older booklets of the *Li chi*, the *Chung yung* and the *Ta hsüeh* possess the disadvantage of representing a system (although Confucius seems clearly never to have reduced his teaching to a system), and consequently of providing us with ideas reconsidered and worked over again by his disciples. Moreover, the *Lun yü* itself does not have the value which an original work by Confucius would have had, for it is a relatively late compilation. It represents, however, the most archaic form in which we can lay hold upon Confucian doctrine.

15   *Lun yü*, XII, 17, p. 258.

16   Ibid., XIII, 6, p. 266.

17   Ibid., II, 20, 152.

18   Ibid., XII, 18, 19, pp. 258–59. The preceding quotation is taken from the same passage.

19   European commentators have attributed to Confucius the theory that the prince's example would reform the people (cf. Legge, *Ch. Cl.*, I, *Prolegomena*, p. 106; Dvorak, *China's Religionen*, I, p. 188 ff.; and so on). No passage in the *Lun Yü* (nor in the later works, the *Chung yung, Ta hsüeh*, and so on) shows the example of the prince as an agency for reforming the people. The theory of Confucius derives from that of the *Hung fan* and in a general way from the religious ideas of the time regarding the Royal Virtue, and the example has nothing to do with that. It is with Mo-tzu that the theory of the people's imitating of superiors as a means of transforming them appears. It was then adopted by the Confucianists. It is set forth in the *Fang chi* of the *Li chi* (Couvreur, II, pp. 406–9, etc.). But see the *Shu ching, Shao kao* (Legge, p. 432): 'It is for him who is in the position of king to overtop all with his virtue. In this case the people will imitate (*hsing* = *fa*) him throughout the whole empire, and the king will become more illustrious.'

20   *Lun yü*, II, 1, p. 145.

21   Ibid., XVII, 2, 3, p. 318. The preceding quotation is from the same passage.

22   Ibid., VI, 25, p. 193.

23   Ibid., II, 16, p. 150. For the meaning of this much discussed sentence, see Haas, 'Lun yü', II, 16, in *Asia Major*, Prelim. Vol., pp. 145–64.

24   Ibid., II, 15, 16, p. 150; XVI, 13, p. 315.

25   Ibid., VIII, 8, p. 211.

26   Ibid., XII, 22, p. 260. Usually *jen* is translated as 'humanity', probably in the hope of preserving a trace of the Chinese play upon

words between *jen* 'man' and *jen* 'the virtue of altruism'; but this translation renders many of the passages of the *Lun yü* unintelligible. I have borrowed from Father Wieger, *Histoire des croyances religieuses et des opinions philosophiques en Chine*, p. 134, the translation 'altruism', which is the best that can be given for this term.

27 *Lun yü*, IV, 5, p. 166.
28 Ibid., XII, 2, p. 251; V, 11, p. 177; XV, 23, p. 301. The aphorism in the last two passages was uttered by the disciple Tzu-kung.
29 Ibid., I, 2, p. 138.
30 Ibid., IV, 3, p. 166.
31 Ibid., XII, 1, p. 250.
32 Ibid., XIV, 2, p. 276.
33 Ibid., XII, 1, p. 250.
34 Ibid., III, 3, p. 155.
35 Ibid., IV, 2, p. 165.
36 Ibid., I, 6, p. 140.
37 Ibid., XIV, 45, p. 292.
38 Ibid., XVI, 9, p. 313.
39 Ibid., XIV, 45, p. 292.
40 Ibid., VIII, 9, p. 211.
41 Ibid., XIII, 12, p. 267.
42 He was said to have been born in Sung, which is probably wrong, or even in Ch'u, for which there is no evidence. That he came from Lu, though not absolutely certain, is the most likely and with good reason the most generally held opinion. See Sun Yi-jang, *Mo-tzu hou yü*, ch. 1, 1*b*; cf. Forke, op. cit., p. 29. Mo was probably his family and Ti his personal name; but this is not certain. Chiang Yung considers Ti to be the family name. Cf. Ch'en Chu, op. cit., pp. 5–8.
43 *Kuo yü*, ch. 18, 3*a* (*Ch'u yü*). The real name of this person is not known: Wen-tzu is only a posthumous title. Sun Yi-jang in his *Mo-tzu hou yü*, ch. 1, 5*a* (cf. Forke, op. cit., p. 8) has suggested that it was the Minister of War, K'uan, who succeeded to the post of his father, Tzu-ch'i, in 478; but this suggestion is unlikely, and Wen-tzu was more probably one of K'uan's brothers.
44 *Mo-tzu*, ch. 12, p. 552. Usually the interview is placed in 438, a date taken from a passage of Hsü Chih-ku's *Ku chu kung chiu shih* (of T'ang times), ch. 2, 15*a* (ed. *P'ing-chin kuan ts'ung shu*). That passage seems to be a quotation from *Mo-tzu*, ch. 12, more complete than the present text. But the date is in the beginning of the introduction and must have been added by the author, for none of the anecdotes in ch. 12 of the *Mo-tzu* contains a single date. Nevertheless, though far from certain, it is not improbable; for the text speaks of the great age of King Hui, who died in 430.
45 One anecdote shows him recalling from Ch'i his disciple Sheng Cho, who had a post there, because this state had attacked his native state three times, in 412, 411 and 408 (*Mo-tzu*, ch. 13, 10*a–b*, p.

581); two others associate him with T'ai-kung of Ch'i and his general Hsiang Tzu-niu regarding a projected attack against Lu (ibid., p. 579). These probably relate to the incursions of 412-403, for T'ien Ho governed Ch'i a long time before usurping the throne, and the posthumous title of T'ai-kung is simply due to the late composition date of this chapter, a collection of anecdotes and recollections compiled by his disciples long after the Master's death. These dates are not inconsistent with the passages of the chapter 'Against War', *Fei kung*, where he states that 'now' the empire is divided into four between Ch'i, Chin, Ch'u and Yüeh; for although Chin had disappeared from the political scene after the murder of the Count of Chih in 453, the final division of the principality was not officially recognized until fifty years later, and in the interval its prestige could remain great in the eyes of a man living at a distance.

46   The passage in the authentic parts of the *Mo-tzu* alluding to the most recent event is the one referring to the people of Cheng as 'having killed their princes three times'. This refers to the murder of Ai (456), Yu (423), and Hsü (396). An anecdote (*ch.* 13, sec. 49, Forke, p. 581) tells of a discussion with the Prince of Lu-yang about the people of Cheng who 'in the course of three generations have murdered their princes', which refers to the same three cases. The fact that this Prince of Lu-yang, if he was really the son of a minister who died in 478, can hardly have spoken about an event in 396 (cf. Forke, p. 581, n. 1) is of little importance; section 49 is a recent one and contains numerous anachronisms. The mention of Prince K'ang of Ch'i by his posthumous title (*ch.* 8, sec. 32, Forke, p. 369) is not a sufficiently strong argument for moving the composition date of the chapter on music (one of the authentic chapters) to after his death (379), but must be an interpolation by the editors, his disciples. Nevertheless, as this prince ascended the throne in 404, it is no argument that Mo Ti must have died before the end of the fifth century, as Forke, p. 27, has already shown. As to the passage on Wu Ch'i (*ch.* 1, sec. 1, Forke, p. 162) and his death in 381 B.C., it is of no importance, because it is found in one of the spurious chapters. Moreover, it is contradicted by an anecdote in the *Lü shih ch'un ch'iu*; cf. Ch'en Chu, op. cit., p. 12.

47   A number of quotations from the Classics found in the *Mo-tzu* have been collected by Ch'en Chu, op. cit., pp. 33-77.

48   There were originally 71 sections (*Ch'ien-Han shu*, ch. 30, 15*b*), of which 18 have been lost. Of the remaining 53 only 24 appear to go back — often, unfortunately, in revised form — to Mo-tzu's authentic work (8-39, sections 22-24, 29-30, 33-34, and 38 being lost). Sections 46-48 are a collection of anecdotes and discourses by Mo-tzu (similar to those of the *Lun yü* on Confucius), probably compiled during the fourth century. Sections 49-50 are a collection of the same type but of a later date. Sections 1-7 are also the work of his school (this is also the opinion of Ch'en Chu, op. cit., pp. 21

ff., whose arguments seem to me excellent. Hu Shih and Liang Ch'i-ch'ao believe, wrongly in my opinion, that sections 1–3 do not belong to Mo-tzu's school, which would leave only sections 5–7), and they seem to date from the third century. Sections 40–45, which also belong to the third century, have been attributed by Hu Shih, probably correctly, to that branch of the school which the author of the *Chuang-tzu, ch.* 33, calls Pieh Mo (see below, pp. 333–35 and which was especially concerned with dialectics. Finally, sections 52–71, which deal with the defence and siege of fortified towns, must have come from a special branch of the school. See Hu Shih, *Chung kuo che hsüeh shih ta kang,* I, pp. 151–52, and *The Development of the Logical Method in Ancient China,* pp. 53–54 (the numbers Hu Shih gives for the sections of the *Mo-tzu* differ from my own because, by a regrettable procedure, he has changed the traditional numbering in not counting the lost sections).

49 Chinese scholars usually deny this, because these writings contain the expression 'the Master Mo-tzu said', from which they conclude that it must be the work of his disciples (see for example *Ssu k'u ch'üan shu tsung mu, ch.* 117, 1*a*). But this is a formula which, in all the writings of the philosophers of this period, disciples introduce as a sign of respect when studying or transmitting the words of a master. Anyhow, the argument is a bit weak in itself, since the style of all these chapters is remarkably homogeneous, if not in their entirety, at least in certain passages.

50 Yü Yüeh, *Yü lou tsa tsuan, ch.* 34, 17*b*. Forke, op. cit., pp. 22–23, adopts this quite probable theory; but he adds that there were probably three versions received orally by different students, and that one reason for the difference bore on the necessity of translating spoken into written language. But at this time there was probably little difference between the two. His theory becomes all the less tenable because Forke admits the existence of an original text. It is difficult to see how the poor collections of scraps from student notebooks could have taken over — within the school — the place of the original text written by the Master himself. It seems to me simpler to suppose that after their separation the three schools, transmitting more or less precisely these texts which served as study manuals for their students — and transmitting also the commentaries and reflections of successive teachers — ended by establishing the three markedly different versions that have come down to us. For the three schools of Mo-tzu's disciples, see below, p. 329–30.

51 Comparing these sections with Mo-tzu's own work is of interest since it shows how far the anecdotes truly preserve the Master's doctrine. It may also serve to indicate the value of the *Lun yü* in relation to Confucius's teachings.

52 That is, the love for oneself or one's family rather than for others and their families.

53 *Mo-tzu, ch.* 4, Forke, p. 240; Legge, *Ch. Cl.,* II, *Prolegomena,* pp. 104–5.

A summary of this chapter can be found in Wieger, *Histoire des croyances religieuses*, p. 211.

54   *Mo-tzu, ch.* 6, Forke, p. 301. This is a part of Mo-tzu's teaching that has impressed later generations, steeped in Confucian ritualism; cf. Wu Yü, 'A neglected side of Mo Tzu's Doctrine as seen through Hsün Tzu', in *Shinagaku*, II, vii (1922), 1–18.

55   *Mo-tzu, ch.* 5, 1*b*–2*a*, Forke, p. 267. Cf. Wieger, op. cit., pp.210–11.

56   Ibid., *ch.* 3 (sec. 12), 2*b*, Forke, p. 219; cf. secs. 11 and 13.

57   Ibid., *ch.* 4, 3*a*, Forke, p. 242.

58   Ibid., *ch.* 12, 4*a*; pp. 555, 556 (the four quotations of this paragraph).

59   Ibid., *ch.* 2, 4; p. 173.

60   Ibid., *ch.* 7, sec. 26; p. 315.

61   Ibid., *ch.* 7, p. 315.

62   Ibid., *ch.* 7, secs. 26–28; pp. 314–42.

63   Ibid., *ch.* 12, sec. 48, no. 4, p. 566.

64   Legge, *Yi ching*, introd., p. 46, finds resemblances in style with the *Chung yung* and, as he accepts the tradition that this treatise is by Tzu-ssu, he relegates the *Hsi tz'u* to the second half of the fifth century.

The *yin* and *yang* theory is mentioned in *Mo-tzu, ch.* 7, sec. 27; Forke, p. 324; but, although this passage is found in one of the authentic chapters, it is difficult to draw any definite conclusion from that, because it is found in only one of the three editions in which this chapter, like all the others of the same type, has been preserved; so that it might be a later addition by the school to which this particular edition belonged.

65   This figure is obtained by combinations of numbers symbolizing figures and lines. Cf. Legge, *Yi ching*, pp. 368–69, nn.

66   These were two common words meaning: *yin*, the shady side, and *yang*, the sunny side, of a mountain or valley. It is in the *Hsi tz'u* that they first appear with a philosophical meaning.

67   *Yin* and *yang* have generally been defined as 'forces': see Suzuki, *A brief history of early Chinese Philosophy*, pp. 15–16; Wieger, *Histoire des croyances religieuses et des opinions philosophiques en Chine* Hu Shih, *Chung-kuo che hsüeh shih ta kang, ch.* 1, pp. 78–79; Tucci, *Storia della filosofia cinese antica*, p. 15; etc. This quite unjustifiably introduces modern ideas into Chinese thought — ideas which are entirely alien to it.

68   *Hsi tz'u*, in *Yi ching*, Legge, p. 356.

69   Ibid., pp. 372–73.

70   Ibid., p. 355.

71   Ibid., p. 377. The word *ch'i* actually means 'vase'. I have used the word 'body', because the relation between *ch'i* and *wan-wu* seems to me a little like that of simple chemical bodies to common beings and things. Naturally this comparison must not be pushed too far.

72   'Sum' naturally in time, and not in space, which they occupy completely as they follow each other in turn. The Taoists, who made Tao a reality in itself, were the first to change this way of seeing things.

73   *Hsi tz'u*, pp. 353–54.

Chapter 3.   The Taoist School

1   In the middle of the third century B.C., the school of Chuang-tzu
claimed Lao-tzu and Kuan Yin tzu as the founders of the mystic sect
of Taoism (*Chuang-tzu*, ch. 33, p. 305). A work attributed to the latter
was in circulation at the time and appears to have still existed in
Han times (*Ch'ien-Han shu, ch.* 30, 12*b*). Evidently it is from this that
the anecdote of Lao-tzu's departure for the west and of his
interview with 'Yin of the Pass' Kuan Yin, author of the book, is
derived. The book is unknown to Chuang-tzu, who narrates the
death of Lao-tzu (the name of Kuan Yin tzu indeed appears in an
anecdote of the *Chuang-tzu,* ch. 19, p. 357); but this appears to be an
interpolation reintroduced from the *Lieh-tzu* (ch. 2, p. 85, together
with about a third of chapter 19). However, it was known to the
author of the *Lieh-tzu* (ch. 3, p. 107), so it appears sufficiently
reasonable to place the composition of the *Kuan-yin-tzu* towards the
end of the fourth or the very beginning of the third century. The
story of his departure for the west must be a romantic introduction
to this philosophical work, following a common practice of the
time. The work now bearing the name *Kuan-yin-tzu,* or again *Wen-
shih chen ching,* is a forgery of the eighth century A.D.

2   Absolutely nothing is known regarding the author of the *Lao-tzu.* I
speak of the *Lao-tzu* because, if it is certain that there was a book
with this name, this does not mean that there indeed existed a
person of that name. The case is the same as for the *Lieh-tzu.* The
biography devoted to him by Ssu-ma Ch'ien (*Shih chi, ch.* 63, 1*a*–2*a*,
trans. in Legge, *Sacred Books of the East,* XXXIX, *Texts of Taoism,* I, pp.
34–36; Dvorak, op. cit., pp. 2–3; Federmann, *Lao-tse Tao teh king,* pp.
vii–ix, etc.) is practically without content. For the tales of the Taoist
school at the end of the fourth century B.C., see *Chuang-tzu, ch.* 3, p.
229; *ch.* 7, p. 265; *ch.* 13, pp. 313–15; *ch.* 14, pp. 325–29; *ch.* 21, p.
381; *ch.* 22, p. 393; *Lieh-tzu, ch.* 2, p. 98; *ch.* 3, pp. 107, 115; etc.; cf.
also *Han Fei tzu, ch.* 18, 6*a.* These make Lao-tzu a somewhat older
contemporary of Confucius (*Chuang-tzu, ch.* 14, pp. 325–29). As to
the names attributed to him by Ssu-ma Ch'ien: family name Li,
personal name Erh, the old traditional name of Tan becoming a
posthumous honorific name (the present-day *Shih chi* adds a
surname, Po-yang; but that derives from the spurious commentary
on the *Tao te ching* attributed to Ho-shang kung and appears to be
an interpolation, for the citations of the T'ang period do not
contain it; cf. Chang-huai, commentary on the *Hou-Han shu, ch.* 7,
7*a*), as well as the place of his birth, K'u-hsien in Ch'u. It is known
that in the second century B.C., Li Chieh, tutor of Liu Ang, King of
Chiao-hsi, a grandson of the founder of the Han dynasty, claimed
descent from Lao-tzu (*Shih chi, ch.* 63, 2*a*). These data probably came
from his family register, as the genealogy did, through the

intermediacy of the commentary composed by the exegetical school of the *Tao te ching* deriving from the Man from the Banks of the River, *Ho-shang chang-fu*, a school then very eminent in Ch'i and Chiao-hsi, and one with which Li Chieh was in touch. They thus have little value. In any case, even if accepted, they are not sufficient to make Lao-tzu a man of the south, a representative of the barbarians from the banks of the Yangtze among the northern Chinese; for the Ch'u in question is that of the beginning of Han, in northern Kiangsu; and K'u-hsien, situated near present-day Ch'en-chou, was in ancient times part of the purely Chinese principality of Ch'en. Unfortunately the *Tao te ching*, which is exceedingly short, contains neither any allusion to historical matters nor even a proper name. It is consequently difficult to date. It is quoted, however, very consistently from the end of the fourth century on, in the *Chuang-tzu*, the *Lieh-tzu*, the *Han Fei tzu*, and so on, which thus provides a rough age limit. On the other hand, the oldest quotation from it appears to me that in the *Lun yü*, which carries us back to the end of the fifth or the beginning of the fourth century B.C. (see below, p. 338). From its language and style it cannot be assigned a date older than this period. Ts'ui Tung-pi (1740–1816) in his *Chu tzu k'ao hsin lu*, seems to me to bring it down somewhat too late when he places the work in the time of Yang-tzu and his disciples, and thus makes the author a contemporary of Chuang-tzu. Tsumaki, 'Study on Taoism' in *Tōyō gakuhō*, I (1911), i, p. 9, is satisfied to place it vaguely 'after Confucius and before Han Fei tzu' — that is, between the fifth and third centuries B.C. The authenticity of the work has been challenged by Herbert Giles, whose article 'The Remains of Lao Tzu' has given rise to a whole controversy (summarized in Dvorak, op. cit., p. 17 ff.). Giles believed then that it must be viewed as a forgery of the third century B.C. The arguments are not very convincing. At the most they prove a fact otherwise known: that in the third century one or several other books were in circulation besides the *Tao te ching*, either attributed to Lao-tzu or about him, and that the authors of the time quoted fragments from them.

3   This is all we know of Chuang-tzu. His personal name appears repeatedly in his work. Prince Mou of Chung-shan is named in *ch*. 17, p. 345, and *ch*. 28, p. 461 (see above, pp. 231–32. Allusion is made to the journey to Ch'u in *ch*. 18, p. 353; King Hui of Wei (370–318) is designated by his personal name, Ying (alongside a king of Ch'i whose unknown name, Mou, should doubtless be rectified), at the same time as the *hsi-shou* (Kung-sun) Yen, of whom the *Shih chi* speaks in about the years 314–310, in *ch*. 25, p. 431 (the proper names are not transcribed in the translation). This chapter is consequently from the last quarter of the fourth century. *Ch*. 17, p. 341, recounting the abdication of King K'uai of Yen (320–314) in favour of his minister (316), his death and the ruin of Yen, which the King of Ch'i conquered in 314 (*Shih chi*, IV, 142), takes us back to

the same period. There is a much-disputed passage of *ch.* 10, p. 277, where it is said that, after the prince of Ch'i was assassinated by Ch'eng-tzu of T'ien (Heng, see above, p. 235) in 481, the latter's descendants occupied the throne for twelve generations. But since King Min, a contemporary of Chuang-tzu, was only the descendant in the eighth generation after Heng, this has been regarded as an interpolation, or the whole chapter has even been considered non-authentic. But the last king of Ch'i, Chien (264–221), was himself only the representative of the tenth generation, so that the number twelve was not correct for any period; and all that can be said is that, if this is not a textual inaccuracy, the author (whoever he was) was mistaken. As against that, chapter 30 in its entirety, commencing, 'Formerly, King Wen of Chao ...' and thus placing in the past a prince who reigned from 298 to 266 B.C., should be attributed, it appears to me, not to Chuang-tzu himself, but to his disciples and probably with it the three last chapters, 31–33. Chapter 29, 'the robber Chih', often questioned without reason, is certainly authentic. As to chapter 19, about a third of it consists of anecdotes drawn from chapter 2 of the *Lieh-tzu*, the style of which in no way recalls Chuang-tzu's. It is probably necessary to regard this as filling in a gap. To sum up, Chuang-tzu appears to have written in the last years of the fourth century, but additions were made to his work throughout the following half-century. It is already quoted in the *Lü shih ch'un ch'iu*, *ch.* 33, *7a*, *ch.* 14, *21b*, *22a* (third century B.C.).

4   The present *Chuang-tzu* comprises 33 chapters. Under the Han there were 52, but it is impossible to determine whether this reflected another way of dividing the work, or whether 19 chapters were actually lost between the first and fourth centuries of our era. It is likewise difficult to ascertain what epoch the division into *nei ching* (*ch.* 1–7), *wai ching* (*ch.* 8–22), and *tsa ching* (*ch.* 23–33) goes back to. In 742 A.D. the work received the honorary title of *Nan-hua chen ching*.

5   G. von der Gabelentz, *Beiträge zur chinesischen Grammatik, Die Sprache des Cuang-tsi* (*Abhandl. d. Sächsischen Gesellsch d. Wiss.*, 1888).

6   The existence of an actual personage called Lieh-tzu is highly problematical. The preface attributed to Liu Hsiang gives him the personal name of Yü-k'ou, and his birth is given as in the state of Cheng at the end of the seventh century. If he actually existed, he had nothing to do with the book which bears his name and which is much more recent. This was already recognized under the T'ang by Liu Tsung-yüan, *Lieh tzu pien*, when he suggested that, in the preface, Prince Mu of Cheng (627–606) should be replaced by Prince Mu of Lu (407–377). The present *Lieh-tzu* comprises eight chapters, but the seventh, introduced here by mistake, probably by the editors of the Han period, is a fragment from the works of Yang-tzu (see below pp. 317–21), and the eighth is a collection of anecdotes of all kinds, some simply variants of passages from the *Chuang-tzu* or from the first chapters of the *Lieh-tzu*, others without any clear

philosophical import; only the first six chapters are of any real significance. The *Lieh-tzu* cites fragments: *ch.* 1 (p. 73) from the *Kuo yü*, *ch.* 15, 8*a* (*Chin yü*) or more precisely from one of the sources of this work; and p. 77 and p. 161 from the *Yen-tzu ch'un ch'iu*, *ch.* 1, 20*b*, and *ch.* 1, 19*b*; *ch.* 3, 105–7 alludes to the *Mu t'ien-tzu chuan*; and p. 109 cites a passage of the *Chou li*. These texts are, however, too poorly dated to be able to serve as reliable landmarks. Tsou Yen, who is mentioned therein (*ch.* 5, p. 143), lived in the second half of the fourth century and the first half of the third. The latest date is in *ch.* 2, p. 103, the mention of King K'ang of Sung (328–286) under his posthumous name. Furthermore, the work is cited in the *Lü shih ch'un ch'iu*, *ch.* 9, 7*b*–8*a*, *ch.* 16, 5*b*–6*a* (second half of the third century). Quite lately Ma I-ch'u, Professor at Peking University, in his 'Study on the authenticity of the *Lieh-tzu*', *Lieh-tzu wei shu k'ao* (*Kuo ku*, 1919, nos. 1 and 3) has attempted to prove that the *Lieh-tzu* was a forgery, composed towards the end of the third century A.D. by Wang Pi or his school. This article has been easily refuted by Takenouchi, 'A Textual Criticism of the Lieh-tzu', in *Shinagaku* (*Sinology*), I (1920), iv, pp. 1–16.

7   It forms chapter 33 of the present-day *Chuang-tzu*.

8   *Lieh-tzu*, *ch.* 4, p. 128; *Chuang-tzu*, *ch.* 33, p. 505. The work was in five sections (*Ch'ien-Han shu*, *ch.* 30, 12*b*).

9   The *Tao te ching* is so short that it is quite difficult to obtain from it an exposition of a 'doctrine of Lao-tzu'. The efforts of Dvorak, Strauss, and Grill are hardly encouraging. I have preferred to study, as a whole which developed in a consistent manner, the Taoist school during the approximate century and a half which passed between the composition of the *Lao-tzu* and that of the *Lieh-tzu*.

10   Henri Maspero, *Le Saint et la vie mystique chez Lao-tseu et Tchouang-tseu* (I refer to this article for any references not found herein). Hu Shih, *The Development of the Logical Method in Ancient China*, pp. 142–48, has recently attempted the paradox of explaining Chuang-tzu's doctrine as a system of logic.

11   *Chuang-tzu*, *ch.* 12, pp. 296–97.

12   Ibid., *ch.* 13, p. 317.

13   Ibid., *ch.* 22, p. 395.

14   *Lao-tzu*, sec. 52, 49; cf. *Hsün-tzu*, *ch.* 1, 17*a*.

15   Illumination, a spontaneous act, cannot be required upon entrance into the school, as a kind of formality. It develops in due course, sooner or later according to the individual. Chuang-tzu was already a teacher and had numerous disciples when his conversion took place (op. cit., *ch.* 20, p. 377).

16   *Chuang-tzu*, *ch.* 4, p. 233.

17   Ibid., *ch.* 20, p. 373.

18   Ibid., *ch.* 7, p. 267.

19   *Lao-tzu*, sec. 59, p. 53; Father Wieger's interpretation, like Strauss's (p. 264) and Dvorak's (p. 119), using the commentary of Ho-shang kung, is entirely different and makes a political aphorism out of

this passage. Legge's (p. 102), on the contrary, is about the same as mine.

20 *Chuang-tzu*, ch. 2, p. 215; ch. 24, p. 421.

21 Ibid., ch. 23, p. 391.

22 *Lieh-tzu*, ch. 2, p. 85.

23 *Lao-tzu*, sec. 41, p. 45.

24 *Chuang-tzu*, ch. 13, p. 309.

25 Masson-Oursel, 'Etudes de logique comparée: II, Evolution de la logique chinoise', in *Revue philosophique*, LXXXIV (1917), p. 71, has already established 'the connection of Taoist doctrine with the theories of the *I ching*'.

26 *Lao-tzu*, sec. 42, pp. 45–47. I translate according to the quotation of the *Huai-nan-tzu*. The present-day editions add three words: 'The Tao produced the One', which, with the majority of modern Chinese critics, I reject as an interpolation.

27 *Chuang-tzu*, ch. 25, p. 437.

28 *Lao-tzu*, sec. 25, p. 36.

29 Ibid., sec. 34, p. 41.

30 *Chuang-tzu*, ch. 22, p. 394.

31 I have borrowed the translation of the word *chün* from Father Wieger, who was the first to draw attention to this notion of 'continuity' and to show its importance in Taoism.

32 *Lieh-tzu*, ch. 3, p. 109.

33 Ibid., ch. 1, p. 73.

34 Ibid., ch. 1, p. 77.

35 Ibid., ch. 1, p. 75.

36 *Chuang-tzu*, ch. 22, p. 395.

37 Ibid., ch. 3, p. 229.

38 Ibid., ch. 6, p. 261.

39 Ibid., ch. 2, p. 227.

40 *Lieh-tzu*, ch. 3, p. 111.

41 *Chuang-tzu*, ch. 6, p. 251.

42 *Lieh-tzu*, ch. 1, p. 71.

43 *Chuang-tzu*, ch. 6, p. 257.

44 Ibid., ch. 6, p. 259.

45 Ibid., ch. 6, p. 261.

46 It can be seen how, despite certain similarities in detail, the Ego differs from the *âtman* of the Hindus (see La Vallée-Poussin, "Indo-européens et Indo-iraniens, L'Inde vers 300 av. J. C.', *Histoire du Monde*, III, p. 272). Two philosophical systems both based upon mystical experience must have points of contact, because this experience is the same everywhere and at all times. Tucci, *Storia della filosofia cinese antica* (Bologna, 1922), app., 'Lao Tze e l'India', pp. 110–18, has already developed with much justice this idea that any close connection between Lao-tzu's philosophy and Indian doctrines is completely unfounded.

47 *Lao-tzu*, sec. 59, p. 53.

48 *Chuang-tzu*, ch. 17, p. 343.

49 Ibid., *ch.* 8, p. 269.
50 Ibid., *ch.* 23, p. 411.
51 Ibid., *ch.* 11, p. 287.
52 *Lao-tzu*, sec. 3, p.20.
53 *Chuang-tzu*, *ch.* 9, p. 275.

Chapter 4.   Schools Derived from Taoism: Yang-tzu and the Legalists

1 His contemporaries were in no doubt as to the Taoist tendencies of some of his teachings: 'Ch'in-tzu said to him: "I don't know how to reply to you. But if one were to report your words to Lao Tan and Yin of the Pass and ask them questions about it, your words would be in full agreement [with their replies]. But if my words were reported to Yü the Great or to Mo Ti and their opinion were asked, my words would be in full agreement [with their replies]." ' (*Lieh-tzu*, *ch.* 7, 10*b*; Wieger, p. 173).

2 Yang-tzu mentions the usurpation of the T'ien family in Ch'i as an accomplished fact (*Lieh-tzu*, *ch.* 7, p. 163); mention is made of his audience with the King of Liang, a title which appeared only in 336 (ibid., p. 170); his discussion with Ch'in-tzu (Ch'in Hua-li), a direct disciple of Mo-tzu (ibid., p. 173; cf. p. 171) carries us back a little earlier; once, Mo-tzu appears (ibid., p. 173). On the other hand, the name of Yang-tzu is mentioned in the *Mencius* (pp. 282, 464, 491, etc.) and in the *Chuang-tzu* (pp. 269, 279, etc.). An anecdote from the *Chuang-tzu*, *ch.* 27, p. 453, relating the interview between Lao-tzu and a certain Yang Tzu-chü is attributed to Yang Chu in the *Lieh-tzu*, *ch.* 2, p. 99, through confusion of names or perhaps simply through a copyist's error; cf. Giles, *Biographical Dictionary*, no. 2370.

3 It forms chapter 7 of the *Lieh-tzu*.

4 *Lieh-tzu*, *ch.* 7, p. 165.

5 For want of a better expression, I translate *chiu sheng* as 'eternal life', though this is only approximately correct. Yang-tzu does not admit that it is possible not to die, and says so expressly. *Chiu sheng* is life prolonged to an extreme limit, for ages.

6 Lieh-tzu, *ch.* 7, p. 173, as also for the preceding quotation.

7 Ibid., p. 173.

8 Ibid., p. 165.

9 Ibid., p. 175.

10 Ibid., p. 179.

11 Ibid., p. 177.

12 A *Sung-tzu* in 18 sections existed in Han times and was ascribed to him (*Ch'ien-Han shu*, *ch.* 30, 18*a*). The end of section 18 of the *Sung-tzu* (*ch.* 12, *Cheng lun*) seems to be part of a disputation with Sung K'eng (also known as Sung Hsing and Sung Yung) and to have got into this work by mistake. In it he is repeatedly called 'Master Sung-tzu'. Two of Sung K'eng's theories are discussed and refuted there, but both of them deal with psychology (cf. also *Chuang-tzu*, sec. 33: (1) If one shows that to be insulted is not dishonorable, all strife ceases.

(2) Human nature has few desires, but everyone commits the error of believing that his own nature has many desires). The author seems to have insisted on a universal union and the suppression of war, which is a doctrine of Mo-tzu, but with a Taoist tinge.

13 On the historical use of this work, see below, p. 259.

14 *Yin Wen tzu*, trans. Masson-Oursel and Chu Chia-chien, pp. 592–593.

15 Yin Wen tzu had conversations with King Hsüan of Ch'i (342–324) before Kung-sun Lung (*Ch'ien-Han shu*, ch. 30, 15a). The catalogue of Liu Hsiang (end of the first century B.C.) made him one of the 'Masters of the Chi Gate' (ibid.); while the *Shih chi*, ch. 46 (V, p. 259) and *ch.* 74, does not mention him among the members of that society. The *Shuo yüan* (also by Liu Hsiang) places him in touch with King Hsüan of Ch'i, the *Lü shih ch'un ch'iu* (middle of the third century B.C.) with King Min (323–84); an anecdote in the *Kung-sun Lung tzu*, 2b, makes him older than Kung-sun Lung. All this agrees well enough to place him in the second half of the fourth and the beginning of the third century. No attention should be paid to the statement in Chung-ch'ang's preface, which makes him a disciple of Kung-sun Lung, as this preface is a forgery.

16 The ancient *Yin Wen tzu* was a tiny work of one section (*Ch'ien-Han shu*, loc. cit.). It seems to have grown considerably during the first centuries A.D., for an edition of two chapters existed at the end of the sixth century (*Sui shu*, ch. 34, 3a). This edition, from which numerous quotations exist, was current in the T'ang dynasty. It had a preface attributed to Chung-ch'ang (T'ung) (third century A.D.) and a commentary attributed to Liu Hsin (*Yi lin, ch.* 2, 18a); but the preface contains an anachronism that betrays the forgery. It was lost about the tenth century, and the modern work is a clumsy reconstruction probably dating from the eleventh century. Wei Cheng (eighth century) was still acquainted with the ancient work (*Ch'ün shu chih yao*, ch. 37, 14a–21a), as was his contemporary Ma Tsung (*Yi lin, ch.* 2, 18a–19a), and a little later Chao Jui (*Ch'ang-tuan ching*), for they cite long fragments from it; so does the *T'ai-p'ing yü lan*, an encyclopedia published in 984. On the other hand, in 1151 Ch'ao Kung-wu had already seen the modern work (*Chün chai tu shu chih*, ch. 11, 17b); likewise a little later Kao Ssu-sun (*Tzu-lüeh*, ch. 3, 3a) and his contemporary Hung Mai (*Yung chai hsü pi*), etc. This reconstituted text of Sung times is all that has come down to us, either through the great Taoist collection *Tao tsang*, where it was inserted, or through independent editions (an edition from the end of the Sung, which was reproduced at the beginning of the Ming, is the original for the re-edition of the *Ssu pu ts'ung k'an*) or in more recent collections (*Shou-shan ko ts'ang shu*, *Po tzu*, etc.). The compiler placed extracts from the *Ch'ün shu chih yao*, the *Yi lin*, the *T'ai-p'ing yü lan*, etc., end to end, his arrangement being rather poor. He suppressed the title of the second chapter, probably so as to make it correspond to the data in the *Ch'ien-Han shu*. He completed in his

own way the fragment of Chung-ch'ang's preface which is preserved in the *Yi lin*; but he does not seem generally to have added anything to the fragments which he assembled. Thus the work in its present form on the one hand contains numerous interpolations of the Six Dynasties period and, on the other, represents an arrangement due to the Sung compilers. There are, to be sure, some genuine parts (for example the passage, sec. 2, 9*b*, p. 591, with its variant in the quotation of the *Tao te ching*), but they are not always easily recognizable.

17   *Lun yü*, XIII, p. 263. The *Lun yü* on the whole dates from the fifth and fourth centuries B.C. But this passage, which has no analogue in the rest of the work and alludes to a doctrine that could have been known only towards the end of the fourth century, must be a later interpolation by the school. In my opinion it is because they realized the difficulty of dating this theory back to the time of Confucius himself, and also because they wanted to safeguard their text, that modern Chinese scholars have been led to look for an interpretation that leaves out the theory of the 'rectification of names' and attempts to explain the word *ming* by written characters. Cf. Chavannes, *Les Mémoires historiques*, V, pp. 378–85, 440–42.

18   The work quoted by Han Fei tzu, *ch*. 17, sec. 43, 7*b*, still existed towards the beginning of our era (*Shih chi, ch*. 68, 4*b*; *Ch'ien-Han shu, ch*. 30, 14*b*); it disappeared no doubt towards the end of the Han dynasty. The present *Shang-tzu* is a forgery.

19   The books which are current today under the titles *Teng Hsi-tzu*, *Shen-tzu*, and *Shang-tzu* are forgeries of the Six Dynasties period. The present *Shih-tzu* is an attempt by Chang Tsung-yüan to reconstruct the ancient work, which was lost about the tenth or eleventh century. It contains extensive extracts from sixteen of the twenty original sections (*Ch'ien-Han shu, ch*. 30, 17*a*), almost all of them from the *Ch'ün shu chih yao, ch*. 36, and the *Chu tzu hui han*, which form chapter 1, as well as many short fragments which it has been impossible to classify, which form chapter 2. Two revised and enlarged recensions of it exist, one by Sun Hsing-yen (1799, reissued in 1806 in his *P'ing-chin-kuan ts'ung shu*); the other, and better, one is by Wang Chi-p'ei. What remains is unfortunately too incomplete to enable one to form a clear idea of the author's theories. An abridgement will be found in Wieger, *Histoire des croyances religieuses et des opinions philosophiques en Chine*, pp. 238–39. The *Shih-tzu* cannot go back further than the middle of the third century: its preserved fragments allude to Tsou Yen's theories about the world, without mentioning him by name (*ch*. 2, 12*a*). They mention the conquest of Ch'i by Yo Yi in 286 (*ch*. 2, 4*b*). Finally, the name of the *Lieh-tzu*, a work compiled in the third quarter of the third century, is mentioned in it. Cf. Pelliot, 'Meou-tseu ou les doutes levés', *T'oung Pao*, XIX (1918–19), pp. 353–54.

20   *Shih chi, ch*. 63, 3*a*, 5*b*; cf. *Chan kuo ts'e, ch*. 3, 80*a–b*. Ssu-ma Ch'ien

gives no date in this chapter; but in the annals of Ch'in he indicates that in 237 'the king of Han formed plans with Han Fei to weaken Ch'in'; then he mentions his death in 233 (*ch.* 5, II, pp. 114, 116); and in the annals of Han he gives the date of his embassy to Ch'in, 234 (*ch.* 45, V, p. 222). These are the dates I have used. Wieger, *Histoire des croyances religieuses*, places his death in 230, following the *Ch'i lu* of Juan Hsiao-hsü (sixth century), in *Shih chi cheng yi, ch.* 63, 3*a*.

21   The extant *Han Fei tzu* is composed of 55 sections, as was that of the Han period (*Ch'ien-Han shu, ch.* 30, 14*b*); but a number of sections which had been lost were replaced in rather haphazard fashion, probably in the time of the Six Dynasties. The first section, 'The first interview with the king of Ch'in' (*Ch'u chien Ch'in*) is the outline of a discourse attributed to Chang Yi in the *Chan kuo ts'e, ch.* 3. It is from these lost sections that certain ancient quotations would probably come, ones which are not found in the modern text (cf. Wang Hsien-ch'ien, *Han Fei tzu chi chieh*, preliminary chapter, pp. 12–16, *Yi-wen*). Other sections contain numerous interpolations; some offer an only partly intelligible text (e.g., sec. 48, *ch.* 18, 12*b* and 20*b*, which is moreover incomplete as well). Some chapters are so badly arranged and have so many variants among the manuscripts followed that in many cases the editors have not dared choose among the different readings and have contented themselves to reproduce them one after the other (e.g., *ch.* 14, 3*a*–4*b*, 6*b*, 12*a*, 12*b*, etc.). On the whole, the work appears to date from the second half of the third century, but it is not entirely by Han Fei. As with Chuang-tzu, Mo-tzu, and most of the philosophers of that period, a large part is due to the Master's disciples. For instance, section 6 speaks of the kingdoms of Ch'i, Yen, Ch'u, and Wei as being already destroyed, though this took place only after Han Fei's death (*ch.* 2, p. 1). Only rarely is it possible to distinguish between the parts that can be traced to the Master and those that must be attributed to his school. In my opinion, Hu Shih exaggerates when he regards only seven sections as authentic (40, 41, 43, 45, 46, 49, 50), cf. *Chung kuo che-hsüeh shih ta kang*, I, p. 365. Except for a few clear cases, his selection seems to me to be largely arbitrary. Moreover, he himself attaches little importance to it, as he quotes passages from sections which are, by his own witness, spurious (e.g., p. 381, sec. 54, etc.).

22   *Han Fei tzu, ch.* 2, 10, 11 (sec. 7); 10, 2 (sec. 31).

23   Ibid., *ch.* 1, 29 (sec. 5).

24   Ibid., *ch.* 17, 13, 14 (sec. 43).

25   Ibid., *ch.* 17, 12 (sec. 43).

26   Ibid., *ch.* 19, 1–2 (sec. 49). Cf. Wu, *Ancient Chinese Political Theories*, p. 202.

27   Ibid., *ch.* 20, 14 (sec. 54). This change is attributed, not to Progress, as Hu Shih believes, op. cit., p. 381, introducing a modern Western idea, but to universal instability. Only Tao is unchangeable; all

other things change, and laws are variable things like everything else.

28 *Han Fei tzu*, ch. 19, 2–4 (sec. 49); cf. G. Tucci, *Storia della filosofia cinese antica*, pp. 88–89, and Wu, op. cit., p. 202.

29 *Han Fei tzu*, ch. 19, 11–12 (sec. 49). The importance of efficiency in Han Fei's doctrine has been well brought out by Hu Shih, op. cit., pp. 382–84.

Chapter 5.   The School of Mo-tzu and the Sophists

1 For the successors of Mo-tzu, see Sun Yi-jang, *Mo hsüeh ch'uan shou k'ao* [Investigation of the transmission of Mo-tzu's doctrines], a supplementary work to his *Mo-tzu hsien ku*; cf. Forke, *Me Ti*, p. 75; Hu Shih, *Chung kuo che hsüeh shih ta kang*, I, pp. 184–86. Besides the scarcity of information, the chief difficulty arises from the fact that the third century compilers of Han Fei and the unknown author of chapter 33 of the *Chuang-tzu* are only partly in agreement.

2 He is also called Ch'in Hua-li; cf. Forke, *Me Ti*, pp. 76–77.

3 *Han Fei tzu*, ch. 19, 12b.

4 He died, it would appear, during the lifetime of Chuang-tzu (*Chuang-tzu*, ch. 24, pp. 419–21), with whom he is associated in various anecdotes (ibid., ch. 5, p. 249; ch. 17, pp. 347–49; ch. p. 18, 351; ch. 26, p. 445; ch. 27, pp. 449–51).

5 *Chuang-tzu*, ch. 33, p. 509.

6 Ibid., ch. 2, p. 221.

7 Ibid., ch. 33, p. 507.

8 There is a list of ten paradoxes specifically assigned to him in the *Chuang-tzu*, ch. 33, p. 507. For their interpretation I rely mainly upon the theories of Chang Ping-lin, op. cit., pp. 191–94, and of Hu Shih in his article on the philosophy of Hui Shih and Kung-sun Lung, and in his two great works, *The Development of the Logical Method in Ancient China*, pp. 111–17, and *Chung kuo che hsüeh shih ta kang*, I, p. 228 ff. Nevertheless, my reconstruction of the system differs in some respects from theirs, as I have attempted to eliminate the influence of Western philosophical ideas as far as possible. Cf. Tucci, op. cit., pp. 57–58; Forke, *The Chinese Sophists*.

9 In this paradox I am unable to discern, as Hu Shih does in his *Hui Shih Kung-sun Lung chih che hsüeh*, p. 91, 'striking and indubitable' proof that Hui Shih admitted the earth to be round. All he meant to say was that, space being illimitable and infinite, any point could be considered the centre of the earth.

10 There is no reason to suppose that Hui-tzu believed 'space to be in constant motion' (Hu Shih, *The Development of the Logical Method in Ancient China*, p. 114) and still less that either he or the Reformed School of Mo-tzu (Pieh Mo) based this theory of space on the 'bold hypothesis verging on belief that the earth, and not the sun, moved' (p. 115). It was not because space 'was in constant motion' that high and low, large and small were the same, but because

finite measurements could have no relation to the infinite. In support of his theory Hu Shih cites a passage from the *Mo-tzu* (ch. 10, p. 468) which he rightly connects with Hui-tzu but, wrongly in my opinion, interprets as alluding to a movement of space (this would be meaningless, for Hui-tzu held space to be infinite, and I do not see how Hu Shih conceives a perpetual displacement of infinite space), when he is discussing the relations between space and time.

11 Huan T'uan is quoted in the *Chuang-tzu*, ch. 33; Ti Chien is mentioned in the *Lü shih ch'un ch'iu*, ch. 13, 8b; ch. 18, 15a.

12 *Lü shih ch'un ch'iu*, ch. 13, 8b; ch. 18, 2b, 16b; *Chuang-tzu*, ch. 17, p. 345; *Lieh-tzu*, ch. 4, p. 127; *Chan kuo ts'e*, ch. 20. The dates which I adopt here are approximately those of Hu Shih, op. cit., pp. 110–11. He has been identified with the Kung-sun Lung also known as Tzu-shih, a disciple of Confucius, born in 499 (*Shih chi*, ch. 67, 9b) and also with the head of a school designated by the name of Ping in the *Chuang-tzu*, ch. 24, p. 419; these identifications are without any basis.

13 This is the very basis of Zeno of Elea's theory: it is thus not startling that their systems resemble one another in certain points. These resemblances must not, however, be exaggerated, as they would perhaps appear less striking to us if we knew the work of Kung-sun Lung better.

14 *Kung-sun Lung tzu*, 3b, 5b (sec. 2, 'Discussion on the White Horse'). Cf. translation in Tucci, op. cit., pp. 146–48. To understand Kung-sun Lung's reasoning, it is necessary to recall that this phrase 'white horse is not (the same thing as) horse' signifies also 'a white horse is not a horse', and that Kung-sun Lung passes constantly from one meaning to the other.

15 *Kung-sun Lung tzu*, 9b, 12a (sec. 5, 'Discussion on Hard and White'); translation in Tucci, op. cit., pp. 148–51 (cf. Hattori, 'Confucianism and its Opponents', in *Cosmopolitan Student*, April–May 1916, p. 138; Hu Shih, op. cit., p. 125). The final passage on the operation of the mind is very corrupt, but by comparing the two parallel passages with the analogous passage in *Mo-tzu*, ch. 10, 3b, 17b, it can be reconstituted. Cf. Henri Maspero, *Notes sur la logique de Mo-tseu et de son école*, pp. 58–64.

16 Certain distinctions appear purely verbal, such as the paradox, 'An orphan calf never had a mother', which is explained, 'At the time it had a mother, it was not an orphan calf' (*Lieh-tzu*, ch. 4, p. 129; cf. *Chuang-tzu*, ch. 33, p. 509: 'A colt ...'). In reality Kung-sun Lung's oddness arises because to the distinction of the elementary terms, 'colt', 'orphan', 'to have a mother', he adds here a time element, which is also divisible. To me the paradox 'A puppy is not a dog' belongs to this same category, in which are introduced the notions of division in time; and consequently it differs from 'A white horse is not a horse', to which Hu Shih, op. cit., p. 119, p. 5n, compares it, but into which this notion does not enter.

17 *Chuang-tzu*, ch. 33, pp. 507–9. The translations of these paradoxes

are not always very happy nor very precise. Legge, op. cit., p. 230, translates: 'Swift as the arrowhead is, there is a time when it is neither flying nor at rest'; and Hu, op. cit., p. 119 has: 'The arrow has moments of simultaneous motion and rest.' (Cf. also R. Wilhelm's translation, *Dschuang dsï*, introd., p. xviii.) In my opinion this interpretation renders the paradox unintelligible, since, if there are only *certain* moments when it is both at rest and in motion, in the interval between these instants it *is* either at rest or in motion, and it is no longer possible to prove anything. It is necessary that all the moments during which the movement lasts be moments of both rest and motion. That is why I insist on adding the word 'succession'. The arrow, properly speaking, is neither at rest nor in motion, because in reality it is at the same time both, according to the division of space one is considering.

No matter how one attempts to translate this sentence, in order to understand it an idea must be introduced which is not explicitly given in the text itself, since the word *shih* signifies 'some moments' as well as 'the moments'. One can express this idea implicitly, as Hu does by omitting the article which makes it possible (in English only) to use two words as in Chinese (*yu … shih* = has moments), or as Legge does, 'a moment', explicitly by using the indefinite article; or, as above, still more explicitly by a particular word. Whatever method is adopted, it will carry with it a personal contribution which is not in the text, since the laws of the European translator's language require him to make a choice between the two meanings which the Chinese sentence presents.

18   The order of these short phrases is quite unclear. It would appear nevertheless that the disarrangement was originally less than it is nowadays. The text appears to have been arranged initially in two columns, one above and the other below, on bamboo slips, each containing an ordered sequence of connected subjects; and it was undoubtedly the Han editors who neglected this arrangement and mixed up the two columns. Nevertheless, even in re-establishing the original arrangement as far as possible (which is often extremely difficult), the order arrived at is still most uncertain. Moreover, the text of these propositions, already so obscure in themselves, has suffered enormously in transmission and, notwithstanding all the efforts of the Chinese critics, many passages remain unintelligible or of more or less doubtful meaning. Cf. Hu Shih, *Chung kuo che hsüeh shih ta kang*, I, p. 189. There is a special critical edition by Liang Ch'i-ch'ao, published in 1913 under the title of *Mo ching chiao shih*.

19   *Mo-tzu, ch.* 10, 15*a*, sec. 43, p. 477. Teng-ling-tzu and the Reformed School, Pieh Mo, are mentioned in *Chuang-tzu, ch.* 33, p. 501; but this is one of the chapters which were composed within the school towards the middle of the third century.

20   *Mo-tzu, ch.* 10, 12*a*, sec. 43, p. 485; cf. *Kung-sun Lung tzu*, 11*b*; p. 469, 'Hardness and Whiteness', cf. *Kung-sun Lung tzu*, 9*b* (sec. 5); *ch.* 10,

3*b*, 17*b*, p. 485, 'the eye and the fire', cf. *Kung-sun Lung tzu*, 11*b*–12*a*.
21 *Mo-tzu, ch.* 10, 1*a*, sec. 40/1 p. 413.
22 Ibid., *ch.* 10, 6*a*, sec. 42, p. 441; Hu Shih, *Chung kuo che hsüeh shih ta kang*, I, p. 199, and *The Development of the Logical Method in Ancient China*; H. Maspero, op. cit., pp. 39–40.
23 *Mo-tzu, ch.* 10, 9*a*, sec. 42/65, p. 454.
24 Ibid., *ch.* 10, 2*b*, sec. 40/76, 78, pp. 420–21; *ch.* 10, 10*b*, sec. 42/78–79, pp. 459–60.
25 Ibid., *ch.* 10, 1*a*, sec. 40/18, 20, p. 415, etc.
26 It forms sections 45 of the modern *Mo-tzu* text, *ch.* 11, p. 526. Hu Shih has edited it separately, as *Mo-tzu Hsiao ch'ü p'ien hsin ku*, in the monthly review of Peking University (*Pei-ching ta-hsüeh yüeh k'an*) no. 3, and has reproduced it in his collection of articles published in 1923 under the title *Hu Shih wen ts'un*, I, ii, pp. 35–74.
27 *Mo-tzu, ch.* 11, sec. 45, pp. 527 ff. Cf. H. Maspero, *Notes sur la logique de Mo-tseu et de son école*, pp. 41–53.

Chapter 6.   The School of Confucius in the Fourth and Third Centuries

1 Mo-tzu agrees with the Confucian tradition in showing some of the disciples serving various princes; he accuses them of having always caused troubles wherever they were (*ch.* 9, 22*b*).
2 For the disciples of Confucius, see especially *Shih chi, ch.* 67; the *Chia yü, ch.* 9 (a forgery of the third century A.D.) is strongly influenced by it. Cf. Legge, *Ch. Cl.*, I, *Prolegomena.*, p. 113 ff., for a good summary of the official teaching. The traditional chronology of these persons is full of errors. The inconsistency of the dates for Confucius's grandson, Tzu-ssu (see below, pp. 338–39) has long been commented upon by Chinese critics; but there are numerous other cases. Tzu-hsia was forty-four years younger than Confucius (*Shih chi, ch.* 67, 5*b*): therefore he would have been born in 508 B.C. But the *Shih chi* elsewhere adds that he was teaching the classics to Prince Wen of Wei in the eighteenth year of that prince's reign: he would then have been 101 years old. Another passage places this fact in the twenty-fifth year of Prince Wen's reign (401), when Tzu-hsia would have been 108. Or again Wu-ma Ch'i is described as thirty years younger than Confucius, and thus born in 521; so it is unlikely that he would have lived beyond 450, and impossible beyond 421. But in the *Mo-tzu, ch.* 11, 17*a*, p. 547, he is shown as a contemporary of Mo Ti and of the Lord of Yang-wen, who was minister in Lu in 396. It seems thus that he should be placed about fifty years later. But there is a difficulty about that for, according to the *Lun yü*, VII, xxx, 2 (Legge, pp. 204–5), he appears as having been with Confucius in Ch'en; and the traditional arrangement of the life of Confucius sets his sojourn there from 495 to 490 (cf. Legge, *Ch. Cl.*, I, *Prolegomena.*, p. 79). In fact, the whole of this chronology is artificial and has even less value than that of Confucius himself.
3 *Li chi*, I, p. 146 (*T'an kung*); *Shih chi*, V, p. 427. It is a moot question

whether the disciples of Confucius wore mourning clothes, as Ssu-ma Ch'ien relates, or were content with the 'mourning of the heart', as the *Li chi* says.

4   This was the second section of the building, the houses of patricians having only two halls — one behind the other, and each with its own court — and not three like the palaces of princes. See above, p. 289.

5   *Shih chi*, V, p. 428.

6   These are the disciples whose discourses make up chapter 19 of the *Lun yü*. This fact seems to me to indicate clearly the importance of the schools which claimed descent from them in that period.

7   An echo of this is found in the criticisms which the leaders of the various schools directed at one another, *Lun yü*, ch. 19.

8   The *Lun yü* is anterior to the other Confucian works, *Ta hsüeh* and *Chung yung*, which cite passages from it. Quotations are also found in the *Mencius* and, less often, in the *Chuang-tzu* and *Lieh-tzu*; and finally, in two small, late works of the school of Mo-tzu (*ch.* 9, sec. 39, and *ch.* 11, sec. 46). The *Lun yü* cites a passage from the *Lao-tzu*, but the latter work is too poorly dated to serve as a guide. On the other hand, Legge (op. cit., *Prolegomena.*, p. 15) has already noted that the classification of the disciples in chapter 11 (p. 237 ff.) could only have been made after their deaths. Though I am not so convinced as he that the tradition which has Tzu-hsia dying in 406 is accurate, that date would certainly make it impossible to fix the compilation of this work earlier than the fourth century B.C.

9   Two different editions of the *Lun yü* appear to have existed at the end of the Chou dynasty: that of Lu in twenty sections, and that said to be of Ch'i, in twenty-two sections and divided into a greater number of paragraphs. At the end of the first century B.C. Chang Yü established a definitive text, taking as his basis the Lu edition, with some additions and corrections from the Ch'i version as well as from a third edition called '*Lun yü* in ancient characters', which was believed to be one of the books discovered in Confucius's house when King Kung of Lu had it pulled down in order to enlarge his palace, in the second century B.C. (See the list of variants in these two texts by Hsü Yang-yüan, *Lun yü Lu tu k'ao*, in *Hu-chou ts'ung shu*; it is the source of all modern editions.) The twenty-first section of the Ch'i edition seems to have been a dissertation on jade (its title, given as *Wen wang*, 'Questions regarding the king', should presumably be altered to *Wen yü*, 'Questions regarding jade', the two characters *wang* and *yü* differing only in a dot); some fragments of it have been preserved. Of the twenty-second section, *Chih tao*, nothing remains. On the question of the establishment of the *Lun yü* text under the Han dynasty, cf. Takenouchi, 'A Textual Criticism on the *Lun yü*', in *Shinagaku*, V, i, (1929), pp. 19–63.

10   Chinese philologists who have subjected the *Lun yü* to critical analysis have been able to identify some of these documents, although such study has been hampered by Chang Yü's work.

There are two and a half chapters (10, 16, and the beginning of 17, and additionally 2, pars. 21–24) in which Confucius is always designated by his family name, 'Master K'ung', *K'ung-tzu* (whereas in the others he is called simply 'the Master', *tzu*), and the style of these also presents common features. There would seem to have been a special source for these. Apart from this document, chapter 11, the style of which shows characteristic differences, must be placed in a class by itself. On the other hand, a certain number of scattered passages in the work (1, par. 10; 10) contain words peculiar to the Ch'i dialect (cf. Takenouchi, op. cit., pp. 46–50). Finally, it is likely that at least parts of chapters 1, 4, 8, 14, and 19, where Tseng Shen is called 'Master Tseng', *Tseng-tzu*, derived from a collection belonging to his school, and the three passages of chapter 1 which call Yu Jo 'Master Yu', *Yu-tzu* (contrasting with 12, 225, where he is simply called Yu Jo) from a collection belonging to his school. The greater part of the work, however, has resisted analysis.

11 The greater part of the texts relating to Confucius in the *Tso chuan* and the *Li chi* are evidently traditions of the school even later than the *Lun yü*.

12 Today they form chapters twenty-eight and twenty-nine of the *Li chi* (Couvreur, II, pp. 427–79; pp. 614–35); from there they were taken to be included in the small collection of classic books which is called the Four Books, *Ssu shu*.

13 Since Confucius's son, K'ung Li (Po-yü) died before his father at the age of fifty in about 480 (*Shih chi*, V, p. 430, and n. 1), Tzu-ssu, who lived sixty-two years (ibid., p. 431), would have to have died in 420 at the latest if he was the master's son. But the dates for Confucius himself are far from certain and should probably be made later by twenty to thirty years, which would make the chronology and the genealogy agree. Cf. above, note 1 to Book V, ch. 2, pp. 449–50.

14 Further details are found in the *K'ung-ts'ung-tzu*; but this work, which is said to be the work of K'ung Fu, a descendant of K'ung Chi in the Ch'in era, is a forgery compiled by Wang Su in the middle of the third century A.D.

15 *Mencius*, pp. 385–86; 388–89; 336; *Han Fei tzu*, ch. 16, 1a. An anecdote of the *K'ung-ts'ung-tzu*, ch. 1, 53b (ed. *Ssu pu ts'ung k'an*) places the death of Mu of Lu (377) during his sojourn in Wey.

16 A small collection on questions of ritual was extant in Han times; in 23 *p'ien*, it was entitled *Tzu-ssu-tzu* (*Ch'ien-Han shu*, ch. 30, 9b). It had been made up by assembling all the scattered pamphlets on the rites which had not been included in other collections and by combining them with four little works from the *Li chi* which are ascribed to Tzu-ssu: the *Chung yung*, the *Piao chi*, the *Fang chi*, and the *Tzu yi* (*Sui shu*, ch. 13, 2b, citing a statement by Shen Yüeh in 502 A.D.). As to this work, several phrases from which are inserted in the *Yi lin*, ch. 2, in the *T'ai-p'ing yü lan*, etc. (they have been pulled together by Hung Yi-hsüan, *Ching tien chi lin* (1811 edition), ch. 19, by excluding the chapters in the *Li chi*), see Takenouchi, *On Tzu szu tzu*,

pp. 78–84. It disappeared at the beginning of the Sung, and the book which today bears this title is a reconstruction made in the thirteenth century by Wang Cho.

17 Takenouchi, *A Textual Criticism of the Chung yung*, pp. 24–27.

18 Erkes, *Zur Textkritik des Chung yung*, has effectively brought out the importance of Taoist ideas in the *Chung yung*; but in my opinion he has dated the work too late by setting its composition at the end of the third century.

19 *Chung yung*, Legge, *Ch. Cl.*, I, p. 247.

20 Ibid., p. 248. Legge translates, 'is watchful over himself when he is alone'. But this passage is quoted in two small works of later date in the *Li chi*, the *Ta hsüeh* and the *Li ch'i*, and there the context makes clear that the meaning is the one I have adopted.

21 The traditional modern attribution to Tzu-ssu rests on a spurious quotation from an author of the first century A.D., in a forged inscription attributed to the middle of the third century and fabricated in the fifteenth. It should thus be set aside. On the other hand, Chu Hsi proposed attributing it to Tseng-tzu, though without sufficient reason. Recently, Takenouchi, 'When Was the Ta Hsüeh Written?', pp. 26–27, has believed that its composition could be brought down to the first century A.D.; but his arguments are far from convincing.

22 The commentary quotes some phrases from the *Chung yung*: it is therefore of later date. On the other hand, Mencius (p. 295) refers to it.

23 A whole section of the present-day text is merely a collection of unconnected quotations from the classics, the remnants of a bundle of documents which have fallen apart and into complete disorder, and which the editors of Han times were unable to put in order again.

24 This is what the Chinese commentators call the Three Rules of the *Ta hsüeh*, and the paragraph following it includes the Eight Articles which enable the Three Rules to be put into practice. Takenouchi, op. cit., pp. 23–26, has attempted to demonstrate that the Three Rules are inspired by a passage from a little work of the second century B.C., and the Eight Articles partly from a passage from Mencius and partly from a phrase of Tung Chung-shu, a writer in the end of the second century B.C.; but his comparisons, which deal with the ideas and not with the texts, prove only that the ideas which the author of the *Ta hsüeh* expressed rapidly became commonplaces within the Confucian school.

25 *Ta hsüeh*, pp. 357–58.

26 His native village was called Tsou; it is not certain whether this was the region so named in the principality of Lu, or to the small principality of Tsou, also called Chu, which was very near it.

27 The dates officially adopted for the birth and death of Mencius are 372–288. Official sanction has led Legge to adopt them, *Ch. Cl.*, II, *Prolegomena.*, p. 17, as well as Herbert Giles, *Biographical Dictionary*,

no. 1522, and Grube, *Geschichte der chinesischen Literatur*, pp. 95–97, etc. But they are not universally recognized by Chinese scholars: Jen Chao-lin prefers 374–291; the *Ssu shu lei tien fu nien hsüeh* gives 375–299; and so on. In fact, all these dates are the result of more or less fortuitous calculations, which offer no certainty, and it is best to reject their factitious precision. Mencius himself asserts that he lived 'seven hundred years and more' after the beginning of the Chou (that is to say, before the year 350 B.C., according to the chronology which seems to have been that of all his contemporaries). He mentions kings Hui of Wei (370–319), Hsüan of Ch'i (319–c. 300), K'uai of Yen (320–314), and Prince P'ing of Lu (314–296). He may be placed, consequently, in the second half of the fourth century, an approximation which is quite sufficient for a writer of this period. Cf. Henri Maspero, 'La Chronologie des rois de Ts'i au 4e siecle a.C.', in *TP*, XXV (1927), pp. 367–86.

28 Ssu-ma Ch'ien appears to have taken this information from the *Meng tzu wai shu*, par. 1, in which Mencius, giving the series of masters separating him from Confucius, asserts that he was a disciple of K'ung Po, surnamed Tzu-shang, son of Tzu-ssu. The *Meng tzu wai shu*, a compilation attributed to Mencius, was not authentic but perhaps derived from his school.

29 *Mencius*, p. 185. Legge places the journey to Ch'i before 324 because, according to Mencius, it was then over 700 years since the beginning of the Chou dynasty, and because, that dynasty having begun in 1122 according to the modern official chronology, 800 years would have elapsed by 323. But Mencius, like all his contemporaries, placed the beginning of Chou in 1050: thus any date after 350 makes more than 700 years, and nothing can be deduced from this evidence.

30 See above, p. 322. [Tr. note: The text has been altered here to correspond with another Maspero work, 'La Chronologie des Rois de Ts'i au IVe Siecle avant notre Ere' (TP, vol. 25, 1928, pp. 367–86). A brief discussion of the chronological problem is Kierman, *Four Late Warring States Biographies* (Wiesbaden: Harrassowitz, 1962), pp. 60–1]

31 Legge, p. 215, translates 'silver', but the word *chin* can only be used for gold or copper. The amounts 2.400 or 1.680 ounces of gold seem to me too large, although Katō Shigeru in *Researches on the Precious Metals in the T'ang and Sung Dynasties* (Tokyo, 1925; in Japanese) II, p. 627 ff., in similar instances unhesitatingly accepts that in analogous cases gold is meant.

In the inscriptions of the Chou dynasty *chin* always means bronze. Cf. the inscription on the Fu-tzu bell: 'Having received some of the auspicious metal, I have made a bell'; or the inscription on the *kuei* of the scribe Sung: 'The auspicious metal I have used to make a cauldron for cooking'; etc. It is particularly interesting to find this meaning of the word *chin* confirmed in the inscriptions from Ch'i contemporaneous to Mencius. Cf. *Tso chuan*, eighteenth year of Hsi (Legge, p. 174). In 642 the Lord of Ch'u gave the Count of Cheng metal (*chin*), but afterwards repented having done so and made him take an oath that he would not make arms with it; he made three bells.

32　'That was about the time when Ch'i was fortifying Hsieh' (*Mencius*, p. 174), that is, in 323 (*Chu shu chi nien*, in *Shih chi so yin*, ch. 75, 1*b*).

33　Mencius, pp. 169, 170.

34　Mencius, p. 219, himself declares that his post was purely honorary and (p. 233) that he did not receive a regular salary, which in my opinion indicates, not that he never received anything from King Min (how could he then have become rich, as is stated on p. 178?), but that he preferred occasional presents, which seemed to him less likely to cost him his freedom. The mission to T'eng is recalled on p. 219; the death of his mother, p. 220. I have followed the most usual interpretation of Chinese scholars, though it is far from certain. It is often impossible to distinguish between events relating to the two sojourns in Ch'i.

35　*Mencius*, pp. 282–83.

36　Ibid., pp. 147, 240.

37　Ibid., p. 148. The expression 'an enlightened prince', *ming-chün*, is one of the favourite expressions of the Legalist school.

38　For the *ching* system, see pp. 67–68 and 403–4 above.

39　Mencius, p. 200.

40　Ibid., pp. 242–43.

41　One need only compare this passage of Mencius with the *Lun yü*, p. 267, to see how he develops the theories of Confucius, forcing his own ideas into the framework outlined by the Master. As far as the short aphorisms can be recognized as his, the ideas of Confucius on the people's education are the more broad-minded. See, for instance, the distinction between the good who are to be rewarded and the incapable who must be instructed (*Lun yü*, p. 152), and also the statement that 'to put to death without having instructed is called cruelty' (p. 353). Confucius seems to have envisioned a perfect system of moral instruction.

42　Mencius, p. 483.

43　Ibid., p. 357.

44　*Shu ching*, p. 292. That chapter of the present-day *T'ai-shih* is a spurious one; the forger has interpolated the famous passage of Mencius there.

45　*Mencius*, p. 355.

46　Ibid., p. 167.

47　Ibid., p. 392.

48　Ibid., p. 313.

49　Ibid., pp. 126, 429–30. An aphorism already attributed to Confucius put Justice, *yi*, and Utility, *li*, in opposition to one another (*Lun yü*, p. 166). This was perhaps a reaction by the Confucian school against the theories of Mo-tzu, which were very popular at the time when the *Lun yü* was being compiled.

50 *Lun yü*, p. 250. See above, pp. 290–92.

51 *Mencius*, pp. 397–98.

52 See above, pp. 313–14. Wieger, in his *Histoire des croyances religieuses et des opinions philosophiques en Chine*, p. 234, has already drawn attention to a 'Taoist tendency' in the psychology of Mencius.

53 *Mencius*, pp. 310–11.

54 This is the reading in the *Shih chi*; but to make it correspond to the dates given by Liu Hsiang, some Chinese scholars have suggested altering 'fifty' to 'fifteen' (in Chinese, by reversing the order of the two characters 'five' and 'ten', this correction is very simply effected); and Pelliot, *J. As.* XI, ii (1913), pp. 403–4, is inclined to accept this correction, the advantages of which I do not clearly see.

On the other hand, one correction of the *Shih chi* is absolutely necessary: the suppression of about a line concerning Tsou Yen and his disciples, which has been inserted into the beginning of the Hsün-tzu biography, owing to an inversion of the slips. Cf. Hu Shih, op. cit., I, p. 303.

55 *Shih chi, ch.* 74, 2b. The exact dates for the birth and death of Hsün-tzu are not given by Ssu-ma Ch'ien. Liu Hsiang, the great editor of ancient literature under the Han, in his report to the throne (which is merely a copy of the *Shih chi*, with some additions and alterations due to borrowings from the *Chan kuo ts'e*), attempts to prove Ssu-ma Ch'ien's assertion that Hsün-tzu was very old in the time of King Hsiang (283–265): he makes him arrive in Ch'i under kings Wei (376–343) and Hsüan (342–323), then go to Ch'u, to the court of the Lord of Ch'un-shen, until the latter's death (238). This would make him at least 160 years old at his death. This text, a poor amalgam of fragments of various origins, does not merit the importance which Chinese scholars attach to it, even if it is genuine.

Some excellent biographical studies have been produced on Hsün-tzu. In the eighteenth century, there was the *Hsün-ch'ing tzu t'ung lun*, followed by a *Hsün-ch'ing tzu nien piao*, by Wang Chung (*Shu hsüeh pu i*, 5b–14a; this is a posthumous work printed in 1814 and published in 1815, twenty years after the author's death). It places Hsün-tzu's arrival in Ch'i in 283 and his death a little after 238. More recently, Wang Hsien-ch'ien, in his edition of the *Hsün-tzu* (1891) has him live until 213, partly because of a passage in the *Yen t'ieh lun*, partly because Liu Hsiang places him a hundred years after Mencius. Finally, Hu, op. cit., I, p. 305, proposes the dates of about 315–235: he has him reach Ch'i about 265–260, places his interview with Fan Sui about 260–255 and one with King Hsiao-ch'eng of Chao about 260–250, and sets his residence at Lan-ling between 250 and 238. Cf. Homer H. Dubs, *Hsüntze, the Moulder of Ancient Confucianism* (London, 1927); J. J. L. Duyvendak, 'The Chronology of Hsün tzu', in *TP*, XXVI (1927), pp. 73–95.

56 *Hsün-tzu, ch.* 11, 11b (sec. 16). Fan Sui was minister to King Chao (306–251) from 266 to 255 (*Shih chi, ch.* 79, 4b–6b). Hsün-tzu's visit to Ch'in must have taken place during this period.

57   Ibid., *ch.* 10.

58   This event is generally placed in the year 255 B.C. Cf. Duyvendak, op. cit., p. 75.

59   *Shih chi*, *ch.* 87, 1*a*. Li Ssu is mentioned in the *Hsün-tzu*, *ch.* 10, 14*b* (sec. 15).

60   This is the title given it by Liu Hsiang, except that the character *hsün* is replaced by *sun* to avoid the personal name of the Emperor Hsüan (73–48 B.C.). The name was changed to *Hsün-tzu* by the commentator Yang Liang in the ninth century.

61   His works are extant and form 32 sections (in 20 *chüan*) with a commentary by Yang Liang (ninth century), except for sections 12 and 20 (as well as the end of section 9), for which this commentary is missing (for the history of the text, see Pelliot, 'Notes de Bibliographie chinoise', in *BEFEO*, II, 320). Sections 8 (*ch.* 4), 15 (*ch.* 10), and 16 (*ch.* 11), which contain anecdotes about Hsün-tzu's travels, and in which he is called Hsün-ch'ing-tzu, are probably school texts. Section 27 (*ch.* 19) is a collection of loose sentences which no doubt come from a bundle that had come undone. The last five sections (28–32) are a mixture of fragments having no relation to Hsün-tzu. Some are to be found elsewhere (e.g., sec. 31), partly in the *Ta Tai li chi*, sec. 40. The other sections are probably authentic. Hu Shih, *Chung kuo che hsüeh shih ta kang*, I, p. 306, says that he accepts only four (17, 21, 22, 23); but as he quotes important passages from sixteen sections, it would seem that his definitive judgement is less strict than it seemed at first. The bundle of slips from which the *Ta Tai li chi* was compiled contains sections 1 and 12 of the *Hsün-tzu* (*Ta Tai li chi*, *ch.* 7, sec. 64; *ch.* 1, sec. 42), which does not seem a reason why we should reject them.

62   *Yin Wen tzu*, 2*a*, trans. Masson-Oursel, p. 328.

63   *Hsün-tzu*, *ch.* 16, 6*b* (sec. 22), trans. Duyvendak, p. 234; *Hsün-tzu chi chieh*, *ch.* 16, p. 9. The text has *ming yu ku shan,* which must be read *ming wu ku shan.* This correction is imperative in view of the similar expressions that precede it.

64   *Hsün-tzu*, *ch.* 17, 1*a* (sec. 23). The preceding quotation is taken from the same section.

65   *Hsün-tzu*, *ch.* 13, 1*a* (sec. 19).

66   Ibid., *ch.* 5, 12*b*–13*b* (sec. 9).

67   Ibid., *ch.* 3, 6*a*–*b* (sec. 5).

68   Ibid., *ch.* 2, 17*b* (sec. 4); *ch.* 3, 5*b* (sec. 5).

69   I translate the word *hsing* by 'human nature' to conform to established usage. In reality the word *hsing* here has its technical meaning in Chinese philosophy; and it would be much more accurate to translate it by 'essence', as it is 'that which makes man a man'. And the example from *ch.* 3, 5*b*, states Hsün-tzu's thought precisely: 'That wherein men are men,' he says, 'is not that they have two legs and no hair' (a mere coincidence with Plato's celebrated saying), that is to say, their physical qualities, for the animal called *hsing-hsing* has the form and the laugh of man, and he

also has two legs and no hair. It is their essence, *hsing*, which distinguishes them from other things; each thing is separated from others by its own essence, *hsing*.

70 *Hsün-tzu, ch.* 15, 1*a* (sec. 21): the summary of the 'errors' of Mo-tzu, Sung-tzu, Chuang-tzu, Hui-tzu, etc., and, a little further on, ibid., 5*a*.

71 Ibid., *ch.* 15, 9*a*.

72 Ibid., *ch.* 15, 7*b*–8*a*.

73 Ibid., *ch.* 16, 1*b*–2*a* (sec. 22), trans. Duyvendak, p. 225; *ch.* 17, 2*b*–3*a* (sec. 23), trans. Legge, p. 83; *ch.* 4, 19*b*.

74 Ibid., *ch.* 4, 14*b*; *ch.* 11, 18*a*.

75 Ibid., *ch.* 1, 12*a*–13*b*; *ch.* 2, 1*a*–2*a*.

76 Ibid., *ch.* 1, 12*a*–12*b*.

77 The *Han Fei tzu*, ch. 19, 12*b*, names eight Confucian schools which were flourishing in his day: those of Tzu-chang, Tzu-ssu, Yen, Meng (Mencius), Ch'i-tiao, Chung-liang, Sun (Hsün-tzu), and Yüeh-cheng. The last is the school of Yüeh-cheng K'o, a disciple of Mencius; I have found no data on Chung-liang; and to Ch'i-tiao Ch'i is attributed a work which still existed in the first century B.C. (*Ch'ien-Han shu, ch.* 30, 9*b*; cf. *Mo-tzu, ch.* 9, sec. 39, Forke, f. 412).

78 *Hsün-tzu, ch.* 3, 17*a*, violently criticizes the school of Tzu-hsia.

79 Ibid., *ch.* 3, 15*a*. See the ideal education of a young prince, as described by a writer of the third century, in *Kuo yü, ch.* 17, 1*b*–2*a* (*Ch'u yü*).

80 *Mo-tzu, ch.* 9, sec. 39, Forke, p. 404; *Hsün-tzu, ch.* 3, 17*a*.

81 Takenouchi Yoshiō, 'A Textual Criticism of the *Chung yung*', in *Shinagaku*, II (1922), ix, pp. 24–27, suggests — with good reason, it seems to me — attributing the Confucian work on the *Yi ching* to the school of Tzu-ssu.

82 Part of the composite work which bears the name *Tso chuan* seems to have been taken from an ancient ritual commentary on the *Ch'un ch'iu* which was written about this time. Moreover, the *Ch'ien-Han shu, ch.* 30, 5*b*, mentions others which were already lost by the first century B.C. A chapter of Franke's *Das konfuzianische Dogma und die chinesische Staatsreligion*, pp. 56–88, is devoted to the commentaries on the *Ch'un ch'iu*.

83 Takenouchi Yoshiō, 'The Relation between Meng Tzu and Ch'un Ch'iu', in *Shinagaku*, IV, ii (1927), pp. 44–45, has shown that the *Ku-liang chuan* contains at least three word-for-word quotations from the *Kung-yang chuan*, which he calls 'another commentary' and that it is therefore the more recent. Both of them, having the same lacunae and moreover expressing almost identical views, derive not only from the same verbal teaching but also, in my opinion, from the same original written text. The *Kung-yang chuan* may come from the school of Tseng-tzu (cf. the study of the names of the masters mentioned in it and their relation to this school, ibid., pp. 38–41), and in any case would have come under the influence of the peculiar Ch'i culture (even the influence of Tsou Yen), which would

explain how he came to be known to Mencius. The *Ku-liang chuan*, on the other hand, being more modern, would have come under the influence of Hsün-tzu and his school.

84   *Ch'ien-Han shu*, ch. 30, 7*a*; it is today scattered and partly lost. A section remains in the *Hsün-tzu*, ch. 20, 16*b*–24*b*, sec. 31; two sections (one of which is the same as the foregoing) are in the *Ta Tai li chi*, ch. 1, 5*a*–10*a*, secs. 40–42; and three other sections in the *Li chi*, II, pp. 362–75 and 600–613 — that is, five sections out of seven. A fragment of one of the others is perhaps preserved in chapter 20 of the *Chung yung* (Legge, p. 268), but this is more doubtful. Ma Kuo-han believed he had found the whole of⁻it in the *Ta Tai li chi*, secs. 68–71, 74–76 (*Yü han shan fang chi yi shu*). But it seems to me difficult to overlook the assertion of Yen Shih-ku (*Ch'ien-Han shu*, loc. cit.) that one of the sections of this work forms part of the *Li chi*, because the San ch'ao chi still existed in his day. There is an edition, with commentary by Hung Yi-hsüan, with the title *K'ung-tzu san ch'ao chi*, in Yen Chieh, *Ching yi ts'ung ch'ao*, ch. 29–30 (*Huang Ch'ing ching chieh*, 178th *chung*).

85   In Han times there was in circulation a *Tseng-tzu* in eighteen sections, which is now lost. The *Ta Tai li chi*, ch. 4–5, secs. 49–58, has ten sections which seem to me to belong to the school of Tseng-tzu and to date from the third century; also perhaps chapters 5, 10, and 21 of the *Li chi*. The *Tseng-tzu* in one modern chapter is a reconstruction from the beginning of the thirteenth century A.D. by Wang cho, the author of the spurious *Tzu-ssu tzu*. Cf. Takenouchi, op. cit., p. 465. A reconstruction, which is slightly different (as regards the order of the material) in four chapters with a commentary, has been attempted by Juan Yüan, *Tseng-tzu chu shih*, in *Huang Ch'ing ching chieh*, 106th *chung*.

86   *Ta Tai li chi*, ed. Ssu pu ts'ung k'an, ch. 7 (secs. 62–63).

87   Ibid., ch. 9 (secs. 68–71); ch. 11 (secs. 74–76).

88   Ibid., ch. 9, 5*a*.

89   Most of them seem to belong to the third century. A small number may possibly go back to the fourth; others, such as the *Wang chih*, are of the second century.

Chapter 7.   Historical Romance and History

1   Trans. Eitel in *China Review*, XVII, pp. 223–40, 247–58. See also Chavannes, *Mémoires historiques*, V, app. 2; Kume, 'Konron Seiōbō kō' [Inquiry into Hsi-wang-mu of K'un-lun], in *Shigaku Zasshi*, IV, pp. 197–214; L. de Saussure, 'Le Voyage du roi Mou au Turkestan', in *J. As.*, 1920, pp. 151–56; 'La relation des voyages du roi Mou', in *J. As.*, 1921, pp. 247–80; 'The Calendar of the Muh t'ien tsz chuen', in *New China Review*, 1920, pp. 513–16; 'Le Voyage du roi Mou et l'hypothèse d'Ed. Chavannes', in *TP*, 1920–21, pp. 19–31.

In my opinion all these authors are wrong in treating this

romance as a factual historical chronicle and in trying to locate a barbarian kingdom or tribe of Hsi-wang-mu in central Asia.

2 The *Tso chuan*, pp. 186–87, has preserved a summary of these years of adventure; fragments are to be found in various passages of the *Han Fei tzu*, the *Lü shih ch'un ch'iu*, and so on; lastly, several anecdotes in the 'Discourses of Chin' of the *Kuo yü* must have been taken from these adventures. But as there was also an ancient Chronicle of Chin (which has likewise been lost), it is often difficult to decide the origin of these fragments.

3 The *Shang shu ta chuan* was lost about the fourteenth century A.D. Fragments of it have been reassembled and published by several scholars since the eighteenth century.

4 Sections 12–31 and 36–50 of the *Yi Chou shu* certainly belong to this romance (secs. 13–20 and 41–42 have been lost). But sections 51–59, though referring to the Duke of Chou, are by other authors and obviously stem from different sources. The author has a precise chronology of months and days, which does not always agree with that of the *Shu ching*, and a study of which would perhaps enable one to date the work quite exactly.

5 Though of little literary value, this romance is a document of great importance, especially from a religious viewpoint. Less retouched than the *Shu ching*, it gives a less tendentious picture of customs in the later centuries of the Chou dynasty.

6 There is a work in existence today called *Kuan-tzu*, in 24 *chüan* divided into 86 sections (of which about ten have been lost), which claims to be the work of Kuan Yi-wu. But even if it is not completely spurious, the ancient portions are buried in a mass of chapters which were forged probably in the fourth or fifth century A.D. It quotes (*ch.* 5, 6a, ed. *Ssu pu ts'ung k'an*) the *T'ai shih*, a spurious chapter of the *Shu ching* from the third century, and it copies (*ch.* 7, 3a) the *Tso chuan*, p. 388, even to its chronology of the princes of Lu, which is absurd for a minister of Ch'i: 'In the ninth year Kung-sun Wu-chih attacked Yung-lin; Yung-lin killed Wu-chih. Duke Huan, coming from Chü, was the first to enter Ch'i. The men of Lu attacked Ch'i in order to put Chiu on the throne ...,' etc. The ninth year is that in the reign of Prince Chuang of Lu, and the whole passage is made up of phrases taken from the *Tso chuan*. This work was already in existence under the T'ang, as quotations from that period prove, and the division of it into only 19 sections in the *Sui shu* must be indicative merely of some other arrangement of the sections. At the top was placed a report by Liu Hsiang on his revision of the text in the first century B.C., which is entirely apocryphal, since he mentions the 86 sections of the modern work, although his own authentic catalogue knew only a *Kuan-tzu* of 18 sections (commentary, *Cheng yi*, of Chang Shou-chieh in the *Shih chi*, *ch.* 62, 2b; this passage shows that in the *Ch'ien-Han shu*, *ch.* 30, 12a, the number '86 sections' is due to an interpolation under the influence of the modern forgery).

7   The ancient *Kuan-tzu*, since lost and replaced by a forgery in the fourth or fifth century A.D., still existed in the first century B.C. It was composed of 18 sections (*Shih chi, ch.* 62, 2*b*; see preceding note). There are some passages from it in the *Kung-yang chuan*, the *Ku-liang chuan*, the *Mencius*, the *Shih chi*, etc. One of the same passages has been abridged independently in the *Tso chuan* and the *Kuo yü*, and comparison shows what the original may have been like. These quotations prove that it was written before the end of the fourth century B.C. On the other hand, the mention of 72 kings who performed the *feng* and *shan* sacrifices (*Shih chi, ch.* 28, III, p. 423), which recalls a passage in the *Shan hai ching, ch.* 5, and the two very clear allusions to some of its episodes in the *Lun yü*, show that it hardly goes back beyond the beginning of that century.

     G. Haloun, 'Seit wann kannten die Chinesen Tocharer oder Indogermaner überhaupt', in *Asia Major*, thought he could establish a series of older prototypes, which he would have made to disappear and be replaced, and he has even tried to draw up a table of them. But I do not think his point of view is correct: cf. *J. As.*, 1927.

8   There exists today a *Yen-tzu ch'un ch'iu* in eight chapters, but it underwent important changes towards the end of the Sung and the beginning of the Yüan dynasty (the Yüan edition, which was republished with a commentary, *Yen-tzu ch'un ch'iu yin yi*, by the scholar Sun Hsing-yen, was already, with a few insignificant variations, the same as the modern editions), if indeed it is not a reconstruction done in that period to replace the authentic work, which has also been lost. Luckily the original had often been quoted in Han and T'ang times (not to mention long extracts or summaries made by the author of the *Tso chu*; cf. *Han Fei tzu, ch.* 15, sec. 37, 10*b*). Wei Cheng, in his *Ch'ün shu chih yao, ch.* 33, reproduced nearly half of the first six chapters; the *Yi lin* (*ch.* 1, 4*b*–6*b*) also gives quite a few extracts from it; the commentary of Li Shan in the *Wen hsüan* often quotes short fragments from it; that of Prince Chang-huai in the *Hou-Han shu* mentions a dozen complete anecdotes; and so on. I have used only passages which are certified by pre-Sung quotations, which in the present state of affairs seems to me the only safe method. For the sake of convenience I add, for this quotation, a reference to the Ming edition reproduced in the *Ssu pu ts'ung k'an*.

9   The frequent references in the *Yen-tzu ch'un ch'iu* to the name of Mo-tzu (Liu Tsung-yüan, 773–819 A.D., *Pien Yen-tzu ch'un ch'iu*, in *Tseng kuang chu shih yin pien T'ang Liu hsien-sheng chi, ch.* 4, 6*a*, Yüan dynasty edition reproduced in *Ssu pu ts'ung k'an*; cf. *Yen-tzu ch'un ch'iu, ch.* 3, 7*b*; *ch.* 5, 8*a*), who lived in the second half of the fifth and the first years of the fourth century, and the predictions (in *Tso chuan*, p. 589; cf. *ch.* 4, 38*b*) regarding the T'ien family's usurpation in Ch'i in 386 B.C. and regarding the ruin of the princely house of Chin (403 or 375, whichever occurrence one chooses) make it

impossible to place the date for the compilation of the *Yen-tzu ch'un ch'iu* earlier than the middle of the fourth century. On the other hand, the *Tso chuan* has made great use of it (see, for example, the anecdote about the assassination of Prince Chuang in 548, commentary to the *Hou-Han shu, ch.* 58a, 5b–6a; *Tso chuan,* p. 514); Mencius (Legge, pp. 158–59) cites a passage from it; the *Lü shih ch'un ch'iu* also was aware of it (*ch.* 20, 7a, etc.). It was therefore well known at the end of the fourth century, and is thus well dated. The few quotations in *Mo-tzu, ch.* 9 (Forke, p. 407), do not invalidate this conclusion, for they are all in the *Fei ju* section, which must be attributed to later work of his school and is of relatively late date.

10   That is the arrangement of modern editions, but it is authenticated by the fact that Wei Cheng already followed it, and he too divided each section into two chapters.

11   *Hou-Han shu, ch.* 90A, 4b; *Yen-tzu, ch.* 2, 20b–22a.

12   *Wen hsüan, ch.* 13, 2a; *ch.* 28, 3a; *ch.* 48, 4a; *Yen-tzu, ch.* 1, 19b–20a.

13   *Tso chuan,* p. 514; *Hou-Han shu, ch.* 58A, 5b–6a; *Yen-tzu, ch.* 5, 4b–5b.

14   The *Shih chi, ch.* 65, is a summary of this romance; the *Lü-shih ch'un ch'iu* alludes to it. There exists today a *Wu-tzu* that is not altogether spurious. The romance of Wu Ch'i contains anachronisms which quickly show up its non-historical character; see above, bk. 4, ch. 1, n. 10, and bk. 4, ch. 2, n. 11.

15   H. Maspero, 'Le Roman de Sou Ts'in' in *Etudes asiatiques publiées par l'Ecole française d'Extrême-Orient à l'occasion de son 25e anniversaire,* II, 141; and cf. above, bk. 4, ch. 3, n. 14.

16   *Mencius,* IV, ii, p. 21, Legge, p. 327.

17   *Shih chi, ch.* 75–78.

18   *Mo-tzu, ch.* 8, Forke, p. 192.

19   The *Chou li* in its present form has unfortunately been subjected to serious alterations. Not only has one whole portion, the 'Winter Ministry' (which was already lost in Han times) been replaced by a document of the same era or a little later, as has also been done with other shorter passages. (One such is the paragraph about the Director of Music, which was a work presented to Emperor Hsiao-wen of the Han, 179–157 B.C. by a certain Tou, who claimed to be 180 years old and to have been Director of Music to Prince Wen of Wei in the fourth century; cf. *Ch'ien-Han shu, ch.* 30, 5a.) There also seem to have been a number of detailed interpolations. The *Chou li* has been violently attacked by Chinese and Japanese scholars who regard it as a forgery of Han times. On the other hand, tradition ascribes it to the Duke of Chou, brother of King Wu, the founder of the Chou dynasty. Both of these opinions seem to me equally exaggerated.

20   The most recent European studies on the *Tso chuan* are the first part of Franke's *Das konfuzianische Dogma und die chinesische Staatsreligion* (1920), pp. 1–86; and especially Bernhard Karlgren's important study, 'On the nature and authenticity of the *Tso chuan*', in *Göteborgs Högskolas Arsskrift,* XXXII (1926).

21 A prophecy made to the Prince of Wei when he set up his capital in Ti-ch'iu in 629 promised that it would remain there for 300 years (*Tso chuan*, p. 219); but in 320 Prince Ssu renounced his title for that of overlord, *chün*, because his territory had been reduced to the single city of P'u-yang (*Shih chi*, IV, p. 211). Another passage (*Tso chuan*, p. 293) recalls that, when King Ch'eng set up the tripods at Chia-ju, it was predicted that his dynasty would last thirty reigns and over 700 years. But the tripods had been set up at Chia-ju in 1027 (*Chu shu chi nien*, Legge, p. 146) and were lost in the River Ssu in 327 (ibid., pp. 174–75). (It need scarcely be said that the date when the tripods had been set up was fixed after their disappearance, so as to conform to the prophecy which the *Tso chuan* reports, and which must have been well known; the date has no historical reality.) Moreover, thirty reigns after King Ch'eng bring us to King Hsien (367–319). Thus the *Tso chuan* can have been written, at the earliest, about the end of the fourth century. On the other hand, it cannot be later than the middle of the third century, because after that time the prophecy that Ch'in could not carry out a victorious campaign in the east (p. 244) could not have been made. It is interesting to note that by linguistic arguments Karlgren (op. cit., p. 65) arrives independently at a date for the compilation of the *Tso chuan* much the same as the one I have deduced.

22 I will sum up in a few lines the conclusions I have come to from a study of the *Tso chuan* and its sources which will be published shortly [see Henri Maspero, 'La Composition et la date du *Tso chuan*', in *Religion chinoise et bouddhique*, I (Brussels, 1932), pp. 137–215]. Karlgren, op. cit., p. 65, from his examination of the *Tso chuan* has come to the conclusion that it was the work of 'one or more persons of the same school and speaking the same dialect'. This conclusion seems to me to go beyond the results of his enquiry, which prove at the very most that the third century compiler has touched up the style of the documents to standardize the language in the same way as he believes (ibid., p. 50) the editors of the *Shu ching* to have done.

As is known, the majority of contemporary Chinese critics, following K'ang Yu-wei, have returned to the theory enunciated at the beginning of the nineteenth century by Liu Feng-lu, that the *Tso chuan* is a forgery by Liu Hsin, a famous scholar of the Han dynasty, in the first century B.C. Franke, op. cit., has adopted this theory and has summed up the main arguments very well. Moreover, Iijima, 'The *Tso chuan* Criticized from the Viewpoint of the Calendar System of the Han Dynasty', in *Tōyō Gakuhō*, II (1912), pp. 28–57, 181–210; and 'A Further Discussion on the Date When the *Tso chuan* Was Written', ibid., IX (1919), pp. 155–94, has tried to bolster this theory with astronomical arguments. None of these has succeeded in making it plausible. On the contrary, Karlgren, op. cit., has shown that there is a strong presumption in favour of its being an ancient work.

23 The *Shih ch'un* was a collection of prophecies which was found in the tomb of Chi about 279 A.D. It was found that the stories were textually almost exactly the same as those in the *Tso chuan*, from which it was concluded that the *Shih ch'un* was made up of extracts from the *Tso chuan*. Actually, in view of the probable date of the Chi tomb, it must have been one of the sources of the *Tso chuan*. It is lost today.

Chapter 8. The New Chinese Poetry of the Fourth and Third Centuries: Ch'ü Yüan

1 Bushell, 'The Stone Drums', in *Journal of the North China Branch of the Royal Asiatic Society*, VIII (1873), p. 133 ff.
2 The *Shih chi, ch.* 84, gives no date for Ch'ü Yüan's birth. Giles, *Chinese Literature*, pp. 50–53, follows it; Chavannes, 'Le calendrier des Yn' (*J. As.*, 1890, pp. 489–91) makes the date 332 (but afterwards abandons it again, with good reason), from a verse near the beginning of the *Li sao*; and Grube, *Geschichte der chinesischen Literatur*, p. 173, has followed him. Unfortunately, the calendar indications of the *Li sao* are too unclear, despite their precision, to determine the date exactly. On the other hand, leaving aside this passage, Ch'ü Yüan calls himself old in the *Hsi sung* (*Chiu chang*, in *Ch'u tz'u*, ch. 4, 7a), a poem belonging to a series that dates from his last disgrace (297), in which are mentioned his third (295) and ninth (289) years of exile. Moreover, although he might possibly have held an important hereditary post at court as a young man, it is hardly likely that such a difficult embassy as that of 312 would have been entrusted to a young man. He can hardly have been born later than 350 B.C. Lu K'an-ju in *Ch'ü Yüan*, pp. 4–5, using the same passage from the *Li sao* in which the poet declares that he was born in a *yin* year, but finding that 331 would make him too young for the embassy to Ch'i in 313, fixes his birth a dozen years earlier, in 343 (355 would make him too old at the time of his death) and his death at fifty-four years of age in 290. These dates are possible, but the calculations upon which they are based are valueless and remain hypothetical. Chih Wei-ch'eng, op. cit., p. 3, who is more careful, places the birth 'around 340'. Chang Wei-huan, in the *Yi nien lu hui pien* of 1925 (*ch.* 1, 2a, a paragraph which is a personal addition), fixes his life as 343 to 277 B.C., but does not state his reasons. Kuo Mo-jo, *Ch'ü Yüan*, p. 15, points out that the *Lü shih ch'un ch'iu* makes the eighth year of Ch'in Shih-huang-ti (239) a *shen* year and that therefore the *yin* year mentioned in the *Li sao* must be 341. But, as he does not find the date given in the *Li sao* correct for 341, he sets the date back to 340 by a perfectly arbitrary piece of juggling with the calendar, and places Ch'ü Yüan's death in 278.

Hu Shih in *Tu Ch'u tz'u*, pp. 139–43, has picked out a number of doubtful passages in the biography contained in the *Shih chi* and concludes therefrom that Ch'ü Yüan never really existed, but that it was a fictitious name to which were attributed in Han times famous pieces of poetry of diverse origin, 'in the same way as with Homer in Greece'. The defects of the biography cannot be denied; but they are not enough to justify this theory, which Kuo Mo-jo has taken the trouble to refute point by point in his *Ch'ü Yüan*. A local tradition ascribed to the sixth century in the *Shui ching chu* places the ancient domain of Ch'ü Yüan some dozens of *li* northeast of the sub-prefecture of Tzu-kuei (Kweichow, in Ch'ing times) on the Yangtze in Hupei, and the funerary temple of his sister Nü-hsü up-river from the Ch'u capital, which was near modern Chiang-ling.

3   *Shih chi, ch.* 84, 1*a*. The biography of Ch'ü Yüan by Ssu-ma Ch'ien (*Shih chi, ch.* 84) has been translated by G. Margouliès, *Le Kou-wen chinois*, (Paris, 1926), pp. 83–89.

This title is not mentioned in his works, but from the way he talks about the post he held it is certain that for some time he was one of the Ch'u king's trusted advisers: 'I miss the days when I had the Prince's trust, when it was my duty to enlighten him, when I carried on the meritorious tradition of my ancestors by enlightening my inferiors, when I explained the difficulties and uncertainties of the laws — the state was rich and powerful, the laws were strict.' (*Hsi wang jih,* in *Chiu ko, Ch'u tz'u, ch.* 4, 31*b*). Even if there was some personal exaggeration, this cannot all be made up.

4   The poem *Ai Ying* is dated to the ninth year of his exile: 'Alas! I wanted to see the prince again; it was not permitted. ... Now it is nine years that I have been away.'

5   *She chiang* (*Ch'u tz'u, ch.* 4, 7*a*): 'Young, I loved this strange costume [court dress]; I am old and can't console myself [to have given it up].'

6   The tradition that he drowned himself in the Mi-lo River is probably a dramatic interpretation of the poetic suicide theme in *Hsi wang jih* (*Ch'u tz'u,* ch. 4, 25*a*).

7   The *Li sao* is usually regarded as dealing with his first disgrace; there is no reason to separate it thus from the other poems. Moreover, it appears to me to contain a very clear allusion, not only to King Huai but also to King Ch'ing-hsiang.

8   Hu Shih, op. cit., pp. 144–45, distributes these poems over a period of some centuries, the *Chiu ko* being the most ancient, together with the *Li sao* and part of the *Chiu chang*, which he considers approximately contemporary, being the earliest. Then come 'The Fisherman', *Yü fu*, and 'The Divination', *Pu chü*, which would be after Ch'u was conquered by the state of Ch'in and would thus date from the end of the third century at the earliest; and finally the 'Distant Journey', *Yüan yu*, part of the *Chiu chang*, and the *T'ien wen* would be dated from the Han period. The discussion, which takes up barely eight lines, consists merely of a number of assertions, almost none of which can be seriously supported. It is strange that Hu, himself a poet, has not perceived the unity and the quite personal character of several pieces which he separates in this way, and that the Han imitations (such as Ssu-ma Hsiang-ju's *Ta jen,*

which is an imitation of the *Yüan yu*, or the pieces which fill up the last chapters of the *Ch'u tz'u*) have not convinced him that none of the poems attributed to Yüan of Ch'ü or his group could come down to so late a date.

9   Tradition ascribes the causes of Ch'ü Yüan's misfortunes to this vanity: 'Shang-kuan slandered Ch'ü P'ing, saying: "The king has Ch'ü P'ing make the decrees; there is nobody who does not know it every time a decree is issued." P'ing boasts about his merit and says: "but for me nobody could have done this!" The king was angry and dismissed Ch'ü P'ing.' (*Shih chi, ch.* 84, 1*a*; Margouliès, *Le Kou-wen*, p. 83).

10   The rhythm of poetic prose among contemporary writers of the north and centre, Chuang-tzu, for example (who, for reasons I do not understand, is often regarded as a southerner, although he lived in Wei), is of a very different character, much freer and, above all, much more oratorical, often achieving a pulse like regular poetry. On rhythm in Chuang-tzu, see Georg von der Gabelentz, 'Beiträge zur chinesischen Grammatik: Die Sprache des Cuang-tsi', in *Abhandl. Philol.-hist. Cl. k. Sächs. Ges. Wiss.*, VIII (1888), pp. 629–35.

11   *She chiang* (*Ch'u tz'u, ch.* 4, 7*a*–8*a*).

12   *Ch'u tz'u, ch.* 4, 4*b*, 19*b*.

13   *Chuang-tzu*, p. 223.

14   *Ch'u tz'u, ch.* 1, 7*a*–8*a*, Legge, p. 848.

15   The various interpretations of Chinese scholars differ. Nevertheless, they agree on the general lines, especially that by 'women', princes are meant. I deviate from them only in bringing these allegories into closer touch with the real occurrences of the poet's life.

16   *Yüan yu* (*Ch'u tz'u, ch.* 5, 10*b*).

17   *Li sao* (*Ch'u tz'u, ch.* 5, 24*a*).

18   *Yüan yu* (*Ch'u tz'u, ch.* 5, 5*b*–6*a*. In this second journey his guide is Ch'ih-sung, an immortal, *hsien*, and Perfect Man, *chen-jen* (ibid., 2*a*).

19   Ibid., 4*a*; cf. *Chuang-tzu*, p. 331; ibid., 5*b*, cf. *Lao-tzu*, p. 26, sec. 10.

20   Little is known about Sung Yü (see Erkes, *Das Zurückrufen der Seele*, p. 3), and still less about Ching Ch'a.

21   This poem has been translated by Erkes. For the rite of summoning the souls of the dead, see above, p. 107.

22   *Hsün-tzu, ch.* 18, 11*b*–15*a*, and the *Ch'ien-Han shu, ch.* 30, 20*b*, mention 'the ten sections of *fu* by minister Sun' — i.e., Hsün-tzu. One of these *fu* contains verbal imitations of passages from the *Chiu ko* and *Chiu chang* (ibid., p. 12*a*). The first two pieces in this section are in regular four-character verse (in the style of the *Shih ching*) intermixed with prose passages.

23   *Ch'ien-Han shu, ch.* 30, 19*a*; ibid., 20*b*, Ch'in shih tsa fu. Nothing remains of these works.

24   The *fu* is ordinarily regarded as a prose form, keeping the name of poetry for what the Chinese call *shih*, the ancient model for which is the pieces in the *Shih ching*, while the modern type is made up of

poems in regular verse of five or seven words. Although good reasons could be given for using this classification, it seems difficult to speak meaningfully of pieces which are rhythmic and rhymed (much less free than our free verse) by calling them prose.

Chapter 9. *The Scientific Movement and Foreign Influences*

1 *Shu ching*, Legge, p. 127.

2 Kanda, 'Mountain-Worship in Ancient China, as seen in the *Shan hai ching*', in *Shinagaku*, II (1922), pp. 332–48. The present-day *Shan hai ching* is a collection of texts of varying origin which were included within it at different periods. Its foundation is the *Wu tsang ching* in twenty-six sections, each section corresponding to a mountain chain (today in five chapters, one for each point of the compass), which was edited for publication by Liu Hsiang towards the end of the first century B.C. His son Liu Hsin published this in 6 B.C., together with three other works: the *Hai wai ching* (*ch.* 6–9), the *Hai nei ching* (*chs.* 10–13), and a treatise on rivers (end of *ch.* 13) which dates from some time around the end of the second century B.C. (for this work, see *TP* (1925), p. 377). To these the commentator Kuo P'u added the *Ta mang ching* (*ch.* 14–17) and another *Hai nei ching* (*ch.* 18) in the fourth century A.D. The latter was really made up out of bits and pieces dislodged from the *Ta mang ching* (see especially Ogawa Seiki, op. cit., though I would not accept all of his opinions).

3 Eight of the twelve mountain ranges of the centre, or almost a third of those given for all of China, lie between the Yellow River and the Han. The smallest hills and streams of the region are noted, none of the tiny affluents of the Lo being omitted. The distances between ranges are about fifteen *li*, though outside this region they increase to hundreds of *li*.

4 The author of the *Wu tsang ching* was unacquainted with the lands beyond the sources of the Wei and Ching rivers, since their conquest was completed by the counts of Ch'in between the years 310 and 265, when the Jung of Yi-chü submitted. On the other hand, he was familiar with the mountains of Shu, which the king of Ch'in conquered in 316. But, as Ch'in was on friendly terms with the Chou court after 334, it seems to me that the work should be placed towards the end of the fourth century. The vague understanding of central Asia which it shows does not contradict this date, for knowledge of that region is of a different sort, being the contribution of foreign merchants speaking of foreign lands.

5 The loss of the Tripods in 327 drew attention to them and brought them back into favour towards the end of the fourth century B.C. This explains why the drawings were called by their name.

6 Laufer, 'Ethnographische Sagen des Chinesen' (*Festschrift für Kuhn*, pp. 199–210).

7 Tsou Yen must have resided in Wei for some time under King Hui (370–318), *Shih chi*, V, p. 158. From there he proceeded to Yen about

the time when King Chao acceded (312–279), ibid., IV, p. 145. He was one of the scholars of the Chi Gate at Lin-tzu under King Hsüan of Ch'i (319-c. 300), ibid., V, p. 258. He was associated with the Lord of P'ing-yüan, a minister of Chao (died in 251), who got him to debate with his favourite, the sophist Kung-sun Lung (*Shih chi, ch.* 76, 2b). He must thus have lived in the second half of the fourth century, and died during the first years of the second quarter of the third century. There is no life of him in the *Shih chi,* but only a short passage devoted to him at the end of the biography of Mencius (*ch.* 74, 1b–2a). His works are lost. His theories have been expounded by Conrady, *Indischer Einfluss,* pp. 342–43, who has pointed out that they contain important elements of Indian influence.

8   *Shu ching,* Legge, pp. 19–21 (*Yao tien*). Four stars are named there, only three of which have been identified rather vaguely by the ancient tradition. The very precise modern identifications are due to the work of the astronomer-priest Yi Hang at the beginning of the eighth century A.D. — that is, at a time when the knowledge of the precession of the equinoxes made possible an exact picture of the skies at any given date. The date chosen was, of course, that which the historians of those days assigned to Yao.

   The hour of the observations is not given, but the regular custom in Chou times was to observe the stars at dawn or dusk, *hun,* though in this case it can only be the latter. The records of the *Yao tien* are made quite unclear because the twilight hour varies with the season.

9   *Yao tien,* p. 21.

10 *Hsi tz'u* (in *Yi ching,* Legge, p. 365). I do not think, despite the late date of this text, that the five-year period had been invented (or introduced from abroad) at such a late date as towards the end of the fifth century, for example; for one of the elements which served to establish it, the imprecise reckoning of the year as 366 full days, is to be found already in the *Yao tien,* a treatise in the *Shu ching* which it would be difficult to bring down to so late a period. We have:

$$5 \times 366 = 1{,}830 \text{ days}, \quad 5 \times 12 + 2 = 62 \text{ lunations}.$$

If it is granted that the long (30-day) and the short (29-day) lunations alternate regularly, and that the two intercalary lunations are both long, we have:

$$(30 \times 29) + (30 \times 30) + (2 \times 30) = 1{,}830 \text{ days}.$$

Thus was established an apparent agreement, though actually incorrect, between the movements of the sun and the moon.

11 It is known that the Chinese *hsü* are the equivalent of the Hindu *nakshatra* and the Arab *manâzil.* There is not the slightest doubt that these three systems have a common origin, though the place where

and the time when they were invented remain highly controversial. For the bibliography and a discussion of the various opinions, see L. de Saussure, who concludes in favour of a Chinese origin. Since then the thesis of their common origin in a different centre altogether (Babylonia) has been upheld by Oldenburg in his *Nakshatra und Sieou*. Despite the interest of Saussure's articles, I feel bound to reject his conclusions. Knowledge of the twenty-eight *hsü* appeared late in Chinese literature: about the end of the fourth century in the *Tso chuan* and the *Chou li*. Nevertheless, the fragments which remain from the great astrological works of the fourth century show that those works were in use a century earlier. Before the fifth century certain stars and constellations are mentioned which were used in that system (the Pleiades and Aquarius in the *Yao tien*, the Herdsman and the Weaving Maiden in the *Shih ching*, etc.), though these isolated references do not prove that the whole system existed.

12 L. de Saussure, *Le Cycle de Jupiter*, proves clearly that this cycle was introduced into China about 375 B.C. Shinjō has independently, but more recently, reached the same conclusion, which seems correct to me. Iijima, *A Further Discussion on the Date When the Tso chuan Was Written*, pp. 155–94, tries to show that the anecdotes from the *Tso chuan* and the *Kuo yü*, in which this cycle is mentioned, date from Han times and more precisely reveal the influence of Liu Hsin on this subject. In my view, the relationship he establishes is correct, but his conclusions should be reversed: contrary to what Iijima says, Liu Hsin based his theory on the pre-existing ideas of the *Tso chuan* and *Kuo yü*, which were incorrect but which he believed to be true.

13 *Shih chi*, III, pp. 402–3.

14 *Ch'ien-Han shu*, *ch.* 26, 6*a*. Knowledge of the apparent motion of Mars seems to have been still rudimentary in Han times (ibid., *ch.* 21 B, 5*b*). Cf. L. de Saussure, 'Les Origines de l'astronomie chinoise', *TP*, XV (1914), 647.

15 Iijima, *Further Notes on the Chinese Astronomical Knowledge*, has observed that the duodenary cycle originally began with the character *yin* (now the third), and that various considerations later caused the character *tzu* to be placed first, a position it has retained. Thus the Yin calendar, which, registering this displacement, sets the first day of the calendar and of the cycle under the symbols *chia-tzu*, is subsequent to the calendar of Chuan-hsü, which places that day under the symbols *chia-yin*. Shinjō, *The Kan Chih Wu Hsing Theory*, p. 12, locates the introduction of the Chuan-hsü and the Yin calendars in the same period as that of the Jovian cycle.

16 This is at least what seems to emerge from the *Ch'in chi* (*Shih chi*, *ch.* 5, Chavannes, II, pp. 90 ff.), in which, from 265 B.C. on, the tenth month always seems to mark the beginning of the year.

17 *Mo-tzu*, *ch.* 10, sec. 40, par. 18, p. 415; ibid., *ch.* 11, sec. 44, par. 29, p. 513; ibid., sec. 43, par. 58, p. 491; ibid., sec. 42, par. 52, p. 452.

Appendix 1
Guide to Pronunciation: Simplified Wade-Giles Romanization

No romanization of Chinese is really satisfactory, since all systems must use sounds or signs conventionally in ways that are not standard to the language into which they are transcribing Chinese, or to represent sounds which do not exist in that language at all. Wade-Giles is of course based upon nineteenth century English and tends perhaps to be influenced by the South China-*cum*-treaty port milieu in which it was devised, though that influence has been largely massaged out of it in recent years. The following is a table of standard vowels, diphthongs, and consonants. It does not cover every possible vocable, but those omitted are comprehensible on the basis of common English orthography. Samples of live Wade-Giles are furnished where certain English words are directly reproducible in Wade-Giles: e.g. (WG: *shen*), (WG: *yen*).

Vowels:

a   as in f*a*ther
e   like the *u* in sh*u*n (WG: *shen*), except after *ü*, *i*, or *y*, when it is like e in yen (WG: *yen*)
i   like the *ie* in bel*ie*f or *ee* in l*ee* (WG: *li*)
o   as in *o*ld, but without the *oo*-'vanish' normal in English; often modified to the *o* of c*o*rk
u   as in r*u*de, but again without the *oo*-'vanish', or with a very light one. After *ss* or *tz*, *u* represents an almost vestigial schwa (undifferentiated mid-vowel), *uh*, but hardly vocalized except as a continuation of the consonant buzz.
ü   is like German *ü* or French *u*, generally described as shaping the mouth to say *oo* and then saying *ee*

Diphthongs:

ie or ieh   like American colloquial *yeh* (WG: *yeh*)

ai   like English *I* or the *igh* in h*igh* (WG: *hai*)
ei   like the *ay* in h*ay* (WG: *hei*)
ia   as in nostalg*ia*, but with more *a* than in common English pronunciation.
ao   like the *ow* in h*ow* (WG: *hao*)
ou   like the *ow* in t*ow* (WG: *t'ou*), i.e., with oo-'vanish', unlike *o* above
ih   like *ir* in st*ir*, but with the *r* muted
iu   like *you*
ui and *uei*   like *way* (WG: *wei*)
ua   something like *ua* in q*ua*lity, except that *a* is sounded as in h*a*rd (Think of how people imitate a baby's protest: 'Wah!')
uai   like *ui* in q*ui*et, or the way we say Y. English *why* (WG: *huai*)

Consonants

Note: The first five sets of 'paired' sounds are formed the same way in the mouth but distinguished by whether or not they are aspirated (that is, by whether or not the sound is produced by a quick puff of air without vibration of the vocal cords. The distinction is readily noted by placing a hand on the Adam's Apple and then noting the perceptible buzz when the unaspirated sound is made).

ch   like the *g* in *g*in (WG: *chin*)
ch'   like *ch* in *ch*ew (WG: *ch'u*)
k   like *g* in *g*un (WG: *ken*)
k'   like *k* in *k*ing or *c* in *c*ow (WG: *k'ao*)
p   like *b* in *b*uy (WG: *pai*)
p'   like *p* in *p*ie (WG: *p'ai*)
t   like *d* in *d*o (WG: *tu*)
t'   like *t* in *t*o (WG: *t'u*)
ts and *tz*   like *ds* in Win*ds*or
ts' and *tz'*   like *ts* in ou*ts*ide
sh   like *sh* in *sh*oe (WG: *shu*)
hs   like the *ss* in mi*ss*ion or like *sh* in *sh*y (WG: *shai*)
j   is an intermediate sound between English *r* and the *zh* sound of *s* in vi*s*ion

Appendix 2
Chronology

	Hsia dynasty, founded by Ch'i, son of the Great Yü. Last king of the Hsia, Chieh
	Shang (Yin) dynasty, founded by T'ang the Victorious, with his minister Yi Yin, 15th-13th century B.C. Thirty kings. Great clans and domains. Last king Tsou (Tsou-hsin)
C. 1100 B.C.	Chou dynasty founded by King Wu, son of 'King' Wen, aided by the Duke of Chou. First three principalities: Sung (carrying on the sacrifices of Shang), Wey, Lu.
827-782	Reign of King Hsüan, the eleventh king of the Chou, under whom consecutive history commences rather sparsely.
822	Hao, the capital of the Chou, pillaged.
771	Hao pillaged again, this time ruined. King Yu killed, but Chou line re-established at Lo-yi, eastern capital. Royal power effectively ended, however; real strength from then on in the principalities.
722	Ch'un ch'iu (Spring and Autumn) period begins, so called from title of the chronicle of Lu, first year of which chronicle is 722. More appropriately, era of the great principalities, including those quite near the new capital (Chin, Yü, Kuo, Wey, Cheng, Ts'ai, Ch'en, Lu, and Shen) which were ruled by relatives of the royal family. In longer run the larger principalities (Chin, Ch'i, Ch'u, and Ch'in), mainly outside this group of 'central states', emerge to prominence.
680	Duke Huan of Ch'i (r. 685-643), with his minister Kuan Chung, becomes first of hegemons, *pa*: that is, chief of a league of states precariously joined to sustain the ceremonial primacy of the Chou house, at first chiefly by fending off the 'semi-barbarian' southern state of Ch'u.

632	Symbolic victory over Ch'u at Ch'eng-p'u wins hegemony for Chin and Duke Wen (r. 636–628), second *pa*.
584	Wu-ch'en, originally from Ch'u, arrives in Wu as agent of Chin to train Wu army and provide a military power on the Ch'u flank.
c. 550-c. 480	Confucius If he existed, Lao-tzu was apparently contemporary with Confucius
481	Ch'un ch'iu period ends, since the *Ch'un ch'iu* ends in this year.
453	After assassination of Count of Chih, Chin divides into 'Three Chin' (Han, Wei, and Chao), commencing Warring States period, and also offering a more logical end to the Ch'un ch'iu period. Second half of fifth century: Mo-tzu
403	The 'Three Chin' are ceremonially recognized by the Chou king. Second half of fourth century: Mencius (Meng-tzu); Chuang-tzu 4th-3rd centuries: Hsün-tzu; Ch'ü Yüan
314	Ch'i intervenes in succession crisis in Yen and occupies that state.
312	Ch'i expelled from Yen by uprising.
297	King Chao-hsiang of Ch'in kidnaps King Huai of Ch'u during meeting at Wu Pass.
286	King Min of Ch'i attacks the 'Three Chin' but draws counterattack from six states under Yen general Yo Yi; and Yen occupies all of Ch'i except two strongholds, Chü and Chi-mo.
279	T'ien Tan of Ch'i drives Yen out and reconstitutes state of Ch'i. These wars inaugurate many-sided conflict culminating in final Ch'in victory.
249	Ch'in destroys last vestige of the Chou royal state.
230	Ch'in destroys Han.
228	Ch'in destroys Chao.
227	Prince Tan of Yen sends Ching K'o to attempt assassination of King Cheng of Ch'in, who is to become First Emperor of Ch'in.
226	Ch'in destroys state of Yen, seizing capital and forcing king to flee into Liao-tung, and executes Prince Tan.
225	Ch'in destroys Wei.
223	Ch'in destroys Ch'u.
222	Ch'in destroys last remnant of Yen, in Liao-tung. Ch'in drives down Yangtze River and forces submission of Yüeh princes.
221	Ch'in destroys Ch'i and unifies China as empire.

General Bibliography

This selected list includes works used throughout *La Chine antique*: chiefly those listed in Maspero's *Bibliographie générale*, rather than the more specialized bibliographical lists placed at the beginnings of Book II, chapters 1 and 2; Books III and IV; and all nine chapters of Book V.

Classics and Commentaries

Maspero used the French translations of Biot and Couvreur, and Legge's English translations. Where there was no such translation available, he referred to Juan Yüan's 阮元 *Sung-pen Shih-san-ching chu-shu* [Sung editions of the Thirteen Classics and sub-commentaries] 宋本十二經注疏, published 1816, reproduced in 1887 by the Mo-wang-hsien kuan 眽望仙館.

Chou-li, 周禮 [Rites of the Chou], translated by Edouard Biot as *Le Tcheou-li ou Rites des Tcheou*, 1851. Reprinted by the Ch'eng-wen Book Co., Taipei, 1970.

Ch'un ch'iu 春秋 ['Spring and Autumn' Annals], translated by James Legge as *The Ch'un Ts'ëw with the Tso Chuen*, Hong Kong, 1872, Book v of *The Chinese Classics (Ch.Cl.)*. Reprinted in Hong Kong: the Hong Kong University Press, 1960. The volume includes a translation of the *Tso chuan* and samples from the Kung-yang and Ku-liang commentaries.

Huang Ch'ing ching chieh 皇清經解 [Exegetical Works on Classics from the Imperial Ch'ing Era], published at Canton, 1829, under the editorship of Juan Yüan.

Huang Ch'ing ching chieh hsü pien 續編 (Continuation of the above work), published at Kiangyin, 1888, under the direction of Wang Hsien-ch'ien 王先謙.

Kung-yang chuan 公羊傳 and *Ku-liang chuan* 穀梁傳, commentaries on the *Ch'un-ch'iu, Ssu-pu ts'ung-k'an,* 四部叢刊, (SPTK) edition.

Li chi 禮記 [Collected Rituals], translated as *Li-ki ou Mémoires sur les Bienséances et les Cérémonies* by Father S. Couvreur (which Maspero used) and by Legge as *Li ki*, vols. 27–28. In *Sacred Books of the East*, 1885.

Shih ching 詩經 [Classic of Poetry], translated by Legge as *The She King*, vol. 4 of *Ch.Cl.*, Hong Kong, 1871.

Shu ching 書經, also called *Shang shu* 尚書 [Classic of Documents], translated by Legge as *The Shoo King*, vol. 3 of *Ch.Cl.*, Hong Kong, 1865. Reprint, edited by Clae Waltham. Chicago: H. Regnery, 1971.

Ta-Tai li chi 大戴禮記 [Elder Tai's Treatise on Rites], SPTK edition. Translated into German by R. Wilhelm as *Li Gi, das Buch der Sitte des älteren und jüngeren Dai*, 1930.

Tso chuan 左傳 [Tso commentary], historical narrative cut up to serve as commentary to the *Ch'un ch'iu* (*q.v.*, above).

Yi ching 易經 [Classic of Change], translated by Legge as vol. 16 of *Sacred Books of the East*, 1899. Reprint. New York: Dover, 1963. Reprinted with teaching aids and introduction by Ch'u Chai and Winberg Chai. New Hyde Park, New York: University Books, 1964. Retranslated many times, most authoritatively into German by R. Wilhelm (1923), then set into English from German by Cary F. Baynes, London: Routledge & Kegan Paul, 1951.

Yi li 議禮 [Ceremony and Ritual], translated into French by S. Couvreur as *Cérémonial* (1928), which Maspero used, and translated into English by J. Steele as *The I-Li* (1917).

Taoist Texts

Tao te ching 道德經 [The Book of the Way and Its Power], also called *Lao-tzu* 老子.

Chuang tzu 莊子.

Lieh-tzu 列子.

[Maspero cites no Chinese edition for the Taoist texts. He says that he worked from Father Léon Wieger's translation of these three texts contained in *Les Pères du système taoïste*, vol. 2 of Taoïsme (1913). The *Tao te ching* and the *Chuang tzu* have exerted an enormous fascination for Westerners, attracting a horde of translators, a short list of whom is in Hightower, *Topics in Chinese Literature*. (Harvard-Yenching Institute Studies, vol. 3, rev. ed., 1953. Maspero too was drawn to Taoism and spent much of his years after *La Chine antique* studying Taoism and its place among Chinese religions. His work on this was pulled together by Professor Max Kaltenmark, *Le Taoïsme et les religions chinoises*. Paris: Gallimard, 1971. An English translation is in preparation.]

Histories

Chan kuo ts'e 戰 國 策 [Records of the Warring States, or Strategies of the Warring States], SPTK edition. Translated by James I. Crump, *Chan-Kuo Ts'e*. London: Oxford, 1970.

Chu shu chi nien 竹 書 紀 年 ['Bamboo Annals'], translated by Legge in the Prolegomena to *Ch.Cl.*, vol. 3, *The Shoo King*. Also by Biot in *J.As.*, 1841–42.

Kuo yü 國 語 [Discourses of the Principalities], SPTK edition. Abridged translation into French by C. de Harlez, *J.As.* 1893–94. Later published in book form. Louvain, 1895.

Shih chi 史 記 [Historical Records, or Records of the Historian], by Ssu-ma Ch'ien 司 馬 遷 , Ch'ien-lung (1739) edition of the *Twenty-four Histories*. About half (chaps. 1–47) translated into French by Edouard Chavannes, *Les Mémoires historiques de Se-ma Ts'ien*. Paris: Leroux, 5 vols., 1895–1905. [Large blocks of the *Shih chi* and many individual chapters have been translated into various Western languages, covering virtually the entire work but varying greatly in quality. T. Pokora lists these translations, published and unpublished to that date, in *Oriens Extremus* 9:2, December 1962.]

Cordier, Henri. *Histoire générale de la Chine et de ses relations avec les pays étrangers depuis les temps les plus anciens jusqu'à la chute de la dynastie mandchoue*. Paris, 1920–21. [This is largely derived from Father J. A. M. de Mailla's *Histoire générale de la Chine*, 13 volumes, Paris, 1777–85, which is a translation of the *T'ung-chien kang-mu* 通 鑑 綱 目 and its continuations.]

Hirth, Friedrich. *The Ancient History of China to the End of the Chou Dynasty*. New York, 1908.

Tchang, Father Mathias. *Synchronismes chinois, chronologie complète et concordance avec l'ère chrétienne de toutes les dates concernant l'histoire de l'Extrême-Orient (Chine, Japon, Annam, Mongolie, etc.) 2357 av. J. C.-1904 ap. J. C.* In *Var. Sin.* 24, 1905.

Tschepe, Father Albert. *Histoire du Royaume de Ou*. Shanghai, *Var. Sin*. 10, 1896.

———. *Histoire du Royaume de Tch'ou*. Shanghai, *Var. Sin*. 22, 1903.

———. *Histoire du Royaume de Ts'in*. Shanghai, *Var. Sin*. 27, 1909.

———. *Histoire du Royaume de Tsin*. Shanghai, *Var. Sin*. 30, 1910.

———. *Histoire des trois royaumes de Han, Wei et Tchao*. Shanghai, *Var. Sin*. 31, 1910.

Social Sciences and Humanities

Chavannes, Edouard. *Le Dieu du Sol dans la Chine antique*. App. to *Le T'ai chan*. Paris: Guimet, 1910.

DeGroot, J. J. M. *The Religious System of China*. 6 vols. Leyden, 1921. Reprinted. Taipei Literature House, 1964.

Granet, Marcel. *Fêtes et Chansons anciennes de la Chine*. Paris, 1919. Translated as *Festivals and Songs of Ancient China*. New York: Dutton, 1932.

———. *La Polygynie sororale et le sororat dans la Chine antique*. Paris, 1920.

———. *Danses et Légendes de la Chine ancienne*. Paris, 1926.

Hu Shih. *The Development of the Logical Method in Ancient China*. Doctoral dissertation, Columbia University, 1917, later translated by Dr Hu as part of Volume 1 in his never completed *Chung-kuo che-hsüeh shih ta kang* 中國哲學史大綱. Shanghai, 1919. [*Development*, published in Shanghai, 1922, was reprinted by Paragon, New York, 1963.]

Laufer, Berthold. *Jade, a Study in Chinese Archaeology and Religion*. Chicago: Field Museum, 1912.

Wieger, Father Léon. *Histoire des croyances religieuses et des opinions philosophiques en Chine depuis l'origine jusqu'a nos jours* (Hsien-hsien, 1917). Translated by E. C. Werner as *A History of the Religious Beliefs and Philosophical Opinions in China*. Peking, 1927. Reprint. New York: Paragon, 1969.

Bibliographies

Cordier, Henri. *Bibliotheca Sinica*. Paris: Guilmoto, 1904–8. Supplemental Volume, 1924. [Reprinted in five volumes New York: Burt Franklin, 1968. Also Taipei: Ch'eng-wen, 1965–6. Last volume includes Author Index compiled by East Asia Library of Columbia University, New York, 1953.]

Wieger, Father Léon. *La China à travers les âges* (Index bibliographique). Hsien-hsien, 1920.

Wylie, Alexander. *Notes on Chinese Literature*. Shanghai: 1867. Reprinted with Introduction by Howard S. Levy. New York: Paragon, 1964.

[Translator's Note: There are a number of modern bibliographies which are useful guides to various fields. Two general ones, both containing sections on bibliographical works as well as other categories, are Charles O. Hucker's *China: A Critical Bibliography* (Tucson: Arizona, 1962) and Chang Chun-shu's *Pre-Modern China*. Michigan Papers in Chinese Studies, no. 11. Ann Arbor, 1971. Also Chang Kwang-chih's *The Archaeology of Ancient China*, 2d ed., rev. and enlarged. New Haven: Yale, 1968. Contains copious bibliography for reviewing the changing assessment of ancient Chinese civilization, especially from the view of recent archaeology.]

Chinese and Japanese Journals Frequently Cited in Notes

I shu ts'ung pien 藝術叢編. Chinese archaeological review. Shanghai, since 1916.

Shinagaku 支那學 [*Sinology*]. Japanese sinological review. Tokyo, from 1920, to c. 1940.

Tōyō gakuhō 東洋學報 [Reports of the Oriental Society]. Tokyo, since 1911.

Bibliography of the Writings of Henri Maspero

1905

Les finances de l'Egypte sous les Lagides, Paris, XII + 252 pages.

1908

Reviews

Albert Maybon, *La politique chinoise, étude sur les doctrines des partis en Chine* (Paris, 1908), *BEFEO*, VIII, pp. 252–9.
Frank H. Chalfant, *Early Chinese Writing*, n. d., *ibid.*, pp. 264–7.
Jeremiah Curtin, *The Mongols* ... (Boston, 1908), *ibid.*, pp. 571–3.

1909

'Le monastère de la *Kouan-yin qui ne veut pas s'en aller*', in collaboration with Noël Peri, *BEFEO*, IX, pp. 797–807.

Reviews

Edouard Driault, *La question d'Extrême-Orient* (Paris, 1908), *ibid.*, pp. 588–92.
Commandant Harfeld, *Opinions chinoises sur les Barbares d'Occident* (Paris-Brussels, 1909), *ibid.*, pp. 592–3 [cf. *ibid.*, X (1910), pp. 282–3].
L Woitsch, *Zum Pekinger Suhua* ... (Peking, 1908), *ibid.*, p. 593.
H.A. Giles, *Adversaria Sinica*, nos. 2–7 (Shanghai, 1906–9), *ibid.*, pp. 593–600.
A. Vissière, *Premières leçons de chinois* ... (Leiden, 1909), *ibid.*, pp. 808–9.
Sekino Tei, *Stone mortuary Shrines* ... (Tokyo, 1909), *ibid.*, pp. 809–10.
St. Millot, *Dictionnaire des formes cursives des caractères chinois* (Paris, 1909), *ibid.*, p. 811.

1910

'Le songe et l'ambassade de l'empereur Ming. Etude critique des sources', *BEFEO*, X, pp. 95–130. [Japanese tr., *Tōyō-gakuhō*, II (Tokyo, 1912), pp. 100–19.]

'Communautés et moines bouddhistes chinois aux IIe et IIIe siècles', *ibid.*, pp. 222–32.

'Le Protectorat général d'Annam sous les T'ang. Essai de géographie historique', *ibid.*, pp. 539–84, 665–82, one map.

'Sur la date et l'authenticité du *Fou fa tsang yin yuan tchouan*', *Mélanges d'indianisme offerts par ses élèves à M. Sylvain Lévi* (Paris), pp. 129–49.

Reviews

G. E. Gerini, *Researches on Ptolemy's Geography of Eastern Asia* ... (London, 1909), *BEFEO*, X, pp. 422–23.

Hoang-cao-Khai, *Gu'o'ngsu' nam* [*Miroir de l'histoire d'Annam*] (Hanoi, 1910), *ibid.*, pp. 612–17.

Ed. Chavannes, *Le T'ai chan* ... (Paris, 1910), *ibid.*, pp. 627–9.

O. Franke, *Zur Frage der Einführung des Buddhismus in China* ... (Berlin, 1910), *ibid.*, pp. 629–36.

1911

'Contribution à l'étude du système phonétique des langues thai', *BEFEO*, XI, pp. 153–69.

1912

'Etudes sur la phonétique historique de la langue annamite. Les initiales', *BEFEO*, XII, I, pp. 1–127.

Reviews

M. Grammont et Le-quang-Trinh, *Etudes sur la langue annamite* (Paris, 1912), *ibid.*, XII, IX, pp. 15–17.

C. B. Bradley, *Graphic Analysis of the Tone Accents in the Siamese Language* (*J.A.O.S.*, 1911), *ibid.*, pp. 21–2.

Tai Tō seiiki-ki ... (Tokyo, 1911), *ibid.*, pp. 132–6.

1913

Reviews

Ed. Chavannes, *Les documents découverts par Aurel Stein* ... (Oxford, 1913), *BEFEO*, XIII, VII, pp. 25–7.

L. Wieger, *Taoïsme*, II ..., *Buddhisme*, II ... (Ho-kien-fou, 1913), *ibid.*, pp. 27–33.
S. Lévi, *Le 'tokharien B'*, *langue de Koutcha* (*J.As.*, 1913), *ibid.*, pp. 73–9.
L. de La Vallée-Poussin, *Documents sanscrits* ... (London, 1913), *ibid.*, pp. 78–81.
P. Pelliot, *Un fragment du Suvarnaprabhāsasūtra en iranien-oriental* (Paris, 1913), *ibid.*, p. 81.

1914

'Sur quelques textes anciens de chinois parlé', *BEFEO*, XIV, IV, pp. 1–36.
'Rapport sommaire sur une mission archéologique au Tchökiang', *ibid.*, XIV, VIII, pp. 1–75, 21 pl., 35 figs. [Cf. L. Finot, 'Manuscrits sanskrits de Sādhana's retrouvés en Chine', *J. As.*, CCXXV (1934), pp. 1–86.]
[Entretiens avec des moines bouddhistes de Canton concernant Hārītī cited in N. Peri, 'Hārītī, la Mère-de-démons',] *BEFEO*, XVII, III, pp. 62–63.

Reviews

G. Cordier, *Littérature annamite* ... (Hanoi-Haiphong, 1914), *BEFEO*, XIV, IX, pp. 1–6.
T. C. Hodson, *Numeral Systems of Tibeto-Burman Dialects* (*J. Roy. As. Soc.*, 1913), *ibid.*, pp. 6–7.
Lieut-Col. Waddell, *The so-called Mahāpadāna Suttanta* ... (*J. Roy. As. Soc.*, 1914), *ibid.*, pp. 66–7.
R. F. Johnston, *Buddhist China* (London, 1913), *ibid.*, pp. 72–5.
M. Courant, *La langue chinoise parlée* ... (Paris-Lyon, 1914), *ibid.*, pp. 75–8.
Torii Ryūzō, ... *Populations primitives de la Mongolie orientale* ... (Tokyo, 1914), *ibid.*, pp. 79–80.

1915

Reviews

P. Broemer, *L'Indochine du Nord* ... (*Revue Indochinoise*, 1915), *BEFEO*, XV, IV, pp. 13–14.
B. Laufer, *Optical Lenses* ..., *Asbestos and Salamander* ... (*TP*, *ibid.*, pp. 41–6).
Nishi-Hongwan-ji, Seiiki kōko zufu ... (Tokyo, 1915), *ibid.*, pp. 57–64.

1916

'Etudes d'histoire d'Annam. I. La dynastie des Lí antérieurs',
BEFEO, XVI, I, pp. 1–26.
'II. La géographie politique de l'empire d'Annam sous les Lí, les
Trân et les Hô (ve, xve siècles)', *ibid.*, pp. 27–48.
'III. La commanderie de Siang', *ibid.*, pp. 49–55.
'De quelques interdits en relation avec les noms de famille chez
les Tai-noirs', *ibid.*, XVI, III, pp. 29–34.
'Quelques mots annamites d'origine chinoise', *ibid.*, pp. 35–9.

Reviews

B. Karlgren, *Etudes sur la phonologie chinoise* (Uppsala, 1915–16),
BEFEO, XVI, V, pp. 61–73.
Sten Konow, *Fragments of a Buddhist work in the ancient Aryan
Language of Chinese Turkestan* (Calcutta, 1914), *ibid.*, pp. 73–4.

1918

'Etudes d'histoire d'Annam. IV. Le royaume de Van-lang',
BEFEO, XVIII, III, pp. 1–10.
'V. L'expédition de Ma Yuan', *ibid.*, pp. 11–28.
'VI. La frontière de l'Annam et du Cambodge du VIIIe au XIVe
siècle', *ibid.*, pp. 29–36.

1919

'La prière du bain des statues divines chez les Cams', *BEFEO*,
XIX, V, pp. 1–6.
[Note sur des vestiges d'art cam et des fouilles exécutées dans la
région de Kontum], *ibid.*, pp. 103–6 [cf. *ibid.*, XX, IV, pp. 198–9].

Reviews

Lieut-Col. Bonifacy, *Cours d'ethnographie indochinoise* (Hanoi-
Haiphong, 1919), *BEFEO*, XIX, V, pp. 26–9.
M. Granet, *Fêtes et chansons anciennes de la Chine* (Paris, 1919), *ibid.*,
pp. 65–75.
The New China Review (Hong Kong, 1919), *ibid.*, pp. 75–8.

1920

'Le dialecte de Tch'ang-ngan sous les T'ang', *BEFEO*, XX, II,
p. 1–124. [Awarded a *prix ordinaire* by the Academy of
Inscriptions and Belles-Lettres, 1921; cf. *TP*, XX, p. 372.]

1922

'Etudes sur le taoïsme. Le saint et la vie mystique chez Lao-tseu et Tchouang-tseu', *Bull. de l'Assoc. fr. des Amis de l'Orient*, no. 3, Paris, pp. 69–89. [*II, pp. 225–42.]

'Edouard Chavannes', *TP*, XXI, pp. 43–56.

'La Sinologie', *Société asiatique, Le Livre du Centenaire, 1822–1922* (Paris), pp. 261–83.

1923

'Les coutumes funéraires chez les Tai-noirs du Haut-Tonkin', *Bull. de l'Assoc. fr. des Amis de l'Orient*, no. 6, pp. 13–26. [*I, pp. 215–26; † pp. 268–76]

[Communication on 'Les anciennes légendes chinoises dites du déluge', Société Asiatique, 9 March], *J. As.*, CCII, p. 178.

1924

'Légendes mythologiques dans le *Chou king*', *J. As.*, CCII, pp. 1–100.

Review

L. Aurousseau, *La première conquête des pays annamites ...* (*BEFEO*, 1923), *TP*, XXIII, pp. 373–93.

1925

'Le roman de Sou Ts'in', *Etudes Asiatiques publiées à l'occasion du 25 anniversaire de l'Ecole française d'Extrême-Orient* (Paris), II, pp. 127–42.

1926

'Les origines de la civilisation chinoise', *Annales de Géographie*, no. 194, pp. 135–54, 1 map. [Eng. tr., 'The origins of Chinese Civilization', *Smithsonian Institute Report for 1927* (Washington, 1928), pp. 433–52.]

1927

La Chine antique (Paris), XV + 624 pages, 3 maps.

'Notes sur la logique de Mö-tseu et de son école', *TP*, XXV, pp. 1–64.

'Chine et Asie centrale', *Histoire et historiens depuis cinquante ans* (Paris), pp. 517–59.

Reviews

Jean Escarra, ... *Recueil des sommaires de la Cour Suprême de la République de Chine* ... (Shanghai, 1924–25), *J. As.*, CCX, pp. 125–7.

Tchang Fong, *Recherches sur les os du Ho-nan et quelques caractères de l'écriture ancienne* (Paris, 1915), *ibid.*, pp. 127–9.

Takata Tadasuke, *Kou tcheou p'ien* ... (Tokyo, 1925), *ibid.*, pp. 129–42.

G. Haloun, *Die Rekonstruktion der chinesichen Urgeschichte durch die Chinesen* (Berlin, 1925), *ibid.*, pp. 142–4.

Id., *Seit wann kannten die Chinesen die Tocharer oder Indogermanen überbaupt?* (Leipzig, 1925), *ibid.*, pp. 144–52.

M. Granet, *Danses et légendes de la Chine ancienne* (Paris, 1926), *ibid.*, pp. 152–5.

1928

'La chronologie des rois de Ts'i au IVe siècle avant notre ère', *TP*, XXV, pp. 367–86.

'Mythologie de la Chine moderne', *Mythologie asiatique illustrée* (Paris), pp. 227–362, one gravure print, 11 half-tone plates, 80 figs. [†, pp. 87–220.]

'Chinese Sepulchral Inscriptions from Astāna, Turfān', and other translations and notes in French, in Aurel Stein, *Innermost Asia* (Oxford), pp. 983–7 and *passim*.

Reviews

B. Karlgren, *On the Authenticity and Nature of the* Tso chuan (Göteborg, 1926), *J. As.*, CCXII, pp. 159–65.

Memoirs ... of the Tōyō Bunko ... (Tokyo, 1926), *ibid.*, pp. 165–70.

Katō Shigeru, *Researches into the Precious Metals of the T'ang and Sung Dynasties* ... (Kyoto, 1925), *ibid.*, pp. 170–2.

Y. W. Wong, *Wong's System of Chinese Lexicography* ... (Shanghai, 1926), *ibid.*, pp. 173–4.

G. Margouliès, *Le Kouwen chinois...*, *Le 'Fou' dans le Wen-siuan* ... (Paris, 1925), *ibid.*, pp. 174–7.

Homer Dubs, *Did Confucius study the 'Book of Changes'?* (*TP*, 1927), *ibid.*, pp. 178–80.

B . Laufer, *Archaic Chinese Jades* (New York, 1927), *ibid.*, pp. 180–1.

Yūchiku-saizō-Kogyofu, or The Early Chinese Jades ... (n.p., 1925), *ibid.*, pp. 181–3.

M. Muccioli, ... *Sulle 'conoscenze chemiche dei Cinesi'* ... (Rome, 1927, *ibid.*, pp. 183–4.

M.-J. Ballot, *Les laques d'Extrême-Orient* ... (Paris, 1927), *ibid.*, pp. 184–6.

1929

'L'astronomie chinoise avant les Han', *TP*,XXVI, pp. 267–356.

'Les commencements de la civilisation chinoise', *Shina-gaku* (Kyoto), V, II, pp. 1–16. [*III, pp. 79–92.]

['Les influences occidentales en Chine avant les Han', in Japanese] *Tōa-kenkyū* (Tokyo), no. 4.

'Langues' [of French Indochina], *Un empire colonial français, l'Indochine,* work published under the direction of Georges Maspero (Paris-Brussels), I, pp. 63–80, one map.

'Mœurs et coutumes des populations sauvages', *ibid.*, pp. 233–55.

1930

'Préfixes et dérivation en chinois archaïque', *M.S.L.P.*, XXIII, pp. 313–27.

1931

[Communication on 'La question de la parenté des langues dans les langues de l'Asie extrême-orientale', Geneva, 25 August,] *Actes du IIe Congrès International des Linguistes* (Paris, 1933), pp. 225–27.

[Communication entitled: 'Quelques observations sur les classiques et les commentaires chinois', Leiden, 11 September] *Actes du XVIIIe Congrès International des Orientalistes* (Leiden, 1932), p. 142.

1932

'La composition et la date du *Tso tchouan'*, *Mél. chinois et bouddhiques,* I (Brussels), pp. 137–215.

'La vie privée en Chine à l'époque des Han', *R.A.A.*, VII, pp. 185–201, 13 figs., 4 half-tone plates.

'Sur quelques objets de l'époque des Han', *Etudes d'orientalisme publiées par le Musée Guimet à la mémoire de Raymonde Linossier* (Paris), pp. 403–18, pl. xli-xliv.

Review

Chiu Bien-ming [Tcheou Pien-ming], *The Phonetic structure and Tone Behaviour of Hagu* ... (Hamburg, 1930), *B.S.L.P.*, XXXIII, pp. 220–24.

1933

'Le mot *ming* 明 ', *J. As.*, CCXXIII, pp. 249–56.

'La chaire de Langues et Littératures chinoises et tartares-mandchoues', *Livre jubilaire composé à l'occasion du 4e Centenaire du Collège de France* (Paris), pp. 355–66, one plate.

[Communication on 'Une communauté bouddhiste du 11e siècle en Chine', Société Asiatique, 8 June,] *J. As.*, CCXXIII, p. 347.

Reviews

Tong Tso-pin, *Sin hou pou ts'eu sie pen* (Nan-yang, 1928), *J. As.*, CCXXII, fasc. appended, pp. 1–2.

Kouo Mo-jo, *Kia-kou wen-tseu yen-kieou* [*Recherches sur les caractères des inscriptions sur écaille de tortue et sur os des Yin*] (Shanghai, 1930), *ibid.*, pp. 2–11.

Id., *Tchong-kouo kou-tai che-houei yen-kieou* [*Recherches sur la Société de l'Antiquité chinoise*] (Shanghai, 1930), *ibid.*, pp. 11–18.

Note: the two publications immediately above were translated into Chinese by Lou K'an-jou, with a reply by Kouo Mo-jo, *Wen hio nien pao (Chinese Literature,* published by the Society of Chinese Literature of Yenching University), Peking, II (June 1936), pp. 1–4, 61–72.]

B. Karlgren, *Some Fecundity Symbols in Ancient China* (Stockholm, 1930), *ibid.*, pp. 18–21.

Shin Kan ga-sen shūroku (Tokyo, 1929), *ibid.*, pp. 22–3.

Sekino Tei ..., *Archaeological Researches on the ancient Lo-lang District* (Tokyo, 1927), Harada Yoshito, *Lo-lang* ... (Tokyo, 1930), *ibid.*, pp. 23–6.

Arvid Jongchell, *Huo Kuang och hans tid, täxter ur Pan Ku's Ch'ien Han shu* (Göteborg, 1930), *ibid.*, pp. 26–9.

Nancy Lee Swann, ... *Biography of the Empress Têng* ... (*J.A.O.S., 1931*), *ibid.*, pp. 29–33.

R. des Rotours, *Le Traité des Examens* ... (Paris, 1932), *ibid.*, pp. 33–7.

B. Karlgren, *The Authenticity of Ancient Chinese Texts* (Stockholm, 1929), *ibid.*, pp. 38–48.

J. J. L. Duyvendak, *The Book of Lord Shang* ... (London, 1928), *ibid.*, pp. 48–59.

A Conrady and Ed. Erkes, *Das älteste Dokument zur chinesischen Kunstgeschichte, T'ien wen* ... (Leipzig, 1931), *ibid.*, pp. 59–74.

Walter Simon, *Tibetisch-chinesische Wortgleichungen* ... (Berlin-Leipzig, 1930), *ibid.*, pp. 74–9.

Sir Alexander Hosie, *Philip's Commercial Map of China* ... (London, n. d.), *ibid.*, pp. 79–81.

Wang Li, *Une prononciation chinoise de Po-pei* ... (Paris, 1932), *B.S.L.P.*, XXXIV, pp. 223–5.

Walter Simon, *Tibetisch-chinesiche Wortgleichungen* (Berlin-Leipzig, 1930), *ibid.*, pp. 225–8.

F.-M. Savina, *Lexique dày-français* ... (Hanoi, 1931), *ibid.*, pp. 228–36.

Sung-nien Hsü [Siu Song-nien], *Anthologie de la littérature chinoise* ... (Paris, 1931), *Revue critique d'histoire et de littérature* (Paris), pp. 376–8.

1934

'Les origines de la communauté bouddhiste de Lo-yang', *J. As.*, CCXXV, pp. 88–107.

'La langue chinoise', *Conférences de l'Institut de Linguistique de l'Université de Paris*, 1933 (Paris, 1934), pp. 33–70.

Preface to E. Backhouse et J.-O.-P. Bland, *Les empereurs mandchous, Mémoires de la Cour de Pékin*, translated by L. M. Mitchell (Paris), pp. 7–24.[*III, pp. 209–27 under title 'Comment tombe une dynastie chinoise: la chute des Ming']

Reviews

Lo Tch'ang-p'ei, *Examen des initiales* ... (Pei-p'ing, 1930), *B.S.L.P.*, XXXV, pp. 205–12.

Nguyen-van-Huyên, *Les chants alternés des garçons et des filles en Annam* ... (Paris, 1934), *ibid.*, pp. 213–17.

1935

'Le Serment dans la procédure juridique de la Chine antique', *Mél. chinois et bouddhiques*, III (Brussels), pp. 257–317.

[Communications on 'La doctrine des Taoïstes relative à l'anatomie du corps humain dans ses relations avec la circulation du souffle', Société Asiatique, 12 April and 10 May], *J. As.*, CCXXVII, pp. 149–50.

Preface to Ching-chi Young, *L'écriture et les manuscrits lolos*, Publications of the Bibliothèque Sino-Internationale, no. 4 (Geneva), one page.

Reviews

Sueji Umehara, *Etude sur la poterie blanche* ... *des Yin* ... (Kyoto, 1932), *J. As.*, CCXXVI, pp. 158–60; id., *Etude archéologique sur le Pien-chin* ... (Kyoto, 1933), *ibid.*, pp. 160–3.

Chōsen sōtokufu ... [*Government General of Korea, Report on Excavations* ...] (Seoul, 1933), *ibid.*, pp. 163–5.

Government General Museum of Chōsen ... (Seoul, 1933), *ibid.*, p. 165.

A. Conrady, *Yih-king Studien* ... (*Asia Major*, 1931), *ibid.*, pp. 166–70.

Arthur Waley, *The Book of Changes* ... (Stockholm, 1934), *ibid.*, pp. 170–73.

Esson M. Gale, *Discourses on Salt and Iron* ... (Leiden, 1931), *ibid.*, pp. 173–6.

James R. Ware, *The Wei Shu and the Sui Shu on Taoism* (*J.A.O.S.*, *1933–4*), *ibid.*, pp. 313–17.

[*Yin-tö*] (Peiping, 1931–2), *ibid.*, pp. 318–19.

Suzuki Ryūichi, *Kokugo-sakuin* (Kyoto, 1934), *ibid.*, pp. 320–1.

B. Karlgren, *Word families in Chinese* ... (Stockholm, 1934), *B.S.L.P.*, XXXVI, pp. 175–83.

K. Wulff, *Chinesisch und Tai* ... (Copenhagen, 1934), *ibid.*, pp. 185–7.

J. Margouliès, *Petit précis de grammaire chinoise écrite* (Paris, 1934), *ibid.*, pp. 187–8.

Walter Simon, *Die Bedeutung der Final-partikel i* ... (Berlin, 1934), *ibid.*, pp. 189–90.

1936

'Le régime féodal et la propriété foncière dans la Chine antique', *Revue de l'Institut de Sociologie* (Brussels), XVI, 1, pp. 3–36. [*III, 109–46.]

Discours prononcé ... *à la distribution solennelle des prix faite aux élèves du Petit Lycée Janson-de-Sailly* (Paris), 3 pages.

[Communication on 'L'organisation d'un domaine foncier en Chine au temps de Tcheou Occidentaux'], *Acad. des Inscr. et B.-L., C. r* ..., January–March, pp. 80–2.

[Communication on 'Les dieux et leur rôle dans la religion taoïste avant les T'ang', Société Asiatique, 3 April], *J. As.*, CCXXVIII, pp. 483–4.

[Communication on 'L'aspect dans la langue chinoise parlée', Copenhagen, 21 September], *IVe Congrès International des Linguistes* (Copenhagen, 1938), p. 209.

Review

Jean Lartigue, *Mission archéologique en Chine, 1914, I* ... (Paris, 1935), *J. As.*, CCXXVIII, pp. 520–5.

1937

Institut de France. Académie des Inscriptions et Belles-Lettres. Les dieux taoïstes: comment on communique avec eux. Lecture faite dans la séance publique du vendredi 19 novembre 1937, Paris, 17 pages [= *Acad. des Inscr. et B.-L., C. r* ..., pp. 361–74]. [†pp. 467–8.]

'Les procédés de 'nourrir le principe vital' dans la religion taoïste ancienne', *J. As.*, CCXXIX, pp. 177–252, 353–430 [†pp. 479–589.]

'Les régimes fonciers en Chine', *Recueil de la Société Jean Bodin*

(Brussels), II, pp. 265–314. [*III, pp. 147–92.]

'Les langues d'Extrême-Orient', *Encyclopédie Française*, vol. I, L'outillage mental (Paris), I° 40, 1 to 16, I° 42, 1 to 15.

'Un texte chinois inconnu sur le pays de Ta-ts'in (Orient romain)', *Mélanges Maspero, II, Mém. de l'Institut Français*, LXVII (Le Caire), pp. 377–87. [*III, pp. 91–108 under the title 'Un texte taoiste sur l'Orient Romain'.]

1938

'Les termes désignant la propriété foncière en Chine', *Recueil de la Société Jean Bodin* (Brussels), III, pp. 287–301. [*III, pp. 193–208.]

Preface to Ting-Ming Tchen [Tch'en Ting-ming], *Etude phonétique des particules de la langue chinoise* (Paris, n. d.), pp. I-VI.

[Observations sur l'emploi de la houe et de la charrue dans la Chine antique, à propos d'une communication de M. Hrozny sur la charrue en Sumer-Akkad, en Egypte et en Chine,] *Acad. des Inscr. et B.-L., C. r* ... , pp. 519–21.

Reviews

R. Schäfer, *Sino-Tibetica* ... (Berkeley, 1938), *B.S.L.P.*, XXXIX, pp. 206–7.

Wang Li, *Relations entre le vocalisme et le ton en chinois* ... (Peking, 1930), *ibid.*, p. 208.

Walter Simon, *Has the Chinese Language Parts of Speech?* (London, 1937), *ibid.*, pp. 209–13.

1939

'Les instruments astronomiques des Chinois au temps des Han', *Mél. chinois et bouddhiques*, VI (Bruges), pp. 183–370, 13 figs. [Distributed in 1942.]

'Les Ivoires chinois et l'Iconographie populaire', *Les Ivoires religieux et médicaux chinois d'après la collection Lucien Lion*, text by Henri Maspero, René Grousset, Lucien Lion (Paris), pp. 5–18; résumé in English, pp. 83–6. [*I, pp. 227–39.]

'Rapport sur l'activité de l'Ecole française d'Extrême-Orient ... lu dans la séance du 7 juillet 1939', *Acad. des Inscr. et B.-L., C. r* ..., pp. 348–60.

Reviews

Herrlee Glessner Creel, *The Birth of China* ... (London, 1936), *J. As.*, CCXXXI, pp. 299–304.

A. C. Moule and P. Pelliot, *Marco Polo* ... (London, 1938), *ibid.*, pp. 304–7.

O. Siren, *History of early Chinese Painting* ... (London, 1933), *ibid.*, pp. 307–13.

Basil Alexeiev, *La littérature chinoise* ... (Paris, 1937), *ibid.*, pp. 313–16.

P. Masson-Oursel, *La philosophie en Orient: la Chine* ... (Paris, 1938), *ibid.*, pp. 455–9.

W. Eberhard and R. Müller, *Contributions to the Astronomy of the San-kuo Period* ... (Peking, 1936), *ibid.*, pp. 459–68.

Ecole Française d'Extrême-Orient. Questionnaire linguistique (Hanoi, 1938), *ibid.*, pp. 468–70.

J. Siguret, *Territoires et populations des Confins du Yunnan* ... (Peiping — Leipzig, 1937), *O. L. Z.*, XLII, cols. 126–7.

R. H. Van Gulik, *Mi Fu on Ink-Stones* ... (Peking, 1938), *ibid.*, cols. 559–61.

1940

[Communication on 'L'organisation administrative et religieuse de l'église taoïque au temps des Six Dynasties', Société Asiatique, 8 March], *J. As.*, CCXXXII, p. 305.

1941

[Communication on 'Le monde des morts et les funérailles chez les Tai-noirs', Société Asiatique, 9 May], *J. As.*, CCXXXIII, p. 224.

1942

O. Franke, *Geschichte des chinesischen Reiches* ... (Berlin, 1936–7), *O.L.Z.*, XLV, cols. 260–6. [The manuscript of this review had been submitted early in 1939.]

1943

[Communication on 'La technique du labour à la houe et sur l'organisation de l'agriculture dans la Chine antique', Société Asiatique, 12 November], *J. As.*, forthcoming.

1944

[Speech delivered at the meeting of 7 January, in assuming the Presidency of the Academy of Inscriptions and Belles-Lettres], *Acad. des Inscr. et B.-L., C. r* ..., pp. 2–4.

[Funeral oration for Mr Lo Tchen-yu, correspondent of the Academy, same meeting], *ibid.*, pp. 11–13.

[Funeral oration for Mr Thureau-Dangin, member of the Academy, meeting of 24 January], *ibid.*, pp. 53–67.

[Funeral oration for Mgr Joseph Wilpert, correspondent of the Academy, meeting of 25 February], *ibid.*, pp. 101–5.

[Funeral oration for Count Alexandre de Laborde, member of the Academy, read at the meeting of 11 August by Mr Gustave Dupont-Ferrier], *ibid.*, pp. 322–6.

Posthumous Publications

Mélanges posthumes sur les réligions et l'histoire de la Chine (Paris, 1950); vol. I, *Les religions chinoise*; vol. II, *Le Taoïsme*; vol. III, *Etudes historiques*. These volumes include the following items previously unpublished:

Vol. I

   (a) 'La religion chinoise dans son développement historique,' (I, pp. 1–138), also reprinted in *Le Taoïsme*, pp. 7–86.

   (b) 'La société et la religion des chinois anciens et celles des Tai modernes' (I, pp. 139–94) [Lectures given in Tokyo, 1929], also reprinted in *Le Taoïsme*, pp. 221–67, together with 'Les coutumes funéraires chez les Tai-noirs du Haut-Tonkin' (pp. 268–76).

   (c) 'Comment le Bouddhisme s'est introduit en Chine' (I, pp. 195–211) [Lecture given in Brussels, 1940, edited by Paul Demiéville], also reprinted in *Le Taoïsme* pp. 277–91.

Vol. II

   (d) 'Le Taoïsme dans les croyances religieuses des chinois à l'époque des Six Dynasties' (II, pp. 13–57) [Lecture given in Brussels, 1940], also reprinted in Le *Taoïsme*, pp. 293–330.

   (e) 'Le Poète Hi K'ang et le club des sept sages de la forêt de bambous' (II, pp. 59–69) [Lecture given in Brussels, 1940], also reprinted in *Le Taoïsme*, pp. 331–40.

   (f) 'Essai sur le Taoïsme aux premiers siècles de l'ère chrétienne' (II, pp. 71–222), also reprinted in *Le Taoïsme*, pp. 341–466.

Vol. III

   (g) 'L'astronomie dans la Chine ancienne: histoire des instruments et des découvertes' (III, pp. 13–34) [probably written between 1932 and 1939].

   (h) 'Influences occidentales en Chine avant les Han' (III, pp. 35–51) [Lecture given in Tokyo, 1929].

   (i) 'Le roman historique dans la littérature chinoise de

l'antiquité' (III, pp. 53–62) [Lecture given in Tokyo, 1929].
(j) 'La vie courante dans la Chine des Han: à propos d'une exposition du Musée Cernuschi' (III, pp. 63–76) [written shortly before 1938].

'Le Taoïsme', *Hommes et Mondes* (Paris, 1950), pp. 567–81.

'Le Ming-t'ang et la crise religieuse avant les Han', *Mélanges chinois et bouddhiques*, 9 (1951), pp. 1–171.

'Langues de l'Asie du Sud-Est', in *Les Langues du Monde*, new edition (Paris, 1954), pp. 523–644.

Les institutions de la Chine, completed by Jean Escarra (Paris, 1952).

Les documents chinois de la troisième expédition de Sir Aurel Stein en Asie Centrale (London, 1953).

'Contribution à l'étude de la société chinoise à la fin des Chang et au début des Tcheou', *BEFEO*, 46,2 (1954), pp. 335–403.

La Chine antique, new edition revised from corrections and additions left by the author (Paris, 1955); reprinted 1965.

Henri Maspero and Etienne Balazs, *Histoire et institutions de la Chine ancienne, des origines au XIIe siècle après J.C.* (Paris, 1967).

Le Taoïsme et les religions chinoises, preface by Max Kaltenmark (Paris, 1971).

NOTE:

In the bibliography, studies reprinted in the *Mélanges posthumes* are indicated by an asterisk*; articles reproduced in *Le Taoïsme et les religions chinoises* by a dagger†, followed by vol. (in case of the *Mélanges*) and page numbers. Articles printed in *Le Taoïsme* have for some strange reason been changed to employ *pinyin* romanization, which may well create some confusion for the reader.

Index

The Index is keyed to the romanized Chinese terms, arranged alphabetically, with a minimum of cross-reference; thus the pertinent entries are under *fa-chia*, not Legalists (although in that and other potentially confusing cases there are cross-references). Also, Maspero's form of personal names is observed; thus, Chung of Kuan, not Kuan Chung. Alternate names (honorifics, appellations, personal names, etc.) are given in parentheses with the primary name: e.g. Confucius (K'ung Ch'iu, K'ung-tzu, Chung-ni).

There are three forms of group entries: (*a*) sovereigns of principalities (sov.) who share the same formal name (e.g., Hui 惠 Wen 文); (*b*) families (fam.) of obvious importance in the principalities (e.g., the Chao, Wei, and Hsün families in Chin); and (*c*) special groups: the disciples of Confucius, hexagrams, and trigrams.